本卷受海南省人大常委会法制工作委员会委托编译

CHINESE-ENGLISH COLLECTION OF
REGULATIONS OF CHINA HAINAN FREE TRADE PORT
(2020-2021)

海南自由贸易港法规
（2020-2021）
选 编

（中英对照）

屈文生 主编

法律出版社
LAW PRESS · CHINA
北京

图书在版编目(CIP)数据

海南自由贸易港法规(2020-2021)选编:汉英对照/屈文生主编. -- 北京:法律出版社,2023
ISBN 978-7-5197-8206-1

Ⅰ.①海… Ⅱ.①屈… Ⅲ.①自由贸易区-法律-汇编-海南-汉、英 Ⅳ.①D922.299.9

中国国家版本馆CIP数据核字(2023)第153660号

海南自由贸易港法规(2020-2021)选编
(中英对照)
HAINAN ZIYOU MAOYIGANG FAGUI (2020-2021) XUANBIAN
(ZHONG-YING DUIZHAO)

屈文生 主编

策划编辑 解 锟
责任编辑 朱 峰 韩泓宇
装帧设计 李 瞻

出版发行 法律出版社
编辑统筹 辞书·融出版编辑部 法律翻译与出版研发中心
责任校对 马秋婧
责任印制 吕亚莉
经 销 新华书店

开本 787毫米×1092毫米 1/16
印张 48.5 **字数** 1180千
版本 2023年11月第1版
印次 2023年11月第1次印刷
印刷 三河市龙大印装有限公司

地址:北京市丰台区莲花池西里7号(100073)
网址:www.lawpress.com.cn
投稿邮箱:info@lawpress.com.cn
举报盗版邮箱:jbwq@lawpress.com.cn

销售电话:010-83938349
客服电话:010-83938350
咨询电话:010-63939796

书号:ISBN 978-7-5197-8206-1
定价:398.00元

卷首语

在海南建设中国特色自由贸易港，是党中央新时代改革开放的重大举措，是我国加快建立开放型经济新体制的重大举措，展现出我国坚定不移全面扩大开放、构建对外开放新格局、推动建设开放型世界经济的意志和决心，对于统筹国内国际两个大局和推动中国特色社会主义创新发展有着重要意义。

对外翻译对于推动构建中国法治话语体系发挥着重要作用。海南自由贸易港建设过程中，外国主体对我国相关法律法规的了解需求与日俱增，海南自由贸易港法规体系的外译应属构建海南自由贸易港法治话语体系乃至中国法治话语体系的题中之义。

海南自由贸易港法规体系的外译有助于包括"一带一路"沿线国家在内的世界各国把握海南自由贸易港投资自由便利的法律环境，更好地开展国际交流与合作，最终提升海南自由贸易港吸引外资、国内外投资者共享新机遇的能力。事实上，包括海南自由贸易港法律法规在内的中国法的外译是将中文法律语言转换为普通法、大陆法、伊斯兰法等法系中主要法律语言的跨语际、跨法系、跨文化的"一对多"实践。海南自由贸易港必然是法治的，这一法治的内容和形象需要以独立且包容的姿态向外界呈现，实现具有中国特色的海南自由贸易港法规体系的自我表达，并取得更加深远的影响。

基于上述考量，受海南省人大常委会法制工作委员会的委托，本卷收录了 2020—2021 年海南省人民代表大会通过的部分海南自由贸易港法规以及相应的英译版本，以期世界各国充分了解海南自由贸易港的内部运作和对外往来规则，畅通"引进来"战略的有效实施。

一、海南自由贸易港法规体系

海南自由贸易港高质量发展，离不开完备的法律法规规范的支撑。海南自由贸易港正在高效有序推进以《中华人民共和国海南自由贸易港法》（以下简称《海南自由贸易港法》）为基础的自由贸易港法规体系建设，将海南自由贸易港战略逐渐从"政策推动"转向"法治引领”，确保各项重大改革于法有据，推动自由贸易港建设行稳致远。[1]

《海南自由贸易港法》的颁布施行，以及一批海南自由贸易港法规的相继出台，为海南自由贸易港建设夯实了法治之基，让各项改革于法有据。《海南自由贸易港优化营商环境条例》从优化市场环境、政务环境、法治环境等方面作出规范，为打造一流营商环境提供了制度保障。《海南自由贸易港公平竞争条例》从国际合作、竞争政策等方面推进公平竞争制度集成创新，致力于建立海南自由贸易港统一开放、竞争有序的市场体系。《海南自由贸易港反消费欺诈规定》重点打击在旅游消费市场欺客、“宰客”等典型欺诈消费者的行为，加大惩戒力度，遵循过罚相当原则，分类分档设定处罚。二者在公平竞争和反消费欺诈领域属全国首创。《海南省多元化解纠纷条例》明确建立多元化国际商事纠纷解决机制，为投资者解决民商事纠纷提供便利基础。[2]

《海南省大数据开发应用条例》标志着海南在推进大数据开发应用和产业发展方面进入新阶段，为规范大数据开发应用，促进大数据产业发展，服务海南自贸区、自贸港建设具有十分重要的战略意义和现实意义。《海南自由贸易港社会信用条例》属于信用体系建设的基础性法规，以维护信用主体合法权益为宗旨，为社会信用信息的管理提供了制度性基础。《海南省反走私暂行条例》秉持“以防为主、打防结合、综合治理”原则，运用信息化手段创新走私货物物品监管机制，为海南构建既放得开又管得住的对外开放格局提供了法治保障。《海南自由贸易港消防条例》开创了自由贸易港专项消防立法先河，推动消防法治和体制机制深层次变革，是消防安全和自由贸易港融合发展的最新实践。

除上述基础性法规外，海南自由贸易港在园区建设、市场准入、投资贸易、海关港务、数据保护、商业信托、医疗养老、国际仲裁等方面有着诸多细化规定。《中国（海南）自由贸易试验区商事登记管理条例》《中国（海南）自由贸易试验区重点园区极简审批条例》在全国率先推行商事登记“全岛通办”和“全网通办”，改变传统分级属地登记模式，由海南省市场监督管理部门作为商事主体的登记机关进行统一登记，申请人通过电子化登记平台自主申报，登记平台自动审核商事登记申请信息，实现登记注册“办事不求人”和“一次都不用

〔1〕 参见《海南加快构建自由贸易港法律法规体系》，载《海南日报》2022年4月27日；参见李猛、孙鸽平：《探索构建中国自由贸易试验区与海南自由贸易港法治保障体系——以完善国家立法为主要视角》，《西北民族大学学报（哲学社会科学版）》2021年第4期，第92页。

〔2〕 参见管斌：《海南自由贸易港建设的金融法治创新——一个空间视角》，《经济法论丛》2021年第1卷，第116—119页。

跑”。[1]与上述两部条例配套的是《海南自由贸易港市场主体注销条例》，该条例进一步优化注销程序，尤其为个体工商户等市场主体退出减负。

此外，《海南自由贸易港科技开放创新若干规定》为打造“陆海空”科技创新高地出台多项措施，对于促进海南自由贸易港和国家开放创新具有重要意义。《海南自由贸易港博鳌乐城国际医疗旅游先行区条例》为建设世界一流的国际医疗旅游目的地和医疗科技创新平台，在产业政策、招商引资、医疗创新、旅游服务、跨境服务贸易等方面先行先试提供支撑。《海南自由贸易港安居房建设和管理若干规定》等一些管用的“民生小法”，着力解决人民群众关心的热点、难点问题。《海南经济特区禁止一次性不可降解塑料制品规定》将“禁塑”作为海南建设国家生态文明试验区的标志性工程和先导性项目之一，成为海南经济特区一张靓丽的名片。

“立出良法，调出优法，以法制促法治”。上述基础性法律法规和细则形成海南自由贸易港加快构筑起优良营商环境的“四梁八柱”。法治是最好的营商环境。公开透明、可预期的法治化环境，有利于各类市场主体放心投资、安心经营、专心创业，有助于吸引全世界投资者来海南投资兴业。[2]

总之，海南自由贸易港的法治建设和法治创新致力于创建我国开放程度最高、体制机制最新、政策措施最惠、营商环境更优、创新程度最强的法治建设新制度。[3]海南自由贸易港全面贯彻实施《海南自由贸易港法》，将充分运用自贸港法规制定权，紧贴自贸港建设急需，坚持立法创新，提升立法质量和效率，加快建设具有世界影响力的、法治的中国特色自由贸易港。[4]

二、海南自由贸易港法规体系的英译需求与意义

“一带一路”倡议自提出至今，对海南自由贸易港立法的外译提出了更高要求。只有切实做好法律外译，外国主体才能更明晰地了解和运用海南自由贸易港的法律制度、改革措施，才能将海南作为“新时代改革和法治双轮驱动、协同发展的新高地”“法治化自由贸易

[1] 参见邢东伟、张维炜：《海南人大：加快构建自由贸易港法律法规体系》，载中国人大网 2021 年 4 月 20 日，http://www.npc.gov.cn/npc/c30834/202104/f1124d668a7a45c89ac6b9c113875d4b.shtml。

[2] 参见金昌波：《海南加快构建自由贸易港法律法规体系》，载《海南日报》2022 年 5 月 7 日。

[3] 参见刘云亮：《中国特色自由贸易港法治创新研究》，《重庆理工大学学报（社会科学）》2021 年第 5 期，第 130 页。

[4] 参见邢东伟、翟小功：《运用自贸港法规制定权构建相关法规体系　海南自由贸易港法颁布实施一周年成果亮点纷呈》，载《法治日报》2022 年 6 月 22 日。

港的新典范”“新时代法治中国建设的新标杆”等形象向世界传播。[1]目前，相较于外国法的汉译，中国法的外译尚不成体系，翻译方法亦不甚科学。外译时不盲目效仿外国法术语、概念，重视中国法特色及其传递的话语，正是海南自由贸易港法规走向世界的关键。

海南自由贸易港立法的外译工作在很长一段时间内须依靠我们自身完成。一方面，外方因受意识形态、立场与法律汉语能力等因素限制，常对特色中国法术语、话语贯以外文固有表述方式或其他容易引发联想的翻译，折损其表达效果，不利于中国法话语的输出。另一方面，中国法须以独立、统一并体谅受众的方式呈现。在这一过程中还可通过比较中外制度差异，构建视野更开阔的话语体系。这都要求中国法主动对外翻译，实现自我表达，而非被塑造成“他者”。[2]

翻译作为一种跨文化的交流活动，受到政治、经济、文化等因素共同作用。[3]翻译活动从来都具有很强的目的性，涉及“为什么翻译”的根本问题。[4]美国注重向全球输出美国法，曾两次推出“法律与发展运动”（Law and Development Movement）。美国法律输出的前提是将美国法译成接收对象可以理解的语言，在第二次运动中，美国加大对法律翻译的投入。例如，1993 年，美国福特基金会资助翻译关于人权的各类规则、研究，向东南亚各国发送。[5]参与者梅里曼（John H. Merryman）提到，法律与发展运动的手段之一就是制定美国法，然后翻译成当地语言。[6]可见，美国开展的两轮法律与发展运动促使美国法在国际经济规范中取得主导地位，作为基础工作的法律翻译发挥了重要作用。

中国政府自 20 世纪初开始推动重大法律翻译实践工程。中国首次主动向西方国家全面展示中国法发生于一百余年前的“五四”运动前后，特别是为 1926 年法权会议（Commission on Extraterritoriality in China）开启了若干重要立法司法翻译工程，旨在废除治外法权，争取民族独立，向各国证明中国立法、司法已经“与各西国律例改同一律”，敦促其

〔1〕 参见刘云亮：《中国特色自由贸易港建设法治先行论》，《上海政法学院学报》2022 年第 2 期，第 81 页。

〔2〕 参见万立：《中国法的对外翻译——以欧盟法的翻译策略、实践及经验为镜鉴》，《外语与外语教学》2020 年第 6 期，第 23 页。

〔3〕 See Li Chen, *Chinese Law in Imperial Eyes: Sovereignty, Justice, and Transcultural Politics*, Columbia University Press, p. 87.

〔4〕 参见许钧：《从翻译出发：翻译与翻译研究》，复旦大学出版社 2014 年版，第 100、103 页。

〔5〕 See Carol Rose, “The ‘New’ Law and Development Movement in the Post-Cold War Era: A Vietnam Case Study,” *Law & Society Review*, No. 1, 1998, p. 119.

〔6〕 See John Henry Merryman, “Comparative Law and Social Change: On the Origins, Style, Decline & Revival of the Law and Development Movement,” *The American Journal of Comparative Law*, No. 3, 1977, p. 483.

履行废除治外法权的承诺。[1]百年沧海桑田，世界今非昔比，如今中国特色社会主义法律体系已经形成，中国特色社会主义法治体系正迈向新时代。

回顾历史，立足现实，展望未来。法律在世界范围传播、流动，是法律发展的规律之一。法律外译对海南自由贸易港法治本身及其形象的构建和传播等具有重要意义。它的外译既不能削足适履，完全“同化”于目标语场，亦不能特立独行，完全“外化”于目标语域。二者构成高效沟通的需求和表达概念的需求之间的持续张力，如何衡诸二者，是海南自由贸易港法规外译必须解决的问题。因此，它的外译需要以更科学的外译方法，使外方精准理解的同时，更完整地传递海南自由贸易港的法治内容和形象。

三、海南自由贸易港立法的英译原则

历史地看，立法文本的对外翻译活动，往往是应法律移植、对外投资、对外宣传与法治形象塑造、开展比较法研究以及进行诉讼或非诉讼法律服务等现实需求而启动。对于实践资源丰富的立法文本英译活动而言，研究者可以对其进行技术意义上的基础翻译研究。这里所指的技术意义上的立法文本英译，主要是中文立法文本的外译活动。但不管是外文立法的汉译，还是中文立法的外译，都面临一个不借助译入语便无法表达，然而借助译入语又未必能准确表达的困境。技术意义上的立法翻译者在面临类似问题时，必然要寻求解决问题的有效且实用途径。

我国立法文本的英译应该是以原文为中心（即以我为主）的翻译行为。立法文本的翻译不能以译文为中心，即使是以法律移植为目的的立法文本翻译，即专门为了满足完善译入国立法需求的翻译行为，也不例外。立法文本的翻译须高度忠实于原文本，无论是译入语文本中的字、词（含实词和虚词）、短语、句子、段落还是篇章，均须在内容和形式方面全面忠实于原文。“忠实”主要借助技术意义上的立法文本英译活动实现，技术意义上的立法文本英译研究因而同样重要，也是法律翻译研究的重点。技术意义上的立法翻译活动所形成的翻译文本，往往就成为跨语际立法和司法的研究对象。[2]

中文立法文本英译宜遵守对等律（law of equivalence）、同一律（law of identity）和等效律（law of equal authenticity）三大翻译原则，形成一个有机原则体系。在这一原则体系中，

---

〔1〕 参见屈文生、万立：《“五四”时期的法律外译及其意义》，《外国语》2019年第5期，第98—100页。

〔2〕 参见屈文生：《中国立法文本对外翻译的原则体系——以民法英译实践为中心》，《中国外语》2022年第1期，第11页。

对等律和同一律是立法文本英译的基本原则，等效律是终极目标和最高原则。

法律翻译中的对等律也称等值和最切近的自然对等（the closest natural equivalence），包含文本类型对等（equivalence of text types）、语义对等（semantic equivalence）和形式对等（formal equivalence）三项次级原则（secondary principles）。

同一律概念可以理解为同一意义原则，即 principle of identity。所谓“同一”（identity），既非指“一致”也非指“关联”（correlation）。

等效律是指效力相等原则（the principle of equal authenticity）。所谓“等效”（equal authenticity），是源语立法文本和译本具有同等的法律效力（equal legal effect）——原文本和译本产生一致效果。

立法文本分为宪法、法律、行政法规、地方性法规、自治条例、单行条例、规章及规范性文件等主要类型，因此在翻译不同类型的立法文本时，要选择英美法上可以表述相同立法文本类型的专业术语。海南自由贸易港法规的翻译，宜在上述三大原则指引下开展，并依据立法语境及目的并兼顾所处的法律体系，做出恰当的翻译，从而将法治海南自由贸易港法规的内容更准确、有效地向外传播，并为法治海南自由贸易港的法治形象的构建提供基础。对等律和同一律是法律翻译主要适用的原则，而等效律主要针对双语或多语立法国家的立法文本，在一些关键法律术语的翻译上也可能需要采用这一原则。[1]

法律法规翻译受对等律指引，意味着译者需将立法文本中大量具有鲜明格式性特征的立法常用字或单词、词语、短语、句子、段落乃至篇章与译入语进行对等。这一点在法律法规名称，国家机关、机构、单位名称的翻译上有显著体现，对于这些专有名称，要寻找真正对等的而非看似对等的译名。

比如，《海南自由贸易港法》译成 Law/Act on Hainan Free Trade Port，《中国（海南）自由贸易试验区商事登记管理条例》译成 Regulations of China (Hainan) Pilot Free Trade Zone on the Administration of Commercial Registration，《海南经济特区道路旅游客运管理若干规定》译成 Rules of Hainan Special Economic Zone on the Administration of Road Passenger Transport。

上述“法”“条例”“规定”由高到低属于不同层级的立法：“法”一般由全国人民代表大

〔1〕 参见屈文生：《“一带一路”国家立法文本的翻译——国家需求、文本选择与等效原则》，《外语与外语教学》2020 年第 6 期，第 7—8 页。

会或其常务委员会颁布，而 law/act 在英美法上也表示国会或议会颁布的法律，与“法”成立对等关系；条例一般是国务院或地方人民代表大会或其常务委员会颁布的行政法规或地方性法规，而 regulations 在英美法上主要也是由中央政府或地方立法机关颁布；规定与条例的颁布部分主体一致，包括国务院的职能部门或地方政府，因而与英美法上的 rules 比较对等。

比如，《海南省大数据开发应用条例》所称“大数据管理机构”可能被译成 big data management institution，但这并不是最为对等的翻译。首先，management 更多是指具体的管理、经营、运营，而 administration 则更多是指政府部门的管理。其次，institution 的含义非常广泛，大多是指社会机构或研究所，而 office 更能表示大数据管理机构中的“机构”。《海南省大数据开发应用条例》将大数据管理机构定义为“不以营利为目的、履行相应行政管理和公共服务职责的法定机构”，换言之，它是以服务为目的具有公共职能的机构，而常用来表示政府内设部门的 office 可以很好地对应这一点。

此外，商事主体登记平台、行政审批信息管理平台、企业信用信息公示系统等不属于行政机构，是公共服务的载体，它们的翻译也需要符合对等原则，不可轻易简化。上述三例宜分别译成 market entity registration platform，administrative review management platform，以及 enterprise credit information publicity system。

立法语言中既有专业术语，又有通俗词语；既有意义准确的词语，也有意义模糊的用语。因而，立法语言翻译有四大策略，即专业对专业（术语对术语）、通俗对通俗、准确对准确、模糊对模糊。关于准确对准确，切不可误将法律术语视作通俗语来加以翻译。比如，在海南自由贸易港立法中，滥用职权、玩忽职守、徇私舞弊是高频出现的法律术语，但在日常生活中也有使用。三者比较准确的译法分别是 abuse of position，dereliction of duty，playing favoritism and committing irregularities。其中，徇私舞弊容易被译成 nepotism，但这种表述是指任人唯亲，范围小于徇私舞弊，因为徇私舞弊是指国家工作人员利用职务便利和权力实施违法行为。

在《海南自由贸易港市场主体注销条例》等海南自由贸易港立法中，“依职权”多次出现，可能常常被译作 on its own initiative 或 by virtue of an office/ex officio，但二者都不对等于中文立法中的“依职权”，即行政主体直接依法律、法规、规章规定的行政职权，而无需以行政相对人先行申请作为启动条件实施的行政处理。by virtue of an office/ex officio 主要指当一个团体（比如董事会、委员会）的成员由于担任另一个职务而当然地成为该团体的成员，即由于担任一个职务而依职权担任另一职务，因而并不完全对应中国法上的依职权。

在翻译过程中，我们发现拉丁语 motu proprio 是依职权的等效译名。该词原指教皇自行签署而非盖印颁布的文件，今指非经正式申请而采取的职务行为。因此，motu proprio 是依职权的对等译名。

法律法规翻译的最高目标是实现效力等值，所有经过作准认证或通过立法程序审议的平行文本具有同等法律效力。就英汉这一语对而言，中国香港特区是世界上唯一以中英双语立法的地区，中国香港特区双语立法和翻译的最大特点就是中英两个文本具有同等法律意义和法律效力，因为译文本身就是法律。对于立法文本翻译而言，这是最高要求，是终极目标和最高原则。海南自由贸易港法规英译本，并非官本，并不具有同等法律效力，但翻译时仍可将其作为最高原则去尽力遵守。[1]英译海南自由贸易港的主要立法文本，旨在满足外国日益增长的对法律文本的获取需求，拆除语言障碍，助力中国海南与各国的法律沟通合作，降低中外法律冲突环节的交涉成本，提高对外合作效率。

海南自由贸易港制度是贸易自由便利、投资自由便利、财政税收制度等一整套制度集成创新，而法治是这一创新的基础。以《海南自由贸易港法》为基础，以各项法规、规章及政策为展开的海南自由贸易港法规体系是这一创新的重要保障，而这一法治体系的对外翻译可以促进世界了解海南法治化、国际化、便利化的营商环境和公平统一高效的市场环境，了解有中国特色的世界一流自由贸易港，并促使海南自由贸易港法规体系树立良好的国际形象，与新加坡、迪拜等自由贸易港形成双向互动。

我们不仅要将新加坡、迪拜等世界顶级自由贸易港的主要立法文本译成中文，以供海南自由贸易港法规体系建设借鉴，还要将海南自由贸易港法规体系翻译出去，以供世界各国了解海南自由贸易港是法治的自由贸易港，有着逐渐完善的法律法规体系保障的一流营商环境，也能服务于讲好海南故事，彰显海南乃至中国的法治形象。

事实上，要建设有世界影响力的中国特色海南自由贸易港，法律对话交流至关重要，但中国法律规范体系的外译不同于文学、科学、外交外译。立法文本是法律概念、法律制度、法律文化及法律方法的载体，反映国家治理理念、体系、模式，彰显中国法治的新理解和新

[1] 参见屈文生：《“一带一路”国家立法文本的翻译——国家需求、文本选择与等效原则》，《外语与外语教学》2020 年第 6 期，第 8 页。

实践，而其英译质量的高低关乎中国法治自我表达的效果、参与国际事务的自我表达、中国法治话语权的提升等重要问题。

随着“一带一路”倡议、人类命运共同体构建等的深入展开，要求以更开放的姿态对外传递中国法治话语。如何做到法律翻译和法治话语不被异化或边缘化，便成为中文立法文本英译要考虑的核心问题。从这个意义上讲，立法文本的翻译又不只是技术意义上的翻译问题，我们须将其视作一种法治话语传播和法治话语实践加以考察。不夸张、不菲薄、不盲从、不迎合、以我为主等五项原则，可以成为中国法律话语对外翻译的基本原则。[1]

2023 年 2 月，中共中央办公厅、国务院办公厅印发《关于加强新时代法学教育和法学理论研究的意见》，要求“加强与共建‘一带一路’国家法治学术交流合作。完善外国法查明机制，推进世界主要国家法律法规数据库建设，注意组织搜集筛选、翻译国外法律信息资料，加强世界法学名著的汉译工作和中国法学优秀成果的外译工作”。海南自由贸易港法规的外译不仅有助于呈现海南自由贸易港法治化、国际化、便利化和公平、透明、可预期的营商环境，使外国主体把握海南自由贸易港的制度集成创新、市场体系建设、优化政务服务、便利贸易投资、优化法治环境等一系列政策措施，还有助于讲好海南自由贸易港的法治故事，提升中国特色社会主义法治体系和法治理论的国际影响力和话语权。

国家社会科学基金重大项目“‘一带一路’沿线
国家法律文本翻译、研究及数据库建设”课题组
2023 年 6 月 2 日于上海

〔1〕 参见屈文生：《中国立法文本对外翻译的原则体系——以民法英译实践为中心》，《中国外语》2022 年第 1 期，第 18 页。

目　录

海南自由贸易港公平竞争条例

Regulations of Hainan Free Trade Port on Fair Competition

海南自由贸易港公平竞争条例

（2021 年 9 月 29 日海南省第六届人民代表大会常务委员会
第三十次会议通过）

第一章　总　则

第一条　为了加快建设高水平海南自由贸易港，促进和保护公平竞争，保障经营者和消费者的合法权益，根据《中华人民共和国海南自由贸易港法》《中华人民共和国反不正当竞争法》《中华人民共和国反垄断法》等法律法规，结合海南自由贸易港实际，制定本条例。

第二条　海南自由贸易港借鉴国际通行规则完善公平竞争制度，强化竞争政策的基础性地位，依法平等保护各类市场主体的合法权益，建设统一开放、竞争有序的市场体系。

第三条　海南自由贸易港保障经营者依法公平参与市场竞争，扩大经营规模，提高市场竞争力。

经营者在生产经营活动中应当遵守法律、法规和商业道德，遵循诚实守信、公平竞争原则，履行安全、质量、劳动者权益保护、消费者权益保护、生态环境保护等方面的法定义务，在国际经贸活动中遵循国际通行规则。

第四条　县级以上人民政府市场监督管理部门依据职责负责本行政区域内的公平竞争监督管理工作，查处影响公平竞争的行为，对经营者依法依规开展商业竞争进行事前指引，开展公平竞争宣传。

县级以上人民政府发展改革、商务等有关主管部门依据职责做好公平竞争监督管理的相关工作。

Regulations of Hainan Free Trade Port on Fair Competition

(Adopted at the 30th Session of the Standing Committee of the 6th Hainan Provincial People's Congress on September 29, 2021)

Chapter I General Provisions

Article 1 These Regulations are enacted pursuant to the Hainan Free Trade Port Law of the People's Republic of China, Anti-Unfair Competition Law of the People's Republic of China, Anti-Monopoly Law of the People's Republic of China, and other applicable laws and regulations, and based on the actual circumstances of Hainan Free Trade Port to expedite the development of a high-end Hainan Free Trade Port, improving and protecting fair competition, and protecting the legal rights of business operators and consumers alike.

Article 2 The Hainan Free Trade Port shall improve fair competition by drawing on internationally accepted rules, improving the basic fundamental status of competition policy, protecting legal rights for all kinds of market entities equally pursuant to law, and developing a standardized and orderly competitive open market system.

Article 3 The Hainan Free Trade Port shall guarantee business operators lawful and fair participation in market competition, expansion of business scale and improved market competitiveness in accordance with the law.

Business operators shall abide by laws, regulations, and business ethics, follow the principles of honesty, trustworthiness, and fair competition, fulfill safety, quality, employee and consumer rights protection statutory obligations, and ecological environment protection, and abide by international trade practices when conducting business internationally.

Article 4 The market regulation agency of the people's government at or above the county level shall be responsible for fair competition oversight and administration within their respective administrative areas, investigate and penalize acts that impair fair competition, provide *ex ante* guidance on commercial competition for operators pursuant to law, and conduct fair competition awareness to the extent of their duties.

The development and reform, commerce, and other people's government agencies at or above the county level shall effectively conduct fair competition oversight and administration work subject to their duties.

第五条　县级以上人民政府建立公平竞争议事协调机制，负责下列事项：

（一）制定和发布对推进公平竞争政策实施和公平竞争审查工作产生重大影响的规划、计划、制度、办法及其他文件等；

（二）加强竞争政策实施的统筹协调、指导推进工作，组织对涉及市场主体经济活动的重大政策措施进行会审；

（三）统筹、协调、监督、指导有关部门和单位开展公平竞争审查工作；

（四）组织、指挥、监督有关部门和单位开展影响公平竞争治理的联合执法和专项执法，协调、督促查处跨地区或者跨部门的重大、复杂案件；

（五）组织开展公平竞争治理信息化建设，提高公平竞争治理工作智能化水平；

（六）组织调查、评估市场总体竞争状况，组织宣传有关公平竞争的法律法规和政策措施，做好讲解答疑工作，回应社会关切；

（七）政府交办的其他涉及公平竞争的事项。

第六条　海南自由贸易港应当建立健全公平竞争社会共治机制，培育公平竞争文化，鼓励、引导经营者建立竞争合规制度。

行业协会等经营者组织应当加强行业自律，开展对经营者的竞争政策宣传、指导、培训等，引导、规范经营者依法竞争，维护市场公平竞争秩序；消费者组织应当努力提升消费者维权意识和维权能力，加强对影响公平竞争行为的社会监督。

第七条　县级以上人民政府应当推动运用互联网、大数据、区块链等

Article 5 The people's government at or above the county level shall establish a fair competition deliberation and coordination institution which shall be responsible for the following matters:

(a) preparing and issuing plans, schemes, rules, methods, and other documents that significantly impact the implementation of fair competition policies and reviews;

(b) improving the overall coordination, guidance, and optimization of competition policy implementation, and organizing joint reviews of major policies and actions concerning economic activities of market entities;

(c) integrating, coordinating, overseeing, and guiding the appropriate agencies and organizations to conduct fair competition reviews;

(d) organizing, directing, and overseeing the appropriate agencies and organizations to conduct joint and specific law enforcement against activities that affect fair competition governance, and coordinating and encouraging the investigation and resolution of major and complicated cases across areas or agencies;

(e) organizing the information system development for fair competition governance to improve smart fair competition governance;

(f) organizing the investigation and evaluation of overall market competition, organizing the publicity of fair competition laws, regulations, and policies to explain and answer questions and respond to public concerns; and

(g) other fair competition work as assigned by the government.

Article 6 The Hainan Free Trade Port shall establish and improve the fair competition social co-governance system, develop a fair competition culture, and encourage and guide business operators to establish competition compliance programs.

Industry associations and other business operator organizations shall improve self-discipline, announce competition policies, guide and train business operators, guide and standardize lawful competition among business operators, and maintain the market fair competition order. Consumer organizations shall strive to improve their awareness and capacity to defend their rights and improve social oversight over actions that may impair fair competition.

Article 7 The people's government at or above the county level shall encourage the use of modern information technologies such as the Internet, big data, and blockchain to implement

现代信息技术进行智能化监管，认定竞争违法行为、预警识别影响公平竞争的市场运行风险，提升监管效能，预防和制止不正当竞争行为和垄断行为。

第八条 县级以上人民政府应当推动与国内其他地区在公平竞争领域的工作协作，实现联动执法、信息共享。

第九条 海南自由贸易港应当在制定竞争政策、执法协同、交流培训、宣传教育、竞争文化促进等方面加强公平竞争国际合作。

第十条 县级以上人民政府及有关部门应当建立健全影响公平竞争行为的举报制度和举报人奖励、保护制度，畅通举报通道，鼓励、支持和保护一切单位和个人依法对影响公平竞争的行为进行社会监督。

国家机关及其工作人员不得支持、包庇影响公平竞争的行为。

第二章 公平竞争政策

第十一条 县级以上人民政府及有关部门在制定与市场主体经济活动密切相关的政策措施时，应当尊重市场经济规律，最大限度减少政府对市场资源的直接配置，最大限度减少政府对市场活动的直接干预，促进商品和要素自由便利流动，充分发挥市场在资源配置中的决定性作用。

第十二条 县级以上人民政府及有关部门应当推动产业政策向普惠化和功能性转型，强化对技术创新和结构升级的支持，加强产业政策和竞争政策协同。

县级以上人民政府及有关部门在制定具体的产业政策时，应当坚持以

smart oversight, identify acts of illegal competition, identify and warn of market operation risks that may affect fair competition, improve oversight efficiency, and prevent and curb unfair competition and monopolies.

Article 8 The people's government at or above the county level shall encourage fair competition and collaboration with other Chinese regions to achieve joint law enforcement and information sharing.

Article 9 The Hainan Free Trade Port shall improve international collaboration for fair competition policy creation, law enforcement coordination, communication and training, education and awareness, and competition culture improvement.

Article 10 The people's government at or above the county level and the appropriate agencies shall establish and improve the reporting system and the incentive and protection systems for whistleblowers, clear the reporting channels, and encourage, support, and protect all entities and individuals to lawfully conduct social oversight on acts that impair fair competition.

Government agencies and their employees shall not support or cover up acts that may impair fair competition.

Chapter II Fair Competition Policies

Article 11 When issuing policies and actions closely related to economic activities of market entities, the people's government at or above the county level and appropriate agencies shall respect the market economy rules, minimize the direct allocation of market resources, and direct intervention in market activities by the government, encourage the free and unrestricted flow of merchandise and factors, and take full advantage of the market's decisive role in resource allocation.

Article 12 The people's government at or above the county level and appropriate agencies shall encourage the transformation of industrial policies to generalization and functionality, improve the support for technological innovation and structural upgrades, and optimize coordination between industrial and competition policies.

The people's government at or above the county level and appropriate agencies should abide by the competition policies as the basis when issuing industrial policies, coordinate industrial

竞争政策为基础，统筹协调产业政策和其他经济政策，充分发挥各类政策在推动经济高质量发展中的相互促进作用，增强产业竞争力，集聚全球优质生产要素。

第十三条 政府及有关部门应当依法平等对待各类市场主体，保障各类市场主体在准入许可、经营运营、要素获取、标准制定、优惠政策等方面享受平等待遇。

没有法律、法规或者国务院决定和命令依据的，政府及有关部门不得制定减损市场主体合法权益或者增加其义务的政策措施；政府及有关部门不得滥用行政权力，制定含有排除、限制竞争内容的政策措施。

第十四条 县级以上人民政府及有关部门推进自然垄断行业改革，开放竞争性业务，加快竞争性环节市场化，加强自然垄断行业和垄断环节监管。

第十五条 海南自由贸易港实行放宽市场准入特别清单（特别措施）、外商投资准入负面清单等管理制度。负面清单以外的领域，各类市场主体均可以依法平等进入、公平竞争。

海南自由贸易港实行跨境服务贸易负面清单管理制度。负面清单以外的领域，境内外服务提供者依法平等参与市场竞争。

第十六条 海南自由贸易港支持数字经济依法创新健康发展，对平台经济、共享经济等新业态领域不正当竞争行为和垄断行为进行规范治理，保护市场公平竞争。

第三章 公平竞争审查

第十七条 行政机关以及法律、法规授权的具有管理公共事务职能的

policies, and other economic policies together, and take full advantage of the mutual improvement of different high-end economic development policies, optimize industrial competitiveness, and gather global high-quality production factors.

Article 13 The government and appropriate agencies shall treat different market entities equally pursuant to law and ensure that different market entities enjoy equal treatment in access permissions, business operations, factor acquisition, standards issuance, and preferential policies.

The government and appropriate agencies shall not issue policies and actions that may infringe upon market entities' legal rights or increase their obligations without basing such on laws, regulations, or State Council decisions and orders. Such government and appropriate agencies shall not abuse their administrative powers to issue policies and actions that exclude or restrict competition.

Article 14 The people's government at or above the county level and appropriate agencies shall encourage the reform of natural monopoly industries, open up businesses for competition, expedite the commercialization of areas open to competition, and improve the oversight of natural monopoly industries and monopolized portions.

Article 15 The Hainan Free Trade Port shall implement a specific list to ease market access (special actions) and the Foreign Investment Negative List. All market entities may enter and compete equally in all sectors other than those specified in the Negative List pursuant to law.

The Hainan Free Trade Port shall implement a negative list management system for cross-border service transactions. Domestic and foreign service providers may participate and compete equally in all sectors other than those provided by the negative list pursuant to law.

Article 16 The Hainan Free Trade Port shall support the lawful, innovative, and sound development of the digital economy, regulate unfair competition and monopolies in new business areas such as platform and shared economies, and protect fair competition in the market.

Chapter III Fair Competition Review

Article 17 The administrative agencies and organizations authorized to manage public

组织，在起草市场准入和退出、产业发展、招商引资、招标投标、政府采购、经营行为规范、资质标准等涉及市场主体经济活动的地方性法规、政府规章、行政规范性文件、其他政策性文件以及“一事一议”形式的具体政策措施时，应当体现和贯彻公平竞争原则，按照国家和本省的有关规定进行公平竞争审查，并形成书面审查结论。

涉及市场主体经济活动的地方性法规、政府规章和以政府名义印发的行政规范性文件草案，未经公平竞争审查的，不得提交政府审议；在提交政府审议前还应当向同级市场监督管理部门征求公平竞争审查意见。

第十八条 涉及市场主体经济活动的地方性法规、政府规章、行政规范性文件、其他政策性文件以及“一事一议”形式的具体政策措施实施后，制定机关或者实施机关应当依照有关规定对其影响统一市场和公平竞争的情况进行评估。经评估认为妨碍统一市场和公平竞争的，应当及时废止或者修改。

第十九条 政府及有关部门在开展公平竞争审查工作中，可以依照有关规定引入第三方评估。

第二十条 县级以上人民政府应当将公平竞争审查工作纳入营商环境、法治政府等考核评价体系。

县级以上人民政府应当建立政策措施抽查机制，重点抽查市场主体反映比较强烈、问题比较集中、滥用行政权力排除限制竞争行为多发的行业和地区的政策措施，抽查结果依法适时向社会公布。对抽查发现的排除、限制竞争问题，被抽查单位应当及时整改；未及时整改或者未达到整改要求的，依照有关规定处理。

affairs pursuant to law shall implement the principle of fair competition and conduct fair competition reviews pursuant to provisions of the state and this Province when drafting local regulations, government rules, regulatory standards, other policy documents, and specific policies and ad hoc actions involving market access and withdrawal, industrial development, investment attraction, bidding, government procurement, business practice standards, qualification standards, and other economic activities of market entities.

Local regulations, government rules, and draft administrative normative documents concerning economic activities issued on behalf of the government shall not be submitted to the government for deliberation without a fair competition review. A fair competition review from the administration for market regulation at the same level must also be obtained before such regulations, rules, or regulatory standard drafts are submitted for deliberation.

Article 18 The issuing or implementing agency shall evaluate their influence on the standardized market and fair competition pursuant to law after the implementation of local regulations, government rules, regulatory standards, other policy documents, and specific policies, or ad hoc actions relating to economic activities of market entities. Any such regulations, government rules, regulatory standards, other policy documents, specific policies, or ad hoc actions deemed to impair the market regularization and fair competition by the evaluation shall be promptly revoked or revised.

Article 19 The government and the appropriate agency may introduce a third party evaluation in accordance with applicable law when conducting a fair competition review.

Article 20 The people's government at or above the county level shall include a fair competition review when assessing and evaluating the business environment, law-based governance, and other systems.

The people's government at or above the county level shall implement an internal review plan for policies and actions, focus on policies and actions for industries and sectors which often receive complaints, have extensive problems, or abuse administrative authority to preclude or restrict competition from market entities. The results of the internal review shall be publicly announced in due course pursuant to law. Any entity found to exclude or restrict competition in the internal reviews shall promptly make the appropriate corrections, and those who fail to promptly make such corrections or fail to meet correction requirements shall be penalized pursuant to law.

第四章　影响公平竞争的行为

第二十一条　禁止经营者实施下列法律法规规定的扰乱市场竞争秩序，损害其他经营者或者消费者合法权益的不正当竞争行为：

（一）实施混淆行为，引人误认为是他人商品、服务或者与他人存在特定联系；

（二）采用财物或者其他手段贿赂以谋取交易机会或者竞争优势；

（三）直接或者帮助其他经营者对商品、服务作虚假或者引人误解的商业宣传，欺骗、误导消费者；

（四）侵犯商业秘密；

（五）从事违法有奖销售；

（六）编造、传播虚假信息或者误导性信息，损害竞争对手的商业信誉、商品声誉；

（七）利用技术手段，通过影响用户选择或者其他方式，妨碍、破坏其他经营者合法提供的网络产品或者服务正常运行；

（八）其他扰乱市场竞争秩序，损害其他经营者或者消费者合法权益的不正当竞争行为。

第二十二条　禁止经营者从事下列法律规定的垄断行为：

（一）具有竞争关系的经营者达成垄断协议或者经营者与交易相对人达成垄断协议，行业协会组织本行业的经营者达成垄断协议；

（二）具有市场支配地位的经营者从事滥用市场支配地位的行为；

（三）实施违反法律规定的具有或者可能具有排除、限制竞争效果的

Chapter IV Acts Impairing Fair Competition

Article 21 Business operators shall be prohibited from committing any of the following acts that disturb the order of market competition and infringe upon the rights of other operators or consumers as provided by laws and regulations:

(a) committing acts that mislead others to believe that they offer the products or services provided by another business operator or have a particular connection with another operator;

(b) seeking transaction opportunities or competitive advantages through bribery or other means;

(c) directly or indirectly assisting other business operators to create false or misleading commercial advertising materials for goods and services to deceive and misinform consumers;

(d) infringing upon trade secrets;

(e) engaging in illegal sales promotions;

(f) creating and sharing false or misleading information that damages competitor business or product reputation;

(g) using technical means or other means to influence user choices to impair or stop the regular operation of networked products or services legally provided by other operators; or

(h) committing other acts that disrupt the market competition order and infringe upon the rights of other operators or consumers.

Article 22 Business operators shall be prohibited from engaging in any of the following monopolistic practices as provided by law:

(a) entering into monopoly agreements with competing business operators or transaction counterparties, or the industry association coordinates the operators in the same industry to enter into monopoly agreements;

(b) abusing the business operator's dominant market position;

(c) implementing the specific actions that may illegally exclude, restrict, or may exclude or restrict competition; or

经营者集中；

（四）法律规定禁止经营者从事的其他垄断行为。

第二十三条 行政机关和法律、法规授权的具有管理公共事务职能的组织不得滥用行政权力实施下列排除、限制竞争行为：

（一）限定或者变相限定单位或者个人经营、购买、使用其指定的经营者提供的商品或者服务；

（二）妨碍商品或者服务在地区之间的自由流通；

（三）排斥或者限制经营者参加招标投标、土地使用权出让、工程建设、房地产开发、金融信贷、物资采购等经济活动；排斥或者限制外地经营者在本地投资或者设立分支机构；

（四）强制或者变相强制经营者从事法律规定的垄断行为；

（五）制定、发布含有排除、限制竞争内容的涉及市场主体经济活动的政府规章、行政规范性文件、其他政策性文件以及“一事一议”形式的具体政策措施；

（六）其他滥用行政权力排除、限制竞争行为。

第五章 对影响公平竞争行为的调查

第二十四条 县级以上人民政府市场监督管理部门及有关主管部门应当严格按照法律法规和部门职责规定，落实监管责任，对涉嫌影响公平竞争的行为进行调查。

举报影响公平竞争的行为，采用书面形式并提供相关事实和证据的，县级以上人民政府市场监督管理部门及有关主管部门应当依法及时处理。

(d) committing other monopolistic acts provided by law.

Article 23 The administrative agencies and organizations authorized by laws and regulations to manage public matters shall not abuse their administrative power to exclude or restrict competition as follows:

(a) explicitly or implicitly require entities or individuals to operate, purchase, or use products or services provided by designated operators;

(b) hindering the free, inter-regional circulation of products or services;

(c) excluding or restricting business operators from participating in bidding, land use rights grants, construction projects, real estate development, financing, procurement, and other economic activities; excluding or restricting foreign business operators from investing or setting up local offices;

(d) explicitly or implicitly forcing operators to engage in monopolistic acts provided by law;

(e) issuing and publishing government rules, regulatory standards, other policy documents, and specific policies and ad hoc actions involving economic activities of market entities and excluding and restricting competition; or

(f) other acts involving the abuse of administrative power to exclude or restrict competition.

Chapter V Investigating Acts Infringing Upon Fair Competition

Article 24 The market regulation agency of the people's government at or above the county level and the appropriate agencies shall abide by laws and regulations and agency responsibilities when performing their oversight responsibilities and investigating acts suspected of impairing fair competition.

The market regulation agency of the people's government at or above the county level and the appropriate agencies shall promptly resolve any reports of acts suspected of impairing fair competition made in writing and supported by appropriate documentation and information.

第二十五条 单位和个人认为政府规章、行政规范性文件、其他政策性文件以及“一事一议”形式的具体政策措施未进行公平竞争审查或者违反审查标准出台的，可以向制定机关反映，也可以向备案审查机关提出审查要求或者审查建议，或者向制定机关的上级机关、市场监督管理部门举报，有关部门应当及时处理。核实存在未进行公平竞争审查或者违反审查标准出台政策措施行为的，制定机关应当及时进行整改，并依法向社会公开。涉嫌违反《中华人民共和国反垄断法》的，由反垄断执法机构依法调查。

单位和个人认为地方性法规违反公平竞争原则的，可以依法向备案审查机关提出审查要求或者审查建议。

第二十六条 县级以上人民政府市场监督管理部门及有关主管部门在调查过程中，应当保障被调查的经营者、利害关系人的陈述权和申辩权，并在法律法规规定的时限内完成调查；法律法规没有规定调查时限的，调查应当在合理期限内完成。

县级以上人民政府市场监督管理部门及有关主管部门在调查过程中，可以采取约谈被调查的经营者等方式，依法进行告诫并提出整改要求。

第二十七条 县级以上人民政府市场监督管理部门及有关主管部门调查涉嫌影响公平竞争的行为，可以依照有关规定采取下列措施：

（一）进入涉嫌影响公平竞争行为的经营场所进行检查；

（二）询问被调查的经营者、利害关系人及其他有关单位、个人，要求其说明有关情况或者提供与被调查行为有关的其他资料；

（三）查询、复制与涉嫌影响公平竞争行为有关的协议、账簿、单据、文件、记录、业务函电和其他资料；

Article 25 Entities or individuals deeming government rules, regulatory standards, administrative normative documents, other policy documents, and specific ad hoc policies or actions issued have not gone through fair competition review or violate the review standards may submit a report to the issuing agency, request review, or offer review recommendations to the filing and review agency, or report to a higher level of the issuing agency and the market regulation agency. The appropriate agencies shall promptly manage such and the issuing agency shall promptly correct and announce such pursuant to law if the appropriate agencies confirm that the issuance of such have not gone through fair competition review or violate the review standards. Anyone suspected of violating the Anti-Monopoly Law of the People's Republic of China shall be investigated by anti-monopoly law enforcement agencies pursuant to law.

Where the entities or individuals believe that local regulations violate the principle of fair competition, they may request review or offer review recommendations to the filing and review agency pursuant to law.

Article 26 The market regulation agency of the people's government at or above the county level and the appropriate agencies shall, ensure the investigated operators' and stakeholders' rights to representation and defense during the investigation, and complete the investigation within the time limit provided by laws and regulations; the investigation shall be completed within a reasonable time limit where the law does not provide a time limit for the investigation.

The market regulation agency of the people's government at or above the county level and the appropriate agencies may issue warnings to the operators and recommend corrections during the investigation through interviews and other methods pursuant to law.

Article 27 The market regulation agency of the people's government at or above the county level and the appropriate agencies may take the following actions in accordance with the regulations when investigating acts suspected of impeding fair competition:

(a) entering and inspecting the premises of the business suspected of impairing fair competition;

(b) questioning the operators, stakeholders, and other entities and individuals, and requiring them to provide information or other materials related to the acts being investigated;

(c) inquiring about and copying agreements, account books, bills, documents, records, business correspondence, and other materials related to the acts suspected of impairing fair competition;

（四）查封、扣押与涉嫌影响公平竞争行为有关的财物；

（五）查询涉嫌影响公平竞争行为的经营者的银行账户；

（六）法律、法规规定的其他措施。

第二十八条 县级以上人民政府市场监督管理部门及有关主管部门对涉嫌影响公平竞争行为的调查，确需公安机关协助的，公安机关应当依法予以配合。

调查涉嫌影响公平竞争的行为，被调查的经营者、利害关系人及其他有关单位、个人不得拒绝、阻碍执法机构的调查。

第二十九条 监察机关、人民法院、人民检察院、行政执法机关在办理案件过程中，发现涉嫌影响公平竞争行为线索的，可以将线索移交县级以上人民政府市场监督管理部门及有关主管部门。县级以上人民政府市场监督管理部门及有关主管部门应当依法处理。

第六章 法律责任

第三十条 行政机关和法律、法规授权的具有管理公共事务职能的组织及其工作人员在公平竞争监督管理工作中滥用职权、玩忽职守、徇私舞弊的，依法给予处分；构成犯罪的，依法追究刑事责任。

第三十一条 行政机关和法律、法规授权的具有管理公共事务职能的组织滥用行政权力，实施排除、限制竞争行为的，由上级机关责令改正，并对直接负责的主管人员和其他直接责任人员依法给予处分。

县级以上人民政府市场监督管理部门可以向有关上级机关提出依法处理的建议。

(d) seizing or confiscating assets related to acts suspected of impairing fair competition;

(e) inquiring about the bank accounts of operators suspected of impairing fair competition; or

(f) other actions provided by laws and regulations.

Article 28 Where the market regulation agency of the people's government at or above the county level and the appropriate agencies require assistance from public security agencies when investigating acts suspected of impairing fair competition, the public security agency shall cooperate pursuant to law.

Where the acts suspected of impairing fair competition are under investigation, the business operators, stakeholders, and other entities and individuals shall not refuse or impede the law enforcement agencies in their investigation.

Article 29 Where the supervisor commission, people's courts, people's procuratorates, and administrative law enforcement agencies find evidence of acts suspected of impairing fair competition when managing cases, they may hand over such evidence to the market regulation agency of the people's government at or above the county level and the appropriate agencies. The market regulation agency of the people's government at or above the county level and the appropriate agencies shall manage such pursuant to law.

Chapter VI Legal Liability

Article 30 Any administrative agencies or organizations authorized by laws and regulations to manage public affairs or their employees who abuse of position, commit dereliction of duty, or play favoritism and commit irregularities in the oversight and administration of fair competition shall be penalized pursuant to law. Those committing crimes shall be held criminally liable pursuant to law.

Article 31 Administrative agencies or organizations authorized by laws and regulations to administrate public affairs abuse their administrative power and commit acts that exclude or restrict competition shall be ordered to make corrections by their higher-level agencies, and the person directly in charge and other directly liable employees shall be penalized pursuant to law.

The market regulation agency of the people's government at or above the county level may submit penalty recommendations to the appropriate higher-level agency pursuant to law.

第三十二条 对于破坏竞争秩序、损害消费者合法权益的行为，消费者可以依法举报或者提起诉讼。

影响公平竞争的行为侵害众多消费者合法权益的，法律规定的机关和有关组织可以依法向人民法院提起公益诉讼，各级市场监督管理部门依法给予支持。

第三十三条 有本条例规定的违法行为的，依照有关规定纳入公共信用信息，依法予以公示；对严重失信企业和个人，由有关部门依照有关规定予以惩戒。

第三十四条 违反本条例规定的行为，本条例未设定处罚但其他法律、法规已设定处罚规定的，依照有关法律、法规的规定处罚；有关法律、法规的规定严于本条例的，依照有关法律、法规的规定执行。

第七章 附 则

第三十五条 本条例自 2022 年 1 月 1 日起施行。

Article 32 Consumers may report or bring litigation against acts that disrupt the order of competition or infringe upon consumer rights pursuant to law.

Where acts impairing fair competition infringe upon the legal rights of many consumers, the authorities and appropriate organizations as provided by law may file public interest litigation in the people's court pursuant to law, and the market regulation agencies at all levels shall provide support pursuant to law.

Article 33 Any illegal act provided in these Regulations shall be included in the public credit information system pursuant to applicable regulations and announced pursuant to law; those entities and individuals on the list of untrustworthy entities shall be penalized by the appropriate agencies pursuant to law.

Article 34 Where other laws and regulations provide penalties for violations of these Regulations not provided in these Regulations, or provide more severe penalties than these Regulations, such laws and regulations shall control.

Chapter VII Supplementary Provision

Article 35 These Regulations shall come into force as of January 1, 2022.

海南自由贸易港国际船舶条例

Regulations of Hainan Free Trade Port on International Ship

海南自由贸易港国际船舶条例

（2021 年 6 月 1 日海南省第六届人民代表大会常务委员会第二十八次会议通过）

第一章 总 则

第一条 为提升海南自由贸易港国际船舶检验、登记、营运等活动的便利化和服务保障水平，促进海运业及相关产业发展，根据《中华人民共和国海上交通安全法》《中华人民共和国船舶登记条例》等有关法律、法规，结合海南自由贸易港实际，制定本条例。

第二条 本条例所称国际船舶，是指在海南自由贸易港登记的航行国际航线的船舶。

国际船舶的船籍港为中国洋浦港。

第三条 海南海事管理机构负责海南自由贸易港国际船舶检验、安全监督、污染防治和船员权益保障等服务管理工作。

与国际船舶登记相关具体工作由国家海事管理机构确定的国际船舶登记机构（以下简称国际船舶登记机构）负责。

省人民政府交通运输主管部门负责国际船舶的营运等服务管理工作，其他有关部门依据职责做好国际船舶的相关服务管理工作。

第四条 海南海事管理机构、国际船舶登记机构和省人民政府交通运输等主管部门应当通过全省统一的政务信息资源共享开放基础设施，实现互联互通和信息共享，加强执法协同。

Regulations of Hainan Free Trade Port on International Ship

(Adopted at the 28th Session of the Standing Committee of the 6th Hainan Provincial People's Congress on June 1, 2021)

Chapter I General Provisions

Article 1 These Regulations are enacted pursuant to the Maritime Traffic Safety Law of the People's Republic of China, the Regulations of the People's Republic of China on Ship Registration, and other applicable laws and regulations, together with the actual circumstances in the Hainan Free Trade Port to improve the facilitation and service assurance of international ship survey, registration, and operation activities in the Hainan Free Trade Port, and encourage the development of the maritime industry and related industries,.

Article 2 "International ships" in these Regulations refer to the ships registered in the Hainan Free Trade Port and sailing international routes.

The port of registry for these international ships is China's Yangpu Port.

Article 3 The Hainan maritime administration office shall be responsible for the surveying, safety oversight, pollution prevention, protection of seamen rights, and other services and administration for international ships within the Hainan Free Trade Port.

The international ship registration agency determined by the state maritime administration (hereinafter referred to as "the international ship registration agency") shall be responsible for the specific work concerning international ship registration.

The competent provincial people's government transportation agency shall be responsible for the services and administration of international ships, and other appropriate agencies shall effectively perform their international ship service and administration duties.

Article 4 The Hainan maritime administration office, the international ship registration agency, provincial people's government transport agency, and other appropriate agencies shall achieve integration and information sharing, and improve law enforcement coordination through the centralized provincial government information resource sharing and open-access platform.

第五条　海南海事管理机构、国际船舶登记机构和省人民政府交通运输等主管部门应当对国际船舶有关活动的组织和个人加强信用管理，依照有关规定予以联合激励和联合惩戒。

第二章　船　舶

第六条　经授权的船舶检验机构可以开展国际船舶法定检验及相应证书的签发工作。

外国船舶检验机构可以根据国际船舶业务发展需要，在海南自由贸易港依法设立企业法人、分支机构或者常驻代表机构等。

第七条　取得法定检验授权的船舶检验机构可以开展国际船舶入级检验。

外国船舶检验机构开展国际船舶入级检验的具体管理办法，由省人民政府制定，经国务院交通运输主管部门同意后实施。

第八条　在海南自由贸易港设立且从事国际船舶法定检验、入级检验的船舶检验机构或者分支机构及其船舶检验活动的监督管理由海南海事管理机构负责。

第九条　下列船舶可以办理国际船舶登记：

（一）在海南自由贸易港有住所的中国公民所有或者融资租赁、光船租赁的船舶；

（二）在海南自由贸易港依法成立的法人所有或者融资租赁、光船租赁的船舶；

（三）在海南自由贸易港依法成立的非法人组织所有或者融资租赁、光船租赁的船舶。

国际船舶登记主体外资股比不受限制。

Article 5 The Hainan maritime administration office, the international ship registration agency, provincial people's government transport agency, and other appropriate agencies shall improve credit administration for organizations and individuals engaging in international ship activities, and jointly reward or penalize them pursuant to applicable regulations.

Chapter II Ships

Article 6 Authorized ship classification societies may carry out statutory surveys of international ships and issue the certificates.

Foreign ship classification societies may establish juristic persons, branch offices, or local representative offices in the Hainan Free Trade Port based on the development of international ship business.

Article 7 Ship classification societies with statutory authority to conduct surveys may conduct international ship classification surveys.

Specific administration guidelines for foreign ship classification societies to conduct international ship classification surveys shall be issued by the provincial people's government and implemented with the approval of the State Council transport agency.

Article 8 The Hainan maritime administration office shall be responsible for oversight and administration when ship classification societies or their branches are incorporated in the Hainan Free Trade Port to conduct statutory international ship surveys, classification surveys, and other ship classification activities.

Article 9 Any of the following ships may apply for international ship registration:

(a) ships owned or leased via financial lease or bareboat charter by Chinese citizens domiciled in the Hainan Free Trade Port;

(b) ships owned or leased via financial lease or bareboat charter by juristic persons registered in the Hainan Free Trade Port ; or

(c) ships owned or leased in means via financial lease or bareboat charter by unincorporated entities legally set up in the Hainan Free Trade Port.

There are no restrictions on the proportion of foreign investment in international ship registration entities.

第十条 申请办理国际船舶登记应当先行取得船舶识别号、中文名称和英文名称，英文名称可以使用英文单词。

第十一条 国际船舶登记种类包括：

（一）船舶所有权登记；

（二）船舶国籍登记；

（三）船舶抵押权登记；

（四）光船租赁登记；

（五）船舶变更登记；

（六）船舶注销登记；

（七）国家规定的其他种类。

第十二条 国际船舶登记申请材料应当使用格式文本。

申请人提交的国际船舶登记申请材料是外文的，应当同时提供中文译本，中文译本与外文不一致的，以中文为准。

通过国家或海南自由贸易港政务服务平台能够核验的证照类材料，免于提交原件。

第十三条 国际船舶登记机构应当审查国际船舶登记申请材料是否齐全，申请材料是否符合法定形式，申请书内容与所附材料是否一致，格式文本填写是否完整，并核实申请材料是否为原件或者与原件一致。

第十四条 经国际船舶登记机构审查，船舶登记申请符合规定要求的，予以登记，制作并发放相应船舶登记证书。

国际船舶登记机构应当建立国际船舶登记信息记录簿，记载国际船舶各项登记信息。

Article 10 The ship identification number, Chinese name, and English name (English words are allowed) shall be obtained before the application for international ship registration.

Article 11 International ship registration types shall include:

(a) registration of ship title;

(b) registration of ship nationality;

(c) registration of ship mortgage;

(d) registration of bareboat charter;

(e) ship registration changes;

(f) ship deregistration; and

(g) other types as provided by the state.

Article 12 The application shall use standard forms for international ship registration.

Applicants submitting materials for international ship registration in foreign languages shall also submit a Chinese version. The Chinese version shall prevail in the event of any conflicts with the foreign language version.

Applicants submitting license materials that can be verified through the national or the Hainan Free Trade Port government service platform are exempt from submitting the originals.

Article 13 The international ship registration agency shall inspect whether the international ship registration application materials are complete, whether the application materials are in the statutory format, whether the application contents match the attached materials, whether the standard forms are complete, and whether the application materials are original or match the original.

Article 14 Where the application for ship registration satisfies the requirements provided after review by the international ship registration agency, the registration shall be permitted, and the ship registration certificate shall be produced and issued.

The international ship registration agency shall keep a record of the international ship registration information to record international ship registration information.

第十五条 有下列情形之一的，国际船舶登记机构不予登记并书面告知理由：

（一）申请人不能提供权利取得证明文件或者申请登记事项与权利取得证明文件不一致的；

（二）第三人主张存在尚未解决的权属争议且能提供证据的；

（三）申请登记事项与已签发的登记证书内容相冲突的；

（四）违反法律、行政法规规定的。

第十六条 船舶所有人申请办理船舶所有权登记时，应当提交以下申请材料：

（一）申请人合法身份的证明文件；

（二）船舶所有权取得的证明文件；

（三）经授权的船舶检验机构签发的船舶技术参数证明。

现有船舶申请前款登记时，还应当提交上一船籍港船舶登记机关出具的船舶抵押情况证明和船舶注销登记证明书。

国际船舶所有权取得的证明文件，对于新造船舶是指建造证明和船舶交接文件；对于购买取得的船舶是指买卖证明和船舶交接文件；对于仅改变船籍港、所有权不变的船舶是指上一船籍港船舶所有权登记证书。

第十七条 船舶所有人暂时无法提交船舶所有权取得的证明文件原件时，可以使用复印件或者扫描件申请办理临时船舶所有权登记。船舶所有人应当对复印件或者扫描件的真实性、合法性、有效性负责。

已办理临时船舶所有权登记的国际船舶，申请办理国际船舶抵押权登记的，抵押权人应当提交确认书，确认其持有尚未提交给船舶登记机关的船舶所有权证明文件原件。

Article 15 Under any of the following circumstances, the international ship registration agency shall not register the ship, and shall inform the applicant of the reasons for such in writing:

(a) the applicant fails to provide documentation supporting the acquisition of rights or the items included in the registration application do not match the documentation supporting the acquisition of rights;

(b) a third party claims that there are unresolved title disputes and is able to provide evidence;

(c) the items included in the registration application do not match the information on the issued registration certificate; or

(d) laws or administrative regulations are violated.

Article 16 When applying for ship title registration, the shipowner shall submit the following application materials:

(a) documentation certifying the applicant's legal identity;

(b) documentation certifying the passage of ship title; and

(c) certificate of ship technical parameters issued by the authorized ship classification society.

When applying for ship title registration, the ship mortgage certificate and deregistration certificate issued by the ship registration agency in the previous port of registry shall be submitted.

Documentation supporting the passage of the international ship title refers to the shipbuilding certificate and ship delivery document for newly-built ships, the sales certificate, and ship delivery document for purchased ships, and the title registration certificate from the previous port of registry for ship changing their port of registry without change of title.

Article 17 Where the shipowner is unable to submit the original documentation supporting the acquisition of ship title at the time of registration, the shipowner may request temporary ship title registration using a photocopy or scanned copy. The shipowner shall be responsible for the authenticity, legality, and validity of the photocopy or scanned copy.

Where an international ship mortgagee requests mortgage registration after temporary title registration, the mortgagee shall submit a confirmation letter to prove to the ship registration agency that the original supporting documentation for the certificate of ship title is actually in their possession.

第十八条 船舶所有人申请办理国际船舶国籍登记，暂时无法提交船舶注销登记证明书的，可以使用上一船籍港船舶登记机关出具的同意注销证明；或者原船舶所有人在临时船舶国籍登记有效期届满前，将上一船籍港船舶注销登记证明书交付给新船舶所有人的承诺文件，申请办理临时船舶国籍登记。

第十九条 符合办理船舶临时登记条件的，国际船舶登记机构审核后颁发临时证书。

临时船舶所有权登记证书、临时船舶国籍证书的有效期均为一个月。

船舶所有人可以在临时船舶所有权登记证书、临时船舶国籍证书有效期届满前向国际船舶登记机构申请延续，并提交相关证明材料。符合条件的，国际船舶登记机构应当作出准予延续的决定，延续时间最长不得超过一个月。

船舶所有人在临时船舶所有权登记证书、临时船舶国籍证书有效期内可以持国际船舶所有权取得证明材料原件和船舶注销登记证明书，申请办理国际船舶所有权登记和船舶国籍登记。完成国际船舶所有权登记和船舶国籍登记的同时，临时登记终止。

第二十条 国际船舶具有下列情形之一的，国际船舶登记机构应当注销其国际船舶国籍登记：

（一）申请人提交虚假国际船舶登记申请材料的；

（二）不再符合本条例规定的国际船舶登记资格要求的；

（三）船舶检验证书失效三个月以上的；

（四）临时船舶国籍登记有效期届满，未提交上一船籍港船舶登记机关出具的船舶注销登记证明书的；

Article 18 Where the shipowner applies for international ship nationality registration and is unable to submit the ship deregistration certificate at the time of registration, the shipowner may use the deregistration approval certificate issued by the ship registration agency in the previous port of registry, or the shipowner may request temporary ship nationality registration using a commitment letter from the original shipowner to deliver the ship deregistration certificate from the previous port of registry to the new shipowner before the expiration of the temporary ship nationality registration.

Article 19 Where the requirements for temporary ship registration are met, the international ship registration agency shall issue a temporary certificate after review.

The temporary ship title registration certificate and the temporary ship nationality certificate shall be valid for 1 month.

The shipowner may apply for renewal with the international ship registration agency before the expiration of the temporary ship title registration certificate and temporary ship nationality certificate, and submit the appropriate certification materials. Where the requirements are met, the international ship registration agency shall make a decision on whether to grant the renewal, and the renewal shall be for a maximum of 1 month.

The shipowner may apply for international ship title registration and ship nationality registration with the original international ship title acquisition and ship deregistration certificates within the temporary ship title and ship nationality certificate validity periods. The temporary registration shall then be terminated after the international ship title registration and ship nationality registration is complete.

Article 20 Where an international ship falls under any of the following circumstances, the international ship registration agency shall deregister its international ship nationality:

(a) the applicant submits falsified international ship registration application materials;

(b) the ship is no longer eligible for international ship registration as provided in these Regulations;

(c) the ship survey certificate is over 3 months expired;

(d) the ship deregistration certificate issued by the previous port of registry's ship registration agency is not submitted before the expiration of the temporary ship nationality registration;

（五）光船租赁合同期满或者光船租赁关系终止之日起十五日内未办理注销登记的；

（六）国际船舶质量评价连续三年达不到规定标准的；

（七）其他不再符合船舶登记要求的。

第二十一条　单位和个人可以按照有关规定查询、复制国际船舶登记信息记录簿中的船舶技术资料、船舶登记种类等基本信息。国际船舶登记机构应当根据单位和个人的需要，对查询、复制的信息资料予以盖章确认。

单位和个人不得非法使用国际船舶登记信息。

第二十二条　国际船舶登记机构和船舶检验机构可以按照有关规定核发国际船舶电子证书，电子证书与纸质证书具有同等法律效力。

第二十三条　超出国家规定的进口船舶船龄限制的国际船舶，经国务院交通运输主管部门同意，并经授权的船舶检验机构检验合格后，可以申请办理国际船舶登记。

第二十四条　国际船舶应当同时持有船舶检验证书和（临时）船舶国籍证书，方可航行、停泊和作业。

第二十五条　经国家授权的机构应当依照国际通行做法设置国际船舶质量、企业安全和防污染管理、船舶检验机构等评价指标，定期开展评价。

评价分值较低的，经国家授权的机构应当开展海事特别安全检查并提出整改意见。

(e) the deregistration is not completed within 15 days of the date of expiration of bareboat charter contract or termination of bareboat charter relationship;

(f) fails to meet international ship quality inspection criteria for 3 consecutive years; or

(g) other circumstances under which ship registration requirements are no longer met.

Article 21 Entities and individuals may inquire and copy the basic information such as ship technical data and ship registration types in the record book of international ship registration information in accordance with applicable provisions. The international ship registration agency shall, based on the needs of entities and individuals, seal and confirm the inquired and copied information.

Entities and individuals shall not unlawfully use international ship registration information.

Article 22 The international ship registration agency and ship classification society may issue an electronic international ship certificate pursuant to applicable provisions, and the electronic certificate shall have the same legal effect as a paper certificate.

Article 23 International ships exceeding the age limit for imported ships provided by the state may apply for international ship registration with approval from the State Council competent transportation agency after passing a classification conducted by the authorized ship classification society.

Article 24 International ships must shall have both the ship survey certificate and the (temporary) ship nationality certificate before sailing, berthing, and other operations.

Article 25 The state-authorized agency shall establish evaluation metrics, including international ship quality, entity safety, pollution prevention administration, and ship classification societies based on leading international practices, and shall conduct regular evaluations.

Where the evaluation score is comparatively low, the agency authorized by the state shall conduct specialized maritime safety inspections and provide correction recommendations.

第三章 船 员

第二十六条 持有工作证明材料并在国际船舶任职的境外船员及其家属，按照相关法律法规和工作要求入境海南。

第二十七条 与海南自由贸易港船员用人单位签订劳动合同的境外船员的社会保险，应当按照法律法规和海南自由贸易港有关规定办理，船员所在国（地区）与我国签订社会保险双边或者多边协议的除外。

第二十八条 境外企业和个人可以按照有关规定在海南自由贸易港开办或者合作开办船员培训机构，从事船员培训业务。开设国家规定的船员培训项目，应当经海南海事管理机构批准。

境外人员在海南自由贸易港参加国家规定的船员培训项目，经考试合格的，可以按照有关规定申请相应的船员适任证书和培训合格证书。

第四章 营 运

第二十九条 经营国际客船、国际散装液体危险品船运输业务，应当符合国家有关法律法规规定，并经省人民政府交通运输主管部门批准。

省人民政府应当制定具体管理办法，经国务院交通运输主管部门同意后实施。

第三十条 国内水路运输经营者使用国际船舶从事省内沿海水域水路运输业务，应当经省人民政府交通运输主管部门批准。

国际船舶经批准可以从事省内沿海水域水上施工作业。

Chapter III Seamen

Article 26 Overseas seamen holding employment certificates and employed on international ships and their families shall enter Hainan in compliance with applicable law, regulations, and employment requirements.

Article 27 Social insurance for overseas seamen who entered employment contracts with employers in the Hainan Free Trade Port shall be administrated pursuant to law and Hainan Free Trade Port regulations, except when the countries (regions) where seamen are located have entered into bilateral or multilateral social insurance agreements with China.

Article 28 Overseas entities and individuals may open or jointly open seaman training centers to conduct seaman training in the Hainan Free Trade Port pursuant to law. The creation of seaman training projects provided by the state must be approved by the Hainan maritime administration office.

Any foreigner who has participated in seaman training projects provided by the state within the Hainan Free Trade Port and passed the examination may apply for the seaman competency and proficiency certificates pursuant to applicable provisions.

Chapter IV Operations

Article 29 The operation of international passenger ships and international ships carrying hazardous bulk liquids must comply with applicable national laws and regulations and be approved by the provincial people's government transport agency.

The provincial people's government shall issue specific administrative regulations and implement them upon the consent of the State Council transport agency.

Article 30 Domestic waterway transport operators shall obtain approval from the provincial people's government transport agency before using international ships to conduct waterway transport operations within provincial coastal waters.

International ships may participate in offshore construction projects within provincial coastal waters after receiving approval.

第三十一条 达到国家强制报废船龄的国际船舶，经国务院交通运输主管部门同意，并经授权的船舶检验机构检验合格后，在证书有效期内可以继续从事水路运输。

第三十二条 国际船舶所有人或者经营人应当在海南自由贸易港设立联络机构，代表该企业与行政主管机关就有关管理及法律事务等进行联络。联络机构可以由国际船舶所有人或者经营人自行担任，也可以委托注册在海南自由贸易港的法人或者非法人组织担任。

联络机构应当向海南海事管理机构和省人民政府交通运输主管部门备案。

第五章 进 出 境

第三十三条 公安机关应当优化审批方式、简化审批流程，为需要办理《合资船船员登陆证》的船员提供网上办理等便利服务。

第三十四条 船舶检验、维修和物料供应的相关人员可以在国际船舶办理进口岸手续前上船开展服务，但应当提前取得相关口岸检查机关许可。

第三十五条 从境外购买或者通过其他合法途径取得且拟申请办理国际船舶登记的旧船舶，按照有关规定免于办理重点旧机电产品进口许可证。

第六章 税费和海运服务

第三十六条 对境外进口和境内建造的国际船舶，船用备件以及在船自用的燃料，按照有关规定免税或者退税。

Article 31 Any international ship reaching compulsory scrapping age may continue to provide waterway transport within its certificate's validity period with the consent of the State Council transport agency and after passing a survey conducted by an authorized ship classification society.

Article 32 International shipowners or operators shall set up branch offices in the Hainan Free Trade Port to communicate with administrative authorities on applicable administrative and legal matters on behalf of the organization. The branch office may be operated by the international shipowner or operator, or may be authorized to a juristic person or an unincorporated entity registered in the Hainan Free Trade Port.

The branch office shall register with the Hainan maritime administration office and the provincial people's government transport agency.

Chapter V Entry and Exit

Article 33 Public security agencies shall optimize the review and approval methods, simplify the process, and provide convenient services such as online applications for seamen in need of Joint Venture Ship Seamen Landing Certificates.

Article 34 Ship survey, maintenance, and material supply staff may board international ships to provide services before completing port entry procedures, provided that advance permission has been obtained from the appropriate port survey agencies.

Article 35 Old ships purchased from overseas or obtained by other legal means planning to apply for international ship registration are exempt from applying for import licenses for used major mechanical and electrical products pursuant to applicable law.

Chapter VI Taxes and Maritime Transport Services

Article 36 International ships imported from abroad or built in China, spare parts for ships, and fuel for the ships' own use shall be exempt from taxes or such taxes shall be refunded pursuant to applicable regulations.

第三十七条 对注册在海南自由贸易港并实质性运营的国际船舶及其辅助性业务经营者、船员服务机构和船舶检验机构，按照有关规定享受企业所得税优惠；其高级管理人员、船员等按照有关规定享受个人所得税优惠。

第三十八条 在海南自由贸易港内设立的企业因开展国际船舶融资借用外债涉及跨境担保的，可以自行办理担保合同签约，无需事前审批，合同签约后，按照有关规定办理登记。

符合条件的国际船舶融资，外债资金可以意愿结汇。

第三十九条 支持在海南自由贸易港注册的国际船舶企业通过保单融资、仓单质押贷款、应收账款质押贷款、知识产权质押贷款等方式开展融资业务。

第四十条 在海南自由贸易港内注册的企业申请银行提供境外船舶融资担保的，可以以购买保险的方式取代保证金。

第四十一条 在海南自由贸易港设立的融资租赁企业开展境内融资租赁业务，可以按照有关规定收取外币租金。

第四十二条 在海南自由贸易港内注册的国际海运及其辅助性企业向境外支付运费及相关费用，符合规定的免于办理税务备案。

第四十三条 支持境内外企业和机构在海南自由贸易港开展航运保险、船舶融资租赁、海损理算、船舶交易和航运仲裁等服务。

鼓励在海运业开展跨境人民币结算再保险业务。

第四十四条 鼓励在海南自由贸易港设立的海运企业依照有关规定成立相互保险组织和自保公司。

Article 37 International ships registered and substantially operated within the Hainan Free Trade Port together with their auxiliary business operators, seaman service providers, and ship classification societies shall be entitled to preferential enterprise income tax pursuant to applicable provisions; their executives and seamen shall be entitled to preferential personal income tax pursuant to applicable provisions.

Article 38 Where a business entity incorporated within the Hainan Free Trade Port takes on foreign debt for international ship financing involving cross-border guarantees, it may independently perform the guarantee contract without prior approval and register in compliance with applicable provisions once the contract is signed.

Foreign debt funds for eligible international ship financing may be paid through at-will foreign exchange transactions.

Article 39 International shipping organizations registered in the Hainan Free Trade Port shall receive support to conduct financing operations through policy financing, warehouse receipt pledge loans, accounts receivable pledged loans, and intellectual property pledge loans.

Article 40 If an organization registered within the Hainan Free Trade Port applies for a bank guarantee when financing overseas ships, it may purchase insurance in place of the deposit.

Article 41 Financial lease organizations incorporated in the Hainan Free Trade Port may charge for leases in foreign currency pursuant to applicable provisions when conducting domestic financial lease operations.

Article 42 International maritime transport organizations and supporting organizations registered in the Hainan Free Trade Port shall be exempt from filing tax records when paying freight and other similar expenses to overseas parties if they comply with applicable provisions.

Article 43 Domestic and foreign businesses and organizations shall receive support to provide services such as shipping insurance, ship financing, average adjustments, ship transactions, and shipping arbitration within the Hainan Free Trade Port.

Reinsurance for overseas payments made in RMB in the shipping industry shall be encouraged.

Article 44 Maritime entities incorporated within the Hainan Free Trade Port are encouraged to set up mutual insurance organizations and self-insurance companies pursuant to applicable provisions.

第四十五条 建立国际船舶商事纠纷化解机制，与境内外仲裁机构、调解机构等争议解决机构开展合作，提高化解商事纠纷服务水平。

第七章 法律责任

第四十六条 未按照本条例第二十五条规定对海事特别安全检查意见所列问题进行整改的，应当限期整改；经限期整改仍不符合要求，存在严重安全隐患的，可以按照以下规定处理：

（一）对国际船舶签发短期船舶安全管理证书或者取消船舶安全管理证书；

（二）对企业签发短期符合证明或者取消符合证明；

（三）对船舶检验机构取消部分或者全部授权。

第四十七条 国家机关工作人员违反本条例规定滥用职权、徇私舞弊、玩忽职守的，依法给予处分；构成犯罪的，依法追究刑事责任。

第四十八条 违反本条例规定，本条例未设定处罚而法律法规另有处罚规定的，从其规定。

第八章 附 则

第四十九条 在海南自由贸易港登记的航行港澳航线的船舶参照适用本条例。

第五十条 本条例自 2021 年 9 月 1 日起施行。

Article 45 A commercial dispute resolution mechanism for international ships shall be created, and collaborations with domestic and foreign arbitration, mediation, and other dispute resolution institutions shall be conducted to improve commercial dispute resolution services.

Chapter VII Legal Liability

Article 46 Where problems listed in maritime safety survey opinions are not corrected pursuant to Article 25 of these Regulations, corrections shall be made within a specified time limit. The following shall apply where the correction made within the time limit fails to meet the requirements and there are material potential safety hazards:

(a) short-term ship safety administration certificates will be issued to the international ship, or ship safety administration certificates will be revoked;

(b) short-term compliance certificates will be issued to the enterprise, or compliance certificates will be revoked; and

(c) the ship classification society authorization will be revoked in full or in part.

Article 47 Any government agency functionary who abuses the position, commits dereliction of duty, or plays favoritism and commits irregularities in violation of these Regulations shall be penalized pursuant to law, and held criminally liable should such acts constitute a crime.

Article 48 Where other laws and regulations provide penalties for violations of these Regulations not provided in these Regulations, such laws and regulations shall prevail.

Chapter VIII Supplementary Provisions

Article 49 These Regulations shall apply *mutatis mutandis* to ships registered in the Hainan Free Trade Port sailing Hong Kong and Macao routes.

Article 50 These Regulations shall come into force as of September 1, 2021.

海南自由贸易港企业破产程序条例

Regulations of Hainan Free Trade Port on Business Bankruptcy Procedures

海南自由贸易港企业破产程序条例

（2021年12月1日海南省第六届人民代表大会常务委员会第三十一次会议通过）

第一章　总　则

第一条　为了优化企业破产程序，公平、高效、便利地清理债权债务，依法保护境内外债权人、债务人及其他利害关系人的合法权益，根据《中华人民共和国海南自由贸易港法》的规定，遵循有关法律、行政法规的原则，结合海南自由贸易港实际，制定本条例。

第二条　住所地位于海南自由贸易港的债务人不能清偿到期债务，并且资产不足以清偿全部债务或者明显缺乏清偿能力的，依照本条例规定清理债务。

债务人有前款规定情形，或者有明显丧失清偿能力可能的，可以依照本条例规定进行重整。

本条例所称债务人包括企业法人、合伙企业、个人独资企业。

第三条　海南自由贸易港的破产案件，由债务人住所地的人民法院管辖，海南自由贸易港破产审判机构实行专门管辖的案件除外。

人民法院之间因管辖权发生争议，由争议双方协商解决；协商解决不成的，报请共同的上级人民法院指定管辖。

Regulations of Hainan Free Trade Port on Business Bankruptcy Procedures

(Adopted at the 31st Session of the Standing Committee of the 6th Hainan Provincial People's Congress on December 1, 2021)

Chapter I General Provisions

Article 1 These Regulations are enacted under the Hainan Free Trade Port Law of the People's Republic of China, following the principles of applicable laws and administrative regulations, and based on actual circumstances in the Hainan Free Trade Port to optimize the business bankruptcy procedures, fairly, efficiently and conveniently pay off creditor claims and debts, and protect legal rights of creditors, debtors, and other stakeholders domestic and abroad.

Article 2 If debtors domiciled in the Hainan Free Trade Port are unable to pay off due debts and their assets are insufficient to pay off all the debts or they clearly lack solvency, their debts shall be liquidated pursuant to these Regulations.

If the debtor falls under any of the circumstances specified in the above paragraph or there is a possibility of obvious loss of solvency, it may be subject to reorganization pursuant to these Regulations.

Debtors as referred to in these Regulations include business juristic persons, partnerships, and sole proprietorships.

Article 3 Hainan Free Trade Port bankruptcy cases shall be resolved by the people's court having jurisdiction over the debtor's domicile, except when the cases are subject to the jurisdiction of specific Hainan Free Trade Port bankruptcy judicial bodies.

Any dispute over jurisdiction between the people's courts shall be resolved by the disputing courts through negotiation, or shall be submitted to the superior people's court of the two courts for the designated jurisdiction if such negotiation fails.

第四条 县级以上人民政府应当与人民法院建立行政与司法协调机制，统筹推进破产处置工作，保障破产工作所需相关经费，加强企业债务风险监测预警和破产信息共享，协调处理破产处置涉及的重大问题，建立并完善相关配套制度。

县级以上人民政府发展改革、市场监管、财政、税务、人力资源和社会保障、自然资源和规划、住房和城乡建设、国有资产监督管理、公安等有关部门应当按照职责分工，协调或者处理破产程序中涉及的社会稳定、职工权益、财产接管、资产处置、税收征管、注销登记、信用修复、费用保障、打击逃废债等相关事务，并推动和支持管理人依法履职。

人民法院应当推进破产审判机制改革，加强破产审判专业化建设，提高破产案件办理的质量和效率。

第五条 省人民政府确定的工作部门或机构（以下称破产事务管理部门）负责行使破产事务的行政管理职能，承担行政与司法协调机制的日常工作。市、县、自治县人民政府根据实际需要确定破产事务管理部门。

第二章 申请与受理

第六条 债务人有本条例第二条规定的情形，可以向人民法院提出重整、和解或者破产清算申请。

债务人不能清偿到期债务，债权人可以向人民法院提出对债务人进行重整或者破产清算的申请。

Article 4 The people's governments at or above the county level shall establish an administrative and judicial coordination system together with the people's courts to comprehensively improve bankruptcy management, ensure the necessary funding for bankruptcy work, improve business debt risk monitoring, early warning, and bankruptcy information sharing, coordinate the management of major bankruptcy management issues, and create and improve appropriate support systems.

The development and reform, market oversight and administration, finance, tax, human resources and social security, natural resources and planning, housing and urban-rural development, state-owned assets oversight and administration, law enforcement, and other appropriate agencies under the people's governments at or above the county level shall coordinate the work on and manage social stability, employee rights and interests, asset takeover, asset management, tax administration, deregistration, credit repair, expense guarantees, crack down on debt evasion, and other issues involved in bankruptcy proceedings based on the division of responsibilities and encourage and support bankruptcy administrators to lawfully perform their duties.

The people's court shall encourage bankruptcy trial system reform, improve professional expertise for bankruptcy trials, and improve the quality and efficiency of bankruptcy case management.

Article 5 The agency or body designated by the provincial people's government (hereinafter referred to as the "bankruptcy administrative agencies") shall be responsible for exercising the administrative functions over bankruptcy matters and performing routine administrative and judicial coordination system work. The city, county, and autonomous people's governments shall appoint the bankruptcy administrative agencies on a case by case basis.

Chapter II Petition and Acceptance

Article 6 Debtors may submit a petition for reorganization, settlement or bankruptcy liquidation with the people's court under the circumstances provided in Article 2 of these Regulations.

Where debtors fail to pay off their due debts, creditors may file a petition for debtor reorganization or bankruptcy liquidation with the people's court.

债务人已解散但未清算或者未清算完毕，资产不足以清偿债务的，依法负有清算责任的主体应当向人民法院申请破产清算。

债务人的董事、监事、高级管理人员知道或者应当知道债务人有本条例第二条规定情形的，应当及时书面提请债务人向人民法院提出重整、和解或者破产清算申请，避免债务人状况继续恶化和财产减损。

人民法院受理破产申请前，申请人可以书面请求撤回申请。

第七条 人民法院在接收破产申请材料后、裁定受理破产申请前，债权人、债务人或者其他利害关系人因情况紧急，不立即申请财产保全将会使其合法权益受到难以弥补的损害的，可以向人民法院申请对债务人的全部或者部分财产采取保全措施。

债权人或者其他利害关系人申请采取前款保全措施的，应当提供担保；不提供担保的，人民法院应当裁定驳回保全申请。

人民法院采取保全措施后，裁定不予受理破产申请的，应当一并解除相应的保全措施。

第八条 关联企业成员之间存在关联企业成员因人员、经营、财产等混同导致法人人格高度混同的，或者区分各关联企业成员财产的成本过高、严重损害债权人公平清偿利益的，管理人或者符合本条例第六条的申请人可以向人民法院申请适用关联企业实质合并破产方式进行审理。

第九条 债权人或者债务人提起破产申请的，人民法院应当接收材料并登记，符合受理条件的，应依法受理。

Where a debtor is dissolved without any liquidation or is pending liquidation and its assets are not sufficient to pay off the debts, the individuals liable for the liquidation shall file a petition for bankruptcy liquidation with the people's court.

The directors, supervisors, or executives of the debtor shall submit a written petition to the debtor asking them to file a petition for reorganization, settlement, or liquidation bankruptcy with the people's court to avoid additional worsening of the debtor's conditions and asset impairment should any of the debtor's directors, supervisors, or executives know or should have known that the debtor falls under any of the circumstances provided in Article 2 of these Regulations.

The petitioner may submit a written petition to withdraw their petition before the people's court accepts bankruptcy filings.

Article 7 Before the people's court rules to accept the bankruptcy filing after it receives the documents for such filing, the creditor, debtor, or any other stakeholder may petition the people's court for an injunction of all or part of the debtor's property due to emergency if the failure to take an immediate injunction may lead to irrevocable damages to legal rights of the parties concerned.

Any creditor or stakeholder who petitions for the injunction mentioned in the above paragraph shall provide a guarantee; otherwise, the people's court shall dismiss the petition.

The people's court shall terminate the injunction should it decide not to accept the bankruptcy filings after taking the injunction.

Article 8 Administrators or petitioners meeting the requirements provided in Article 6 of these Regulations may petition the people's court to consolidate the bankruptcy of the debtors and its affiliates in the same court should the affiliates and the debtor intermingle in personal, business operation, and corporate assets, or the cost to distinguish the corporate assets between the affiliates and the debtor is comparatively high, which would harm the creditor's right for equitable compensation.

Article 9 Where a creditor or debtor submits bankruptcy filings, the people's court shall accept the documents and complete case registration. The court shall then accept the case pursuant to law if it meets the necessary requirements.

债权人提出破产申请的，人民法院应当自收到申请之日起五日内通知债务人。债务人及其相关人员无法取得联系的，人民法院可以公告通知，公告期为七日。债务人对申请有异议的，应当自收到人民法院的通知之日或者公告期满之日起七日内向人民法院提出。人民法院应当自异议期满之日起十日内裁定是否受理。

除本条第二款规定的情形外，人民法院应当自收到破产申请之日起十五日内裁定是否受理。

有特殊情况需要延长前两款规定的裁定受理期限的，经上一级人民法院批准，可以延长十五日。相关部门审批期间以及当事人补充、补正相关材料的期间，不计入申请审查期限。

第十条 人民法院在受理破产申请前，可以根据案件实际情况组织债务人、债权人听证，并应当自发出听证通知之日起十五日内完成听证。出资人、实际控制人、意向重整投资人等利害关系人及相关政府部门可以参加听证。

存在下列情形之一的，人民法院应当组织听证：

（一）债务人为上市公司的；

（二）债务人为非上市公众公司的；

（三）债权债务关系复杂、债务规模较大的破产案件；

（四）适用关联企业实质合并破产方式进行审理的破产案件；

（五）法律法规规定应当听证的其他情形。

听证结束后，人民法院应当根据听证笔录，依照本条例规定，作出是否受理破产申请的裁定。

听证期间不计入申请审查期限。

Where the creditor petitions for bankruptcy, the people's court shall notify the debtor within 5 days from the day the petition is received. The people's court may issue a publication notice for 7 days if the debtor or its appropriate employees cannot be contacted. The debtor shall submit any objections to the petition to the people's court within 7 days of the day on which the court notice is received or the court's publication expires. The people's court shall decide whether or not to accept the case within 10 days from the day the objection expires.

Except for the circumstances provided in Paragraph 2 of this Article, the people's court shall decide whether or not to accept the bankruptcy case within 15 days from the day the petition is received.

The time limit for deciding whether to accept a case as provided in the two paragraphs above may be extended by 15 days under special circumstances and after the approval of the higher people's court. The approval period for the agencies involved and the period during which the parties concerned supplement and correct documents shall not be counted as part of the petition review period.

Article 10 Before accepting the bankruptcy case, the people's court may organize a hearing for the debtor and creditor based on actual case conditions and shall complete the hearing within 15 days from the day on which the hearing notice is issued. Capital contributors, shareholders, controlling beneficiaries, prospective reorganization investors, other stakeholders, and the government agencies involved may participate in the hearing.

The people's court shall organize a hearing under any of the following circumstances:

(a) the debtor is a listed company;

(b) the debtor is an unlisted public company;

(c) the case involves a significant debt and complex creditor's rights and debts are involved;

(d) the case involves the consolidated bankruptcy of the debtor and its affiliate; or

(e) other circumstances requiring a hearing as provided by laws and regulations.

After the hearing, the people's court shall decide on whether or not to accept the bankruptcy filing based on the minutes of the hearing and these Regulations.

The hearing period shall not be counted as part of the petition review period.

第十一条 人民法院裁定受理破产申请的，应当同时指定管理人。受理裁定书以及指定管理人决定书应当在作出之日起五日内送达申请人、被申请人、管理人，并通知破产事务管理部门。

第十二条 人民法院应当自裁定受理破产申请之日起二十五日内通知已知债权人，并予以公告。

通知和公告应当载明下列事项：

（一）申请人、被申请人的名称或者姓名；

（二）人民法院受理破产申请的时间和适用程序；

（三）申报债权的期限、地点和注意事项；

（四）管理人的名称或者姓名、联系方式及其处理事务的地址；

（五）债务人的债务人或者财产持有人应当向管理人清偿债务或者交付财产的要求；

（六）第一次债权人会议召开的时间、地点和召开方式；

（七）人民法院认为应当通知和公告的其他事项。

第十三条 人民法院受理破产申请后，管理人对破产申请受理前成立而债务人和对方当事人均未履行完毕的合同有权决定解除或者继续履行，并书面通知对方当事人。

管理人自接受指定之日起二个月内未书面通知对方当事人，或者自收到对方当事人书面催告之日起三十日内未答复的，视为解除合同。

管理人决定继续履行合同的，对方当事人应当履行；但是，对方当事人有权要求管理人提供担保。管理人不提供担保的，视为解除合同。

第十四条 人民法院受理破产申请后，有关债务人财产的保全措施应当解除，执行程序应当中止。

Article 11 The people's court shall appoint an administrator when it decides to accept the bankruptcy case. The petitioner, respondent, and administrator shall receive the acceptance decision and administrator appointing decision within 5 days of the day when the decision is made, and the bankruptcy administrative agency shall also be notified.

Article 12 The people's court shall notify the known creditors within 25 days of the day of making a decision on the bankruptcy case and issue a public notice.

The notice shall specify the following:

(a) the names of the petitioner and the respondent;

(b) the time when the people's court accepts the bankruptcy case and procedures;

(c) period, address, and notes in the declaration of claims;

(d) name and contact methods for the bankruptcy administrator, as well as the office address;

(e) requirements for the debtor or the debtor's property holders to pay the debts or deliver the property;

(f) the time, place, and manner for the first meeting of creditors to be held; and

(g) any other matters the people's court deems necessary to be included in the notice.

Article 13 After the people's court accepts the bankruptcy petition, the administrator shall have the right to terminate or continue the performance of a contract entered into before acceptance, yet has not been fully performed by both parties concerned, and shall notify the counterparty of its decision in writing.

The contract shall be deemed terminated where the bankruptcy administrator fails to inform the counterparty in writing within 2 months of the day they are appointed or fails to reply to a written demand letter requirement made by the counterparty within 30 days.

Where the bankruptcy administrator decides to continue a contract, the counterparty shall continue to perform the contract and has the right to require the administrator to provide a guarantee or the contract shall be deemed terminated.

Article 14 After the people's court accepts a bankruptcy case, any action preserving the debtor's property shall be removed and the enforcement performance procedures shall be suspended.

对债务人财产采取保全措施或者执行措施的相关机关，在收到人民法院破产案件受理裁定后，应当及时解除对债务人财产的保全措施，中止有关执行程序。

第十五条 人民法院受理破产申请后，有关债务人的民事诉讼，只能向受理破产申请的人民法院提起。当事人之间在破产申请受理前订立有仲裁条款或者仲裁协议的，应当向选定的仲裁机构申请仲裁。

人民法院受理破产申请后，相关主体根据本条例第二十条及第六十四条对管理人提起的损害赔偿诉讼，应当向受理破产申请的人民法院提起。

第三章 破产事务管理部门和管理人

第十六条 破产事务管理部门履行下列职责：

（一）配合人民法院确定管理人资质，建立和调整管理人名册，支持和推动管理人行业自律组织建设；

（二）监督管理人履行职责；

（三）提供破产事务咨询和援助服务；

（四）协助调查破产欺诈和相关违法行为；

（五）实施破产信息登记和信息公开制度；

（六）统筹协调各相关部门处理破产事务；

（七）其他与破产事务有关的行政管理职责。

第十七条 管理人可以由有关部门、机构的人员组成的清算组或者依法设立的律师事务所、会计师事务所、破产清算事务所等社会中介机构或者符合条件的个人担任。管理人的条件、任用、履职管理办法由人民法院会同破产事务管理部门制定。

After receiving the decision of the people's court on the acceptance of the bankruptcy case, the appropriate agencies that took injunction or enforcement action against the debtor's property shall promptly remove the injunction actions against the debtor's property and suspend any enforcement.

Article 15 After the people's court accepts the bankruptcy case, any civil action related to the debtor may only be filed with the people's court that accepted the case. If an arbitration clause or arbitration agreement before the bankruptcy case is accepted, they shall initiate arbitration with the agreed arbitration institution.

After the people's court accepts the bankruptcy case, indemnification litigation brought by the appropriate entities against the administrator in accordance with Articles 20 and 64 of these Regulations shall be filed with the people's court that accepted the bankruptcy case.

Chapter III Bankruptcy Administrative Agencies and Administrators

Article 16 Bankruptcy administrative agencies shall:

(a) cooperate with the people's court to determine the eligibility of the administrator, create and adjust a list of administrator names, and support and encourage the development of administrator industry self-regulation;

(b) supervise the administrator's performance of its duties;

(c) provide bankruptcy advice and assistance;

(d) assist in investigating bankruptcy fraud and similar offenses;

(e) implement a bankruptcy information registration and information disclosure system;

(f) coordinate with all applicable agencies to resolve bankruptcy matters; and

(g) perform other administrative duties for bankruptcy matters.

Article 17 The position of bankruptcy administrator may be held by a liquidation group comprised of employees from appropriate agencies and organizations by professional service providers such as legally incorporated law firms, accounting firms, or bankruptcy liquidation firms, or by individuals qualified to do so. The requirements and rules for the administrator's appointment and performance of duties shall be issued jointly by the people's court and bankruptcy administrative employees.

有下列情形之一的，不得担任管理人：

（一）因故意犯罪受过刑事处罚；

（二）曾被吊销相关专业执业证书；

（三）与本案有利害关系；

（四）已破产企业的实际控制人以及曾担任已破产企业的董事、监事、高级管理人员并对破产负有主要责任的人员，自该企业破产程序终结之日起未逾三年；

（五）已经被人民法院宣告破产且尚未恢复信用的个人；

（六）人民法院认为不宜担任管理人的其他情形。

管理人应当按照国家有关规定参加执业责任保险。

第十八条　管理人由人民法院指定。

破产事务管理部门可以向人民法院推荐管理人人选；经审查符合管理人条件并适宜担任本案管理人的，人民法院可以指定该推荐人选为管理人。

债务人与债权额占已知债权总额四分之一以上的债权人协商一致，可以向人民法院推荐管理人人选；经审查符合管理人条件并适宜担任本案管理人的，人民法院可以指定该推荐人选为管理人。

破产申请受理前，根据有关规定已经成立清算组的，人民法院可以指定该清算组为管理人。

重大、复杂破产案件，人民法院一般应当通过竞争方式指定管理人。

第十九条　债权人会议、经债权人会议授权的债权人委员会认为管理人不能依法、公正执行职务或者有其他不能胜任职务情形的，可以申请人民法院予以更换并推荐管理人人选。

Anyone who falls under any of the following shall not act as an administrator:

(a) has received a criminal penalty for an intentional crime;

(b) the qualification has been revoked;

(c) has an interest in the case;

(d) a controlling beneficiary of a bankrupted business, or a person assuming main responsibility for a bankrupted business, including its directors, supervisors, and executives, for at least three years following the day when the business bankruptcy proceedings end;

(e) is declared bankrupt and their credit has not yet been repaired; or

(f) other circumstances under which the people's court deems it inappropriate to act as an administrator.

The administrator shall purchase practice liability insurance pursuant to applicable national law.

Article 18 A bankruptcy administrator shall be designated by the people's court.

The bankruptcy administrative agencies may submit a nomination for an administrator to the people's court. The people's court may designate the nominated candidate as the administrator if they meet the requirements and are deemed suitable to serve as the case administrator after consideration.

If the debtor and a creditor owed more than a quarter of the total known claims reach an agreement through negotiation, they may submit their nomination for the administrator to the people's court. The people's court may designate the nominated candidate as the administrator if they meet the requirements and are deemed suitable to serve as the case administrator after consideration.

Before accepting the bankruptcy case, if a liquidation group has been created as required, the people's court may designate the liquidation group as the administrator.

The people's court shall generally appoint an administrator through competition for important and complex bankruptcy cases.

Article 19 If the meeting of creditors or the creditors' committee authorized by the meeting of creditors believes that the administrator has failed to perform or fulfill its duties and functions in a lawful and impartial manner, or is incompetent, it may submit a petition for replacement to the people's court and recommend a new administrator.

人民法院同意更换管理人且前款被推荐人选符合本条例规定的，人民法院应当指定其为管理人。

第二十条 管理人应当勤勉尽责，忠实履行下列职责，向人民法院报告工作，并接受人民法院、破产事务管理部门、债权人会议和债权人委员会的监督：

（一）接管债务人的财产、印章和账簿、文书等资料；

（二）调查债务人财产状况，制作财产状况报告；

（三）决定债务人的内部管理事务；

（四）决定债务人的日常开支和其他必要开支；

（五）在第一次债权人会议召开之前，决定继续或者停止债务人的营业；

（六）管理和处分债务人的财产；

（七）以债务人名义履行法律规定的纳税申报等相关义务；

（八）代表债务人参加诉讼、仲裁或者其他法律程序；

（九）提议召开债权人会议；

（十）列席债权人会议，向债权人会议报告职务执行情况，并回答询问；

（十一）发现债务人、债权人或者其他相关人员涉嫌恶意逃废债、虚假破产等违法犯罪行为的，及时向有关机关报告；

（十二）人民法院、破产事务管理部门依照本条例和有关规定，要求管理人履行的其他职责。

本条例对管理人的职责另有规定的，适用其规定。

If the people's court approves a change in administrator and the nominated candidate in the preceding paragraph meets the requirements provided in these Regulations, the people's court shall designate them as the administrator.

Article 20 Bankruptcy administrators shall be diligent and responsible and faithfully perform the following duties, report to the people's court, and accept the supervision of the people's court, the bankruptcy administrative agencies, the meeting of creditors, and the creditor committees:

(a) take control of the property, seals, account books and documents, and other material belonging to the debtor;

(b) investigate the financial status of the debtor and prepare the financial reports;

(c) decide on debtor internal management matters;

(d) decide on daily and other necessary expenditures of the debtor;

(e) decide whether to continue or suspend the debtor's business before the first meeting of creditors;

(f) manage and dispose of the debtors' property;

(g) perform applicable obligations such as tax returns on behalf of the debtor as required by law;

(h) participate in lawsuits, arbitrations, or any other proceedings on behalf of the debtor;

(i) recommend the convening of meetings of creditors;

(j) attend meetings of creditors, report the performance of their duties and functions, and answer any relevant questions;

(k) report to the appropriate agencies if it suspects or discovers the debtor, creditor, or other staff to be involved in malicious debt evasion, false bankruptcy claims, and other illegal or criminal acts; and

(l) perform other duties as required by the people's court and the bankruptcy administrative agencies in compliance with these Regulations and other applicable rules.

If these Regulations have requirements otherwise on the duties of bankruptcy administrators, these Regulations shall apply.

第二十一条 管理人凭人民法院作出的破产案件受理裁定书、指定管理人决定书依法履行职责，公安、自然资源和规划、人力资源和社会保障、市场监管、税务、不动产登记、银行及其他有关单位和个人应当依法予以配合；有关单位和个人不予配合的，管理人可以申请人民法院出具协助执行通知书。

占有和管理债务人印章和账簿、文书等资料的有关人员，应当在管理人指定期限内将印章和账簿、文书等资料交付给管理人，逾期未交付的，管理人可以申请人民法院强制执行。

管理人向人民法院、公安、自然资源和规划、人力资源和社会保障、市场监管、税务、不动产登记、银行及其他有关单位申请查询债务人财产信息的，有关部门和单位应当依法及时提供所掌握的债务人财产相关信息。

第四章　债务人财产和债权人权利行使

第二十二条 破产申请受理时属于债务人的全部财产、破产申请受理后至破产程序终结前债务人取得的财产，为债务人财产，包括债务人在境内外所有的货币、实物以及依法享有的可以用货币估价并可以依法转让的债权、股权、知识产权、用益物权、虚拟财产等财产和财产权益。

第二十三条 债权人应当在人民法院确定的债权申报期限内向管理人申报债权。

Article 21 The administrator shall perform the duties based on the decisions made when the people's court accepts bankruptcy cases and appoints administrators. Appropriate organizations, including public security, natural resources and planning, human resources and social security, market oversight, taxation, real estate registration agencies, banks, and individuals, shall cooperate in accordance with law. The administrator may petition the people's court for enforcement if such organizations or individuals refuse to cooperate.

Anyone who holds and controls the debtor's seals, account books, documents, and other files shall deliver said seals, account books, documents, and other files to the administrator within the time limit specified by the administrator. The administrator may petition the people's court for enforcement in the event of a failure to deliver within the time limit.

The people's court, public security, natural resources and planning, human resources, social security, market oversight, taxation, and real estate registration agencies, banks, and other government agencies and organizations involved shall promptly provide any debtor property information as requested by the administrator pursuant to law.

Chapter IV Debtor Property and Exercise of Creditor's Rights

Article 22 Debtor property refers to all property owned by the debtor at the time the bankruptcy case is accepted, as well as property obtained by the debtor between the time the bankruptcy case is accepted to the conclusion of bankruptcy proceedings, including all the currency and physical items owned by the debtor domestically and overseas, as well as creditor's rights, stock shares, intellectual property rights, usufruct rights, virtual property, and other property and property rights that have a monetary value and may be assigned pursuant to law.

Article 23 Creditors shall declare their creditor's rights to the administrator within the term for claims declaration determined by the people's court.

债务人所欠职工的工资和医疗、伤残补助、抚恤费用，所欠的应当划入职工个人账户的基本养老保险、基本医疗保险费用，以及法律、行政法规规定应当支付给职工的补偿金属于职工债权，不必申报，由管理人调查后列出清单并予以公示。第三方垫付的上述费用、债务人欠缴的住房公积金及劳务合同、劳务派遣合同中应当支付给劳动者的报酬，参照职工债权处理。

第二十四条 在人民法院确定的债权申报期限内，债权人未申报债权的，可以在破产财产最后分配前补充申报；但是，此前已进行的分配，不再对其补充分配。为审查和确认补充申报债权的费用以及与清偿补充申报债权有关的提存费用，由补充申报人承担。

第二十五条 管理人收到债权申报材料后，应当对所申报的债权进行登记造册；管理人应当对申报债权的性质、数额、担保财产、是否超过诉讼时效期间、是否超过强制执行期间等情况进行审查，编制债权表，并提交第一次债权人会议核查。

债务人、债权人对债权表记载的债权无异议的，由人民法院裁定确认。

债务人、债权人对债权表记载的债权有异议的，应当自收到债权表之日起十五日内向管理人提交异议书并说明理由。经管理人复核，异议人仍然不服的，应当自收到管理人复核意见之日起十五日内向裁定受理破产申请的人民法院起诉；当事人在破产申请受理前订立有仲裁条款或者仲裁协议的，应当向选定的仲裁机构申请确认债权债务关系。

第二十六条 债权人会议设主席一人，由有表决权的债权人协商推选后报人民法院指定，或者由人民法院从有表决权的债权人中指定。

债权人会议主席主持债权人会议。

Any wages, subsidies for medical treatment, disability allowances, workplace injury compensation owed by a debtor, basic pension insurance premiums, and basic medical insurance premiums that should have been transferred to employees' personal accounts, as compensation for the employees provided by applicable law and administrative regulations are not required to be declared, and the bankruptcy administrator shall produce and publish a checklist for such. Any of the above expenses advanced by a third party, the housing accumulation fund owed by the debtor, and the remuneration payable to independent contractor staff and temporary staff shall be deemed as staff claims.

Article 24 Within the time limit for declaration of the creditor's rights as determined by the people's court, where a creditor fails to declare their creditor's rights, they may make up their declaration before the final allocation of the bankruptcy assets. However, no more distribution may be made if the allocation has already been made. Expenses for examining and confirming supplementary declarations of creditor's rights and the escrow expenses to pay creditors' rights in the supplementary declaration shall be assumed by the party submitting the supplementary declaration.

Article 25 Where a bankruptcy administrator receives the claims declaration documents, it shall record them in a book. The administrator shall then review the nature, amount, declared creditor's rights secured property, and whether the declared creditor's rights exceed the statute of limitations or the enforcement period, and prepare a claims form to submit to the first creditor's meeting for confirmation.

The people's court shall issue a ruling if the debtors and creditors have no objection to what is recorded on the claims form.

Where there are objections, either of them shall state the objection in writing to the administrator and explain the reasons for such within 15 days of the day the form is received. If the objection is not resolved following administrator review, litigation may be filed with the people's court accepting the bankruptcy case within 15 days of the receipt of the administrator's review opinions. Where the parties have entered into an arbitration clause or agreement before the bankruptcy case is accepted, the parties shall request the designated arbitration institution to affirm the creditor's rights.

Article 26 The meeting of creditors shall have a chairman elected by the creditors with voting rights through negotiation and reported to the people's court for appointment, or designated by the people's court from among the creditors with the voting rights.

The chairman shall preside over the meeting of creditors.

第二十七条 第一次债权人会议由人民法院召集，自债权申报期限届满之日起十五日内召开。

以后的债权人会议，在人民法院认为必要时，或者管理人、债权人委员会、占已知债权总额四分之一以上的债权人向债权人会议主席提议时召开。债权人会议主席拒绝召开的，前述主体可以申请人民法院决定召开。

第二十八条 召开债权人会议，管理人应当提前十五日通知已知的债权人。

债权人的联系方式、通信地址、住所地变更的，债权人应当及时书面或以双方约定的其他方式告知管理人；未及时告知的，管理人根据变更前信息作出的通知有效。

第二十九条 债权人会议可以采用现场方式或者书面、网络等非现场方式召开和表决。

债权人会议涉及表决事项的，管理人应当妥善保管记载表决内容的相关资料，并盖章或者签字确认。

管理人应当在债权人会议表决结果确定后三日内，向全体债权人公布表决结果。

第三十条 债权人会议的决议，由出席会议的有表决权的债权人过半数通过，并且其所代表的债权额占无财产担保债权总额的二分之一以上。但是，法律或者本条例另有规定的除外。

债权人会议的决议具有下列情形之一，损害债权人利益的，债权人可以自管理人公布债权人会议决议之日起十五日内，书面请求人民法院裁定撤销全部或者部分事项决议，责令债权人会议依法重新作出决议：

Article 27 The first meeting of creditors shall be convened by the people's court within 15 days of the expiration of the time limit for the declaration of the creditor's rights.

Subsequent meetings of creditors may be held whenever deemed necessary by the people's court, or where the bankruptcy administrator, creditors' committee, or any creditor whose claims account for more than a quarter of the total known claims advises the chairman to convene a meeting of creditors. If the chairman of the meeting of creditors refuses to convene the meeting, the above entities may petition the people's court for a decision to convene.

Article 28 Where a meeting of creditors is convened, the administrator shall notify the known creditors 15 days in advance.

If the creditor's contact information, mailing address, or domicile changes, the creditor shall promptly inform the administrator of such changes in writing or in any other way agreed upon by the parties. If not notified in time, the notice provided by the administrator based on the information submitted prior to the change shall be deemed valid.

Article 29 The meeting of creditors may be convened and voted on-site, in writing, or online.

If the meeting of creditors involves voting, the administrator shall properly maintain voting information and confirm such via seal or signature.

The administrator shall announce voting results to all creditors within 3 days of the day the meeting of creditors voting results are determined.

Article 30 A resolution of the meeting of creditors may be passed only upon the consent of the majority of the creditors with voting rights attending the meeting and representing the majority of the total amount of the unsecured claims, except as otherwise provided by law or these Regulations.

If a resolution of the meeting of creditors is passed under any of the following circumstances and infringes upon creditor's rights, the creditors may petition the people's court in writing to rule for the cancellation of all or part of the resolution and require the meeting of creditors to pass a new resolution pursuant to law within 15 days of the day on which the administrator announces the resolution of the meeting of creditors:

（一）债权人会议的召开、表决违反法定程序；

（二）债权人会议的决议内容违法；

（三）债权人会议的决议超出债权人会议的职权范围。

债权人会议的决议，对于全体债权人均有约束力。

第三十一条 债权人会议可以决定设立债权人委员会。债权人委员会由债权人会议选任的债权人代表和一名债务人的职工代表或者工会代表组成。债权人委员会成员总数一般为单数，不得超过九人。

债权人委员会成员应当经人民法院书面决定认可。

第五章 重 整

第三十二条 自人民法院裁定债务人重整之日起至重整程序终止，为重整期间。重整期间，债务人符合下列条件的，经债务人申请，人民法院可以批准债务人在管理人的监督下自行管理财产和营业事务：

（一）债务人的内部治理机制仍正常运转；

（二）债务人自行管理有利于债务人继续经营；

（三）债务人不存在隐匿、转移财产的行为；

（四）债务人不存在其他严重损害债权人利益的行为。

经人民法院批准由债务人自行管理财产和营业事务的，依照本条例规定已接管债务人财产和营业事务的管理人，应当向债务人移交财产和营业事务，本条例规定的管理人职权中有关财产管理和营业事务的职权应当由债务人行使。

(a) the convening and voting of the meeting of creditors violate statutory procedures;

(b) the resolution passed by the meeting of creditors violates the law; or

(c) the resolution passed by the meeting of creditors exceeds the meeting of creditors' range of duties.

Resolutions passed at the meeting of creditors shall be binding on all creditors.

Article 31 The meeting of creditors may decide to establish the creditors' committee, which shall comprise creditor representatives elected during the meeting of creditors, as well as a debtor employee representative or labor union representative. The total number of members of the creditors' committee shall in general be an odd number and shall not exceed 9 members.

The creditors' committee members shall be confirmed by the people's court in writing.

Chapter V Reorganization

Article 32 The period of reorganization shall be calculated from the day on which the people's court rules that a debtor shall go through reorganization to the day when the reorganization procedures are terminated. During the reorganization, if a debtor meets the following conditions, the debtor may manage its property and business operations under the supervision of its bankruptcy administrator upon filing a petition and obtaining approval from the people's court:

(a) the debtor's internal management is still functional;

(b) the debtor's internal management aligns with future operations;

(c) the debtor has no recorded misconduct, such as concealing and assigning property; and

(d) the debtor has no other recorded conduct that may materially infringe upon creditor rights.

Where the people's court approves the debtor to independently manage its property and operations, the administrator who has taken over the debtor's property and operations in compliance with these Regulations shall hand over the property and operations to the debtor. The administrators' duties and powers for asset management and operations management provided in these Regulations shall be exercised by the debtor.

管理人、债权人等利害关系人发现债务人存在严重损害债权人利益的行为或者有其他不适宜自行管理情形的，可以申请人民法院作出终止债务人自行管理的决定。人民法院决定终止的，应当通知管理人接管债务人财产和营业事务。

第三十三条　债务人或者管理人应当自人民法院裁定债务人重整之日起六个月内，同时向人民法院和债权人会议提交重整计划草案；期限届满，经债务人或者管理人请求，有正当理由的，人民法院可以裁定延期三个月。

债务人自行管理财产和营业事务的，由债务人或管理人制作重整计划草案；管理人负责管理财产和营业事务的，由管理人制作重整计划草案。

债务人、管理人未按期提出重整计划草案的，人民法院应当裁定终止重整程序，并宣告债务人破产。

第三十四条　根据重整实际需要，重整计划草案可以包括下列内容：

（一）重整投资人退出机制；

（二）重整计划执行期间债权人对特定财产享有的担保权的行使；

（三）需要约定的其他事项。

重整投资人对债务人财产、债权债务和经营状况享有知情权，有权查阅债务人有关资料，并承担保密义务。

第三十五条　下列各类债权的债权人参加讨论重整计划草案的债权人会议，依照下列债权分类，分组对重整计划草案进行表决：

（一）对债务人的特定财产享有担保权的债权；

If the debtor has materially infringed upon creditor's rights or when circumstances not conforming to internal management occur any administrator, creditor, or other stakeholders who discover such may petition the people's court for a decision to terminate the internal management. If the people's court decides to terminate such, it shall notify the administrator to take over the debtor's property and operations.

Article 33 A debtor or bankruptcy administrator shall submit a draft reorganization plan to both the people's court and the meeting of creditors within 6 months of the day the people's court approves the reorganization. When the time limit expires, the people's court may, upon the reasonable request of the debtor or the administrator, rule for a 3-month extension.

If the debtor independently manages the property and operations, the debtor or the administrator shall prepare the draft reorganization plan. Where the administrator manages the property and operations, the administrator shall prepare the draft reorganization plan.

If the debtor or the administrator fails to submit the draft reorganization plan on time, the people's court shall issue a ruling to terminate the reorganization proceedings and declare the debtor bankrupt.

Article 34 The draft reorganization plan may include the following based on actual reorganization requirements:

(a) the withdrawal plan for investors in the reorganization;

(b) the exercise of creditors' security rights in specific property during the implementation of the reorganization plan; and

(c) other issues to be agreed upon.

Reorganization investors shall have the right to be informed of the property, creditor's rights, debts, and debtor business conditions, consult the debtor's records, and maintain confidentiality.

Article 35 Creditors having the following types of claims shall participate in the meeting of creditors to discuss the draft reorganization plan and vote on it in groups:

(a) the secured creditor's rights in specific debtor property;

（二）债务人所欠职工的工资和医疗、伤残补助、抚恤费用，所欠的应当划入职工个人账户的基本养老保险、基本医疗保险费用，以及法律、行政法规规定应当支付给职工的补偿金；

（三）债务人所欠税款；

（四）普通债权。

人民法院在必要时可以决定在普通债权组中设小额债权组对重整计划草案进行表决。

第三十六条 人民法院应当自收到重整计划草案之日起三十日内召开债权人会议，对重整计划草案进行表决。

管理人应当在债权人会议表决重整计划草案十五日前，通过会议、信件、传真、电子邮件等有效方式向债权人、出资人及其他利害关系人披露重整计划草案的相关信息。

出席会议的同一表决组的债权人过半数同意重整计划草案，并且其所代表的债权额占该组债权总额的三分之二以上的，即为该组通过重整计划草案。

重整计划草案制作人应当向债权人会议就重整计划草案作出说明，并回答询问。

第三十七条 各表决组均通过重整计划草案的，重整计划即为通过。自重整计划通过之日起十日内，债务人或者管理人应当向人民法院提出批准重整计划的申请。

部分表决组未通过重整计划草案的，债务人或者管理人可以同该表决组协商。该表决组可以在协商后再表决一次，再次表决应当在第一次表决后的二个月内完成。双方协商的结果不得损害其他表决组的利益。

(b) wages, subsidies for medical treatment, disability allowance, and workplace injury compensation owed by the debtor, basic pension insurance premiums, and basic medical insurance premiums transferred to the individual accounts of employers as well as employee compensation as required by laws and administrative regulations;

(c) the taxes owed by the debtor; and

(d) the ordinary creditor's rights.

The people's court may decide, if necessary, to set up a group of small claims creditors under the ordinary creditor's rights to vote on the draft reorganization plan.

Article 36 The people's court shall convene a meeting of creditors to vote on the draft within 30 days of the day the draft reorganization plan is received.

The administrator shall disclose the information of the draft reorganization plan to creditors, investors, and other stakeholders through meetings, letters, faxes, e-mails, and other valid means 15 days before the meeting of creditors votes on the draft.

Where the majority of the creditors in the same voting group have claims representing two-thirds or more of the total amount of claims group at the meeting of creditors, and approve the draft reorganization plan, the draft shall be adopted by such group.

The drafter of the reorganization plan shall explain the draft plan and answer any inquiries at the meeting of creditors.

Article 37 If all voting groups approve the draft reorganization plan, the draft shall be adopted. The debtor or the administrator shall submit a petition for the people's court to approve the reorganization plan within 10 days of the day the reorganization plan is adopted.

The debtor or the administrator may negotiate with any of the voting groups that do not agree with the draft. The group may vote again after the negotiation within 2 months of the date of the first vote. Negotiation results shall not infringe upon the rights of any other voting group.

未通过重整计划草案的表决组拒绝再次表决或者再次表决仍未通过重整计划草案，但重整计划草案符合法律规定的条件的，债务人或者管理人可以申请人民法院批准重整计划草案。

人民法院审查时，应当充分听取各方意见；认为重整计划草案符合法律规定的，应当自收到申请之日起三十日内裁定批准，终止重整程序，并予以公告。

第三十八条 重整计划草案未获得通过且未依照本条例第三十七条的规定获得批准，或者已通过的重整计划未获得批准的，人民法院应当裁定终止重整程序，并宣告债务人破产。

第三十九条 重整计划由债务人负责执行。人民法院裁定批准重整计划后，已接管财产和营业事务的管理人应当向债务人移交财产和营业事务。

债务人在重整计划执行完毕后，应当向人民法院申请裁定确认重整计划执行完毕。按照重整计划减免的债务，自重整计划执行完毕时起，债务人不再承担清偿责任。

第四十条 人民政府及其相关部门和金融机构应当加强对债务人重整的支持，可以通过依法落实相关税收优惠、提供信贷支持等方式帮助债务人恢复正常生产经营；重整计划执行期间及执行完毕后，不得对其在市场准入、招投标、行政审批、公共服务等方面额外设置限制性条件，法律、行政法规另有规定的除外。

重整计划执行期间，债务人可以依据国家和本省有关规定，凭人民法院出具的相应裁定书向县级以上人民政府社会信用主管部门或者作出失信行为认定的单位申请信用修复。

Where any of the voting groups that do not agree with the draft refuse to re-vote or disagree with the draft after re-voting, the debtor or the administrator may petition the people's court to approve the draft plan, provided it meets legal requirements.

The people's court shall fully consider the opinions of all parties during their review. Where the people's court deems that the draft reorganization plan complies with the law, it shall grant an approval, terminate the reorganization procedures, and issue a public notice of such within 30 days of the day the petition for approval is received.

Article 38 Where a draft reorganization plan fails to be adopted and approved pursuant to Article 37 of these Regulations, or where an adopted draft fails to be approved, the people's court shall issue a ruling to terminate the reorganization procedures and declare the debtor bankrupt.

Article 39 The debtor shall be responsible for carrying out the reorganization plan. After the people's court approves the reorganization plan, the administrator that has taken over the property and operations shall transfer such to the debtor.

After the implementation of the reorganization plan is completed, the debtor shall petition the people's court to issue a ruling to confirm the completion. The debtor shall no longer be liable to pay debts reduced or exempted in accordance with the reorganization plan after the completion of the implementation of the reorganization plan.

Article 40 The people's government, its appropriate agencies, and financial institutions shall improve their support for the debtor's reorganization, and may help the debtor resume operations by implementing appropriate preferential tax policies and providing credit loan support pursuant to law. No additional restrictive requirements including market access, bidding, administrative approval, or public service restrictions shall be imposed during and after the implementation of the reorganization plan, except as otherwise provided by laws and administrative regulations.

During the implementation of the reorganization plan, the debtor may submit a request for credit repair to the competent social credit agency of the people's government at or above the county level or to the institution that made the decision to deem them untrustworthy pursuant to applicable national and provincial laws, and the decision made by the people's court.

债务人在重整计划执行过程中，相关单位和个人不予配合的，债务人可以申请人民法院协助执行。

第四十一条 申请重整前，债务人可以预先制定重整计划草案并征求相关债权人、出资人等利害关系人的意见，或者与债权人、出资人等利害关系人就债务清偿、出资人权益调整等协商签订协议。

重整程序中，申请人或者管理人可以将预先制定的重整计划草案提交债权人会议表决，或者将预先达成的协议内容直接纳入重整计划草案。

重整程序中，管理人可以根据案件实际情况沿用预重整已有的工作成果。

第四十二条 相关权利人在重整前已经同意债务人预先制定的重整计划草案或者已经达成相关协议，在重整程序中制定的重整计划草案未减损相关权利人权益的，经相关权利人向管理人明示，相关权利人可以不参与重整程序中制定的重整计划草案表决，视为其同意重整程序中制定的重整计划草案。但存在下列情形的，相关权利人应当对重整计划草案进行表决：

（一）重整计划草案对预先制定的重整计划草案或者预先达成的协议内容进行了修改，并对相关权利人产生不利影响的；

（二）债务人隐瞒重要信息、披露虚假信息的；

（三）客观情况发生重大变化的；

（四）人民法院认为应当进行表决的其他情形。

If any of the organizations or individuals involved fails to cooperate while carrying out the reorganization plan, the debtor may petition the people's court for enforcement.

Article 41 Before petitioning for reorganization, the debtor may prepare a draft reorganization plan and collect the opinions of creditors, investors, and other stakeholders, or negotiate and sign an agreement with creditors, investors, and other stakeholders on matters including debt repayments and adjustment of investor rights.

During the reorganization procedure, the applicant or the administrator may submit the draft reorganization plan prepared in advance to the meeting of creditors for voting, or directly include the agreement in this draft plan.

With regard to the reorganization proceedings, the administrator may use existing pre-reorganization results as the case may be.

Article 42 If any rights holder involved agrees to the draft reorganization plan prepared in advance by the debtor or has entered into agreements before the reorganization, and the draft plan prepared in the reorganization proceedings does not infringe upon their rights, such rights holders may opt not to participate in the votes for the draft plan prepared in the reorganization proceedings based on the grounds that the rights holders have expressly informed the administrator of such, it shall be deemed that such rights holders have agreed with the draft reorganization plan prepared during the reorganization proceedings. However, rights holders involved must vote on the draft reorganization plan if:

(a) the draft reorganization plan changes the plan prepared in advance or the agreement consented to in advance, which materially affects right holder's rights;

(b) the debtor conceals important information or provides falsified information;

(c) substantial changes in actual circumstances have taken place; or

(d) other circumstances where the people's court deems it necessary to vote.

第六章　和　解

第四十三条　人民法院经审查认为和解申请符合本条例规定的，应当裁定和解，予以公告。自人民法院裁定债务人和解之日起至和解程序终止，为和解期间。

和解期间，经债务人申请，人民法院可以批准债务人在管理人的监督下自行管理财产和营业事务。

第四十四条　债务人直接向人民法院申请和解的，人民法院应当在债权申报期届满后一个月内，召开债权人会议，对和解协议草案进行表决。

债务人在人民法院受理破产申请后、宣告债务人破产前申请和解，人民法院同意对和解协议草案进行表决的，应当在和解协议草案提出后一个月内召开债权人会议，对和解协议草案进行表决，债权申报期不计入该期间。案件复杂的，可以延长一个月。

管理人和债务人应当在债权人会议上就和解协议草案作出说明，并回答债权人的提问。

第四十五条　债务人在和解期间有下列情形之一的，管理人应当及时向人民法院报告：

（一）债务人隐匿账簿、文书、财产或者虚报财务状况的；

（二）债务人拒绝回答管理人询问或者故意隐瞒重大事项的；

（三）债务人经通知后，无正当理由不出席债权人会议的；

（四）债务人有欺诈、恶意减少债务人财产或者其他显著不利于债权人的行为的；

Chapter VI Settlement

Article 43 Where the people's court deems that a request for settlement complies with these Regulations following a review, it shall issue a ruling on such settlement and publish such ruling. The period between the day on which the people's court issues a ruling on the debtor's settlement and the termination of the settlement procedures is the settlement period.

During the settlement negotiations, a debtor may manage its property and operations under the supervision of its bankruptcy administrator upon filing a petition and obtaining approval from the people's court.

Article 44 If the debtor directly submits a petition for settlement with the people's court, the people's court shall convene a meeting of creditors to vote on the draft settlement agreement within 1 month of the expiration of the creditor's rights declaration period.

If the debtor petitions settlement after the people's court accepts the bankruptcy case and before the declaration of debtors' bankruptcy, and the people's court agrees to vote on the draft settlement agreement, a meeting of creditors shall be convened to vote on the draft within 1 month of the draft being proposed, and the debt declaration period shall not be counted as part of such period. Complex cases may be extended for 1 month.

The administrator and the debtor shall explain the draft settlement agreement at the meeting of creditors and respond to creditor inquiries.

Article 45 The administrator shall, during the settlement, promptly report to the people's court if:

(a) the debtor conceals account books, documents, and property, or falsely reports its financial status;

(b) the debtor refuses to respond to administrator inquiries or deliberately conceals major issues;

(c) the debtor fails to attend the meeting of creditors without valid reason after being notified of such;

(d) the debtor is recorded committing any fraudulent act or maliciously under-declaring property, or any other acts that clearly infringe upon creditor's rights; or

（五）导致和解程序无法继续进行的其他情形。

人民法院接到报告后，应当传唤债务人，如债务人无正当理由不到场或者不能就上述行为说明正当理由时，人民法院可以终止和解程序并宣告债务人破产。

第四十六条 债权人会议通过和解协议的决议，由出席会议的有表决权的债权人过半数同意，并且其所代表的债权额占无财产担保债权总额的三分之二以上。

经对债务人的特定财产享有担保权的债权人同意，和解协议草案可以对该债权人的权益进行约定。

债务人与债权人在债权人会议召开前达成未损害其他债权人利益的债务清偿协议，和解协议草案规定的债务清偿安排不低于该书面协议约定且不低于同类债权的清偿比例的，视为该债权人出席债权人会议，并同意和解协议草案。

第四十七条 自债权人会议表决通过和解协议之日起五日内，债务人或者管理人应当向人民法院提出认可和解协议的申请。人民法院经审查认为符合本条例规定的，应当自收到申请之日起十五日内裁定认可，终止和解程序，并予以公告。

和解协议草案未获得债权人会议表决通过，或者已经债权人会议表决通过的和解协议未获得人民法院认可的，人民法院应当裁定终止和解程序，并宣告债务人破产。

第四十八条 经人民法院裁定认可的和解协议，对债务人、全体和解债权人及同意和解协议的担保债权人均有约束力。

(e) other circumstances that discontinue the settlement procedures' exist.

After receiving the report, the people's court shall summon the debtor. If the debtor fails to appear without valid reason or raise valid reason for the above acts, the people's court may terminate the settlement procedures and declare the debtor bankrupt.

Article 46 Resolutions passed by the meeting of creditors on the settlement agreement must be approved by the majority of the creditors with voting rights present at the meeting, and whose claims account for more than two-thirds of the total amount of claims free from property security.

The draft settlement agreement may specify the rights and interests of creditors having equity security in their property with the creditors' consent.

If the debtor and the creditor reach a debt payment agreement that does not infringe upon the rights of any other creditors before the meeting of creditors, and the payment provided in the draft settlement agreement is not lower than that agreed in the agreement or the payment proportion of similar claims, the creditor shall be deemed to have attended the meeting of creditors and agreed to the draft settlement agreement.

Article 47 Within 5 days of the day on which the settlement agreement is approved by the meeting of creditors' votes, the debtor or the administrator shall petition the people's court to approve this agreement. If the people's court considers upon review that this agreement conforms with these Regulations, it shall issue a ruling for approval, terminate the settlement procedures, and issue a public notice within 15 days of receiving the petition.

If the draft settlement agreement is not approved by the meeting of creditors' votes, or the settlement agreement approved by the meeting of creditors is not approved by the people's court, the people's court shall issue a ruling to terminate the settlement procedures and declare the debtor bankrupt.

Article 48 A settlement agreement approved by the people's court shall have binding force on the debtor, all the creditors in the settlement, and all creditors holding security interests that approved the agreement.

因债务人的欺诈或者其他违法行为而成立的和解协议，人民法院应当裁定撤销协议或者确认协议无效，并宣告债务人破产。

第四十九条 债务人与全体债权人可以就债务清理在庭外自行委托人民调解委员会、调解员、调解组织或者破产事务管理部门等进行和解，达成和解协议的，可以请求人民法院裁定认可和解协议。

第七章 破产清算

第五十条 人民法院受理破产清算申请后，第一次债权人会议上无人提出重整或和解申请的，管理人应当在债权审核确认和必要的审计、资产评估后，及时向人民法院提出宣告破产的申请。

人民法院受理破产和解或重整申请后，债务人出现应当宣告破产的法定原因时，人民法院应当依法宣告债务人破产。

人民法院宣告债务人破产的，应当自裁定作出之日起五日内送达债务人和管理人，自裁定作出之日起十日内通知已知债权人，并予以公告。

债务人被宣告破产后，债务人称为破产人，债务人财产称为破产财产，人民法院受理破产申请时对债务人享有的债权称为破产债权。

第五十一条 变价出售破产财产应当通过拍卖进行，债权人会议决议直接变价出售的除外。所拍卖的破产财产价格，可以以委托评估确定的价格、债权人会议决定、网络询价、定向询价等方式合理确定底价。

处置破产财产前，管理人可以确定有相应资质的审计、评估机构对破产财产进行审计、评估。债权人会议对破产财产的市场价格无异议的，可以不进行评估，但国有资产除外。

The people's court shall revoke the agreement or rule it invalid and declare the debtor bankrupt should the settlement agreement be created through debtor fraud or any illegal act.

Article 49 The debtor and all creditors may independently entrust a people's mediation committee, mediator, mediation organization, or bankruptcy administrative agency to settle the debts out of court. If a settlement agreement is reached, they may petition the people's court to issue a ruling to approve the agreement.

Chapter VII Bankruptcy Liquidation

Article 50 After the people's court accepts the bankruptcy case, if no petition for reorganization or settlement is submitted at the first meeting of creditors, the administrator shall promptly petition the people's court to declare bankruptcy after all claims are reviewed and confirmed and any necessary audits and asset appraisal are completed.

Where there is statutory reason to declare the debtor bankrupt after the people's court accepts the bankruptcy settlement or reorganization petition, the people's court shall declare the debtor bankrupt pursuant to law.

Where the people's court declares the debtor bankrupt, the court shall serve the declaration on the debtor and the administrator within 5 days of the day on which the ruling is made, notify the known creditors and issue a public notice within 10 days of the date the ruling is made.

Where a debtor is declared bankrupt, the debtor shall be named as the bankrupt party and their property taken as the bankruptcy assets. Claims against the debtor when the people's court accepts the bankruptcy case shall be the bankruptcy creditor's rights.

Article 51 Bankruptcy assets shall be sold via auction unless the meeting of creditors decides to make direct sales of the assets. The reserve price of the bankruptcy assets may be reasonably determined through third party valuation, the decision made by the meeting of creditors, online inquiry, directional inquiry, and other methods.

Before selling the bankruptcy assets, the administrator may decide upon a qualified audit and appraisal organization to audit and appraise the bankruptcy assets. Unless for state-owned assets, an appraisal may not be required if the meeting of creditors does not object to the market price of the bankruptcy assets.

第五十二条 破产财产数额巨大，即时变现存在困难且严重影响整体债权人利益的，经债权人会议决议，管理人可以委托有资质的资产管理公司或者其他机构管理财产，并制定变现计划。财产的变现所得，扣除必要费用后，剩余部分向债权人清偿。

第五十三条 破产费用和共益债务由债务人财产随时清偿。债权人、管理人、债务人的出资人、实际控制人或者其他利害关系人垫付破产费用和共益债务的，垫付款项按照破产费用和共益债务的顺序从债务人财产中向垫付人随时清偿。

破产申请受理后，经债权人会议决议通过，或者第一次债权人会议召开前经人民法院许可，自行管理的债务人或者管理人可以为债务人继续营业借款。该借款产生的债务列入共益债务。经对债务人特定财产享有担保权的债权人同意，债权人会议可以决议上述借款的清偿顺序优先于该担保债权。

债务人财产不足以清偿破产费用，管理人应当提请人民法院终结破产程序。人民法院应当自收到请求之日起十五日内裁定终结破产程序，并予以公告。

第五十四条 对破产人的特定财产享有担保权的权利人，对该特定财产享有优先受偿的权利。

破产财产在优先清偿破产费用和共益债务后，依照下列顺序清偿：

（一）破产人所欠职工的工资和医疗、伤残补助、抚恤费用，所欠的应当划入职工个人账户的基本养老保险、基本医疗保险费用，以及法律、行政法规规定应当支付给职工的补偿金；

Article 52 If the price of the bankruptcy assets is high, thus making it difficult to be sold and may seriously affect overall creditor interests, the administrator may hire a qualified asset management company or other agency to manage the assets and prepare a realization plan upon the resolution of the meeting of creditors. After deducting the necessary expenses from the income gained from the assets, the remaining part shall be paid off to the creditors.

Article 53 Bankruptcy expenses and mutual benefits debts shall be paid off at any time by the debtor's property. If any creditor, administrator, shareholders, controllers, or other stakeholders advance bankruptcy expenses and mutual benefits debts, such advance payments shall be deemed as bankruptcy expenses and mutual benefits debts and be paid off from the debtor's property at any time.

After the bankruptcy case is accepted, and upon the adoption of the resolution of the meeting of creditors or with the approval of the people's court before the first meeting of creditors, debtors or administrators independently managing property may borrow money to continue debtor operations. Any debt arising from such borrowing shall be included as mutual benefits debt. The meeting of creditors may decide the loan repayment order to take priority over the secured creditor's rights with the consent of creditors having equity in specific debtor property.

Where debtor's property is not sufficient to pay off bankruptcy expenses, the administrator shall petition the people's court to terminate the bankruptcy procedures. The people's court shall, within 15 days of the day the petition is received, decide to terminate bankruptcy procedures and issue a public notice.

Article 54 Creditors with security interests in specific property shall be prioritized when payment for such property is distributed.

After paying off the prioritized bankruptcy proceedings expenses and mutual benefits debts, the remaining bankruptcy assets shall be liquidated in the following order:

(a) wages and subsidies for medical treatment, disability allowance, and workplace injury compensation expenses in default, basic pension insurance premiums, basic medical insurance premiums to be transferred to employee personal accounts, and compensation for employees as required by laws and administrative regulations;

（二）破产人欠缴的除前项规定以外的社会保险费用和破产人所欠税款；

（三）普通破产债权。

享有本条第一款规定权利的债权人行使优先受偿权利未能完全受偿的，其未受偿的债权作为普通债权；放弃优先受偿权利的，其债权作为普通债权。

破产财产不足以清偿同一顺序的清偿要求的，按照比例分配。

债务人的董事、监事和高级管理人员的工资按照该债务人职工的平均工资计算。

第五十五条 债务人被人民法院宣告破产后，管理人应当及时拟订并提交债权人会议讨论通过破产财产分配方案，经人民法院裁定认可后，由管理人执行。无财产可供分配的，或者管理人在最后分配完结且提交破产财产分配报告后，管理人应当请求人民法院裁定终结破产程序。人民法院裁定终结的，应当予以公告。

破产宣告前，第三人为债务人提供足额担保或者为债务人清偿全部到期债务的，或者债务人已清偿全部到期债务的，人民法院应当裁定终结破产程序，并予以公告。

第五十六条 管理人应当自破产程序终结之日起十日内，持人民法院终结破产程序的裁定，向破产人的原税务机关、原登记机关办理注销登记，相关部门应当予以办理。

破产程序终结后，管理人可以依照国家档案管理的有关规定将接管的破产人的账册、文书等卷宗材料移交档案馆保存，保管费用由管理人在破产财产分配时预留。

(b) social insurance premiums and taxes defaulted on, other than those provided in the preceding paragraph; and

(c) ordinary creditor's bankruptcy rights.

If creditors enjoying the rights provided in Paragraph 1 of this Article are not fully repaid after exercising the payment priority, any unpaid claims shall be deemed common claims. Where a party waives such priority, their creditor's rights shall be deemed as common claims.

Where the bankruptcy assets are insufficient to cover liquidation requirements in a similar sequence, it shall be distributed according to the proportion.

Wages owed to directors, supervisors, and executives of the debtor shall be calculated based on average debtor employee wages.

Article 55 After the debtor is declared bankrupt by the people's court, the administrator shall promptly prepare and submit the bankruptcy assets distribution plan to the meeting of creditors for discussion and approval. After being approved by the people's court, the administrator shall implement the distribution plan. If there are no assets available for distribution, or after the administrator has completed the final distribution and submitted the distribution report, the administrator shall petition the people's court to issue a ruling to terminate the bankruptcy proceedings. The people's court shall issue a public notice if the court decides to terminate the proceedings.

Before bankruptcy is declared, if a third party provides the debtor with sufficient security or pays off all debts owed by the debtor, or the debtor has paid off all due debts, the people's court shall issue a ruling to terminate the bankruptcy proceedings and issue a public notice.

Article 56 The administrator shall, within 10 days of the date on which the bankruptcy procedures are terminated by the decision of the people's court to terminate bankruptcy proceedings, deregister the company through the original tax authority and registration agency, which shall be managed by the appropriate agencies.

After the bankruptcy proceedings are terminated, the administrator may, in accordance with applicable rules of the national archives administration, transfer the accounts, documents, and other files belonging to the bankrupt taken over to the archives for preservation, and preservation expenses shall be kept in advance by the administrator during the distribution of the bankruptcy assets.

第八章　简易程序

第五十七条　对于债权债务关系明确、债务人财产状况清晰且具备下列情形之一的破产案件，由审判员一人适用简易程序独任审理；确有必要的，可以由合议庭审理：

（一）债权人人数较少的；

（二）债务人为中小企业的；

（三）债务人无财产或者财产较少，可能不足以支付全部破产费用的；

（四）债务人财产易于变价、无需变价或者已经处置变现的；

（五）债务人经过自行清算或者强制清算，资产和负债均已确认完毕的；

（六）债务人成立时间较短，经营活动较少的；

（七）债务人已经歇业或者停工停产，且不存在职工安置问题的；

（八）人民法院认为适宜适用简易程序的其他情形。

适用简易程序审理的破产案件，人民法院可以指定个人管理人。

第五十八条　人民法院在裁定受理破产申请时，应当同时决定是否适用简易程序并进行公告。

适用简易程序审理的破产案件，人民法院应当在裁定受理之日起四个月内审结。因特殊情况需要延长审理期限的，可以延长不超过二个月。

适用简易程序审理的破产案件，除申报债权期间外，不受本条例关于破产程序各节点期限的限制，但应当妥善保护破产参与人的合法权利。

Chapter VIII Simplified Procedures

Article 57 If a bankruptcy case has a clear obligation relationship with a clear condition of debtor's property and falls under any of the following circumstances, the case shall be tried by one judge through simplified procedures; it may also be tried by a panel of judges when necessary:

(a) there is a small number of creditors;

(b) the debtor is a small or medium-sized business;

(c) the debtor has no property or little property, which may not be sufficient to cover bankruptcy expenses;

(d) the debtor's property is easy to appraise at the current rate, there is no need to appraise at the current rate, or has been disposed of and money received;

(e) the debtor's assets and liabilities have been confirmed through self-liquidation or compulsory liquidation;

(f) the debtor has been established for only a short time and has only conducted a few business activities;

(g) the debtor has closed down or stopped operations, and there are no issues concerning employee resettlement; or

(h) other circumstances under which the people's court deems it appropriate to implement simplified procedures.

With regard to bankruptcy cases tried through simplified procedures, the people's court may designate an individual as the administrator.

Article 58 When deciding to accept the bankruptcy case, the people's court shall also decide whether to implement simplified procedures and issue a public notice.

The people's court shall conclude bankruptcy cases tried under simplified procedures within 4 months from the day on which the cases are accepted. If special circumstances deem it necessary to extend the trial time limit, it may be extended for no more than 2 months.

Any bankruptcy case tried through simplified procedures shall not be subject to the bankruptcy proceeding time limit restrictions provided in these Regulations, except for the period to declare claims. However, the legal rights of bankruptcy participants shall be sufficiently protected.

第五十九条　适用简易程序审理的破产案件，一般采用传真、电子邮件等简便方式送达相关文书，但民事裁定书、决定书除外。

债权人会议一般采用视频会议等灵活方式召开，优先采取网络投票、书面信函、电子邮件等形式进行表决。

适用简易程序的破产案件，一般不设立债权人委员会。

第六十条　适用简易程序审理的破产案件，在第一次债权人会议召开时，已经形成重整计划草案的，可以一并提交债权人会议表决。

适用简易程序审理的破产案件，在第一次债权人会议召开时已能够确认债务人符合宣告破产条件的案件，管理人可以在第一次债权人会议上申请人民法院宣告债务人破产，并将债务人财产处置方案、分配方案以及破产程序终结后可能追加分配的方案一并提交债权人会议表决。

第六十一条　债务人、债权人、管理人及其他利害关系人认为不宜适用简易程序的，最迟应当在第一次债权人会议上提出异议，由人民法院决定是否将简易程序转为普通程序。

人民法院在审理破产案件时发现存在不宜适用简易程序情形的，应当及时决定将案件转为普通程序审理，并将转换审理程序决定书送达管理人，予以公告。管理人应当通知已知债权人、债务人、破产事务管理部门和有关单位。

案件转为普通程序审理的，除有证据证实确有错误或有侵害当事人实体合法权益的，已经进行的破产程序继续有效。

Article 59 Documents for bankruptcy cases tried through simplified procedures shall be generally served by simple methods, such as fax or e-mail, except for civil judicial rulings and decisions.

Meetings of creditors shall generally be convened flexibly, using methods such as video conference, and online voting, written letters, and e-mail shall be given priority in voting.

A creditors' committee will not be established in bankruptcy cases tried through simplified procedures usually.

Article 60 Where draft reorganization plans in bankruptcy cases tried through simplified procedures are prepared by the time the first meeting of creditors is held, such drafts may be submitted to the meeting of creditors for voting.

Where it can be verified that the debtor meets the requirements to declare bankruptcy at the first meeting of creditors in bankruptcy cases tried through simplified procedures, the administrator may petition the people's court to declare the debtor bankrupt at the first meeting of creditors. The management and distribution plan for the debtor's property and the plan for potential additional allocation after the termination of bankruptcy proceedings shall also be submitted to the meeting of creditors for voting.

Article 61 If the debtor, creditor, administrator, or other stakeholder believes it is inappropriate to implement simplified procedures, they shall raise an objection no later than the first meeting of creditors, and the people's court shall decide whether or not to change the simplified procedures into general procedures.

Where the people's court finds that it is inappropriate to implement simplified procedures when adjudicating bankruptcy cases, the court shall promptly decide whether to change the case into general procedures, notify the administrator of the decision to change, and issue a public notice. The administrator shall inform the creditors, debtors, bankruptcy administrative agencies, and other organizations involved.

Where the case is changed into general procedures, the proceedings conducted shall continue to be valid unless there is proof of an error or the legal rights of the parties concerned have been infringed upon.

第九章　法律责任

第六十二条　债务人及债务人的有关人员违反本条例规定，有下列行为之一的，由人民法院依法予以训诫、拘传、罚款、拘留；造成损失的，应当依法承担赔偿责任；构成犯罪的，依法追究刑事责任：

（一）拒不配合管理人调查债务人的财产，拒不回答相关问题，或者作虚假陈述、误导性陈述的；

（二）拒不提交相关资料或隐匿、毁弃、伪造、变造财务账簿等资料的；

（三）依照本条例规定应当向管理人移交财产、印章和账簿、文书等但拒不移交的；

（四）故意隐匿、转移、毁损、不当处分债务人财产或者其他不当减损债务人财产的；

（五）虚构债务，或者承认不真实债务的；

（六）故意逃避债务的；

（七）以不正当手段妨碍管理人执行职务的；

（八）擅自离开住所地或者出境的；

（九）有义务列席债权人会议的债务人的有关人员，经人民法院传唤，无正当理由拒不列席债权人会议的；

（十）其他妨害破产程序的行为。

债务人的董事、监事或者高级管理人员违反忠实义务、勤勉义务，致使所在企业破产的，依法承担民事责任，并自破产程序终结之日起三年内不得担任任何企业的董事、监事、高级管理人员。

Chapter IX Legal Liability

Article 62 Any debtor or their employees who violate these Regulations and commit any of the following acts shall be admonished, forcibly summoned, fined, or arrested by the people's court pursuant to law, shall assume indemnification liability pursuant to law if damages are caused, and held criminally liable pursuant to law if they:

(a) refuse to cooperate with the administrator during the investigation of the debtor's property, answer appropriate questions, or provide falsified or misleading statements;

(b) refuse to submit the necessary documents or conceal, destroy, discard, counterfeit, forge, or alter financial account books;

(c) refuse to transfer the property, seals, account books, documents, and anything else to be transferred to the administrator in compliance with these Regulations;

(d) deliberately conceal, transfer, damage, or improperly dispose of the debtor's property, or commit other acts that damage the debtor's property without valid reason;

(e) falsify debts or claim false debts;

(f) deliberately evade debts;

(g) obstruct the administrator from performing their duties without valid reason;

(h) leave their domicile or cross national borders without official permission;

(i) debtor employees obliged to attend the meeting of creditors refuse to attend without valid reason after being summoned by the people's court; or

(j) other acts that hinder the bankruptcy procedures.

Any of the debtor's directors, supervisors, or executives who violate their duty of loyalty and diligence, causing the bankruptcy of the business, shall assume civil liability pursuant to law, and shall not serve as the director, supervisor, or executive for any business within 3 years from the day the bankruptcy proceedings are concluded.

债务人的董事、监事、高级管理人员因故意或者重大过失违反本条例第六条第四款规定，造成债务人财产损失的，应当依法承担赔偿责任。

第六十三条　债权人、利害关系人和其他第三人违反本条例规定，由人民法院依法予以训诫、拘传、罚款、拘留；造成损失的，依法承担赔偿责任；构成犯罪的，依法追究刑事责任：

（一）申报虚假债权，或者主张虚假的取回权、抵销权，损害债权人利益的；

（二）人民法院受理破产申请后，与债务人恶意串通企图通过诉讼等方式侵害其他债权人合法权益的；

（三）明知债务人处于破产程序中，与债务人恶意串通转移债务人财产，损害债权人利益的；

（四）妨碍管理人执行职务的；

（五）其他损害债权人利益、妨害破产程序的行为。

第六十四条　管理人未依照本条例规定勤勉尽责、忠实执行职务，由人民法院责令改正，可以处以罚款、训诫，并可以采取降低管理人报酬、依职权更换管理人、暂停或者取消其管理人资格等措施；给债权人、债务人或者第三人造成损失的，依法承担赔偿责任。

管理人与他人恶意串通，妨害破产程序的，由人民法院依法予以训诫、拘传、罚款、拘留；构成犯罪的，依法追究刑事责任。

第十章　附　则

第六十五条　本条例没有规定的，适用《中华人民共和国民事诉讼法》《中华人民共和国企业破产法》和其他法律、行政法规的有关规定。

Any of the debtor's directors, supervisors, or executives who, either intentionally or through gross negligence, violates Paragraph 4 of Article 6 hereof and causes the debtor to suffer property loss(es) to the debtor shall be liable for indemnification pursuant to law.

Article 63 Any debtor, stakeholder, or related party who violates these Regulations and commits any of the following acts shall be admonished, forcibly summoned, fined, or arrested by the people's court pursuant to law, shall assume indemnification liability if damages are caused, and held criminally liable pursuant to law if they:

(a) declare false claims, claim false reclamation rights or rights of offset damaging creditors' interests;

(b) collude with the debtor to infringe upon creditor's rights through litigation after the people's court accepts the bankruptcy case;

(c) collude with the debtor to transfer the debtor's property with full knowledge that the debtor is undergoing bankruptcy proceedings and infringing upon creditor's rights;

(d) hinder the administrator from performing their duties; or

(e) commit other acts that infringe upon creditor's rights or hinder bankruptcy proceedings.

Article 64 Any administrator who fails to perform their duties diligently and faithfully in compliance with these Regulations shall be corrected, fined, or admonished by the people's court, and may be *motu proprio* replaced, suspended, made disqualified, or have their payment reduced. Administrators shall also be liable to indemnify any creditors, debtors, or third parties who suffer losses as a result of their actions.

Any administrator who conspires with others to hinder bankruptcy proceedings shall be admonished, forcibly summoned, fined, or arrested by the people's court pursuant to law and held criminally liable pursuant to law if a crime is committed.

Chapter X Supplementary Provisions

Article 65 Unless otherwise provided in these Regulations, the Civil Procedure Law of the People's Republic of China, the Enterprise Bankruptcy Law of the People's Republic of China, and other laws and administrative regulations shall control.

第六十六条 住所地位于海南自由贸易港的合伙企业、个人独资企业依照本条例规定清理债务，合伙人、投资人对企业存续期间的债务应当依法承担偿还责任。

第六十七条 本条例自2022年3月1日起施行。

Article 66 The partners and investors of any partnership or sole proprietorship domiciled in Hainan Free Trade Port that liquidate their debts in compliance with these Regulations shall be liable for repayment of the debts while the business is in operation pursuant to law.

Article 67 These Regulations shall come into force as of March 1, 2022.

海南自由贸易港社会信用条例

Regulations of Hainan Free Trade Port on Social Credit

海南自由贸易港社会信用条例

（2021 年 9 月 29 日海南省第六届人民代表大会常务委员会第三十次会议通过）

目 录

第一章 总 则

第一条 为了规范社会信用信息管理，维护信用主体合法权益，加快社会信用体系建设，优化营商环境，推进海南自由贸易港高质量发展，根据有关法律、行政法规，结合海南自由贸易港实际，制定本条例。

第二条 本条例所称社会信用，是指自然人、法人和非法人组织等信用主体在社会和经济活动中履行法定义务或者约定义务的行为和状态。

社会信用信息，是指可用以识别、分析、判断信用主体遵守法定义务或者履行约定义务状况的客观数据和资料。社会信用信息分为公共信用信息和市场信用信息。

公共信用信息是指国家机关以及法律、法规授权具有管理公共事务职能的组织等，在履行法定职责、提供公共服务过程中产生或者获取的社会信用信息。

Regulations of Hainan Free Trade Port on Social Credit

(Adopted at the 30th Session of the Standing Committee of the 6th Hainan Provincial People's Congress on September 29, 2021)

Contents

Chapter I General Provisions

Article 1 These Regulations are enacted to govern social credit information administration, protect entity's legal interests, accelerate the establishment of the social credit system, optimize the business environment, and encourage high-quality development in the Hainan Free Trade Port pursuant to laws, administrative regulations, as well as realities of the Hainan Free Trade Port.

Article 2 Social credit as mentioned in these Regulations refers to the conduct and circumstances of entities including individuals, juristic persons, and unincorporated entities when performing their statutory or agreed obligations in social and economic activities.

Social credit information refers to the information and material that can be used to identify, analyze, and confirm compliance with statutory obligations or the performance of agreed obligations by the entities. Social credit information is classified as public credit information and business credit reports.

Public credit information refers to social credit information generated or obtained by state agencies authorized by laws and regulations to manage public affairs when performing statutory duties or offering public services.

市场信用信息是指行业协会商会、信用服务机构及其他企业事业单位等，在生产经营和社会服务活动中产生或者获取的社会信用信息。

第三条　社会信用信息的采集、归集、披露、共享、查询和应用等活动应当依法进行，不得危害国家安全、公共安全和公共利益，不得泄露国家秘密、商业秘密与个人隐私，确保信息安全。

第四条　县级以上人民政府应当将社会信用体系建设纳入国民经济和社会发展规划，建立健全社会信用体系建设的协调机制、目标责任制和考核制度，统筹推进本行政区域社会信用体系建设。

县级以上人民政府社会信用主管部门负责社会信用管理的综合协调、规划编制、政策制定及监督管理等工作，统筹建设、运营、管理本级信用信息共享平台。

县级以上人民政府自然资源和规划、旅游文化、生态环境、商务、教育、卫生健康、公安、住房和城乡建设、交通运输、市场监督管理等有关部门，监察委员会、人民法院、人民检察院等，应当按照职责分工做好相关社会信用工作。

第五条　国家机关以及法律、法规授权具有管理公共事务职能的组织应当加强信用应用，建立健全以信用为基础的监管机制，对监管对象进行分级分类监管。

第六条　社会信用体系建设应当注重发挥行业协会商会以及其他社会组织的作用，鼓励、引导社会力量参与信用管理、服务和监督。

第七条　鼓励发展信用服务业，支持信用服务机构通过征信、信用咨询、信用评级、信用保险、信用担保等，为社会提供信用产品和服务。

A business credit report refers to the social credit information generated or obtained by industry associations, chambers of commerce, credit service providers, and other enterprises and public institutions during business production, operation, and social service.

Article 3 The collection, classification, disclosure, sharing, inquiry, and use of social credit information shall be conducted pursuant to law, and shall not harm national security, public security, or the public interest, and shall not disclose state secrets, trade secrets, or personal privacy, and information security shall be ensured.

Article 4 The people's governments at or above the county level shall include the establishment of the social credit system into the national economic and social development plan, create and optimize coordination, goal-oriented accountability, and assessment systems for establishing the social credit system, and comprehensively encourage the establishment of the social credit system in their administrative areas.

The competent social credit agencies of the people's governments at or above the county level shall be responsible for social credit comprehensive coordination, plan preparation, policy creation, oversight, and administration, and shall conduct overall administration for the building, operation, and management of the credit information sharing platform at the same level.

The agencies of the people's governments at or above the county level, such as the natural resources and planning, tourism and culture, ecological environment, commerce, education, health, public security, housing and urban-rural construction, transportation, market regulation and administration agencies, as well as the oversight commissions, people's courts, and people's procuratorates, shall fully perform their social credit duties.

Article 5 State agencies authorized by laws and regulations to manage public affairs shall enhance the use of credit, create and optimize a credit-based oversight system, and conduct hierarchical and categorized oversight over those subject to credit oversight.

Article 6 The establishment of the social credit system shall focus on the role of trade associations, chambers of commerce, and other social organizations, and shall encourage and guide the private sector to participate in credit administration, service, and oversight.

Article 7 Credit service industry development shall be encouraged and the credit service providers are supported to provide credit products and services to the public through credit investigation, credit consultation, credit rating, credit insurance, and credit guarantees.

鼓励在市场交易、企业管理、行业自律、金融服务等活动中查询社会信用信息和使用信用报告等信用产品。

鼓励信用服务机构利用大数据、云计算、区块链、人工智能等现代技术开发具有自主知识产权的信用产品，拓展信用应用服务领域。

鼓励信用评级机构对接国际评级市场，积极参与国际竞争和制定国际标准，增强评级机构国际影响力。

第八条 海南自由贸易港建立健全社会信用体系，加强政务诚信、商务诚信、社会诚信和司法公信等重点领域诚信建设。

第九条 县级以上人民政府应当加强诚信文化建设，开展信用知识教育，提高公众守法诚信意识。

信用服务机构、其他企业事业单位应当加强自身信用管理，引导本单位增强诚信经营意识。

电视、广播、报刊、网络等媒体应当开展诚信文化宣传教育，营造诚信和谐的社会氛围。

社会公众应当守信自律，增强诚信意识，积极参与信用教育和信用监督活动。

第十条 县级以上人民政府及有关部门可以开展跨地区的信用体系建设合作，推进社会信用信息共享、信用产品互认、守信激励和失信惩戒合作。

Social credit information inquiries and the use of credit products such as credit reports in business transactions, business management, industry self-regulation, financial services, and other activities shall be encouraged.

Credit service providers are encouraged to use modern technologies such as big data, cloud computing, blockchain, and artificial intelligence to develop credit products with proprietary intellectual property rights and expand the credit application service industry.

Credit rating agencies are encouraged to benchmark the international rating market, actively participate in international competition and create international standards, and strengthen international influence.

Article 8 The Hainan Free Trade Port shall create and optimize a comprehensive social credit system and improve credit development in key areas including government administration, business operations, social credit reports, and judicial agency authority.

Article 9 The people's governments at or above the county level shall improve the development of the integrity culture, conduct credibility knowledge awareness, and improve public awareness of the rule of law and integrity.

Credit service providers, enterprises, and public institutions shall improve their credit administration and guide themselves to improve their awareness of compliant business operations.

Media, including television, radio, newspapers, and the internet, shall be used to advertise and encourage awareness of the culture of credibility and create a harmonious social atmosphere of creditworthiness.

Individual persons shall keep their promises and exercise self-regulation, improve their awareness of good faith, and actively participate in credit education and credit oversight activities.

Article 10 The people's government at or above the county level and its agencies may conduct interregional collaboration in credit system establishment, and advance social credit information sharing, mutual recognition of credit products, and collaboration in trustworthiness incentives and penalties.

第二章　社会信用信息管理

第十一条　公共信用信息实行目录制管理。海南自由贸易港执行全国公共信用信息基础目录。

省人民政府社会信用主管部门会同有关部门依法编制海南自由贸易港公共信用信息目录，报省人民政府批准后执行。

海南自由贸易港公共信用信息目录应当向社会公布，并适时更新。

第十二条　国家机关以及法律、法规授权具有管理公共事务职能的组织在办理登记注册、资质审核、日常监管、公共服务等过程中，应当按照公共信用信息目录以及相关标准规范要求记录、存储公共信用信息，并及时、准确、完整地将其归集到信用信息共享平台。

第十三条　县级以上人民政府及有关部门应当建立健全信用承诺制度。

鼓励市场主体主动向社会作出信用承诺，在政府门户网站或者其他渠道上自愿公示其登记注册、生产经营、合同履约、社会公益等信用信息，并对信息真实性公开作出信用承诺。真实、合法、完整的信用承诺信息，可以作为办理行政许可、进行事中事后监管、开展信用评价和生成信用报告等的重要依据。

第十四条　行业协会商会、信用服务机构、其他企业事业单位在生产经营和社会服务活动中，可以依法采集相关信用主体的市场信用信息。

采集市场信用信息，涉及自然人个人信息的，应当经信用主体同意，并告知信用主体采集内容、采集方式、信息用途以及信用主体所享有的权利和应当承担的义务。依照法律、行政法规规定应当公开的信息除外。

Chapter II Social Credit Information Administration

Article 11 Public credit information shall be administered as a list and the Hainan Free Trade Port shall be subject to the national credit report list.

The competent provincial people's government social credit agency shall, together with other appropriate agencies, formulate the Hainan Free Trade Port public credit information list pursuant to law, which shall not be done until it has been submitted to and approved by the provincial people's government.

The Hainan Free Trade Port public credit information shall be published and updated periodically.

Article 12 State agencies authorized by laws and regulations to manage public affairs shall record and store public credit information according to the public credit information list and applicable standards and specifications, and shall promptly collect and record accurate and complete public credit information to the credit information sharing platform when performing registration, eligibility review, daily oversight, and public services.

Article 13 The people's government at or above the county level and its agencies shall create and optimize the credit commitment system.

The market entities are encouraged to take initiative to make public credit commitments, voluntarily publish their credit information, including registration, production and operation, contract performance, and social public welfare on government portals or other channels, and commit to the authenticity of the credit information. The authentic, valid, and complete credit commitment information may be used as an important reference for matters such as administrative licensing, regulatory oversight conducted during and after the request, credit evaluation, and generating credit reports.

Article 14 Trade associations, chambers of commerce, credit service providers, and other enterprises and public institutions may collect business credit for entities involved in production, operation, and social service activities pursuant to law.

Entities' consent shall be acquired before collecting their business credit involving personal data belonging to natural persons, and the entity shall be informed of the description, method, purpose of the collection, and entity rights and obligations unless such information is required to be published pursuant to laws and administrative regulations.

采集市场信用信息，不得采集自然人的收入、存款、有价证券、商业保险、不动产信息和纳税数额信息。但是，明确告知可能产生的不利后果、取得信用主体书面同意并约定用途的除外。

采集市场信用信息，禁止采集自然人的宗教信仰、血型信息，疾病、病史信息，基因、指纹等生物识别信息以及法律、行政法规规定禁止采集的其他信息。

支持行业协会商会建立健全行业内信用承诺制度，鼓励会员以自主申报、自主承诺等形式提供自身社会信用信息。

第十五条 县级以上人民政府应当建立健全社会信用信息共享机制，促进公共信用信息和市场信用信息互动融合。省人民政府社会信用主管部门、司法机关、实行垂直管理单位等应当加强沟通与协作，推进海南自由贸易港信用信息共享平台与金融信用信息基础数据库等相关信用信息系统开发合作。

金融信用信息基础数据库和实行垂直管理单位的信用信息服务系统可以与信用信息共享平台实现信息共享与数据交换。

第十六条 公共信用信息通过公开公示、授权查询、政务共享等方式披露。

依法应当公开的公共信用信息，公共信用信息平台应当按照规定向社会公开公示。依法不能公开的公共信用信息，经信用主体自身实名认证或者书面授权可以查询，并按照约定的用途使用。

第十七条 县级以上人民政府及有关部门应当制定并公布服务规范，合理设置社会信用信息查询窗口，通过互联网等向社会提供便捷的查询服务。

Information on natural person income, deposit, securities, commercial insurance, real estate, and taxes paid shall not be collected when collecting business credit, provided that the entity has been expressly informed of potential adverse consequences in advance, agrees to such collection in writing, and the collection purpose was provided.

Information including the individual's religious beliefs, blood groups, diseases, medical histories, genetic and fingerprint biometric information, and other information prohibited to be collected by laws and administrative regulations shall not be collected when collecting business credit.

Trade associations and chambers of commerce are supported to create and optimize the credit commitment system, and their members are encouraged to independently provide their own social credit information and independent commitment.

Article 15 The people's government at or above the county level shall create and optimize a social credit information sharing system and encourage the integration of public credit information with business credit reports. The social credit agencies, judicial agencies, and government agencies under the direct administration of the provincial government shall improve communication and coordination to encourage development and collaboration between the Hainan Free Trade Port credit information sharing platform and basic financial credit information databases, or other relevant credit information systems.

Information sharing and data exchange may be conducted between basic databases of financial credit information, the credit information service system used by the government agencies under the direct administration of the provincial government, and the credit information sharing platform.

Article 16 Public credit information shall be disclosed through publications, authorized access, government sharing or in other means.

The public credit information platform shall publish any public credit information required to be published by law. Public credit information that cannot be disclosed pursuant to law may be accessed, provided that entity identity verification is completed or authorization is obtained and may be used in compliance with the agreed purpose.

Article 17 The people's government at or above the county level and its agencies shall formulate and publish service specifications, set up a reasonable social credit information inquiry portal, and provide convenient online services for the public.

第三章　守信激励与失信惩戒

第十八条　海南自由贸易港建立守信激励和失信惩戒制度，加强对守信行为的倡导和褒扬，依法对失信行为进行惩戒和约束。

县级以上人民政府及有关部门应当组织实施守信激励和失信惩戒。

第十九条　县级以上人民政府及有关部门应当建立守信激励机制，对信用状况良好的信用主体，可以在法定权限范围内实施下列激励措施：

（一）在行政管理和公共服务中，给予优先办理、简化程序等便利服务措施；

（二）在公共资源交易中，予以信用加分、提升信用等次；

（三）在日常监管中降低抽查比例，减少检查频次，更多适用非现场检查方式；

（四）在政府优惠政策实施中，同等条件下列为优先选择对象或者予以重点支持；

（五）在信用门户网站或者相关媒体上进行宣传推介；

（六）国家和海南自由贸易港规定的其他激励措施。

第二十条　海南自由贸易港结合建设实际需要，依照法律、法规和国家有关规定，确定严重失信主体名单领域范围。国家对设列严重失信主体名单领域范围有规定的执行国家规定。

第二十一条　严重失信主体名单的认定标准依照法律、法规和国家有关规定确定的标准执行。地方性法规规定严重失信主体名单制度，应当同时规定严重失信主体名单认定标准和惩戒措施。

Chapter III Trustworthiness Incentives and Penalties

Article 18 The Hainan Free Trade Port shall create a system for trustworthiness incentives and a penalty system, and shall improve the advocacy and praise of trustworthiness and the penalization and restriction of dishonest conduct pursuant to law.

The people's government at or above the county level and its agencies shall organize and perform work related to trustworthiness incentives and penalties.

Article 19 The people's government at or above the county level shall create a trustworthiness incentive system and perform the following incentive policies for good credit entities within their statutory authority:

(a) provide service facilitations such as priority service and simplified administrative management and public service procedures;

(b) increase credit points and upgrade credit levels in public resource transactions;

(c) reduce the proportion of random inspections in daily oversight, reduce inspection frequency, and conduct more off-site inspections;

(d) prioritize or offer additional support for government preferential policies compared to other entities when they meet all other requirements;

(e) advertise and promote on credit portal websites or relevant media; and

(f) implement other national and Hainan Free Trade Port incentive policies.

Article 20 The Hainan Free Trade Port determines the coverage of the list of entities committing material untrustworthy acts pursuant to law and development circumstances. If the coverage of the list of entities committing significant untrustworthy acts is provided by the national regulations, the national regulations shall apply.

Article 21 Standards for the list of entities committing material untrustworthy acts shall be implemented pursuant to the standards determined by applicable national laws and regulations. Where local regulations provide a system for the list of entities committing material untrustworthy acts, they shall also provide the appropriate standards and penalties for the list of entities committing material untrustworthy acts.

县级以上人民政府有关部门作出认定严重失信主体名单决定前，应当告知信用主体决定的事由、依据和依法享有的权利；信用主体提出异议的，应当予以核实，必要时可以组织听证。处理结果应当在规定时限内反馈。

将信用主体列入严重失信主体名单，应当出具并送达认定严重失信主体名单决定文书，决定文书应当载明事由、依据、失信惩戒措施提示、移出条件和程序以及救济途径等。

第二十二条 本省地方性法规可以规定下列失信惩戒措施：

（一）在行政管理和公共服务中，不适用信用承诺制等便利措施；

（二）在日常监管中，列为重点监管对象；

（三）在公共资源交易中，予以信用减分、降低信用等次；

（四）限制参与政府投资或者政府与社会资本合作的建设项目，或者予以提高保证金比例；

（五）限制享受政府优惠政策支持，限制申请财政性资金项目；

（六）限制参与表彰奖励，取消参加评先评优资格，撤销相关荣誉；

（七）法律、法规规定的其他措施。

对失信主体采取惩戒措施应当与失信主体失信行为相关联，与其失信行为的性质、情节以及社会影响程度相适应，采取轻重适度的惩戒措施，确保过惩相当。

第二十三条 海南自由贸易港执行全国失信惩戒措施基础清单。

省、设区的市人民政府社会信用主管部门应当会同有关部门根据本省地方性法规编制海南自由贸易港失信惩戒措施清单，报本级人民政府审定后向社会公布。

Before the agencies of the people's governments at or above the county level make a decision on the entities committing material untrustworthy acts, they shall inform the entity of the reason and basis of the decision, as well as their legal rights. Any objections raised by the entity shall be verified, and a hearing may be held if necessary. The management results shall be notified within the required time limit.

If an entity is listed as an entity that has committed significant untrustworthy acts, a decision document shall be issued and sent. The decision document shall clarify the reasons, basis, reminders of penalties for untrustworthy acts, conditions, and procedures for removal from the list, and corrections.

Article 22 The provincial local regulations may impose the following penalties for untrustworthy acts:

(a) exclusion from the credit commitment system in administrative management and public services;

(b) listing as a major entity in routine oversight;

(c) reduce credit points and downgrade credit levels in public resource transactions;

(d) restrictions on participation in construction projects invested by the government or through public-private partnerships, or raising the deposit proportion;

(e) restrictions on government preferential policy support and application for financial funding;

(f) restrictions on participating in recommendations and rewards, participating in evaluations, and revoking eligibility for applicable awards; and

(g) other actions provided by laws and regulations.

Penalties imposed against untrustworthy entities shall be proportional to the untrustworthy acts committed by the entity and in conformity with the nature, circumstance, and social impact of such act, and, appropriate penalties shall be imposed to ensure that there is a balance between the untrustworthy acts and penalties.

Article 23 The Hainan Free Trade Port shall be subject to the national basic list of penalties for untrustworthy acts.

The agency with jurisdiction over social credit of the people's governments in provinces and cities with districts shall, together with the appropriate agencies, prepare a list of penalties for untrustworthy acts pursuant to provincial regulations, submit it to the people's governments at the appropriate level for review and approval, and publish it.

海南自由贸易港失信惩戒措施清单应当动态更新。

第二十四条 县级以上人民政府有关部门认定失信行为，应当以下列具有法律效力的文书为依据：

（一）生效的司法裁判文书和仲裁文书；

（二）行政处罚、行政裁决等行政行为决定文书；

（三）法律、法规和国家有关规定中规定的可以作为失信行为认定依据的其他文书。

第二十五条 法人或者非法人组织被列入严重失信主体名单的，有关部门和单位在记录相关失信信息时，应当标明对相关失信行为负有责任的法定代表人、主要负责人、实际控制人和其他直接责任人的信息，并依照有关规定实施相应的惩戒措施。

第四章 信用主体权益保护

第二十六条 县级以上人民政府及有关部门和其他信用信息提供单位应当建立健全社会信用信息安全管理制度，采取安全保密措施，保障社会信用信息采集、归集、披露、共享、查询和应用等过程的安全。

从事社会信用信息管理和服务的机构及人员，不得非法提供、披露和使用信用信息，不得篡改、虚构、泄露、窃取和非法买卖信用信息。

第二十七条 公共信用信息中的失信信息披露期限一般不超过五年。披露期限届满后不得再行披露。披露期限自失信行为认定之日起计算；失信行为处于持续状态的，披露期限自失信行为终止之日起计算。法律、法规另有规定的，从其规定。

The list of penalties for untrustworthy acts in the Hainan Free Trade Port shall be updated from time to time.

Article 24 The agencies of the people's governments at or above the county level shall determine untrustworthy acts based on the following binding documents:

(a) effective judicial judgments and arbitral awards;

(b) decisions issued by administrative agencies such as decisions on administrative penalties or administrative rulings; and

(c) other documents that may be used as the basis to determine untrustworthy acts provided by laws, reglations, and other state provisions.

Article 25 Where a legal entity or an unincorporated entity is included in the list of entities committing material untrustworthy acts, the appropriate agencies shall note the statutory representative, principal person in charge, actual controller, and other persons directly responsible when recording credit breach information and impose the appropriate penalty.

Chapter IV Credit Entity Protection

Article 26 The people's government at or above the county level, its agencies, and other organizations providing credit information shall create and optimize a social credit information security system and adopt confidentiality measures to ensure security during the collection, classification, disclosure, sharing, inquiry, and use of social credit information.

Institutions and employees for social credit information administration and services shall not illegally provide, disclose, or use credit information, and shall not tamper, fabricate, disclose, steal, or illegally buy and sell credit information.

Article 27 The untrustworthy act information in the public credit information disclosure period shall generally not exceed 5 years. No further disclosure shall be made after the expiration of this period. The disclosure period shall be calculated from the date on which the untrustworthy act is verified. The disclosure period shall be calculated from the date on which the untrustworthy act stops if the acts are continuous, except as otherwise provided by laws and regulations.

第二十八条　自然人有权每年从采集、归集其社会信用信息的机构免费获取本人的信用报告。

信用服务机构向信用主体提供相关服务的，不得将该服务与个人社会信用信息采集相捆绑，强迫或者变相强迫信用主体接受。

第二十九条　社会信用信息提供单位发现其提供的社会信用信息存在错误、遗漏的，应当及时更正，并将更正后的信息及时报送信用信息共享平台。

第三十条　信用主体认为其社会信用信息存在错误、遗漏或者侵犯其合法权益的，可以向县级以上人民政府社会信用主管部门、社会信用信息提供单位提出书面异议申请。县级以上人民政府社会信用主管部门、社会信用信息提供单位应当在收到异议材料之日起一个工作日内作出异议标注，并在七个工作日内将核查及处理结果反馈申请人。情况复杂的，异议处理机构可申请延期，经该机构负责人批准可延长核查期限，但整个异议处理期限累计不得超过十五个工作日。

对于核查确实有误的，应当予以更正或者删除，并告知申请人；作出不予变更决定的，应当说明理由。

第三十一条　信用主体的公共信用信息向信用信息共享平台归集后，其公共信用信息被原提供单位撤销或者据以认定其失信状态的行为被生效法律文书撤销的，撤销单位应当及时向县级以上人民政府社会信用主管部门报送变更信息。

Article 28 Natural persons are entitled to obtain their own credit reports free of charge from the institutions that collect and classify their social credit information annually.

Where a credit service provider provides a credit entity with services, it shall not relate such with the collection of personal social credit information, or explicitly or implicitly compel the entity to accept the collection of such credit information.

Article 29 A social credit information provider shall promptly make corrections and submit the corrected information to the credit information sharing platform if it discovers any error or omission in the social credit information it submits.

Article 30 If an entity believes that its social credit information includes mistakes, omissions, or infringes upon its legal rights, it may submit a written objection to the competent social credit agencies of the people's governments at or above the county level and to the social credit information provider. The competent social credit agencies of the people's governments at or above the county level and the social credit information provider shall take note of the objection within 1 business day from the date on which the objection is accepted, and shall report the verification and management results to the entity within 7 business days. The organization managing the objection may request an extension under complex circumstances, and the verification period may be extended with the approval of the person in charge of the organization, but the total objection management period shall not exceed 15 business days.

The government agency or the organization shall correct or remove the incorrect credit report and inform the requester of such a decision once the information is deemed incorrect. The government agency or the organization shall explain any decisions not to make changes to the credit report to the requester.

Article 31 Where entity's public credit information uploaded to the credit information sharing platform is removed, the organization responsible for removing the information shall promptly submit the change to the competent social credit agency under the people's government at or above the county level if the credit information was removed by its original provider or an effective court decision rules that the entity did not perform an untrustworthy act.

县级以上人民政府社会信用主管部门应当在收到变更信息之日起二个工作日内完成信息删除工作。

第三十二条 失信主体纠正失信行为、消除不良影响的，可以向县级以上人民政府社会信用主管部门或者作出失信行为认定的单位申请信用修复。

失信主体开展信用修复可以按照规定通过作出信用承诺、完成信用整改、接受专题培训、参加公益慈善等方式进行。

符合信用修复条件的，县级以上人民政府社会信用主管部门及有关部门应当按照有关规定将其移出严重失信主体名单，终止公开共享相关失信信息，依法对相关失信信息进行处理，并将修复情况告知信用主体。修复完成后，应当按照程序及时终止实施惩戒措施。国家对信用修复有规定的，依照其规定执行。

县级以上人民政府社会信用主管部门可以会同有关部门制定信用修复的具体办法，报本级人民政府批准后实施。

第三十三条 信用主体认为公共信用信息管理活动中的具体行政行为侵犯其合法权益的，可以依法申请行政复议或者提起行政诉讼。

第五章 法律责任

第三十四条 国家机关以及法律、法规授权具有管理公共事务职能的组织及其工作人员实施下列行为之一的，由法律、法规规定的相关主管部门或者纪检监察部门责令改正；情节严重的，依法给予处分；构成犯罪的，依法追究刑事责任。

The competent social credit agencies of the people's governments at or above the county level shall delete the information within 2 business days of receipt of the changed information.

Article 32 If an untrustworthy entity corrects its untrustworthy act and eliminates the adverse effects, it may request its credit to be repaired by the competent social credit agency of the people's governments at or above the county level or from the institution that verified the untrustworthy act.

An untrustworthy entity may repair its credit by making credit commitments, conducting credit rectification, taking part in special training, and participating in public welfare and charity activities.

If credit repair requirements are met, the competent social credit agencies of the people's governments at or above the county level and other agencies shall remove the entity from the list of entities committing material untrustworthy acts, end the publication of information on their untrustworthy act, manage the untrustworthy act information pursuant to law, and inform the credit entity of the repair. After the repair is complete, the penalty shall be terminated within the time required by law, except as otherwise provided by the national laws.

The competent social credit agencies under the people's governments at or above the county level, together with other agencies, may prepare specific rules for credit repair, which shall be implemented after being submitted to the people's government at the appropriate level for approval.

Article 33 If an entity believes that the specific administrative acts concerning public credit information administration infringe upon their legal rights, they may request administrative review or file an administrative lawsuit pursuant to law.

Chapter V Legal Liability

Article 34 Any state agency authorized by laws and regulations to manage public affairs or any of its employees commits any of the following acts, shall be corrected by the competent agency or discipline inspection and oversight agency designated by laws and regulations, imposed penalties pursuant to law if the circumstances are serious, and held criminally liable pursuant to law if a crime is committed:

（一）未按规定采集、归集、披露、共享、查询和应用社会信用信息或者未按规定受理信用异议处理；

（二）篡改、虚构、隐匿、违规删除社会信用信息；

（三）泄露未经授权公开的社会信用信息；

（四）泄露涉及国家秘密、商业秘密、个人隐私的社会信用信息；

（五）违反国家规定获取或者向他人出售、提供社会信用信息；

（六）违法实施信用激励和惩戒措施；

（七）违反信用信息安全管理制度造成信息丢失；

（八）法律法规禁止的其他行为。

第三十五条 行业协会商会、信用服务机构、其他企业事业单位及其工作人员违反本条例规定，有下列行为之一的，由县级以上人民政府社会信用主管部门或者相关监督管理部门按照管理权限责令限期改正、没收违法所得；情节严重的，对单位处五万元以上五十万元以下罚款，并对直接负责的主管人员和其他直接责任人员处一万元以上十万元以下罚款：

（一）提供虚假信用产品；

（二）采集禁止采集的社会信用信息或者未经同意违法采集自然人社会信用信息；

（三）未履行保密义务或者超出法定、约定范围公开、使用社会信用信息；

（四）篡改、虚构、窃取和非法买卖社会信用信息。

(a) collecting, classifying, disclosing, sharing, querying, and using social credit information in a way that does not comply with the requirements, or not accepting credit objections as required;

(b) tampering with, fabricating, concealing, or illegally deleting social credit information;

(c) divulging unauthorized public social credit information;

(d) divulging social credit information involving state secrets, trade secrets, and personal privacy;

(e) obtaining, selling, or providing social credit information in violation of national law;

(f) illegally implementing credit incentives or penalties;

(g) causing the loss of information in violation of the credit information security administration system; or

(h) committing other acts prohibited by laws and regulations.

Article 35 Any trade associations, chambers of commerce, credit service providers, or other enterprises or public institutions or any of their employees who violates these Regulations and commits one of the following acts shall be required by the competent social credit agency under the people's governments at or above the county level or the oversight and administrative agencies, exercising their administrative authority to make corrections within a specific time limit and any illegal gains shall be confiscated. A penalty of not less than 50,000 Yuan but not more than 500,000 Yuan may be imposed under serious circumstances, and a fine of not less than 10,000 Yuan but no more than 100,000 Yuan may be imposed on the persons directly in charge and other directly liable employees:

(a) providing falsified credit products;

(b) collecting prohibited social credit information or illegally collecting personal social credit information without consent;

(c) failing to perform confidentiality obligations, or disclosing or using social credit information beyond the scope of laws and agreements; or

(d) tampering with, fabricating, stealing, or illegally buying or selling social credit information.

第三十六条 在社会信用信息采集、归集、披露、共享、查询和应用等过程中，损害信用主体合法权益的，应当依法承担民事责任；构成犯罪的，依法追究刑事责任。

第六章 附 则

第三十七条 本条例自 2022 年 1 月 1 日起施行。

Article 36 Anyone who infringes upon an entity's legal rights when collecting, classifying, disclosing, sharing, inquiring, or using social credit information shall assume civil liability pursuant to law and shall be held criminally liable pursuant to law if a crime is committed.

Chapter VI Supplementary Provision

Article 37 These Regulations shall come into force as of January 1, 2022.

海南自由贸易港市场主体注销条例

Regulations of Hainan Free Trade Port on Market Entities Deregistration

海南自由贸易港市场主体注销条例

（2021 年 12 月 1 日海南省第六届人民代表大会常务委员会
第三十一次会议通过）

第一条　为了畅通市场主体退出渠道，建立注销便利制度，完善优胜劣汰的市场机制，优化营商环境，根据《中华人民共和国海南自由贸易港法》，遵循有关法律、行政法规的基本原则，结合海南自由贸易港实际，制定本条例。

第二条　省人民政府市场监督管理部门是市场主体注销的登记机关，负责海南自由贸易港市场主体注销登记、监督管理和服务。

市、县（区）、自治县人民政府市场监督管理部门负责本辖区市场主体的监督管理和服务。

第三条　省人民政府市场监督管理部门应当加强与人民法院、自然资源和规划、商务、人力资源和社会保障、公安、国有资产管理、金融监管、税务、海关、大数据等相关单位之间的信息共享和业务协同，建立市场主体注销网上服务专区，制定标准化规则，完善市场主体注销联动服务，提高注销登记效率。

第四条　市场主体因下列情形终止经营活动的，应当依法向登记机关申请注销登记：

（一）章程或者协议约定的解散事由出现，但通过修改章程或者协议约定而存续的除外；

（二）经营期限届满未延期的；

（三）依法被吊销营业执照、责令关闭、撤销的；

Regulations of Hainan Free Trade Port on Market Entities Deregistration

(Adopted at the 31st Session of the Standing Committee of the 6th Hainan Provincial People's Congress on December 1, 2021)

Article 1 These Regulations are enacted pursuant to the Hainan Free Trade Port Law of the People's Republic of China and basic principles of other applicable laws and administrative regulations, and based on the actual circumstances in Hainan Free Trade Port to facilitate withdrawal channels and reduce withdrawal costs for market entities, improve the market system for well-performing businesses to achieve success and for poorly-run businesses to be eliminated, and optimize the business environment.

Article 2 The provincial people's government market regulation agency shall be the market entity deregistration agency, and shall also be responsible for market entity deregistration, oversight and administration, and related services within the Free Trade Port.

The city, county (district), and autonomous county people's government market regulation agency shall be responsible for market entity supervision, administration, and related services within their own administrative areas.

Article 3 The provincial people's government market regulation agency shall improve coordination and communication with the people's courts, natural resources and planning agencies, commerce, human resources and social security, public security, state-owned assets administration, financial oversight, taxation, customs, big data, and other agencies, improve information sharing and service collaboration between different agencies, create a dedicated online service for market entity deregistration, implement standardized rules, and improve interconnection services for market entity to process and improve deregistration efficiency.

Article 4 Market entities terminating their business due to the following circumstances shall submit a deregistration request with the registration agency pursuant to law:

(a) the occurrence of any termination circumstances provided in the articles of incorporation or agreement, except where the articles of incorporation or agreements are amended to allow the market entity to continue operations;

(b) the business period expires and is not renewed;

(c) the business license is revoked pursuant to law, the market entity is ordered to shut down, or its business registration is revoked;

（四）因合并或者分立需要解散的；

（五）经法定程序作出决议解散的；

（六）被依法宣告破产的；

（七）人民法院依法予以解散的；

（八）法律、法规规定的其他情形。

市场主体注销依法须经批准的，应当经批准后向登记机关申请注销登记。市场主体注销前依法应当清算的，应当自清算结束之日起三十日内申请注销登记。

第五条 市场主体申请注销登记，应当向登记机关提交申请书和法律、法规规定的其他材料，并对其真实性、合法性、有效性承担责任，不得提交虚假材料或者采取其他欺诈手段隐瞒重要事实取得注销登记。

登记机关对申请人提交的材料和信息进行形式审查。对申请材料齐全、符合法定形式的予以确认并当场登记。不能当场登记的，应当在三个工作日内予以登记；情形复杂的，经登记机关负责人批准，可以再延长三个工作日。登记机关办理注销登记手续后，市场主体终止。

申请材料不齐全或者不符合法定形式的，登记机关应当一次性告知申请人需要补正的材料。

利害关系人认为登记机关受理的注销登记申请不符合法定条件的，可以通过国家企业信用信息公示系统或者直接向登记机关提出异议，提交相应证明材料，并对证明材料的真实性负责。登记机关应当对利害关系人提出的异议进行审查，作出是否注销的决定。

(d) liquidation due to merger or division;

(e) liquidation due to a resolution made pursuant to statutory procedures;

(f) the market entity is lawfully declared bankrupt;

(g) liquidation by the people's court pursuant to law; and

(h) other circumstances provided by laws and regulations.

The market entity shall request deregistration approval from the registration agency if its deregistration is subject to approval pursuant to law. Market entities subject to liquidation before registration pursuant to law shall request deregistration within 30 days of the liquidation completion date.

Article 5 The market entity requesting deregistration shall submit their request and other materials pursuant to law, and shall be liable for the authenticity, legality, and validity of such, and shall not submit falsified materials or use any other fraudulent methods to conceal important information to complete deregistration.

The registration agency shall conduct a formal review of the materials and information submitted by the requester. Requests shall be confirmed and deregistration shall be completed immediately if the request materials are complete and conform to statutory formats, or within 3 business days if immediate deregistration is not available; the process can be extended for a further 3 business days with the approval of the person in charge of the registration agency under complex circumstances. The market entity shall be terminated after the registration agency completes deregistration procedures.

The registration agency shall inform the requester of any additional materials necessary in one instance should the request materials submitted be incomplete or do not conform to statutory formats.

Any stakeholder claiming the deregistration approved by the registration agency does not meet the statutory requirements may raise their objections to the registration agency's decision through the National Enterprise Credit Information Publicity System or to the registration agency directly by submitting proof of such and shall assume liability for the authenticity of the materials submitted. The registration agency shall then review the objections raised by the stakeholders and make a decision on deregistration.

第六条 市场主体申请注销登记前，应当依法办理分支机构注销登记。

注销分支机构的，应当自注销决议或者决定作出之日起三十日内向该分支机构的登记机关申请注销登记。

市场主体已注销导致其分支机构无法办理注销登记的，该分支机构注销可以由已注销主体的继受主体或者投资主体代为办理。

第七条 市场主体未发生债权债务或者已将债权债务清偿完结的，未发生或者已经结清清偿费用、职工工资、社会保险费用、法定补偿金、应缴纳税款（滞纳金、罚款），并由全体投资人书面承诺对上述情况的真实性承担法律责任的，可以适用简易注销程序。上市股份有限公司和涉及国家规定实施准入特别管理措施的外商投资企业除外。

第八条 市场主体有下列情形之一的，不适用简易注销程序：

（一）依法被吊销营业执照、责令关闭、撤销的；

（二）被列入经营异常名录的；

（三）存在股权或者投资权益被冻结、出质或者动产抵押等情形的；

（四）市场主体的分支机构未办理注销登记的；

（五）有正在被立案调查或者采取行政强制、被予以行政处罚、司法协助等情形的；

（六）注销依法须经批准的；

（七）法律、法规规定的其他情形。

登记机关审查市场主体简易注销登记申请时，发现其存在前款第二项、第三项、第四项规定情形的，应当告知市场主体待上述情形消失后可以再次依程序公示申请简易注销登记。

Article 6 Market entities shall complete deregistration for their branch office(s) before requesting deregistration pursuant to law.

Market entities shall request branch office deregistration with the registration agency within 30 days of the deregistration resolution or decision being made.

Branch deregistration may be managed by the deregistered market entity successor or investors if the market entity has already been deregistered and is unable to deregister the branch.

Article 7 Simplified deregistration procedures may be implemented if a market entity does not benefit from any creditor's rights or owes debts, has already exercised their creditor's rights or discharged debts, does not owe or has already paid liquidation expenses, employee wages, social insurance premiums, statutory compensation, tax payable (late fees or fines), and all investors have issued a written commitment to assume liability for the authenticity of such, except for publicly listed companies and foreign-invested entities under market access administration as required by the state.

Article 8 The market entity may not request simplified deregistration, if:

(a) the business license of the market entity is lawfully revoked, it is ordered to close down, or its business registration is revoked;

(b) the market entity is added to the list of concern;

(c) market entities whose equity or investments are frozen, pledged, or mortgaged;

(d) the market entity branch office has not completed deregistration;

(e) the market entity is under investigation, administrative injunction and administrative enforcement, administrative penalty, or judicial assistance;

(f) market entity deregistration is subject to approval pursuant to law; or

(g) other circumstances provided by laws and regulations exist.

The registration agency shall inform the market entities whether they are eligible to request simplified deregistration again once the circumstances mentioned in Subparagraph (b), (c) or (d) above are resolved.

第九条 市场主体选择申请简易注销登记的，应当通过国家企业信用信息公示系统公示简易注销登记申请及全体投资人承诺书等信息，公示期为七日。公示期届满，相关单位、利害关系人未提出异议的，市场主体应当自公示期届满之日起二十日内向登记机关申请注销登记。

个体工商户通过简易程序申请注销登记的，无需公示。由登记机关将个体工商户的注销登记申请推送至税务等相关单位，相关单位在十日内没有提出异议的，可以直接办理注销登记。

第十条 利害关系人对市场主体公示的简易注销登记申请及全体投资人承诺书等信息有异议的，可以在公示期内通过国家企业信用信息公示系统或者直接向登记机关提出，提交相应证明材料，并对证明材料的真实性负责。

第十一条 市场主体申请简易注销登记，应当向登记机关提交以下材料：

（一）申请书；

（二）全体投资人承诺书或者人民法院终结强制清算程序的裁定、终结破产程序的裁定。

个体工商户通过简易程序申请注销登记的，无需提交承诺书。

第十二条 市场主体因通过其登记的住所或者经营场所无法取得联系被列入经营异常名录满两年的，登记机关可以对其作出除名决定。

第十三条 登记机关作出除名决定前，应当通过国家企业信用信息公示系统公示，公示期为三十日。

公示期届满，相关单位、利害关系人未提出异议的，登记机关应当作出除名决定，以统一社会信用代码代替市场主体名称，并向社会公示，但公示期届满前有下列情形之一的除外：

Article 9 If a market entity chooses to request simplified deregistration, it shall announce all information about the request and its investor commitment on the National Enterprise Credit Information Publicity System for 7 days. The request shall then be submitted to the registration agency within 20 days of the expiration of the announcement period, provided no agencies or stakeholders raise any objections.

Sole proprietorships are not required to announce such when requesting simplified deregistration. The registration agency shall transfer sole proprietorship deregistration requests to tax or other appropriate agencies. Sole proprietorships can then directly request deregistration if no objections are raised within 10 days of the expiration of the announcement period.

Article 10 If a stakeholder raises an objection to the information announced by the market entity, such as the request for simplified deregistration and the commitment made by all investors, the stakeholder may submit the applicable documentation through the National Enterprise Credit Information Publicity System or directly to the registration agency within the announcement period, and the stakeholder shall be liable for the authenticity of any materials submitted.

Article 11 Market entities requesting simplified deregistration shall submit the following materials to the registration agency:

(a) written request; and

(b) a letter of commitment from all investors, or a ruling from the people's court ordering the termination of compulsory liquidation or bankruptcy.

Sole proprietorships going through simplified deregistration procedures are not required to submit a letter of commitment.

Article 12 Registration agencies may delist any commercial enterprises included in the list of concern for 2 years from the registration system if they cannot be contacted through their registered domicile or business premise.

Article 13 The registration agency shall announce its intent to deregister the commercial enterprise via the National Enterprise Credit Information Publicity System for 30 days before making its decision.

Upon the expiration of the announcement period, the registration agency may delist the market entity and announce it by replacing its name with the uniform social credit identifier if no objections are raised by the appropriate agencies or stakeholders, unless:

（一）市场主体已经办理住所或者经营场所变更登记，或者提供的证据能够证明其仍在登记的住所或者经营场所经营的；

（二）登记机关已经受理市场主体的注销登记申请或者市场主体已经被依法注销的；

（三）法律、法规规定的其他情形。

第十四条 市场主体被除名后，应当依法完成清算、办理注销登记，不得从事与清算或者注销无关的活动。被除名期间市场主体存续。

第十五条 市场主体有下列情形之一的，登记机关可以对其作出依职权注销的决定，办理注销登记：

（一）依法被吊销营业执照、责令关闭、撤销满六个月未申请注销登记的；

（二）经营期限届满六个月未延期或者未申请注销登记的；

（三）依法歇业期限届满未恢复营业或者未申请注销登记的；

（四）依法被除名满六个月未申请注销登记的；

（五）法律、法规规定的其他情形。

第十六条 登记机关依职权拟对市场主体注销的，应当通过国家企业信用信息公示系统进行公示，公示期为三十日。

公示期内，登记机关应当向自然资源和规划、人力资源和社会保障、税务、人民法院等相关单位征询市场主体是否涉及不动产权利登记、拖欠职工工资、欠缴社会保险、欠缴税款及未结涉税事项和审理、办理或者执行中的案件等情形以及情况。相关单位收到征询意见函后应当于十个工作日内书面答复。

(a) the market entity has registered a change of domicile or business address, or proves that it is still operating in the registered domicile or business address;

(b) the registration agency has accepted the deregistration request or the market entity was deregistered pursuant to law; or

(c) other circumstances provided by laws and regulations exist.

Article 14 Market entities must complete liquidation and complete deregistration procedures following delisting pursuant to law, and shall not engage in any activities irrelevant to liquidation or deregistration. Market entities shall still exist during the delisting period.

Article 15 The registration agency may complete deregistration *motu proprio* under any of the following circumstances:

(a) the business license is revoked pursuant to law, the market entity is ordered to close, or its business registration is revoked for 6 months without requesting deregistration;

(b) the market entity fails to renew its business term or request deregistration following 6 months after the expiration of the business term;

(c) the market entity fails to restart the business operation or request deregistration following the expiration of the business suspension term pursuant to law;

(d) the market entity fails to request deregistration within 6 months of being delisted; or

(e) other circumstances provided by laws and regulations exist.

Article 16 A registration agency terminating a market entity's registration *motu proprio*, shall publish its decision to the National Enterprise Credit Information Publicity System for 30 days.

The registration agency shall inquire with the appropriate agencies, such as natural resources and planning, human resources and social security, taxation, and people's courts whether the market entity is involved in matters such as the registration of immovable property rights, unpaid wages, unpaid social insurance, unpaid taxes, and outstanding tax-related matters, or cases under court proceedings or enforcement during the announcement period. The appropriate agencies shall issue a written response within 10 business days of receiving the inquiry.

第十七条 公示期届满，登记机关应当作出依职权注销的决定，并向社会公布，但公示期内有下列情形之一的除外：

（一）市场主体在国家企业信用信息公示系统公示清算信息或者申请注销登记的；

（二）利害关系人或者相关单位提出异议的。

市场主体在被注销公示期内主动申请注销登记的，登记机关应当依法为其办理注销登记。

第十八条 存在下列情形之一的，登记机关或者其上级机关，根据利害关系人请求或者依照职权，应当撤销依职权注销决定：

（一）利害关系人提供的人民法院、仲裁机构的生效法律文书或者其他证据能够证明被依职权注销的市场主体债权债务尚未清理完结，需要恢复该市场主体登记进行清算的；

（二）清算义务人依法组织清算并申请办理注销登记的；

（三）违反法定程序作出注销决定的；

（四）根据本条例第十五条第一项、第四项规定作出依职权注销决定的情形被依法撤销的；

（五）为了国家利益或者社会公共利益，需要恢复被依职权注销的市场主体登记的；

（六）其他应当撤销的情形。

第十九条 因市场主体已经注销导致其出资的市场主体无法办理注销登记的，可以由该已经注销主体的继受主体或者投资主体代为办理。

因市场主体之外的其他主体已经撤销或者注销导致其管理或者出资的市场主体无法办理注销登记的，可以由该已经撤销或者注销主体的继受主体或者上级主管单位代为办理。

Article 17 The registration agency shall decide on the deregistration *motu proprio* at the end of the announcement period and shall announce such unless:

(a) the commercial enterprise announces its liquidation or request for deregistration via the National Enterprise Credit Information Publicity System; or

(b) stakeholders or government agencies raise objections.

The registration agency shall process the deregistration pursuant to law if the market entity takes the initiative to request deregistration during the announcement period.

Article 18 The registration agency or its superior agency shall revoke the deregistration decision *motu proprio* or at the request of the stakeholders under any of the following circumstances:

(a) valid legal documents or other evidence from the people's court or arbitral institutions provided by the stakeholders can prove that the credits and debts of the market entity deregistered *motu proprio* have not been settled and the market entity needs to remain registered for liquidation purposes;

(b) the liquidator organizes liquidation pursuant to law and requests deregistration;

(c) the deregistration decision violates statutory procedures;

(d) the decision to deregister *motu proprio* pursuant to Subparagraph (a) or (d) of Article 15 of these Regulations is revoked pursuant to law;

(e) it is necessary to restore the registration of the market entity deregistered *motu proprio* to maintain national or public interests; or

(f) other circumstances under which the decision shall be revoked.

Article 19 A successor or investor may process deregistration on behalf of a market entity unable to process the deregistration due to having capital contributed from a terminated market entity.

A successor or superior competent agency may process the deregistration of a market entity controlled or funded by a deregistered entity if the deregistered entity is not a market entity, thus preventing the deregistration of the market entity controlled or funded by the deregistered agency.

第二十条　清算义务人未依法履行清算、申请注销登记义务，造成损害的，应当依法承担民事责任，并三年内不得担任其他市场主体的董事、监事、高级管理人员；构成犯罪的，依法追究刑事责任。

市场主体未经清算被依法注销的，其清算义务人依法承担的组织清算义务不变。

第二十一条　市场主体提交虚假材料或者采取其他欺诈手段隐瞒重要事实取得注销登记的，由登记机关撤销登记，依照国家有关规定予以处罚，并将市场主体列入严重违法失信名单予以惩戒。

市场主体被撤销简易注销登记的，应当按照一般注销程序申请注销登记。

登记机关撤销市场主体注销登记时，应当将市场主体恢复到注销前的状态。第三人已经注册使用被注销市场主体名称的，登记机关应当恢复被注销市场主体的统一社会信用代码，不再保留原名称。

第二十二条　各级人民政府市场监督管理部门及其工作人员在注销登记管理中滥用职权、弄虚作假、玩忽职守、徇私舞弊的，对直接负责的主管人员和其他直接责任人员依法给予处分；构成犯罪的，依法追究刑事责任。

第二十三条　本条例自 2022 年 3 月 1 日起施行。

Article 20 If the liquidator fails to fulfill obligations of liquidation or applying for deregistration pursuant to law shall assume civil liability pursuant to law, and shall not serve as a director, supervisor, or executive for another market entity within the following 3 years if they fail to fulfill the obligations, thus causing damages. They shall be held criminally liable if their actions constitute a crime.

Any liquidation obligations assumed by the individual responsible for the liquidation shall remain unchanged if the market entity is deregistered pursuant to law without going through liquidation.

Article 21 The registration agency shall revoke the deregistration of any market entity that submits falsified materials or conceals important information in order to complete deregistration, penalize it as required by national regulations, and add it to the list of market entities that committed serious violations.

Where the market entity simplified deregistration is revoked, it shall request deregistration pursuant to general deregistration procedures.

Where the registration agency revokes the deregistration of a market entity, the market entity shall be restored to its original status prior to the deregistration. The registration agency shall restore the uniform social credit identifier for the market entity but not the original name if a third party has already registered such name.

Article 22 If market regulation agency of the people's governments at all levels and their employees are involved in abuse of position, falsification, dereliction of duty, or playing favoritism and committing irregularities concerning the deregistration administration, the person directly in charge and other employees directly liable shall be subject to penalties pursuant to law and held criminally liable if a crime is committed.

Article 23 These Regulations shall come into force as of March 1, 2022.

Article 26 If the liquidator fails to fulfill obligations of liquidation [illegible] deregistration pursuant to law shall assume civil liability pursuant to law [illegible] damages. They shall be held [illegible] liable [illegible]

[illegible]

海南自由贸易港消防条例

Regulations of Hainan Free Trade Port on Fire Protection

海南自由贸易港消防条例

（2020 年 7 月 31 日海南省第六届人民代表大会常务委员会第二十一次会议通过）

目　录

第一章　总　　则

第一条　为了预防火灾和减少火灾危害，加强应急救援工作，保护人身、财产安全，维护公共安全，为海南自由贸易港建设创造良好的消防安全环境，根据《中华人民共和国消防法》等有关法律法规的规定，结合本省实际，制定本条例。

第二条　消防工作贯彻预防为主、防消结合的方针，按照政府统一领导、部门依法监管、单位全面负责、公民积极参与的原则，实行消防安全责任制，建立健全社会化的消防工作网络。

Regulations of Hainan Free Trade Port on Fire Protection

(Adopted at the 21st Session of the Standing Committee of the 6th Hainan Provincial People's Congress on July 31, 2020)

Contents

Chapter I General Provisions

Article 1 These Regulations are enacted pursuant to the Fire Protection Law of the People's Republic of China and other applicable laws and regulations, and based on the actual circumstances of this Province to prevent fire disasters and reduce fire hazards, improve emergency rescue operations, protect personal and property safety, safeguard public safety and develop a favorable fire safety environment for the development of Hainan Free Trade Port (hereinafter referred to as the "HFTP").

Article 2 Fire services shall follow the policy of putting major effort into prevention and combining fire prevention with firefighting, and shall follow the principle of unified leadership by the government and agency regulation pursuant to law, hold organizations fully accountable and actively involve citizens, enforce a fire safety accountability system and implement a proper fire services network that works closely with the community.

第三条 各级人民政府负责本行政区域内的消防工作，将消防工作纳入国民经济和社会发展计划，保障消防工作与经济社会发展相适应。

县级以上人民政府应当将消防和应急救援经费纳入同级财政年度预算，适应经济和社会的发展，保障火灾预防、消防宣传教育培训、消防设施装备建设、灭火和应急救援的实际需要。

各级人民政府成立的消防安全委员会，负责研究、统筹、协调、指导本行政区域内的消防工作。

第四条 县级以上人民政府应急管理部门对本行政区域内的消防工作实施监督管理，并由本级人民政府消防救援机构负责实施。

县级以上人民政府其他工作部门在各自职责范围内，依法做好消防工作。

军事设施的消防工作，由其主管单位监督管理，消防救援机构协助。

矿井地下部分、核电厂、海上石油天然气设施的消防工作，由其主管单位监督管理。

铁路、港口、民航、森林、水上的消防工作按照国家和本省的有关规定执行。

第五条 维护消防安全是全社会的共同责任。单位和个人应当遵守消防法律法规，履行消防安全责任。

鼓励、支持社会力量开展消防公益活动。鼓励单位和个人参与公共消防设施建设，捐赠消防公益事业。

鼓励消防科研创新，推广运用先进科技成果增强火灾预防、灭火和应急救援能力。

Article 3 All levels of local people's governments shall be responsible for fire services within their respective administrative areas and include fire services in the national economic and social development plan to ensure that fire services are appropriate to economic and social development.

The people's governments at or above the county level shall incorporate the funds for fire protection and emergency rescue into the fiscal annual budget at the same level, adapt to the development of the economy and society, and guarantee that it meets community requirements for fire prevention, fire protection awareness, education and training, fire protection facilities and equipment development, and firefighting and emergency rescue.

The fire safety committees created by the people's governments at all levels shall be responsible for studying, planning, coordinating, and guiding the fire services within their respective administrative areas.

Article 4 The emergency administration agencies of the people's governments at or above the county level shall oversee and manage fire services within their administrative areas, and the fire departments of the people's government at the same level shall be responsible for the enforcement of such.

Other agencies of the people's governments at or above the county level shall, within the scope of their respective functions and duties, put effort into fire protection pursuant to law.

Military facility fire services shall be overseen and managed by the competent agency and assisted by fire departments.

The fire services for underground parts of mines, nuclear power plants, and offshore oil and gas facilities shall be overseen and managed by their competent agencies.

Fire services for railways, ports, civil aviation, forests, and water shall be enforced pursuant to applicable national and provincial laws.

Article 5 It is a common responsibility for society as a whole to ensure fire safety. Organizations and individuals shall comply with applicable fire protection laws and regulations in their exercise of fire safety duties.

The private sector is encouraged to conduct fire protection activities for the public interest, and it is also encouraged for organizations and individuals to participate in the development of public fire protection facilities and donate to fire services for the public interest.

It is encouraged to make research and innovation on fire protection and promote the widespread application of advanced achievements in science and technology to improve fire prevention, firefighting, and emergency rescue operations capabilities.

第六条 每年的11月9日为本省消防活动日，当月为消防安全月。各级人民政府及有关部门、单位依法应当组织开展消防宣传、纪念、表彰和奖励等相关活动。

第二章 消防安全职责

第七条 各级人民政府应当依法落实消防工作责任制，其主要负责人是本地区消防工作的第一责任人，分管负责人是消防工作的主要责任人，其他负责人应当落实消防安全“一岗双责”制度。

第八条 县级以上人民政府应当履行下列消防工作职责：

（一）组织编制消防专项规划，将其纳入国土空间规划，并负责组织实施；

（二）保障公共消防设施用地，负责公共消防设施、消防装备建设；

（三）建立国家综合性消防救援队和专职消防队；

（四）组织开展消防宣传教育、消防安全检查和专项治理；

（五）协调解决本行政区域的重大消防安全问题；

（六）法律、法规规定的其他消防工作职责。

第九条 省重点产业园区管理机构应当履行下列消防工作职责：

（一）根据市县消防专项规划或者本园区消防专项规划，建设与园区发展规模等相适应的消防基础设施；

（二）建立消防安全组织，明确专人负责消防工作，根据需要建立专职消防队；

（三）开展园区消防安全检查和消防宣传教育，指导园区企业落实消防安全责任；

Article 6 The annual Fire Protection Day falls on November 9 and the Fire Protection Month falls on November. The people's governments at all levels, as well as all the departments and organizations concerned, shall organize and enforce fire protection awareness, commemoration, commendation and reward, and other related activities pursuant to the rules.

Chapter II Duties on Fire Safety

Article 7 The people's governments at all levels shall enforce the fire protection accountability system pursuant to law. The principal heads of the governments shall be the first persons responsible for fire protection in local areas, and the competent heads as the primary responsible persons for fire protection. Other heads shall exercise the system of Dual Duties out of A Single Post for fire safety.

Article 8 The people's governments at or above the county level shall perform the following fire service duties:

(a) to organize and create special fire protection plans, integrate them into the national spatial planning, and take charge of their enforcement;

(b) to ensure adequate land for public facilities for fire protection, and to take charge of building up public facilities and equipment for fire protection;

(c) to set up the national integrated fire departments and full-time fire brigades;

(d) to organize awareness and education on fire protection and inspection and specific actions for fire safety;

(e) to coordinate and solve major problems on fire safety in their respective administrative areas; and

(f) other fire protection duties pursuant to laws and regulations.

Article 9 The administrative agencies of key industrial parks in the Province shall perform the following fire service duties:

(a) to conduct infrastructure development for fire protection corresponding to the development scale of the park based on ad hoc planning by the city, county, or park concerned;

(b) to set up an organization for fire safety, designate a person in charge of fire protection, and set up a full-time fire brigade as necessary;

(c) to conduct inspection on fire safety and awareness on fire protection in the park, and guide entities in the park in fulfillment of fire safety duties; and

（四）履行当地人民政府委托的其他消防工作职责。

消防救援机构应当支持和保障省重点产业园区的消防工作，根据园区发展的实际需要建立国家综合性消防救援队。

消防救援机构应当指导园区企业依法履行主体责任，强化消防安全自律，推动园区企业间的协作，开展联合宣传教育培训、联合演练、应急联动，推进共建共治共享，构建消防安全新型区域协作机制。

第十条 乡镇人民政府应当履行下列消防工作职责：

（一）建立消防安全组织，明确专人负责消防工作，制定消防安全制度，落实消防安全措施；

（二）安排必要的资金，用于公共消防设施建设和业务经费支出；

（三）将消防安全内容纳入本级规划并组织实施；

（四）根据当地经济发展和消防工作的需要建立专职消防队、志愿消防队；

（五）加强消防宣传教育和应急疏散演练；

（六）部署消防安全整治，组织开展消防安全检查，督促整改火灾隐患；

（七）指导、支持和帮助村民委员会、居民委员会开展群众性的消防工作，对村民委员会、居民委员会履行消防安全职责的情况实施监督检查；

（八）法律、法规规定的其他消防工作职责。

街道办事处应当履行前款第一项、第四项、第五项、第六项、第七项、第八项职责，并保障消防工作经费。

第十一条 县级以上人民政府消防救援机构依法履行下列职责：

（一）贯彻执行消防法律、法规和技术标准；

（二）参与编制城乡消防规划，配合有关部门实施；

(d) other duties entrusted by the local people's government.

The fire departments shall support and guarantee fire services for the key industrial parks in the Province, and set up national integrated fire departments as necessary for the development of the park.

The fire departments shall guide entities in the industrial park to assume their primary responsibility pursuant to law, develop self-regulation on fire safety, promote collaboration among entities in the park, conduct joint awareness, education, and training, joint drills, as well as emergency interconnectivity, promote joint development, governance and sharing, and build up a new regional fire safety coordination system.

Article 10 The township people's government shall perform the following fire service duties:

(a) to set up an organization for fire safety, designate a person in charge of fire protection, develop a system for fire safety, and practice measures for fire safety;

(b) to arrange the necessary funds for the development of public facilities for fire protection and business expenses;

(c) to incorporate fire safety matters into the planning of the township government and organize their exercise;

(d) to set up, a full-time fire brigade and a voluntary fire brigade as necessary for local economic development and fire services;

(e) improve awareness and education on fire protection and emergency evacuation drills;

(f) to implement fire safety regulations, organize fire safety inspections, and require the removal of hidden fire hazards;

(g) to guide, support, and help villagers' committees and residents' committees to organize the public participating in fire services, oversee and inspect the enforcement of duties on fire safety by villagers' committees and residents' committees; and

(h) other fire protection duties pursuant to laws and regulations.

The subdistrict agencies shall perform the duties under Subparagraph (a), (d), (e), (f), (g), or (h) of the preceding paragraph, and guarantee funding for fire services.

Article 11 The fire departments of the people's governments at or above the county level shall perform the following duties pursuant to law:

(a) to enforce fire laws, regulations, and technical standards;

(b) to participate in developing urban and rural planning on fire protection, and cooperate with appropriate agencies;

（三）对公众聚集场所投入使用、营业消防安全检查实行告知承诺制管理；

（四）开展消防监督检查，督促整改火灾隐患，依法查处消防安全违法行为；

（五）组织、指导开展消防宣传教育培训和消防演练；

（六）承担火灾扑救，参加应急救援，调查火灾原因，统计火灾损失；

（七）对其他消防队伍及公安派出所进行业务指导；

（八）法律、法规规定的其他职责。

第十二条 发展和改革、财政、自然资源和规划、住房和城乡建设、旅游和文化广电体育、农业农村、工业和信息化等部门在规划制定、调整和实施中，应当做好消防救援站、训练基地、市政消火栓、消防取水设施、消防信息工程等公共消防设施及消防装备的规划、立项和建设等工作。

市政、供水、供电、通信、交通等负责公共消防设施管理维护的部门和单位，应当保持消防供水、消防通信、消防车通道等公共消防设施的完好有效。

第十三条 县级以上人民政府市场监督管理部门、消防救援机构应当按照各自职责，加强对生产、流通和使用领域消防产品质量的监督检查。

县级以上人民政府应急管理部门依法负责易燃易爆危险化学品相关的安全监督管理，组织编制和协调相关部门实施易燃易爆危险化学品事故应急救援预案。

县级以上人民政府住房和城乡建设主管部门依法负责特殊建设工程的消防设计审查、消防验收以及其他建设工程的备案和抽查；承担城镇燃气设施、建设工程施工现场的消防安全监督管理职责。

(c) to manage public plazas under the notification-commitment system for launching and inspecting facilities for fire safety for the business use;

(d) to enforce fire oversight and inspection, require the removal of hidden fire hazards, and investigate and manage fire safety violations pursuant to law;

(e) to organize and guide the implementation of awareness, education, and training on fire protection as well as fire drills;

(f) to engage in firefighting, participate in emergency rescue, investigate the causes of fire, and count the fire losses;

(g) to give professional guidance to other fire brigades and police stations; and

(h) other duties pursuant to laws and regulations.

Article 12 The development and reform, finance, natural resources and planning, housing and urban and rural development, tourism, culture, radio, television and sports, agriculture and rural affairs, industry, and information technology agencies shall put effort into the planning, creation, and development of public firefighting facilities and equipment in the projects concerning firefighting rescue stations, training bases, municipal fire hydrants, firefighting water intake facilities, firefighting information engineering, and other similar projects.

The municipal, water supply, power supply, communication, transportation, and other agencies and organizations responsible for the management and maintenance of public facilities for fire protection shall maintain public facilities, for fire protection, such as water supply, communication, and fire engine passages, intact and effective.

Article 13 The market regulation and fire departments of the people's governments at or above the county level shall, pursuant to their respective duties, improve the oversight and inspection of the quality of fire protection products with respect to their production, circulation, and utility.

The emergency administration agencies of the people's governments at or above the county level shall be responsible for the safety and regulatory oversight for inflammable and explosive dangerous chemicals pursuant to law, and organize the preparation and coordination of appropriate agencies to enforce the emergency rescue plan for accidents involving inflammable and explosive dangerous chemicals.

The housing and urban and rural competent agencies of the people's governments at or above the county level shall be responsible for fire protection design, review, and acceptance, as well as the reporting for the recordation and inspection of other development projects pursuant to law; perform duties on overseeing and managing urban gas facilities and fire safety at construction sites.

县级以上人民政府农业农村主管部门依法负责渔港、渔排、渔船的消防安全监督管理。

第十四条 教育主管部门应当指导和监督学校、学前教育机构、教育培训机构做好消防安全工作，将消防安全列入教育、教学的内容。

学校应当选聘专兼职消防辅导员，每学年至少组织一次专题消防安全教育和消防演练。学前教育机构应当采取适合幼儿特点的方式，对幼儿开展消防安全常识教育。

人力资源和社会保障主管部门应当指导和监督职业培训机构做好消防安全工作，将消防安全列入职业培训的内容。

旅游和文化广电体育主管部门应当指导和监督旅游经营单位开展消防宣传培训工作，将消防安全知识纳入旅游从业人员的岗位培训内容。

工会、共产主义青年团和妇女联合会等团体应当结合各自工作对象的特点，组织开展消防宣传教育。

第十五条 新闻媒体、政府网站等有关单位，应当定期安排时段或者版面无偿发布公益消防安全信息，宣传消防法律、法规和消防常识。

公共场所应当利用场所内的广播、视频设备、宣传栏等宣传消防安全知识。

鼓励、支持社会力量开展消防职业教育和消防安全培训。

提倡居民家庭配备灭火器、火灾探测报警、逃生自救等消防器材。

第十六条 公安派出所按照国家和本省的有关规定履行消防安全监督管理职责。

第十七条 村民委员会、居民委员会应当确定消防安全管理人，制定消防安全公约，开展经常性防火检查、消防宣传和消防安全区域联防，配备必要的消防器材，组织志愿消防队、成年村民、居民进行消防演练，扑救火灾。

The agricultural and rural competent agencies of the people's governments at or above the county level shall be responsible for overseeing and administering fire safety on fishing ports, fishing rafts, and fishing boats pursuant to law.

Article 14 The education agencies shall guide and oversee schools, preschool education institutions, education, and training institutions to guarantee the appropriate services for fire safety, and integrate fire safety into the curriculum.

The schools shall hire full-time and part-time fire safety instructors and organize special education and fire drills on fire safety at least once every school year. The preschool education institutions shall teach pre-school children basic knowledge on fire safety with acceptable methods appropriate for them.

The human resources and public safety competent agency shall guide and oversee vocational training institutions to guarantee the proper services for fire safety, and integrate fire safety into the vocational training.

The tourism, culture, radio, television, and sports competent agencies shall guide and oversee tourism business organizations to enforce awareness and training on fire protection, and integrate fire safety knowledge into the vocational training of tourism professionals.

Trade unions, Communist Youth League organizations, women's federations, and other organizations shall organize to tailor awareness and education tailored to the needs of the local community.

Article 15 The news media, government websites, and other appropriate organizations shall regularly arrange a periodical or a page to publish public fire safety information free of charge and announce laws, regulations, and basic knowledge on fire protection.

Radio, video equipment, billboards, and others shall be used to announce fire safety knowledge in public places.

The private sector is encouraged and supported to provide fire vocational education and fire safety training.

Households are advised to acquire fire protection equipment including without limitation fire extinguishers, smoke detectors, escape tools, and self-rescue products.

Article 16 The police stations perform their duties of fire safety regulatory oversight pursuant to national and provincial laws.

Article 17 The villagers' committees and residents' committees shall confirm a fire safety administrator, draft fire safety conventions, enforce regular inspections for fire prevention, fire protection awareness, and regional joint activities for fire safety, have necessary firefighting equipment, and organize voluntary fire brigades, adult villagers and residents to conduct fire drills and extinguish fires.

村民委员会、居民委员会应当设置消防宣传栏，利用文化活动站、学习室等场所，开展经常性的消防宣传教育；利用广播、视频设备定时播放消防安全常识；在火灾多发季节、农业收获季节、重大节日和乡村民俗活动期间，有针对性地开展消防宣传教育。

第十八条 机关、团体、企业、事业单位和有固定的生产经营场所且具有一定规模的个体工商户，以及其他社会组织（以下统称单位）是消防安全的责任主体，对本单位、本场所消防安全全面负责，应当履行下列消防安全职责：

（一）落实消防安全责任制，制定本单位的消防安全制度、消防安全操作规程，制定灭火和应急疏散预案；

（二）按照国家标准、行业标准配置消防设施、器材，设置消防安全标志，并定期组织检验、维修、保养，确保完好有效；

（三）对建筑消防设施每年至少进行一次全面检测，检测记录应当完整准确，并存档两年以上备查；

（四）保障疏散通道、安全出口、消防车通道畅通，保证防火防烟分区、防火间距符合消防技术标准；

（五）组织防火检查，及时消除火灾隐患，防火检查及火灾隐患整改记录应当存档两年以上备查；

（六）每年至少组织一次消防演练，演练记录应当存档两年以上备查；

（七）设有消防控制室的，应当保障24小时值班；

（八）法律、法规规定的其他消防安全职责。

单位的法定代表人或者主要负责人，是本单位或者场所的消防安全责任人。

第十九条 消防安全重点单位除应当履行本条例第十八条规定的消防安全职责外，还应当履行下列消防安全职责：

The villagers' committees and residents' committees shall set up a public billboard for fire protection, and enforce regular awareness and education on fire protection at entertainment stations, study rooms, and other places; and regularly organize targeted fire protection awareness and education using radio and video equipment to broadcast knowledge on fire safety; in the fire-prone season, agricultural harvest season, major holidays and during rural folk activities.

Article 18 The state agencies, organizations, entities, public institutions, and sole proprietorships with fixed business places and of a specified size, as well as other social organizations (hereinafter referred to as the "Organization"), are the principal bodies responsible for fire safety and are in charge of overall fire safety of their own Organizations and places so they shall perform the following fire safety duties:

(a) to enforce a fire protection accountability system, develop a system and operation procedures on fire safety, and make plans on firefighting and emergency evacuation;

(b) to be equipped with fire control facilities and equipment, set up fire safety signs, and organize inspection, repair, and maintenance on a regular basis to ensure that they are in good condition and effective under the national standards and industry standards;

(c) to conduct an overall examination on fire protection facilities at least once a year, and the examination record shall be complete and accurate and archived for more than 2 years for future reference;

(d) to ensure passages on evacuation routes, safety exits, and passages for fire engines accessible, and that the space separation plan for fire protection and smoke prevention as well as fire protection intervals meet the technical standards for fire protection;

(e) to organize fire protection inspections to remove fire hazards in a timely manner, and ensure that records for of inspections on fire protection and of rectification on fire hazard are archived for more than 2 years for future reference;

(f) to organize fire drills at least once a year, and ensure that drill records are retained for more than 2 years for future reference;

(g) to ensure a fire control room, if there is one, is on duty around the clock; and

(h) other fire protection duties pursuant to laws and regulations.

A statutory representative or responsible person of an Organization is the person responsible for the fire safety of the Organization or location.

Article 19 The key fire safety organization shall perform the following fire safety duties in addition to those specified in Article 18:

（一）确定消防安全管理人，组织实施本单位的消防安全管理工作；

（二）建立消防档案，确定消防安全重点部位，设置防火标志，实行严格管理；

（三）实行每日防火巡查，并建立巡查记录；

（四）对职工进行岗前消防安全培训，每年对职工至少进行一次消防安全培训，每半年至少组织一次消防演练，消防安全培训和演练记录应当存档两年以上备查；

（五）每年将本单位消防安全管理人的基本情况，消防设施配备、维护情况报消防救援机构备案；

（六）自行组织或者委托消防技术服务机构开展消防安全评估，并将评估结果向社会公开。

县级以上人民政府消防救援机构应当将发生火灾可能性较大以及发生火灾可能造成重大的人身伤亡或者财产损失的单位，确定为本行政区域内的消防安全重点单位，并由应急管理部门报本级人民政府备案。消防安全评估办法由省人民政府消防救援机构会同有关部门制定。

鼓励单位消防安全管理人取得消防职业资格证书。鼓励单位组建或者委托消防专业管理团队开展日常消防管理。

第二十条 下列人员应当参加消防安全培训：

（一）单位的消防安全管理人员；

（二）消防设施监控操作人员、防火巡逻员；

（三）消防技术服务机构的从业人员；

（四）专职消防队、志愿消防队队员；

（五）从事易燃易爆危险物品运输、管理、操作的人员；

（六）人员密集场所的有关从业人员。

(a) to clarify the fire safety administrator responsible for organizing fire safety management for the Organization;

(b) to create fire archives, determine the key parts of fire safety, set fire signs, and enforce strict management;

(c) to enforce the daily fire inspection and set up inspection records;

(d) to organize pre-job training on fire safety for employees, regular training on fire safety for employees at least once a year, and fire drills at least once every 6 months to ensure that the records of training and drills on fire safety are kept on file for more than 2 years for future reference;

(e) to report the basic information of the fire safety administrator of the Organization and the equipment and maintenance of fire facilities to the fire departments for recordation; and

(f) to organize or entrust the fire protection technical service agencies to evaluate fire safety services and publish the results of the evaluation.

The fire departments of the people's governments at or above the county level shall identify the Organization most at risk of a fire that may cause great loss of life or property, as the focal organization for fire safety within their respective administrative areas. The emergency administration agencies shall report to the people's government at the same level for recordation. Procedures for fire safety evaluation shall be enacted by the fire departments of the provincial people's government in conjunction with the appropriate agencies.

The fire safety administrator of the Organization is encouraged to become a certified firefighter. The Organization is encouraged to set up or retain a professional fire management team to enforce daily fire management.

Article 20 The following personnel shall participate in training on fire safety:

(a) the fire safety management personnel of the Organization;

(b) monitoring operators of fire protection facilities and fire patrols;

(c) employees of technical service institutions of fire protection;

(d) full-time fire brigade and voluntary fire brigade members;

(e) personnel engaged in the transportation, management, and operation of inflammable and explosive dangerous goods; and

(f) employees concerned in crowded places.

消防行业特有职业（工种）的从业人员应当依法取得职业资格证书，持证上岗。

第二十一条 实行承包、租赁、委托经营的，业主应当提供符合消防安全的建筑物、场所，并由承包者、租赁者、受委托者履行消防安全管理职责。

同一建筑物由两个以上单位管理或者使用的，村民委员会、居民委员会应当指导建筑物的管理、使用各方共同协商，在签订的协议中明确各方的消防安全责任，并确定责任人对共用的疏散通道、安全出口、建筑消防设施和消防车通道进行统一管理；消防安全责任没有约定或者约定不明确的，由各方共同承担。

同一建筑物有多个产权人的，公共消防安全管理所需经费和共用消防设施设备维护、维修和改造所需经费由产权人按照约定承担；没有约定或者约定不明确的，由各产权人共同承担。

第二十二条 居民住宅区的物业服务企业对物业服务区域内的消防安全管理工作负责，履行下列消防安全职责：

（一）在承接物业服务项目时，应当查验消防设施状况，并告知业主委员会或者全体业主；

（二）确定消防安全管理人；

（三）开展防火检查，消除火灾隐患，发现重大火灾隐患，需要政府协调处理的，应当报告消防救援机构；

（四）定期组织开展应急疏散消防演练；

（五）保障消防设施、器材及消防安全标志完好有效；

（六）保障疏散通道、安全出口、消防车通道畅通；

（七）对业主、使用人违反消防安全管理规定的行为予以劝阻、制止；不听劝阻、制止的，可以向消防救援机构或者公安派出所报告；

（八）物业服务合同约定或者法律、法规规定的其他消防安全职责。

Employees engaged in special occupations (job types) in the fire protection field shall be certified for their jobs pursuant to law.

Article 21 Owners of property subject to contract, lease or trust, shall provide buildings and premises that meet fire safety requirements, and the contractor, lessee, and trustee shall perform fire safety management duties.

If one building is managed or used by two or more Organizations, villagers' committees and residents' committees shall guide the management of the building, negotiate with all parties, clarify duties of all parties on fire safety in the signed contract, and determine that the persons of all parties in charge of fire safety place shared evacuation passages, safety exits, fire control facilities in the building and fire engine passages under uniform management. If the fire safety responsibility is not agreed or not clearly agreed, it shall be shared by all parties.

If there are multiple property owners in one building, the funds needed for public fire safety management and for maintenance, repair, and transformation of shared fire protection facilities and equipment shall be assumed by the property owners under the agreement. If there is no agreement or the agreement is not clear, it shall be shared by all property owners.

Article 22 The entities of residential property are responsible for the fire safety management in the property management area, and perform the following fire safety duties:

(a) to check the status of fire protection facilities and inform the owners' committee or all owners when undertaking property management projects;

(b) to determine the fire safety administrator;

(c) to enforce fire prevention inspection, eliminate fire hazards, find major fire hazards, if necessary for coordination by the government, and report such to the fire departments;

(d) to regularly organize fire drills for emergency evacuation;

(e) to ensure that fire control facilities, equipment, and fire safety signs are in good condition and effective;

(f) to ensure the smooth passage in evacuation routes, safety exits, and passages for fire engines;

(g) to discourage and stop the owners and users from violating the fire safety management regulations; and to report the parties that do not listen to dissuasion or stop to a fire department or a police station; and

(h) other duties provided in the property service agreement or other fire protection duties pursuant to laws and regulations.

第三章　火灾预防

第二十三条　消防救援站、消防供水、消防通信、消防车通道等公共消防设施和消防装备应当纳入基本建设计划，按照国家和本省的有关标准和规范建设。

公共消防设施应当与其他市政设施统一规划、统一设计、同步建设。新建、扩建、改建城区、园区及重大建设项目，应当配套建设公共消防设施。

纳入规划的公共消防设施建设用地，禁止擅自改变用途。

城市基础设施配套费应当统筹安排一定比例，专项用于公共消防设施和消防装备建设及其维护保养。

第二十四条　农村主要道路应当满足消防车通行需要。统一规划建设的农村住宅应当符合防火间距要求。

农村设有生产生活供水管网的，应当设置室外消火栓。城乡利用海、河、湖、池塘等天然水源作为消防水源的，应当设置消防取水设施。取水困难的应当建设消防水池等储水设施。

第二十五条　消防救援机构应当协助有关部门做好渔港、渔排、渔船的消防安全、火灾扑救、海上救援等工作。

渔港码头应当设置室外消火栓或者消防取水设施；渔排、渔船应当配备消防器材。

第二十六条　国家规定的特殊建设工程的消防设计审查应当依照有关规定并入施工图设计文件联合审查。消防验收纳入竣工验收范围，集中统一办理。

依法实行消防设计审查验收的建设工程发生改建、扩建、改变使用性质等重大变更的，应当重新向建设工程所在地住房和城乡建设主管部门申请消防设计审查、消防验收。

Chapter III Fire Prevention

Article 23 The fire rescue stations, fire water supply, fire communication, fire engine passages, and other public fire facilities and fire equipment shall be integrated into the basic development plan, pursuant to applicable national and provincial standards and norms.

The public fire control facilities shall be planned, designed, and constructed simultaneously with other municipal facilities. The new construction, expansion, renovation of urban areas, parks, and major construction projects shall be equipped with public fire protection facilities.

The construction land for the public fire protection facilities, incorporated in the planning, is banned from the unauthorized change of its use.

The supporting fees for urban infrastructure shall be arranged in a certain proportion, which shall be specifically used for the construction and maintenance of public fire protection facilities and equipment.

Article 24 The rural main roads shall facilitate passages for fire engines. Uniform planning and construction of rural residential buildings shall meet the requirements on intervals for fire prevention.

An outdoor fire hydrant shall be installed in rural areas with a water supply network for production and living. If natural water sources such as sea, rivers, lakes, and ponds are utilized as fire water sources in urban and rural areas, water intake facilities for fire protection shall be installed. The water storage facilities, such as fire pools among others, shall be built up in areas difficult for fire water intake.

Article 25 The fire departments shall assist the appropriate agencies in fire safety, firefighting, and rescue at sea in fishing ports and on fishing rafts and fishing boats.

The outdoor fire hydrants or fire water intake facilities shall be installed at fishing port terminals; the fishing rafts and fishing boats shall be equipped with firefighting equipment.

Article 26 The review of the fire protection design of special construction projects as specified by the state shall be included in the joint review of construction drawings and design documents pursuant to law. The fire protection acceptance shall be incorporated into the completion acceptance and shall be processed uniformly.

In case of major changes such as alteration, expansion, change in the nature of utilization, the construction project subject to fire protection design review and fire protection acceptance shall be resubmitted to the competent agency of housing and urban-rural development in the region where the construction project is located.

住房和城乡建设主管部门应当及时将消防验收、备案和抽查情况告知消防救援机构，并与消防救援机构共享建筑平面图、消防设施平面布置图、消防设施系统图等资料。

第二十七条　建设工程施工现场的消防安全由施工单位负责；实行总承包的，由总承包单位负责。

施工现场应当符合下列规定：

（一）施工现场应当设置消防车通道并确保畅通；

（二）施工现场应当按照规定设置消防水源，配备必要的消防设施和灭火器材；

（三）高层建筑应当根据施工进度，同步安装室内消火栓系统或者设置临时消火栓、水泵接合器等，满足施工现场火灾扑救的消防供水要求；

（四）施工现场的电气工程和装置应当符合有关安全规定；

（五）办公、生活区与作业区分开设置，厨房与宿舍保持安全距离；

（六）不得在尚未竣工的建筑物内设置员工集体宿舍。

建设单位、监理单位应当监督施工单位严格按照有关施工规程操作，杜绝火灾隐患。

临时建筑应当符合消防安全要求，不得占用消防车通道。

第二十八条　公众聚集场所在取得营业执照或者依法具备投入使用条件后，应当向消防救援机构提出投入使用、营业消防安全许可申请，在其作出符合消防安全标准的承诺并提供相关材料后，消防救援机构不再进行实质性审查，当场作出许可决定。

消防救援机构应当制定公众聚集场所消防安全标准并向社会公布。

消防救援机构应当对作出承诺的公众聚集场所加强事中事后监管。

The competent agency for housing and urban and rural construction shall promptly inform the fire departments of the fire protection acceptance, filing, and inspection, and share the building plan, fire protection facilities layout, fire protection facilities system diagram, and other data with the fire departments.

Article 27 Developers are responsible for the fire safety of the construction site; general contractors shall be responsible for the fire safety of general contracting.

A construction site shall comply with the following:

(a) passages for fire engines shall be set up at the construction site and kept smooth;

(b) fire water sources shall be set up at the construction site pursuant to law, and the site shall be equipped with necessary firefighting facilities and equipment;

(c) high-rise buildings shall, based on construction progress, be fitted with indoor fire hydrant systems or equipped up temporary fire hydrants, and water pump adapters as provided by fire water supply requirements for firefighting on the construction site;

(d) the electrical engineering and equipment on the construction site shall comply with the applicable safety regulations;

(e) the office, living area, and operation area are set separately, and the kitchen and dormitory are kept at a safe interval; and

(f) no staff dormitory shall be located in an unfinished building.

A project owner and overseeing organization shall oversee the developer in operations under applicable construction regulations, so as to remove fire hazards.

The temporary buildings shall meet the requirements of fire safety and shall not occupy passages of fire engines.

Article 28 After obtaining the business license or meeting the conditions for putting it into use pursuant to law, public plazas shall submit an application for a fire safety license to the fire departments. After issuing the commitment to meet fire safety standards and providing appropriate materials, the fire departments will no longer conduct the substantive review and grant the license on spot.

Fire departments shall draft fire safety standards for public plazas and publish them.

Fire departments shall improve oversight on public plazas as issuers of commitment during and after the event.

公众聚集场所发生改建、扩建、改变使用性质、更换经营者等重大变更的，应当重新向场所所在地消防救援机构作出其符合消防安全标准的承诺。

消防救援机构应当与省信息共享交换平台建立对接，及时获取市场监管部门推送的公众聚集场所商事主体登记信息。

第二十九条 从事建筑消防设施检测维修保养、消防安全监测等消防技术服务机构和执业人员，应当具备相应的从业条件，按照相应的服务标准提供消防技术服务，并对服务质量负责。消防救援机构应当加强对相关从业行为的监督抽查。

消防技术服务机构和执业人员不具备从业条件、弄虚作假的，纳入信用记录，依法实施信用惩戒。

第三十条 本条例规定的消防许可事项可以由集中审批服务部门承担。需要开展技术审查的，集中审批服务部门可以委托专业技术服务机构开展。

第三十一条 对符合国家规定适合海南自由贸易港需求的国际消防技术标准，可以在海南自由贸易港适用。

鼓励具备相应条件的境外消防技术服务机构在海南自由贸易港开展消防技术服务。鼓励具备相应资格的境外消防技术从业人员根据本省规定通过技能认定后到海南自由贸易港执业。境外消防技术服务机构开展消防技术服务的条件和境外消防技术从业人员技能认定的具体办法由省人民政府应急管理部门、消防救援机构制定。

第三十二条 消防产品应当符合质量要求，禁止安装、使用不合格的消防产品以及国家明令淘汰的消防产品。

建筑构件、建筑材料和室内装修、装饰材料的防火性能必须符合国家标准；没有国家标准的，必须符合行业标准。

In case of major changes such as renovation, expansion, change in the nature of use, and replacement of operators, public plazas shall issue the commitment to meet the fire safety standards to the fire department where the place is located.

Fire departments shall establish docking with the provincial information sharing and exchange platform, and promptly obtain the registration information of commercial enterprises in public plazas recommended by market regulation agencies.

Article 29 Fire protection technical service agencies and practitioners engaged in inspection, maintenance, and fire safety monitoring of fire protection facilities for a construction project shall have corresponding employment qualifications, provide fire protection technical services pursuant to corresponding service standards, and be responsible for service quality. The fire departments shall improve the oversight and inspection of the professional operations.

The fire protection technical service agencies and practitioners, not meeting the conditions for employment or involved in falsification shall be listed into the credit record and subject to credit punishment pursuant to law.

Article 30 The fire permit matters specified in these Regulations can be conducted by the centralized approving agencies. The centralized approving agencies may hire professional and technical agencies to enforce the technical review as necessary.

Article 31 The international technical standards for fire protection that meet the standards of the HFTP pursuant to law by the state can be applied in the HFTP.

Foreign fire protection technical institutions with adequate capabilities are encouraged to provide fire protection technical services in the HFTP. Qualified foreign fire technology practitioners are encouraged to practice in the HFTP after being accredited as certified professionals under the regulations of this Province. The specific regulations for overseas fire protection technical institutions to enforce fire protection technical services and the skill certification of overseas fire protection technical employees shall be enacted by the emergency administration agencies and fire rescue institutions of the provincial people's government.

Article 32 Fire protection products shall meet the quality requirements, and it is prohibited to install and use fire protection products that are unqualified or explicitly ousted by the state.

The fire resistance performance of building components, building materials, and interior build-out and decoration materials must meet the national standards. The industry standards shall apply if there is no national standard.

人员密集场所装修装饰工程，应当按照消防技术标准的要求，使用不燃、难燃材料。建设单位、施工单位、监理单位应当依照国家规定对使用的装修、装饰材料进行查验。

第三十三条 禁止人员密集场所在营业期间进行电焊、气焊、气割、砂轮切割、油漆粉刷等具有火灾危险的施工、维修作业。

禁止在加油站、加气站等具有火灾、爆炸危险的场所吸烟和使用明火。

禁止在公共娱乐场所燃放烟花爆竹，禁止在建筑密集区、林区和高铁沿线等区域放飞孔明灯。

禁止在住宅、地下建筑、集贸市场、商场内生产、储存、销售、销毁易燃易爆危险品。

第三十四条 用于居住的出租房屋，应当符合消防安全要求；居住人数较多的出租房屋，应当提高消防安全要求。

出租人应当遵守下列消防安全管理规定：

（一）发现火灾隐患及时消除或者通知承租人消除；

（二）对承租人改变房屋使用功能和结构是否符合消防安全要求进行监督；

（三）发现承租人有消防安全违法行为的，及时制止；

（四）国家和本省的其他消防安全要求。

承租人应当遵守下列消防安全管理规定：

（一）对承租房屋内的消防设施、器材进行日常管理；

（二）改变房屋使用功能和结构的，应当符合消防安全要求；

（三）发现火灾隐患及时消除或者通知出租人消除；

（四）国家和本省的其他消防安全要求。

Combustible and flame-retardant materials shall be used in the build-out project of crowded places under the fire protection technical standards. The project owner, the developer, and the construction supervisor shall inspect the build-out and decorative materials used pursuant to national regulations.

Article 33 Construction and maintenance with fire hazards, such as electric welding, gas welding, gas cutting, grinding wheel cutting, and painting, are banned in crowded places during their business hours.

Smoking and open flames are banned in places with fire and explosion hazards such as gas stations and filling stations.

Fireworks are banned in public places for entertainment, and Kongming lanterns (sky lanterns) are banned from flying in densely built areas, forest areas, and areas along the high-speed railway.

It is forbidden to produce, store, sell or destroy flammable or explosive dangerous goods in residential buildings, underground buildings, fairs, and shopping malls.

Article 34 Rental homes shall meet the fire safety requirements. Rental homes with a large number of residents shall improve the fire safety requirements.

The lessor shall comply with the following regulations on fire safety management:

(a) to remove or notify the lessee to remove any hidden fire hazards in a timely manner;

(b) to oversee whether the change of the function and structure of the property by the lessee meets the fire safety requirements;

(c) to discourage the lessee where the lessee violates any fire safety rules in a timely manner; and

(d) other duties as required by the state and the Province.

The lessee shall comply with the following regulations on fire safety management:

(a) the daily management of fire protection facilities and equipment shall be conducted in the leased house;

(b) the change of the function and structure of the house shall meet the requirements of fire safety;

(c) to remove or notify the lessee to remove any hidden fire hazards in a timely manner; and

(d) others required by the state and the Province.

第三十五条 农家乐、民宿的经营管理者应当按照消防安全标准建设管理，履行本条例第十八条规定的单位消防安全职责；符合消防安全重点单位界定标准的，应当纳入重点单位管理。

第三十六条 飞机、船舶、火车、汽车等交通运输工具应当按照规定配置消防器材，标明紧急疏散标识。

电动汽车充电基础设施应当符合国家有关标准和本省的消防安全要求。

停放电动自行车较多的居民住宅区、集体宿舍和其他场所，应当设置电动自行车集中停放场所和符合用电安全要求的充电设施，采取防火分隔措施。村民委员会、居民委员会、物业服务企业或者其他管理人应当加强日常管理，做好巡查、检查工作。

禁止在疏散通道、安全出口、楼梯间停放电动自行车。

禁止违反用电安全要求给电动自行车充电。

第三十七条 单位、个人敷设电线、燃气管道和使用电器产品、燃气用具应当符合消防安全规定，及时更新老化电气线路，不得违反消防安全规定用电、用气。

供电企业应当定期对公用供电设施、户外电气线路进行检测，及时更换、改造老化供电设施和电气线路；加强用电管理，开展电气消防安全检查，督促电气火灾隐患的整改。

对用电单位和个人超负荷用电、违规拉线接电等可能引发火灾的行为，供电企业应当依法及时予以制止，电力管理部门应当依法处理。

Article 35 Operators and managers of farmhouses and homestays shall, pursuant to the fire safety standards, perform the fire safety duties of the Organization provided in Article 18. Those falling within the scope of key fire safety organizations shall be incorporated in the management of key organizations.

Article 36 Aircrafts, ships, trains, cars, and other means of transport shall be equipped with fire protection equipment pursuant to law and shall be marked with emergency evacuation signs.

The electric vehicle charging infrastructure shall comply with the applicable national standards and the fire safety requirements of this Province.

The residential areas, collective dormitories, and other places where a large number of electric bicycles are parked shall be integrated with centralized parking locations for electric bicycles and charging facilities that meet the safety requirements for electricity use, and fire prevention and separation measures shall be adopted. The villagers' committees, residents' committees, property management entities, or other managers shall improve daily management and conduct inspections.

The parking of electric bicycles in evacuation routes, safety exits, and stairwells is banned.

It is forbidden to charge electric bicycles in violation of electrical safety requirements.

Article 37 Organizations and individuals laying wires, gas pipelines, and using electrical products and gas appliances shall comply with fire safety regulations, update aging electrical lines in a timely manner, and shall not use electricity or gas in violation of fire safety regulations.

Power supply entities shall regularly inspect public power supply facilities and outdoor electrical lines, and replace and transform aging power supply facilities and electrical lines in a timely manner; improve electricity management, enforce electrical fire safety inspection, and require the removal of hidden electrical fire hazards.

The power supply operators shall promptly stop the wrong acts of organizations and individuals that may lead to fire, such as overloading the power consumption and connecting the cables in violation of regulations, and the power management departments shall punish them pursuant to law.

第三十八条 公众聚集场所和生产、储存、运输、销售易燃易爆危险品的企业以及园区的消防安全重点单位按照国家和本省的有关规定投保火灾公众责任保险。对老城区、城中村、偏远农村的居民推行火灾保险，市、县、自治县人民政府可以给予补贴。

鼓励保险公司承保火灾保险，建立火灾风险评价机制，将火灾公众责任保险费率和单位消防安全状况联系浮动，促进投保单位提高消防安全管理水平。

第三十九条 应用新技术、新工艺、新材料的，应当符合国家和海南自由贸易港的有关规定和标准。

第四十条 鼓励互联网、物联网、大数据、云计算、区块链等信息技术在消防安全领域的应用，建设智慧消防综合管理服务平台，实现消防数据归集共享，融入智慧城市一体建设。

鼓励利用智慧消防技术开展内部消防安全管理，监测消防安全状况，评估消防安全风险，实施消防安全预警、预报。

设有自动消防设施的人员密集场所和生产、储存、经营易燃易爆危险品场所应当和城市消防安全远程监控系统联网，加强消防设施的联网监测。

第四章　消防组织

第四十一条 各级人民政府应当统筹规划、合理布局、因地制宜、配套建立国家综合性消防救援队、专职消防队和志愿消防队等多种形式的消防队伍。

Article 38 Public plazas and entities that produce, store, transport and sell flammable and explosive dangerous goods, as well as key fire safety organizations in the park, shall acquire fire public liability insurance pursuant to national and provincial laws. The people's governments of cities, counties, and autonomous counties can provide subsidies for fire insurance for residents in old residential areas, villages in cities, and remote rural areas.

It is encouraged for insurance companies to underwrite fire insurance, establish the fire risk assessment mechanism, connect the fire public liability insurance rate with the fire safety status of an organization, and promote the insured organization for improved and higher-level management on fire safety.

Article 39 The application of new technologies, new processes, and new materials shall comply with applicable national and HFTP regulations.

Article 40 It is encouraged to apply the internet, Internet of Things, big data, cloud computing, blockchain, and other information technologies to fire safety, to build up the integrated management service platform for smart fire to realize the collection and sharing of fire data, and incorporate these technologies into the integrated development of smart cities.

It is encouraged to make use of smart fire technology to enforce internal fire safety management, monitoring fire safety conditions, assessing fire safety risks, and implementing fire safety early warning and forecast.

Crowded places with automatic fire protection facilities and places where inflammable and explosive dangerous goods are produced, stored, and operated shall be interconnected with the remote monitoring system of urban fire safety, and the networked monitoring of fire protection facilities shall be improved.

Chapter IV Fire Protection Organizations

Article 41 The people's governments at all levels shall create a comprehensive plan and rational layout, adjust measures to local conditions, and set up national comprehensive fire departments, full-time fire teams, and volunteer fire teams.

县级以上人民政府根据本行政区域经济社会发展和消防工作需要，可以采取聘用专职消防队员或者消防文员等形式补充消防力量。

第四十二条 县级以上人民政府应当按照国家规定建立国家综合性消防救援队、政府专职消防队，配备消防救援装备，根据实际需要建设消防救援指挥中心、物资储备和训练基地。根据消防救援工作需要，组建机动消防救援力量，建设石化、山岳、水域、地质灾害、空勤、急救、核生化等消防救援专业力量。

市、县、自治县应当根据消防规划，建设水上或者水陆消防救援站。

距离消防救援站较远的全国重点乡镇应当建立政府专职消防队；其他乡镇、街道办事处应当根据当地经济发展和消防工作的需要，建立政府专职消防队或者志愿消防队。

各类园区、国家公园、工矿区、港口、中心渔港、风景名胜区、旅游度假区、环岛旅游公路的驿站，应当根据规划和实际需要建设消防站、配备消防救援力量。

大型商业综合体、超高层建筑和建筑总面积达到五十万平方米的新建住宅小区应当根据规划和实际需要建设消防站。

第四十三条 下列单位应当建立单位专职消防队：

（一）大型核设施单位、大型发电厂、民用机场、主要港口；

（二）生产、储存易燃易爆危险品的大型企业；

（三）储备可燃的重要物资的大型仓库、基地；

（四）第一项、第二项、第三项规定以外的火灾危险性较大、距离消防救援站较远的其他大型企业。

The people's governments at or above the county level may, pursuant to the demands of economic and social development and fire protection in their respective administrative areas, employ full-time firefighters or fire clerks to supplement their fire protection forces.

Article 42 The people's governments at or above the county level shall, pursuant to national regulations, establish national comprehensive fire departments and government full-time fire departments, equip them with fire rescue equipment, and build fire rescue command centers, material reserves, and training bases as demanded in practice. And the governments shall set up mobile fire-rescue forces, and build professional fire rescue forces such as petrochemical, mountain, water, geological disasters, aircrew, first aid, and nuclear biochemistry as demanded in fire rescue services.

The city, county, and autonomous county shall build water or land fire rescue stations under fire planning.

The national key towns far away from fire rescue stations shall establish full-time government fire brigades. Other townships and local sub-district agencies shall establish the full-time government fire brigade or the volunteer fire brigade as required by local economic development and fire protection.

All kinds of parks, national parks, industrial and mining areas, ports, central fishing ports, scenic spots, tourist resorts, and stations of tourist roads around the island shall build fire stations and equip with fire rescue forces as planned and demanded in practice.

Large commercial complexes, super high-rise buildings, and newly built residential quarters with a total development area of 500,000 square meters shall be built as planned and demanded in practice.

Article 43 The following organizations shall set up a full-time fire brigade:

(a) large nuclear facilities, large power plants, civil airports, and major ports;

(b) large entities that produce and store inflammable and explosive dangerous goods;

(c) large warehouses and bases for storing important combustible materials; and

(d) other large entities with greater fire risk and farther from the fire rescue station than those specified in Subparagraph (a), (b), or (c).

消防救援机构可以组织、指导前款规定的相邻或者相近的单位联合建立单位专职消防队。

第四十四条　市、县、自治县人民政府应当鼓励、扶持单位以及村民委员会、居民委员会建立志愿消防队等多种形式的消防组织，开展群众性自防自救工作。

第四十五条　国家综合性消防救援队、专职消防队应当按照国家和本省的有关标准建设。组建单位应当保障消防队的建设经费和业务经费。

专职消防队建成后，应当经当地消防救援机构验收。未经消防救援机构同意，不得随意撤销。

国家综合性消防救援队、专职消防队和志愿消防队等开展灭火救援演练时，相关部门和单位应当予以配合。

第四十六条　消防救援人员依法享受国家和社会给予的各项优待优抚。

国家综合性消防救援队和政府专职消防队应当为其队员购买人身意外伤害保险，所需费用由同级财政承担。

鼓励单位专职消防队、志愿消防队的组建单位为消防队员购买因执行职务发生的人身意外伤害保险。

对因参加火灾扑救或者应急救援受伤、致残或者死亡的人员，人民政府、用人单位和保险机构应当按照有关规定给予医疗、工伤待遇、抚恤和保险金；符合烈士评定条件的，按有关规定办理。

The fire departments may organize and guide the adjacent or similar Organizations specified in the preceding paragraph to jointly create a full-time fire brigade.

Article 44 The people's governments of cities, counties, and autonomous counties shall encourage and support Organizations, villagers' committees, and residents' committees to establish voluntary fire brigades and other forms of fire protection organizations to organize the public participating in self-defense and self-rescue services.

Article 45 The national comprehensive fire departments and full-time fire brigades shall be set up under applicable national and provincial standards. The organization setting up these teams shall guarantee the development funds and business funds for the fire brigade.

The full-time fire brigade shall be acknowledged by the local fire department once set up. Without the consent of fire departments, it shall not be arbitrarily canceled.

Appropriate agencies and organizations shall cooperate with firefighting and rescue drills conducted by national comprehensive fire departments, full-time fire brigades, and voluntary fire brigades.

Article 46 The fire rescue personnel shall have the right to the preferential treatment given by the state and society pursuant to law.

The national comprehensive fire departments and the government full-time fire brigade shall purchase personal accident insurance for their members, and the expenses required shall be assumed by the finance agencies at the same level.

It is recommended that full-time fire brigades and voluntary fire brigades of the Organization purchase personal accident insurance for firefighters performing their duties.

The people's government, employers, and insurance institutions shall give medical treatment, treatment of work-related injuries, pensions, and insurance benefits to those injured, disabled, or killed in firefighting or emergency rescue pursuant to law. The grant of national honorary titles, if any, shall be considered pursuant to law.

第五章　灭火和应急救援

第四十七条　任何人发现火灾及其他灾害事故应当立即报警。任何单位、个人应当无偿为报警提供便利，不得阻拦报警。

严禁谎报火灾、险情。公安机关、消防救援机构核查、处理谎报火灾、险情的行为时，通信企业应当协助。

第四十八条　国家综合性消防救援队、专职消防队应当 24 小时值班备勤，接到报警或者命令立即出动，救助遇险人员，排除险情，扑灭火灾。

专职消防队应当接受消防救援机构的统一调动，参加火灾扑救、应急救援。

消防救援机构应当会同卫生健康等相关部门建立消防救援和院前急救联动机制，实行本省 119 消防报警和 120 急救中心应急合作。

公安派出所接到火灾或者其他灾害事故报警，应当及时向消防救援机构报告，并先行组织群众扑救初起火灾或者实施救援；消防救援队到达后，公安派出所应当配合消防救援队做好警戒等工作。

发生火灾、险情的，单位应当立即启动应急救援预案，采取必要措施，防止危害扩大和次生、衍生灾害发生，并向消防救援队提供相关技术资料、信息和处置方法。

第四十九条　消防车、消防艇等消防交通工具赶赴火场或者灾害事故现场时，可以使用警笛、警灯，其他交通工具和行人应当避让；必要时可以启用平时禁止通行的道路、地段和水域；紧急情况时，对于阻碍消防交通工具通行的其他交通工具和障碍物，可以强制让道和实施破拆。

Chapter V Firefighting and Emergency Rescue

Article 47 Anyone who discovers fire and other disasters and accidents shall report to the police immediately. Any organizations or individuals shall assist them to report the emergency free of charge and shall not prevent them from doing so.

Falsified report of fire and danger is prohibited. The communication entities shall assist public security agencies and fire departments in verifying and resolving false reports of fire and danger.

Article 48 The national comprehensive fire departments and full-time fire brigade shall be on duty around the clock, and shall be dispatched immediately upon receiving an alarm or order to rescue persons in distress, and eliminate dangerous situations and extinguish fires.

The full-time fire brigade shall accept the uniform mobilization of fire departments to participate in firefighting and emergency rescue.

The fire departments shall, in conjunction with health and other appropriate agencies, establish the connectivity mechanism between fire rescue and pre-hospital first aid, and realize emergency cooperation between "119" fire alarm centers and "120" emergency centers in this Province.

Where the police station receives the alarm of fire or other disasters, it shall report to the fire departments promptly and organize the public to put out the initial fire or conduct rescue. After the fire department's arrival, the police station shall cooperate with the fire department to alert.

In case of fire or danger, the Organization shall immediately launch the emergency rescue plan, take necessary measures to prevent the expansion of hazards and secondary and derivative disasters, and provide appropriate technical data, information, and disposal methods to the fire departments.

Article 49 When firefighting vehicles such as fire engines and fire boats rush to the site of a fire or disaster accident, they can use sirens and warning lights, and other vehicles and pedestrians shall make way for them. Inaccessible roads, lots, and waters at ordinary times can be opened (if necessary). In case of emergency, other vehicles and obstacles, hindering the passage of firefighting vehicles, can be forced to make way or torn apart.

消防车、消防艇等消防交通工具使用的警灯、警笛为专用警报设备，禁止其它交通工具使用。

第五十条 国家综合性消防救援队、政府专职消防队扑救火灾、实施应急救援，不收取任何费用。

单位专职消防队、志愿消防队参加本单位以外的火灾扑救或者应急救援的，可以将燃料、灭火剂和器材、装备等的损耗情况，报告火灾或者灾害事故发生地的消防救援机构，经消防救援机构审核后，向市、县、自治县人民政府申请给予补偿。

根据火灾扑救或者应急救援需要，调用和征用社会物资、工程机械的，在使用完毕后应当及时归还。社会物资、工程机械被调用、征用或者调用、征用后毁损、灭失的，县级以上人民政府应当按照有关规定给予补偿。

第五十一条 县级以上人民政府统一领导国家综合性消防救援队、专职消防队参加火灾以外的其他重大灾害事故的应急救援工作。消防救援机构统一组织和指挥火灾现场扑救。

社会救援力量参加火灾扑救、应急救援的，应当接受现场总指挥的统一指挥调度。

第五十二条 根据火灾扑救、应急救援的实际需要，相关部门和单位应当及时、无偿向消防救援机构提供有关数据、资料。

在修建道路以及停电、停水、截断通信线路时有可能影响灭火救援的，有关单位必须事先通知当地消防救援机构。

第五十三条 驻琼部队、供水、供电、燃气、通信、医疗、环卫、环境保护、气象、民航、铁路、港口等相关部门和单位应当参加政府统一领导的火灾扑救、应急救援工作。

Warning lights and sirens used by firefighting vehicles such as fire engines and fire boats are specifically used as warning equipment, and other vehicles are prohibited from using them.

Article 50 The national comprehensive fire departments and government full-time fire departments shall not charge any fees for fighting fires and conducting an emergency rescue.

In respect of the full-time fire brigade and volunteer fire brigade of the Organization to participate in firefighting or emergency rescue outside the Organization, the loss of fuel, fire extinguishing agent and equipment, can be reported to the fire departments where fire or disaster accident occurred, and after the fire department's audit, apply to the people's governments of cities, counties and autonomous counties for reimbursement.

Social materials and construction machinery shall be called and requisitioned, and shall be returned in time after use as demanded in firefighting or emergency rescue. The people's governments at or above the county level shall reimburse if private sector materials and construction machinery are damaged or lost after being called for, expropriated, or requisitioned pursuant to law.

Article 51 The people's governments at or above the county level shall take a leading role in arranging the national comprehensive fire departments and full-time fire brigades to participate in the emergency rescue of major disasters and accidents other than fires. The fire departments shall organize and direct the on-site firefighting.

Private sector rescue forces participating in firefighting and emergency rescue shall accept the unity of command under the on-site commander.

Article 52 Agencies and organizations concerned shall provide appropriate data and materials to fire departments in a timely and free manner as required by firefighting and emergency rescue.

Where the construction of roads, power outages, water cuts, and communication lines may affect firefighting and rescue, organizations concerned must notify the local fire departments in advance.

Article 53 Departments and organizations concerned, such as troops stationed in Hainan, water supply, power supply, gas, communication, medical care, sanitation, environmental protection, meteorology, civil aviation, railways, and ports, shall participate in the firefighting and emergency rescue under the unified leadership of the government.

消防救援指挥应当纳入省人民政府建立的综合应急救援指挥平台，互联共享道路交通、气象、公共卫生、环境监测、海上搜救、电力、三防、抗震救灾、森林防火等信息，实现统一调度、统一指挥、统一协调。

省和市、县、自治县人民政府应当整合消防救援力量和资源，建立区域消防应急联动机制，协调周边省、自治区消防救援力量和资源，建立跨海消防救援增援机制。

第六章　火灾事故调查

第五十四条　消防救援机构负责调查火灾原因，统计火灾损失。

发生下列火灾事故的，由火灾发生地的县级以上人民政府组织事故调查:

（一）造成人员死亡或者产生社会影响的一般火灾事故、较大火灾事故，由市、县、自治县人民政府组织调查处理；

（二）重大火灾事故由省人民政府组织调查处理；

（三）特别重大火灾事故按照国家规定执行。

第五十五条　火灾扑灭后，消防救援机构应当及时调查火灾原因。消防救援机构可以委托依法设立的价格鉴证机构、资产评估机构对火灾直接财产损失进行鉴定或者评估。火灾直接财产损失鉴定意见或者评估报告可以作为消防救援机构统计火灾损失的依据。

第五十六条　消防救援机构有权根据事故调查需要划定现场封闭范围，并可以进入现场及场所进行勘验和检查；有权向火灾发生知情人询问情况，调取资料，扣押物品；有权向有关机关、组织查阅、复制相关文件、资料。

The fire and rescue command shall be incorporated into the comprehensive emergency rescue command platform established by the provincial people's government, and the information of road traffic, meteorology, public health, environmental monitoring, maritime search and rescue, electricity, three defenses (personnel, material, technology), earthquake relief, forest fire-prevention, and the like, shall be interconnected and shared, so as to realize the unified dispatch, unified command, and unified coordination.

The people's governments of provinces, cities, counties, and autonomous counties shall integrate fire rescue forces and resources, establish the regional fire emergency connectivity mechanism, coordinate the fire rescue forces and resources of neighboring provinces and autonomous regions, and establish a cross-sea fire rescue reinforcement mechanism.

Chapter VI Investigation of Fire Accidents

Article 54 Fire departments are responsible for investigating the cause of the fire and figuring out fire losses.

In case of any of the following fire accidents, the people's governments at or above the county level where the fire occurred shall organize an accident investigation:

(a) the common fire accidents and major fire accidents that cause death or social impact shall be investigated and handled by the people's governments of cities, counties, and autonomous counties;

(b) major fire accidents are investigated and handled by the provincial people's government; or

(c) in case of particularly serious fire accidents, national regulations shall control.

Article 55 After the fire is extinguished, the fire departments shall promptly investigate the cause of the fire. The fire departments may retain price appraisal agencies and asset appraisal agencies established pursuant to law to identify or evaluate direct property losses caused by fire. The appraisal opinion or assessment report of direct property loss caused by fire can be used as the basis for fire departments to figure out fire losses.

Article 56 A fire department is entitled to designate the closed scope of the site as demanded in accident investigation, and to enter the site and place for inquest and inspection; to ask the insider of the fire, obtain information and seize articles; to consult and copy appropriate documents and materials from appropriate national agencies and organizations.

消防救援机构应当自火灾发生之日起三十日内完成火灾事故认定，并于七日内告知当事人；情况复杂、疑难的，经消防救援机构负责人批准，可以延长三十日；法律法规另有规定的除外。

火灾事故调查中需要进行检验、鉴定的，检验、鉴定时间不计入调查期限。

第五十七条 火灾扑灭后，发生火灾的单位和有关人员应当按照消防救援机构的要求保护现场，接受事故调查，如实提供与火灾有关的情况。未经消防救援机构同意，任何人不得擅自进入火灾现场，不得擅自清理、移动火灾现场物品。

第五十八条 对造成人员死亡或者重大社会影响的火灾，应当倒查工程建设、中介服务、消防产品质量、使用管理等各方主体责任。

第五十九条 消防救援机构在火灾事故调查中发现有下列情形之一的，应当依法移送有关部门进行调查：

（一）有放火嫌疑以及因爆炸物品爆炸引起火灾事故的，移送公安机关；

（二）车辆在道路上发生火灾，属于道路交通事故的，移送公安机关交通管理部门；

（三）生产、经营、储存、运输、使用危险化学品和处置废弃危险化学品过程中发生火灾，属于安全生产事故的，移送应急管理部门；

（四）因城镇燃气事故引发的火灾，移送住房和城乡建设主管部门；

（五）电力设备、设施因故障引起自身燃烧未蔓延至其他物品的，移送电力主管部门；

（六）港口、船舶、渔港、渔船、水上设施发生的火灾事故，移送农业农村、海事等主管部门。

A fire department shall complete the identification of the fire accident within 30 days of the date of the fire and inform the parties within 7 days. If a circumstance is complicated and difficult, it can be extended for 30 days subject to the approval of the person in charge of the fire department; except as otherwise provided by laws and regulations.

If inspection and identification are required in the fire accident investigation, the inspection and identification time shall not be included in the investigation period.

Article 57 After the fire is extinguished, the Organization on fire and personnel concerned shall protect the scene as required by the firefighting and rescue institutions, accept the accident investigation, and truthfully provide information related to the fire. Without the consent of a fire department, no one is allowed to enter the fire site without authorization, and no one is allowed to clean or move the articles at the fire site without authorization.

Article 58 In case of fire causing death or a significant community impact, the primary liability of all parties, such as engineering development, intermediary services, fire protection product quality, and use management, shall be investigated.

Article 59 Where a fire department finds any of the following circumstances in the investigation of a fire accident, it shall be transferred to the appropriate agencies for investigation:

(a) anyone suspected of arson and any fire accident caused by the explosion of explosives shall be transferred to public security agencies;

(b) any road traffic accident caused by a vehicle catching fire on the road shall be transferred to the traffic administration office of public security agencies;

(c) if the fire occurs during the production, operation, storage, transportation and use of hazardous chemicals and the disposal of abandoned hazardous chemicals, which amounts to the safety production accident, the case shall be transferred to the emergency administration agencies;

(d) any fire accident caused by a gas accident in an urban or township region shall be transferred to the competent agency of housing and urban-rural development;

(e) any case of combustion of power equipment and facilities due to their own fault or defect but causing no damage to other materials shall be transferred to the competent agency of electric power; or

(f) any fire accident in ports, ships, fishing ports, fishing boats, and water facilities, shall be transferred to the competent agency of agriculture, rural affairs, and maritime affairs.

第七章 监督检查

第六十条 各级人民政府应当确定消防工作责任目标，督促本级人民政府有关部门和下级人民政府履行消防工作职责。

各级人民政府应当把消防工作作为政府目标责任考核和领导干部政绩考评的重要内容，纳入社会治安综合治理等考评范围。

市、县、自治县人民政府应当每年向省人民政府专题报告消防工作。

县级以上人民政府有关部门以及行业协会应当根据本系统、本行业的特点，推进消防安全标准化建设，有针对性地开展消防安全检查，及时督促整改火灾隐患。

第六十一条 依法履行消防监督检查工作职责的有关部门和机构应当加强消防安全事中事后监管，制定年度检查计划，明确抽查范围、抽查事项和抽查细则，合理确定抽查比例和频次，将检查计划和检查结果告知被检查单位，并向社会公开。

依法履行消防监督检查工作职责的有关部门和机构发现火灾隐患，应当及时通知有关单位和个人采取措施消除隐患。有关单位和个人应当按照整改意见，在规定期限内整改。依法履行消防监督检查工作职责的有关部门和机构应当对整改情况进行检查。

市、县、自治县人民政府可以将消防执法纳入综合行政执法。

第六十二条 消防救援机构应当推动建立消防诚信体系，及时将消防违法行为纳入信用记录，督促单位和个人遵守消防法律法规。

鼓励金融系统、各类行业组织将单位消防安全相关信息纳入社会信用体系，推动建立行业消防安全自律机制。

Chapter VII Oversight and Inspection

Article 60 The people's governments at all levels shall determine the objectives of fire protection, and urge the appropriate agencies of the people's government at the corresponding level and the people's governments at a lower level to perform their fire protection duties.

The people's governments at all levels shall take fire protection as an important part of their assessment system for evaluating completion of government duties and enforcement of principal cadres, and also for evaluating comprehensive management of public safety.

The city, county, and autonomous county people's governments shall report the fire protection to the provincial people's government annually.

The departments of the people's governments at or above the county level and trade associations concerned shall, in light of the characteristics of the system and the industry, promote the development of fire safety standardization, enforce fire safety inspections in a targeted manner, and promptly urge the rectification of fire hazards.

Article 61 The appropriate agencies and institutions that perform the duties of fire oversight and inspection pursuant to law shall improve the during- and post-event oversight of fire safety, draft annual inspection plans, clarify the scope, inspection items and rules, reasonably determine the proportion and frequency of inspections, and inform the inspected organizations of the inspection plans and results and publish them.

The appropriate agencies and institutions that perform the duties of fire oversight and inspection pursuant to law shall promptly notify Organizations and individuals concerned to take measures to remove hidden dangers. The Organizations and individuals concerned shall, as suggested in rectification, adjust and improve themselves within the prescribed time limit. The appropriate agencies and organizations that perform the duties of fire oversight and inspection shall inspect the corrections pursuant to law.

The city, county, autonomous county people's governments may incorporate fire law enforcement into comprehensive administrative law enforcement.

Article 62 Fire departments shall promote the establishment of a fire integrity system, promptly add fire violations to credit records, and require the Organizations and individuals to comply with fire laws and regulations.

It is recommended that organizations in the financial system and all kinds of industry put fire safety-related information into the social credit system and promoting the establishment of an industry fire safety self-regulatory system.

第六十三条 消防救援机构应当提供火灾风险提示、消防安全咨询、隐患整改指导等便民服务。

聘用的消防文员受消防救援机构委托，协助消防救援机构工作人员开展消防宣传、消防监督等工作。

第六十四条 举办每场预计参加人数在1000人以上大型群众性活动的，承办人应当按照国家有关规定向公安机关申请安全许可。消防救援机构根据公安机关的通知进行消防安全检查，发现火灾隐患的，应当及时指导承办人整改。

大型群众性活动的承办人对其举办活动的消防安全负责，应当制定消防安全工作方案，落实消防安全措施，确保参加活动的人数在消防安全条件允许的范围内。需要临时搭建舞台、看台等建筑物、设施的，应当符合国家和本省的有关消防安全标准。

为大型群众性活动提供场所的单位，应当在活动举办前对其消防设施、设备进行检查，确保正常使用。

第六十五条 消防救援机构发现存在下列重大消防安全隐患的，应当由应急管理部门书面报告本级人民政府：

（一）不符合城乡消防安全布局的重大火灾危险源；

（二）耐火等级低的建筑密集区；

（三）公共消防设施不符合消防安全要求的；

（四）影响公共安全的重大火灾隐患。

接到报告的人民政府应当及时核实情况，组织或者责成有关部门、单位采取措施整改。

对重大火灾隐患单位，人民政府应当列入挂牌督办事项，督促整改。必要时，可以采取责令暂时停产、停业等紧急措施。

Article 63 Fire departments shall provide convenience services such as fire risk warnings, fire safety consultation, and hidden danger rectification guidance.

A fire clerk employed by a fire department shall assist the employees of the fire department to conduct fire protection awareness and oversight.

Article 64 If a large-scale public event is held with more than 1,000 participants, the organizer shall apply to the public security agency for a safety license pursuant to national law. A fire department shall inspect fire safety as notified by the public security agency, and shall promptly guide the contractor to eliminate the fire hazards.

An organizer of a large-scale public event shall take responsibility for the fire safety of their activities, and shall draft fire safety work plans, enforce fire safety measures, and ensure that the number of people participating in activities falls within the quotas permitted by fire safety conditions. The construction of a temporary stage, a stand, or any other building and facilities (if in need) shall comply with applicable national and provincial fire safety standards.

An Organization providing places for a large-scale public event shall inspect their firefighting facilities and equipment to ensure their effective use before the event.

Article 65 Where a fire department finds any of the following major hidden hazards to fire safety, the emergency administration agency shall report to the people's government at the same level in writing:

(a) major fire hazards not in line with the layout of urban and rural fire safety;

(b) densely built areas with low fire-resistance rating;

(c) the public fire control facilities not in conformity with the fire safety requirements; or

(d) major fire hazards to public safety.

The people's government receiving the report shall promptly verify and organize or instruct the appropriate agencies and Organizations to correct.

The people's government shall list an Organization with major fire hazards into the oversight matters and require correction. Emergency measures, if necessary, such as suspension of production or business, may be adopted.

建筑物耐火等级低且公共消防设施不适应防火和灭火需要的建筑密集区，当地人民政府应当有计划地组织实施改造，或者采取防火分隔、提高耐火等级、增设消防车通道和消防供水设施等措施，改善消防安全条件，提高防火、灭火能力。

第六十六条　依法履行消防监督检查工作职责的有关部门和机构及其工作人员在消防监督管理工作中，不得有下列行为：

（一）利用消防设计审查、消防验收和消防安全检查收取费用或者谋取单位、个人利益；

（二）利用职务便利为用户、建设单位指定或者变相指定消防产品、装修装饰材料的品牌、销售单位，或者消防技术服务机构、消防设施施工单位；

（三）组织消防安全教育培训时，向单位和个人收取费用。

任何单位和个人有权对依法履行消防监督检查工作职责的有关部门和机构及其工作人员违反前款规定的行为和其他违法行为进行检举、控告。受理检举、控告的机关和部门应当按照职责及时查处，并应当为举报人保密。

第八章　法律责任

第六十七条　单位有下列行为之一的，责令限期改正；逾期不改正的，对单位处一千元以上五千元以下罚款，并对其直接负责的主管人员和其他直接责任人员依法给予警告：

（一）未制定本单位的消防安全制度、消防安全操作规程、灭火和应急疏散预案的；

The local people's governments shall organize and conduct the transformation in a planned way in the densely built areas where the fire-resistance rating of buildings is low and the public fire control facilities are not suitable for the fire prevention and extinguishing needs, or take measures such as fire separation, fire-resistance rating improvement, the addition of fire engine passages and fire water supply facilities, to improve fire safety conditions and fire prevention and extinguishing capabilities.

Article 66 No agency, office, or their employees who perform their duties of fire oversight and inspection pursuant to law shall have any of the following circumstances in fire regulatory oversight:

(a) taking advantage of fire design review, fire acceptance, and fire safety inspection to solicit fees or dishonestly seek gains of Organizations and individuals;

(b) taking advantage of the position to designate, directly or in any disguised form, brands and vendors of fire protection products and decoration materials for users and developers, or fire protection technical service institutions and fire protection facilities developers; or

(c) collecting fees from Organizations and individuals when organizing fire safety education and training.

Any Organization or individual is entitled to report and accuse the appropriate agencies and institutions and their employees who perform their duties of fire oversight and inspection in violation of the above provisions and other laws pursuant to law. The appropriate agencies accepting reports and accusations shall promptly investigate and resolve them pursuant to their duties, and shall keep all informants confidential.

Chapter VIII Legal Liability

Article 67 Any Organization, under one of the following circumstances, shall be required to correct within the time limit; if overdue, the Organization shall be fined not less than 1,000 Yuan and not more than 5,000 Yuan, and the person directly in charge and other personnel subject to direct liabilities shall be given a warning:

(a) a fire safety system, fire safety operation procedures, firefighting and emergency evacuation plans of the Organization have not been created;

（二）未按照规定组织防火检查的；

（三）未按照规定对建筑消防设施每年至少进行一次全面检测的；

（四）未按照规定组织消防演练的。

设有消防控制室的场所未保证 24 小时值班的，责令改正，对单位处一千元以上五千元以下罚款。

第六十八条 消防安全重点单位有下列行为之一的，责令限期改正；逾期不改正的，处一千元以上五千元以下罚款，并对其直接负责的主管人员和其他直接责任人员依法给予警告：

（一）未确定消防安全管理人的；

（二）未建立消防档案的；

（三）未确定消防安全重点部位，设置防火标志的；

（四）未按照规定开展防火巡查，并建立巡查记录的；

（五）未按照规定开展消防安全培训的；

（六）未按照规定将消防安全管理人员的基本情况、本单位消防设施配备、维护情况报消防救援机构备案的；

（七）未按照规定开展消防安全评估的。

第六十九条 单位有下列行为之一的，责令改正，处五千元以上五万元以下罚款：

（一）消防设施、器材或者消防安全标志的配置、设置不符合国家标准、行业标准，或者未保持完好有效的；

（二）损坏、挪用或者擅自拆除、停用消防设施、器材的；

（三）占用、堵塞、封闭疏散通道、安全出口或者有其他妨碍安全疏散行为的；

（四）埋压、圈占、遮挡消火栓或者占用防火间距的；

(b) any Organization fails to organize fire inspection pursuant to law;

(c) any Organization fails to conduct the comprehensive inspection of fire protection facilities of the building at least once a year pursuant to law; or

(d) any Organization fails to organize fire drills pursuant to law.

Any place with a fire protection room, which is not put on duty around the clock as guaranteed shall be required to correct, and the Organization concerned shall be fined not less than 1,000 Yuan and not more than 5,000 Yuan.

Article 68 Any key fire safety organization, under one of the following circumstances, shall be ordered to remediate within the time limit; if overdue, the Organization shall be fined not less than 1,000 Yuan and not more than 5,000 Yuan and the person directly in charge and other personnel directly liable shall be given a warning:

(a) a fire safety administrator is not appointed;

(b) fire archives are not established;

(c) the key parts of fire safety are not determined, and fire signs are not set;

(d) fire inspections have not been conducted pursuant to law and inspection records are not created;

(e) fire safety training has not been conducted pursuant to law;

(f) the basic information of fire safety management personnel and the equipment and maintenance of fire protection facilities of the Organization are not reported to the fire departments for the record; or

(g) fire safety assessment has not been conducted pursuant to law.

Article 69 Any Organization, under one of the following circumstances, shall be required to correct and fined not less than 5,000 Yuan and not more than 50,000 Yuan:

(a) the configuration and setting of fire protection facilities, equipment, or fire safety signs do not comply with the national standards and industry standards, or are not in good condition and effective;

(b) fire protection facilities and equipment are damaged and misappropriated or are removed and disabled without authorization;

(c) evacuation passages and safety exits are occupied, blocked and sealed, or any other act that obstructs safe evacuation;

(d) fire hydrants are buried, occupied, and blocked, or fire prevention intervals are occupied;

（五）占用、堵塞、封闭消防车通道，妨碍消防车通行的；

（六）人员密集场所在门窗上设置影响逃生和灭火救援的障碍物的；

（七）对火灾隐患经消防救援机构通知后不及时采取措施消除的。

个人有前款第二项、第三项、第四项、第五项行为之一的，处警告或者五百元以下罚款。

有本条第一款第三项、第四项、第五项、第六项行为，经责令改正拒不改正的，强制执行，所需费用由违法行为人承担。

第七十条 违反本条例第二十条第二款规定，未取得职业资格证书人员上岗作业的，责令改正，对单位处一千元以上一万元以下罚款。

第七十一条 违反本条例第二十二条规定，物业服务企业未落实消防安全责任的，责令限期改正；逾期不改正的，处三千元以上三万元以下罚款。

第七十二条 违反本条例第二十七条规定，建设工程施工现场不符合消防安全规定的，责令限期改正；逾期不改正的，责令停止施工，处三千元以上三万元以下罚款，并对其直接负责的主管人员和其他直接责任人员处一千元以上三千元以下罚款。

第七十三条 违反本条例第二十八条第一款规定，未向消防救援机构作出承诺或承诺失实的，责令限期改正；逾期不改正的，责令停止使用或者停产停业，并处三万元以上三十万元以下罚款。

第七十四条 生产、销售不合格的消防产品或者国家明令淘汰的消防产品的，由市场监督管理部门依照《中华人民共和国产品质量法》的规定从重处罚。

(e) passages of fire engines are occupied, blocked or closed, or fire engines are obstructed;

(f) obstacles are put at doors and windows in crowded places and escape from and rescue through these doors windows are affected in case of fire; or

(g) measures are not taken in a timely manner to remove fire hazards after being notified by a fire department.

An individual, under one of the circumstances mentioned in Subparagraph (b), (c), (d), or (e) of the preceding paragraph, shall be given a warning or fined not more than 500 Yuan.

Anyone, in violation of Subparagraph (c), (d), (e), or (f) of Paragraph 1 of this Article, who refuses to rectify after being required to correct, shall be ordered to remediate and assume related expenses.

Article 70 Any organization, in violation of Paragraph 2 of Article 20, whose employees are not certified for special occupations but engage in them, shall be ordered to remediate and fined not less than 1,000 Yuan and not more than 10,000 Yuan.

Article 71 Any property management entities, in violation of Article 22, that fail to perform fire safety duties, shall be ordered to remediate within the time limit, and shall be fined, if overdue, not less than 3,000 Yuan and not more than 30,000 Yuan.

Article 72 The construction site in violation of Article 27 or that does not meet the requirements of fire safety shall be ordered to remediate within the time limit. If overdue, shall be ordered to stop construction, fined not less than 3,000 Yuan and not more than 30,000 Yuan, and the person directly in charge and other personnel directly liable shall be fined not less than 1,000 Yuan and not more than 3,000 Yuan.

Article 73 Whoever, in violation of Paragraph 1 of Article 28 hereof, fails to promise to the fire department or makes an inaccurate promise, shall be ordered to remediate within the time limit. If overdue, shall be ordered to stop using or suspend production or business, and shall be subject to a fine of not less than 30,000 Yuan and not more than 300,000 Yuan.

Article 74 Whoever produces or sells noncompliant firefighting products or firefighting products explicitly ousted by the state shall be penalized more severely by the market regulation agency pursuant to the Product Quality Law of the People's Republic of China.

违反本条例第三十二条规定，安装、使用不合格的消防产品、国家明令淘汰的消防产品，或者安装、使用不符合消防技术标准的室内装修、装饰材料的，责令限期改正，逾期不改正的，处五千元以上五万元以下罚款；情节严重的，责令停止施工、停止使用或者停产停业。

第七十五条 违反本条例第三十三条、第三十四条和第三十六条第四款、第五款规定的，责令停止违法行为，处五百元以下罚款。应当给予治安管理处罚的，依照《中华人民共和国治安管理处罚法》处罚。

第七十六条 本条例规定的行政处罚，由公安机关、住房和城乡建设主管部门、市场监督管理部门和消防救援机构按照各自职权决定，但已经实施相对集中行政处罚权，由综合行政执法部门实施的，从其规定。

第七十七条 依法履行消防监督检查工作职责的有关部门和机构及其工作人员有下列行为之一的，由其所在单位或者上级主管部门对直接负责的主管人员和其他直接责任人员依法给予处分；构成犯罪的，依法追究刑事责任：

（一）对不符合消防安全要求的消防设计文件、建设工程、场所准予审查合格、消防验收合格、消防监督检查合格的；

（二）无故拖延消防设计审查、消防验收、消防监督检查，不在法定期限内履行职责的；

（三）在消防设计审查、消防验收、消防监督检查，以及消防安全教育培训等工作中收取费用的；

（四）利用消防设计审查、消防验收和消防监督检查职务便利谋取单位和个人利益的；

Whoever, in violation of Article 32 hereof, installs or uses noncompliant firefighting products or firefighting products explicitly ousted by the state, or installs or uses interior decoration and decorative materials not in line with the technical standards for fire protection, shall be required to remediate within the time limit. If no remediation is made within the time limit, a fine of not less than 5,000 Yuan and not more than 50,000 Yuan shall be imposed. If the circumstances are serious, they shall be required to stop construction, use, or suspend production or business.

Article 75 Anyone in violation of Article 33, 34, or Paragraph 4, 5 of Article 36 shall be ordered to stop illegal acts, and fined not more than 500 Yuan. If they are subject to public safety administrative penalties, they shall be penalized pursuant to the Law of the People's Republic of China on Public Safety Administration Punishment.

Article 76 The administrative penalties provided in these Regulations shall be decided by public security agencies, the competent agencies of housing and urban-rural development, the market regulation agencies, and the fire departments pursuant to their respective functions and duties. Any administrative penalty imposed by a single administrative law enforcement agency for comprehensive matters shall control in any matter concerning multiple agencies.

Article 77 If the appropriate agencies, institutions, and their employees who perform their duties of fire protection oversight and inspection pursuant to law are under one of the following circumstances, the person directly in charge and other personnel directly liable shall be penalized by their Organization or higher competent agency. If the act constitutes a crime, criminal liability shall be assumed pursuant to law:

(a) the fire design documents, development projects, and places, not in line with the fire safety requirements, are approved to pass the examination, fire acceptance, and fire oversight and inspection;

(b) unjustified delay in fire design review, fire acceptance, fire oversight and inspection, and failure to perform their duties within the statutory time limit;

(c) charged fees for the fire design review, fire acceptance, fire oversight and inspection, and fire safety education and training;

(d) gains of the Organizations and individuals have been made dishonestly via the fire design review, fire acceptance, and fire oversight and inspection duties;

（五）发现火灾隐患不及时通知有关单位或者个人整改的；

（六）利用职务为用户、建设单位指定或者变相指定消防产品、装修装饰材料的品牌、销售单位，或者消防技术服务机构、消防设施施工单位的；

（七）将消防车、消防艇以及消防器材、装备和设施用于与消防和应急救援无关的事项的；

（八）其他滥用职权、玩忽职守、徇私舞弊的行为。

第七十八条 各级人民政府及其有关部门和工作人员有下列情形之一的，由其上级人民政府、上级行政机关责令改正，并根据情节轻重对主要负责人、直接负责的主管人员和其他直接责任人员给予处分；构成犯罪的，依法追究刑事责任：

（一）未落实消防安全责任制的；

（二）未向上一级人民政府专题报告消防工作的；

（三）未组织编制消防专项规划，并组织实施的；

（四）未及时协调解决本行政区域内重大消防安全问题的；

（五）发现本行业、本系统单位存在火灾隐患不采取措施整改的；

（六）其他滥用职权、玩忽职守、徇私舞弊的行为。

未依法履行消防工作职责，致使本地发生重、特大火灾的，对县级以上人民政府主要负责人、分管负责人和其他负责人依照国家和本省有关规定进行问责。

(e) Where a fire hazard is found, but it is not promptly notified to the Organizations or individuals concerned for correction;

(f) anyone taking advantage of the position designates, directly or indirectly, brands and vendors of fire protection products and decoration materials, fire protection technical service agencies, or fire protection facilities developers for users and developers;

(g) anyone uses fire engines, fireboats and firefighting equipment, equipment and facilities for matters unrelated to fire fighting and emergency rescue; or

(h) other acts are found involving abuse of position, dereliction of duty, or playing favoritism and committing irregularities.

Article 78 Where the people's governments at all levels and their agencies and staff concerned are under any of the following circumstances, the people's government at a higher level and the administrative agency at a higher level shall require them to correct, and the principal responsible person, the person directly in charge, and other personnel directly liable shall be punished in accordance with the severity of the circumstances. Where the act constitutes a crime, criminal liability shall be assumed pursuant to law if any of them:

(a) does not enforce the accountability system for fire safety;

(b) does not report fire services to the people's government at a higher level;

(c) does not organize the preparation and implementation of special planning on fire protection;

(d) does not coordinate and solve major fire safety problems within their respective administrative areas in a timely manner;

(e) fails to take measures to correct such hidden fire hazards as found within their respective industry or sector; or

(f) has done any other acts which involves abuse of position, dereliction of duty, or playing favoritism and committing irregularities.

Where any of them who fails to perform duties on fire protection pursuant to law, causes heavy and serious fires in a local area, the principal responsible person, responsible person in charge, and other responsible persons of the people's governments at or above the county level shall be held accountable pursuant to relevant provisions of the nation and the Province.

第九章　附　则

第七十九条　在本省内自由贸易港以外区域的消防工作，参照本条例执行。

第八十条　本条例自2020年11月1日起施行。1998年11月20日海南省第二届人民代表大会常务委员会第四次会议通过的《海南省消防条例》同时废止。

Chapter IX Supplementary Provisions

Article 79 If fire services out of the HFTP but in the Province, these Regulations shall apply *mutatis mutandis*.

Article 80 These Regulations shall come into force as of November 1, 2020. The Regulations on Fire Protection in Hainan Province, adopted at the 4th Session of the Standing Committee of the 2nd Hainan Provincial People's Congress on November 20, 1998, shall be repealed at the same time.

Chapter IX Supplementary Provisions

海南自由贸易港优化营商环境条例

Regulations of Hainan Free Trade Port on Optimizing the Business Environment

海南自由贸易港优化营商环境条例

（2021 年 9 月 29 日海南省第六届人民代表大会常务委员会第三十次会议通过）

第一条　为营造法治化、国际化、便利化的营商环境，激发市场主体活力，建设高水平的中国特色自由贸易港，根据《中华人民共和国海南自由贸易港法》《优化营商环境条例》等有关法律、法规，结合海南自由贸易港实际，制定本条例。

第二条　省和市、县、自治县人民政府应当加强对优化营商环境工作的组织领导，明确营商环境改革引领性目标和营商环境建设年度目标，建立健全优化营商环境统筹推进工作机制，统筹协调深化营商环境改革工作。政府主要负责人是优化营商环境的第一责任人。

省和市、县、自治县人民政府优化营商环境工作主管部门负责组织、指导、督促、协调和推进优化营商环境日常工作，组织开展营商环境考核和监督管理工作。

省和市、县、自治县人民政府工业和信息化、自然资源和规划、商务、市场监督管理、金融监督管理等有关部门依据职责负责优化营商环境相关工作。

第三条　省人民政府参照国际国内营商环境评价指标体系，以市场主体满意度为导向，按照横向可对比、纵向可考核的要求，编制海南自由贸易港营商环境评价指标体系并组织实施。

Regulations of Hainan Free Trade Port on Optimizing the Business Environment

(Adopted at the 30th Session of the Standing Committee of the 6th Hainan Provincial People's Congress on September 29, 2021)

Article 1 These Regulations are enacted pursuant to the Hainan Free Trade Port Law of the People's Republic of China, Regulations on Optimizing the Business Environment and other applicable laws and regulations, and based on actual circumstances in the Hainan Free Trade Port to create a law-based, international and convenient business environment, stimulate the vitality of market entities, and establish a high-end free trade port with Chinese characteristics.

Article 2 The provincial, city, county, and autonomous county people's governments shall improve organization and leadership in optimizing the business environment, specify the leading business environment reform objectives and the annual business environment development objectives, implement and optimize a working system for streamlining the optimization of the overall business environment, and coordinate and improve the business environment reform. The government program director shall be the primary person directly responsible for the optimization of the business environment.

Provincial, city, county, and autonomous county people's government agencies tasked with optimizing the business environment shall be responsible for organizing, guiding, overseeing, coordinating, and implementing daily business environment optimization work, and organizing the assessment, oversight, and administration of the business environment.

The provincial, city, county, and autonomous county's people's government agencies, such as those responsible for industry and information technology, natural resources and planning, commerce, market regulation, financial oversight, and administration, shall be responsible for optimizing the business environment based on their individual authorities and duties.

Article 3 The provincial people's government shall prepare and implement the Free Trade Port evaluation metrics system based on international and domestic business environment evaluation metrics systems, horizontally comparable and vertically assessable requirements, and market entity satisfaction.

政府及有关部门应当根据营商环境评价结果，及时制定或者调整优化营商环境政策措施。省人民政府对未达到国家和本省要求的优化营商环境目标或者在全省营商环境评价中排名靠后的市、县、自治县人民政府及有关部门主要负责人实行约谈，督促其优化营商环境。

第四条 政府及有关部门应当适应国际经济贸易规则发展和全球经济治理体系改革新趋势，以贸易投资自由化便利化为重点，在标准对接、信息共享、人员交流和执法协同等方面加强营商环境国际交流。

制定有关贸易、投资等相关管理活动的法规、规章、行政规范性文件，应当评估是否符合我国参加的国际协议，加强与国际通行规则对接融合。

第五条 单位和个人应当树立人人都是营商环境的理念，积极参与营商环境建设，共同营造开放包容、互利合作、诚实守信、文明和谐、重商护商的社会氛围。

政府及有关部门应当按照构建亲清新型政商关系的要求，增强主动服务市场主体意识，建立有事必应、无事不扰的经营便利政策制度，健全畅通有效的政企沟通机制，依法为市场主体解决生产经营中遇到的困难和问题，保障市场主体正常开展生产经营活动。

政府部门工作人员应当规范政商交往行为，勤勉尽责，依法履职，严格遵守纪律，清正廉洁，不得利用职务之便为本人或者他人谋取私利，不得干扰市场主体正常生产经营活动，不得增加市场主体负担。

省和市、县、自治县人民政府应当建立营商环境考核督察制度和营商环境政务切身体验、专业观察监督制度，通过专项督察、日常督导等方式加强对优化营商环境工作的监督检查，公开曝光营商环境反面典型案例。

The government and its agencies shall promptly issue or amend policies and guidelines to optimize the business environment based on the evaluation results. The provincial people's government may discuss regulation with those directly in charge of city, county, or autonomous county people's governments or their agencies that fail to meet the national or provincial business environment optimization requirements or rank low in the provincial business environment assessment, and encourage them to optimize the business environment.

Article 4 The government and its agencies shall adapt to emerging international economic and trade rules and global economic governance system reform trends, focus on the liberalization and facilitation of trade and investment, and improve international business environment communication in standards sharing, information sharing, employee exchange, and law enforcement coordination.

The issuance of any trade, investment, or related administrative activity regulations, rules, or administrative normative documents shall be assessed to ensure they conform to the international agreements to which China is a party and improve awareness and integration with internationally accepted rules.

Article 5 Entities and individuals shall raise awareness that everyone is a part of the business environment, actively participate in the development of the business environment, and jointly create a social atmosphere of openness, inclusiveness, mutual collaboration, honesty and trustworthiness, civilization and harmony, and valuing and protecting business.

The government and its agencies shall improve market entity service awareness, implement a policy system for business facilitation responsive to market entity needs, improve the free and effective communication between government and business, solve difficulties in production and operation for market entities pursuant to law, and ensure market entities' regular production and operation based on the requirements of developing a cordial and transparent relationship between government and market entities.

Government staffs shall follow best practices to build relationships with business operators, instill a strong work ethic and sense of responsibility, perform their authorities and duties as required by law, strictly abide by disciplinary rules, develop personal integrity, avoid abusing their positions to seek personal gains for themselves or others, not interfere with market entity regular production and operations, and not increase the burden on market entities.

The provincial, city, county, and autonomous county people's governments shall implement a business environment assessment and oversight system, a business environment practical experience system, and a professional observation and oversight system, improve business environment optimization oversight and review through specific oversight and daily inspections, and publish examples of bad business environment optimization.

第六条 县级以上人民政府应当通过设立投诉平台等方式受理市场主体对营商环境问题的投诉、举报，按照统一受理、按责转办、限时办结、跟踪督办的原则，依法依规对投诉、举报事项进行处理，能够解决的应当即时处理，暂时不能解决的，应当提出具体解决方案。处理结果应当及时向投诉、举报人反馈，并依法为投诉、举报人保密。

优化营商环境工作主管部门应当对投诉、举报的重点问题组织专项核查。

对市场主体投诉反映的共性、普遍性问题，政府及有关部门应当建立解决问题的长效机制。

第七条 政府及有关部门应当推进和落实贸易自由化便利化措施，逐步减少企业资质、配额、数量、许可等管理措施。

政府及有关部门应当落实海南自由贸易港跨境服务贸易负面清单管理制度，对清单外事项按照境内外一致原则实施管理，并推进扩大跨境服务贸易对外开放领域。

政府及有关部门应当推进服务贸易创新发展，在服务贸易管理体制、促进机制、发展模式、监管制度等方面先行先试。对在海南自由贸易港注册登记且仅在海南自由贸易港从事商业特许经营活动的特许人不进行商业特许经营备案。

第八条 政府及有关部门应当高标准建设国际贸易“单一窗口”和口岸基础设施，不断丰富和拓展国际贸易“单一窗口”地方特色功能应用，实行口岸收费项目目录清单公示制度，规范口岸合规收费，并逐步推进简并港口收费项目，降低港口收费标准，减少贸易合规成本。

Article 6 The people's governments at or above the county level shall accept complaints and reports on business environment issues filed by market entities by creating complaint platforms and resolving such complaints and reports in a standardized manner, escalating them to the competent agency based on the division of responsibility, resolve them within the specified time limit, and follow up on the results as required by law. Those complaints and reports that can be resolved shall be resolved immediately, and specific solutions shall be brought up for those that cannot be resolved temporarily. The results shall be kept confidential pursuant to law and promptly announced to the complaints and informants.

The competent agency in charge of optimizing the business environment shall organize specific inspections of the main complaint and report issues.

The government and its agencies shall set up a long-term effective system to resolve common issues reported by market entities.

Article 7 The government and its agencies shall improve and implement trade liberalization and facilitation measures, and reduce administrative measures on enterprise qualification, quota, quantity, and license step by step.

The government and its agencies shall create a negative list for cross-border trade in services in the Free Trade Port, treat the items not on the list equally for domestic and foreign entities, and improve the opening up of cross-border trade in services.

The government and its agencies shall improve trade in services innovation and development and conduct trial reforms in government administration, optimization, development methods, and trade in services oversight systems. Concession operators registered in the Free Trade Port and only involved in commercial concessions within the Free Trade Port may be exempted from commercial concessions filing.

Article 8 The government and its agencies shall set up a Single Portal system for international trade and port infrastructure construction following high standards, continue to boost and expand local innovation for the Single Portal, and implement a system to publish the list of port charges, standardize port charges, simplify and consolidate port charges step by step, and lower port charge standards and compliance costs.

海关应当落实通关便利化政策，精简监管证件和随附单证，简化货物流转流程和手续，提升通关效率。除依法需要检验检疫或者实行许可证件管理的货物外，货物进入海南自由贸易港，海关按照有关规定径予放行。

政府及有关部门加强推进海南自由贸易港与其他国家和地区的动植物疫情信息共享，探索认可海南自由贸易港与其他国家和地区间动植物检疫措施的等效性。

第九条　政府及有关部门应当推进和落实海南自由贸易港外商投资准入负面清单、海南自由贸易港放宽市场准入特别清单管理制度，全面推行极简审批投资制度，推行市场准入承诺即入制，提升市场主体准入准营便利度。

第十条　政府及有关部门应当高标准建设国际投资“单一窗口”，对投资咨询、代办服务、设立公司、外汇登记、银行开户、项目建设及其他事项办理等投资全链条，提供全流程服务。

第十一条　政府采购和政府投资工程招标投标等公共资源交易活动，应当公开透明、公平公正，保障各类市场主体依法平等参与，不得违规设置不合理条件，或者以其他任何形式排斥、限制潜在投标人或者供应商。

政府及有关部门应当优化招标投标流程，逐步推行招标投标全流程电子化。招标人、招标代理机构不得因使用电子招标投标方式，额外向投标人收取费用或者不合理地增加潜在投标人参与投标的难度。

投标人应当保证投标的工程项目、商品和服务质量符合规定，不得以相互串标、低于成本报价等违法违规方式参与竞标，扰乱招标投标市场秩序。

Customs authorities shall implement the policies to facilitate customs clearance, simplify or remove certificates and documents required for customs administration, simplify goods transfer procedures and improve customs clearance efficiency. Customs shall release goods into the Free Trade Port as required except for goods requiring inspection and quarantine or those subject to license administration pursuant to law.

The government and its agencies shall improve animal and plant epidemic information sharing between the Free Trade Port and other countries and areas, and explore mutual animal and plant quarantine recognition measures between the Free Trade Port and other countries and areas.

Article 9 The government and its agencies shall improve and implement the Free Trade Port foreign investment access negative list, relax Free Trade Port market access list system, fully implement a simplified investment approval system, implement a market access permission system through commitment, and improve ease of access for market entities entering the market.

Article 10 The government and its agencies shall set up a high standard international investment Single Portal system and provide services for all investment procedures, including investment consultation, agency services, incorporation, foreign exchange registration, bank account opening, project construction, and other matters.

Article 11 Public resource transactions, such as those for government procurement, bidding, and tendering for government-invested projects, shall be open, transparent, fair, and just, and all kinds of market entities shall be guaranteed equal participation pursuant to law. Unreasonable conditions in violation of regulations shall not be set and potential bidders or suppliers shall not be excluded or restricted in any way.

The government and its agencies shall optimize the bidding process and gradually implement electronic bidding. The bid solicitor and bid agency shall not charge extra fees to bidders or unreasonably increase the difficulty for potential bidders to participate in bidding due to the use of electronic bid solicitation and bidding.

Bidders shall warrant that the quality of the projects, goods, and services they bid for meet the requirements and shall not submit bids in violation of the law or commit acts that disturb the bid solicitation and bidding market order, such as bid-rigging or quoting prices below cost prices.

政府及有关部门应当推进公共资源交易全过程在线实时监管，推进市场主体履约行为信用评价和行政处罚结果在公共资源交易过程中的运用，加大打击串通投标、骗取中标、以行贿谋取中标等违法行为。

第十二条 对政府性基金、涉企行政事业性收费、涉企保证金以及实行政府定价的经营服务性收费实行目录清单管理，并向社会公开。禁止擅自收费、越权收费、超标准收费和重复收费。

省人民政府根据发展需要，依照有关规定减少收费项目，降低收费标准，减轻市场主体负担。

第十三条 政府及有关部门应当制定和完善促进引导金融服务实体经济的政策措施，建立健全地方财政扶持中小微企业发展机制和对各类金融机构的激励机制。完善财政扶持产业发展方式，通过政府投资基金、贷款风险补偿、融资担保等方式为中小微企业融资提供支持。推广“评价增信＋金融服务”等有利于中小微企业融资的服务管理模式。

省和市、县、自治县人民政府应当推进企业信用信息服务平台、金融综合服务平台等公共信息平台互联互通，为市场主体提供涉企信用信息服务、融资对接服务等综合金融服务。

第十四条 政府及有关部门应当建立科学合理的人才引进、认定、使用和待遇保障机制，实行以薪酬水平为主要指标的人才评价标准，依托海南自由贸易港人才服务“单一窗口”，实行更加开放便利的人才、停居留、出境入境和工作签证政策。

第十五条 人力资源社会保障部门应当为市场主体提供用工指导、政策咨询、劳动关系协调等服务和指导。鼓励和支持企业组织职工开展各种形式的职业技能培训。

The government and its agencies shall improve online real-time supervision of public resource transactions process, improve the implementation of credit evaluation and administrative penalty results for market entity performance, and step up efforts to crack down on legal violations such as bid-rigging, false bidding, and bribery.

Article 12 Government funding, administrative charges for non-profits over market entities, commercial deposits, and operating service fees subject to government pricing shall also be administered as a list and publicly announced. Any unauthorized charges, *ultra vires* charges, charges over-standard, or duplicate charges are prohibited.

Based on development needs, the provincial people's government may reduce the fees and charges, lower fees and standards, and reduce the burden on market entities pursuant to applicable regulations.

Article 13 The government and its agencies shall implement and optimize policies and measures to lead financial services into the real economy, and set up and optimize local financial support systems for the development of medium, small, and micro businesses and incentive systems for different types of financial institutions. Financial support for industrial development shall be improved to provide support for micro, small and medium businesses through government investment funds, loan loss compensation, and financial guarantees. Credit support financial services and other financing services that benefit micro, small and medium businesses shall be encouraged.

The provincial, city, county, and autonomous county people's governments shall encourage the integration of public information platforms such as business credit report service platform and comprehensive financial service platform, and provide comprehensive financial services such as business credit report, and financial institution connections for market entities.

Article 14 The government and its agencies shall create a scientific and reasonable system to ensure the introduction, identification, employment, and treatment of skilled employees, implement skilled employee evaluation standards using salary levels as the main metrics, and create a "Single Portal" for skilled employee services in the Free Trade Port, implement more open and facilitation policies for skilled employees and their permission of stay, residence, exit and entry, and work visas.

Article 15 Human resources and social security agencies shall provide employment guidelines, policy advice, employment relations coordination, and other services for market entities. Businesses shall be encouraged and receive support to conduct different forms of vocational training.

支持劳动者通过临时性、非全日制、季节性、弹性工作等灵活多样形式实现就业，为劳动者提供社会保障卡一卡通服务。

用人单位因生产经营特点不能实行国家规定的标准工时制度且符合特殊工时制度实行范围，经集体协商实行不定时或者综合计算工时工作制度的，可以实行告知承诺制。

第十六条 政府及有关部门与市场主体签订招商引资、战略合作等合同协议，应当坚持平等协商、依法依规、互利共赢、务实审慎原则并考虑财政支付能力，不得违反国家、海南自由贸易港有关规定承诺优惠条件。

对招商引资过程中以合同协议以外的方式承诺的投资政策和优惠条件，应当依照法定权限和规定程序以书面的形式作出。

第十七条 政府及有关部门应当履行向市场主体依法作出的政策承诺、依法签订的合同以及司法机关作出的生效裁决，不得擅自变更政策承诺或者合同；不得以政府换届、相关责任人调整等为由不履行；行政区划调整、机构或者职能调整的，由承接相应职责的政府及有关部门负责履行；对未依照规定履行承诺、合同或者不履行生效裁决的，应当限期解决。

因国家利益、社会公共利益需要改变政策承诺、合同约定的，应当依照法定权限和程序进行，并依法对市场主体因此受到的损失予以补偿。因政府及有关部门违法违规失信行为给市场主体合法权益造成损失的，应当予以赔偿。

县级以上人民政府应当对本级人民政府部门和下级人民政府的政务履约守诺情况进行考核，建立政务失信责任追究制度，按照规定对政务失信行为予以惩戒。

The unemployed workforce shall receive support to find temporary, part-time, seasonal, and flexible employment, and obtain an integrated social security card.

Employers unable to implement the national standard work hours system due to production and operation needs and implement alternative work schedules instead may implement acknowledgement after joint negotiations to request a flexible work schedule or compressed work schedule.

Article 16 The government and its agencies shall abide by the principles of mutual negotiations, legal and regulatory compliance, mutual benefit, and prudence, and shall consider financial payment capabilities when signing investment incentive and strategic partnership agreements with market entities, and shall not violate the preferential conditions promised by the state and the Free Trade Port.

Investment policies and preferential conditions promised by means other than contracts during the investment attraction shall be made in writing based on statutory authority and specified procedures.

Article 17 The government and its agencies shall fulfill the policy commitments made to market entities, the contracts, and the effective rulings made by the judicial branch, and shall not change policy commitments or contracts without authorization; shall not withhold performance due to government transitions or job transfer of accountable employees; the government and their agencies who assume the power shall perform the original power if there is an adjustment of administrative areas, institutes, or functions and responsibilities; those who fail to fulfill their commitments, contracts, or effective rulings as required shall resolve them within the time limit provided.

Any policy commitment or contractual amendments shall be made based on statutory authority and procedures and the market entities shall be indemnified against any resulting losses pursuant to law if it is necessary to change the policy commitments and contractual provisions due to national interests and public interests. Market entities shall be eligible for indemnification against losses suffered and infringement upon their legal rights due to illegal acts or acts conducted in bad faith by the government or its agencies.

The people’s governments at or above the county level shall assess the performance and compliance of government agencies at the appropriate and lower levels, set up an accountability system for administrative service violations, and issue penalties for such violations as necessary.

第十八条 国家机关、事业单位不得违约拖欠市场主体的货物、工程、服务等账款，不得在合同未作约定的情况下以等待竣工验收批复、决算审计等为由，拒绝或者迟延支付市场主体账款。

省和市、县、自治县人民政府及其有关部门应当加大对国家机关、事业单位拖欠市场主体账款的清理力度，并通过加强预算管理、跟踪审计、绩效考核、严格责任追究等措施，防止和纠正拖欠市场主体账款的行为。

第十九条 省人民政府应当以市场主体需求为导向，依法采取直接取消审批、审批改为备案等方式，持续减少行政许可事项，实行与海南自由贸易港相适应的最简权力清单管理制度。

地方性法规、政府规章原则上不再新设行政许可，但涉及国家安全、社会稳定、生态保护红线、重大公共利益等国家实行准入管理的事项除外。

第二十条 在海南自由贸易港推行行政审批告知承诺制度，但直接涉及公共安全、生态环境保护和直接关系人身健康、生命财产安全的以及依法应当当场作出行政审批决定的行政审批事项除外。实行告知承诺制的具体事项，由政府审批改革主管部门会同有关部门研究后报本级人民政府批准。

对于适用告知承诺制的事项，审批部门一次性告知申请人审批条件和需要提交的材料，申请人自愿签署告知承诺书并按要求提交材料的，审批部门应当直接作出行政许可决定，并依法对申请人履行承诺情况进行监督检查。申请人未履行承诺的，审批部门应当责令其限期整改；整改后仍未满足条件的，应当撤销行政许可决定，按照有关规定予以信用惩戒。

省人民政府政务服务管理机构应当组织编制告知承诺制办事指南、告知承诺书格式文本，并通过相关服务场所、政府网站和全省一体化在线政务服务平台等渠道公布，方便申请人查阅、索取或者下载。

Article 18 State agencies and public institutions shall not delay payment for market entity goods, projects, or services, and shall not refuse or delay such payment on the grounds of waiting for final approval or final accounts auditing in the absence of contractual provisions.

The provincial, city, county, and autonomous county people's governments and their agencies shall improve efforts to settle any late payments owed by national agencies and public institutions to market entities, and prevent and correct late payments by improving budget management, tracking audit, performance appraisals, implementing strict accountability, and other measures.

Article 19 Guided by market entity requirements, the provincial people's government shall continuously relax administrative licensing matters by directly canceling reviews and approvals or changing the approval into filing requirements, and implement a minimalist authority list administration system suitable for the Free Trade Port.

In principle, no new administrative licenses shall be added to local regulations or government rules, except for those involving national security, social stability, ecological conservation boundary, major public interests, or other areas subject to national access administration.

Article 20 An administrative approval acknowledgment shall be implemented in the Free Trade Port, except for those matters directly related to public safety, ecological environment protection, personal health, life and property safety, or administrative approval decisions that shall be made on the spot pursuant to law. Specific matters subject to acknowledgment shall be reported to the people's government at the appropriate level for approval after being jointly analyzed by the competent government approval report department and other agencies.

The approval agency shall inform those requesting items subject to acknowledgment of the approval requirements and materials to be submitted in one go. The approval agency shall directly make an administrative licensing decision and oversee and inspect the requester's performance of the commitments pursuant to law if the requester voluntarily signs the acknowledgment and submits the required materials. If the requester fails to fulfill their commitment, the approval agency shall require them to correct such within a time limit. The administrative licensing decision shall be revoked and a credit penalty shall be imposed pursuant to applicable law if the requester still fails to meet the requirements after correction.

The administrative agency responsible for the provincial people's government administrative services shall organize the preparation of the acknowledgment guidelines and the model version, and announce such in service locations, government websites, and the provincial integrated online administrative service platform to help the requesters with any questions, requests, or downloads.

第二十一条 行政审批实行容缺受理制的，申请人提交的主要申报材料齐全且符合法定形式，非关键性申报材料有欠缺或者存在瑕疵但不影响实质性审核的，经其书面承诺在办理部门作出办理结果前补齐或者补正的，办理部门应当先予受理并进行审查。

申请人在规定时限内补齐容缺容错材料，经审查符合法定要求的，办理部门应当依法作出决定；申请人未按承诺时限补齐所有容缺容错材料的，办理部门应当撤销申请事项并退回其申报材料。在办理过程中有失信行为的，失信年度内不再对其实施容缺受理。

第二十二条 政府有关部门应当持续完善全省统一的工程建设项目审批管理制度，统一审批体系、审批标准和信息平台，精简工程项目全流程涉及的行政许可、技术审查、中介服务、市政公用服务等事项，优化审批流程，推动构建“拿地即开工”的建设项目管理机制，并加强事中事后监管。

第二十三条 供水、供电、供气、通信网络等企事业单位应当推行报装申请全流程网上办理，简化办理流程，精简申报材料，压缩办理时限，全面推行电子账单、电子发票；不得将建设工程规划许可证和建筑工程施工许可证作为办理水、电、气、网络的前置条件。鼓励供水、供电、供气、通信网络等企事业单位为市场主体提供全程代办服务。

第二十四条 政府及有关部门应当以市场主体满意度为检验标准，以市场主体办事“零跑动”为目标，推进政务服务事项网上办、掌上办、就近办、全省通办、跨省通办等，提高政务服务便利度。

政府及有关部门应当建立健全服务市场主体和投资项目服务推进机制，强化跟踪服务，及时解决市场主体经营和投资项目建设中的重大问题，为企业提供全流程服务。

Article 21 The main request materials submitted by the requester shall be complete and conform to the statutory format if the administrative approval is subject to defect system approval, and the processing agency shall preliminarily accept and consider any deficient or flawed non-critical request materials that do not affect the substantive consideration and are promised in writing to be supplied or corrected before the processing agency issues their results.

Where the requester submits or corrects defective materials within the time limit provided and such materials meet statutory requirements after review, the processing agency shall issue a decision pursuant to law; if the requester fails to do so, the processing agency shall revoke the request and return the request materials. The processing agency will not accept additional submissions for the same year if the requester conducts any untrustworthy acts.

Article 22 The agencies shall continuously improve the integrated approval administration system for provincial construction projects, standardize the approval system, approval standards, and information platform, streamline administrative licensing, technical consideration, intermediary services, municipal public services, and other matters involved in the overall project process, optimize the approval process, improve the construction project administration system, that is, "begin construction once the land is granted", and improve oversight both during and after the process.

Article 23 Market entities and public institutions such as water supply, power supply, gas supply, and communication network providers shall conduct online installation request processing, simplify the procedures, streamline the request materials, reduce the processing time, and fully implement electronic bills and tax receipts. Planning permits and construction permits shall not be used as prerequisites for water, electricity, gas, or network provision. Market entities and public institutions such as water supply, power supply, gas supply, and communication network providers shall be encouraged to provide market entities with agency services for the entire process.

Article 24 The government and its agencies shall make market entity satisfaction their target, set market entity "effortlessness" as the goal, and encourage online, portable, close-by, and provincial and inter-provincial integrated administrative services to improve the ease of administrative services.

The government and its agencies shall set up and optimize the service awareness for market entities and investment projects, improve tracking services, resolve major issues in market entity and investment project operations in a timely manner, and provide full-process services for enterprises.

政府及有关部门应当推进相对集中行政许可权改革，实行一枚印章管审批、一件事一次办、证照联办等便利化审批方式，提升审批效能。

省人民政府政务服务管理机构应当统筹推进全省统一的政务服务标准化建设，实现政务服务事项无差别受理、同标准办理；按照统一标准、统一培训、统一组织考核的管理模式，加强和规范对全省政务服务工作人员的管理和培训。

县级以上人民政府政务服务大厅推行综合窗口服务，实行综合受理、分类办理、统一出件。服务窗口应当健全一次告知、首问负责、限时办结等服务制度，完善预约、全程帮办、联办以及错时、延时服务等工作机制。

第二十五条 政府及有关部门应当运用人工智能、大数据、区块链、移动互联网等现代信息技术，加强数据共享与融合，持续优化营商环境中各种公共资源的配置效率和运行状态，推行智能化监管与服务。

政府及有关部门应当依托全省一体化在线政务服务平台，推动全省各政务信息系统整合对接，促进政务服务跨地区、跨部门、跨层级数据共享和业务协同。

政府及有关部门依职能产生的电子证照、电子证明文件、加盖有效电子印章或者数字签名的电子材料等电子证照数据，应当及时共享至电子证照系统。电子证照可以通过依政府职能共享、实人授权使用、社会公示等方式运用。电子证照与纸质证照具有同等法律效力。在全省一体化在线政务服务平台办理政务服务事项，原则上不再要求提交纸质证照。

The government and its agencies shall encourage the reform of centralized administrative licensing authority, implement facilitative approvals, such as setting up a single government agency for all approvals, and one-stop services, and issue business licenses and other certificates at the same time to improve approval efficiency.

The provincial people's government administrative service agency shall coordinate the development of integrated provincial administrative service standardization and achieve non-discriminatory acceptance and standardized administration of administrative services, improve and standardize provincial administrative service official administration and training following a centralized standard, centralized training, and centralized organization and assessment administration method.

The people's governments at or above the county level shall set up the integrated service desks for acceptance, a division of labor, and standardized submission services at their administrative offices. The service desk shall improve the one-time notification service system, and the first government staff who receives the inquiry shall be responsible for resolving it, and the administration shall be completed with a specific time, and improve the appointment, full-time assistant, contact office, out-of-business hour and extended service working systems.

Article 25 The government and its agencies shall use modern information technology such as artificial intelligence, big data, blockchain, and mobile internet to develop data sharing and integration, continuously optimize the allocation efficiency and operating conditions for different public resources in the business environment, and encourage electronic supervision and services.

The government and its agencies shall use the Province's integrated online administrative service platform, improve the integration and interconnection of provincial government information systems, and improve cross-regional, inter-agency, and cross-level data sharing and administrative service collaboration.

Electronic license data such as electronic licenses, electronic certificates, and electronic materials stamped with valid electronic seals or digital signatures generated by competent government agencies based on their functions shall be promptly uploaded to the electronic license system. The electronic license may be shared based on government functions, license holder authorization after identification verification, or by public announcement. Electronic licenses and paper licenses shall have the same legal effect, and it is no longer necessary to submit paper certificates when managing administrative services on the provincial integrated online administrative service platform.

第二十六条 对涉企法规、规章、行政规范性文件，制定机关或者实施机关应当加强宣传解读，根据企业所属行业、规模等主动精准推送政策信息。

政府及有关部门应当通过省政府门户网站、全省一体化在线政务服务平台及其移动客户端、自助终端等渠道及时公开惠企政策，并公布相关负责人及联系方式。省工业和信息化主管部门应当统筹有关部门及时梳理惠企政策、编制兑现事项清单和办事指南，通过全省一体化在线政务服务平台集中公布。

政府及有关部门应当将惠企政策兑现纳入全省一体化在线政务服务平台统一办理。在市场主体办理相关业务时，政务服务管理机构或者审批部门应当主动告知相关惠企政策，进行政策适用指导。

鼓励通过政府部门信息共享等方式，实现符合条件的企业免予申报直接享受惠企政策。对确需企业提出申请的惠企政策，应当合理设置并公开申请条件，简化申报手续，实现一次申报、全程网办、快速兑现。

第二十七条 不动产登记机关应当压缩不动产登记办理时限和优化不动产登记流程，加强与税务、公安、民政、社保等部门和金融机构等单位的信息共享，实施不动产登记、交易和缴税并行办理，提供不动产登记信息网上查询和现场自助查询服务。

推行不动产登记与水、电、气变更联动办理，由不动产登记部门统一受理，一次性收取全部材料并推送至供水、供电、供气等企事业单位并联办理相关业务。

Article 26 Authorities enacting or implementing regulations, rules, or administrative normative documents for enterprise matters shall improve awareness and interpretation, and actively and accurately publish policy information based on the industry and enterprise scale.

The government and its agencies shall promptly announce beneficial policies for market entities through the provincial government portal, the Province's integrated online administrative service platform, mobile applications, self-service devices, and other channels, and announce the government staff directly in charge of such and their contact information. The provincial agency in charge of industry and information technology shall coordinate the relevant agencies to organize beneficial policies for market entities in a timely manner, prepare a list of completed items and guidelines, and announce them through the provincial integrated online administrative service platform.

The agencies shall include beneficial policies for market entities into the integrated provincial online administrative service platform for centralized administration. Where the market entities request services, the administrative service agency or approval agency shall take the initiative to inform market entities of the applicable beneficial policies and issue guidelines upon the implementation of such policies.

Eligible entities may be exempt from the declaration and directly enjoy preferential policies through information sharing among government agencies. Request requirements for market entities preferential policies that need to be requested shall be reasonably set and announced, and the announcement procedures shall be simplified to achieve a one-time declaration, whole-process online operation, and quick implementation.

Article 27 The real estate registration agency shall reduce the registration time limit and optimize the registration process, encourage information sharing with tax, law enforcement, civil affairs, social security, and other agencies and financial institutions, implement parallel processing for real estate registration, transactions, and tax payment, and provide online and on-site real estate registration information self-service inquiry services.

Real estate registration, water, electricity, and gas utility charges shall be integrated and implemented, which shall be accepted by real estate registration agencies, and all materials shall be collected at one time and delivered to water supply, power supply, gas supply, and other organizations and public institutions to manage related services in parallel.

第二十八条　省人民政府及其有关部门应当结合实际情况和市场主体需求，依法推进省级行政管理权限调整由市、县、自治县人民政府及其有关部门和重点园区实施；重点园区所在地市、县、自治县人民政府及其有关部门依法将本级相关管理权限调整由重点园区实施。

调整审批权限的，应当同步调整优化监管层级，实现审批监管权责统一。原实施机关应当对承接机关加强业务培训指导，做好协调对接，强化事中事后监管，切实做到放管结合；承接机关应当周密组织承接工作，做到规范有序，防止出现管理真空。

政府及相关部门以适当的方式支持各类产业园区的管理运营单位设立一站式企业服务受理点，提供开办企业、项目建设、经营管理、人才服务、知识产权管理等政策咨询和代办服务。

第二十九条　政府有关部门应当按照“谁审批、谁监管，谁主管、谁监管”的原则，依法履行监管职责。因行政审批改革，直接取消审批、审批改为备案的，由原审批部门依法承担监管职责；实行告知承诺、优化审批服务的，由审批部门负责依法监管持证经营企业、查处无证经营行为。

实行相对集中行政许可权改革或者综合行政执法改革的市、县、自治县应当按照省人民政府有关规定，实现行业主管部门与行政执法机关之间监管职责明确、监管标准互通、监管信息互联、处理结果互认。

Article 28 The provincial people's government and its agencies shall, based on actual and market demands, improve the adjustment of provincial administrative authority to be implemented by the city, county, autonomous county people's governments, and their agencies and zones as required by law. The people's governments of the cities, counties, or autonomous counties where the zones are located and their agencies shall adjust the applicable administrative authority given to the zones at the appropriate level as required by law.

The oversight level shall be adjusted and optimized at the same time the approval authority is adjusted to achieve the standardization of the approval and oversight authorities and approval and oversight responsibilities. The original implementing agency shall improve service training for the performing agency, properly coordinate and integrate, improve oversight during and after the process, and effectively combine delegation of power with regulations. The performing agency shall carefully organize the work and improve standardization and order to prevent a lack of administration.

The government and its agencies shall support industrial park administration and operation entities to appropriately set up a one-stop service for businesses, and provide policy consultation and agency services, such as starting businesses, project development, operation and administration, and skilled employee services, and intellectual property administration.

Article 29 The government and its agencies shall perform their supervisory duties based on the principle of "the government agency with jurisdiction or approval authority shall be the government agency responsible for supervision." If the approval is directly canceled or changed to filing due to reform, the original approval agency shall assume the supervisory duties as required by law; where the acknowledgment is implemented to optimize the approval service, the approval agency shall be responsible for overseeing the licensed entities as required by law, and investigating and penalizing unlicensed business operations.

The cities, counties, and autonomous counties that implement a reform for centralized administrative licensing or comprehensive administrative law enforcement authority shall specify the regulatory authorities and responsibilities, the exchange of regulatory standards, the integration of regulatory information, and the mutual recognition of processing results between the competent industry and administrative law enforcement agencies pursuant to applicable provincial people's government regulations.

第三十条 省政府有关部门应当对本省法规、规章等设定的行政处罚、行政检查等监管事项进行梳理，形成监管事项目录清单，报省政府批准后按照统一标准接入“互联网＋监管”系统。

对直接涉及公共安全和人民群众生命健康等特殊行业、重点领域，建立重点监管清单，实行重点监管；对其他行业和领域，推行“双随机、一公开”监管，健全随机抽查系统，完善相关细则，确保公平监管；健全跨部门综合监管制度，推进常态化跨部门联合抽查；根据企业信用风险分类结果实施差异化监管措施，实行守信激励、失信惩戒；对新技术、新产业、新业态、新模式等实行包容审慎监管。

第三十一条 行政执法机关应当按照有关规定落实行政执法公示、行政执法全过程记录和重大行政执法决定法制审核制度，通过考核、定期报告、协调指导、执法数据共享等方式，推进行政执法严格、规范、公正、文明。

政府及有关部门应当依法规范、细化量化行政处罚等行政执法自由裁量权标准，确定执法的依据和裁量范围、种类和幅度，统一执法标准和尺度。

第三十二条 行政执法机关和司法机关应当坚持依法保护、平等保护、全面保护的原则，公正高效办理涉及市场主体的各类案件，依法处置扰乱市场主体生产经营活动秩序或者侵害生产经营者人身安全、财产安全等违法行为，防止各类案件超期办理，严格区分经济纠纷与犯罪，严格区分民事责任、行政责任与刑事责任。

Article 30 The provincial government agencies shall organize regulatory matters such as administrative penalties and administrative inspections provided by provincial regulations and rules, and create a list of regulatory matters to be uploaded to the Plus Internet Oversight system after approval from the provincial government.

A list of main oversight and substantive oversight matters for specific industries and main areas directly related to public safety and personal life and health shall be created and implemented. An oversight model using randomly selected inspectors to randomly inspect selected entities and requiring the prompt release of results shall be implemented for other industries and areas, and the random inspection system and rules shall be improved to ensure fair oversight. A comprehensive inter-agency oversight system and standardized inter-agency joint spot checks shall be encouraged. Differentiated oversight measures taking business credit risk classification results, incentives for the honesty, and penalties imposed for violations shall be implemented. Comprehensive and prudent oversight shall be applied to new technologies, new industries, new business forms, and new models.

Article 31 Administrative law enforcement agencies shall conduct administrative law enforcement awareness, record administrative law enforcement, review and approve major administrative law enforcement decisions as necessary, and encourage strict, standardized, fair, and civilized administrative law enforcement through assessments, regular reports, coordination and guidance, and law enforcement data sharing.

The government and its agencies shall standardize and refine administrative law enforcement discretion, such as in administrative penalties, as required by law, determine the basis of law enforcement and the scope, types, and coverage of discretion, and standardize law enforcement standards and coverage.

Article 32 Administrative law enforcement agencies and judicial agencies shall abide by the principles of lawful protection, equal protection, and comprehensive protection, resolve all cases involving commercial enterprises fairly and efficiently, resolve violations that disturb commercial entity production and business activity order, or put producer or operator personal or property safety at risk, resolve all cases within the statute of limitation, strictly distinguish between economic disputes and crimes, and also among civil liability, administrative liability and criminal liability.

行政执法机关和司法机关依法慎重实施查封、扣押、冻结等强制措施；依法需要采取上述强制措施的，不得超标的、超范围查封、扣押、冻结涉案财物，并应当采取措施减轻对市场主体正常生产经营的影响。

第三十三条 制定、修改、废止与市场主体生产经营活动密切相关的法规、规章、行政规范性文件，应当坚持市场主体需求导向，充分听取相关市场主体、行业协会商会的意见，依照法定权限和程序作出，并保持连续性和相对稳定性。与外商投资密切相关的法规、规章、行政规范性文件，制定机关应当提供相应的外文译本或者摘要。

因形势变化或者公共利益需要调整的，应当结合实际设置合理过渡期，为市场主体预留必要的适应调整时间。但因保障国家安全、重大公共利益、海南自由贸易港建设的需要，或者公布后不立即施行将有碍施行的除外。

省和市、县、自治县人民政府应当建立涉企政策的综合协调审查机制，避免政策冲突、不协调或者政策叠加对市场主体正常生产经营活动造成不利影响。

第三十四条 对与市场主体生产经营活动密切相关的法规、规章、行政规范性文件，制定机关或者实施机关应当定期组织开展评估和清理。发现侵害市场主体合法权益或者存在合法性问题的，应当及时修改或者废止。

市场主体认为法规、规章、行政规范性文件侵害其合法权益或者存在合法性问题的，可以依法向备案审查机关书面提出审查建议。备案审查机关应当按照规定处理并反馈处理结果。

Administrative law enforcement agencies and judicial agencies shall carefully implement compulsory measures such as sealing off, seizure and freezing as required by law. Any assets subject to the above methods as provided by law shall not be sealed off, seized, or frozen beyond the specified limit or scope, and precautions shall be taken to reduce the impact on the market entities' regular production and operations.

Article 33 Regulations, rules, and administrative normative documents closely related to market entity production and operation shall favor the market entities, take the opinions of the market entities, industry association, and chambers of commerce into full consideration, and ensure they conform to statutory authority and procedures, and maintain continuity and stability when being issued, amended, or revoked. The enacting agency shall provide the appropriate foreign language translations or abstracts for foreign investment regulations, rules, and administrative normative documents.

A reasonable transition period shall be given based on actual circumstances, and the necessary adjustment time shall be set aside for market entities if the regulations, rules, and administrative normative documents above need to be amended due to the circumstances or for the public interest unless safeguarding national security, major public interests, and the construction of Free Trade Port, or the failure to implement the amendment immediately after the announcement would impair the implementation.

The provincial, city, county, and autonomous county people's governments shall set up a comprehensive coordination and consideration system for policies for market entities to avoid any adverse effects on regular market entity production and operations caused by policy conflicts, in coordination, or overlap.

Article 34 Regulations, rules and administrative normative documents closely related to market entity production and operation shall be regularly evaluated and optimized by the enacting or implementing agencies, and shall be promptly amended or revoked if any legal issues or market entity rights infringement is discovered.

Market entities deeming that regulations, rules and administrative normative documents infringe upon their legal rights or have legal issues may submit a review recommendation in writing to the recording and review agency pursuant to law. The recording and review agency shall process the recommendation and issue its results as required.

第三十五条 省和市、县、自治县人民政府应当推进建设覆盖城乡、便捷高效、均等普惠的公共法律服务体系，建立并完善省、市、县（区）、街道（乡镇）、社区（村）五级公共法律服务平台，为公众和市场主体提供专业化、高水平的公共法律服务。

省和市、县、自治县人民政府司法行政部门应当完善公共法律服务网络、实体、热线平台建设，推动和指导法律专业机构为市场主体提供法律咨询、合同审查等全链条的法律服务。

政府有关部门可以采取发布一般性的指导意见或者提出具体指导建议，制定、发布相关合同示范文本等方式指导市场主体依法合规经营。

第三十六条 鼓励和支持各地区、各部门结合实际情况，在海南自由贸易港法治框架内积极探索原创性、差异化的优化营商环境具体措施；对探索中出现失误或者偏差，符合规定条件的，可以予以免责或者减轻责任。

第三十七条 县级以上人民代表大会常务委员会应当通过听取和审议专项工作报告，组织执法检查，开展专题询问、质询、特定问题调查等方式，对本地区优化营商环境工作进行监督。

第三十八条 政府及有关部门不履行优化营商环境工作职责，有下列情形之一的，由其上级机关、主管部门或者优化营商环境工作主管部门责令改正；对直接负责的主管人员和其他直接责任人员依法给予处理；构成犯罪的，依法追究刑事责任：

（一）拒绝、推诿、拖延履行法定职责的；

（二）违反规定增加或者变相增加办事事项、办事环节、办事材料、办事时限的；

Article 35 The provincial, city, county, and autonomous county people's governments shall implement the development of a public legal service system that is inclusive, convenient, and efficient, covering urban and rural areas, and implement and improve a five-tier public legal service platform in the provinces, cities, counties (or districts), subdistricts (or towns/townships) and communities (or villages) to provide professional and high-quality public legal services for the public and market entities.

The provincial, city, county, and autonomous county people's government judicial agencies shall improve the development of public legal service networks, entities and hotline platforms, and encourage and guide professional legal service providers to provide legal advice, contract reviews, and other full-chain legal services for market entities.

The agencies may guide market entities to operate in compliance with rules and regulations by issuing general guidelines or submitting specific recommendations and preparing or issuing model contracts.

Article 36 All areas and agencies shall be encouraged to actively explore initiatives and differentiated measures to optimize the business environment under the rule of law in Hainan Free Trade Port and based on current conditions; any mistakes or deviations during the exploration under the specified conditions may be exempted or mitigated.

Article 37 The standing committee of the people's congress at or above the county level shall supervise business environment optimization work in the local area by listening to and considering the specific work report, organizing law enforcement inspections, conducting specific inquires, reviews, and investigations of specific issues.

Article 38 If the government and its agencies fail to perform their duties during business environment optimization and any of the following circumstances occur, their superior agencies, competent agencies, or competent agencies responsible for the business environment optimization shall require them to correct such. The employee directly in charge and other directly liable employees shall be penalized pursuant to law, and shall be held criminally liable if a crime is committed:

(a) refusing, avoiding, or delaying the performance of statutory duties;

(b) violating the law to explicitly or implicitly increase the items to be processed, procedures, materials, or time limits;

（三）擅自收费、越权收费、超标准收费和重复收费的；

（四）不履行向市场主体依法作出的政策承诺以及依法订立的各类合同，或者不履行司法机关生效裁决的；

（五）违约拖欠市场主体的货物、工程、服务等账款的；

（六）违反规定不受理投诉、举报或者推诿、拖延办理投诉、举报事项，违规泄露投诉、举报人信息，以及对投诉、举报人打击报复的；

（七）对市场主体故意刁难、吃拿卡要的；

（八）没有法定依据实施行政检查、行政处罚、行政强制等行政行为，妨碍市场主体正常生产经营活动的；

（九）其他损害营商环境或者侵害市场主体合法权益的行为。

司法机关工作人员违反本条例的，依照国家有关规定追究责任。

第三十九条　本条例自 2021 年 11 月 1 日起施行。

(c) charging unauthorized charges, *ultra vires* charges, over-standard charges, or repeat charges;

(d) failing to fulfill the policy commitments made to market entities and contracts made pursuant to law, or failing to perform the effective rulings issued by judicial agencies;

(e) delaying payments for market entity merchandise, projects, and services;

(f) not accepting complaints or reports of regulatory violations, or avoiding or delaying the resolution of complaints and reports, disclosing information about complaints and informants in violation of the law, or retaliating against complainants and informants;

(g) deliberately hindering market entities and asking for favors or bribes;

(h) implement administrative inspections, administrative penalties, administrative injunction and administrative enforcement, and other administrative acts without legal basis to hindering regular market entity production and business activities; or

(i) other acts that harm the business environment or infringe upon market entity rights.

Judicial agency employees in violation of these Regulations shall be investigated and receive penalties pursuant to applicable state regulations.

Article 39 These Regulations shall enter into force as of November 1, 2021.

海南自由贸易港征收征用条例

Regulations of Hainan Free Trade Port on Eminent Domain and Temporary Condemnations

海南自由贸易港征收征用条例

（2021 年 12 月 1 日海南省第六届人民代表大会常务委员会
第三十一次会议通过）

第一章　总　则

第一条　为规范征收征用行为，维护公共利益，保障被征收征用人合法权益，根据有关法律、行政法规的规定，结合海南自由贸易港实际，制定本条例。

第二条　为了公共利益需要征收土地的，经依法批准后，由县级以上人民政府予以公告并组织实施。

市、县、自治县人民政府负责本行政区域的房屋征收与补偿工作。市、县、自治县人民政府确定的房屋征收部门组织实施本行政区域的房屋征收与补偿工作。市、县、自治县人民政府其他有关部门应当依照有关规定和本级人民政府规定的职责分工，互相配合，保障房屋征收与补偿工作的顺利进行。

市、县、自治县人民政府及有关部门（以下简称征用实施单位）依照职责，负责组织实施征用不动产、动产的工作。法律法规另有规定的，从其规定。

第三条　征收应当遵循决策民主、程序合法、结果公开、补偿公平合理的原则。

征用应当遵循效能优先、补偿公平合理的原则。

Regulations of Hainan Free Trade Port on Eminent Domain and Temporary Condemnations

(Adopted at the 31st Session of the Standing Committee of the 6th Hainan Provincial People's Congress on December 1, 2021)

Chapter I General Provisions

Article 1 These Regulations are enacted pursuant to laws and regulations, and based on actual circumstances in the Hainan Free Trade Port to regulate eminent domain and temporary condemnation, protect the public interest, and protect the legal rights of the party concerned.

Article 2 Notice of eminent domain for public interest purposes shall be provided by the people's government at or above the county level subject to approval in accordance with law.

The people's government in cities, counties, and autonomous counties shall be responsible for housing eminent domain and compensation within their administrative areas. The government agencies empowered by the people's government in cities, counties, and autonomous counties for eminent domain in an administrative area shall carry out eminent domain and provide compensation. To ensure a smooth housing eminent domain and compensation process, other city, county, and autonomous county people's government agencies shall cooperate as required by law and follow the division of responsibilities provided by the people's governments at the appropriate levels.

The people's governments in cities, counties, autonomous counties and the appropriate agencies (the agency instituting the temporary condemnation) shall be responsible for organizing and instituting temporary condemnation for immovable and movable assets based on their functions and duties unless otherwise provided by laws and regulations.

Article 3 Eminent domain shall be conducted based on principles of democratic decision-making, legitimate process, openness, and fair and reasonable compensation.

Temporary condemnation shall follow the principles of prioritizing efficiency, and fair and reasonable compensation.

第四条　实施征收征用，应当严格依法保护各类投资者和权利人的合法权益。

第五条　任何组织和个人都有遵守征收征用法律法规的义务，并有权对违反征收征用法律法规的行为提出检举和控告。

第二章　征收与补偿

第六条　县级以上人民政府拟征收农民集体所有土地的，应当在征收预公告发布前，就征收需要是否符合法律规定的公共利益情形进行认定，必要时可以组织有关部门、相关领域专家论证。

在市、县、自治县国土空间规划确定的城镇开发边界内实施成片开发，公共利益情形的认定按照国家有关规定执行。

第七条　对城市更新中旧住宅区拆除重建项目，已签订补偿协议的专有部分面积和业主人数占比均不低于百分之九十的，市、县、自治县人民政府可以按照法律、行政法规及本条例有关规定对未签约部分房屋实施征收。

第八条　不动产所有权人因不动产被征收，导致征收预公告确定范围外相关联的不动产无法实现合理使用的，可以申请将其纳入征收范围。

第九条　征收集体土地、国有土地上房屋的相关程序，按照国家有关规定执行。

第十条　征收集体土地应当依法给予公平合理的补偿，确保被征地农民原有生活水平不降低、长远生计有保障。

市、县、自治县人民政府应当将被征地农民纳入城乡居民基本养老保险、从业人员养老保险和再就业保障等体系。建立被征地农民服务和劳

Article 4 Investors and right holders' legal rights shall be strictly protected pursuant to law when the eminent domain and temporary condemnation action is instituted.

Article 5 All organizations and individuals shall abide by the laws and regulations governing eminent domain and temporary condemnations, and be entitled to file complaints of any violation of the laws and regulations on eminent domain and temporary condemnations.

Chapter II Eminent Domain and Compensation

Article 6 If the people's governments at or above the county level recommend eminent domain on land collectively owned by a rural community, it shall determine whether the eminent domain conforms to the public interest as required by law and designate agencies and experts to conduct any necessary appraisal before notice of the eminent domain is published.

The determination of the public interest when developing plots within the boundaries of urban development delimited by the city and autonomous county land space planning shall be conducted pursuant to national law.

Article 7 The people's governments in cities, counties, and autonomous counties may conduct eminent domain on properties lacking agreements pursuant to applicable laws, administrative regulations, and these Regulations if at least 90% of the property owners have signed compensation agreements and the built-up area they own is no less than 90% of the total area in the old residential area demolition and renovation projects in the urban renewal.

Article 8 The owners of immovable property may request the government agency to add immovable property not within the scope of the eminent domain notice into the scope if such property cannot be reasonably used due to the eminent domain of other immovable property.

Article 9 The appropriate national procedures for eminent domain on buildings on collective or state-owned land shall apply pursuant to national law.

Article 10 Fair and reasonable compensation shall be paid pursuant to law for collective land appropriated under eminent domain to ensure that the lives of farmers whose land was included in the eminent domain (displaced farmers) are not impacted and long-term livelihood is guaranteed.

The people's governments in cities, counties and autonomous counties shall add displaced farmers to the pension for urban and rural residents, employment pension, and employment program. A service and work skills training system for displaced farmers shall be created by

动技能培训机制，对被征地农民建档立册，有针对性地进行实用技能培训。用地企业新增岗位同等条件下应当优先录用被征地农民。支持劳务派遣服务公司派遣有条件的被征地农民异地就业。

第十一条 征收农用地和未利用地的土地补偿费、安置补助费标准由省人民政府制定的区片综合地价确定；征收农村集体建设用地的补偿标准，按照省人民政府规定确定。

征收集体土地涉及农村村民住宅的，应当尊重农村村民意愿，采取重新安排宅基地建房、提供安置房或者货币补偿等方式给予公平合理的补偿。

征收集体土地涉及农村村民住宅以外的其他建筑物、构筑物，重新安排用地的，对其建筑物、构筑物按照重置价格结合成新给予货币补偿；不能重新安排用地的，按照市场价格给予货币补偿。青苗及地上其他附着物补偿费按照省人民政府规定的标准执行。

征收集体土地可以根据被征地农村集体经济组织及农民意愿，采取补贴资金、留用地、留物业等方式，让被征地农村集体经济组织和农民分享土地增值收益。

土地补偿费、安置补助费的分配标准和分配方式由省人民政府制定。

第十二条 对被征收房屋及其他不动产价值的补偿，不得低于征收决定公告之日被征收房屋及其他不动产类似不动产的市场价格。被征收房屋及其他不动产的价值，由具有相应资质的不动产价格评估机构评估确定。

被征收人可以选择货币补偿，也可以选择房屋产权调换。

filing for displaced farmers and conducting targeted skills training. Business entities shall give displaced farmers priority if they have the same skills as other candidates for new jobs. Staffing companies shall receive support to assign eligible displaced farmers to work in different places.

Article 11 Land compensation fees and resettlement subsidies for agricultural land and unused land shall be based on the comprehensive land price of each lot issued by the provincial people's government. The compensation standard for rural collective development land eminent domain shall be determined based on regulations issued by the provincial people's government.

Collective land eminent domain involving rural villager buildings shall respect the willingness of rural villagers and give fair and reasonable compensation by rearranging homesteads to build homes or providing alternate housing or monetary compensation.

Where collective land eminent domain involves other buildings or structures other than rural villager buildings: if the land is rearranged, the buildings and structures shall be given monetary compensation based on the replacement price for an equal building; otherwise, monetary compensation shall be given based on the market price. Compensation for crops and other attachments shall be determined based on the standards provided by the provincial people's government.

The methods for collective land eminent domain may involve subsidy funds, reserved land, and reserved property based on the willingness of the displaced agricultural collectives and farmers to ensure that such displaced agricultural collectives and farmers can share the value-added benefits offered by the land.

The land compensation fee and resettlement subsidy allocation standards and methods shall be issued by the provincial people's government.

Article 12 Compensation for buildings or other immovable properties appropriated under eminent domain shall not be lower than their market price on the date the notice of eminent domain decision is published. The value of homes and other types of real estate appropriated under eminent domain shall be assessed and determined by a qualified real estate valuation agency.

Owners under eminent domain may choose monetary compensation or exchange of title for buildings.

第十三条 因征收造成搬迁和临时安置的，应当支付搬迁补偿费、临时安置费。涉及住宅的，临时安置费按照租赁与被征收房屋面积、地段相当的住宅所需费用平均价格确定，且不低于保障被征收住宅所有权人基本居住条件所需费用。

第十四条 征收非住宅房屋及其他不动产造成停产停业损失的，应当根据房屋被征收前的效益、停产停业期限等给予补偿或者按照市场价格补偿。

第十五条 集体土地、国有土地上房屋的征收补偿费应当在补偿协议约定的期限内或者征地补偿安置决定、房屋征收补偿决定公告发布之日起三个月内全额支付到位。发生迟延的，支付的补偿应当包括法律法规和政策规定的适当利息。

第三章 征用与补偿

第十六条 因抢险救灾、疫情防控等紧急需要，征用实施单位在调用现有储备资源、紧急采购后，仍无法满足紧急需要的，可以依法对组织、个人所有的不动产、动产实施征用。

征用组织、个人的不动产、动产应当与紧急情况可能造成社会危害的性质、程度和范围相适应。征用实施单位有多种方式可以选择应对紧急需要的，应当选择有利于最大限度保护组织、个人权益的方式。

本条例所称征用的不动产、动产包括组织、个人所有或者使用的土地、房屋、场所、设施、运输工具、工程机械和其他物资等。

Article 13 Relocation compensation fees and temporary resettlement fees shall be paid where eminent domain results in relocation or temporary resettlement. Temporary resettlement fees shall be determined based on the average rent prices for the type of building required in the same area and location as the building to be appropriated under eminent domain, and shall not be less than the fees required for ensuring the basic living standards of the owners whose buildings are to be appropriated under eminent domain.

Article 14 Compensation shall be paid based on the benefits prior to the eminent domain, the period of time production or operations are suspended, or the market price where the eminent domain of non-residential buildings or other immovable properties causes production losses or suspension of operations.

Article 15 Compensation for buildings appropriated under collective land and state-owned land eminent domain shall be paid in full within 3 months from the date when the eminent domain compensation resettlement decision and housing eminent domain compensation decision notices are published or within the time limit agreed in the compensation agreement. Otherwise, the compensation to be paid shall include the appropriate interest as provided by laws, regulations, and policies.

Chapter III Temporary Condemnation and Compensation

Article 16 A government agency instituting a temporary condemnation may seize immovable or movable property owned by organizations or individuals as necessary and pursuant to law should there be an urgent need, such as emergency rescue and disaster relief or pandemic prevention and control if the agency instituting a temporary condemnation is still unable to cope with the urgent need after resorting to existing reserve resources and emergency procurement.

The appropriation of immovable and movable property belonging to organizations or individuals shall be reasonable based on the nature, extent, and scope of social harm that may be caused by an emergency. The agency instituting the temporary condemnation shall choose an appropriation method that offers maximum protection of organization or individual rights should alternatives to respond to the emergency not be available.

Immovable and movable properties appropriated under eminent domain as mentioned in these Regulations refer to lands, buildings, places, facilities, vehicles, construction machinery, and other materials owned or used by organizations and individuals.

第十七条 征用实施单位可以在职责范围内对紧急需要可能征用的不动产、动产，通过信息共享或者调查登记了解相关情况。对可能征用的不动产，应当建立征用预备目录，并制定不动产征用预案，报本级人民政府备案。

征用预备目录应当及时更新。

第十八条 征用实施单位应对紧急需要依法征用不动产、动产的，应当向被征用不动产、动产的组织或者个人发出应急征用凭证。

特别紧急情况下无法当场发出应急征用凭证的，应当在实施征用开始后四十八小时内补发。

应急征用凭证应当载明征用依据、事由及被征用不动产、动产的名称、数量、规格、技术保障要求、交付时间和地点、征用期限等。

第十九条 组织或者个人收到应急征用凭证后，应当及时配合交付被征用的不动产、动产，必要时安排相关操作人员、技术指导人员等专业人员及后勤保障人员协助做好征用工作。

征用实施单位应当与被征用不动产、动产的组织或者个人办理交接手续。

第二十条 被征用不动产、动产使用完毕或者应急征用凭证确定的征用期限届满后，征用实施单位应当通知被征用不动产、动产的组织或者个人，凭应急征用凭证办理返还交接手续。

被征用的不动产、动产毁损、灭失的，征用实施单位应当一并出具毁损、灭失证明。

Article 17 The agency instituting a temporary condemnation may know related information on immovable and movable property that may be appropriated under temporary condemnation for emergency purposes through information sharing or investigation and registration based on their functions and duties. A temporary condemnation list shall be created for immovable properties pending appropriation under temporary condemnation, and an appropriation plan for immovable properties shall be prepared and reported to the people's governments at the appropriate level for filing.

The temporary condemnation list shall be regularly updated.

Article 18 The agency instituting a temporary condemnation action may issue a certificate of emergency appropriation to the organization or individual pending appropriation under temporary condemnation.

Certificates must be issued within 48 hours following the start of the appropriation if a certificate of emergency appropriation cannot be issued on the spot due to the nature of the special emergency.

The emergency appropriation certificate shall specify the appropriation basis, reasons, and the name, quantity, specifications, technical support requirements, delivery time and place, and appropriation period for the immovable or moveable property.

Article 19 An organization or individual shall promptly deliver the immovable or movable property pending appropriation upon the receipt of a certificate of emergency appropriation, and if necessary, appropriate operators, technical instructors, or other professionals and logistics support employees may be arranged for assisting in appropriation.

The agency instituting a temporary condemnation shall complete delivery procedures with the organizations or individuals owning the appropriated immovable or movable property.

Article 20 The agency instituting a temporary condemnation shall notify the organization or individual concerned and facilitate the return and delivery under the certificate of emergency appropriation once the appropriated immovable or movable property is no longer necessary or the time limit specified in the certificate of emergency appropriation expires.

The agency instituting a temporary condemnation shall issue a certificate proving damage or loss should the appropriated immovable or movable property become damaged or is lost.

第二十一条 征用实施单位应当自返还交接手续结束后三十个工作日内，主动会同有关部门对被征用不动产、动产的组织或者个人提出征用补偿建议；组织或者个人也可以自返还交接手续结束后，向征用实施单位提出补偿要求。

征用实施单位可以就征用补偿金额与被征用不动产、动产的组织或者个人进行协商，协商一致的，签订征用补偿协议；协商不成的，按照市场价格确定征用补偿金额。

征用实施单位应当在补偿金额确定后十五个工作日内作出征用补偿决定，并及时向被征用不动产、动产的组织或者个人支付补偿费。

第二十二条 造成不动产、动产毁损、灭失的，按下列标准给予补偿：

（一）毁损但经维修能够恢复使用功能的，补偿金额按照必要的维修费用支出确定；

（二）灭失、无法维修、经维修无法恢复使用功能或者维修费用超过财产毁损前价值的，补偿金额应当综合考虑财产重置成本、综合成新率、净残值等因素确定；

（三）法律法规对补偿标准另有规定的，从其规定。

第二十三条 因征用不动产、动产造成组织或者个人停产停业的，应当补偿停产停业期间需要支付的水、电、房租、人员工资等必要费用。

因征用造成个人住宅毁损的，征用实施单位应当及时给予修复，在修复期间，应当保障被征用人的居住条件。

第二十四条 除涉及国家秘密、商业秘密、个人隐私外，征用实施单位应当在政府门户网站或者其他互联网政务媒体、新闻媒体上对征用不动产、动产的补偿标准、补偿金额等予以公告，接受社会监督。

Article 21 The agency instituting a temporary condemnation shall take the initiative to submit a temporary condemnation compensation plan for organizations or individuals owning the appropriated immovable and movable property together with the appropriate agencies within 30 business days of completing the return and delivery. Organizations and individuals may also claim compensation from the appropriation agency after the property is returned and handed over.

The agency instituting a temporary condemnation may negotiate appropriation compensation amount with organizations or individuals owning the appropriated immovable and movable property, and execute an appropriation compensation agreement after negotiating an agreement; if not, the appropriation compensation shall be assessed at market price.

The agency instituting a temporary condemnation shall make a decision on the appropriation compensation within 15 business days of determining the compensation amount and issue payment to the organizations and individuals owning the appropriated immovable and movable property in a timely manner.

Article 22 Compensation for damage(s) or loss(es) caused to immovable and movable property shall be determined based on the following standards:

(a) compensation shall be determined based on the repair expenses if the property is damaged but can be restored to its original function after maintenance;

(b) compensation shall be determined after comprehensive consideration of property replacement costs, weighted residual value, net salvage value, and other factors if the property is lost, cannot be repaired or restored to its original function after repair, or the repair costs will exceed the value of the property; or

(c) any other laws or regulations providing different compensation standards shall control.

Article 23 Expenses such as water fees, electric power charges, rent, and employee wages during the suspension period shall be compensated should the organization or individual be required to suspend production or operations due to the appropriation of immovable or movable property.

The agency instituting a temporary condemnation shall promptly repair any personal residences damaged due to the appropriation, and shall ensure the livelihood of those affected by the appropriation during the repair period.

Article 24 The agency instituting a temporary condemnation shall publish compensation standards and amounts for appropriated immovable or movable property on the government portal or other internet media on government affairs, and news media, except where state secrets, trade secrets, or personal privacy is involved, and shall accept social oversight.

第四章 法律责任

第二十五条 国家工作人员在征收征用工作中滥用职权、玩忽职守、徇私舞弊的，对直接负责的主管人员和其他直接责任人员，依法给予处分。

第二十六条 组织、个人采取暴力、威胁等方法阻碍依法进行的征收征用与补偿工作，构成违反治安管理行为的，依法给予处罚。

第二十七条 违反本条例规定的行为，本条例未设定处罚而相关法律法规另有处罚规定的，从其规定。

违反本条例规定的行为，构成犯罪的，依法追究刑事责任。

第五章 附 则

第二十八条 本条例自 2022 年 1 月 1 日起施行。

Chapter IV Legal Liability

Article 25 The persons directly in charge and other employees directly liable shall be subject to disciplinary action pursuant to law should government staffs commit abuse of position, dereliction of duty, play favoritism and commit irregularities, or other such acts during their eminent domain and temporary condemnation.

Article 26 Organizations or individuals using violence, threats, or other means to obstruct the eminent domain, temporary condemnation, or compensation pursuant to law, constituting a violation of public security administration, shall be penalized pursuant to law.

Article 27 Violations of these Regulations shall be subject to other applicable laws and regulations if these Regulations do not provide penalties for such violations.

Anyone committing a violation of these Regulations that also constitutes a crime shall be held criminally liable pursuant to law.

Chapter V Supplementary Provision

Article 28 These Regulations shall enter into force as of January 1, 2022.

海南自由贸易港知识产权保护条例

Regulations of Hainan Free Trade Port on Intellectual Property Rights Protection

海南自由贸易港知识产权保护条例

（2021 年 12 月 1 日海南省第六届人民代表大会常务委员会第三十一次会议通过）

第一章 总 则

第一条 为了加强知识产权保护，激发创新活力，优化营商环境，打造国际一流的知识产权保护高地，根据《中华人民共和国海南自由贸易港法》的规定，遵循有关法律、行政法规的基本原则，结合海南自由贸易港实际，制定本条例。

第二条 本条例所称知识产权，是指权利人依法就下列客体享有的专有的权利：

（一）作品；

（二）发明、实用新型、外观设计；

（三）商标；

（四）地理标志；

（五）商业秘密；

（六）集成电路布图设计；

（七）植物新品种；

（八）法律规定的其他客体。

第三条 海南自由贸易港开展知识产权保护工作应当遵循全面保护、严格保护、平等保护、依法保护、快速保护、协同保护的原则，对标国际先进标准，创新体制机制，建立制度完备、运转高效的知识产权保护体系。

Regulations of Hainan Free Trade Port on Intellectual Property Rights Protection

(Adopted at the 31st Session of the Standing Committee of the 6th Hainan Provincial People's Congress on December 1, 2021)

Chapter I General Provisions

Article 1 These Regulations are enacted under the Hainan Free Trade Port Law of the People's Republic of China, the basic principles of other laws and regulations, and based on actual circumstances in the Hainan Free Trade Port to improve intellectual property rights protection, encourage innovation, optimize the business environment, and develop a world-class intellectual property rights protection area.

Article 2 Intellectual property rights in these Regulations refer to the proprietary rights of the right holders of the following under law:

(a) works;

(b) inventions, utility models, and designs;

(c) trademarks;

(d) geographical indications;

(e) trade secrets;

(f) integrated circuit layout designs;

(g) new plant varieties; and

(h) other items provided by laws.

Article 3 The Hainan Free Trade Port shall follow the principles of comprehensive, strict, equal, lawful, rapid, and coordinated protection, adopt international advanced standards as benchmarks, innovate the institutions and mechanisms, and create a complete and efficient intellectual property rights protection system.

第四条 县级以上人民政府应当加强知识产权保护工作的组织领导，将知识产权保护工作纳入国民经济和社会发展规划，建立健全知识产权保护考核评价制度。

县级以上人民政府应当建立健全知识产权工作协调机制，研究制定知识产权重大政策，协调解决知识产权工作中的重大问题。

第五条 县级以上人民政府知识产权主管部门（以下简称知识产权主管部门）负责组织实施与统筹协调本区域知识产权保护工作。

作品、发明、实用新型、外观设计、商标、地理标志、商业秘密、集成电路布图设计、植物新品种等知识产权具体管理部门（以下简称知识产权具体管理部门），依法履行各自职责范围内的知识产权保护工作。

发展和改革、工业和信息化、商务、科学技术、财政、公安、司法行政、金融管理、海关等部门，按照各自职责配合做好知识产权保护相关工作。

第六条 县级以上人民政府及有关部门应当加强知识产权法律、法规和知识产权知识宣传教育普及工作，促进全社会尊重和保护知识产权意识的提升。

鼓励新闻媒体和社会公众开展知识产权保护公益宣传，对知识产权违法行为进行舆论监督。

第七条 县级以上人民政府应当综合运用财政、税收、金融、产业、科技、文化、贸易、人才等政策，激励知识产权创造，完善企业为主体、市场为导向的高质量创造机制。

Article 4 The people's governments at or above the county level shall improve intellectual property rights protection organization and administration, integrate intellectual property rights protection into the national economic and social development plan, and create and optimize an intellectual property rights protection review system.

The people's governments at or above the county level shall create and optimize a coordination system for intellectual property rights work, study and issue major intellectual property rights policies, and coordinate and solve major intellectual property rights issues.

Article 5 The intellectual property rights agency of the people's government at or above the county level (hereinafter referred to as "intellectual property rights agency") shall be responsible for organizing the implementation and comprehensive coordination of intellectual property rights protection in their administrative areas.

Intellectual property rights agency responsible for works, inventions, utility models, designs, trademarks, geographical indications, trade secrets, integrated circuit layout design, or new plant varieties (hereinafter referred to as "intellectual property rights agencies") shall conduct intellectual property rights protection within the scope of their authorities and duties as required by law.

The development and reform, industry and information technology, commerce, technology, finance, public security, judicial administration, financial management, customs, and other competent agencies shall cooperate in intellectual property rights protection work based on their specific authorities and duties.

Article 6 The people's governments at or above the county level and their agencies shall improve awareness and education for intellectual property rights laws, regulations, and knowledge, and improve the society's overall awareness of intellectual property rights respect and protection.

News media and the public are encouraged to raise intellectual property rights protection awareness, and facilitate public opinion oversight over intellectual property rights violations.

Article 7 The people's governments at or above the county level shall comprehensively use public funding, taxation, finance, industry, technology, culture, trade, and skilled employee policies to encourage intellectual property rights creation and improve the effective innovation system with businesses as the main entities and the market as the guide.

第八条 支持海南自由贸易港三亚崖州湾科技城建立与国际通行规则相衔接的知识产权制度体系，促进南繁育种和深海科技等领域国际合作，建设具有海南特色、国际认同度较高、知识产权营商环境一流的海南自由贸易港知识产权保护与运用先行区。

第二章 行政保护

第九条 知识产权具体管理部门应当利用互联网、大数据、区块链、云计算和人工智能等现代信息技术，建立知识产权纠纷网上处理机制，运用源头追溯、实时监测、在线识别、网络存证、统计分析、跟踪预警等技术手段，严厉打击知识产权侵权行为。

第十条 鼓励自然人、法人和非法人组织进行作品自愿登记。

版权部门应当加强互联网著作权保护，依法查处网络侵权盗版行为。

第十一条 省知识产权主管部门应当按照国家有关规定，为新一代信息技术、石油化工新材料、现代生物医药、南繁育种、深海科技、航天科技等重点发展产业和战略性新兴产业提供专利优先审查通道。

省知识产权主管部门推动在优势产业集聚区建立知识产权保护中心，开展快速审查、快速确权、快速维权服务，降低知识产权权利人及相关权利人的维权成本。

第十二条 知识产权主管部门应当强化知识产权质量导向，引导自然人、法人和非法人组织依法进行商标注册申请、专利申请，依法查处不以使用为目的的恶意申请商标注册和不以保护创新为目的的非正常专利申请行为。

Article 8 The Hainan Free Trade Port Sanya Yazhou Bay Science and Technology City shall receive support to implement an intellectual property system in line with international rules, encourage international collaboration in plant breeding and deep-sea technology, and develop an internationally recognized intellectual property rights protection and implementation pilot zone in the Hainan Free Trade Port tailored to the Hainan area and a first-class intellectual property business environment.

Chapter II Administrative Protection

Article 9 The designated intellectual property rights agencies shall utilize modern information technology such as the internet, big data, blockchain, cloud computing, and artificial intelligence to create an online intellectual property rights dispute resolution processing platform, and utilize technical means such as source tracking, real-time monitoring, online identification, online registration, statistical analysis, tracking, and early warning to severely crack down on intellectual property rights infringement.

Article 10 Individuals, juristic persons, and unincorporated entities are encouraged to voluntarily register their works.

Copyright administrative offices shall improve online copyright protection and investigate and penalize online infringement and piracy pursuant to law.

Article 11 The provincial intellectual property rights agencies shall provide priority channels of patent review for new-generation key development industries and strategic emerging industries, such as information technology, new petrochemical materials, modern biomedicine, Nanfan plant breeding, deep-sea technology, and aerospace technology.

The provincial intellectual property rights agencies shall encourage the creation of intellectual property rights protection centers in beneficial industrial parks, conduct quick reviews, confirmation, and protection, and reduce protection costs for intellectual property rights and other rights holders.

Article 12 The intellectual property rights agencies shall improve intellectual property rights quality orientation and guide individuals, juristic persons, and unincorporated entities to register trademarks and patents pursuant to law, and investigate and penalize deceptive trademark applications not for real use and unusual patent applications submitted for purposes other than innovation protection.

知识产权代理机构知道或者应当知道委托人存在前款规定的恶意申请商标注册和非正常专利申请行为的，不得接受其委托。

第十三条 在查处侵犯商业秘密行政案件中，商业秘密权利人提供初步证据，证明其已经对所主张的商业秘密采取保密措施，且合理表明商业秘密被侵犯的，知识产权具体管理部门可以要求涉嫌侵权人证明权利人所主张的商业秘密不属于商业秘密或者其不存在侵犯商业秘密的行为。

第十四条 知识产权具体管理部门应当扩大植物新品种权保护范围和保护环节，加大对实质性派生品种的保护，激励育种创新，提升植物新品种保护水平。

第十五条 知识产权具体管理部门应当会同有关部门为中医药、老字号、非物质文化遗产、传统知识、民间文艺和少数民族文化等知识产权的创造和保护提供指导、咨询等服务，引导知识产权相关权利人利用著作权登记、专利申请、商标注册、商业秘密保护等方式和保护规则，维护知识产权权利人合法权益。

第十六条 知识产权具体管理部门应当会同有关部门建立健全新技术、新产业、新业态、新模式知识产权保护规则，提供必要的培训与指导，加强创新成果的知识产权保护。

第十七条 海南自由贸易港依法保护数据收集、存储、加工、使用等活动中形成的知识产权。知识产权具体管理部门建立健全与数据相关的知识产权交易规范，指导市场主体做好数字产品的制造、销售等全产业链知识产权合规经营和侵权风险防范。

Intellectual property rights agencies who know or should have known that their clients have applied for the registration of a deceptive trademark or filed an unusual patent application as provided above shall refuse to work with such clients.

Article 13 If the trade secret holder provides that basic documentation confidentiality measures have been taken to protect trade secrets concerned involved in administrative trade secret infringement investigations and provides reasonable suspicion that the trade secret has been infringed, the competent intellectual property rights agency may require the alleged infringing party to prove that the trade secret concerned is not legally defined as a trade secret or no trade secret infringement has been committed.

Article 14 Intellectual property rights agencies shall expand the coverage and protection processes for new plant variety rights, promote the protection of essentially derived varieties, encourage breeding innovation, and improve the protection of new plant varieties.

Article 15 The designated intellectual property rights agency and other agencies shall provide guidance, advice, and other services for the creation and protection of intellectual property rights related to traditional Chinese medicine, time-honored brands, intangible cultural heritage, traditional knowledge, folk literature and art, and minority cultures, and guide intellectual property rights holders to protect their legal rights through copyright registration, patent applications, trademark registration, trade secret protection, and other applicable methods.

Article 16 The designated intellectual property rights agencies shall create and optimize intellectual property rights protection rules for new technologies, new industries, new business methods, and models, provide the necessary training and guidance, and improve intellectual property rights protection for the innovation-based achievements.

Article 17 The Hainan Free Trade Port shall protect intellectual property rights created through data collection, storage, processing and use pursuant to law. The designated intellectual property rights agencies shall create and optimize standards for intellectual property rights transactions related to data, and guide market entities to conduct effective intellectual property rights compliance and infringement risk prevention throughout the entire industrial chain, such as in the manufacturing and sales of digital products.

第十八条 知识产权具体管理部门、商务部门应当会同贸易促进机构和相关行业组织等，建立健全知识产权涉外风险防控体系和跨境维权援助机制，加大对市场主体境外知识产权维权援助的指导，为市场主体开展贸易、投资等活动及时提供预警和应对服务。

第十九条 省知识产权主管部门应当会同有关部门建立技术调查官制度，配备技术调查官，为专利、植物新品种、集成电路布图设计、技术秘密、计算机软件等行政裁决、行政执法、调解、仲裁、诉讼和维权援助提供专业技术支持。技术调查官受指派或委托参与知识产权案件办理活动，就案件所涉技术问题提出的技术调查意见，作为认定技术事实的参考。

第二十条 海关依照法律、行政法规的规定，加强边境执法与境内执法衔接，在境外与海南自由贸易港进出境环节、全岛封关运作后由海南自由贸易港进入内地环节及其他海关负责监管区域，对与货物有关的专利权、商标专用权、著作权和与著作权有关的权利等知识产权实施保护。

第三章 司法保护

第二十一条 知识产权具体管理部门与公安机关、人民检察院、人民法院应当加强知识产权行政执法与刑事司法衔接，建立健全行政机关和司法机关信息共享、案件移送、协调配合、监督制约、责任追究等工作机制，保证涉嫌知识产权犯罪案件依法及时进入司法程序。

人民法院、人民检察院、公安机关应当依法履行知识产权保护职责，加大知识产权犯罪行为打击力度，重点打击链条式、产业化知识产权犯罪。

Article 18 The designated intellectual property rights agencies and agencies of commerce, together with trade promotion societies and appropriate industry organizations, shall create and optimize a prevention and control system for international intellectual property rights risks and a cross-border rights protection assistance system, improve guidance for market entities to protect their intellectual property rights abroad, and provide prompt warning and response services for market entities to conduct trade and investment activities.

Article 19 Provincial intellectual property rights agencies and other agencies shall set up a system of technical investigation officers and assign them to provide professional technical support for administrative adjudication, administrative law enforcement, mediation, arbitration, litigation, and rights protection assistance in areas such as patents, new plant varieties, integrated circuit layout design, technical secrets, and computer software. Technical investigation officers shall be assigned or authorized to participate in intellectual property rights case trials and submit opinions on the technical issues concerned to serve as references when identifying technical facts.

Article 20 Customs shall improve collaboration between border law enforcement and domestic law enforcement, and protect intellectual property rights, including patent rights for goods, exclusive use of trademarks, copyrights, and other rights related to copyrights, when international goods entering and exiting the Hainan Free Trade Port, goods entering China's mainland via Hainan Free Trade Port after the whole island becomes a free trade port, and in other areas under customs oversight pursuant to laws and administrative regulations.

Chapter III Judicial Protection

Article 21 Intellectual property rights agencies, public security agencies, people's procuratorates, and people's courts shall improve the connection between intellectual property rights administrative law enforcement and criminal procedures, create and optimize working systems for information sharing, case transfer, coordination, oversight and restriction, and accountability between administrative agencies and judicial agencies, and ensure that judicial procedures for cases involving intellectual property rights offenses begin promptly pursuant to law.

The people's courts, people's procuratorates, and public security agencies shall perform their authorities and duties to protect intellectual property rights pursuant to law, intensify the crackdown on intellectual property rights crimes, and focus on cracking down on organized and industrial intellectual property rights crimes.

人民法院、人民检察院、公安机关应当依照有关规定统一知识产权刑事案件的立案、追诉和裁判标准，并向社会公开。

人民法院、人民检察院加强对知识产权纠纷特点和趋势分析，通过发布典型案例、编撰类案办案指南、提出司法建议、检察建议等方式，为市场主体、行政部门、行业协会、科研机构等提供指引。

第二十二条 公安机关应当依法办理知识产权犯罪案件，支持知识产权具体管理部门开展相关行政执法工作，可以根据需要按照有关规定提前介入涉嫌重大犯罪的知识产权行政案件。

第二十三条 人民检察院应当加强知识产权民事、行政、刑事案件法律监督，依法开展知识产权公益诉讼工作。

第二十四条 人民法院应当推进知识产权民事、行政、刑事案件审判“三合一”改革，构建技术调查官、专家陪审员、专家辅助人、技术咨询和鉴定等知识产权多元化技术事实查明机制，健全知识产权纠纷特邀调解制度。

人民法院应当推进知识产权案件诉讼程序繁简分流，强化举证责任分配，鼓励当事人充分利用区块链、电子数据平台等第三方保全证据方式收集、固定证据，提高知识产权案件审判质量和效率。

人民法院应当加大知识产权民事、行政、刑事案件的执行力度，探索知识产权财产性权益的新型执行方法。

第二十五条 人民法院应当完善知识产权侵权损害赔偿制度，综合考虑知识产权市场价值、侵权人主观过错以及侵权行为的持续时间、影响范围、后果严重程度等因素，合理确定赔偿数额；正确适用知识产权惩罚性赔偿制度，加大对重复侵权、故意侵权和规模侵权的惩罚性赔偿，依法惩处严重侵害知识产权行为。

The people's courts, people's procuratorates, and public security agencies shall standardize intellectual property rights criminal case filing, prosecution, and adjudication procedures pursuant to applicable regulations and announce such.

The people's courts and people's procuratorates shall improve analysis of intellectual property rights dispute characteristics and trends, and provide guidance for market entities, administrative agencies, industry associations, and research institutes by publishing typical cases and issuing guidelines for similar cases, or submitting judicial and procuratorial recommendations.

Article 22 Public security agencies shall resolve intellectual property rights crimes pursuant to law, support intellectual property rights agencies performing the related administrative law enforcement, and join intellectual property rights administrative cases involving major crimes early on a case-by-case basis pursuant to applicable law.

Article 23 The people's procuratorates shall strengthen the legal oversight over civil, administrative, and criminal cases of intellectual property rights, and carry out public interest litigation of intellectual property rights pursuant to law.

Article 24 The people's courts shall encourage cross-functional integration between civil, administrative, and criminal intellectual property rights case trials, and develop an alternative means to accomplish technical fact-finding for intellectual property rights, such as technical investigators, expert assessors, expert assistants, technical advice and appraisal, and improve the intellectual property rights dispute court-appointed mediation.

The people's courts shall use different procedures for complex and simple intellectual property rights litigation, improve the allocation of the burden of proof, and encourage the parties involved to make full use of blockchain, electronic data platforms, and other third party evidence preservation methods to collect and provide reliable evidence and improve intellectual property rights case trial quality and efficiency.

The people's courts shall improve the enforcement of civil, administrative, and criminal intellectual property rights judgments and explore new enforcement methods for intellectual property rights involving property and other rights.

Article 25 The people's court shall improve the indemnification system for damages caused by intellectual property rights infringement, comprehensively consider intellectual property rights market value, culpable state of mind, duration, the extent of influence, severity, and other factors, and reasonably determine the indemnification amount; and correctly implement a punitive damages system for intellectual property rights, increase punitive damages for repeat infringements, intentional infringements, and mass tort, and penalize material intellectual property rights infringements pursuant to law.

第二十六条　人民法院依法公正审理涉外知识产权案件，平等保护中外权利人合法权益，妥善处理与国际贸易有关的重大知识产权纠纷，依法妥善处理国际平行诉讼，确保案件裁判符合相关国际公约和国际惯例，促进国际贸易合作。

人民法院应当推进国际司法协助和交流合作，简化跨境文书送达、调查取证等程序，探索在互惠基础上相互承认与执行外国法院民商事判决的途径和方式。

第二十七条　海南自由贸易港知识产权法院应当建立与海南自由贸易港知识产权保护相适应的案件管辖制度和协调机制，加强对植物新品种、关键核心技术、重点领域、新兴产业等知识产权司法保护。

第二十八条　省知识产权主管部门应当会同人民法院、仲裁机构，加强知识产权确权与知识产权侵权纠纷处理程序的协调，建立健全知识产权无效宣告程序与知识产权侵权纠纷行政裁决、民事侵权诉讼、仲裁程序的衔接机制。

第四章　社会共治

第二十九条　就不相同或者不相类似商品或服务使用的未注册商标是复制、摹仿或者翻译他人未在国内注册的驰名商标，误导公众，致使该驰名商标持有人的利益可能受到损害的，在海南自由贸易港内禁止使用。

第三十条　使用注册商标的商品，经商标注册人或者其许可使用注册商标的单位、个人售出后，除该商品使用有关注册商标会对该注册商标的显著特征或者声誉造成损害的以外，任何单位或者个人可以在海南自由贸易港内进口、销售、使用该商品。

Article 26 The people's courts shall adjudicate cases involving foreign intellectual property rights fairly pursuant to law, equally protect Chinese and foreign right holder legal rights, properly resolve major international trade intellectual property rights disputes, properly manage international parallel litigation pursuant to law, ensure court opinions and decisions comply with applicable international conventions and international practices and improve international trade collaboration.

The people's courts shall encourage international judicial assistance, exchanges, and collaboration, simplify cross-border document service procedures, investigation, and evidence collection, and encourage mutual recognition and enforcement of reciprocal civil and commercial judgments by foreign courts.

Article 27 The Hainan Free Trade Port Intellectual Property Rights Court shall align the jurisdiction and coordination systems with intellectual property rights protection in the Hainan Free Trade Port and enhance judicial protection of intellectual property rights such as new plant varieties, and core technologies, key fields, and emerging industries.

Article 28 Provincial intellectual property rights agencies, people's courts, and arbitration organizations shall strengthen coordination between the confirmation of intellectual property rights and intellectual property rights infringement dispute resolution, and create and optimize a connection system between the procedures of invalidation of intellectual property rights and administrative adjudication, civil infringement litigation and arbitration procedures of intellectual property rights infringement disputes.

Chapter IV Social Co-governance

Article 29 Unregistered trademarks created by copying, imitating, or translating other well-known trademarks not registered in China that may mislead the public and infringe upon the rights of the well-known trademark holders, regardless of whether used for the same or different types of goods or services, shall be prohibited in the Hainan Free Trade Port.

Article 30 Any entity or individual may import, sell or use goods with registered trademarks purchased from the trademark registrar or entities or individuals authorized by the trademark registrar to use such registered trademarks in Hainan Free Trade Port unless such goods with registered trademarks may infringe upon the distinctive features or harm the reputation of the registered trademarks.

允许境外注册商标商品在海南自由贸易港内加工并直接出口，但因此容易导致商品来源混淆或者误导公众的除外。

第三十一条 禁止下列侵犯地理标志的行为：

（一）通过使用地理标志或者产品描述，使公众误认为产品来自获得保护的地理标志产地范围的；

（二）在产地范围之外的相同或者类似产品上使用获得保护的地理标志或其意译、音译、字译，或者同时使用“类”“型”“式”“仿”等表述的；

（三）未经批准擅自在产品上使用地理标志专用标志的；

（四）在产品上使用与地理标志专用标志相似的标志，使公众误以为是地理标志专用标志的；

（五）销售本条第（一）项至第（四）项侵犯地理标志的产品的；

（六）法律、法规规定的其他行为。

第三十二条 海南自由贸易港举办展览、交易等展会活动，展会举办单位应当要求参展方提交未侵犯他人知识产权的合规性书面承诺或者知识产权相关证明文件。未按照要求提交的，展会举办单位不得允许其参加展会相关活动。

展会举办单位可以根据展会规模、期限等情况，自行或者与仲裁机构、行业组织、知识产权服务机构等设立展会知识产权纠纷处理机构。

参展项目被权利人递交书面材料投诉侵权的，展会举办单位应当立即要求参展方在限定时间内提供未侵权证明。参展方未提供的，展会举办单位应当责令参展方撤出该参展项目；不能撤出项目的，应当采取遮盖等方式处理。

Goods with overseas registered trademarks may be processed and exported directly in Hainan Free Trade Port unless the origin of such goods is misleading or the goods are likely to mislead the public.

Article 31 The following infringements against geographical indications are prohibited:

(a) utilizing geographical indications or product descriptions to mislead the public into believing that the products originate from areas with protected geographical indications;

(b) utilizing protected geographical indications or their loose translation, transliteration, or direct translation, or expressions such as *lei* (class), *xing* (type), *shi* (mode), *fang* (pattern) on the same or similar products outside their place of origin;

(c) utilizing exclusive geographical indication labels on products without approval;

(d) utilizing labels similar to those used for geographical indications on products to mislead the public to believe that they are specific geographical indication labels;

(e) selling products that infringe upon geographical indications as provided in Paragraphs (a) through (d) of this Article; or

(f) other acts provided by laws and regulations.

Article 32 Organizers of exhibitions, trade shows, and other similar activities in the Hainan Free Trade Port shall require participants to submit a written commitment or similar documents stating that they do not infringe upon third party intellectual property rights, and shall not allow such participants to participate in the exhibition or other exhibits if such documents are not submitted as required.

The exhibition organizer may set up a specific intellectual property rights dispute resolution institution either independently or together with arbitration, industry association, or intellectual property service institutes based on the scale and duration of the exhibitions.

Exhibition organizers shall immediately require participants to submit materials proving non-infringement within a specified time should rights holders submit written complaints claiming said participants infringed upon their rights. The exhibition organizer shall require the participant to withdraw from the exhibition if they fail to submit such materials. If the project cannot be removed, it shall be covered or hidden in other ways.

知识产权具体管理部门认定参展方侵权行为成立的，应当通知展会举办单位责令参展方立即停止侵权行为，依法予以处理。

第三十三条 电子商务平台经营者应当建立知识产权保护内部管理制度和侵权投诉快速处理机制，配合知识产权具体管理部门处理知识产权纠纷和查处违法行为，及时采取删除、屏蔽、断开链接、终止交易和服务等必要措施，制止平台内经营者的侵权行为或者违法行为，维护知识产权权利人合法权益。

第三十四条 自然人、法人和非法人组织参加政府投资项目、政府采购和招标投标等活动，应当向有关主管部门提交不存在侵犯他人知识产权的书面承诺，并明确违背承诺的责任。

鼓励自然人、法人和非法人组织在书面合同中约定知识产权合规性承诺的内容以及相应的违约责任。

第三十五条 知识产权具体管理部门对知识产权纠纷作出行政裁决前，可以根据当事人自愿的原则，先行调解。

支持人民调解、商事调解或者其他具有调解职能的组织依法调解知识产权侵权纠纷。

知识产权侵权纠纷经调解组织调解达成协议的，双方当事人可以向有管辖权的人民法院申请司法确认。

第三十六条 鼓励当事人运用仲裁方式解决知识产权纠纷。对可能进入中国市场的过境货物涉嫌侵犯知识产权的，争议相关当事人可以约定临时仲裁。

海南自由贸易港仲裁机构应当加强知识产权纠纷仲裁专业化建设，广泛吸纳知识产权专业人才参与仲裁工作。

Intellectual property rights agencies shall notify the exhibition organizer to require the participant to immediately cease the infringement and resolve it pursuant to law should the agencies confirm the alleged infringement.

Article 33 E-commerce platform operators shall create an internal intellectual property rights protection management system and a quick response system for infringement complaints, cooperate with the intellectual property rights competent agencies managing intellectual property rights disputes and investigating illegal acts, and promptly take the necessary action, such as deleting, blocking, unlinking, and terminating transactions and services to stop the infringement or violations committed by operators in the platform and protect the intellectual property rights owners' legal rights.

Article 34 Where individuals, juristic persons, or unincorporated entities participate in government investment projects, government procurement, bidding, or other similar activities, they shall submit a written commitment to competent agencies warranting that there is no infringement of third party intellectual property rights and specify liability for the violation of the commitment.

Individuals, juristic persons, and unincorporated entities shall be encouraged to specify the contents of the intellectual property rights commitments and the applicable breach of contract liability in written contracts.

Article 35 The designated intellectual property rights agencies may first conduct a mediation based on the principle of mutual willingness before delivering an administrative ruling on intellectual property rights disputes.

The people's mediation, commercial mediation, or other mediation organizations shall receive support to mediate intellectual property rights infringement disputes pursuant to law.

Either party may request approval from a competent people's court if an intellectual property rights infringement dispute is resolved through mediation by a mediation organization.

Article 36 The parties involved are encouraged to resolve intellectual property rights disputes through arbitration and may agree to an ad hoc arbitration if transit goods that may enter the Chinese market are alleged to infringe on intellectual property rights.

The Hainan Free Trade Port arbitration organizations shall improve intellectual property rights dispute arbitration professional expertise, and extensively include intellectual property rights professionals in arbitration.

支持境外知名仲裁机构及争议解决机构在海南自由贸易港依法开展知识产权纠纷仲裁业务。支持海南自由贸易港仲裁机构与境外知名仲裁机构及争议解决机构开展知识产权纠纷仲裁业务合作。

第三十七条 鼓励和支持公证机构创新公证证明和公证服务方式，依托电子签名、数据加密、区块链等技术，提供知识产权创新创造、运用流转、融资增信、证据保全、权利救济等公证服务。

在海南自由贸易港设立的可以办理涉外公证业务的公证机构，在海南自由贸易港范围内办理知识产权涉外公证业务，不受执业区域限制。

鼓励公证机构开展异地协作，为跨区域知识产权保护提供公证服务。

第三十八条 鼓励知识产权相关服务机构和人员，运用专业知识或者大数据分析技术，对知识产权纠纷事实认定、法律依据、处理结果和损害赔偿额计算等进行中立预判或者评估，为当事人快速解决纠纷提供指引和参考。

第三十九条 知识产权相关行业组织应当加强自律，建立健全知识产权行业服务标准和维权保护机制，配合知识产权具体管理部门开展行政执法工作，协助处理和调解知识产权纠纷，维护会员合法权益。

第五章 运用与服务

第四十条 省知识产权主管部门应当建立知识产权综合服务平台，加强知识产权信息化、智能化建设。

International renowned arbitration and dispute resolution organizations shall receive support to conduct intellectual property rights dispute arbitration in the Hainan Free Trade Port pursuant to law, and arbitration organizations of the Hainan Free Trade Port shall receive support to conduct intellectual property rights dispute arbitration in collaboration with internationally renowned arbitration and dispute resolution organizations.

Article 37 Notary offices shall be encouraged and receive support to create innovative notarial certification and notarial services and to rely on technology such as electronic signatures, data encryption, and blockchain to provide notarial services such as intellectual property rights innovation and creation, implementation, and circulation, finance and credit support, evidence preservation, and rights remedies.

Hainan Free Trade Port notary offices eligible to manage notarization involving foreign intellectual property rights may manage such within the Hainan Free Trade Port, and their operations are not restricted by area.

Notary offices shall be encouraged to collaborate in different areas and provide notarial services for cross-regional intellectual property rights protection.

Article 38 Intellectual property rights service providers and their employees are encouraged to use professional knowledge or big data analysis technology to conduct neutral intellectual property rights dispute prejudgments or evaluations on the fact-finding, legal basis, resolution results, and calculation of damages to provide guidance and reference for the parties involved to quickly resolve disputes.

Article 39 Intellectual property rights industry organizations shall encourage self-discipline, implement and optimize intellectual property rights industry service standards and rights protection systems, cooperate with competent intellectual property rights agencies to carry out administrative law enforcement, assist in resolving and mediating intellectual property rights disputes, and protect their members' legal rights.

Chapter V Application and Service

Article 40 Provincial intellectual property rights agencies shall create a comprehensive intellectual property rights service platform and improve information technology and digitization of intellectual property rights work.

知识产权具体管理部门应当依托知识产权综合服务平台，健全知识产权服务体系，为市场主体和社会公众提供知识产权政策指导、检索查询、维权援助等公共服务。

第四十一条　省知识产权主管部门应当建立专利导航制度。发展和改革、科学技术、工业和信息化、商务等相关部门应当对区域发展规划、重大产业规划、政府投资的重大经济科技项目组织开展专利导航，防范知识产权风险。

鼓励市场主体运用专利导航，提高创新发展决策的精准度和科学性。

第四十二条　单位可以依法处置其职务创新成果的知识产权，促进相关成果的实施和运用。被授予知识产权的单位可以采取股权、期权、分红等产权激励方式，使创新成果完成人合理分享创新收益。

规范和完善高等院校、科研机构等单位的知识产权项目管理制度，建立健全知识产权转移转化机制，鼓励建立专业化知识产权转移转化机构，促进知识产权成果实施和运用。

第四十三条　鼓励和支持高等院校、科研机构、知识产权服务机构、行业组织和企业事业单位等建立知识产权联盟，开展知识产权研究、交流合作、联合维权和协作运用，实施知识产权资源共享，推进知识产权与产业发展深度融合。

第四十四条　支持金融机构创新知识产权质押融资、融资租赁、信托等金融服务模式，完善知识产权融资风险控制和质押财产处置机制，构建知识产权多元化融资模式。

The designated intellectual property rights agency shall improve the intellectual property rights service system and provide public services such as policy guidance, information inquiry, and rights protection assistance for market entities and the public based on the comprehensive intellectual property rights service platform.

Article 41 Provincial intellectual property rights agencies shall create a patent mapping system. The development and reform, technology, industry and information technology, commerce, and other agencies shall organize patent mapping for regional development planning, major industrial planning, and major economic and technological projects receiving government investment to prevent intellectual property rights risks.

Market entities shall be encouraged to implement patent mapping to achieve accurate and science-based innovations and development.

Article 42 Entities may dispose the intellectual property rights from the service information pursuant to law and encourage the implementation and use of related achievements. Entities granted intellectual property rights may adopt equity, options, dividends, and other property rights incentives to reasonably share innovation benefits with those who create them.

The higher learning institutes, research institutions, and other intellectual property rights entities shall standardize and improve the system for intellectual property rights projects management, create and optimize a system for intellectual property rights assignment and transformation, and be encouraged to create specialized intellectual property rights assignment and transformation institutes to promote the implementation and use of intellectual property rights achievements.

Article 43 The higher learning institutions, research institutions, intellectual property rights service providers, industry organizations, businesses, and public institutions shall be encouraged and supported to set up intellectual property rights alliances, conduct intellectual property rights research, exchanges and collaboration, joint rights protection, and coordinated intellectual property rights implementation to share intellectual property rights resources and encourage the deep integration of intellectual property rights and industrial development.

Article 44 A diversified intellectual property rights financing model shall be created to support financial institutes to innovate financial service models such as intellectual property rights pledge financing, financial leases, and trust, and improve intellectual property rights finance risk control and pledged assets disposal systems.

鼓励和支持保险机构开展知识产权境外侵权责任险、专利执行险、专利被侵权损失险等保险业务。

外汇管理部门应当会同知识产权具体管理部门推行跨境知识产权贸易、投融资业务的外汇自由化、便利化政策。

第四十五条 在海南自由贸易港内转让、许可使用知识产权，从事技术开发及相关技术咨询、技术服务等取得的收入，依法享受税收优惠。

第四十六条 推动建设海南国际知识产权交易所，在知识产权转让、运用和税收政策等方面开展制度创新，规范探索知识产权证券化，完善知识产权信用担保机制。

第四十七条 支持知识产权服务业集聚发展，引进知识产权高端服务机构。支持有条件的海南自由贸易港重点园区根据需要建设综合性知识产权运营服务平台，培育国际化、市场化、专业化的知识产权服务机构。

鼓励知识产权评估服务机构开发针对不同应用场景的知识产权评估工具，围绕创新主体、市场主体的转让许可、投资融资等需求，提供规范、便捷的知识产权评估服务。

第四十八条 海南自由贸易港应当拓宽知识产权对外合作交流渠道，加强与世界知识产权组织、国际植物新品种保护联盟等国际组织的合作交流，推动“一带一路”知识产权经济协作发展，构建与国际接轨的知识产权保护体系。

鼓励和支持社会组织依法开展知识产权保护国际交流合作。

The insurance institutions shall be encouraged and receive support to provide overseas intellectual property rights infringement liability insurance, patent execution insurance, and patent infringement loss insurance services.

Foreign exchange agencies and the designated intellectual property rights agencies shall implement foreign exchange liberalization and facilitation policies for cross-border intellectual property rights trading, investment, and financing.

Article 45 Any income arising out of the assignment or licensing of intellectual property rights and involvement in technology development and technical consultation and technical services in the Hainan Free Trade Port shall be entitled to preferential tax policies pursuant to law.

Article 46 The development of the Hainan International Intellectual Property Rights Exchange shall be encouraged to carry out institutional intellectual property rights assignment, implementation and tax policy innovation, standardize intellectual property rights securitization exploration and improve the intellectual property rights credit guarantee system.

Article 47 The consolidation and development of intellectual property rights services and high-end intellectual property rights services shall receive support and be implemented. Eligible Hainan Free Trade Port main zones shall receive support to develop comprehensive intellectual property rights operation service platforms on a case-by-case basis, and develop international, market-oriented, and specialized intellectual property rights service providers.

Intellectual property rights review service providers are encouraged to develop intellectual property rights review toolkits for different use cases, and provide standardized and easy intellectual property rights review services to meet innovator and market entity needs, such as license assignment and investment financing.

Article 48 The Hainan Free Trade Port shall create more channels for foreign intellectual property rights collaboration and exchange, improve collaboration and exchange with international organizations such as the World Intellectual Property Organization and International Union for the Protection of New Plant Varieties, improve the intellectual property rights collaboration and development among countries included in the Belt and Road Initiative, and develop an intellectual property rights protection system in line with international standards.

Private organizations are encouraged and receive support to conduct international intellectual property rights exchanges and collaboration pursuant to law.

第六章 监督管理

第四十九条 县级以上人民政府应当根据法律、法规规定并结合相关部门职责范围，建立由知识产权具体管理部门牵头，旅游和文化、公安、海关、综合执法等相关部门参与的联合执法机制，健全跨部门、跨区域知识产权行政执法联动响应与协作制度，实现违法线索互联、监管标准互通、处理结果互认。

第五十条 权利人或者利害关系人投诉知识产权侵权行为，知识产权具体管理部门对有证据证明存在侵权事实，如不及时制止将使权利人或者利害关系人合法权益受到难以弥补的损害的，经权利人或者利害关系人申请，可以先行发布禁令，责令涉嫌侵权人立即停止涉嫌侵权行为，并依法处理。

发布禁令前，可以要求权利人或者利害关系人提供适当担保。经调查，侵权行为不成立的，应当及时解除禁令。权利人或者利害关系人申请有错误的，应当赔偿被申请人因停止有关行为所遭受的损失。

涉嫌侵权人对禁令不服的，可以依法申请行政复议或者提请行政诉讼。

第五十一条 知识产权具体管理部门或者人民法院作出知识产权侵权行为成立的决定或者判决生效后，同一侵权行为人就同一知识产权再次实施相同类型侵权行为，经权利人或者利害关系人请求，知识产权具体管理部门调查属实的，可以直接责令侵权人立即停止侵权行为，并依法处理。

Chapter VI Oversight and Administration

Article 49 The people's governments at or above the county level and the administrative agencies shall create establish a joint law enforcement system led by intellectual property rights agencies as required by law and based on their authorities and duties, and shall involve other administrative agencies such as tourism and culture, public security, customs, and comprehensive law enforcement agencies and improve the intellectual property rights administrative law enforcement inter-agency and cross-regional collaborative response to achieve sharing of violation leads, regulatory standards, and resolution result recognition.

Article 50 Upon the request of a rights holder or stakeholder, intellectual property rights agencies may issue an injunction to order alleged infringers to immediately cease the alleged infringement and resolve it pursuant to law where rights holders or stakeholders claim intellectual property rights infringement and provide documentation of such, and it would cause the rights holder or stakeholder to suffer irreparable damage to their legal rights if the infringement cannot be ceased in a timely manner.

Before issuing an injunction, the rights holder or stakeholder may be required to provide an appropriate guarantee. The injunction shall be promptly dismissed if the infringement cannot be verified after investigation. If the requester (the rights holder or stakeholder) is found to be at fault, it shall indemnify the respondent against any loss(es) suffered due to the ceased acts.

The alleged infringer may request administrative review or file an administrative suit pursuant to law if they feel wronged by the injunction.

Article 51 The designated intellectual property rights agency may directly require the infringer to immediately cease their infringement and manage it pursuant to law upon the request of the rights holder or stakeholder should the infringer commit the same infringement of the same intellectual property rights after the intellectual property rights agency or the people's court makes a decision or judgment confirming the intellectual property rights infringement.

第五十二条 知识产权具体管理部门应当归集自然人、法人和非法人组织的知识产权失信行为信息，依法纳入信用档案，根据信用风险分类结果实施差异化监管措施。

自然人、法人和非法人组织有下列失信行为之一的，应当将其列入严重失信主体名单：

（一）故意侵犯他人知识产权，构成犯罪的；

（二）故意侵犯他人知识产权或者提交非正常专利申请、恶意商标注册申请损害公共利益，性质恶劣、情节严重、社会危害较大，受到主管部门较重行政处罚的；

（三）在人民法院或者行政机关作出知识产权侵权行为成立的判决或者决定后，有履行能力但拒不履行、逃避执行的；

（四）法律、法规和国家规定应当列入知识产权严重失信主体名单的其他行为。

第五十三条 对列入知识产权严重失信主体名单的失信主体，应当实施下列惩戒措施：

（一）禁止或者限制其承接政府投资项目、参加政府招标投标；

（二）禁止或者限制其享受有关费用减免、政府资金扶持等优惠政策；

（三）取消其进入知识产权专利优先审查、快速授权、快速维权通道资格；

（四）取消其参加政府知识产权表彰评比资格；

（五）法律、法规和国家规定的其他惩戒措施。

Article 52 Intellectual property rights agencies shall collect information on intellectual property rights misuse by individuals, juristic persons, and unincorporated entities, legally include it in their credit records and provide specific oversight based on the credit risk classification.

Individuals, juristic persons, or unincorporated entities committing any of the following acts shall be added to the entity blacklist:

(a) intentionally infringing third party intellectual property rights, thus constituting a crime;

(b) intentionally infringing upon the intellectual property rights of others, filing an abnormal patent application, or maliciously registering a trademark is subject to heavier administrative punishment by the competent agency in case that it is against the public interest, involves grave risks, and causes significant social harm;

(c) refusing to perform or avoiding enforcement after a people's court has made an judgment or an administrative agency has made a decision on the intellectual property rights infringement, despite having the ability to comply; or

(d) other acts that should be included in the entity blacklist provided by laws, regulations and national rules.

Article 53 The following disciplinary action shall be taken against material violations committed by those in the entity blacklist:

(a) ban or restriction on performing government investment projects or participating in government bids;

(b) ban or restriction on benefiting from preferential policies such as fee reductions or government funding;

(c) removal of eligibility for prioritized patent protection review, quick authorization, and fast track;

(d) removal of eligibility to participate in intellectual property rights awards given by governments; and

(e) other disciplinary action provided by laws, regulations and state provisions.

第七章　法律责任

第五十四条　侵权人因侵犯知识产权受到罚款处罚后，自行政处罚决定书生效之日起五年内再次实施同类违法行为的，知识产权具体管理部门可以按照有关法律、法规规定的相应罚款数额予以双倍处罚。

第五十五条　申请人恶意申请商标注册的，由申请人所在地或者违法行为发生地县级以上知识产权具体管理部门给予警告，有违法所得的，可以处违法所得五倍最高不超过五万元的罚款；没有违法所得的，可以处三万元以下的罚款。

第五十六条　对侵犯商业秘密的行为，除依据《中华人民共和国反不正当竞争法》的规定处理外，知识产权具体管理部门应当责令侵权人返还或者销毁载有商业秘密的图纸、软件或者其他有关载体，不得继续披露、使用或者允许他人使用商业秘密。

对侵权人利用权利人的商业秘密生产的产品，尚未销售的，知识产权具体管理部门应当监督侵权人销毁，但是权利人同意收购或者同意侵权人继续销售的除外。

第五十七条　违反本条例第三十一条规定，由违法行为发生地县级以上知识产权具体管理部门责令立即停止侵权行为，没收、销毁侵权产品和伪造地理标志专用标志的工具，违法经营额五万元以上的，可以处违法经营额五倍以下的罚款；没有违法经营额或者违法经营额不足五万元的，可以处二十五万元以下的罚款。

销售不知道是侵犯地理标志的产品，能证明该产品是自己合法取得并说明提供者的，由知识产权具体管理部门责令停止销售。

Chapter VII Legal Liability

Article 54 The designated intellectual property rights agency may double the amount of penalty provided by applicable law if the infringer commits a similar infringement within 5 years of the effective date of the administrative penalty decision and has been penalized once.

Article 55 If an applicant applies for trademark registration in bad faith, the intellectual property rights agency at or above the county level where the applicant is located or where the violation occurs shall issue a warning. Moreover, a penalty equal to five times the amount of any illegal income generated but not more than 50,000 Yuan may be imposed, otherwise, a maximum 30,000 Yuan penalty may be imposed.

Article 56 The designated intellectual property rights agency shall require infringers to return or destroy any drawings, software, or other media containing trade secrets, and shall not continue to disclose, use, or allow others to use such trade secrets unless the infringement involves trade secrets covered by the Anti-Unfair Competition Law.

The designated intellectual property rights agency shall oversee the destruction of any products produced by the infringer using trade secrets belonging to the rights holder that have not yet been sold unless the rights holder agrees to purchase such products or the rights holder authorizes the infringer to sell them.

Article 57 The designated intellectual property rights agency at or above the county level where the violation occurs shall require anyone who violates Article 31 of these Regulations to immediately cease the infringement, confiscate, and destroy the infringing products, as well as any tools used to forge specific geographical indications. A penalty of less than five times the income obtained through illegal business shall be imposed if the income generated exceeds 50,000 Yuan. A penalty of less than 250,000 Yuan may be imposed if no income is earned from the illegal business or less than 50,000 Yuan is earned.

Intellectual property rights agencies shall order sales to be stopped if the infringer is not aware that the product sold or to be sold infringes upon geographical indications and can prove that the product was legally obtained, and is able to indicate the supplier.

第五十八条 展会举办单位违反本条例第三十二条第一款、第三款规定，不履行管理义务的，由违法行为发生地县级以上知识产权主管部门责令改正，可以处三万元以上十万元以下的罚款。

第五十九条 涉嫌侵权人违反本条例第五十条第一款规定，拒不执行禁令停止涉嫌侵权行为，经认定构成侵权的，由发布禁令的知识产权具体管理部门按照有关法律、法规规定的相应罚款数额予以双倍处罚。

第六十条 除法律、法规另有规定外，知识产权侵权行为违法经营额按照下列方法计算：

（一）侵权产品已经销售的，按照实际销售价格计算；

（二）侵权产品尚未销售的，按照已经销售的同类产品的实际销售价格或者标示价格从高计算；

（三）没有实际销售价格或者标示价格的，或者标示价格明显与产品价值不符的，按照与侵权产品相同或者相似的同类产品的市场中间价格计算；

（四）侵权产品只在境外销售的，按照离岸价格计算。无法查明离岸价格的，可以参考同类合格产品的国际市场中间价格或者国内市场中间价格计算；

（五）多次实施侵权行为且未经行政处理的，其违法经营额应当累计计算；

（六）违法经营额应当扣除已经依法缴纳的税费，但不扣除实施该侵权行为过程中实际支出的合法成本；

（七）法律、法规规定的其他能够合理计算侵权产品价格的方法。

Article 58 If an exhibition organizer violates Paragraph 1 or 3 of Article 32 of these Regulations and fails to fulfill its management obligations, competent intellectual property rights agencies at or above the county level in the place where the violation takes place shall require the organizer to make corrections and may impose a penalty of not less than 30,000 Yuan and not more than 100,000 Yuan.

Article 59 If infringers who allegedly violate Paragraph 1 of Article 50 of these Regulations do not comply with injunctions to stop the alleged infringements, the designated intellectual property rights agencies issuing injunctions may double the amount of penalty provided by applicable laws and regulations once the infringements are confirmed.

Article 60 Unless otherwise provided by laws and regulations, income obtained through intellectual property rights infringement shall be calculated according to the following methods:

(a) the actual selling price if the infringing product has been sold;

(b) the higher of the actual selling price or market price of similar products already sold if the infringing product has not yet been sold;

(c) the average market price of similar products equal to or similar to the infringing products if no actual selling or market price can be found or if the market price clearly does not match the product value;

(d) the FOB price if the infringing products are only sold overseas, or the average international or domestic market price of similar eligible products if the FOB price cannot be determined;

(e) the total income earned from the illegal business if the infringement has been committed repeatedly with no administrative penalty;

(f) taxes and fees already paid pursuant to law shall be deducted from the total illegal business income, but legal costs actually incurred during the infringement process shall not be deducted; and

(g) other methods to reasonably calculate the price of the infringing products as provided by laws and regulations.

第六十一条 违反本条例规定，本条例未设定处罚而法律、法规另有处罚规定的，从其规定。

违反本条例规定的行为，依法决定由市、县、自治县综合行政执法机构实施处罚的，从其规定。

省负责专利执法的部门可以根据需要，委托具有专利执法条件的市、县、自治县综合行政执法机构实施专利行政处罚。

第八章 附 则

第六十二条 本条例自 2022 年 1 月 1 日起施行。

Article 61 Other laws and regulations shall control if they provide penalties for the violation of these Regulations.

Other laws shall control if they provide that comprehensive administrative law enforcement agencies of cities, counties, and autonomous counties must enforce the penalties for violations of these Regulations.

The provincial agency responsible for patent law enforcement may, as the case may be, authorize the comprehensive law enforcement agencies of cities, counties, and autonomous counties eligible for patent law enforcement to enforce administrative penalties for patent violations.

Chapter VIII Supplementary Provision

Article 62 These Regulations shall enter into force as of January 1, 2022.

[illegible] shall control [illegible] provide penalties for the [illegible]

[illegible]

[illegible]

海南自由贸易港反消费欺诈规定

Provisions of Hainan Free Trade Port on Deceptive Trade Practices

海南自由贸易港反消费欺诈规定

（2021年9月29日海南省第六届人民代表大会常务委员会第三十次会议通过）

第一条 为严厉打击消费欺诈行为，维护市场秩序，保护消费者合法权益，优化营商环境，遵循《中华人民共和国消费者权益保护法》等法律、法规的基本原则，结合海南自由贸易港实际，制定本规定。

第二条 经营者为消费者生活消费提供其生产、销售的商品或者服务时，采取故意告知消费者虚假情况或者隐瞒真实情况等手段损害消费者合法权益的行为，适用本规定。

第三条 经营者向消费者提供商品或者服务的质量、性能、用途、有效期限等信息，应当真实、全面，不得作虚假或者引人误解的宣传。

经营者应当在经营场所的醒目位置设立提示牌，对海鲜、水果、旅游特产等特色产品的品种、价格及季节性特征进行介绍并作出消费提示。

鼓励经营者在国家规定的无理由退货方式、期限、范围外，作出更有利于消费者的退货承诺。

第四条 交易市场开办者应当加强对本交易市场内经营者的规范管理，审查入场经营者的市场主体登记证明，与入场经营者签订反消费欺诈承诺书，定期对入场经营者进行检查，发现入场经营者有违反本规定行为的，应当及时制止并报告所在地市、县、自治县人民政府市场监督管理部门。

Provisions of Hainan Free Trade Port on Deceptive Trade Practices

(Adopted at the 30th Session of the Standing Committee of the 6th Hainan Provincial People's Congress on September 29, 2021)

Article 1 These Provisions are enacted based on the basic principles of the Law of the People's Republic of China on the Consumers' Rights Protection and other laws and regulations, and based on actual circumstances in the Hainan Free Trade Port to crack down on deceptive trade practices, maintain market order, protect consumer rights and interests, and optimize the business environment.

Article 2 These Provisions shall apply where business operators provide products or services that they produce or sell for consumer daily use and intentionally falsify information to mislead consumers or conceal the truth to the detriment of consumer rights.

Article 3 Product or service quality, performance, utilization, or expiration information provided by business operators to consumers shall be true and comprehensive, and no falsified or misleading advertisements shall be made.

Business operators shall set up notice boards in prominent places throughout their premises to display the varieties, prices, and seasonal characteristics of specialty products such as seafood, fruits, and specialties for tourists, and provide consumption tips.

Business operators are encouraged to create warranty policies beneficial to consumers to return products for any reason and that exceed legal requirements for time limits and type of product.

Article 4 Market operators shall improve the regulation of business operators, review business operator registration certificates, sign written commitments against deceptive trade practices with business operators, regularly inspect business operators, and promptly stop any business operators in violation of these Provisions and report them to the local municipal, county, or autonomous county people's government market regulation agencies.

集贸市场开办者应当统一配置供消费者称量所购商品份量是否准确的公平秤，每个独立销售区域的设置数量不少于一台。

本条第一款所称交易市场开办者，包括在海南自由贸易港设立的电子商务平台经营者。

第五条 县级以上人民政府应当加强对反消费欺诈工作的领导，加强市场监管智能化建设，采取措施制止消费欺诈行为，营造安全放心的消费环境。

县级以上人民政府应当建立反消费欺诈工作协调机制，由市场监督管理部门会同旅游文化、商务、公安等有关部门开展反消费欺诈联合执法、宣传和监督检查工作，及时查处消费欺诈行为。

第六条 消费者委员会和其他消费者组织依法对经营者提供商品或者服务进行社会监督，适时发布消费预警，保护消费者合法权益，倡导消费者理性消费。

有关行业组织应当加强行业自律，建立健全行业规范，推动行业诚信建设，引导、督促本行业经营者依法经营。

新闻媒体应当做好维护消费者合法权益的宣传工作，对消费欺诈行为进行舆论监督。

第七条 任何单位和个人可以向县级以上人民政府市场监督管理等有关部门投诉、举报消费欺诈行为。有关部门接到投诉、举报后应当按照有关规定及时处理，将处理结果告知投诉、举报人，并依法为投诉、举报人保密。

Farmers' market operators shall provide fair scales for consumers to accurately weigh their purchased goods, and each independent sales area shall have at least one fair scale.

The market operators referred to in Paragraph 1 of this Article include e-commerce platform operators incorporated in the Free Trade Port.

Article 5 People's governments at or above the county level shall improve deceptive trade practice prevention administration, improve electronic market oversight, and take action to stop deceptive trade practices to create a safe and secure consumption environment.

People's governments at or above the county level shall create a deceptive trade practice prevention coordination system, and the market regulation agency shall collaborate with the appropriate tourism and culture, commerce, and public security agencies to conduct joint deceptive trade practice prevention law enforcement, awareness, oversight, and inspection, and promptly investigate and penalize any instances of deceptive trade practice.

Article 6 The consumer council and other consumer organizations shall conduct social oversight over the products or services provided by business operators, issue early warnings in a timely manner, protect consumer rights, and advocate rational consumption methods pursuant to law.

The appropriate industry organizations shall encourage industry self-discipline, implement and optimize industry standards, develop industry integrity, and guide and urge industry operators to operate pursuant to law.

News media shall improve awareness of the protection of consumer rights and report on and uncover deceptive trade practices.

Article 7 Any entity or individual shall be entitled to file a complaint or report deceptive trade practice to the market regulation agency of the people's government at or above the county level. The appropriate agencies shall then promptly process the complaints and reports received pursuant to applicable law, send notice of the results to the complainants and whistleblowers, and keep their identities confidential pursuant to law.

县级以上人民政府市场监督管理等有关部门应当将受理投诉、举报的电话、信箱、微信公众号或者电子邮件地址向社会公布。对实名举报并查证属实的，由查处消费欺诈行为的部门对举报人给予奖励。举报奖励办法由省人民政府制定。

鼓励消费者通过在线消费纠纷解决机制、消费维权服务站、消费维权绿色通道、第三方争议解决机制等方式与经营者协商解决消费者权益争议。

第八条 经营者销售海鲜、水果、旅游特产及其他商品时，使用不合格的计量器具、破坏计量器具准确度、将包装物重量作为商品重量或者以作弊的方式称量商品，短斤缺两的，由县级以上人民政府市场监督管理部门责令改正，给予警告，没收违法所得，对经营者处二千元以下的罚款；情节较重或者社会影响恶劣的，处二千元以上五万元以下的罚款；情节严重或者社会影响特别恶劣的，处五万元以上五十万元以下的罚款，并可以处不少于三个月的责令停产停业，直至依法吊销营业执照。

经营者为单位、有前款规定的行为情节严重或者社会影响特别恶劣的，除依照前款规定处罚外，对其法定代表人、主要负责人和其他直接责任人员，处一千元以上三万元以下的罚款。

第九条 经营者有下列欺诈行为之一的，由县级以上人民政府市场监督管理部门责令改正，给予警告，没收违法所得，对经营者处一万元以下的罚款；情节较重或者社会影响恶劣的，处一万元以上十万元以下的罚款；情节严重或者社会影响特别恶劣的，处十万元以上五十万元以下的罚款，并可以处不少于三个月的责令停产停业，直至依法吊销营业执照：

The market regulation agencies of the people's government at or above the county level shall announce the telephone number, address, official WeChat subscription, or email address for sending complaints and reports. The agency investigating the deceptive trade practices shall reward the whistleblower should they use their real name and the report or complaint submitted is verified to be true. The reward guidelines shall be issued by the provincial people's government.

Consumers are encouraged to negotiate and resolve disputes with business operators through online dispute resolution services, consumer rights protection platforms, consumer rights protection fast track platforms, and third party dispute resolution services.

Article 8 Where a business operator sells seafood, fruit, specialties for tourists, and other products, and such operator uses non-conforming scales, tampers with the accuracy of the scales, includes the package weight in the product weight, or intentionally misweighs products, the market regulation agency of the people's governments at or above the county level shall require the operator to make the necessary corrections, issue a warning, confiscate any illegal income earned, and impose a penalty under 2,000 Yuan. If the circumstances are serious or have an adverse impact on the public, a penalty of not less than 2,000 Yuan and not more than 50,000 Yuan shall be imposed. If the circumstances are serious or have a significantly adverse impact on the public, a penalty of not less than 50,000 Yuan but not more than 500,000 Yuan may be imposed, and the operator may be required to suspend production or business for a minimum of 3 months, or its business license will be revoked pursuant to law.

Where the business operator is an entity in violation of the preceding paragraph and the circumstances are serious or the violation has a significantly adverse impact on the public, its statutory representative, the person directly in charge, and other employees subject to direct liability shall receive a penalty of not less than 1,000 Yuan and not more than 30,000 Yuan.

Article 9 If a business operator commits any of the following deceptive acts, the market regulation agency of the people's government at or above the county level shall require the operator to correct such act, issue a warning, confiscate the illegal income, and impose a penalty of less than 10,000 Yuan. If the circumstances are serious or have an adverse impact on the public, a penalty of not less than 10,000 Yuan and not more than 100,000 Yuan shall be imposed. If the circumstances are serious or have a significantly adverse impact on the public, a penalty of not less than 100,000 Yuan and not more than 500,000 Yuan shall be imposed, and the business operator may be required to suspend production or business for a minimum of 3 months, or its business license is revoked pursuant to law:

（一）在提供海鲜代客加工、汽车维修、装饰装修等服务中，采用谎报用工用料、偷换材料、偷工减料等方式欺诈消费者的；

（二）在销售的商品中掺杂、掺假，以假充真，以次充好，以不合格商品冒充合格商品欺诈消费者的；

（三）在经营场所内设置相对封闭、独立区域，诱骗或者强迫旅游者购买旅游商品的；

（四）在销售商品或者提供健身、美容、培训、餐饮等服务中，采用预收款等方式骗取消费者费用而不提供或者不按照约定提供商品、服务的。

经营者为单位、有前款规定的行为情节严重或者社会影响特别恶劣的，除依照前款规定处罚外，对其法定代表人、主要负责人和其他直接责任人员，处五千元以上五万元以下的罚款。

第十条 经营者有下列欺诈行为之一的，依照《中华人民共和国反不正当竞争法》的规定处罚：

（一）借助免费或者不合理低价旅游、组织讲座、现场体验、公益活动等名义和形式进行虚假宣传，误导、欺骗消费者的；

（二）发布虚假免税或者零关税商品信息，误导、欺骗消费者的；

（三）以虚构交易、编造用户评价等方式进行虚假或者引人误解的商业宣传，误导、欺骗消费者的；

（四）在提供婚纱摄影、海鲜餐饮、汽车租赁、房屋租赁等服务中，对其服务作虚假或者引人误解的商业宣传，误导、欺骗消费者的；

（五）在提供高空、高速、水上、潜水、探险等旅游娱乐服务中，对其服务作虚假或者引人误解的商业宣传，误导、欺骗消费者的；

（六）销售伪造或者冒用知名商品特有的名称、包装、装潢商品的。

(a) when providing seafood processing, vehicle maintenance, renovation, and other services, using falsified materials, surreptitiously switching materials, cutting corners, or using other methods to cheat consumers;

(b) bulking or adulterating products sold, selling fake products as genuine products, selling inferior products as superior products, or selling defective products as conforming products to deceive consumers;

(c) setting up relatively closed and independent areas in the business premises to induce or force tourists to buy tourist products; or

(d) when selling commodities or providing services such as fitness, beauty treatment, training, catering, and other services, deceiving consumers by charging advance or other fees and failing to provide the products or services as agreed.

Where a business operator is an entity and materially violates the above paragraph or has an adverse impact on the public, its statutory representative, the person directly in charge, and other employees directly liable shall receive a penalty of not less than 5,000 Yuan and not more than 50,000 Yuan.

Article 10 Business operators who commit any of the following deceptive acts shall be penalized pursuant to the Anti-Unfair Competition Law of the People's Republic of China:

(a) false advertising under the guise of or by means of free or unrealistically low-cost travel, classes, in-person experiences, or activities for the public interest to mislead or deceive consumers;

(b) publishing false information about duty-free or zero-duty products to mislead or deceive consumers;

(c) issuing false or misleading commercial advertisements through fictitious transactions or false customer reviews to misguide or deceive consumers;

(d) issuing false or misleading commercial service advertisements to misguide or deceive consumers when providing services such as wedding photography, seafood catering, car rental, or accommodation rental;

(e) issuing false or misleading commercial service advertisements to misguide or deceive consumers when providing high-altitude, high-speed, water, diving, or exploration tourism and recreational services; or

(f) selling counterfeit or fake products using the distinctive name, packaging, or designs of well-known products.

第十一条 经营者发布医疗、药品、医疗器械、保健食品等方面的虚假广告，误导、欺骗消费者的，依照《中华人民共和国广告法》的规定处罚。

第十二条 经营者销售伪造产地，伪造或者冒用他人的厂名、厂址，伪造或者冒用认证标志等质量标志，篡改生产日期的商品，或者假冒他人注册商标销售商品或者提供服务的，分别依照《中华人民共和国产品质量法》《中华人民共和国商标法》的规定处罚。

第十三条 经营者向消费者提供商品或者服务时，利用虚假或者使人误解的价格手段，诱骗消费者与其进行交易的，依照《中华人民共和国价格法》等有关规定处罚。

第十四条 交易市场开办者未依照规定履行审查、检查、制止、报告等管理义务，同一交易市场一年内出现两次以上经营者因消费欺诈受到行政处罚的，由县级以上人民政府市场监督管理部门对交易市场开办者处二万元以上十万元以下的罚款；交易市场开办者为单位的，同时对其法定代表人、主要负责人和其他直接责任人员，处一万元以上三万元以下的罚款。

第十五条 经营者利用网络实施消费欺诈行为的，依照本规定处罚。

第十六条 县级以上人民政府市场监督管理等部门调查涉嫌消费欺诈行为时，有关单位或者个人应当配合，不得弄虚作假或者拒绝、阻挠。涉嫌消费欺诈的有关单位和个人在接受调查时弄虚作假或者拒绝、阻挠的，由实施调查的部门责令改正；拒不改正的，处一千元以上五万元以下的罚款。

Article 11 Business operators who publish false advertisements on medical treatment, drugs, medical devices, or dietary supplements to mislead or deceive consumers shall be penalized pursuant to the Advertisement Law of the People's Republic of China.

Article 12 Business operators who sell products with forged origins, forged or falsified factory names and addresses belonging to others, forged or falsified use of quality marks such as certification marks, falsified product production dates, or forged registered trademarks belonging to others to sell products or provide services shall be penalized pursuant to the Product Quality Law of the People's Republic of China or Trademark Law of the People's Republic of China.

Article 13 When providing products or services to consumers, business operators who use false or misleading prices to induce consumers into transactions shall be penalized pursuant to the Price Law of the People's Republic of China or other applicable provisions.

Article 14 Where a market operator fails to perform its administrative obligations such as review, inspection, stoppage, and reporting as required and is subject to administrative penalties for deceptive trade practice twice or more in one year in the market, they shall receive a penalty of not less than 20,000 Yuan and not more than 100,000 Yuan imposed by the market regulation agency of the people's governments at or above the county level. If the market operator is an entity, its statutory representative, the person directly in charge, and directly liable employees shall receive a penalty of not less than 10,000 Yuan and not more than 30,000 Yuan.

Article 15 Business operators who commit deceptive trade practices online shall be penalized pursuant to these Provisions.

Article 16 When the market regulation agency of the people's governments at or above the county level investigate suspected deceptive trade practice, the entities or individuals under investigation shall cooperate and shall not falsify information, refuse, or obstruct the investigation. The investigating agency shall require them to correct their actions, and may impose a fine of not less than 1,000 Yuan and not more than 50,000 Yuan should the investigated entities or individuals refuse to comply.

第十七条 对因消费欺诈受到行政处罚的经营者，有关部门应当依法记入信用档案，通过信用信息平台进行公示。因消费欺诈情节严重或者社会影响特别恶劣受到行政处罚的，依照国家有关市场监督管理严重违法失信惩戒的规定以及本省的有关规定实施相应的惩戒措施。

第十八条 违反本规定的行为，本规定未设定处罚但其他法律、法规已有处罚规定的，依照有关法律、法规的规定处罚；《中华人民共和国食品安全法》《中华人民共和国药品管理法》《中华人民共和国消费者权益保护法》等法律、法规的规定严于本规定的，依照有关法律、法规的规定执行；构成违反治安管理行为的，依照《中华人民共和国治安管理处罚法》予以处罚；构成犯罪的，依法追究刑事责任；造成人身、财产损害的，依法承担民事责任。

消费欺诈违法行为，依法决定由市、县、自治县综合行政执法部门或者乡镇人民政府、街道办事处实施处罚的，从其规定。

第十九条 履行反消费欺诈工作职责的行政管理部门及其工作人员违反本规定，有下列情形之一的，由其上级机关、主管部门责令改正；对直接负责的主管人员和其他直接责任人员依法给予处理；构成犯罪的，依法追究刑事责任：

（一）不依法受理或者不及时处理投诉、举报的；

（二）对监督检查过程中发现的消费欺诈行为不制止或者拖延查处的；

（三）其他滥用职权、玩忽职守、徇私舞弊的行为。

第二十条 本规定自2021年11月1日起施行。

Article 17 Business operators subject to administrative penalties for deceptive trade practice shall be recorded by the appropriate agencies in the credit report pursuant to law and announced via the credit information platform. Appropriate disciplinary action shall be taken against those subject to administrative penalties for material deceptive trade practice or material adverse impact on the public pursuant to applicable national market regulation and administration regulations and applicable provincial regulations.

Article 18 Where other laws and regulations provide penalties for violations of these Provisions not provided in these Provisions, such laws and regulations shall control. The Food Safety Law of the People's Republic of China, the Drug Administration Law of the People's Republic of China, or the Consumer Rights Protection Law of the People's Republic of China shall control should one provide stricter penalties than these Provisions. Those who violate the administration of public security shall be subject to penalties pursuant to the Law of the People's Republic of China on Administration of and Penalties for Public Security, and shall be held criminally liable pursuant to law should such violation commit a crime. Those who cause harm to a person or property shall assume the appropriate civil liability pursuant to law.

The laws shall control if they provide that the comprehensive law enforcement agencies at the city, county, or autonomous county level, the town or township government, or subdistrict office shall penalize those involved in deceptive trade practice.

Article 19 The administrative agencies and their employees with deceptive trade practice prevention duties found to be in violation of these Provisions or involved in any of the following circumstances shall be required by higher authorities and the appropriate agencies to correct such. The persons directly in charge and other directly liable employees shall be penalized pursuant to law and held criminally liable if a crime is committed:

(a) failing to accept or resolve complaints and reports in a timely manner pursuant to law;

(b) deceptive trade practice discovered during oversight and inspection is not stopped or its management is delayed; or

(c) other acts of abuse of position, dereliction of duty, or playing favoritism and committing irregularities.

Article 20 These Provisions shall come into force as of November 1, 2021.

海南自由贸易港安居房建设和管理若干规定

Several Provisions of Hainan Free Trade Port on the Construction and Administration of Affordable Housing

海南自由贸易港安居房建设和管理若干规定

（2021 年 12 月 1 日海南省第六届人民代表大会常务委员会第三十一会议通过）

第一条 为了构建与海南自由贸易港相适应的住房保障体系，改善本地居民家庭和引进人才住房条件，根据有关法律法规，结合海南自由贸易港实际，制定本规定。

第二条 本规定所称安居房，是指由政府提供政策优惠，按照有关标准建设，限定销售对象、销售价格、套型面积和转让年限，实行政府与购房人按份共有产权，面向符合条件的本地居民家庭和引进人才供应的共有产权住房，纳入保障性住房统一管理。

第三条 本省户籍居民家庭或者引进人才同时符合以下条件的，可以申请购买一套安居房：

（一）在本省城镇无住房和无购房记录，或者家庭人均住房建筑面积低于所在市、县、自治县上一年度城镇居民家庭人均住房建筑面积；

（二）本省户籍居民家庭成员至少一人或者引进人才已在海南连续两年缴纳城镇职工基本养老保险或者个人所得税，且每年在海南实际居住时间不少于一百八十三天；

（三）省和市、县、自治县人民政府规定的其他条件。

省人民政府和市、县、自治县人民政府可以对安居房保障对象的范围作适当调整，并向社会公布。

本条第一款所称家庭成员包括居民本人、配偶及未成年子女。

Several Provisions of Hainan Free Trade Port on the Construction and Administration of Affordable Housing

(Adopted at the 31st Session of the Standing Committee of the 6th Hainan Provincial People's Congress on December 1, 2021)

Article 1 These Provisions are enacted pursuant to applicable laws and regulations, and based on actual circumstances in the Hainan Free Trade Port to create an affordable housing system for the Hainan Free Trade Port and improve housing conditions for local residents and arriving professionals.

Article 2 The affordable housing in these Provisions refers to common housing, specifically for eligible local residents and arriving professionals as necessary. Such housing, co-owned by shares by the purchasers and the government, shall be provided by the government through preferential policies and restrictions on target residents, price, housing area, and transfer terms shall be set, with the housing being constructed as required and integrated into the centralized affordable housing administration.

Article 3 Local residents or arriving professionals may request an affordable housing unit if they meet all the following requirements:

(a) the local residents or arriving professional does not own a house, nor are they included in any housing purchase records within Hainan Province, or the average living space per household member is less than the average living space per person in the city, county or autonomous county for the previous year;

(b) at least one family member or the arriving professional has paid basic pension insurance for urban employees or individual income tax in Hainan Province for two consecutive years and has been domiciled in Hainan Province for at least 183 days per year for the two years; and

(c) other requirements provided by the provincial, city, county, and autonomous county people's governments.

The provincial, city, county, and autonomous county people's governments may make and publish appropriate adjustments to the scope of individuals eligible for affordable housing.

The families referred to in Paragraph 1 of this Article shall include the residents themself, their spouses, and minor dependent children.

第四条 省人民政府负责全省安居房建设和管理的指导、督促和监督检查工作，对市、县、自治县人民政府安居房建设情况实施评价考核。

市、县、自治县人民政府负责组织实施本行政区域内安居房的建设和管理工作。

市、县、自治县人民政府应当明确安居房保障实施机构，负责安居房轮候、分配、代持政府产权、上市交易、换购等具体工作。

第五条 省人民政府住房和城乡建设部门应当会同相关部门根据城镇居民住房现状和总体需求、人口增长、住房保障预期目标等，编制全省住房发展规划，明确全省及各市、县、自治县安居房建设目标任务。

市、县、自治县人民政府根据建设目标任务编制本市、县、自治县住房发展规划，制定年度建设计划，明确安居房建设规模、项目选址、土地供应等内容，并向社会公布。

县级以上人民政府应当积极采取措施，创新机制，加大安居房的建设和供给力度，提高安居房保障率。

第六条 安居房建设项目的选址应当根据国土空间规划、城市功能定位和产业布局，优先安排在交通便捷、生活和工作便利、配套设施完善的区域，促进职住平衡、产城融合。项目配套建设的基础设施和公共服务设施，应当与主体工程同步规划、同步建设、同步交付使用。

第七条 市、县、自治县人民政府应当将安居房项目用地纳入土地利用年度计划，单列指标，优先安排，做到应保尽保。

Article 4 The provincial people's government shall be responsible for the guidance, oversight, and inspection of the construction and administration of affordable housing, and for the evaluation and assessment of the construction of affordable housing implemented by the people's governments in the city, county, and autonomous county level.

The city, county, and autonomous county people's government shall be responsible for organizing the construction and administration of affordable housing within their own administrative areas.

The city, county, and autonomous county people's governments shall designate the agency in charge of affordable housing. The agency in charge shall be responsible for publishing the waiting list, allocation, holding property titles on behalf of the government, transactions, larger house purchases, and other specific affordable housing matters.

Article 5 The provincial housing and urban-rural development agency, along with other agencies involved, shall prepare the housing development plan for the whole province and determine objectives and tasks for the construction of affordable housing within the Province, city, county, and autonomous county based on actual circumstances and overall urban resident, population growth, and expected housing protection goal requirements.

The city, county, and autonomous county people's government shall be responsible for preparing housing development plans for their own respective administrative areas, preparing annual construction plans, specifying the scale of construction, project site selection, land supply, and other affordable housing matters based on construction goals and tasks, and make such available to the public.

People's governments at or above the county level shall proactively take action and create systems to improve housing construction and supply to improve affordable housing rates.

Article 6 Site selection for affordable housing construction projects shall prioritize areas with convenient transportation, living, working, and comprehensive support facilities based on land and space planning, urban functional positioning, and industrial layout planning to improve the working and housing balance and industry-city integration. The supporting infrastructure and public service facilities shall be planned, built, and delivered together with the housing construction project.

Article 7 The city, county, and autonomous county people's governments shall include the land for affordable housing projects in the annual land-use plan as separate metrics, prioritize arrangements, and ensure that as much land as necessary is guaranteed.

鼓励在符合规划的条件下将在城镇规划区、产业园区等人口聚集区域已供应的工业、仓储、商业、办公等存量非住宅建设用地依法改变用途用于建设安居房。

鼓励开发企业利用存量住宅用地建设安居房，并在项目融资、商品住宅建设计划安排等方面给予政策支持。

划拨住宅用地可以依法补办出让手续用于建设安居房。

第八条　新供应的安居房建设用地，采取招标、拍卖、挂牌方式出让。市、县、自治县人民政府应当建立房价地价联动和土地出让价格熔断机制，按照“限房价、控地价、竞品质”的原则确定新供应安居房项目建设用地竞得人。

利用新供应用地和存量用地建设的安居房项目，应当纳入市、县、自治县安居房年度建设计划统筹管理，并由市、县、自治县人民政府对房源进行统一分配。鼓励探索创新安居房建设筹集方式和供地方式，可通过集中新建、配建、收购、存量市场化商品住房转化等方式多渠道筹集安居房房源。

第九条　省人民政府住房和城乡建设部门应当会同相关部门制定安居房建设技术导则。安居房建设应当坚持绿色、低碳、节能、环保理念，推行绿色建筑、装配式建筑和全装修建设方式。

安居房套型面积以一百平方米以下中小套型为主。各种套型房源供应应当与基本住房需求相匹配，并根据家庭人口数量增长和人口结构变化情况，逐步满足改善型住房需求。

Non-residential development land located in urban planning areas, industrial zones, and other densely populated areas, including existing industrial, warehousing, commercial, and office, is encouraged to be converted into affordable housing construction pursuant to law and based on planning conditions.

Development entities are encouraged to build affordable housing on existing residential land and may be entitled to preferential policies for project financing, commercial housing construction planning and arrangement, and other matters.

Allocated residential land may be used for affordable housing after finishing the post-registering procedures pursuant to law.

Article 8 Newly supplied land for affordable housing construction shall be assigned through bidding, auctions, and listing. The city, county, and autonomous county people's governments shall link house and land prices and add market-wide circuit breakers for land transfer prices, and select bidders for newly supplied development land for affordable housing projects based on the goals of "limiting house prices, controlling land prices, and competitive quality."

The construction of affordable housing projects using both new and existing land shall be included in the city, county, and autonomous county people's government annual construction plan for comprehensive administration, and the housing shall be allocated by the appropriate people's governments. People's governments shall be encouraged to explore and innovate means to raise and supply land. New affordable housing may be supplied through new construction projects, designated construction in commercial housing projects, purchasing, and converting existing houses and commercially homes into affordable housing.

Article 9 The provincial housing and urban-rural development agency shall, together with the agencies involved, prepare technical guidelines for the construction of affordable housing. Affordable housing construction shall abide by the principles of green, low-carbon, energy conservation, and environmental protection construction, and green building, prefabricated building, and full renovation construction methods shall be used.

Small and medium-sized housing units under 100 square meters shall be the main type of affordable housing units. Different types of housing units shall be supplied based on basic housing requirements, and requirements for improved housing shall be gradually met based on household member growth and changes to the population structure.

第十条 安居房项目建设严格执行规划和施工许可、质量监督、工程监理、竣工验收等建设程序和国家、本省有关保障性住房建设的技术标准及强制性规定，落实建设、勘察、设计、施工、监理等参建各方主体责任。

县级以上人民政府住房和城乡建设等主管部门应当加强对安居房项目建设全过程的监督管理，确保工程质量安全。

第十一条 安居房项目享受以下政策：

（一）按照国家和海南自由贸易港有关规定，减免行政事业性收费和政府性基金，享受税收优惠政策；

（二）按照国家规定取得住房公积金贷款、金融机构开发性、政策性融资支持及贷款利率优惠；

（三）简化项目审批流程，优先办理土地、规划、建设和销售等审批手续；

（四）国家和海南自由贸易港的其他优惠政策。

第十二条 安居房实行现房销售制度，其每平方米销售均价按照项目所在市、县、自治县上一年度城镇居民家庭房价收入比不超过十倍确定，或者不得高于所在市、县、自治县上一年度市场化商品住房销售均价的百分之六十，具体价格由市、县、自治县人民政府结合当地市场化商品住房均价、居民家庭收入等因素确定。安居房购房人的产权份额按照百分之七十确定，并在购房合同中约定。

第十三条 安居房实行轮候分配制度，综合考虑工作和居住就近、便利等因素，合理分配房源。市、县、自治县人民政府应当根据安居房房源数量、申购人数等情况制定轮候规则，做到公平公正公开。

Article 10 Affordable housing construction projects shall strictly follow procedures such as planning and construction licensing, quality supervision, project supervision, and completion inspections, national and provincial technical standards and mandatory regulations on affordable housing construction, and specify the responsibilities of all parties involved in the construction, exploration, design, and supervision.

The housing and urban-rural development agency of the people's governments at or above the county level shall improve supervision of the entire construction project process to ensure project quality and safety.

Article 11 Affordable housing projects may benefit from the following policies:

(a) administrative charges and government fees shall be reduced or exempted and preferential tax policies shall apply pursuant to applicable national laws and Hainan Free Trade Port regulations;

(b) construction projects may obtain housing provident fund loans, developmental and policy financial support from financial institutions, and applicable preferential loan interest rates pursuant to national laws;

(c) the approval process shall be simplified and land, planning, construction, and sales approval procedures shall be prioritized; and

(d) other preferential policies of the state and Hainan Free Trade Port may also apply.

Article 12 The system used for sales of newly built housing shall restrict the average selling price per square meter for affordable housing to a maximum of 10 times the price calculated based on the urban resident housing price to income ratio in the previous year in the city, county, or autonomous county where the construction project is located, or shall not exceed 60% of the average commercial housing selling price in the previous year in the city, county, or autonomous county where the construction project is located. The specific price shall be determined by the city, county, and autonomous county people's government based on the average commercial housing selling price and household income. Purchasers shall own 70% of the title to the affordable housing unit, which shall be specified in the housing purchase contract.

Article 13 An affordable housing waiting list system shall be adopted and the housing supply shall be reasonably allocated by comprehensively considering the distance between the workplace and residence, and convenience. The city, county, and autonomous county people's governments shall prepare and publish waiting list provisions based on the number of houses available and applicants based on the principles of fairness, impartiality, and openness.

对法律、法规或者国家规定应优先保障且符合购房条件的家庭，以及无住房、人均住房建筑面积相对小、收入相对低、落户时间早、居住时间长、未成年子女多的家庭予以优先安排。

第十四条　安居房自签订购房合同之日起满十年的，可以上市交易，购房人和政府按照产权份额获得出售住房总价款的相应部分。省人民政府可以根据法律法规和国家政策对政府持有的安居房产权份额的处置适时作出规定。

符合本省规定换购条件的，购房人可以申请换购一次较大户型的安居房。换购人按照评估价格补交差价，原购安居房由政府收回。具体办法由省人民政府制定。

安居房在未达到上市交易年限内实行封闭流转制度。购房人确需转让安居房的，应当向符合安居房购房条件和轮候规则的对象转让。回购或者转让价格最高不超过原购房价格与按照中国人民银行同期对应期限存款基准利率计算的利息之和。

第十五条　省人民政府应当根据本规定制定安居房管理办法。

市、县、自治县人民政府应当结合本地区实际，制定实施办法或者细则，明确安居房申请、审核、公示、轮候、分配、定价、封闭流转、上市交易和换购等制度。

省人民政府住房和城乡建设部门应当建立全省住房保障和房地产信息化管理平台，将安居房建设和管理工作纳入信息化管理平台进行规范管理。

Families in need that meet the purchasing requirements provided by laws, regulations, or state provisions shall be prioritized, along with families lacking housing, families having a comparatively small average residential space per person, low-income households, long-term Hainan residents, long-term resident families, and households with several minor children.

Article 14 Affordable housing shall not be sold until 10 years has passed from the date the housing purchase contract was signed, and the purchaser and government shall receive their portion of the total price of the sold house based on the share of the title held. The provincial people's government may gradually issue regulations governing the management of the government's share of affordable housing pursuant to law and national policies.

The purchaser may request to trade in a small housing unit for a larger affordable housing unit pursuant to the specific provincial regulations. The purchaser shall make up the price difference based on the assessed price, and the previously purchased affordable housing unit shall be recovered by the government. Specific procedures shall be formulated by the provincial people's government.

A closed system shall be implemented for affordable housing before the expiration of the listing and sale period. Purchasers in real need to transfer their affordable housing shall transfer it to another purchaser eligible for purchasing the affordable housing pursuant to the waiting-list provisions. The maximum repurchase price or transfer price shall not exceed the sum originally paid for the housing unit, and interest shall be calculated based on the base deposit interest rate provided by the People's Bank of China during the same period.

Article 15 The provincial people's government shall prepare the provisions for the administration of affordable housing in accordance with these Provisions.

The city, county, and autonomous county people's governments shall prepare implementation guidelines or detailed provisions to implement the application, examination, awareness, waiting list, allocation, pricing, closed circulation, listing and sale, and large affordable housing unit purchase price systems based on the actual circumstances in their administrative areas.

The provincial housing and urban-rural development agency shall create an information platform for provincial housing protection and real estate administration where the affordable housing construction and administration is subject to regulated administration.

第十六条 购房人在提供户籍、住房、城镇职工基本养老保险、个人所得税、在海南实际居住时间等材料时弄虚作假，或者采取贿赂等不正当手段申请购买安居房的，由市、县、自治县人民政府住房和城乡建设部门驳回其申请，自驳回申请之日起五年内不予受理其安居房申请；已购买安居房的，由市、县、自治县人民政府决定收回安居房，并由住房和城乡建设部门或者综合行政执法机构处一万元以上五万元以下罚款，已办理不动产权证的，依法注销不动产权证，且五年内不得再次申请购买安居房，并在个人征信记录中作不良行为记录。

购房人擅自改变安居房居住用途用于生产、经营等活动的，由市、县、自治县人民政府住房和城乡建设部门或者综合行政执法机构没收违法所得，责令限期改正；逾期未改正的，由市、县、自治县人民政府决定收回安居房，已办理不动产权证的，依法注销不动产权证。

住房和城乡建设部门和其他相关管理部门的工作人员在安居房建设管理工作中滥用职权、玩忽职守、徇私舞弊的，依法给予处分；构成犯罪的，依法追究刑事责任。

第十七条 本规定自2022年1月1日起施行。

Article 16 If any purchaser falsifies information or documents about the registered household, housing conditions, basic pension for urban employees, individual income tax, and the actual time spent as a resident of Hainan, or purchases housing illegally, such as through bribery, his request to purchase affordable housing shall be rejected by the city, county, or autonomous county housing and urban-rural development agency, and such request shall not be accepted again for a further five years from the date of rejection. If the affordable housing has already been purchased, the city, county, or autonomous county people's governments shall recover the housing unit, and the housing and urban-rural development agency or the comprehensive administrative law enforcement agency shall impose a penalty of not less than 10,000 Yuan and not more than 50,000 Yuan. If the real estate title certificate has already been issued, such certificate shall be revoked pursuant to law, and another request to purchase affordable housing shall not be made for a further five years. Such misconduct shall also be recorded in such individual's credit report.

If the purchaser arbitrarily changes the use of the affordable housing for production, business activities, or any other purposes, the housing and urban-rural development agency of city, county, or autonomous county people's government or the comprehensive administrative law enforcement agency where the house is located shall confiscate any illegal income and order the purchaser to make corrections within a specified time limit; if the purchaser fails to make such corrections within the time limit, the purchased affordable housing unit shall be recovered by the city, county or autonomous county people's government and the real estate title certificate shall be revoked pursuant to law.

Any employee of housing and urban-rural development agency or other administrative agency who abuses their positions, neglects their duties, or plays favoritism and commits irregularities during the construction and administration of affordable housing projects shall be penalized pursuant to law and held criminally liable pursuant to law where a crime is committed.

Article 17 These Provisions shall come into force as of January 1, 2022.

海南自由贸易港科技开放创新若干规定

Several Provisions of Hainan Free Trade Port on Science and Technology Open-Access and Innovation

海南自由贸易港科技开放创新若干规定

（2021 年 12 月 1 日海南省第六届人民代表大会常务委员会第三十一次会议通过）

第一条 为了实施科技创新发展战略，构建开放型科技创新体制机制，根据《中华人民共和国海南自由贸易港法》等有关法律法规，结合海南自由贸易港实际，制定本规定。

第二条 省和市、县、自治县人民政府应当建立科技开放创新统筹协调工作机制，科技主管部门负责本行政区域科技开放创新的统筹协调和监督管理工作。

省和市、县、自治县人民政府发展改革、自然资源和规划、农业农村、工业和信息化、财政、人力资源和社会保障、教育、卫生健康、金融监管等有关部门，在各自职责范围内负责科技开放创新相关工作。

第三条 省和市、县、自治县人民政府应当将科研基础设施和科技创新平台建设、科技人才保障、高新技术产业发展、国际科技合作等科技开放创新工作，纳入国民经济和社会发展规划。

鼓励科研机构、高等院校、企业在海洋、航天、生物医药、信息技术、清洁能源、节能环保、热带高效农业等领域进行科技创新。

第四条 政府及有关部门应当加大科技开放创新财政投入，通过资助、奖励、补贴等多种方式引导社会资金投入科技开放创新，推动全社会科技研究开发经费持续稳定增长。

Several Provisions of Hainan Free Trade Port on Science and Technology Open-Access and Innovation

(Adopted at the 31st Session of the Standing Committee of the 6th Hainan Provincial People's Congress on December 1, 2021)

Article 1 Several Provisions are enacted under the Hainan Free Trade Port Law of the People's Republic of China and other applicable laws and regulations, in combination with actual circumstances in the Hainan Free Trade Port to advance the strategy of innovation and development of science and technology and develop an open scientific and technological innovation system.

Article 2 The provincial, city, county, and autonomous county people's governments shall create an overall coordination system for science and technology open-access and innovation, and the competent science and technology agency shall be accountable for the overall coordination, oversight, and administration of the open-access science technology innovation in their administrative areas.

The provincial, city, county, and autonomous county government agencies in charge of development and reform, natural resources and planning, agriculture and rural affairs, industry and information technology, finance, human resources and social security, education, health, and the finance oversight shall be accountable for work related to the science and technology open-access and innovation within the scope of their authorities and duties.

Article 3 The provincial, city, county, and autonomous county people's governments shall include scientific research infrastructure and scientific innovation platform development, scientific and technological skilled employee assurances, high-tech industry development, international science and technology collaboration, and other scientific and technological open-access and innovation into the national economic and social development plan.

The research institutes, higher learning institutions, and businesses are encouraged to conduct scientific and technological innovation in fields such as ocean, aerospace, biomedicine, information technology, clean energy, energy conservation and environmental protection, and productive tropical agriculture.

Article 4 The government and its agencies shall increase financial investment in science and technology open-access and innovation, and invest in science and technology open-access and innovation through subsidies, awards, grants, and other financial funding, and improve the continuous and steady growth of funding for whole society scientific and technological research and development.

政府及有关部门应当支持企业及其他社会力量通过捐赠方式投入基础研究、应用基础研究、高新技术开发和转化应用，其捐赠支出可以按照有关规定享受公益捐赠有关优惠待遇。

第五条 政府及有关部门应当引导境内外资本对科技企业提供融资支持，推动科技创新基金体系建设，拓宽创新创业项目境外融资渠道。

支持金融机构创新科技金融产品和服务，鼓励银行依法开展投贷联动业务、设立科技金融专营机构，鼓励银行、保险、担保等各类金融机构开展知识产权质押融资、股权质押融资、信贷保险等业务，为科技企业提供融资便利。

推动在海南自由贸易港设立全国性金融科技基础设施运营机构、金融科技子公司、金融科技创新实验室等。

第六条 省和市、县、自治县人民政府应当在国土空间规划、土地供应、海域使用等方面，支持种业、深海、航天、生物医药、热带高效农业等领域的国家级科技创新平台、国家科技创新基地、国家重大科学装置、重大科研基础设施和条件平台建设。

鼓励以出让、出租等方式利用农村集体经营性建设用地建设国家级科技创新平台、重大科研基础设施和重大科技项目。

利用财政资金、国有资本购置和建设的重大科研基础设施、大型科学仪器设备等应当按照有关规定向社会开放共享。支持融资租赁企业引进国外先进高端科研仪器设备，开展融资租赁服务。

第七条 政府及有关部门应当积极培育科技型中小企业、高新技术企业、科技型领军企业。支持高新技术企业牵头组织实施重大科技项目，通过资助、奖励、补助等多种方式鼓励企业加大研发投入，落实支持企

The government and its agencies shall support businesses and other private sectors to invest in basic and applied research and high-tech development through donations. Donators may benefit from appropriate preferential policies for public philanthropy.

Article 5 The government and its agencies shall guide domestic and foreign capital to provide financial support for science and technology businesses, improve the development of a funding system for science and technology innovation, and broaden overseas financing channels for innovation and entrepreneurship projects.

Financial institutions shall receive support to innovate technology and finance products and services, banks will be encouraged to integrate investment and loan operations, set up fin-tech concession entities, and banks, insurance, guarantee, and other financial institutions will be encouraged to conduct intellectual property rights pledge financing, equity pledge financing, credit insurance, and other activities to provide financing facilities for technology organizations.

The creation of national fin-tech infrastructure operators, fin-tech subsidiaries, and fin-tech innovation laboratories within the Hainan Free Trade Port will be improved.

Article 6 The provincial, city, county, and autonomous county people's governments shall support land planning, land supply, and sea area used for the construction of national-level scientific and technological innovation platforms, technological innovation bases, major national scientific facilities, and major scientific research infrastructure platforms in fields such as seed industry, deep sea, aerospace, biomedicine, and productive tropical agriculture.

Registered rural collective land for development purposes is encouraged to be used via assignment or lease for the construction of national scientific and technological innovation platforms, major scientific research infrastructure, and major scientific and technological projects.

Major scientific research infrastructure, large scientific instruments, and equipment purchased or built using financial funding and state-owned capital shall be shared with the public as necessary. Financial lease organizations shall receive support to add foreign advanced high-end scientific research instruments or equipment and conduct financial lease services for such.

Article 7 The government and its agencies shall actively develop small and medium-sized scientific and technological businesses, high-tech businesses, and leading scientific and technological businesses. High-tech businesses shall receive support to take the lead in organizing the implementation of major scientific and technological projects, businesses shall be encouraged

业技术创新的固定资产加速折旧、股权激励、技术入股、技术服务和转让、设备进口等优惠政策和分红激励政策。

鼓励企业、科研机构和社会组织等在海南自由贸易港设立科技企业孵化器，推动建立海南自由贸易港科技企业孵化器网络。

第八条 政府及有关部门应当通过政策支持、财政扶持等方式，鼓励国内外各类创新主体采取多种方式设立新型研发机构。在科技计划项目承担、科研设备进口采购、高新技术企业认定等方面对新型研发机构给予支持。

政府及有关部门对实行报备员额制的新型研发机构，依照有关规定赋予其在财政资金使用、科技项目管理、科技成果转化、实验室资产使用等方面充分的自主权，适用灵活的用人机制、薪酬制度和社会保险制度。

第九条 政府及有关部门应当鼓励设立研发设计、中试熟化、检验检测认证、技术转移、创业孵化、知识产权、科技咨询等科技服务机构和科技公共服务平台，促进科技服务业发展。

第十条 省和相关市、县、自治县人民政府应当推动打造南繁种业科技创新高地，加快建设国家南繁科研育种基地、崖州湾种子实验室和全球动植物种质资源引进中转基地等创新平台，支持三亚崖州湾南繁科技城建设国家热带农业科学中心、现代种业示范区和国际种业贸易中心。

省和相关市、县、自治县人民政府应当推动打造深海技术科技创新高地，支持三亚崖州湾深海科技城承接深海领域国家科技创新重大项目、引入国家大科学装置，建设深海科技创新中心、国家深海基地南方中心、深海科技中试基地和深海科技成果孵化与转化基地。

to increase research and development (hereinafter referred to as "R&D") investment through different means including funding, awards and subsidies, and preferential policies and dividend incentive policies shall be issued, such as for the accelerated depreciation of fixed assets, equity incentives, technology shareholding, technical services and assignment, and equipment imports that may support technological innovation among businesses.

Organizations, research institutes, and private organizations shall be encouraged to set up science and technology business incubators in the Hainan Free Trade Port, and the creation of a network of technology business incubators in the Hainan Free Trade Port shall also be encouraged.

Article 8 The government and appropriate agencies shall issue policies and offer financial support to encourage domestic and foreign innovative entities to set up new R&D institutes. They shall support new R&D institutes in conducting science and technology planning projects, importing and purchasing scientific research equipment, and identifying eligible high-tech businesses.

The government and its agencies shall authorize new R&D institutes subject to employee quotas to independently make decisions on fund utilization, scientific and technological project management, scientific and technological achievement transformation, and laboratory assets, and to use flexible employment, salary, and social insurance systems as required.

Article 9 The government and its agencies shall encourage the creation of scientific and technological service providers and public service platforms in areas such as research, development and design, experimentation and awareness, inspection and certification, technology transfer, business development, intellectual property rights, and scientific and technological consultation to improve the development of the scientific and technological service industry.

Article 10 The provincial, city, county, and autonomous county people's governments shall support Nanfan seed technology and innovation development, and expedite the construction of the national Nanfan Scientific and Research Breeding Base, Yazhou Bay Seed Laboratory, and Global Animal and Plant Germplasm Introduction and Transfer Base, and support the Nanfan Technology Zone of Sanya Yazhou Bay to build a national tropical agricultural science center, a modern seed industry demonstration zone and an international seed industry trade center.

The provincial, city, county, and autonomous county people's governments shall encourage the creation of leading deep-sea technological innovation, support the Sanya Yazhou Bay Deep-sea Technology Zone to conduct major national deep-sea scientific and technological innovation projects, improve access to scientific facilities, and build the deep-sea technology innovation center, the Southern Base of the National Deep Sea Center, the deep-sea technology pilot base and the deep-sea technology achievement development and transformation base.

省和相关市、县、自治县人民政府应当推动打造航天科技创新高地，支持文昌国际航天城建立星箭研制、航天先进制造、发射、航天应用的航天科技创新平台，开展关键技术研发和成果转化应用，发展空间大数据、空间信息应用、航天科普等产业。

第十一条 鼓励重点园区设立国际离岸创新创业试验区，依照有关规定提供外币兑换、利润汇回等便利，建设离岸企业孵化器、创新创业基地、技术转移中心等平台，在产学研用结合、知识产权保护、离岸数据外包服务等方面进行创新。

国际离岸创新创业试验区应当推动境外科技成果在海南自由贸易港转移转化，鼓励境外科技人才在海南自由贸易港创新创业，支持跨国公司、境外研发机构在海南自由贸易港依法设立研发机构和技术转移中心。

国际离岸创新创业试验区内可以建设国际科技大数据平台，为国内外科研人员提供专门的国际科技信息和跨境数据流动服务。

第十二条 省和市、县、自治县人民政府应当推动设立国际科技合作项目，建立国际科研合作平台和联合攻关机制，推进气候变化、重大疾病、生物多样性保护等人类共同议题的国际科技合作。

政府及有关部门应当鼓励各类创新主体与境外机构合作开展前瞻性、战略性技术研究，建立财政科研资金跨境使用管理机制，依法支持相关设备、材料、样品、样本跨境使用。

The provincial, city, county, and autonomous county people's governments shall encourage the creation of leading science and technology innovation space, support the Wenchang International Space City to develop a science and technology innovation platform for satellite and rocket research and development, advanced space manufacturing, launches, and space applications, main technology research and development and achievement transformation implementation, and develop industries such as space big data, space data utilization, and space science awareness.

Article 11 The main industrial parks shall be encouraged to set up international offshore innovation and entrepreneurship pilot zones, provide foreign currency exchange services, profit repatriation, and other services as required, create offshore business development centers, innovation and entrepreneurship bases, technology transfer centers, and other platforms, and encourage innovation in businesses, universities, research institutes, and end-user integration, intellectual property rights protection, and offshore data outsourcing services.

The international offshore innovation and entrepreneurship pilot zone shall improve the transfer and transformation of overseas scientific and technological achievements within the Hainan Free Trade Port, encourage overseas scientific and technological skilled employees to innovate and start businesses in the Hainan Free Trade Port, and support multinational companies and overseas R&D institutes to set up R&D facilities and technology transfer centers in the Hainan Free Trade Port in accordance with the law.

The international scientific and technological big data platform may be added to the international offshore innovation and entrepreneurship pilot zone to provide specialized international scientific and technological information and cross-border data flow services for domestic and overseas researchers.

Article 12 The provincial, city, county, and autonomous county people's governments shall encourage the creation of international scientific and technological collaboration projects, create international scientific research collaboration platforms and joint research systems, and encourage international scientific and technological collaboration on common concerns such as climate change, major diseases, and biodiversity protection.

The government and its agencies shall encourage all kinds of innovative entities to collaborate with overseas institutes to conduct forward-looking and strategic technical research, set up a management system for cross-border use of financial research funding, and legally support cross-border use of equipment, materials, samples, and specimens.

政府及有关部门应当推进技术贸易自由化便利化，扩大技术进出口经营者资格范围，取消对外贸易经营者备案登记，加强对禁止类和限制类技术进出口的安全管控。

鼓励科研机构、高等院校、企业以及科技交流专业机构通过举办国际性学术会议、科技创新展会、创新创业大赛等方式开展国际科技合作交流工作。

第十三条 省和市、县、自治县人民政府应当推动建立与国际接轨、体现中国特色、符合海南定位的国际人才管理服务体制机制。推行国际人才管理服务一卡通制度。

放宽境外人员参与政府科研任务限制，允许符合条件的外国人兼职创新创业。对外国人工作许可实行负面清单管理，推行以薪酬水平为导向的外国高层次人才认定标准，提供出境入境和停居留便利。

完善事业单位聘用外国人工作制度，符合条件的外国人依照有关规定考核评价后可以免于考试，直接予以聘用。

第十四条 省和市、县、自治县人民政府应当根据旅游业、现代服务业、高新技术产业、热带高效农业等重点产业的发展需求，推动与粤港澳大湾区和科技创新发达省市合作，推动重点园区与其他省市国家高新技术产业开发区、国家级新区等园区合作，促进人员、资金、技术、信息等创新要素高效便捷流动，打造开放创新引领区。

鼓励国内高等院校、科研机构、企业和社会组织在海南自由贸易港重点园区设立科研机构、研发基地和成果转化基地。

The government and its agencies shall encourage the liberalization and facilitation of the technology trade, expand the scope of eligibility for technology import and export operators, cancel the registration or recordation requirement for foreign industry operators, and improve controls for the import and export of prohibited and restricted technologies.

The research institutes, higher learning institutions, businesses, and professional science and technology institutes are encouraged to conduct international science and technology collaboration and exchanges by holding events such as international academic seminars, science and technology innovation exhibitions, and innovation and entrepreneurship competitions.

Article 13 The provincial, city, county, and autonomous county people's governments shall encourage the creation of an international-standard skilled employee service system adapted for circumstances in China and conforming to Hainan's positioning, and implement a one-card system for international employee management and services.

The limitation on overseas employees is eased to allow them to participate in government scientific research tasks and allow qualified foreigners to work part-time in innovation and entrepreneurship. A negative list is implemented for foreigner work permits and salary-oriented standards for foreign high-end professionals, and facilitate entry, exit, and residence.

The employment system for foreigners working in public institutions is improved to facilitate direct employment by exempting qualified foreigners from testing after being assessed as required.

Article 14 The people's governments in provinces and cities, counties, and autonomous counties shall encourage collaboration with the Guangdong-Hong Kong-Macao Greater Bay Area and other provinces and cities encouraging advanced scientific and technological innovation, encouraging collaboration with main zones and other provinces and cities, national high-tech industrial development zones, new national zones, and other zones, encourage the efficient and easy flow of innovative elements such as employees, capital, technology, and information, and create leading openness and innovation areas based on the development needs of main industries such as tourism, modern service industries, high-tech industries, and productive tropical agriculture.

Domestic higher learning institutions, research institutes, businesses, and private organizations are encouraged to set up research institutes, R&D bases, and achievement transformation bases in key zones of the Hainan Free Trade Port.

第十五条 省和市、县、自治县人民政府应当建立完善以信任为前提的财政科研经费管理机制，扩大科研项目承担单位和科研人员的经费管理自主权，优化科研项目经费拨付、管理以及成果评价方式，加大科研人员激励力度，调动科研人员的创造性和创新活力。

对人才类和基础研究类科研项目实行财政经费包干制，对从事基础性、前沿性、公益性研究的独立法人科研机构逐步推行财政经费包干制。横向科研项目资金按照委托方要求或者合同约定进行管理。

第十六条 省和市、县、自治县人民政府应当完善技术交易市场体系建设，加强成果应用示范和场景创新。建立国内外科技成果转移转化的技术与信息服务平台，健全科技成果转化有关资产评估管理机制，推动科技成果转化和产业化。

政府及有关部门应当推动建设国家科技成果转移转化示范区，鼓励重大新药成果等科技成果优先在海南转移转化。

技术开发、技术咨询、技术服务等活动的奖励报酬提取，按照科技成果转化有关规定执行。

第十七条 利用财政性资金形成的归单位所有的职务科技成果，高等院校、科研机构可以赋予科技成果完成人共同所有权或者长期使用权，但是可能影响国家安全、公共利益、社会稳定的除外。

依据前款规定，赋予科技成果完成人共同所有权的，科技成果完成人与单位可以约定共同共有或者按份共有。按份共有的，科技成果完成人的份额可以不低于 70%。赋予科技成果完成人长期使用权的，使用权限可以不低于 10 年。

对于同一职务科技成果，科研人员获得职务科技成果所有权或者长期使用权的，其单位可以不再给予其成果转化收益和奖励。

Article 15 The provincial, city, county, and autonomous county people's governments shall create and optimize an administration system for financial scientific research funding based on trustworthiness, expand independent funding for participating institutes and scientific research employees, improve funding allocation for scientific research projects, increase incentives for scientific research employees, and improve their creativity and innovation vitality.

A lump-sum funding system shall be implemented for skilled employees and basic research projects, and be gradually implemented for research institutes with independent juristic persons involved in basic, cutting-edge, and public welfare research. Funding for horizontal scientific research projects shall be managed based on the delegating party or contract requirements.

Article 16 The provincial, city, county, and autonomous county people's governments shall improve the development of a technology trade market system, strengthen the demonstration of technological achievements and innovation of technology implementation, create a technology and information service platform for domestic and overseas science and technology achievement transfers and transformations, improve the asset appraisal management system for the transformation of science and technology achievements, and promote the transformation and industrialization of science and technology achievements.

The government and its agencies shall improve the construction of national demonstration zones for science and technology achievement transfers and transformations, and encourage the prioritization of the transfer and transformation of major new pharmaceutical achievements and other science and technology achievements in Hainan.

Rewards and fees for activities such as technology development, technical consultation, and technical services shall be paid in compliance with regulations on the transformation of science and technology achievements.

Article 17 Higher learning institutions and research institutes may grant joint title or long-term use rights to the individual who creates scientific and technological work for hire using fiscal funds provided that they would affect national security, the public interest, or social stability. The work for hire's ownership belongs to the employer.

As required by the preceding paragraph, if the work for hire is granted joint ownership, the individual and employer may agree on either joint or proportional ownership. When choosing proportional ownership, the proportion owned by the individual shall not be less than 70%. The long-term use rights period shall not be less than 10 years.

If the individual obtains ownership or long-term use rights for the same work for hire, the employer may not grant them the benefits and rewards arising from the transfer.

第十八条　政府及有关部门应当支持新技术、新产业、新业态、新模式健康发展。采用政府首购、订购以及购买服务等方式促进技术创新产品的规模化应用，实行颠覆性创新产品市场准入特别措施，促进新技术、新产品产业化、商品化。

政府及有关部门应当建立符合新技术、新产业、新业态、新模式的包容审慎监管体系，健全新技术、新产品应用安全监测机制，分类实行监管规则和标准，加强事中事后监管。

第十九条　对利用财政性资金或者国有资本设立的探索性强、不确定性高的科技项目，能够充分证明承担项目的单位和科技人员已经履行了勤勉尽责义务仍未能形成预期科技成果的，经立项主管部门组织专家论证后，可以允许该项目结题，不影响相关单位和个人再次申请利用财政性资金或者国有资本设立的科技项目。

第二十条　本规定自 2022 年 1 月 1 日起施行。

Article 18 The government and its agencies shall support the sustainable development of new technologies, new industries, new business operations, and new models. They shall encourage the large-scale use of technological and innovative products through initial purchases, government ordering or procurement services, and implement special actions to enable market access for disruptive innovative products to improve the industrialization and commercialization of new technologies and new products.

The government and its agencies shall create an inclusive and prudent oversight system in line with new technologies, new industries, new business operations, and models, improve the application safety monitoring system for new technologies and new products, implement oversight rules and standards through classification, and enhance oversight during and after the process.

Article 19 Where the entities and science and technology employees conducting highly experimental and uncertain technology projects set up using fiscal funding or state-owned capital can prove that they have fulfilled their duty of diligence but still failed to achieve the expected results, the project competent agency may allow the projects to be terminated after organizing expert review by the competent agency. This termination shall not affect the entities and individuals to apply for other science and technology projects using financial funding or state-owned capital.

Article 20 These Regulations shall come into force as of January 1, 2022.

海南自由贸易港免税购物失信惩戒若干规定

Several Provisions of Hainan Free Trade Port on Duty-Free Shopping Untrustworthy Acts Penalties

海南自由贸易港免税购物失信惩戒若干规定

（2021 年 12 月 1 日海南省第六届人民代表大会常务委员会第三十一次会议通过）

第一条 为了预防和惩戒海南自由贸易港免税购物严重失信行为，根据《中华人民共和国海南自由贸易港法》《海南自由贸易港社会信用条例》等法律、法规和国家有关规定，结合海南自由贸易港实际，制定本规定。

第二条 反走私综合治理工作牵头部门负责免税购物严重失信主体的认定工作。

海关、海警依法履行失信惩戒相关职责。

公安、发展改革、市场监督管理、交通运输、商务、邮政管理、人民银行、人民法院等有关部门和单位，应当按照各自职责做好免税购物信用监管和失信惩戒相关工作。

第三条 自然人、法人和非法人组织违反海南离岛旅客免税购物、海南岛内居民消费的“零关税”进境商品等有关监管规定，有下列情形之一的，列入免税购物严重失信主体名单：

（一）构成犯罪，被处以刑罚或者免予刑事处罚的；

（二）被处以行政处罚且情节严重或者被处以两次及以上行政处罚的；

（三）其他违反免税购物监管规定，依照法律、法规以及国家相关政策规定应当列入免税购物严重失信主体名单的。

Several Provisions of Hainan Free Trade Port on Duty-Free Shopping Untrustworthy Acts Penalties

(Adopted at the 31st Session of the Standing Committee of the 6th Hainan Provincial People's Congress on December 1, 2021)

Article 1 These Provisions are enacted pursuant to the Hainan Free Trade Port Law of People's Republic of China, Regulations of Hainan Free Trade Port on Social Credit, and other laws, regulations and state provisions combined with the actual circumstances in the Hainan Free Trade Port to prevent and penalize material violations when purchasing duty-free products in the Hainan Free Trade Port.

Article 2 The leading coordinated anti-smuggling agency shall be responsible for identifying untrustworthy entities for duty-free shopping.

Customs and maritime police agencies shall perform duties related to penalties for violations pursuant to law.

The agencies in public security, development and reform, market regulation, transportation, commerce, and postal administration, together with the people's bank and the people's courts shall be responsible for duty-free shopping credit oversight and penalties for violations in compliance with their duties.

Article 3 Any individual, juristic person, or unincorporated entity that violates duty-free shopping regulations for tourists leaving Hainan or regulations for duty-free imported goods used by Hainan residents shall be added to the list of untrustworthy entities for duty-free shopping under any of the following circumstances:

(a) he has committed a crime and has been penalized or exempt from criminal penalties;

(b) he has been assessed administrative penalties for major untrustworthy acts, or has been assessed two or more administrative penalties; or

(c) he has been listed as untrustworthy entities pursuant to law and applicable national policies due to violating other duty-free shopping regulations.

第四条 因违反免税购物监管规定被处以行政处罚或者刑罚以及免予刑事处罚的，海关、海警、市场监督管理、交通运输和人民法院等部门和单位，应当在行政处罚决定书或者司法裁判文书生效之日起十五日内将相关信息推送至县级以上人民政府反走私综合治理工作牵头部门。

第五条 海南自由贸易港免税购物严重失信主体名单，由县级以上人民政府反走私综合治理工作牵头部门按照国家和本规定确定的标准认定，并将经认定的免税购物严重失信主体名单告知同级人民政府发展改革、市场监督管理等相关管理部门，失信自然人所在单位以及有关金融机构和企业。

县级以上人民政府发展改革、市场监督管理部门应当在信用中国（海南）、国家企业信用信息公示系统（海南）等网站上公示严重失信主体名单，公示期三年。

第六条 对列入免税购物严重失信主体名单的法人和非法人组织，有关机关和单位应当在公示期内对其实施以下惩戒措施：

（一）约谈其主要负责人；

（二）列为重点监管对象，加大日常监管和查验力度，提高随机抽查的比例和频次；

（三）限制参与政府投资或者政府与社会资本合作的建设项目，或者予以提高保证金比例；

（四）在行政管理和公共服务中，不适用告知承诺制等便利措施、不享受守信激励措施；

（五）限制享受政府优惠政策支持、限制申请财政性资金项目；

（六）在公共资源交易中予以信用减分、降低信用等次；

Article 4 Where an administrative penalty or criminal penalty is imposed for violation of duty-free shopping oversight regulations, or the entity is exempt from criminal penalty, the customs, maritime police, market regulation, transportation, people's court, and other agencies shall notify the leading anti-smuggling administrative agency of the people's government at or above the county level within 15 days of the date on which the decision to impose the administrative penalty or court judgment comes into force.

Article 5 The list of untrustworthy entities in the Hainan Free Trade Port shall be determined by the leading coordinated anti-smuggling administrative agency of the people's government at or above the county level in compliance with the standards and these Provisions, and the development and reform and market regulation agencies of the people's government at the same level, the individual's employer, and related financial institutions and businesses shall be notified of the determined list.

The development and reform and market regulation agencies of the people's governments at or above the county level shall publish the list online, including on websites such as Credit China (Hainan) and the National Enterprise Credit Information Publicity System (Hainan) for 3 years.

Article 6 The appropriate agencies and entities shall implement the following disciplinary action and penalties within the publication period for those juristic persons or unincorporated entities listed as untrustworthy entities for duty-free shopping:

(a) meet with the main person in charge;

(b) list the entities as the main entity subject to oversight, improve daily oversight and inspections, and increase the proportion and frequency of random inspections;

(c) restrict the entities from participating in construction projects invested by the government or collaborations between the government and private sector, or increase the deposit amount;

(d) the entity shall not be entitled to benefit from acknowledgment or compliance incentives during administration and public service;

(e) restrict the entities from benefiting from government preferential policy support and applying for public funding;

(f) lower the entity's credit score and downgrade their credit level in public resource transactions;

（七）限制参与表彰奖励、取消参加评先评优资格、撤销相关荣誉；

（八）依照国家纳税信用管理的有关规定进行税收管控；

（九）法律、法规规定的其他措施。

第七条　对列入免税购物严重失信主体名单的自然人，有关机关和单位应当在公示期内对其实施以下惩戒措施：

（一）不得享受免税购物政策；

（二）在日常监管中列为重点监管对象，在其离开海南自由贸易港时作为重点查验对象；

（三）不得从事免税商品经营相关工作；

（四）取消其评优、评奖、获得荣誉称号、推荐保送升学等资格，并按照所在单位有关规定予以处理；

（五）在行政管理和公共服务中，不适用告知承诺制等便利措施、不享受守信激励措施；

（六）法律、法规规定的其他措施。

第八条　征信机构可以依法采集免税购物严重失信行为信息，并向金融机构提供查询。

商业银行、保险公司和证券公司等金融机构可以按照风险定价原则，对免税购物严重失信主体提高贷款利率、财产保险费率和交易佣金，或者依法限制向其提供贷款、保险、保荐、承销等服务。

第九条　免税购物失信信息归集、共享、公开、异议处理和信用修复等工作，按照《海南自由贸易港社会信用条例》有关规定办理。

第十条　本规定自2022年1月1日起施行。

(g) restrict the entity's participation in awards and rewards and cancel their eligibility to participate in excellence evaluations and awards;

(h) subject the entity to tax controls pursuant to applicable national tax credit management regulations; and

(i) other measures provided by laws and regulations.

Article 7 The agencies and entities shall implement the following disciplinary actions and penalties within the publication period for those individuals listed as untrustworthy entities for duty-free shopping:

(a) restrict the entity from benefiting from duty-free shopping policies;

(b) list the entity as the main entity subject to routine oversight, and shall be regarded as the main entity subject to inspection when leaving the Hainan Free Trade Port;

(c) the entity shall not be permitted to participate in business related to duty-free products;

(d) revoke the entity's qualification to participate in awards, rewards, and further education award and commendation evaluation shall be revoked and manage the violation in compliance with its employer's related guidelines;

(e) the entity shall not be entitled to benefit from acknowledgment or compliance incentives during administration and public service; and

(f) other measures provided by laws and regulations.

Article 8 Credit investigation institutions may collect information on material duty-free shopping violations pursuant to law and provide inquiry access for financial institutions.

Commercial banks, insurance companies, securities companies, and other financial institutions may increase loan interest rates, property insurance premium rates, and trading commission rates based on risk-based pricing for any entity that commits material duty-free shopping violations or restrict such entities from acquiring loans, guarantees, underwriting, insurance, and other services pursuant to law.

Article 9 The collection, sharing, disclosure, objection resolution, and credit restoration for duty-free shopping penalties shall be conducted pursuant to the Regulations of Hainan Free Trade Port on Social Credit.

Article 10 These Provisions shall come into force as of January 1, 2022.

海南自由贸易港闲置土地处置若干规定

Several Provisions of Hainan Free Trade Port on Unused Land Management

海南自由贸易港闲置土地处置若干规定

（2021 年 12 月 1 日海南省第六届人民代表大会常务委员会第三十一次会议通过）

第一条 为了有效处置闲置土地和充分利用土地，促进节约集约用地，根据《中华人民共和国海南自由贸易港法》《中华人民共和国城市房地产管理法》等法律、法规，结合海南自由贸易港实际，制定本规定。

第二条 本规定所称闲置土地，是指具有下列情形之一的国有建设用地：

（一）超过动工开发日期满一年未动工开发的；

（二）超过动工开发日期满两年未完成项目总投资额百分之二十五的；

（三）已动工开发但开发建设用地面积占应动工开发建设用地总面积不足三分之一或者已投资额占总投资额不足百分之二十五，中止开发建设满一年的；

（四）以出让方式取得国有建设用地使用权，超过出让合同约定的竣工日期一年未竣工的；

（五）法律、法规规定的其他情形。

依法通过转让取得的国有建设用地使用权，具有前款规定情形之一的，可根据本规定处置。

前款第四项所称竣工是指建设项目依法取得《工程竣工报告》等法定竣工验收文件。

Several Provisions of Hainan Free Trade Port on Unused Land Management

(Adopted at the 31st Session of the Standing Committee of the 6th Hainan Provincial People's Congress on December 1, 2021)

Article 1 These Provisions are enacted to effectively manage unused land, make full use of such land and encourage economical and intensive land use pursuant to law, including the Hainan Free Trade Port Law of the People's Republic of China and Urban Real Estate Administration Law of the People's Republic of China, and based on actual circumstances in the Hainan Free Trade Port.

Article 2 Unused land as referred to in these Provisions means state-owned development land meeting any of the following conditions:

(a) no construction has taken place on the land for 1 year since the development commencement date;

(b) less than 25% of the total project investment has been invested into the project for 2 years since the development commencement date;

(c) development on the land has started but less than 1/3 of the total area to be developed has been built; or less than 25% of the total investment required has been invested and development has been suspended for 1 year;

(d) the state-owned leasehold estate is assigned, but the project is still incomplete for more than 1 year since the completion date agreed upon in the assignment contract; or

(e) other circumstances as provided by laws and regulations.

Unused land for which the state-owned leasehold estate has been obtained through assignment pursuant to law and meeting the conditions provided in this Article may be managed pursuant to these Provisions.

Completion as referred to in the fourth item of Paragraph 1 of this Article refers to the process where construction projects obtain statutory completion inspection documentation, such as the Project Completion Report.

第三条 县级以上人民政府组织和统筹本行政区域内闲置土地认定和处置工作。

省人民政府自然资源和规划主管部门对市、县、自治县人民政府自然资源和规划主管部门调查认定和处置闲置土地工作进行监督管理。市、县、自治县人民政府自然资源和规划部门负责本行政区域内闲置土地认定、处置以及土地闲置费核定等工作的组织实施。税务部门负责土地闲置费具体征收工作。市、县、自治县人民政府发展改革、住房和城乡建设等部门按照各自职责协同做好闲置土地认定和处置工作。

闲置土地所在地乡镇人民政府、街道办事处协助做好闲置土地认定和处置工作。

第四条 有下列情形之一的，可以认定为政府或者政府有关部门原因（以下统称政府原因）造成土地闲置：

（一）因未按照国有建设用地使用权有偿使用合同或者划拨决定书约定、规定的期限、条件将土地交付给国有建设用地使用权人，致使项目不具备动工开发条件的。但出让人和受让人已经签订交地确认文件、确认土地具备开发条件的不视为政府原因；

（二）因国土空间规划依法修改，造成国有建设用地使用权人不能按照国有建设用地使用权有偿使用合同约定或者划拨决定书规定的用途、规划和建设条件动工开发的；

（三）因国家和本省出台相关政策，需要对国有建设用地使用权有偿使用合同约定或者划拨决定书规定的规划和建设条件进行修改或者政策内容影响土地开发，导致无法动工开发的；

（四）因行政机关未依法实施涉及土地开发建设相关行政许可，导致无法动工开发的；

Article 3 The governments at or above the county level shall organize and coordinate the identification and management of the unused land within their administrative areas.

The provincial people's government natural resources and planning agencies shall be responsible for overseeing and managing natural resources and planning agencies under the people's governments in cities, counties, and autonomous counties in the identification and management of unused land. Natural resources and planning agencies under the people's governments in cities, counties, or autonomous counties shall be responsible for organizing the implementation of the identification and management of unused land and the determination of unused land fees within their administrative areas. The local tax authority shall be responsible for collecting unused land fees. The development and reform, housing, and urban-rural development agencies under the city, county, or autonomous county people's governments shall cooperate with and coordinate the identification and management of unused land based on their duties.

Town-level people's governments and subdistrict agencies where the unused land is located shall assist in the identification and management of the unused land.

Article 4 Any of the following circumstances is deemed that the land is unused due to the fault of the government or government agencies (hereinafter collectively referred to as "government fault"):

(a) the project is unable to meet the construction requirements for the state-owned leasehold estate due to the land not being delivered to the state-owned leasehold estate owner within the time limit or under the conditions provided and agreed upon in the state-owned leasehold estate lease contract or a government allocation decision. However, it shall not be deemed as a government fault if the assignor and assignee have signed a land transfer confirmation document and confirmed that the land meets development requirements;

(b) the state-owned leasehold estate owner fails to develop the land pursuant to the function, planning, and construction conditions provided in the state-owned leasehold estate lease contract or the government allocation decision due to changes in national land and space planning pursuant to law;

(c) the unused land cannot be developed due to changes in newly enacted national or Hainan provincial policies on state-owned leasehold estate lease contracts, government allocation decisions, or if such policies impact the development;

(d) the development cannot be started due to the failure of the administrative agencies to issue administrative permissions for land development and construction pursuant to law;

（五）因行政行为引起处置土地上相关群众信访事项等，导致无法动工开发的；

（六）因军事管制、文物保护等无法动工开发的；

（七）法律、法规规定的其他情形。

国有建设用地使用权人认为属于政府原因造成土地闲置的，应当向市、县、自治县人民政府自然资源和规划主管部门提供土地闲置原因说明材料，由市、县、自治县人民政府或者造成土地闲置的政府有关部门书面确认。

第五条 闲置土地按照下列方式处置，但因政府原因或者不可抗力等其他法定原因造成土地闲置的除外：

（一）超过出让合同约定的动工开发日期满一年未满两年不动工开发的，以及已动工开发但开发建设用地面积占应动工开发建设用地总面积不足三分之一或者已投资额占总投资额不足百分之二十五，中止开发建设满一年的，国有建设用地使用权人应当按土地出让金的百分之二十缴纳土地闲置费。

（二）超过动工开发日期满两年未完成项目总投资额百分之二十五的，无偿收回国有建设用地使用权。

（三）以出让方式取得国有建设用地使用权，超过出让合同约定的竣工日期一年未竣工的，应当在竣工前按照下列标准征收土地闲置费：

1. 超过出让合同约定的竣工日期一年未竣工，但未超过三年的，每年按土地现值百分之五征收。

2. 超过出让合同约定的竣工日期三年未竣工，但未超过五年的，每年按土地现值百分之十征收。

(e) the development cannot be started due to complaints caused by administrative action;

(f) the development cannot be started due to military controls or the protection of cultural relics; or

(g) other circumstances provided by laws and regulations.

Any state-owned leasehold estate owner who believes that unused land is a result of government fault shall provide an explanation of the reasons for the unused land to the natural resources and planning agency at the city, county, or autonomous county people's government. The statement shall be verified in writing by the city, county, or autonomous county people's government or the agencies that caused the unused land.

Article 5 Except for unused land due to statutory reasons such as government fault or *force majeure*, the unused land shall be managed in the following ways:

(a) The state-owned leasehold estate owner must pay 20% of the land transfer fee as an unused land fee if no construction has taken place on the land for more than 1 year but less than 2 years since the development commencement date provided in the contract, or if development on the land has started but less than 1/3 of the total area to be developed has been built, or less than 25% of the total investment required has been invested and development has been suspended for 1 year.

(b) The state-owned leasehold estate shall be recovered without compensation if less than 25% of the total project investment has been invested into the project for 2 years since the development commencement date.

(c) Unused land fees shall be collected before the project completion date based on the following standards, if the state-owned leasehold estate is obtained through assignment but the project remains incomplete for 1 year of the completion date provided in the contract:

(i) 5% of the current value of the land shall be charged for every year the project remains incomplete if the project is incomplete for more than 1 year but less than 3 years since the Date;

(ii) 10% of the current value of the land shall be charged for every year if the project remains incomplete for more than 3 years but less than 5 years from the Date;

3．超过出让合同约定的竣工日期五年未竣工，但未超过七年的，每年按土地现值百分之十五征收。

4．超过出让合同约定的竣工日期七年未竣工的，每年按土地现值百分之二十征收。

同时符合第二条规定的两种及以上闲置土地情形的，从重适用前款规定的处置方式。

闲置土地现值应当以综合考虑土地原用途、土地资源条件、土地产值、土地区位、土地供求关系、人口以及经济社会发展水平等因素测算出的基准地价为依据。

第六条　因政府原因造成土地闲置的，市、县、自治县人民政府自然资源和规划主管部门应当与国有建设用地使用权人协商，选择下列方式处置：

（一）延长动工开发期限、竣工期限。对在一年内有条件消除政府原因，具备动工开发条件的闲置土地，可签订补充协议，重新约定动工开发、竣工期限和违约责任。从补充协议约定的动工开发日期起，延长动工开发期限最长不得超过一年。市、县、自治县人民政府应当自签订补充协议后一年内消除土地闲置的政府原因；

（二）调整土地用途、规划条件。因政府或者政府有关部门调整土地用途、规划条件造成土地闲置的，在符合国土空间规划的前提下，可以按照新用途或者新规划条件重新办理相关用地手续，并按照新用途或者新规划条件核算、收缴或者退还土地价款；

(iii) 15% of the current value of the land shall be charged for every year if the project remains incomplete for more than 5 years but less than 7 years since the Date; and

(iv) 20% of the current value of the land shall be charged for every year if the project remains incomplete for more than 7 years from the Date.

Unused land fees shall be charged based on the higher rate provided above if the unused land meets two or more of the circumstances provided in Article 2.

The current value of the unused land may be assessed based on the benchmark land price calculated by comprehensively considering original land use, land resources, land output value, land location, land supply and demand, population, and economic and social development.

Article 6 If the land is unused due to government fault, the natural resources and planning agency of the city, county or autonomous county people's government shall negotiate with the state-owned leasehold estate owner and choose any one of the following management methods:

(a) extension of the construction and completion periods. An amendment for the construction and completion periods, and liability for breach of contract may be signed for unused land suitable for the construction contract if the government fault can be eliminated within 1 year. The construction period shall be extended for a maximum of 1 year from the commencement date provided in the amendment. The city, county, and autonomous county people's governments shall eliminate all governmental fault on the unused land within 1 year of signing the amendment;

(b) adjustment of the land use and planning conditions. Applicable land use procedures may be redone pursuant to the new land use or planning conditions in compliance with national space planning if the unused land is a result of changes to land use or planning conditions by the government or appropriate government agencies. Land price may be calculated, collected, or refunded based on the new use or new planning conditions;

（三）安排临时使用。因政府原因造成项目尚不具备动工开发条件导致土地闲置的，在不具备动工开发条件期间，可以安排国有建设用地使用权人临时使用其闲置土地。从安排使用之日起，临时使用期限最长不得超过两年。市、县、自治县人民政府应当在安排临时使用期限内消除造成土地闲置的政府原因，使项目具备动工开发条件；

（四）置换土地。对已缴清土地价款、落实项目资金，但因国土空间规划依法修改造成土地闲置的，可以为国有建设用地使用权人置换其他价值相当的国有建设用地进行开发建设。涉及出让土地的，应当重新签订土地出让合同，并在合同中注明为置换土地；

（五）协议有偿收回国有建设用地使用权；

（六）法律、法规等规定的其他处置方式。

按照前款第二项和第四项规定的方式处置，涉及商品住宅用地的，必须符合国家和我省房地产管理有关政策规定。

因不可抗力导致土地闲置的，依照本条规定的方式处置。

第七条 因生态环境保护、基础设施和公共服务项目建设、军事管制等公共利益需要导致土地无法开发利用，造成土地闲置的，经市、县、自治县人民政府批准，可以收回国有建设用地使用权，并按照有偿收回闲置土地补偿标准对国有建设用地使用权人给予适当补偿。有偿收回闲置土地补偿标准由省人民政府另行制定。

第八条 市、县、自治县人民政府自然资源和规划主管部门发现有涉嫌构成闲置土地的，应当向国有建设用地使用权人下发闲置土地调查通知书，经调查认定为闲置土地的，应当拟定闲置土地处置方案，报本级人民政府批准后，向国有建设用地使用权人下达征缴土地闲置费决定书

(c) grant of temporary use. State-owned development land owner may be granted temporary use of unused land if government fault leads to the project failing to meet construction requirements until such requirements are fulfilled. The maximum temporary use period shall not exceed 2 years from the date of the grant and the people's governments in the cities, counties, or autonomous counties shall eliminate the government fault that caused the unused land within the temporary use grant period to allow project construction to continue;

(d) land replacement. The state-owned leasehold estate owner may be granted another state-owned leasehold estate of equal value, provided that the land price was already paid and project funding is in place if the unused land is due to the change of national land space planning pursuant to law. The land assignment contract shall be re-signed and the contract shall specify it as replacement land if land assignment is involved;

(e) recovery of state-owned leasehold estate rights through agreement; or

(f) other management methods provided by laws and regulations.

If commercial residential land is involved pursuant to the second and fourth items of Paragraph 1 of this Article, the management shall be subject to the applicable national and Hainan Province property management policies and regulations.

Unused land resulting from *force majeure* may be managed pursuant to this Article.

Article 7 If the land cannot be developed due to the public interest, such as for ecological environment protection, the construction of infrastructure and public service facilities, or military controls, the state-owned leasehold estate rights may be recovered with the approval from the city, county, or autonomous county people's government, and state-owned development land owner shall be appropriately compensated in compliance with the compensation standards for recovering unused land. The standards shall be issued separately by the provincial people's government.

Article 8 If the competent natural resources and planning department under the city, county, or autonomous county people's government finds that a land plot might constitute unused land, the department shall issue an investigation notice to the state-owned development land owner. If the land is determined to be unused after investigation, the appropriate agency shall formulate a management plan for it and submit it to the people's government at the same level for approval, and issue a management decision, such as a decision document to pay unused land fees or to recover the state-owned development land leasehold estate from the owner after obtaining government approval. The state-owned development land owner shall be issued a written notice informing them that they are entitled to request a hearing pursuant to law before

或者收回国有建设用地使用权决定书等处置决定文书。作出处置决定文书前，应当书面告知国有建设用地使用权人依法享有申请听证的权利，国有建设用地使用权人要求举行听证的，应当依法组织听证。

征缴土地闲置费决定书应当同时抄送税务部门。

第九条 本规定第五条第一款第三项规定的土地闲置费按年计征和缴交。起征日为国有土地出让合同约定的竣工期限届满一年之次日，计征截止日为市、县、自治县人民政府自然资源和规划主管部门向国有建设用地使用权人送达《闲置土地调查通知书》之日。征期不足一年的部分，按照征缴标准和计征天数折算。

本规定施行前已出让的土地，已逾期未竣工或未逾期但距约定竣工日期不满两年，且自本规定施行之日起两年内未竣工的，自本规定施行满三年之次日按照本规定第五条第一款第三项规定开始征缴土地闲置费。

第十条 国有建设用地使用权人逾期不申请行政复议、不提起行政诉讼，也不履行相关义务的，市、县、自治县人民政府自然资源和规划主管部门、税务部门可以采取下列措施：

（一）逾期不办理国有建设用地使用权注销登记，不交回土地权利证书的，直接公告注销国有建设用地使用权登记和土地权利证书；

（二）逾期不缴纳土地闲置费或者不交回国有建设用地使用权的，申请人民法院强制执行。

第十一条 造成闲置土地政府原因的相关人民政府及相关部门应当依法履职，消除政府原因。省人民政府和有关部门可采取扣减新增建设用地计划指标、暂停农转用审批等措施，对市、县、自治县人民政府闲置土地处置工作实施考核和奖惩。

the management decision is made. A hearing shall be organized pursuant to law if the state-owned development land owner requests a hearing.

A copy of the written decision on collecting the unused land fees shall also be sent to the tax authority.

Article 9 Unused land fees shall be calculated and collected annually if collected and paid pursuant to the third item of Paragraph 1 of Article 5. The commencement date to collect the fees shall be the second day of the end of the first year after the completion date specified in the state-owned leasehold estate assignment contract. The due date for the calculation and collection of unused land fees shall be the date on which the competent city, county, or autonomous county people's government natural resources and planning agency issues the Notice on Unused Land Investigation to the state-owned development land owner. If the collection period is less than 1 year, the fees due shall be calculated based on the collection standards and collection days.

If land assigned before the implementation of these Provisions remains incomplete or the land development period has not expired but has less than 2 years left and the development is not completed within 2 years of the date these Provisions came into force, the commencement date to collect shall be the second day of the end of the third year of the effectiveness of these Provisions and unused land fees shall be collected and paid in accordance with the third item of Paragraph 1 of Article 5.

Article 10 If the state-owned leasehold estate owner fails to request an administrative review, file an administrative lawsuit, or fulfill its obligations within the time limit, the competent natural resources and planning agency and taxation agencies of the city, county, and autonomous county people's government may take the following actions:

(a) the appropriate agencies may directly publish the deregistration of the state-owned leasehold estate registration and land title certificate, if the state-owned leasehold estate owner does not complete deregistration and does not return the land title certificate; and

(b) petition the people's court for enforcement if the state-owned leasehold estate owner does not pay the unused land fees owed or does not return the right to use the development land.

Article 11 Where the land is unused due to governmental fault, the appropriate people's governments and agencies shall perform their duties and eliminate such fault pursuant to law. The provincial people's government and appropriate agencies may take action such as reducing the expansion index of planned new development land, suspending review and approval for converting agricultural land to development land, and conducting assessments and issuing rewards and penalties to the city, county, or autonomous county people's government related to work managing unused land.

第十二条 县级以上人民政府应当通过依法调整规划、改变土地用途等措施，鼓励和引导闲置土地盘活利用。

第十三条 县级以上人民政府及其有关部门工作人员违反本规定，有下列情形之一的，依法给予处分；对当事人造成损失的，应当依法承担赔偿责任；构成犯罪的，依法追究刑事责任：

（一）违反本规定不如实核定和征缴土地闲置费的；

（二）擅自决定减缴、免缴、缓缴土地闲置费的；

（三）坐支、截留或挪用土地闲置费的；

（四）不依法履行闲置土地监督检查职责的；

（五）未依法履职造成土地闲置或者故意长期拖延未消除导致土地闲置的政府原因的；

（六）其他在闲置土地调查、认定和处置工作中徇私舞弊、滥用职权、玩忽职守的。

第十四条 闲置土地的认定和处置，本规定未作规定的，适用国家和本省的有关规定。

第十五条 本规定自 2022 年 1 月 1 日起施行。

Article 12 The people's government at or above the county level shall encourage and guide the revitalization and utilization of unused land through methods such as adjusting planning and changing land use pursuant to law.

Article 13 If any employee of the people's government at or above the county level or its agencies violates these Provisions and such violation falls under any of the following circumstances, the employee shall be penalized pursuant to law. Any employee of the above agencies that causes losses to a party shall be liable for indemnification pursuant to law and shall be held criminally liable pursuant to law if it constitutes a crime:

(a) failure to truthfully confirm and collect unused land fees in violation of these Provisions;

(b) unauthorized approval of reductions, exemptions or deferment of unused land fees;

(c) spending, keeping, or misappropriating unused land fees;

(d) failure to perform unused land oversight and inspection duties pursuant to law;

(e) failure to perform duties in accordance with the law, thus resulting in unused land, or deliberate long-term delays and failure to eliminate the governmental fault causing unused land; or

(f) other misconduct for playing favoritism and committing irregularities, abuse of position, or dereliction of duty in the investigation, determination, or disposal of unused land.

Article 14 Other provisions of the state and the Hainan Province shall apply if these Provisions do not provide for the determination and management of the unused land.

Article 15 These Provisions shall come into force as of January 1, 2022.

海南自由贸易港博鳌乐城国际医疗旅游先行区条例

Regulations of Hainan Free Trade Port on Bo'ao Hope Pilot Zone of International Medical Tourism

海南自由贸易港博鳌乐城国际医疗旅游先行区条例

（2020 年 6 月 16 日海南省第六届人民代表大会常务委员会第二十次会议通过）

第一章 总 则

第一条 为了促进海南自由贸易港博鳌乐城国际医疗旅游先行区（以下简称先行区）发展，根据有关法律、行政法规，结合本省实际，制定本条例。

第二条 先行区应当按照海南自由贸易港建设的有关要求，对标国际最高标准，创新体制机制，在产业政策、招商引资、医疗创新、旅游服务、跨境服务贸易等方面先行先试，以高水平开放推动国际医疗旅游和高端医疗服务发展，建设世界一流的国际医疗旅游目的地和医疗科技创新平台。

第三条 省人民政府应当加强对先行区建设的组织领导，决定先行区建设中的重大事项，建立考核和评估机制。

省人民政府推进先行区建设领导机构负责先行区建设的指导、督导、推进和协调工作，研究先行区建设中的重大问题。

省人民政府有关部门按照职责分工负责先行区建设的具体指导、协调和服务工作。

Regulations of Hainan Free Trade Port on Bo'ao Hope Pilot Zone of International Medical Tourism

(Adopted at the 20th Session of the Standing Committee of the 6th Hainan Provincial People's Congress on June 16, 2020)

Chapter I General Provisions

Article 1 For the purposes of promoting the development of Bo'ao Hope Pilot Zone of International Medical Tourism (hereinafter referred to as the "Pilot Zone") in Hainan Free Trade Port (hereinafter referred to as "HFTZ"), the Regulations on Bo'ao Hope Pilot Zone of International Medical Tourism are enacted pursuant to applicable laws and administrative regulations and in the light of the actual circumstances of this Province.

Article 2 Pursuant to the applicable requirements for the development of the HFTZ, the Pilot Zone shall adhere to the highest international standards, engage in governance innovation, and be a leader in industry policies, investment promotion, medical innovation, tourism services, and cross-border service trade, so as to promote the development of international medical tourism and high-end medical services with a high level of openness and build a world-class international medical tourism destination and medical science and technology innovation platform.

Article 3 The provincial people's government shall improve the organization and leadership of the development of the Pilot Zone, decide on major issues, and implement an assessment and evaluation system.

The provincial people's government shall enable the lead agency of the Pilot Zone to be responsible for guiding, overseeing, promoting, and coordinating the development of the Pilot Zone, and studying major issues.

The appropriate agencies of the provincial people's government shall be responsible for the guidance, coordination, and service of the development of the Pilot Zone pursuant to their respective functions and duties.

第四条　在先行区设立管理机构。管理机构是在先行区履行相应行政管理和公共服务职责的法定机构，具体负责先行区综合协调、开发建设、运营管理、产业发展、投资促进、制度创新、企业服务等工作，依照授权或者委托行使相应的行政审批权和行政处罚权。

先行区管理机构按照精简高效的原则，在薪酬总额范围内，自主决定机构设置、岗位设置、人员聘用、薪酬标准等，依照有关规定任命的人员除外。

先行区管理机构的高级管理人员及其他工作人员可以从境外选聘。

第五条　先行区管理机构可以依法组建开发运营公司，委托开发运营公司负责先行区内的产业投资、基础设施和公共服务设施的建设及运营，参与园区管理服务的组织与实施。

第六条　琼海市人民政府及其有关部门负责行使先行区的社会管理职能，具体范围由省人民政府规定。

琼海市人民政府及其有关部门应当在规划编制、招商引资、基础设施建设、体制创新、政策实施等方面支持先行区的发展。

第七条　省和琼海市人民政府及其有关部门应当依法将相关管理权限下放或者委托先行区管理机构行使。

不宜下放或者委托行使的管理权限，省和琼海市人民政府有关部门可以按照规定在先行区设立驻区机构。

省人民政府有关部门、先行区管理机构、驻区机构应当明确在先行区的管理权限，依法编制权力清单、责任清单，经批准后向社会公布。

Article 4 An administrative agency shall be created in the Pilot Zone. The administrative agency shall be the statutory agency that performs the appropriate administrative duties and provides public services in the Pilot Zone and is specifically responsible for the integrated coordination, development and construction, operation management, industrial development, investment promotion, institutional innovation, service for entities in the Pilot Zone, and shall exercise the administrative review and penalty authority through the authorization or delegation of power.

Under the principle of streamlining and efficiency, the administrative agency shall independently determine the organization, positions, employment, and salary standards as limited by the salary cap, except for those appointed pursuant to applicable regulations.

The senior administrative officers and other administrative agency employees in the Pilot Zone may be hired from other countries or regions.

Article 5 The administrative agency of the Pilot Zone may incorporate a development and operations company pursuant to law, delegate the development and operations company to be responsible for the development and operation of industrial investment, infrastructure, and public services facilities in the Pilot Zone, and participate in the organization and enforcement of the industrial park administration.

Article 6 The Qionghai Municipal People's Government and its appropriate agencies shall be responsible for the social administration of the Pilot Zone, which shall be specified by the provincial people's government.

The Qionghai Municipal People's Government and its appropriate agencies shall support the development of the Pilot Zone in planning, attracting investment, infrastructure development, institutional innovation, and policy enforcement.

Article 7 The provincial and Qionghai municipal people's governments and their appropriate agencies shall devolve or delegate the appropriate administrative powers to the administrative agency of the Pilot Zone pursuant to law.

If it is not appropriate to devolve or delegate the administrative powers, the appropriate agencies of the provincial and Qionghai municipal people's governments may establish local branch offices in the Pilot Zone pursuant to the rules.

The appropriate agencies of the provincial people's government, the administrative agency of the Pilot Zone, and the local branch offices shall clarify the administrative powers in the Pilot Zone, prepare the list of powers and duties pursuant to law, and publish such upon approval.

第二章 开发建设

第八条 先行区管理机构负责组织编制先行区控制性详细规划以及产业发展规划等，经批准后实施。

先行区周边地区相关规划应当与先行区控制性详细规划以及产业发展规划等相衔接。

第九条 先行区应当严格落实生态环境保护制度和生态保护红线管理制度，严格资源节约利用和环境准入门槛，完善生态环境保护基础设施和措施，坚持绿色低碳循环发展。

第十条 先行区应当加强路网、电网、光网、气网、水网、生产和生活配套服务等基础设施的整体规划和同步建设，促进产城融合发展。

琼海市人民政府和先行区管理机构应当建立开发建设协调机制，统筹先行区与周边地区基础设施、公共服务设施和其他配套设施的建设与管理，推动区域一体化布局和联动发展。

第十一条 省人民政府应当通过债券资金、专项资金、补助等多种方式对先行区予以财政扶持。

第十二条 先行区土地利用应当符合先行区控制性详细规划和产业发展需要，实施严格的节约集约用地制度，提升土地利用效益。

第十三条 省人民政府应当统筹安排先行区年度新增建设用地计划指标，优先保障重点产业、重点项目年度新增建设用地计划指标。

Chapter II Development and Construction

Article 8 The administrative office of the Pilot Zone shall be responsible for organizing the preparation of the detailed regulatory planning and industrial development planning of the Pilot Zone, and the enforcement of such plans upon approval.

The appropriate planning of the surrounding areas of the Pilot Zone shall be connected with the detailed regulatory planning and industrial development planning of the Pilot Zone.

Article 9 The Pilot Zone shall strictly enforce the environmental protection system and the bright-line administrative rules for environmental protection, strictly enforce the resource conservation and utilization and minimum requirements for environmental protection, improve the environmental protection infrastructure and measures, and adhere to pursuing green, low-carbon, and circular development.

Article 10 The Pilot Zone shall improve the comprehensive planning and development of infrastructure such as road networks, power grids, optical networks, gas networks, water networks, production and living supporting services, and promote the integrated development of the industry and city.

The Qionghai Municipal People's Government and the administrative agency of the Pilot Zone shall establish the development and construction coordination system, coordinate the development and management of infrastructure, public services facilities, and other supporting facilities in the Pilot Zone and its surrounding areas, and promote regional integration layout and inter-connective development.

Article 11 The provincial people's government shall give financial support to the Pilot Zone through issuing bonds, special funds, and allowances.

Article 12 The land use in the Pilot Zone shall meet the needs of detailed regulatory planning and industrial development in the Pilot Zone, and enforce the strict land conservation rules to improve land use efficiency.

Article 13 The provincial people's government shall make comprehensive and coordinated arrangements for land use quota for the Pilot Zone, and give priority to the land use quota for the key industries and the annual increased land needs for key projects.

在先行区可以采取划拨、出让、租赁、作价出资或者入股等灵活多样的供地方式。允许以出让、租赁、作价出资或者入股等方式利用农村集体经营性建设用地进行产业项目建设。

第十四条 在先行区有偿供应的土地上配建的属于先行区管理机构资产的产业用房、办公、商业、公寓、停车位等物业，用于先行区的产业扶持、公共服务设施、人才住房等。

第三章 产业发展

第十五条 支持将公立医院品牌、商标、专利、技术、服务、管理等以特许经营的形式提供给先行区医疗机构使用，鼓励公立医院入驻先行区。

第十六条 鼓励境内外资本在先行区投资举办医疗机构，放宽境外资本股比限制。民办医疗机构在医疗服务准入、社会保险定点、职称评定、等级评审、科研教学和学科建设等方面与公立医院享有平等待遇。

支持在先行区引进和培育具有国际先进水平的健康管理机构、医疗旅游保健中心、第三方医学检测机构等医疗机构。

第十七条 支持在先行区建设先进技术临床医学研究中心、临床试验机构和重点实验室等医学科研机构，联合世界知名医学院设立医学院校。鼓励国内外重点科研院所和医学院校、国家重点实验室、知名企业在先行区设立分支机构。

支持在先行区引进和培育医疗健康领域国际学术交流平台、国际性医疗组织，鼓励举办医疗健康领域国际会议和会展活动。

The flexible and diverse land supply methods such as allocation, transfer, lease, capital contribution, or shareholding can be adopted in the Pilot Zone. It is allowed to use rural collective development land for industrial project development by means of transfer, lease, capital contribution, or shareholding.

Article 14 The industrial buildings, office buildings, commercial buildings, apartments, parking spaces, and other properties that belong to the administrative agency of the Pilot Zone, which are paid and built in the Pilot Zone, are used for industrial support, public services facilities, and talent housing in the Pilot Zone.

Chapter III Industrial Development

Article 15 The brands, trademarks, patents, technology, services, management of public hospitals shall be supported to be franchised to the health care institutions in the Pilot Zone. The public hospitals are encouraged to provide services in the Pilot Zone.

Article 16 The domestic and foreign capital shall be encouraged to invest in the health care institutions in the Pilot Zone, and the restrictions on the share ratio of foreign capital shall be relaxed. Private health care institutions enjoy equal treatment with public hospitals in terms of medical service access, social insurance designation, professional title evaluation, grade evaluation, scientific research and teaching, and discipline development.

The international advanced health care institutions, medical tourism health care centers, third-party medical testing institutions, and other health care institutions shall be introduced and cultivated in the Pilot Zone.

Article 17 Construction of clinical research centers with advanced technology, clinical trial institutions and key laboratories, and other medical research institutions in the Pilot Zone shall be supported, as shall achieve establishment of medical colleges in joint efforts with world-renowned medical schools. Domestic and international key scientific research institutes and medical colleges, national key laboratories, and well-known companies shall also be encouraged to set up branches in the Pilot Zone.

International medical and health academic exchange platforms and international medical organizations shall receive support to be introduced and developed in the Pilot Zone, and the international medical care and health conferences and exhibitions shall also be encouraged to be held in the Pilot Zone.

第十八条 支持在先行区建设国家医药成果转移转化试点示范基地，探索开展重大新药创制国家科技重大专项成果转移转化试点，鼓励建设产业化生产基地、医药技术成果转移转化服务平台和交易中心。

第十九条 先行区医疗机构可以在先行区进行干细胞、免疫细胞治疗、单抗药物、基因治疗、组织工程等新技术研究和转化应用。

第二十条 鼓励开展先行区临床真实世界数据应用研究，探索将临床真实世界数据用于药品、医疗器械产品注册，缩短上市时间。

第二十一条 先行区可以建立区域性制剂中心，承担或者接受委托开展先行区医疗机构制剂的配制。

医疗机构制剂可以在先行区调剂使用，具体办法由省人民政府药品监督管理部门制定。

对医疗机构中药制剂委托配制、应用传统工艺配制的中药制剂实施备案管理。

省人民政府药品监督管理部门应当对先行区医疗机构制剂的注册、配制、使用等加强管理，确保制剂安全有效。

第二十二条 旅游文化主管部门应当会同先行区管理机构、卫生健康管理等部门促进医疗与旅游的融合发展，依托全省旅游资源，指导发展高端体检、健康管理、医疗服务、中医养生保健、特色康养等医疗健康产品服务，加强医疗健康养生产品开发和旅游路线设计，发展医养结合、休闲养生、健康农业等医疗旅游延伸项目。

鼓励国内外旅行社等机构为先行区开展专业化医疗旅游中介服务，加大医疗旅游宣传推介力度，提供医疗旅游全流程服务。

Article 18 The national pilot bases for the transfer and transformation of medical achievements shall be supported to be established in the Pilot Zone. The pilot projects for the transfer and transformation of national major scientific and technological achievements for the creation of major new drugs shall be explored, and the industrialized production bases, service platforms, and trading centers for the transfer and transformation of medical technological achievements shall also be encouraged to be established in the Pilot Zone.

Article 19 The health care institutions in the Pilot Zone may carry out research, transformation, and application of new technologies such as stem cells, immune cell therapy, monoclonal antibody drugs, gene therapy, and tissue engineering in the Pilot Zone.

Article 20 The real-world clinical data application research shall be encouraged to be conducted in the Pilot Zone to explore the use of real-world clinical data in the registration of drugs and medical devices and shorten the time to market.

Article 21 The Pilot Zone may establish regional preparation centers and undertake or accept the delegation to compound the preparations in health care institutions in the Pilot Zone.

The finished medical products can be prepared within the Pilot Zone, and specific rules shall be enacted by the medical products administration agency of the provincial people's government.

The drug master file administration shall be implemented for finished traditional Chinese medicine products produced by other entities or prepared via traditional methods.

The medical products administration agency of the provincial people's government shall improve the administration of the registration, compound, and use of the finished medical products in the Pilot Zone to ensure the safety and effectiveness of preparations.

Article 22 The competent agency for tourism and culture shall promote the integration of medical treatment and tourism in collaboration with the administrative agency of the Pilot Zone and health administration agencies, and guide the development of high-end medical examination, health management, medical services, health care with traditional Chinese medicine, special health care and other medical and health products and services, improve the development of medical and health care products and the design of tourism routes, and develop medical tourism extension projects such as a combination of medical care, leisure and health care, and healthy agriculture.

The domestic and foreign travel agencies and other organizations shall be encouraged to carry out specialized medical tourism intermediary services for the Pilot Zone to enhance the promotion of medical tourism and provide full-range medical tourism services.

第二十三条 先行区应当促进中医药传承与文化传播，推进中医药科研和创新，推动中医药国际合作和服务贸易发展。

第二十四条 拟在先行区使用的临床急需进口药品（不含疫苗）、医疗器械，可以在获批前批量储存先行区保税仓库，一次入库、多次通关，保障获批后即提、即用。

允许先行区医疗机构患者经备案承诺，按照本省有关规定将符合条件的进口药品带离先行区使用。

允许先行区扩大境外进口保健食品、保健用医疗器材范围。在符合有关规定的条件下，允许先行区进口使用境外上市但境内未上市的特医食品。

第二十五条 外籍医务人员、患者及陪同人员到先行区诊疗，享受海南自由贸易港出入境、停留居留便利化政策措施。

第二十六条 先行区建立保险业金融机构与先行区医疗机构的合作机制，鼓励开发多样化、特色化、个性化商业健康保险产品，简化理赔手续，探索建立与国际商业保险付费体系相衔接的商业健康保险服务。

支持保险业金融机构与境外机构在先行区合作开发跨境商业健康保险产品。

第二十七条 在先行区依照海南自由贸易港有关规定实行跨境资金流动自由化便利化制度，放宽外商直接投资、跨境融资、个人跨境交易等方面限制，简化外汇登记、外债登记、资金汇出入和结购汇等手续。

第二十八条 先行区的企业和个人依照海南自由贸易港税收制度的有关规定，享受关税、企业所得税及个人所得税等方面的优惠政策。

Article 23 The Pilot Zone shall promote the inheritance and dissemination of traditional Chinese medicine to facilitate scientific research and innovation of traditional Chinese medicine, and promote the development of international cooperation and service of traditional Chinese medicine.

Article 24 The imported medical products (vaccines excluded) and medical devices urgently needed for clinical use in the Pilot Zone may be stored in batches in the bonded warehouse of the Pilot Zone before being approved. Customs declaration of the imported medical products and devices may be made separately after stored in the bonded warehouse altogether, so that they may be picked up and used immediately once being approved.

The patients in health care institutions in the Pilot Zone shall be allowed to take conforming imported medical products out of the Pilot Zone pursuant to the applicable laws of this Province.

The Pilot Zone shall be allowed to increase the variety of imported health food and medical equipment for health care. Pursuant to applicable rules, it shall also be allowed to import food for special medical purposes used overseas but not in China.

Article 25 The foreign medical personnel, patients, and their accompanying personnel, going to the Pilot Zone for medical treatment, shall enjoy the facilitated policies and measures with regard to entry and exit, and stay and residence in the HFTZ.

Article 26 The Pilot Zone shall establish a collaboration system between insurance financial institutions and health care institutions in the Pilot Zone, encourage the development of diversified, featured, and personalized commercial health insurance products, simplify the procedures for claims settlement, and explore the establishment of commercial health insurance services interconnected with the international commercial insurance payment system.

The insurance financial institutions and foreign institutions shall receive support to cooperate in respect of cross-border commercial health insurance in the Pilot Zone.

Article 27 In the Pilot Zone, the system of liberalization and facilitation of cross-border capital flows shall be enforced pursuant to applicable rules in the HFTZ. The restrictions on foreign direct investment, cross-border financing, and cross-border transactions by individuals shall be relaxed. The procedures for foreign exchange registration, foreign debt registration, capital remittance, and purchase of foreign exchange shall be simplified.

Article 28 The entities and individuals in the Pilot Zone shall enjoy preferential policies in terms of customs duties, corporate income tax, and personal income tax pursuant to the applicable rules of the tax system of the HFTZ.

第二十九条 执业医师（含境外）主要执业机构在先行区的，可以直接在先行区其他医疗机构执业。

护士（含境外）可以在先行区多点执业。

第三十条 先行区应当引进境内外高层次人才和急需紧缺人才，自主认定先行区高层次人才，可以对急需紧缺人才结合实际适当放宽文凭、年龄、职称等条件限制。

相关管理部门应当优化人才保障机制，在人才签证、停留和居留、人才移民、住房、医疗、就业、项目与奖励申报、教育等方面提供便利。

先行区依据国家和本省有关规定自主开展卫生系列高级专业技术职称评审工作。

国有企业事业单位医疗卫生、旅游等专业技术和管理人才可以在先行区按规定兼职兼薪。

第四章 服务管理

第三十一条 在先行区实施和深化极简审批改革，鼓励先行区管理机构结合实际需要，探索改革做法，创新管理模式。

先行区管理机构对权限范围内的审批事项，应当简化审批流程，压缩审批时限，提高行政审批服务效能。

先行区管理机构应当建立招商项目落地保障机制，实行项目全程跟踪服务责任制，对重大招商项目提供全程代办协办等优质便捷服务，及时协调解决项目审批、开工建设和生产经营中的问题。

Article 29 The medical practitioner (non-China's mainland medical practitioners included), whose major practicing institution is within the Pilot Zone, may directly practice in other health care institutions in the Pilot Zone.

The nurses (non-China's mainland nurses included) may practice in one or more institutions in the Pilot Zone.

Article 30 The Pilot Zone shall introduce domestic and foreign high-level talents and urgently needed talents, independently evaluate high-level talents in the Pilot Zone, and appropriately relax restrictions on diploma, age, professional title, and other conditions for urgently needed talents in consideration of reality.

The appropriate administrative departments shall optimize the talent guarantee system and provide convenience in talent visa, stay and residence, migration, housing, medical care, employment, project and reward application, and education.

Pursuant to state provisions and rules of this Province, the Pilot Zone independently carries out the evaluation of senior titles in respect of the health professionals.

The professionals and managers of the state-owned entities and institutions, such as in medical, health care, or tourism, may have part-time jobs and part-time remunerations pursuant to the rules in the Pilot Zone.

Chapter IV Service Management

Article 31 The reform of expedited review shall be enforced and improved, and the administrative agency of the Pilot Zone shall be encouraged to explore reforms and innovate administration in light of actual needs.

The administrative agency of the Pilot Zone shall simplify the review procedures, reduce the time limit, and improve efficiency.

The administrative agency of the Pilot Zone shall establish the guarantee system for investment projects, enforce the responsibility system for tracking services throughout the project, provide high-quality and convenient services such as full-time agency or co-sponsorship for major investment projects, and coordinate and solve the problems in project approval, development, production, and operation in a timely manner.

第三十二条 省人民政府卫生健康管理部门应当会同先行区管理机构制定先行区医疗机构设置标准及实施办法。

先行区管理机构会同省人民政府卫生健康管理、药品监督管理等部门，根据各自职责对入驻项目进行产业合规审查和医疗技术先进性评估。

先行区管理机构应当建立先行区不良市场主体退出机制，保障医疗旅游产业健康发展。

第三十三条 对在先行区兴办的医疗机构，不再核发《设置医疗机构批准书》，仅核发《医疗机构执业许可证》。

对先行区医疗机构设置申请和甲类大型医用设备配备申请，可以一并审批。

第三十四条 先行区应当完善医学伦理审查体系，加强临床研究与应用的伦理审查。

省人民政府卫生健康和药品监督管理部门驻区机构应当加强对先行区医疗机构及从业人员遵守医学伦理规范行为的监管。

第三十五条 省人民政府知识产权管理部门应当会同先行区管理机构及其他有关部门加强先行区医疗健康领域知识产权保护，健全多元化知识产权争端解决与维权援助机制和涉外知识产权执法协作机制，鼓励医疗机构积极申请国际专利，注册国际商标。

第三十六条 先行区医疗机构应当建立医疗废物管理责任制，全面落实医疗废物管理责任。

省人民政府卫生健康和药品监督管理部门驻区机构、琼海市人民政府生态环境管理部门按照职责分工对先行区医疗废物管理实施监督管理。

Article 32 The health administration agency of the provincial people's government shall, together with the administrative office of the Pilot Zone, enact standards and rules for health care institutions in the Pilot Zone.

The administrative agency of the Pilot Zone shall, jointly with the health administration agency, medical products administration agency of the provincial people's government, conduct industrial compliance review and medical technology advancement evaluation on the projects pursuant to their respective functions and duties.

The administrative agency of the Pilot Zone shall establish an exit system for noncompliant organizations in the Pilot Zone to ensure the healthy development of the medical tourism industry.

Article 33 In respect of the health care institutions in the Pilot Zone, the Approval for Establishing Health Care Institution shall be no longer issued, and only the Practice License of Health Care Institution shall be issued.

The application for setting up health care institutions in the Pilot Zone and the application for Class A large medical equipment may be jointly reviewed.

Article 34 The Pilot Zone shall improve the medical ethics examination system and improve the ethics examination of clinical research and application.

The local branch office of the health administration agency and medical products administration agency of the provincial people's government shall improve the oversight of the health care institutions' and employees' adherence to the medical ethics in the Pilot Zone.

Article 35 The intellectual property administrative agency of the provincial people's government shall, in collaboration with the administrative agency of the Pilot Zone, and other appropriate agencies, improve the protection of intellectual property rights concerning the medical treatment and health in the Pilot Zone, improve the diversified dispute resolution and protection assistance system and collaboration system for foreign intellectual property law enforcement, and encourage health care institutions to actively apply for international patents and register international trademarks.

Article 36 The health care institutions in the Pilot Zone shall establish the accountability system for medical waste management and completely enforce the accountability system for medical waste management.

The local branch office of the health and medical products administration agency of the provincial people's government, and the environmental administration agency of the Qionghai Municipal People's Government shall oversee and manage the medical waste in the Pilot Zone according to their respective functions and duties.

第三十七条 省人民政府卫生健康和药品监督管理部门驻区机构应当加强对先行区药品、医疗器械的监督检查，及时查处违法行为，确保药品和医疗器械质量安全。

先行区建立药品和医疗器械追溯管理平台，对药品和医疗器械进口、审批、使用、监管等全流程实行追溯管理，实现卫生健康管理部门、药品监督管理部门、海关及先行区内所有医疗机构联网共享。

第三十八条 省人民政府卫生健康和药品监督管理部门驻区机构应当对先行区医疗机构运行、医疗健康从业人员、医疗技术临床应用、医疗卫生服务行业秩序、医疗健康产业等实施全方位监管，保障医疗质量和医疗安全。

省人民政府卫生健康和药品监督管理部门驻区机构应当加强对先行区医疗机构业务合作的监管，建立先行区医疗机构对外合作备案管理制度。

第三十九条 先行区管理机构应当会同省和琼海市人民政府有关部门按照国家有关规定建立医疗机构及从业人员信用记录，依法及时公布、公示和共享医疗机构及从业人员的信用信息，实行守信联合激励和失信联合惩戒。

鼓励医疗行业协会对先行区医疗机构开展医疗质量、服务能力等评价。

第四十条 省人民政府卫生健康管理、药品监督管理等部门应当会同先行区管理机构建立防范医疗风险为主的预警体系，健全突发事件应急预案及处置机制，监督指导医疗机构加强医疗风险管理和完善医疗风险的识别、评估和防控措施，防范各类风险。

Article 37 The local branch office of the health and medical products administration agency of the provincial people's government shall improve the oversight and inspection of medical products and medical devices in the Pilot Zone, investigate and punish illegal acts in a timely manner, and ensure the quality and safety of medical products and medical devices.

The Pilot Zone shall establish a traceability management platform for medical products and medical devices, and enforce traceability management for the whole process of import, review, usage, and oversight of drugs and medical devices, so as to achieve interconnectivity and sharing among health administration agencies, medical products administration agencies, customs, and all health care institutions in the Pilot Zone.

Article 38 The local branch office of the health and medical products administration agency of the provincial people's government shall oversee the operation of health care institutions, medical and health practitioners, clinical application of medical technology, medical and health service industry order, and medical and health industry in the Pilot Zone in an all-round way to ensure medical quality and safety.

The local branch office of the health and medical products administration agency of the provincial people's government shall improve the oversight of the business collaboration of health care institutions in the Pilot Zone and establish the record management system for foreign collaboration of health care institutions in the Pilot Zone.

Article 39 The administrative office of the Pilot Zone shall jointly with the appropriate agencies of the provincial people's government and Qionghai Municipal People's Government establish credit records for health care institutions and practitioners pursuant to state provisions, issue, publish, and share the credit information on health care institutions and providers in a timely manner pursuant to law, and enforce joint incentives for honesty and joint punishment against dishonesty.

The medical industry association is encouraged to evaluate the medical service quality and capability of health care institutions in the Pilot Zone.

Article 40 The health and medical products administration agencies of the provincial people's government shall, jointly with the administrative office of the Pilot Zone, establish the warning system prioritizing medical risk prevention, improve emergency response plans and emergency response system, oversee and guide health care institutions to improve medical risk management, improve the identification, evaluation, prevention, and control measures concerning medical risks, and prevent various risks.

第五章　法律责任

第四十一条　先行区管理机构、省和琼海市人民政府有关部门及其工作人员在先行区服务管理工作中有滥用职权、玩忽职守、徇私舞弊等行为的，对直接负责的主管人员和其他直接责任人员依法给予处分；构成犯罪的，依法追究刑事责任。

第四十二条　先行区建立创新容错机制，对有下列情形之一的，可以按照国家和本省有关规定从轻、减轻处理或者免除责任：

（一）在推进先行区改革创新中因缺乏经验、先行先试出现的失误；

（二）尚无明确限制的探索性试验中的失误；

（三）为推动改革发展的无意过失；

（四）法律法规规定的其他从轻、减轻或者免除责任的情形。

第六章　附　则

第四十三条　本条例自公布之日起施行。

Chapter V　Legal Liability

Article 41　If the administrative agency of the Pilot Zone, the appropriate agencies of the provincial people's government and Qionghai Municipal People's Government, and their employees commit abuse of position, dereliction of duty, or play favoritism and commit irregularities, the person directly in charge and other employees subject to direct liability shall be penalized pursuant to law. If a crime is constituted, criminal liability shall be imposed pursuant to law.

Article 42　The Pilot Zone shall establish the innovative fault-tolerant system. Under any of the following circumstances, the punishment may be attenuated, mitigated, or exempted pursuant to state provisions and rules of this Province:

(a) fault in promoting reform and innovation in the Pilot Zone results from inexperience and pilot trial;

(b) fault in explorations that are not clearly limited;

(c) negligence for the purpose of promoting reform and development; or

(d) other circumstances subject to extenuated, mitigated, or exempt from liability pursuant to law.

Chapter VI　Supplementary Provision

Article 43　These Regulations shall come into force as of the issuance date.

海南自由贸易港海口江东新区条例

Regulations of Hainan Free Trade Port on Haikou Jiangdong New Area

海南自由贸易港海口江东新区条例

（2020年12月30日海南省第六届人民代表大会常务委员会第二十五次会议通过）

第一章 总 则

第一条 为了促进海南自由贸易港海口江东新区（以下简称江东新区）建设和发展，根据有关法律、行政法规，结合海南自由贸易港实际，制定本条例。

第二条 《海口江东新区总体规划》确定的区域适用本条例。

第三条 江东新区应当按照海南自由贸易港建设的有关要求，对标世界高水平的开放形态，建设成全面深化改革开放试验区的创新区、国家生态文明试验区的展示区、国际旅游消费中心的体验区、国家重大战略服务保障区的示范区。

第四条 江东新区应当鼓励和保护公民、法人和其他组织开展创新活动，建立与海南自由贸易港相适应的制度集成创新体系。

第二章 管理体制

第五条 海口市人民政府在江东新区依法设立管理机构。管理机构是在江东新区履行相应行政管理和公共服务职责的法定机构，具体负责江东新区的综合协调、开发建设、运营管理、招商引资、产业发展、制度创新、投资促进、企业服务等工作，依照授权或者委托行使相应的行政审批权和行政处罚权。

Regulations of Hainan Free Trade Port on Haikou Jiangdong New Area

(Adopted at the 25th Session of the Standing Committee of the 6th Hainan Provincial People's Congress on December 30, 2020)

Chapter I General Provisions

Article 1 These Regulations are enacted based on applicable laws and regulations and the actual circumstances of Hainan Free Trade Port to improve the construction and development of the Hainan Free Trade Port Haikou Jiangdong New Area (hereinafter referred to as the "Jiangdong New Area").

Article 2 These Regulations shall govern the areas determined by the Master Plan of the Haikou Jiangdong New Area.

Article 3 The Jiangdong New Area shall, based on the applicable Port construction requirements, benchmark international high-end open areas and build it into a pilot innovation area to further develop the reform and opening up, an exhibition area for the national ecological conservation pilot zone, an experience area for international tourism expenditure destination, and a demonstration area supporting specific national development strategies.

Article 4 The Jiangdong New Area shall encourage and protect citizens, juristic persons, and other organizations to conduct innovation activities and create an integrated innovation system appropriate for the Port.

Chapter II Administrative Institutions

Article 5 The Haikou Municipal People's Government shall set up an administrative agency in the Jiangdong New Area pursuant to law. As the statutory agency providing administrative and public service duties for the Jiangdong New Area, the administrative agency is specifically responsible for the overall coordination, development and construction, operation and management, attracting investments, industrial development, institutional innovation, investment development, business services, and other functions in the Jiangdong New Area, and exercise the corresponding administrative approval authority and administrative penalty authority based on their authorized or delegated powers.

江东新区的社会管理职责由海口市人民政府另行规定。

第六条 江东新区管理机构按照精简高效的原则，在依照有关规定确定的薪酬总额范围内，自主决定机构设置、岗位设置、人员聘用、薪酬标准等，依照有关规定任命的人员除外。

江东新区管理机构的负责人、高级管理人员及其他工作人员可以从境外选聘。

第七条 省和海口市人民政府及其有关部门应当依法将有关管理权限授权或者委托江东新区管理机构行使。

不宜授权或者委托行使的管理权限，省和海口市人民政府及其有关部门可以按照规定在江东新区设立驻区机构。

省和海口市人民政府有关部门、江东新区管理机构、驻区机构应当明确在江东新区的管理权限，依法编制权力清单、责任清单，经批准后向社会公布。

第八条 江东新区管理机构可以依法设立企业，委托企业负责江东新区内的土地开发、基础设施、产业投资、招商引资和公共服务设施的建设及运营，参与江东新区管理服务的组织与实施。

江东新区管理机构根据海口市人民政府授权对所出资企业履行出资人职责，依法享有资产收益、参与重大决策和选择管理者等出资人权利。

第九条 海口市在江东新区建立廉政监督机制，依法对江东新区开发、建设、运营和管理等活动进行廉政监督。

The social administrative responsibilities for the Jiangdong New Area shall be specified separately by the Haikou Municipal People's Government.

Article 6 The Jiangdong New Area administrative agency shall, based on the principles of streamlining and efficiency, independently decide on the organization setup, position setup, employment, salary standard, and other matters within the salary cap pursuant to applicable provisions, except those appointed pursuant to applicable provisions.

The person in charge, senior administrative employees and other Jiangdong New Area administrative agency employees may be selected and employed from overseas.

Article 7 The Provincial and Haikou Municipal People's Governments and agencies shall authorize or delegate the administrative authority to the Jiangdong New Area administrative agency pursuant to law.

The Provincial and Haikou Municipal People's Governments and agencies may set up resident offices in the Jiangdong New Area in compliance with the regulations if the administrative authority shall not be authorized or delegated.

The Provincial and Haikou Municipal People's Government agencies, Jiangdong New Area administrative agencies, and resident offices shall specify the administrative authority in the Jiangdong New Area, prepare the list of authorities and responsibilities pursuant to law, and announce it publicly upon approval.

Article 8 The Jiangdong New Area administrative agency may set up enterprises and hire enterprises to be responsible for the construction and operation of land development, infrastructure, industrial investment, investment attraction, and public service facilities in the Jiangdong New Area, and to engage in the organization and implementation of administrative services in the Jiangdong New Area pursuant to law.

The Jiangdong New Area administrative agency may perform investor duties for the enterprises to which it contributes in compliance with the authorization granted by the Haikou Municipal People's Government, and may enjoy the investor rights such as asset income, participation in major decisions, and selection of executives pursuant to law.

Article 9 The Haikou Municipal People's Government shall implement a clean government oversight system within the Jiangdong New Area, and conduct clean government oversight on the development, construction, operation and administrative activities of the Jiangdong New Area pursuant to law.

第三章 开发建设

第十条 海口市人民政府可以在省人民政府规划主管部门的指导下，依照法定程序对江东新区总体规划进行部分调整，并报省人民政府备案。

江东新区管理机构负责组织编制江东新区控制性详细规划等，经批准后实施。

江东新区周边地区相关规划应当与江东新区控制性详细规划以及产业发展规划等相衔接。

第十一条 江东新区应当加强智慧园区建设，布局智能基础设施，提供服务全域智能化应用，推进园区数字化、智能化管理。

第十二条 江东新区应当加强路网、电网、光网、气网、水网、生产和生活配套服务等基础设施的整体规划和同步建设。

海口市人民政府和江东新区管理机构应当建立开发建设协调机制，统筹江东新区与周边地区基础设施、公共服务设施和其他配套设施的建设与管理，推动区域一体化布局和联动发展。

第十三条 海口市人民政府可以授权江东新区管理机构负责江东新区范围内土地的监督、管理和开发，但土地征收事项除外。

江东新区管理机构可以根据授权开展土地储备，可以通过出租、临时使用等方式对江东新区范围内未供应的政府储备土地加以利用，但不得影响土地正常供应。

Chapter III Development and Construction

Article 10 The Haikou Municipal People's Government may, based on instructions provided by the Provincial People's Government agency, adjust part of the Jiangdong New Area master plan subject to statutory procedures, and report it to the Provincial People's Government for filing.

The Jiangdong New Area administrative agency is responsible for organizing the preparation of the Jiangdong New Area detailed regulatory plan and implementing it upon approval.

Planning for the surrounding areas of the Jiangdong New Area shall match the detailed regulatory plan and industrial development planning in the Jiangdong New Area.

Article 11 The Jiangdong New Area should improve the construction of smart industrial parks, develop intelligent infrastructure, provide intelligent application of services in the overall area, and improve the digital and intelligent administration of the parks.

Article 12 The Jiangdong New Area shall improve the integrated planning and concurrent construction of infrastructure, such as road networks, power grids, optical networks, gas networks, water networks, production, and living facilities.

The Haikou Municipal People's Government and Jiangdong New Area administrative agency shall implement a coordination system for development and construction, coordinate the construction and management of infrastructure, public service facilities, and other supporting facilities in the Jiangdong New Area and surrounding areas, and improve the regional integration layout and development.

Article 13 The Haikou Municipal People's Government may authorize the Jiangdong New Area administrative agency to be responsible for the oversight, administration and development of land within the Jiangdong New Area, with the exception of eminent domain land.

The Jiangdong New Area administrative agency may conduct land banking based on the authorization, and use government banked land not supplied within the Jiangdong New Area via lease or temporary use, but the regular supply of land shall not be affected.

第十四条 省和海口市人民政府应当统筹安排江东新区年度新增建设用地计划指标，优先保障重点产业、重点项目年度新增建设用地计划指标。

在江东新区可以依法采取划拨、出让、租赁、作价出资或者入股等灵活多样的供地方式。允许以出让、租赁、作价出资或者入股等方式利用农村集体建设用地进行产业项目建设。

在江东新区推进差别化土地供应，加强对地下空间开发利用与管控，探索城市地下空间分层出让等土地管理改革创新，提高土地精细化、集约化管理水平。

第十五条 江东新区应当建立健全区内居民搬迁和生产生活安置的保障机制，创新乡村土地征收和居民就业模式，加强安置社区服务体系建设，推动城乡一体化融合发展。

第十六条 江东新区开发建设应当统筹考虑环境承载能力、应对气候变化、污染物排放和经济社会生态发展目标，严守资源利用上限、环境质量底线和生态保护红线，实行严格的环境安全准入管理和环保信用评价制度，加强碳排放管理，坚持低碳、绿色发展。

江东新区应当严格保护东寨港红树林等核心生态资源，加强生态系统修复与环境整治，保护历史文化资源，探索园区、美丽乡村、生态田园和谐共生的建设模式。

第十七条 江东新区管理机构应当创新江东新区开发建设的体制机制，探索多层次、多渠道的投融资新模式。

鼓励江东新区管理机构通过引导和支持企业采取股权合作、公建民营、民办公助等多种形式，参与江东新区基础设施和重点设施建设运营。

Article 14 The Provincial and Haikou Municipal People's Government shall coordinate the arrangements for the annual newly added development land targets for the Jiangdong New Area, and prioritize ensuring the annual newly added development land targets for main industries and projects.

Flexible and diverse land supply methods may be implemented within the Jiangdong New Area, such as allocation, grants, lease, investment at a fixed price or shareholding. The use of rural collective development land for industrial project construction through assignment, lease, investment at a fixed price, or shareholding is permitted.

The Jiangdong New Area shall encourage differentiated land supply, improve the development, utilization, and control of underground space, explore land management reform and innovation such as the layered transfer of urban underground space, and improve the level of refined and intensive land management.

Article 15 The Jiangdong New Area shall set up and optimize a system to safeguard resident relocation and production and living resettlement in the area, innovate rural land eminent domain and resident employment methods, improve the development of the service system for resettled communities, and improve the integration and development of urban and rural areas.

Article 16 In the development and construction of the Jiangdong New Area, comprehensive consideration shall be given to the environmental carrying capacity, climate change, pollutant discharge and economic, social and ecological development goals, and the government shall strictly maintain the upper limits of resource utilization, the environmental quality bottom line, and ecological protection red lines, strictly implement environmental safety access management and an environmental credit assessment system, improve carbon emission management, and follow low-carbon and green development.

The Jiangdong New Area shall strictly protect core ecological resources, such as mangroves in Dongzhaigang, improve ecosystem restoration and environmental remediation, protect historical and cultural resources, and explore development methods that integrate the park, beautiful countryside, and ecological farmland.

Article 17 The Jiangdong New Area administrative agency shall innovate the development and construction system and mechanism, and explore new multi-level and multi-channel investment and financing models.

The Jiangdong New Area administrative agency shall be encouraged to participate in the construction and operation of infrastructure and key facilities in the Jiangdong New Area by guiding and supporting enterprises to adopt different methods, such as equity collaboration, privately operated governmental construction, and private construction with governmental support.

第四章　产业发展

第十八条　江东新区管理机构应当根据江东新区总体规划和发展定位，编制专项规划、产业规划和实施导则，依法经批准后实施，并向社会公布。

第十九条　江东新区推动现代服务业集聚发展，构建创新型、外向型现代服务体系。

鼓励在江东新区开展符合江东新区发展定位、有利于促进产业结构优化升级、加快经济发展方式转变的创新业务。

第二十条　支持江东新区建设临空经济区，重点发展保税航油、飞机租赁、飞机维修、飞机拆解、航空物流、临空商业商贸、临空高端制造等产业集群。

支持江东新区利用航权开放政策开展保税航油业务。鼓励境内外市场主体平等参与保税航油供应、航油基础设施建设使用和飞机维修业务。

支持飞机租赁企业在江东新区开展境外融资业务，取消飞机境外融资限制。鼓励保险资金支持飞机租赁业发展，丰富保险投资工具，探索以保险方式取代保证金。

第二十一条　江东新区应当推动旅游与相关产业融合发展，培育旅游消费新业态，建设具有国际影响力的大型综合性消费商圈，打造国际旅游消费中心体验区。

Chapter IV Industrial Development

Article 18 Based on the overall Jiangdong New Area planning and development direction, the Jiangdong New Area administrative agency shall prepare special planning, industrial planning, and implementation guidelines, which shall be implemented upon approval pursuant to law and announced to the public.

Article 19 The Jiangdong New Area shall encourage the modern service industry cluster development and develop an innovative and export-oriented modern service system.

The Jiangdong New Area is encouraged to support innovative businesses that conform to the Jiangdong New Area development direction, are conducive to improving the optimization and upgrading of industrial structure, and expediting the transformation of the economic development model.

Article 20 The Jiangdong New Area shall receive support to construct the airport economic zone in the Jiangdong New Area, focusing on the development of industrial clusters such as bonded aviation fuel, aircraft leasing, aircraft maintenance, aircraft dismantling, aviation logistics, airport commerce and trade, and advanced aviation manufacturing.

The Jiangdong New Area shall receive support to develop a bonded aviation fuel industry by using the open policy of the freedoms of the air. Domestic and foreign market entities are encouraged to participate equally in bonded aviation supply, construction and use of aviation fuel infrastructure, and aircraft maintenance.

Aircraft leasing companies shall receive support to conduct overseas financing operations in the Jiangdong New Area, and restrictions on overseas aircraft financing shall be lifted. The Jiangdong New Area shall encourage insurance funding to support the development of the aircraft leasing industry, improve insurance investment tools, and explore methods to replace the conventional deposit system with an insurance policy.

Article 21 The Jiangdong New Area shall improve the integration and development of tourism and related industries, develop new tourism consumption methods, develop a large-scale comprehensive consumption business circle with international influence, and build an international tourism consumption center experience zone.

支持在江东新区建设全球消费精品展示交易中心，利用境外展品免税政策举办国家级展会。支持免税品经营企业在江东新区开展经营免税品、建设免税店等相关业务。

支持江东新区设立国际文化艺术品交易场所，鼓励具备资质的企业在江东新区开展面向全球的保税文化艺术品展示、拍卖、交易业务。

江东新区应当融合生态资源，建设国际高端旅游度假区，发展健康养生、休闲农业、民俗文化等旅游延伸产业。

第二十二条 支持境内外投资者在江东新区设立跨国公司总部、区域性（综合型）总部、高成长型总部和专业子公司等法人或分支机构，发展总部经济。

第二十三条 支持在江东新区率先落实金融业扩大开放政策，加快发展离岸贸易和跨境服务贸易，探索发展离岸金融，推动跨境资金流动自由便利。

江东新区应当根据海南自由贸易港发展要求，依法合规建设对接国际交易平台的航运等交易场所及结算中心。交易主体可以按照规定在上述交易场所参与交易和进行资金结算。

江东新区应当构建科技创新投融资服务体系，有序推进人工智能、大数据、云计算、区块链等金融科技领域研究成果推广应用。

第二十四条 江东新区应当培育和引进国际化的会计、法律、管理咨询、培训等专业服务机构，推进服务要素集聚。

具有境外职业资格的境外人员可以按照海南自由贸易港有关规定，经认定后直接在江东新区依法提供服务，其境外从业经历可以视同境内从业经历。

The construction of the global exhibition and exchange center for international boutiques shall be supported in the Jiangdong New Area, where the duty-free policy for overseas exhibits may be used to hold national exhibitions, and business entities entitled to duty-free goods shall receive support to operate duty-free goods and duty-free store construction in the Jiangdong New Area.

The Jiangdong New Area shall receive support to set up an international culture and artwork exchange center, and shall encourage eligible enterprises to hold global exhibitions, auctions, and trade bonded cultural and art pieces in the Jiangdong New Area.

The Jiangdong New Area shall integrate ecological resources, build international high-end tourist resorts, and develop the tourism industries such as health care, leisure agriculture, and folk culture.

Article 22 Domestic and foreign investors shall receive support to set up juristic persons or branch offices, such as headquarters for multinational corporations headquarters, regional (comprehensive) headquarters, high-growth headquarters, and specialized subsidiaries within the Jiangdong New Area to develop the headquarters economy.

Article 23 The Jiangdong New Area shall receive support to take the initiative in adopting policies to expand and open up the financial industry, accelerate the development of offshore trade and cross-border services, explore and develop offshore finance, and improve the freedom and ease of cross-border capital flow.

The Jiangdong New Area shall build shipping and other exchange sites and settlement centers that connect with international trading platforms in compliance with Port development requirements and pursuant to law. Transacting parties may make exchanges and payments in the above locations pursuant to applicable provisions.

The Jiangdong New Area shall develop a scientific and technological innovation investment and finance service system, and encourage the orderly awareness and implementation of research achievements in financial technology fields such as artificial intelligence, big data, cloud computing, and blockchain.

Article 24 The Jiangdong New Area shall develop and introduce international professional service providers, including accounting, law, management consulting, and training, and encourage the consolidation of service elements.

Overseas employees with foreign professional qualifications may provide services directly in the Jiangdong New Area in compliance with Port guidelines, and their overseas employment experience may be recognized as domestic employment experience.

第二十五条 江东新区应当在保障海南自由贸易港数据安全可控的条件下，推动数字贸易、数字安全、数字通信等数字产业发展。

第二十六条 江东新区应当结合产业优势，扶持跨境电商业务发展，在通关、税收征管和支付结算等方面依法给予便利，推进线上线下渠道零售业务融合发展。

第二十七条 鼓励江东新区建设设计产业园，举办国内外设计创意产品展览会、专业论坛等活动。

第二十八条 支持江东新区建设面向国内国际的学研产创一体化平台。鼓励境外理工农医类高水平大学、职业院校在江东新区独立办学，建设引领国际前沿的科教智慧高地。

第二十九条 对于利用财政性资金形成的归单位所有的职务科技成果，高等院校、科研机构可以赋予科技成果完成人共同所有权或者长期使用权，但是可能影响国家安全、公共利益、社会稳定的除外。

依据前款规定，赋予科技成果完成人共同所有权的，科技成果完成人与单位可以约定共同共有或者按份共有。按份共有的，科技成果完成人的份额应当不低于百分之七十。赋予科技成果完成人长期使用权的，科技成果使用权限不得少于十年。

对于同一职务科技成果，科研人员获得职务科技成果共同所有权或者长期使用权的，其单位可以不再给予成果转化收益和奖励。

第三十条 江东新区应当引进境内外高层次人才和急需紧缺人才，按照海南自由贸易港高层次人才认定办法和分类标准自主认定高层次人才，可以对急需紧缺人才结合实际适当放宽文凭、年龄、职称等条件限制。

Article 25 The Jiangdong New Area shall encourage the development of digital industries such as digital commerce, digital security, and digital communications, provided it can ensure data security and controllability within the Port.

Article 26 The Jiangdong New Area shall combine industrial advantages to support the development of cross-border e-commerce business, facilitate customs clearance, tax collection and management, payment and settlement pursuant to law, and encourage the integrated development of online and offline retail businesses.

Article 27 The Jiangdong New Area is encouraged to build a design industrial park, host exhibitions for domestic and international design and creative products, professional forums, and other activities.

Article 28 The Jiangdong New Area is supported to develop an integrated platform for domestic and international industry-university-research-innovation. Overseas high-quality science, technology, agriculture, and medical universities and vocational colleges are encouraged to run independent schools in the Jiangdong New Area, to create a leading international science, education, and wisdom education area.

Article 29 Where job-related scientific and technological achievements using public funding are owned by organizations, higher learning institutions, and research institutes, such entities may grant joint ownership or long-term use rights to those who accomplished the achievements, except those that may affect national security, public interest, and social stability.

Pursuant to the above paragraph, where scientific and technological achievements are given joint ownership, those who have accomplished the achievements and the institute may agree on joint ownership or co-ownership by shares. Where the achievements are co-owned by shares, the share of the accomplishers shall not be less than 70%. Where the long-term use rights are granted to the accomplishers, the use period for scientific and technological achievements shall not be less than 10 years.

Where scientific researchers have obtained joint ownership or long-term use rights for work-related scientific and technological achievements, their institutes may no longer give proceeds from the commercialization of the same achievements and rewards.

Article 30 The Jiangdong New Area shall hire domestic and foreign high-end skilled employees and critically-lacking skilled employees, independently identify workers with exceptional ability based on identification method and classification standard for high-quality skilled employees in the Port, and appropriately relax qualifications such as educational background, age, and professional titles for critically-lacking skilled employees.

支持江东新区建立人才服务“单一窗口”，对在江东新区工作的高层次人才、急需紧缺人才以及其他人才，江东新区在科研、住房、医疗、就业、教育等方面提供便利。

江东新区支持离岸创新人才引进及使用，鼓励江东新区各类单位在港澳台地区及国外建立前端孵化基地、离岸研发中心并聘请使用高层次创新人才。

第五章　服务管理

第三十一条　在江东新区实施和深化极简审批改革，探索在具有强制性标准领域建立“标准制 + 承诺制”的投资制度，简化审批程序，提高审批服务效能。

江东新区管理机构应当建立招商项目落地保障机制，实行项目全程跟踪服务责任制，对重大招商项目提供全程代办协办等优质便捷服务，及时协调解决项目审批、开工建设和生产经营中的问题。

第三十二条　江东新区建立健全以信用监管为基础、与负面清单管理方式相适应的过程监管体系，明确加强过程监管的规则和标准，依法对投资经营活动实施有效监管。

江东新区管理机构按照国家和本省有关规定建立区内市场主体及其从业人员信用记录，依法及时公布、公示和共享其信用信息，实行守信激励和失信惩戒。

江东新区管理机构应当依法建立不良市场主体退出机制，保障产业健康发展。

The creation of a single window for skilled employee services in the Jiangdong New Area is supported to facilitate scientific research, housing, medical care, employment, and education for high-end skilled employees, critical needs skilled employees, and other skilled employees working in the Jiangdong New Area.

The Jiangdong New Area shall support the recruitment and use of overseas innovative skilled employees, and encourage various entities within the Jiangdong New Area to create front-end development bases, offshore research and development centers, and employ high-end innovative skilled employees from Hong Kong, Macao, and Taiwan areas, and overseas.

Chapter V Service Management

Article 31 The Jiangdong New Area shall implement and improve simplified approval reform, explore the implementation of a Standard System Plus Commitment System investment system in areas with mandatory standards, simplify the review and approval procedures, and improve the efficiency of review and approval services.

The Jiangdong New Area administrative agency shall establish safeguards for the establishment of investment projects, implement a responsibility system for tracking services throughout the project, provide effective and convenient services, such as agency and co-ordination throughout the major investment projects, and coordinate and promptly resolve problems during project approval, construction initiation, production, and operation.

Article 32 The Jiangdong New Area shall set up and optimize a process supervision system based on credit monitoring and compatible with international investment negative list administration, specify rules and standards for improving process supervision, and effectively supervise investment and business activities pursuant to law.

The Jiangdong New Area administrative agency shall develop a credit record system for market entities and their employees in the Area in compliance with national regulations, promptly publish, announce and share their credit information pursuant to law, and implement joint compliance incentives and joint penalties for noncompliance.

The Jiangdong New Area administrative agency shall create an exit system for noncompliant market entities to ensure sound industrial development.

第三十三条 江东新区管理机构应当建立营商环境投诉机制，构建统一工作平台，对损害营商环境行为的投诉及时处理，并将处理结果及时反馈投诉人。

第三十四条 省和海口市人民政府及江东新区管理机构应当加强风险防控体系建设，建立健全风险防控配套制度，有针对性地防范化解贸易、投资、金融、数据流动、生态等领域重大风险。

第六章 法律责任

第三十五条 省和海口市人民政府有关部门、江东新区管理机构及其工作人员在江东新区服务管理工作中有滥用职权、玩忽职守、徇私舞弊等行为的，对直接负责的主管人员和其他责任人员依法给予处分；构成犯罪的，依法追究刑事责任。

第三十六条 江东新区建立创新容错机制，对在改革创新、先行先试等工作中出现失误错误的，可以按照国家和本省有关规定从轻、减轻处理或者免除责任。

第七章 附 则

第三十七条 本条例自 2021 年 1 月 1 日起施行。

Article 33 The Jiangdong New Area administrative agency shall implement a compliant business environment system, develop a centralized work platform, promptly resolve complaints about conduct that damage the business environment, and instantly report the results of the resolution to the complainants.

Article 34 The Provincial and Haikou Municipal People's Governments and the Jiangdong New Area administrative agency shall improve the development of the risk prevention and control system and set up and optimize a support risk prevention and control system to prevent and resolve targeted major risks in trade, investment, finance, data flow, ecology, and other fields.

Chapter VI Legal Liability

Article 35 Where the Provincial and Haikou Municipal People's Government agencies, Jiangdong New Area administrative agency and their employees abuse the position, commit dereliction of duty, play favoritism and commit irregularities, or commit other similar acts while managing services in the Jiangdong New Area, the person directly in charge and other employees liable shall be penalized pursuant to law and held criminally liable pursuant to law should such act constitute a crime.

Article 36 The Jiangdong New Area shall implement an innovative fault-tolerant system, and where mistakes are made in improving reform, innovation and other pilot projects, the liability may be lightened, mitigated, or exempted in compliance with national and provincial regulations.

Chapter VII Supplementary Provision

Article 37 These Regulations shall come into force as of January 1, 2021.

海南自由贸易港三亚崖州湾科技城条例

Regulations of Hainan Free Trade Port on Sanya Yazhou Bay Science and Technology City

海南自由贸易港三亚崖州湾科技城条例

（2020 年 12 月 2 日海南省第六届人民代表大会常务委员会第二十四次会议通过）

第一章　总　则

第一条　为了促进海南自由贸易港三亚崖州湾科技城（以下简称科技城）建设和发展，根据有关法律、行政法规，结合海南自由贸易港实际，制定本条例。

第二条　科技城包括《三亚崖州湾科技城总体规划》确定的南山港、深海科技城、南繁科技城、科教城、全球动植物种质资源引进中转基地等区域以及省人民政府确定的其他区域。

第三条　科技城应当按照海南自由贸易港建设的有关要求，对标国际先进标准，创新体制机制，在科技城开放合作、开发建设、产业发展、投资促进、科技创新、知识产权保护和运用等方面先行先试，高水平推进深海科技、南繁科技、动植物种质资源引进中转研发、科教研发、遥感等产业发展。

第四条　科技城应当鼓励和保护公民、法人和其他组织开展创新活动，建立与海南自由贸易港相适应的制度集成创新体系。

Regulations of Hainan Free Trade Port on Sanya Yazhou Bay Science and Technology City

(Adopted at the 24th Session of the Standing Committee of the 6th Hainan Provincial People's Congress on December 2, 2020)

Chapter I General Provisions

Article 1 These Regulations are enacted pursuant to applicable laws and regulations and the Free Trade Port's actual circumstances to improve the construction and development of the Sanya Yazhou Bay Science and Technology City (hereinafter referred to as the "Sci-Tech City") in the Hainan Free Trade Port.

Article 2 The Sci-Tech City includes Nanshan Port, Deep-Sea Sci-Tech Town, Nanfan Breeding Sci-Tech Town, Scientific Research and Education Town, and the Global Introduction and Transfer Base for Animal & Plant Germplasm Resources in accordance with the Overall Plan for the Sanya Yazhou Bay Science and Technology City, and other areas determined by the Provincial People's Government.

Article 3 Pursuant to the applicable Hainan Free Trade Port development requirements, the Sci-Tech City shall benchmark international advanced standards, innovate systems and mechanisms, conduct trials in the fields of open collaboration, development and construction, industrial development, attracting investments, scientific and technological innovation, and the protection and registration of intellectual property rights, and urge the high-quality development of industries such as deep-sea science and technology, and breeding technologies in Nanfan, research on the introduction and transfer of animal and plant germplasm resources, scientific and educational research and development, and remote sensing.

Article 4 The Sci-Tech City shall encourage and protect citizens, juristic persons, and other organizations to conduct innovative activities, and shall implement an institutional integration innovation system appropriate for the Hainan Free Trade Port.

第二章　治理结构

第五条　省和三亚市人民政府应当加强对科技城的领导，协调解决建设发展中的重大问题，决定科技城建设中的重大事项和重大项目，建立考核和评估机制。

省和三亚市人民政府有关部门应当按照职责分工做好科技城建设发展相关工作。

三亚市崖州区人民政府及其有关部门负责行使科技城的社会管理职能，具体范围由三亚市人民政府规定。

第六条　三亚市人民政府在科技城依法设立管理机构。管理机构是在科技城履行相应行政管理和公共服务职责的法定机构，具体负责科技城的综合协调、开发建设、运营管理、招商引资、产业发展、制度创新、投资促进、企业服务等工作，依照授权或者委托行使相应的行政审批权和行政处罚权。

第七条　科技城管理机构按照精简高效的原则，在依照有关规定确定的薪酬总额范围内，实行企业化、市场化的用人机制和薪酬体系，自主决定机构设置、岗位设置、人员聘用、薪酬标准等，依照有关规定任命的人员除外。

科技城管理机构的负责人、高级管理人员及其他工作人员可以从境外选聘。

第八条　科技城管理机构可以依法设立或者引进开发运营企业，委托企业负责科技城内的土地开发、基础设施、产业投资、招商引资和公共服务设施的建设及运营，参与科技城管理服务的组织与实施。

Chapter II Governance Structure

Article 5 The Provincial and Sanya Municipal People's Government shall improve their administration over the Sci-Tech City, coordinate and solve major construction and development issues, make decisions on major issues and projects during the development of the Sci-Tech City, and implement an assessment and evaluation system.

The appropriate Provincial and Sanya Municipal People's Government agencies shall play major roles in the construction and development of the Sci-Tech City based on the division of responsibilities.

The District People's Government of Sanya Yazhou and its appropriate agencies shall be responsible for Sci-Tech City administration, to the extent mandated by the Sanya Municipal People's Government.

Article 6 The Sanya Municipal People's Government shall set up administrative agencies in the Sci-Tech City pursuant to law. The administrative agencies shall be the statutory agencies responsible for performing the corresponding administrative and public service duties in the Sci-Tech City. They shall be specifically responsible for the comprehensive coordination, development and construction, operation and management, investment attraction, industrial development, institutional innovation, investment promotion, business services, and other Sci-Tech City work and exercise corresponding administrative review, approval, and penalty authorities as authorized or delegated.

Article 7 The Sci-Tech City administrative agencies shall implement enterprise and market-oriented employment and salary systems based on the principles of simplicity and high efficiency and within the salary cap determined pursuant to applicable law, and shall independently determine the organizational and position configurations, employee recruitment, and salary standards, with the exception of employees appointed pursuant to law.

The Sci-Tech City administrative agency persons in charge, executives, and employees may be selected and employed from overseas.

Article 8 The Sci-Tech City administrative agencies may include or introduce development and operation enterprises pursuant to law, hire them to be responsible for the construction and operation of Sci-Tech City land development, infrastructure, industrial investment, investment attraction, and public service facilities, and participate in the organization and implementation of Sci-Tech City administrative services.

科技城管理机构根据三亚市人民政府授权对所出资企业履行出资人职责，依法享有资产收益、参与重大决策和选择管理者等出资人权利。

第九条　省和三亚市人民政府及其有关部门应当依法将有关管理权限下放或者委托科技城管理机构行使。

不宜下放或者委托行使的管理权限，省和三亚市人民政府及其有关部门可以按照规定在科技城设立驻城机构。

省和三亚市人民政府有关部门、科技城管理机构、驻城机构应当明确在科技城的管理权限，依法编制权力清单、责任清单，经批准后向社会公布。

第十条　科技城管理机构建立科技城业界共治机制，建设科技城业界共治、社会参与和协商讨论的公共平台。

第十一条　三亚市在科技城建立廉政监督机制，依法对科技城开发、建设、运营和管理活动进行廉政监督。

第三章　开发建设

第十二条　三亚市人民政府可以在省人民政府规划主管部门的指导下，依照法定程序对科技城总体规划进行部分调整，并报省人民政府备案。

科技城管理机构负责根据科技城总体规划组织编制科技城控制性详细规划以及产业发展规划等，经批准后实施。

科技城周边地区相关规划应当与科技城控制性详细规划以及产业发展规划等相衔接。

The Sci-Tech City administrative agencies shall perform investor duties for investor enterprises in compliance with authorization from the Sanya Municipal People's Government and entitles investor rights such as asset income, participation in major decisions, and selection of executives pursuant to law.

Article 9 The Provincial and the Sanya Municipal People's Government and appropriate agencies shall delegate administrative authority to lower-level entities or delegate such to the Sci-Tech City administrative agencies pursuant to law.

The Provincial and the Sanya Municipal People's Government and the appropriate agencies may set up resident administrative agencies within the Sci-Tech City pursuant to law should they be unable to delegate or authorize certain administrative authorities.

Provincial and the Sanya Municipal People's Government agencies, Sci-Tech City administrative agencies, and resident administrative agencies shall specify their administrative authorities within the Sci-Tech City, prepare a list of authorities and a list of responsibilities pursuant to law, and publicly announce such following approval.

Article 10 The Sci-Tech City administrative agencies shall establish a Sci-Tech City industry co-governance system, and develop a public platform for industry co-governance, social participation, and consultation and discussion.

Article 11 The Sanya Municipal People's Government shall implement an anti-corruption government oversight system within the Sci-Tech City and conduct anti-corruption government oversight on Sci-Tech City development, construction, operation, and administration pursuant to law.

Chapter III Development and Construction

Article 12 The Sanya Municipal People's Government may, under the guidance of the Provincial People's Government planning agency, adjust part of the Sci-Tech City's master plan pursuant to statutory procedures, and report such to the Provincial People's Government for filing.

The Sci-Tech City administrative agencies are responsible for organizing the preparation of detailed regulatory and industrial development planning for the Sci-Tech City subject to the Sci-Tech City master plan, which shall be implemented after approval.

Planning for the areas surrounding the Sci-Tech City shall conform to the Sci-Tech City detailed regulatory and industrial development planning.

第十三条 科技城开发建设应当严守资源利用上限、环境质量底线和生态保护红线，严格落实生态环境保护制度，加强生态修复与环境整治，严格进出境环境安全准入管理，坚持绿色发展。

科技城开发建设应当保护自然山水格局和历史文化资源，体现自然、传统和现代融合的城市特色风貌。

第十四条 科技城应当加强路网、电网、光网、气网、水网、生产和生活配套服务等基础设施的整体规划和同步建设，推动产城融合、港城融合、城乡融合与农旅融合发展。

三亚市人民政府应当统筹科技城与周边地区基础设施、公共服务设施和其他配套设施的建设与管理，推动区域一体化布局和联动发展。

第十五条 三亚市人民政府可以授权科技城管理机构负责科技城范围内土地的监督、管理和开发，但土地征收事项除外。

科技城管理机构可以根据授权开展土地储备，可以通过出租、临时使用等方式对科技城范围内未供应的政府储备土地加以利用，但不得影响土地正常供应。

第十六条 省人民政府应当统筹安排科技城年度新增建设用地计划指标，优先保障重点产业、重点项目年度新增建设用地计划指标。

在科技城可以采取收购、置换、入股、合作开发等方式整合土地资源，综合运用规划、地价、容积率、贡献率、奖励等手段，创新土地储备机制。

在科技城可以采取划拨、出让、租赁、作价出资或者入股等灵活多样的供地方式。允许以出让、租赁、作价出资或者入股等方式利用农村集体建设用地进行产业项目建设。

在科技城可以按照规定采用划拨或者协议出让方式供应科研用地和教育用地。

Article 13 The development and construction of the Sci-Tech City shall strictly follow the resource utilization upper limit, minimum environmental quality standards, and categorical ecological protection rules, strictly implement an ecological environmental protection system, improve ecological restoration and environmental remediation, implement a strict environmental safety management system at the border entry and exit, and abide by green development.

The development and construction of the Sci-Tech City shall protect the natural landscape pattern and historical and cultural resources, and encompass urban characteristics that integrate nature, tradition, and modernity.

Article 14 The Sci-Tech City shall improve comprehensive planning and concurrent construction of infrastructure such as road networks, power grids, optical networks, gas networks, water networks, production and living support services, and encourage the development of industry-city integration, port-city integration, urban-rural integration, and agriculture-tourism integration.

The Sanya Municipal People's Government shall coordinate construction and management of infrastructure, public service facilities and other supporting facilities in the Sci-Tech City and the surrounding areas, and promote the integrated layout and linked development of the region.

Article 15 The Sanya Municipal People's Government may authorize the administrative agencies of the Sci-Tech City to be responsible for the supervision, management and development of land within the Sci-Tech City, with the exception of land acquisition matters.

The Sci-Tech City administrative agencies may conduct land banking to the extent authorized, and use land banked by the government within the Sci-Tech City but not yet provided to others either through a lease or a temporary occupancy, but shall not affect the regular supply of land.

Article 16 The Provincial People's Government shall coordinate arrangements for annual Sci-Tech City newly added development land targets and prioritize the achievement of annual newly added development land targets for main industries and projects.

Land resources within the Sci-Tech City may be integrated through acquisition, replacement, shareholding and cooperative development, and the land banking system may be implemented via planning, land price, floor area ratio, contribution rate, and rewards.

Flexible and diverse ways of land supply may be adopted within the Sci-Tech City, such as allocation, grants, lease, fixed-price investment, or shareholding. Rural collective development land may be used for industrial project development through grants, lease, fixed-price investment, or shareholding.

Land for scientific research and education within the Sci-Tech City may be supplied through allocation or assignment agreements pursuant to law.

在科技城依法保障教学、科研、水产育种等项目的海域使用需求。

第十七条 在科技城有偿供应的土地上配建的属于科技城管理机构资产的，或者由科技城管理机构统筹建设的产业用房、办公、商业、住宅、停车位等物业，可用于科技城的产业扶持、社区配套和公共服务、人才住房等。科技城管理机构统筹上述资产的规划、配置和管理。

第十八条 科技城管理机构应当创新科技城开发建设的体制机制，探索多层次、多渠道的投融资新模式。

科技城管理机构探索创新建设项目工程咨询、造价、保险、审批、监管、评价等机制，支持境外工程建设领域相关专业机构以及人员依照海南自由贸易港的有关规定参与科技城开发建设。

第四章 产业促进

第十九条 科技城管理机构应当根据科技城发展定位，编制产业发展规划和指导目录，经三亚市人民政府批准后实施，并向社会公布。

鼓励在科技城开展符合科技城发展定位、有利于促进产业结构优化升级、加快经济发展方式转变的创新业务。企业可以自行确定创新业务范围，但国家另有规定的除外。

第二十条 科技城应当推动信息技术在港口管理和物流系统建设中的应用，增强港口在科考服务、船舶维修以及基地保障方面的功能，先行先试深海、南繁科研等设备的保税研发、保税维修等业务。

Sea area within the Sci-Tech City for teaching, scientific research, aquatic breeding, and other projects shall be guaranteed pursuant to law.

Article 17 Properties built on the land leased by the Sci-Tech City belonging to the Sci-Tech City administrative agencies, or properties built by the Sci-Tech City administrative agencies, such as industrial buildings, administrative agency offices, businesses, residences, and parking spaces may be used for Sci-Tech City industry support, community facilities and public services, and employee housing. The Sci-Tech City administrative agencies shall coordinate the planning, allocation, and management of the above assets.

Article 18 The Sci-Tech City administrative agencies shall pioneer the Sci-Tech City development and construction system and mechanism and explore new multi-level and multi-channel investment and financing models.

The Sci-Tech City administrative agencies shall explore construction project systems for engineering consultation, cost, insurance, approval, supervision, and assessment, and support the overseas engineering construction professional agencies and employees to participate in the development and construction of the Sci-Tech City in compliance with Hainan Free Trade Port regulations.

Chapter IV Industry Development

Article 19 Sci-Tech City administrative agencies shall, based on the Sci-Tech City developmental positioning, prepare the Sci-Tech City industrial development planning and guidance manual, which shall be implemented after being approved by the Sanya Municipal People's Government and publicly announced.

The development of innovative businesses consistent with the Sci-Tech City's developmental positioning, conducive to improving industrial structure optimization and upgrading, and expediting the transformation of the economic development model shall be encouraged. Enterprises may determine their own innovative business scope except as otherwise provided by the state.

Article 20 The Sci-Tech City shall encourage the implementation of information technology in port management and logistics system development, enhance the functions of ports in scientific research services, ship maintenance and base support, and pilot activities such as the exemption of R&D items from import duty and duty-free equipment maintenance for the deep-sea and Nanfan scientific research.

第二十一条 科技城围绕深海科研、资源开发利用和现代服务等领域，重点发展深海科技和海洋产业，聚焦全球深海科技创新资源，建设具有国际水准的国家深海科技创新中心。

第二十二条 科技城围绕国家南繁科研育种基地建设，重点发展南繁科研、种业科技及热带农科产业，加强南繁科研育种用地保护，建设集科研、生产、销售、科技交流、成果转化为一体的现代种业示范区和国际种业贸易中心。支持科技城试行种业开放相关政策，在外资市场准入、生物育种审批、知识产权保护、技术出境服务等领域开展创新。

支持科技城建设国家热带农业科学中心，推动热带农业科技创新、生物育种科技创新，探索实施热带农业对外开放和国际合作新模式，推进全球热带农业中心建设。

第二十三条 支持科技城建设全球动植物种质资源引进中转基地，鼓励在种质资源引进、检验检疫、鉴定评价、保存繁育、研发创新、生物安全防控、品种交易及具有较高科技含量、符合绿色农业发展要求的农业投入品的引进、研发、生产等方面建立更加灵活、高效的管理体制和监管模式。

第二十四条 支持科技城发展科研教育、公共科技研发及创新创业孵化，探索高校科研体制机制改革，开放共享科技资源，促进科技成果转化，推动教育、科研、产业协同发展。

科技城应加大科教城内的公共教学楼、公共活动区等设施建设，推行办学机构聚集、学科交叉融合、办学资源共享的科教发展模式。

Article 21 The Sci-Tech City shall prioritize the development of the deep-sea technology and marine industries in the fields of deep-sea scientific research, resource development and utilization and modern services, focusing on global deep-sea technology innovation resources, and building a national deep-sea technology innovation center that conforms to international standards.

Article 22 Focusing on the construction of the National Nanfan Scientific and Research Breeding Base, the Sci-Tech City shall prioritize the development of Nanfan scientific research, seed science and technology, and tropical agricultural industry, improve the protection of land for Nanfan research and breeding, and develop a modern seed industry demonstration zone and international seed industry trade center integrating scientific research, production, sales, scientific and technological exchanges, and achievements. The Sci-Tech City shall receive support for trial policies related to the seed industry opening up and developing innovations in fields such as foreign market access, plant breeding approval, intellectual property protection, and technology export services.

The Sci-Tech City is supported to build a national tropical agricultural science center, encourage tropical agriculture and plant breeding technological innovation, explore and implement new models to open up and collaborate internationally on tropical agriculture, and encourage the construction of a global tropical agricultural center.

Article 23 The Sci-Tech City is supported to build a global introduction and transfer base for animal and plant germplasm resources and encourage the implementation of a more flexible and efficient management system and oversight model for germplasm resource introduction, inspection and quarantine, appraisal and evaluation, preservation and breeding, research and innovation, biosafety prevention and control, variety trading, as well as the introduction, research and development, and production of high-tech agricultural materials in line with green agriculture development requirements.

Article 24 The Sci-Tech City is supported to the development of scientific research and education, public scientific research and development, and innovation and entrepreneurship development within the Sci-Tech City, explore systemic scientific research reform in colleges and universities, release and share technological resources, encourage the transformation of technological achievements, and improve coordinated development in education, scientific research, and industry.

The Sci-Tech City shall focus on the construction of public educational buildings, public activity areas, and other facilities within the Sci-Tech City and implement the science and education development model of consolidating education institutions, interdisciplinary integration, and the sharing of educational resources.

第二十五条 科技城应当按照海南自由贸易港国际教育岛全省布局，支持国内重点高校在科技城设立分支机构或者与国外知名院校合作办学，支持境外理工农医类高水平大学、职业院校在科技城独立办学，设立国际学校。

支持境内外高等院校、职业院校、科研院所和企业按照市场化机制在科技城建立新型研发机构、创新创业基地和职业培训基地；鼓励境外科研组织、科技服务机构在科技城内设立分支机构，参与国家和地方科技计划。

新型研发机构在承担政府项目、职称评审、引进和培养人才、申请建设用地、投资融资服务等方面可以参照适用科研事业单位相关优惠政策。

支持在科技城探索科技项目立项和组织方式、科研经费使用、人才评价等方面的改革。

第二十六条 支持科技城发展卫星导航、测绘和相关产业及服务，建设卫星遥感信息产业园区。

第二十七条 支持科技城设立跨境电子商务展示展销中心、服务中心和区域总部基地。鼓励跨境电子商务相关专业配套服务发展，形成集孵化、研发、运营、客服、设计于一体的综合服务载体。

第二十八条 科技城应当引导主导产业资产数字化，建立数字资产确权、流动以及交易的技术标准和模式，推动人工智能、大数据、云计算、区块链、物联网等新一代的信息技术应用。

支持与科技城主导产业相配套的金融服务业发展，建设多层次的产业金融服务体系。

Article 25 Based on the provincial planning of the Hainan Free Trade Port International Education Island, the Sci-Tech City shall support top domestic universities to set up satellite campuses within the Sci-Tech City or collaborate with well-known foreign universities to run schools and support renowned high-quality foreign science, technology, agriculture and medical universities, as well as vocational colleges to independently run schools within the Sci-Tech City and set up international schools.

Domestic and foreign higher learning institutions, vocational colleges, research institutes, and enterprises are supported to establish new research and development institutions, innovation and entrepreneurship bases, and vocational training bases within the Sci-Tech City following a market-oriented system, encourage foreign scientific research organizations and technology service providers to set up branches within the Sci-Tech City and participate in national and local science and technology plans.

New research and development institutions may refer to the appropriate preferential policies for scientific research institutes when conducting government projects, assessing professional titles, hiring and developing skilled employees, requesting development land, and investment and finance services.

Researches on reforming the science and technology project implementation and organization model, the use of scientific research funds, and skilled employee assessment are supported within the Sci-Tech City.

Article 26 The Sci-Tech City is supported to develop satellite navigation, surveying and mapping, and related industries and services and build a satellite remote sensing information industrial park.

Article 27 The Sci-Tech City is supported to set up the cross-border e-commerce exhibition and sales center, service center, and regional headquarters, encourage the development of professional services supporting cross-border e-commerce to create an integrated service carrier integrating development, research and development, operations, customer service, and design.

Article 28 The Sci-Tech City shall guide the digitalization of assets for leading industries, develop technical standards and models for the confirmation, flow, and trading of digital assets, and improve the implementation of new-generation information technology such as artificial intelligence, big data, cloud computing, blockchain, and the Internet of Things.

The Sci-Tech City is supported to the development of the financial service industry to support the leading industries in the Sci-Tech City, and develop a multi-level industrial financial service system.

第二十九条 科技城应当探索建立与国际通行规则相衔接的国际化知识产权制度体系，建设海南自由贸易港知识产权保护与运用先行区。

科技城应当围绕推进海洋科技、南繁种业发展及科技创新关键领域、核心技术知识产权保护和运用，建立知识产权快速审查、快速授权、快速维权机制。鼓励科技城推动知识产权证券化，完善知识产权交易体系与交易机制。支持科技城高新技术企业利用股权、知识产权开展质押融资。

鼓励科技城引进高端国际化知识产权服务机构，加强国际知识产权人才培养和引进。

第三十条 支持科技城探索建立国际离岸创新创业试验区，引进境外科研机构、科技企业、科技人员开展国际离岸创新创业。

第三十一条 对于利用财政性资金形成的归单位所有的职务科技成果，高等院校、科研机构可以赋予科技成果完成人共同所有权或者长期使用权，但是可能影响国家安全、公共利益、社会稳定的除外。

依据前款规定，赋予科技成果完成人共同所有权的，科技成果完成人与单位可以约定共同共有或者按份共有。按份共有的，科技成果完成人的份额应当不低于百分之七十。赋予科技成果完成人长期使用权的，科技成果许可使用权限不得少于十年。

对于同一职务科技成果，科研人员获得职务科技成果共同所有权或者长期使用权的，其单位可以不再给予成果转化收益和奖励。

Article 29 The Sci-Tech City shall explore and establish an international intellectual property system in line with international rules, and create an intellectual property protection and implementation pilot zone within the Hainan Free Trade Port.

The Sci-Tech City shall establish a system for the rapid review, authorization, and protection of intellectual property rights by focusing on improving marine science and technology, Nanfan seed industry development and technological innovation, and the protection and implementation of intellectual property rights in key technological innovation areas and core technologies. The Sci-Tech City is encouraged to improve intellectual property securitization and the intellectual property trading system and mechanism, and high-tech enterprises within the Sci-Tech City shall receive support to use equity and intellectual property rights to provide financing secured by asset pledges.

The Sci-Tech City is encouraged to introduce high-end international intellectual property service providers and improve the training and recruitment of international intellectual property skilled employees.

Article 30 The Sci-Tech City shall receive support to explore and set up an international offshore innovation and entrepreneurship pilot zone, and introduce overseas research institutes, technology enterprises and scientific and technological employees to conduct international offshore innovation and entrepreneurship.

Article 31 Higher learning institutions and research institutes may grant joint ownership or long-term use rights to individuals accomplishing work-related technological achievements using public funds, except for those that may affect national security, the public interest, and social stability.

Pursuant to the above paragraph, where technological achievements are granted joint ownership, those who have accomplished such achievements may negotiate joint ownership or co-ownership by shares with their institutes. Where the achievements are co-owned by shares, those accomplishing the achievements shall hold at least 70% of the shares. Where long-term use rights are granted to those accomplishing the achievement, the technological achievement use right term shall be at least 10 years.

Institutes whose scientific researchers obtain joint ownership or long-term use rights for work-related scientific and technological achievements may no longer give proceeds and rewards from the commercialization of the same achievements.

第三十二条 科技城应当引进境内外高层次人才和急需紧缺人才，自主认定科技城高层次人才，可以对急需紧缺人才结合实际适当放宽文凭、年龄、职称等条件限制。

对在科技城工作的高层次人才、紧缺人才以及其他人才，科技城在科研、住房、医疗、配偶就业、子女教育等方面提供便利。

鼓励科技城各类单位在境外建立前端孵化基地、离岸研发中心，聘请使用高层次创新人才。

支持国有企业、事业单位的专业技术和管理人才按规定在科技城兼职兼薪、按劳取酬。

第三十三条 符合条件的港澳台地区人才以及经认定取得我国永久居留权资格的国外人才可以用其境内合法收入在科技城内直接设立科技型企业。

第三十四条 省和三亚市人民政府及科技城管理机构应当综合运用财政后补助、间接投入等方式，通过资助、贷款贴息、奖励、基金等多种形式支持科技城的高等院校、科研机构、企业以及科技人员开展科技创新活动。

科技城的企业或个人依照国家和本省有关规定享受关税、企业所得税、个人所得税等方面的税收优惠政策。

第五章 服务管理

第三十五条 在科技城实施和深化极简审批改革，探索在具有强制性标准领域建立“标准制＋承诺制”的投资制度，简化审批条件和程序，提高审批服务效能，加强事中事后监管。

Article 32 The Sci-Tech City shall introduce domestic and foreign workers with exceptional ability and critical needs skilled workers, independently identify workers with exceptional ability within the Sci-Tech City, and appropriately relax qualification requirements, such as educational background, age, and professional titles for critical needs skilled employees.

The Sci-Tech City shall facilitate scientific research, housing, medical care, spouse employment, children's education, and more for workers with exceptional ability, critically-lacking skilled employees, and other skilled employees working within the Sci-Tech City.

All types of entities in the Sci-Tech City are encouraged to set up front-end development bases and offshore research and development centers and employ workers with exceptional ability.

Professional, technical, and managerial skilled employees of state-owned enterprises and public institutes are supported to work part-time and be paid based on their work in the Sci-Tech City.

Article 33 Qualified skilled employees from the Hong Kong, Macao, and Taiwan areas and foreign skilled employees eligible for permanent residency in China may use their legal domestic income to directly set up scientific and technological enterprises within the Sci-Tech City.

Article 34 The Provincial and Sanya Municipal People's Government and the Sci-Tech City administrative agencies shall comprehensively use the post-financial subsidies and indirect investment to support higher education, research institutes, enterprises, and scientific and technological employees within the Sci-Tech City to conduct scientific and technological innovation activities through various forms such as subsidies, loan interest subsidies, awards, and public funding.

Enterprises or individuals in the Sci-Tech City enjoy preferential tax policies on tariffs, enterprise income tax, and personal income tax pursuant to national and provincial law.

Chapter V Service Management

Article 35 The Sci-Tech City shall establish and improve the minimal review and approval reform within the Sci-Tech City, explore the implementation of a Standard System Plus Commitment System investment system in areas with mandatory standards, simplify review and approval conditions and procedures, improve the efficiency of review and approval services, and improve post-implementation oversight.

省人民政府有关部门在科技城对种质资源引进中转和出口实行“多审合一、多检合一”的审批制度。省人民政府有关部门及海关主管部门建立跨部门间信息互通、监管联动、执法互助、考核互认等工作机制，提高全球动植物种质资源引进便利化水平。

第三十六条 科技城管理机构应当建立和完善招商项目和引进人才全程跟踪服务责任制，为科技城的企业、组织和个人提供优质、高效、便捷的服务。

第三十七条 科技城建立健全以信用监管为基础、与负面清单管理方式相适应的过程监管体系，明确加强过程监管的规则和标准，依法对投资经营活动实施有效监管。

科技城管理机构按照国家有关规定建立科技城内市场主体及其从业人员信用记录，依法及时公布、公示和共享其信用信息，实行守信联合激励和失信联合惩戒。

科技城管理机构应当建立不良市场主体退出机制，保障科技城产业健康发展。

第三十八条 科技城应当完善科技伦理审查制度，对相关科研活动加强审查和监管。

第三十九条 省和三亚市人民政府及科技城管理机构应当加强生物安全风险防控和治理体系建设，建立外来动物、农作物病虫害、外来物种生态安全监测评估预警体系，加强进口农业转基因生物安全监管，确保动植物疫病防控安全。

科技城应当配合国家和省人民政府监管部门建立健全种业信息监测、种业安全预警和种业安全应急处理等种业安全管理机制。

The appropriate Provincial People's Government agencies shall introduce the Multi-review and Multi-inspection Review and Approval Integrated System for the addition, transportation, and export of germplasm resources within the Sci-Tech City. The appropriate Provincial People's Government and customs agencies shall establish working systems such as inter-departmental information exchange, oversight and interaction, mutual assistance in law enforcement, and mutual assessment recognition to improve the level of facilitation when introducing overseas animal and plant germplasm resources.

Article 36 The Sci-Tech City administrative agencies shall establish and optimize a full-process accountability system for investment projects and skilled employee recruitment and provide high-quality, efficient, and convenient services for enterprises, organizations, and individuals in the Sci-Tech City.

Article 37 The Sci-Tech City shall establish and optimize a credit oversight-based process oversight system compatible with negative list management, specify the rules and standards for improving process oversight, and effectively oversee investment and business activities pursuant to law.

The Sci-Tech City administrative agencies shall establish a credit record system for market entities and their employees in the Sci-Tech City pursuant to national regulations, promptly publish, publicize, and share their credit information pursuant to law, and implement joint good credit incentives and joint penalties for bad credit.

The Sci-Tech City administrative agencies shall establish an exit system for bad credit market entities to ensure the healthy development of Sci-Tech City industries.

Article 38 The Sci-Tech City shall improve the science and technology ethics review system and improve the review and oversight of such scientific research activities.

Article 39 The Provincial and Sanya Municipal People's Government and the Sci-Tech City administrative agencies shall improve the development of the biosafety risk prevention and management system, create an ecological safety monitoring, assessment, and early warning system for non-native animals, crop pests and diseases, and non-native species, improve the safety oversight of imported agricultural genetically modified organisms, and ensure the safety in the prevention and management of animal and plant diseases.

The Sci-Tech City shall cooperate with national and the Provincial People's Government regulatory authorities to establish and optimize seed industry safety management systems, such as seed industry information monitoring, seed industry safety early warning, and seed industry emergency management.

第六章 法律责任

第四十条 科技城管理机构、省和三亚市人民政府有关部门及其工作人员在科技城服务管理工作中有滥用职权、玩忽职守、徇私舞弊等行为的，对直接负责的主管人员和其他责任人员依法给予处分；构成犯罪的，依法追究刑事责任。

第四十一条 科技城建立创新容错机制，对有下列情形之一的可以按照国家和本省有关规定从轻、减轻处理或者免除责任：

（一）在推进改革创新中因缺乏经验先行先试出现的失误；

（二）尚无明确限制的探索性试验中的失误；

（三）为推动改革发展的无意过失；

（四）法律法规规定的其他从轻、减轻或者免除责任的情形。

第七章 附 则

第四十二条 本条例自 2021 年 1 月 1 日起施行。

Chapter VI Legal Liability

Article 40 Where the Sci-Tech City administrative agencies, Provincial and the Sanya Municipal People's Government agencies, and their employees abuse the position, commit dereliction of duty, or play favoritism and commit irregularities, and other similar acts while managing Sci-Tech City services, and the persons directly in charge and other liable employees shall be penalized pursuant to law. Those committing crimes shall be held criminally liable pursuant to law.

Article 41 The Sci-Tech City shall create an innovative fault-tolerant system, and liability may be reduced, mitigated, or exempted pursuant to national or provincial law under any of the following circumstances:

(a) mistakes caused by lack of experience in encouraging reform and innovation;

(b) mistakes in exploratory experiments without explicit restrictions;

(c) unintentional negligence to encourage reform and development; or

(d) other circumstances that may reduce, mitigate, or exempt liability as provided by laws and regulations.

Chapter VII Supplementary Provision

Article 42 The Regulations shall come into force as of January 1, 2021.

Chapter VI Legal Liability

海南自由贸易港洋浦经济开发区条例

Regulations of Hainan Free Trade Port on the Yangpu Economic Development Zone

海南自由贸易港洋浦经济开发区条例

（2021 年 12 月 30 日海南省第六届人民代表大会常务委员会第三十二次会议通过）

第一章 总 则

第一条 为促进海南自由贸易港洋浦经济开发区（以下简称洋浦经济开发区）高水平开放和高质量发展，根据有关法律法规，结合洋浦经济开发区实际，制定本条例。

第二条 国务院和省人民政府批准的洋浦经济开发区管理区域（含规划控制范围）及邻接海域的规划、建设、管理和服务，适用本条例。

第三条 洋浦经济开发区的建设和发展应当遵循开放创新、区域协调、绿色低碳等原则，对接国际高水平经贸规则，以制度集成创新为核心，率先实施和创新海南自由贸易港政策制度，形成具有国际竞争力的开放政策和制度体系，发挥海南自由贸易港先行区示范区、高质量发展增长极作用。

第四条 在洋浦保税港区率先实行“一线”放开、“二线”管住的进出口管理制度。在依法有效监管基础上，有序推进开放进程，支持洋浦经济开发区全域实施“一线”放开、“二线”管住的进出口管理制度，推进贸易投资自由化便利化。

第五条 洋浦经济开发区应当围绕海南自由贸易港建设战略定位，服务“一带一路”建设和海洋强国、西部陆海新通道等国家重大战略，推进高水平对外开放。

Regulations of Hainan Free Trade Port on the Yangpu Economic Development Zone

(Adopted at the 32nd Session of the Standing Committee of the 6th Hainan Provincial People's Congress on December 30, 2021)

Chapter I General Provisions

Article 1 These Regulations are enacted pursuant to applicable laws and regulations, together with the actual circumstances in the Yangpu Zone to encourage the high-level opening-up and high-quality development of the Hainan Free Trade Port Yangpu Economic Development Zone (hereinafter referred to as "Yangpu Zone").

Article 2 These Regulations apply to the planning, construction, administration, and administrative services of the Yangpu Zone (including the planning control scope) and its adjacent waters as approved by the State Council and the provincial people's government.

Article 3 The construction and development of the Yangpu Zone shall follow the principles of openness and innovation, regional coordination, green and low-carbon industries, and shall conform to high-quality international economic and trade policies, consider the system of innovation as the core, take the initiative to implement and improve policy management in the Hainan Free Trade Port, devise an internationally competitive open policy and system, and take full advantage of the role of the pilot zone and high-quality development of the Hainan Free Trade Port.

Article 4 The open in first-line and control in second-line import and export administration system shall be first implemented in the Yangpu Bonded Port. The opening-up process shall be organized based on lawful and effective oversight, and the open in first-line and control in second-line import and export administration shall be implemented throughout the Yangpu Zone to improve trade and investment liberalization and facilitation.

Article 5 The Yangpu Zone is encouraged, under a well-established management system, to focus on the strategic positioning of the Hainan Free Trade Port and serve national critical Belt and Road Initiative, maritime development strategies, and new land and marine routes for west China.

第二章　管理体制

第六条　省人民政府设立洋浦经济开发区管理委员会（以下简称洋浦管委会）。洋浦管委会根据授权行使省级行政管理权，与儋州市人民政府合署办公、一体化运作，对洋浦经济开发区统一规划、统一开发、统一建设、统一管理。

第七条　省人民政府应当加强对洋浦经济开发区建设的组织领导，对洋浦经济开发区内重大项目安排、政策先行先试、体制机制创新等给予积极支持，研究解决洋浦经济开发区建设中的重大事项和问题。

省人民政府有关部门应当按照各自职责，推进洋浦经济开发区的建设和发展，相关市县人民政府应当予以支持和配合。

海关、海事、边检、税务等中央驻琼单位设立在洋浦经济开发区的工作机构（以下统称驻区机构），在各自法定职责范围内与洋浦经济开发区共同推进有关制度创新措施落实。洋浦经济开发区应当为驻区机构履行职责提供便利和协助。

第八条　省人民政府应当按照有利于推进海南自由贸易港建设、有利于区域协调发展的原则，在洋浦经济开发区构建更具活力、更加高效的行政管理体制。

第九条　在洋浦经济开发区可以依法设立法定机构，探索实行企业化、市场化的人事管理制度。

第十条　洋浦经济开发区应当按照激励与约束并重原则，实行体现工作绩效和分级分类管理的工资薪酬制度。

Chapter II Administrative Institutions

Article 6 The provincial people's government shall establish the Administration Committee of Yangpu Zone (hereinafter referred to as "Yangpu Administration Committee"). The Yangpu Administration Committee shall exercise provincial-level administrative power in accordance with their authorization, work with Danzhou Municipal People's Government in an integrated manner, and implement standardized planning, development, construction, and administration in the Yangpu Zone.

Article 7 The provincial people's government shall improve management when organizing construction in the Yangpu Zone and shall actively support the operation of major projects, policy trials, and institutional innovation in the Yangpu Zone in order to study and resolve major issues and problems in the construction of the Yangpu Zone.

The municipal and county people's governments shall support and cooperate with provincial people's government agencies who shall, in conformity with their respective duties, promote the construction and development of the Yangpu Zone.

Agencies of customs, maritime affairs, border inspection, taxation, and other agencies established by the central government located in Hainan within the Yangpu Zone (hereinafter referred to as "local agencies") shall, within the scope of their respective statutory duties, jointly establish an appropriate innovation system within the Yangpu Zone. The Yangpu Zone shall provide access and assistance for the local agencies to exercise their duties.

Article 8 The provincial people's government shall create a more dynamic and competent system of administration in the Yangpu Zone conducive to improving the construction of the Hainan Free Trade Port and coordinating regional development.

Article 9 Statutory agencies in the Yangpu Zone may be created in accordance with the law to implement business-oriented and market-oriented employee management systems.

Article 10 The Yangpu Zone shall implement a salary system that reflects performance, and hierarchical and classification administration pursuant to the principle of treating incentives and constraints equally.

第三章 开发建设

第十一条 洋浦管委会负责编制、批准和实施洋浦经济开发区国土空间规划，报省人民政府备案。

省人民政府和儋州市人民政府应当加强对洋浦经济开发区周边地区的规划衔接与管控，推动基础设施互联互通、城市功能互助互济、产业发展协调联动。

第十二条 洋浦经济开发区应当加强路网、电网、光网、气网、水网、生产和生活配套服务等基础设施的整体规划和同步建设，促进港产城融合发展，建设现代化国际滨海产业新城。

第十三条 洋浦管委会可以组建开发运营公司，委托其负责洋浦经济开发区内的土地开发、招商引资、产业投资等，参与洋浦经济开发区管理服务的组织与实施。

第十四条 省人民政府及其有关部门应当支持洋浦经济开发区发展，在安排年度新增建设用地指标、耕地林地跨区域占补平衡、海域使用、能耗、排放等方面应当充分考虑洋浦经济开发区的发展需求。

省人民政府及其有关部门在安排项目和省重点园区资金、产业引导基金、中央预算内资金、地方政府债券、土地储备计划以及争取纳入国家发展规划等方面，应当充分考虑洋浦经济开发区的发展需求。

第十五条 洋浦管委会可以根据授权开展土地储备，通过出租、临时使用等方式对洋浦经济开发区范围内未供应的政府储备土地加以利用，但不得影响土地正常供应。

Chapter III Development and Construction

Article 11 The Yangpu Administration Committee shall be responsible for the preparation, approval, and implementation of the Yangpu Zone regional spatial plan, which shall be recorded by the provincial people's government.

The provincial people's government and Danzhou Municipal People's Government shall improve their connections and control for purposes over the adjacent areas of Yangpu Zone, and encourage infrastructure integration, mutual assistance of urban functions, and coordinated industrial development.

Article 12 The Yangpu Zone shall improve the overall planning and construction of infrastructure including road, power grid, optical fiber network, gas, water, production, and residential support services, improve the overall development of the port, industries, and the city, and build a city with modern international coastal industries.

Article 13 The Yangpu Administration Committee may incorporate a developmental and operational company to assume responsibility for land development, investment attraction, and industrial investment in Yangpu Zone, and to participate in the administration and provision of services in the Yangpu Zone.

Article 14 The provincial people's government and other appropriate agencies shall support and devote substantial attention to the development and needs of Yangpu Zone in arranging land use metrics for annual new construction, compensating and balancing the cross-regional cultivated and forest land, the use of sea areas, energy consumption, and emissions.

The provincial people's government and its appropriate agencies shall provide adequate consideration on the development needs of Yangpu Zone in arranging funds for projects and provincial main industrial zones, industrial guidance funds, funds in the central budget, local government bonds, land reserve plans, and the pursuit of integrating them in national development plans.

Article 15 The Yangpu Administration Committee may conduct land banking based on their authority and use ungranted government reserve land within the Yangpu Zone either by lease or temporary use. The use of such shall in no case affect the normal supply of land.

洋浦经济开发区可以采取划拨、出让、租赁、作价出资或者入股等多种方式供应土地。允许以出让、租赁、作价出资或者入股等方式利用农村集体经营性建设用地进行产业项目建设。支持洋浦经济开发区开展新型产业用地试点，推进实施标准地制度。

支持洋浦经济开发区创新存量建设用地处置方式。洋浦经济开发区可以根据授权，自行编制、颁布实施基准地价及标定地价。

第十六条　洋浦经济开发区应当优化生态环境空间布局，构筑与资源环境承载力相匹配的生态安全、新型城镇化和产业发展格局，创新绿色监管体系，建立现代生态环境和资源保护监管体制，严守生态保护红线、环境质量底线、资源利用上线、生态环境准入清单的管控要求，确保发展不超载、底线不突破。

洋浦经济开发区应当遵循“减量化、再利用、资源化”原则，发展循环经济，统筹社会经济与生态环境协调发展。

第十七条　洋浦经济开发区应当推广清洁能源和节能减排降碳等环境保护技术的应用，推行清洁生产，支持企业节能、减排、降耗、增效，发展低碳绿色产业。

第十八条　洋浦经济开发区应当推进集中供热、工业污水集中处理、工业固废集中处置、公共事故应急等配套公用工程和环保基础设施建设，降低能源价格和废渣、废水、废气处置成本，提升服务产业发展能力。

The Yangpu Zone may supply the land by means of grants, assignments, leases, contributions, or equity. The use as a rural collective operating development land for industrial project construction shall be allowed through assignment, lease, contribution, or equity. The new industrial land supply trial shall be implemented, and a standardized land system is encouraged.

The Yangpu Zone shall support modern management methods for existing development land and may prepare, issue, and implement the benchmark land price and calibrated land price based on their authority.

Article 16 The Yangpu Zone shall improve the ecological planning, develop ecological security and a new urbanization and industrial development model that complies with the resource and environment capacity, innovate the green oversight system, set up a modern oversight system for ecological and resource protection, strictly abide by categorical ecological conservation requirements, environmental quality minimums, resource use caps, and a list of environmental permits for human activities, and ensure that development is not overloaded and the baseline is maintained.

The Yangpu Zone shall abide by the principles of reduction, reuse, and resource recovery, develop a circular economy and produce an overall plan to coordinate the development of the private sector economy and ecological environment.

Article 17 The Yangpu Zone shall encourage the utilization of clean energy, energy conservation, emission reduction, carbon reduction, and other environmental protection technologies, encourage clean production, support enterprises to save energy, reduce emissions, reduce consumption and increase efficiency to develop low-carbon green industries.

Article 18 The Yangpu Zone shall encourage the construction of sustainable public facilities and environmental protection infrastructures such as centralized heating, centralized industrial sewage treatment, centralized industrial solid waste disposal, and public emergency management, lower energy prices and the cost of waste residues, wastewater, and waste gas disposal, and improve service industry capacities.

第四章　产业促进和人才支撑

第十九条　洋浦经济开发区全面放开投资准入，涉及国家安全、社会稳定、生态保护红线、重大公共利益等由国家实行准入管理的领域除外。

洋浦经济开发区对外商投资实行准入前国民待遇加负面清单管理制度。

第二十条　支持洋浦经济开发区创新港口管理体制机制，推动港口资源整合，加强港口基础设施建设，加快建设我国面向太平洋和印度洋的门户港、国际集装箱枢纽港、港口型国家物流枢纽，建设西部陆海新通道国际航运枢纽。

第二十一条　支持洋浦经济开发区建设“中国洋浦港”船籍港和多功能国际海事服务基地，优化运输来往自由便利相关政策，增加内外贸航线，促进船舶以及航运相关服务业等要素集聚。

支持发展洋浦港国际中转业务。

第二十二条　洋浦经济开发区推动建设与海南自由贸易港建设相适应的临港产业体系，集约发展高附加值、低环境负荷的石化新材料、清洁能源、智能装备制造、海工装备制造等高新技术产业。

第二十三条　支持洋浦经济开发区实施全球贸易商计划，加快培育贸易新业态新模式，做强集装箱物流、大宗商品物流、冷链物流、石化物流等专业物流，建设国际航运中心、供应链服务中心、大宗商品集散交易基地和海南自由贸易港进出口贸易基地。

Chapter IV Industry Promotion and Professional Support

Article 19 The Yangpu Zone shall provide liberalized access to investments, except for matters involving national security, social stability, ecological conservation bright lines, the public interest, and other areas subject to national access administration.

The Yangpu Zone shall implement a system of pre-admission national treatment plus a foreign investment negative list.

Article 20 The Yangpu Zone shall receive support to innovate the port administration system, encourage the integration of port resources, improve the construction of port infrastructure, accelerate the construction of China's gateway port, international container hub port, and port-type national logistics hub capable of accessing the Pacific and the Indian Oceans, and to build an international shipping hub with a new land and marine route for west China.

Article 21 The Yangpu Zone shall receive support to build China's Yangpu Port of registry and a multi-functional international maritime service base, to improve liberalization and facilitation policies for transportation, to increase domestic and foreign trade routes, and to encourage the clustering of factors including ships and shipping services.

The development of the international transit business within the Yangpu Port shall be supported.

Article 22 The Yangpu Zone shall encourage the construction of a port industry system suitable for the development of the Hainan Free Trade Port, and the intensive development of high-tech industries including high-value-added and environmental-friendly petrochemical materials, and clean energy, intelligent equipment manufacturing, and marine equipment manufacturing.

Article 23 The Yangpu Zone shall receive support to implement the global trader plan, accelerate the development of new business methods and models, improve professional container, bulk commodity, cold chain, and petrochemical logistics, and establish an international shipping center, supply chain service center, commodity distribution, and trading base, and import and export trade base in the Hainan Free Trade Port.

第二十四条 洋浦经济开发区依照有关规定扩大金融业对外开放，支持贸易投资自由化便利化。支持离岸贸易和跨境服务贸易有序发展，建设海南自由贸易港新型离岸国际贸易先行区。支持洋浦经济开发区跨境投融资等改革。

支持洋浦经济开发区发展航运金融、融资租赁、商业保理等产业。支持培育发展法律服务、会计审计、资产评估、信用评级、融资担保、投资咨询等商务服务业。

第二十五条 洋浦经济开发区内企业或者符合条件的金融机构从境外募集的资金及其提供跨境服务取得的收入，可以在依法合规的前提下自主用于海南自由贸易港内及境外的经营投资活动。

第二十六条 设立儋州洋浦发展投资基金，引导社会资本共同参与儋州洋浦开发建设。

洋浦经济开发区设立政府产业发展引导基金，吸引金融机构、投资机构等社会资本参与，采用股权投资等市场化方式，对投资符合洋浦经济开发区产业规划、安全生产和环保标准的鼓励类产业，以及有收入来源的基础设施、公共设施等项目予以支持。

洋浦经济开发区设立产业发展资金，统筹用于区内各类产业扶持、创新创业支持、市场拓展支持、人才引进培养、基础设施和公共设施建设等，逐步建立健全符合国际惯例的财政保障体系。

第二十七条 省人民政府支持洋浦经济开发区加大科技创新投入，优化创新创业生态，建设产业技术平台和企业孵化机构，建设智慧洋浦。

洋浦经济开发区应当强化创新驱动，培育高新技术企业。

Article 24 The Yangpu Zone shall broaden the market access to the financial industry pursuant to applicable law, and support the liberalization and facilitation of trade and investment. The Yangpu Zone shall maintain the systematic development of offshore and cross-border service trade, and build a new offshore international trade pilot zone in the Hainan Free Trade Port. The reform of cross-border investment and financing in the Yangpu Zone shall receive support.

The Yangpu Zone shall receive support for the development of shipping finance, financial lease, factoring, and other industries. It shall likewise be supported for the creation and development of business services such as legal services, accounting and auditing, asset appraisal, credit rating, financing guarantee, and investment consulting in the Yangpu Zone.

Article 25 Funds raised abroad by the entities or eligible financial institutions in the Yangpu Zone, and income gained from cross-border services may be utilized for operations and investment within or out of the Hainan Free Trade Port pursuant to law.

Article 26 The Danzhou-Yangpu development investment fund shall be set up in order to attract private capital for the development and construction of Danzhou-Yangpu.

The Yangpu Zone shall set up a government industrial development guidance fund to encourage the involvement of financial institutions, investment institutions, and other private capital to adopt market-oriented methods such as equity investment and to support investment in encouraged industries that meet the requirements of industrial planning, safety production, and environmental protection standards of the Yangpu Zone, as well as the infrastructure, public facilities and other projects with sources of income.

The Yangpu Zone shall set up industrial development funds to support industries of all kinds, innovation, and entrepreneurship, market expansion, skilled employee employment and training, infrastructure, and public facility construction to progressively establish and improve the financial security system in line with international practices.

Article 27 The provincial people's government shall support the Yangpu Zone to increase the investment for the innovation and optimization of technology and entrepreneurship ecology, build an industrial technology platform and business incubator, and build a smart Yangpu.

The Yangpu Zone shall improve the innovation and development of high-tech enterprises.

第二十八条 洋浦经济开发区可以根据产业发展需要，制定急需紧缺人才目录，自主出台高层次人才认定标准，相关标准和政策在洋浦经济开发区内执行。按照控制总量、急需紧缺原则，在洋浦管委会的专业岗位设置高端特聘职位，实行灵活人事制度，吸引国内外一流专业人才。

洋浦经济开发区按照海南自由贸易港有关规定，制定符合本区域实际的国内外高层次人才和紧缺人才的人才落户、住房保障、子女入学、医疗保障、配偶就业等优惠政策，根据需要自主引进人才。

第二十九条 支持洋浦经济开发区引入国内外高校和职业院校，探索创新国内外教育合作新模式，建立职业教育培训学校和实训基地，为产业发展培养人才。

第三十条 洋浦经济开发区实行更加开放便利的停居留政策，实施外国人工作许可负面清单管理，按照有关规定对外国人工作许可进行审批，依法简化外国人在洋浦经济开发区工作、出入境等手续。

第五章 监管服务

第三十一条 在洋浦经济开发区实施和深化极简审批改革，在具有强制性标准领域建立“标准制＋承诺制”的投资制度，简化审批条件和程序，提高审批服务效能。

洋浦管委会应当建立招商项目落地保障机制，实行项目全程跟踪服务责任制，及时协调解决项目审批、开工建设和生产经营中的问题。

Article 28 The Yangpu Zone may prepare a list of urgently needed professionals based on actual industry development needs, and independently issue certification standards for high-level professionals. Appropriate standards and policies shall be implemented within the Yangpu Zone. Based on the principles of total amount management and urgent need, high-end specialized jobs for professional posts of the Yangpu Administration Committee may be created and a flexible employee system shall be adopted in order to attract local and foreign first-class professionals.

In compliance with Hainan Free Trade Port regulations, the Yangpu Zone shall prepare preferential policies for the settlement, housing security, children's enrollment, medical security, and spousal employment for local and foreign high-level professionals and urgently needed talents based on actual social circumstances in the areas, and autonomous introduction of talents as the case may be.

Article 29 The Yangpu Zone shall be supported to introduce local and foreign universities and vocational colleges, explore and improve new methods of international education collaboration, establish vocational education and training schools and bases, and develop skilled employees for industry development.

Article 30 The Yangpu Zone shall implement a more accessible and convenient residential policy, implement a negative list for the administration of foreigners' work permits, approve foreigners' work permits pursuant to law, and simplify foreigners' work, entry and exit procedures in the Yangpu Zone pursuant to law.

Chapter V Oversight and Administrative Services

Article 31 The reform of simplified review and approval procedures in the Yangpu Zone shall be implemented and developed. A standard investment system with a commitment to the mandatory standards shall be established, and approval requirements and procedures shall be simplified to improve the efficiency of review and approval services.

The Yangpu Administration Committee shall create a safeguard system for the actual implementation of investment projects, implement a tracking and service responsibility system for the overall project development, and promptly coordinate and resolve the project approval, construction, production, and operation issues.

第三十二条 洋浦经济开发区应当建立健全以信用监管为基础、与负面清单相适应的过程监管体系，依照有关规定制定过程监管的规则和标准，对新技术、新产业、新业态、新模式实施包容审慎监管。

第三十三条 在洋浦经济开发区创新口岸服务体制机制，推行统一高效的口岸服务，简化进出境监管手续，推动各监管部门一次性联合执法。

支持洋浦经济开发区完善对外开放口岸和“二线”口岸查验设施及综合指定监管场地建设。

第三十四条 洋浦经济开发区应当进一步完善洋浦公共信息服务平台建设，促进监管信息的归集、交换和共享。洋浦管委会、驻区机构和省人民政府有关部门应当及时主动提供信息，参与信息交换和共享。

第三十五条 洋浦经济开发区应当加强安全生产监督管理，落实生产经营单位安全生产主体责任，建立完善安全风险评估与论证机制，按照安全风险管控要求进行产业规划和空间布局，严格项目安全准入，建立完善重大风险源管控制度。

第三十六条 洋浦经济开发区应当加强贸易投资、公共卫生、生态环境等领域的风险防控，完善应急管理体系，强化应急处置能力建设，健全重大风险隐患预警与应急处置制度。

第六章　附　则

第三十七条 本条例自 2022 年 1 月 1 日起施行。2010 年 6 月 1 日海南省第四届人民代表大会常务委员会第十五次会议通过的《洋浦经济开发区条例》同时废止。

Article 32 The Yangpu Zone shall create and improve a process-oversight system based on credit oversight and adapted to the negative list, issue rules and standards for process-oversight in compliance with applicable law, and implement a comprehensive and prudent oversight on new technologies, industries, business methods, and models.

Article 33 The port service system and mechanism in Yangpu Zone shall be innovated, the port services shall be standardized and efficient, and the entry and exit oversight procedures shall be simplified in order to improve the comprehensive joint law enforcement of various oversight agencies.

The Yangpu Zone shall receive support for the improvement of the construction of inspection facilities and comprehensive designated oversight sites located at the open and second-line ports.

Article 34 The Yangpu Zone shall optimize the Yangpu public information service platform and improve the collection, exchange, and sharing of regulatory information. The Yangpu Administration Committee, local agencies, and provincial people's government appropriate agencies shall promptly and proactively provide information and participate in information exchange and sharing.

Article 35 The Yangpu Zone shall improve oversight and administration of production safety, implement a production safety accountability system for business entities, establish and improve the safety risk assessment and survey systems, conduct industrial planning and spatial layout based on risk control requirements, strictly enforce project implementation safety standards, and establish and improve the management system for major risk sources.

Article 36 The Yangpu Zone shall improve risk prevention and control in trade and investment, public health, and the ecological environment, improve the emergency administration system, improve emergency response capacity development, and improve the pre-warning and emergency response system for major potential risks.

Chapter VI Supplementary Provision

Article 37 The Regulations shall come into force as of January 1, 2022. The Regulations on the Yangpu Economic Development Zone passed at the 15th Session of the Standing Committee of the 4th Hainan Provincial People's Congress on June 1, 2010, shall be repealed simultaneously.

[illegible]

Chapter VI Supplementary Provisions

[illegible]

中国（海南）自由贸易试验区商事登记管理条例

Regulations of China (Hainan) Pilot Free Trade Zone on the Administration of Commercial Registration

中国（海南）自由贸易试验区商事登记管理条例

（2018 年 12 月 26 日海南省第六届人民代表大会常务委员会第八次会议通过）

第一章 总 则

第一条 为了规范商事登记管理活动，保护商事主体合法权益，加快形成法治化、国际化、便利化的营商环境和公平开放统一高效的市场环境，遵循国家法律、行政法规的基本原则，结合本自由贸易试验区实际，制定本条例。

第二条 本自由贸易试验区内商事登记以及相关管理活动适用本条例。

本条例所称商事登记，是指申请人为设立、注销商事主体资格及变更相关事项，向登记机关提出申请，由登记机关依法登记并公示的行为。

第三条 本条例所称商事主体，是指经登记机关依法登记，以营利为目的从事经营活动的企业法人、其他经济组织和自然人。

商事主体包括公司、非公司制企业法人、合伙企业、个人独资企业及上述企业分支机构、农民专业合作社及其分支机构、个体工商户等。

第四条 商事登记应当遵循规范统一、公开透明、便捷高效、诚实守信的原则。

Regulations of China (Hainan) Pilot Free Trade Zone on the Administration of Commercial Registration

(Adopted at the 8th Session of the Standing Committee of the 6th Hainan Provincial People's Congress on December 26, 2018)

Chapter I General Provisions

Article 1 The Regulations of China (Hainan) Pilot Free Trade Zone on the Administration of Commercial Registration (hereinafter referred to as "these Regulations") are enacted in order to standardize commercial registration development, protect the legitimate rights of commercial enterprises, and accelerate the creation of a law-based, internationalized and convenient environment for doing business and the fair, open, unified, and efficient market environment, pursuant to the basic principles of national laws and administrative regulations, and in the light of the actual circumstances of this Pilot Free Trade Zone (hereinafter referred to as the "PFTZ").

Article 2 These Regulations shall apply to commercial registration and management in the PFTZ.

"Commercial registration", for the purpose of these Regulations, refers to the act of the applicant submitting to the registering office for the incorporation or cancellation of a commercial enterprise or alteration of related matters, and the registering office grants and publishes such pursuant to the rules.

Article 3 "Commercial enterprise", for the purpose of these Regulations, refers to enterprises with legal personality, other economic organizations, and natural persons engaged in for-profit business and registered by the registering office pursuant to the rules.

Commercial enterprises include enterprises, non-incorporated enterprises with legal personality, partnerships, or sole proprietorship enterprises and their branches, farmers' cooperatives and their branches, and self-employed individuals.

Article 4 Commercial registration shall follow the principles of standardization, openness, transparency, convenience, efficiency, honesty, and trustworthiness.

第五条　省人民政府市场监督管理部门是商事主体的登记机关，负责本自由贸易试验区内的商事主体登记、监督管理和服务。

市、县（区）、自治县人民政府市场监督管理部门负责本辖区内商事主体的监督管理和服务，不再核发营业执照。

第六条　本自由贸易试验区实行商事主体自主申报登记制度，全面推行全程电子化商事登记。

申请人通过登记机关的电子化登记平台，以电子文档的形式向登记机关自主申报名称、住所（经营场所）、经营范围、信息变更、注销等事项，登记机关在网上受理、审查、核准、发照和存档。

市、县（区）、自治县市场监督管理部门应当为商事主体提供登记咨询、引导、协助办理等服务。

第七条　本自由贸易试验区实行全岛通办的注册官制度，注册官在商事登记中依法独立行使受理、审查、核准等职责，并承担相应的法律责任。

前款所称注册官是指市场监督管理部门具体负责商事登记的工作人员。

第八条　登记机关对申请人提交的文件实行形式审查。

对申请人填报的格式化登记信息，由登记平台自动审核；对申请人申报的非格式化电子文件，登记机关从本自由贸易试验区范围内随机选派注册官依法审核。

第九条　申请人填报的登记信息和提交的申请材料应当真实、有效，并对其真实性、合法性承担责任。

Article 5 The market regulation agency of the provincial people's government is the registering office for commercial enterprises and is responsible for the registration, oversight, management, and service of commercial enterprises in the PFTZ.

The market regulation agency in cities, counties (districts), autonomous counties people's governments are responsible for the oversight, management, and services for commercial enterprises within their respective jurisdictions, and no longer issue business licenses.

Article 6 The PFTZ has launched the commercial enterprise self-declaration system and digital commercial registration platform for the whole process.

The applicant fills a digital registration platform form with the name, domicile (place of business), business scope, information alteration, cancellation, and other items with the registering office, and the registering office reviews such applications, issues licenses and permits, and keeps records online.

The market regulation agency in cities, counties (districts), autonomous counties shall provide consultation channels, guidance, assistance, and other services for commercial enterprises.

Article 7 The PFTZ has launched an island-wide registrar system. The registrar independently exercises the power of acceptance, examination, and approval in commercial registration pursuant to the rules, and assumes such liability.

The registrar in the preceding paragraph refers to the staff of the market regulation agency specifically responsible for commercial registration.

Article 8 The registering office shall conduct a formal examination of the documents submitted by the applicant.

The standardized forms submitted by the applicant shall be automatically reviewed by the registration platform. The registering office shall randomly appoint registrars from the PFTZ to lawfully review the information on any non-standardized forms submitted by the applicant.

Article 9 The registration information and application materials submitted by the applicant shall be true and valid, and the applicant shall be responsible for their authenticity and legality.

第十条 省人民政府应当建立和完善商事主体登记平台、行政审批信息管理平台和企业信用信息公示系统，实行商事登记机关、有关行政审批机关、监管部门以及有关单位信息共享，健全信息公示制度。

县级以上人民政府应当建立监管执法协作配合机制，实现对商事主体的许可、监管等方面的执法联动。

第二章 登记程序

第一节 设立登记

第十一条 设立商事主体应当依法向登记机关申请设立登记，符合设立条件的，由登记机关依法确认其商事主体资格和一般经营资格，核发营业执照；未经登记，不得以商事主体名义从事经营活动。营业执照签发日期为商事主体的成立日期。

依照法律、法规的规定，在设立登记前需要取得许可的，应当自许可之日起在法定期限内向登记机关申请商事登记；未经许可，不予登记。

依照法律、法规的规定，在设立登记后需要取得许可方可开展特定经营活动的，未经许可，不得开展特定经营活动。

第十二条 省人民政府应当依法向社会公布本自由贸易试验区商事登记实施前置行政许可事项和后置行政许可事项的目录。

第十三条 商事主体申请商事登记涉及后置许可事项的，登记机关在办理登记时，应当告知商事主体依法取得有关行政许可部门的许可后方可经营；在办理登记后，应当将商事主体的登记信息通过信息共享平台告知同级有关行政许可部门。

Article 10 The provincial people's government shall establish and improve the market entity registration platform, administrative review management platform, and enterprise credit information publicity system, enforce information sharing among commercial registration office, administrative review agencies, oversight agencies, and other appropriate agencies, and improve the information publicity system.

The people's governments at or above the county level shall establish a collaboration system for oversight and law enforcement to realize the connectivity of law enforcement in the approval and oversight of market entities.

Chapter II Registration Procedures

Section 1 Registration of Incorporation

Article 11 Market entities shall lawfully apply to the registering office for registration of incorporation. If the requirements for incorporation are met, the registering office shall confirm the qualification to act as a market entity and to undertake general business lawfully, and issue the business license. Without registration, they shall not be allowed to start business in the name of the market entity. The issuance date of the business license is the incorporation date of the market entity.

Pursuant to law, if it is necessary to obtain permission before the registration of incorporation, the party concerned shall apply to the registering office for commercial registration within the statutory time limit from the date of permission. No registration shall be allowed without permission.

No such activities can be conducted without permission where it is necessary to obtain permission before carrying out specific business after the incorporation registration pursuant to law.

Article 12 The provincial people's government shall lawfully publish the catalog of pre-administrative permission and post-administrative permission for commercial registration in the PFTZ.

Article 13 If the application for commercial registration by the market entity involves post-permission matters, the registering office shall inform the market entity to obtain permission from the appropriate administrative approving agency pursuant to the rules before starting. After the registration, the registration information of the market entity shall be transferred to the administrative approval agency at the same level through the information sharing platform.

有关行政许可部门应当在信息共享平台获取商事主体的登记信息，依法办理相关商事登记后置许可，并依法履行后续监管职责。

第十四条　商事主体登记事项包括：

（一）名称；

（二）住所（经营场所）；

（三）类型；

（四）经营范围；

（五）法定代表人或者负责人姓名；

（六）注册资本；

（七）营业期限；

（八）投资人姓名或者名称及其出资额；

（九）法律、法规规定的其他事项。

登记机关应当按照商事主体类型，分别规定商事主体登记事项的具体内容，制定格式化文本。

第十五条　商事主体下列事项应当向登记机关办理备案，登记机关予以存档备查并按照规定公示：

（一）章程或者合伙协议；

（二）董事、监事、高级管理人员；

（三）商事登记联络员；

（四）清算组成员及负责人；

（五）法律、法规规定的其他事项。

登记机关应当按照商事主体类型，分别规定商事主体备案事项的具体内容。

The administrative approval agency shall obtain the registration information of the market entity through the information sharing platform, process the post-permission for such commercial registration pursuant to the rules, and perform the follow-up oversight pursuant to the rules.

Article 14 The items required for registration of market entities include:

(a) name;

(b) domicile (business place);

(c) form;

(d) business scope;

(e) name of the statutory representative or responsible person;

(f) registered capital;

(g) business term;

(h) name of the investor and its capital contributions; and

(i) others specified by laws and regulations.

The registering office shall specify the items requiring registration for market entities and create standardized forms based on the structures of market entities.

Article 15 The following matters of market entities shall be recorded by the registering office, who shall file for future reference and publish it pursuant to the rules:

(a) the articles of association or partnership contract;

(b) directors, supervisors, and senior managers;

(c) commercial registration liaison officer;

(d) members and responsible person(s) of the liquidation committee; and

(e) others specified by laws and regulations.

The registering office shall specify the requirements for the record of market entity based on the structure of the market entities.

第十六条 设立商事主体，申请人应当按照商事主体类型，分别向登记机关提交下列相应的申请材料：

（一）申请书；

（二）公司章程（合伙协议、农民专业合作社章程）。

需要取得前置许可的，应当提交相关许可文件。

登记机关应当按照商事主体类型，制定登记申请材料目录及文书格式规范并向社会公布。

第十七条 申请人可以通过登记平台自主申报商事主体名称，登记机关不对名称进行预先核准。申请人凭申报后生成的名称保留单办理前置许可、商事登记等相关业务。

第十八条 不需要取得前置许可的商事主体名称保留期为三十日；保留期届满前，申请人可以申请延期一次，期限为三十日。

需要取得前置许可的商事主体名称保留期为六个月，保留期届满前，申请人可以申请延期一次，期限为六个月。

期限届满，登记机关不再保留该商事主体名称。

第十九条 登记机关应当放宽商事主体名称限制，制定并公布本自由贸易试验区商事主体名称规则，开放商事主体名称数据库，依法向公众提供可供使用的商事主体名称的查询比对服务。

申请人申请名称不得违反名称规则的规定，不得与本自由贸易试验区已登记的商事主体名称相同。申请人选择使用与他人近似或者可能侵犯他人在先权利的名称登记的，应当承担相关法律责任。

Article 16 To incorporate a market entity, the applicant shall submit the following materials to the registering office based on the structure of the market entities:

(a) the written application; and

(b) the articles of association (partnership contract, the articles of association of farmers' cooperatives).

If it is necessary to obtain the pre-permission, the appropriate documents shall be submitted.

The registering office shall enact and publish the catalog of application materials and the formats pursuant to the structure of the market entities.

Article 17 The applicant may declare the name of the market entity independently through the registration platform, and the registering office shall not pre-approve the business name. The applicant shall process pre-permission, commercial registration, and other related matters with the name under reservation generated after declaration.

Article 18 The reservation period of the name of the market entity that does not need to obtain the pre-permission is 30 days. Before expiration, the applicant may apply for another 30-day extension.

The reservation period of the name of the market entity that needs to obtain the pre-permission is 6 months. Before expiration, the applicant may apply for another 6-month extension.

Upon expiration, the registering office will no longer reserve the name of the market entity.

Article 19 The registering office shall ease the restrictions on the naming of market entity, enact and publish the naming rules of market entity in the PFTZ, disclose the database of the naming of market entity, and provide accessible inquiry and comparison services concerning the naming of market entity pursuant to the rules.

The name declared by the applicant shall not violate the naming rules and not resemble the registered market entity's name in the PFTZ. If the applicant registers for a similar name with others or may infringe upon others' prior rights, it shall assume liability.

第二十条 申请人自主申报住所（经营场所）信息，可不提交使用证明。住所（经营场所）应当是固定场所，并符合法律、法规的有关规定。

多个商事主体可以共用同一地址登记为住所（经营场所）。

登记机关应当对申报的住所（经营场所）与相关部门提供的信息在线进行核对。核对通过的，登记机关根据申请人申报的信息予以记载；核对未通过的，在电子档案中予以备注。

第二十一条 住所（经营场所）依法应当经规划、住建、公安、应急管理、生态环境、文化、卫生健康等相关部门许可方可开展相关经营活动的，开展经营活动前应当依法办理许可。

县级以上人民政府应当公布经营场所的禁设区域目录，商事主体不得以禁设区域目录所列的场所作为住所（经营场所）。

第二十二条 申请人应当按照有关规定自主选择申报经营范围。

登记机关应当按照商事主体的类型，分别规定经营范围填写方式。

第二十三条 登记机关应当按照有关规定和技术标准对申请人等相关人员身份信息进行验证。使用符合法律规定的电子认证服务机构发行的数字证书进行的电子签名与纸质签名具有同等效力。

外国（地区）投资者主体资格和自然人身份按照国家有关规定验证。

第二十四条 登记机关通过登记平台自动审核商事登记申请信息。符合条件的，当场登记并生成加载统一社会信用代码的电子营业执照；不符合条件的，不予登记并说明理由；需要注册官审核的，自提交之日起三个工作日内作出是否准予登记的决定。

Article 20 The applicant may declare its domicile (business place) information independently without submitting the certificate of utilization. The domicile (business place) shall be a fixed place and not violate applicable law.

Multiple market entities can share the same address and register at the domicile (business place).

The registering office shall verify the declared domicile (business place) with the information provided by the appropriate agency online. If verified, the registering office shall record it according to the information declared by the applicant. If not, digital notes shall be made.

Article 21 Domicile (business place) shall be checked by the appropriate agency, such as planning agency, housing agency, public security agency, emergency management agency, ecology and environment agency, cultural agency, and health agency before it can be used for business operation. Market entities shall apply for approval before conducting business operations pursuant to law.

The people's governments at or above the county level shall publish the catalog of banned areas of business places, and market entities shall not be resident at any domicile (business place) listed in the catalog of banned areas.

Article 22 The applicant shall independently declare the business scope pursuant to the applicable rules.

The registering office shall specify the requirements to fill in the business scope according to the structures of market entities.

Article 23 The registering office shall verify the identities of the applicant and other relevant personnel pursuant to regulations and technical standards. The digital signatures made with digital certificates issued by digital certification agencies pursuant to the law shall have the same legal effect as the physical signatures.

The investors' qualifications and their identities as the natural person of foreign (regional) investors shall be verified pursuant to national regulations.

Article 24 The registering office shall automatically examine the application of commercial registration through the registration platform. If it meets the requirements, such agency shall register and produce the electronic business license filled with the unified social credit code on the spot. If not, such agency shall not register and state the reasons. If it needs to be examined by the registrar, the decision on whether to grant the registration shall be made within 3 business days from the date of submission.

第二十五条 电子营业执照与纸质营业执照具有同等法律效力。商事主体可以凭电子营业执照办理有关手续，开展经营活动。

经过申请人电子签名的电子档案与纸质档案具有同等法律效力。

第二十六条 依法无需前置许可的商事主体在其住所（经营场所）所在同一市、县（区）、自治县区域内设立分支机构，或者依法需要前置许可的商事主体，前置许可证上已经记载分支机构住所（经营场所）的，登记机关可以直接在该商事主体营业执照上加注分支机构住所（经营场所），不再另行办理分支机构登记。商事主体自愿申请办理分支机构登记的，登记机关应当予以办理。

第二节 变更登记

第二十七条 商事主体登记事项或者备案事项发生变化的，应当自作出变更决议或者法定变更事项发生之日起三十日内向登记机关申请变更登记或者变更备案。法律、法规规定在变更登记或者变更备案前须经许可的，应当自许可决定之日起三十日内向登记机关申请变更登记或者变更备案。登记机关应当自收到申请后当场作出是否予以变更的决定；需要注册官进行审核或者核验的，应当于收到申请之日起三个工作日内作出是否予以变更的决定，但预约核验时间不计算在列。

未经变更登记的，不得对抗善意第三人。

第二十八条 商事主体的名称、住所（经营场所）和经营范围的变更登记适用本条例第二章第一节的有关规定。

第二十九条 商事主体申请变更登记，应当向登记机关提交下列材料：

Article 25 The electronic business license and paper business license are equally legally binding. The market entity can process relevant procedures using the electronic business license in order to carry out business activities.

The files digitally signed by the applicant are equally legally binding as the paper files.

Article 26 If the market entity, not in need of pre-permission pursuant to the rules, establishes the branch in the same city, county (district) or autonomous county where its domicile (business place) is located, or if the market entity, lawfully requiring pre-permission, has already recorded the domicile (business place) of the branch, the registering office may directly add the domicile (business place) of the branch to the business license of the market entity, and no separate branch registration is required. If the market entity voluntarily applies for the registration of the branch, the registering office shall accept it.

Section 2 Registration of Alteration

Article 27 In case of any alteration of the registration or record of the market entity, such entity shall apply to the registering office for alteration of registration or record within 30 days of the date of making the alteration or the changes of the statutory alternation items. If the law requires pre-permission before the alteration of registration or record, the market entity shall apply to the registering office for the alteration of registration or record within 30 days of the date of the decision to permission. The registering office shall decide on whether to alter it on the spot upon receiving the application. If the registrar is required to carry out examination or verification, it shall decide on whether to alter within 3 business days of the date of receiving the application, but the time for reservation for verification is not included.

Without the registration of alteration, it does not bind upon the *bona fide* third party.

Article 28 The registration of alteration in respect of the name, domicile (business place) and business scope of market entities shall be subject to Section 1 of Chapter II of these Regulations.

Article 29 When applying for registration of alteration, the market entity shall submit the following materials to the registering office:

（一）申请书；

（二）依照法律、法规规定作出的变更决议或者决定。

涉及前置许可的，应当提交相关许可文件。

变更登记事项涉及修改章程的，应当提交修改后的章程或者章程修正案。

商事主体的相关信息以登记机关留存的电子档案为准。

第三十条 商事主体变更类型的，应当按照变更后的商事主体类型填报登记信息并提交相应的材料。

第三十一条 商事主体变更法定代表人、变更投资人、变更注册资本导致投资人组成或者投资人出资比例发生变化的，由登记机关选派商事主体住所（经营场所）所在地注册官依法进行核验，独立出具审查意见。

第三节 注销登记

第三十二条 商事主体因下列情形解散或者终止商事活动的，应当依法向登记机关办理注销登记，终止商事主体资格：

（一）章程或者协议规定的解散事由出现；

（二）经营期限届满，不再申请延期；

（三）被依法吊销营业执照、被责令关闭或者被撤销；

（四）投资人决定解散；

（五）因合并或者分立需要解散；

（六）被依法宣告破产；

（七）人民法院依法予以解散；

(a) the written application; and

(b) the resolution or decision of alteration adopted pursuant to law.

Permission documents shall be submitted as necessary.

If the alteration registration involves revision of the articles of association, the revised copy or draft shall be submitted.

The information of market entity filed through digital records by the registering office shall prevail.

Article 30 If the market entity changes its type, it shall declare the registration information and submit the appropriate materials pursuant to the new type.

Article 31 If the market entity changes its statutory representative, investor, or registered capital, resulting in alteration of the composition of investors or the proportion of investors' contribution, the registering office shall lawfully appoint the registrar at the place where the commercial enterprise's domicile (business place) is located for verification, and independently issue examination opinions.

Section 3 Registration of Cancellation

Article 32 If the market entity dissolves or terminates commercial activities due to the following circumstances, it shall lawfully cancel the registration through the registering office so as to terminate the qualification as a market entity:

(a) the circumstance for dissolution specified in the articles of association or contract appears;

(b) after the expiration of the operating period, no longer applies for further extension;

(c) the business license has been lawfully rescinded, or such entity is ordered to close down or voided;

(d) the investor decides to dissolve;

(e) dissolution due to merger or separation;

(f) has been declared insolvent pursuant to law;

(g) the people's court decides to lawfully dissolve it; or

（八）法律、法规规定的其他情形。

商事主体注销前依法应当清算的，应当自清算结束之日起三十日内申请注销登记。商事主体申请注销登记前，应当办理分支机构注销登记。

第三十三条 对领取营业执照后未开展经营活动、申请注销登记前未发生债权债务或者已将债权债务清算完结的有限责任公司、非公司制企业法人、个人独资企业、合伙企业以及上述企业分支机构，由其自主选择适用简易注销程序或者一般注销程序。法律、法规另有规定的除外。

第三十四条 商事主体选择申请简易注销登记的，应当通过企业信用信息公示系统向社会公告拟申请简易注销登记以及全体投资人承诺等信息，公告期为七日。

第三十五条 登记机关应当自公告之日起一个工作日内将商事主体拟申请简易注销登记信息推送给省税务机关。税务机关按照要求查询商事主体涉税情况，对于存在未办结涉税事宜的商事主体，应当在公告期届满次日前向登记机关提出异议；逾期未提出的，视为无异议。

税务机关可以对下列情形的商事主体不提出异议：

（一）未办理涉税事宜的；

（二）办理涉税事宜但未领取发票、没有欠税和没有其他未办结事项的；

（三）在公告期届满之日前已办结缴销发票、结清应纳税款等清税手续的。

第三十六条 商事主体选择简易注销的，应当在公告期届满次日起三十日内，向登记机关提出简易注销申请。申请简易注销登记，应当向登记机关提交下列材料：

(h) other circumstances as provided by laws and regulations.

If the market entity should be liquidated lawfully before cancellation, it shall apply for the registration of cancellation within 30 days of the date of completion of liquidation. Before the market entity applies for the registration of cancellation, it shall process the registration of cancellation for its branch.

Article 33 The limited liability company, unincorporated enterprise with legal personality, sole proprietorship, partnership, and local branch offices that have not carried out business activities after obtaining the business license, with no creditor's rights and obligations before applying for the registration of cancellation or having settled the creditor's rights and obligations, shall either adopt expedited cancellation or general cancellation, except as otherwise provided by laws and regulations.

Article 34 If the market entity applies for expedited cancellation, it shall publish the information such as the proposed application for expedited cancellation and the commitment of all investors through the enterprise credit information publicity system, and the notice period shall be 7 days.

Article 35 The registering office shall, within 1 business day from the date of publish, transfer the information (the market entity's application for expedited cancellation) to the provincial tax agency. The tax agency shall inquire about the taxation of the market entity according to the requirements and raise objection to the registering office before the expiration of the notice period if the market entity has not cleared tax-related affairs. The overdue objection is deemed as not raising such objection.

The tax agency may raise no objection to the market entity in respect of the following circumstances:

(a) fail to clear tax-related affairs;

(b) process tax-related matters but not receive a receipt, no overdue tax, and no other outstanding matters; or

(c) the tax clearance has been completed such as surrendering receipt and settling the tax payable before the expiration of the notice period.

Article 36 If the market entity chooses expedited cancellation, such entity shall apply to the registering office for expedited cancellation within 30 days after the expiration of the notice period. When applying for expedited cancellation, the following materials shall be submitted to the registering office:

（一）申请书；

（二）全体投资人承诺书；

（三）强制清算终结的企业提交人民法院终结强制清算程序的裁定，破产程序终结的企业提交人民法院终结破产程序的裁定；

登记机关应当在三个工作日内按照有关规定作出是否准予注销的决定。

第三十七条 商事主体不再从事经营活动，又不适用简易注销情形的，应当按照有关规定办理一般注销手续，并依法申请核验。

第三十八条 商事主体申请一般注销登记，应当向登记机关提交下列材料：

（一）申请书；

（二）清算报告；

（三）法律、法规规定提交的其他材料。

第四节 特别规定

第三十九条 商事主体申请办理变更法定代表人、变更投资人、变更注册资本导致投资人组成或者投资人出资比例发生变化和一般注销登记等需要核验的事项的，申请人应当自申请之日起三十日内通过登记平台自主选择核验方式、预约核验时间。登记机关不得设置预约核验的条件。

未经核验，登记机关对申请事项不予办理。

第四十条 商事主体住所（经营场所）所在地注册官应当对法定代表人或者投资人等相关人员的身份信息和意思表示等进行核验。

(a) the written application;

(b) the commitment of all investors; and

(c) entities facing compulsory liquidation shall submit the people's court decision to cancel such, and entities facing insolvency shall submit the people's court decision to cancel such.

The registering office shall decide on whether to grant the cancellation within 3 business days pursuant to applicable rules.

Article 37 If the market entity is no longer engaged in business activities and cannot apply for expedited cancellation, it shall adopt general cancellation pursuant to applicable rules and lawfully apply for verification.

Article 38 The market entity shall submit the following materials to the registering office regarding general cancellation of registration:

(a) the written application;

(b) liquidation report; and

(c) other materials as provided by laws and regulations.

Section 4 Special Provisions

Article 39 If the market entity applies for matters requiring verification, such as altering the statutory representative, the investor, the registered capital, causing changes in the investor composition or the investor's contribution ratio, and general registration of cancellation, the applicant shall independently adopt the verification method and reserve for verification through the registration platform within 30 days of the date of application. The registering office shall not set the conditions for applicants requesting verification.

Without verification, the registering office shall not accept the application.

Article 40 The registrar at the place where the market entity's domicile (business place) is located shall verify the identity information and expression of the intent of relevant personnel such as the statutory representative or investors.

相关人员的意思表示应当符合法律、法规的规定。

登记机关应当对核验过程予以记录并留存。

第四十一条 经注册官核验，符合条件的，登记机关自核验开始之日起三个工作日内应当予以确认；不符合条件或者拒不配合核验的，应当自核验开始之日起三个工作日内驳回并说明理由。

第四十二条 商事登记联络员是指由商事主体指定，由本自由贸易试验区内常住居民担任，负责文件接收、保管、商事登记、年度报告及其他信息公示等事务的工作人员。

商事登记联络员发生变动的，商事主体应当向登记机关备案。

第四十三条 律师事务所、会计师事务所等中介机构及其从业人员在代理登记业务过程中，应当遵守法律、法规的规定，提供的信息、资料以及出具的书面文件应当真实、合法，不得提供虚假信息、资料，不得出具虚假验资报告、评估报告、证明文件以及其他文件。

第四十四条 人民法院和仲裁机构的生效法律文书涉及投资人变更的，商事主体应当向登记机关申请办理相应的登记手续。人民法院依照执行程序通知登记机关协助执行的，登记机关应当办理相应登记手续，并记载公示。

商事主体申请投资人变更登记时，利害关系人已经就投资人变更登记申请材料的真实性、合法性提起民事诉讼或者仲裁的，登记机关不予受理；已经受理的，不予登记。未提起民事诉讼或者仲裁直接向登记机关提出异议的，登记机关应当书面告知其通过民事诉讼、仲裁解决，利害关系人在三十日内不提起民事诉讼、仲裁的，登记机关依法办理变更登记。

The expression of the intent of persons referred to in the preceding paragraph shall comply with the law.

The registering office shall record and keep the verification process.

Article 41 If the registration meets the requirements after verification by the registrar, the registering office shall confirm it within 3 business days of the date of verification. If not or the applicant refuses to cooperate with the verification, the registering office shall reject within 3 business days of the date of the start of the verification and specify the reasons.

Article 42 The commercial registration liaison officer refers to the permanent resident of the PFTZ, designated by the market entity, who accounts for documents acceptance, keeping, commercial registration, annual report, and other information disclosures.

If the commercial registration liaison officer is changed, the market entity shall record such change with the registering office.

Article 43 Law firms, accounting firms, other intermediaries, and their employees shall abide by commercial registration law. The information, data, and written documents provided shall be true and lawful. They shall not falsify information, documents, capital verification reports, evaluation reports, certification documents, and other documents.

Article 44 If the effective legal documents of the people's courts and arbitration agencies involve the alteration of investors, the market entity shall apply to the registering office to register such registration. If the people's court notifies the registering office to record an enforcement action according to the execution procedures, the registering office shall process such registration, and keep it on record and make it known to the public.

Before the market entity applies for registration of investors altered, the interested party has filed the civil lawsuit or arbitration on the authenticity and legality of the application materials for such registration, the registering office shall not accept it. If accepted, the registering office shall not grant registration. If no civil lawsuit or arbitration proceeds but the interested party objects to the registration directly, the registering office shall inform the party in writing that it shall be resolved via civil lawsuit or arbitration. If the interested party does not file the civil lawsuit or arbitration within 30 days, the registering office shall process such registration lawfully.

第三章　监督管理

第四十五条　省人民政府市场监督管理部门负责建设和管理企业信用信息公示系统，建立服务保障机制，为社会公众提供方便快捷的商事主体信息查询服务。

省人民政府各部门应当按照规定的归集路径、方法和内容，将商事主体有关信息统一归集到企业信用信息公示系统，记于商事主体名下，并与相关政务信息系统共享。

第四十六条　省人民政府相关部门应当按照有关规定通过企业信用信息公示系统公示商事主体的登记、行政许可、行政处罚等监管信息以及其他相关信息，供社会公众查询。

商事主体应当通过企业信用信息公示系统依法公示其出资、行政许可、股权变更等信息。

商事主体应当按照有关规定于每年1月1日至6月30日，通过企业信用信息公示系统填报并公示上一年度年度报告；个体工商户、农民专业合作社可以自主选择填报、公示年度报告信息。

商事主体和有关单位可以按照有关规定申请查询电子档案。

第四十七条　县级以上人民政府市场监督管理部门应当加强商事主体的监督管理，随机抽取检查对象、随机选派执法检查人员，并及时公开抽查、检查结果。

商事主体在市场监督管理部门开展检查过程中应当配合询问调查，如实反映情况，并根据检查需要，提供会计资料、审计报告、行政许可、行政处罚决定书、场所使用证明等相关材料。

Chapter III Oversight and Administration

Article 45 The market regulation agency of the provincial people's government takes responsibility for the development and management of the enterprise credit information publicity system and shall establish a service guarantee system in order to provide the public with a convenient and fast query service for market entity information.

All agencies under the provincial people's government shall collect and integrate market entity information into the enterprise credit information publicity system, keep such information under the name of corresponding market entity, and share with relevant administrative information systems pursuant to the prescribed collection channels, methods, and contents.

Article 46 The appropriate agency of the provincial people's government shall publish the regulatory information such as registration, administrative license, and administrative punishment of market entity through the enterprise credit information publicity system and other relevant information for public inquiry pursuant to applicable rules.

The market entity shall publish its capital contribution, administrative license, equity structure changes, and other information lawfully through the enterprise credit information publicity system.

The market entity shall fill in and publish the annual report of the previous year through the enterprise credit information publicity system from January 1 to June 30 annually pursuant to applicable rules. The self-employed individuals and farmers' cooperatives may fill in and publish the annual report information voluntarily.

The market entity and relevant entity may request the digital files pursuant to applicable rules.

Article 47 The market regulation agency of the people's governments at or above the county level shall strengthen the oversight and administration of market entities, randomly select inspection targets, randomly designate law enforcement inspectors, and publish spot check and inspection results in a timely manner.

The market entity shall cooperate with the inquiry and investigation, truthfully state the facts, and provide accounting information, audit reports, administrative license, administrative sanction decision, certificate of place utilization, and other related materials (if necessary) during inspections conducted by the market regulation agency.

省人民政府市场监督管理部门应当加强对市、县（区）、自治县人民政府市场监督管理部门的指导和监督。

第四十八条 人民法院或者登记机关认定商事主体名称应当停止使用的，商事主体应当自收到人民法院生效的法律文书或者登记机关处理决定之日起十五日内办理名称变更登记；名称变更前，以统一社会信用代码代替其名称。

第四十九条 县级以上人民政府市场监督管理部门应当加强对商事主体住所（经营场所）的检查和抽查，对电子档案中有备注的商事主体增加抽查比例和频次。商事主体登记的住所（经营场所）无法联系、地址不存在或者违反法律、法规禁止性规定的，市场监督管理部门应当按照有关规定将其列入经营异常名录。

第五十条 对依法实行注册资本实缴登记制的商事主体，县级以上人民政府市场监督管理部门应当依法对其注册资本缴付情况进行检查，对存在虚报注册资本、虚假出资、抽逃出资的行为依法进行处罚，并对相关责任人实施信用约束。

对其他商事主体的注册资本缴付行为，县级以上人民政府市场监督管理部门应当依法对其公示的出资信息进行检查、核实。

第五十一条 商事主体有下列情形之一的，县级以上人民政府市场监督管理部门将其列入经营异常名录，并在企业信用信息公示系统上予以公示：

（一）未按照规定期限公示年度报告或者未按照规定公示有关信息的；

（二）公示信息隐瞒真实情况、弄虚作假的。

The market regulation agency of the provincial people's government shall improve the guidance and oversight of the market regulation agency of the people's governments of cities, counties (districts), and autonomous counties.

Article 48 Where the people's court or the registering office determines that the name of the market entity cannot continue to be used, the market entity shall process the registration of name alteration within 15 days of the date of receiving the legal documents of the people's court or the decision of the registering office. Before alteration, the unified social credit code shall be used as a replacement.

Article 49 Market regulation agencies of the people's governments at or above the county level shall strengthen the inspection on the domicile (business place) of the market entity, and increase the proportion and frequency of inspections on market entities with notes in digital files. If the registered domicile (business place) of the market entity cannot be accessed, the address does not exist or violates the prohibitive rules of the laws and regulations, the market regulation agency shall put it in the suspicious activities list pursuant to applicable rules.

Article 50 The market regulation agency of the people's governments at or above the county level shall inspect the payment of the registered capital of the market entity for which the registered capital paid-in registration system is applied pursuant to the rules, lawfully punish the false reporting of the registered capital, making false capital contribution, or unjustifiably withdrawing capital contribution, and impose credit limits on the relevant accountable persons.

In case of the payment of registered capital of other market entities, the market regulation agency of the people's governments at or above the county level shall inspect and lawfully verify the disclosed investment information.

Article 51 If the market entity is under any of the following circumstances, the market regulation agency of the people's governments at or above the county level shall put it in the suspicious activities list and publish it on the enterprise credit information publicity system:

(a) fail to publish the annual report within the given time limit or fail to publish relevant information pursuant to the rules; or

(b) disclosed information conceals material facts or is falsified.

第五十二条 被列入经营异常名录的商事主体按照有关规定履行了相关义务的，由县级以上人民政府市场监督管理部门移出经营异常名录。

被列入经营异常名录满三年的商事主体，未按照规定履行相关义务的，由登记机关列入严重违法失信企业名单，并通过企业信用信息公示系统向社会公示。

第五十三条 被列入严重违法失信企业名单的商事主体在相关违法行为未改正前，其法定代表人不得担任其他商事主体的法定代表人、董事、监事和高级管理人员。

县级以上人民政府及其有关部门对被列入经营异常名录或者严重违法失信企业名单的商事主体申请行政许可、政府采购、工程招投标、国有土地出让、授予荣誉等事项，予以限制或者禁入。

第五十四条 因本条例第五十二条第二款规定的情形被列入严重违法失信企业名单的商事主体，自被列入严重违法失信企业名单之日起满三年未再发生该款规定的情形的，可以通过企业信用信息公示系统向社会公告其履行公示义务和拟申请移出严重违法失信企业名单等信息，公告期为三十日。

商事主体可在公告期届满次日起三十日内，向住所（经营场所）所在地人民政府市场监督管理部门申请移出严重违法失信企业名单，市场监督管理部门应当自查实之日起三个工作日内作出移出决定。

公告期间，任何组织和个人可以向市场监督管理部门提出书面异议申请。经核实，异议成立的，市场监督管理部门应当终止移出程序，不再予以信用修复。

Article 52 If the market entity in the suspicious activities list has fulfilled its relevant obligations pursuant to applicable rules, the market regulation agency of the people's governments at or above the county level shall remove it from such list.

If the market entity, having been put in the suspicious activities list for 3 years, fails to fulfill its relevant obligations pursuant to the rules, it shall be put in the list of enterprises with serious illegality and dishonesty by the registering office and publish through the enterprise credit information publicity system.

Article 53 Before the violation is rectified, the statutory representative of the market entity in the list of enterprises with serious violations and dishonesty, shall not serve as the statutory representative, director, supervisor, and senior administrator of other market entities.

The people's governments and their appropriate agency at or above the county level shall limit or ban the market entity in the suspicious activities list or the list of business entities with serious violations and dishonesty from applying for an administrative license, government procurement, project bidding, transfer of state-owned land, and granting of honors.

Article 54 Where the market entity is put in the list of business entities with serious violations and dishonesty due to the circumstance specified in Paragraph 2 of Article 52 of these Regulations which does not occur again within 3 years from the date of being listed, such entity may publish the performance of obligations and apply for the removal from the list of business entities with serious violations and dishonesty through the enterprise credit information publicity system. The notice period is 30 days.

The market entity can apply to the market regulation agency of the people's government where the domicile (business place) is located for the removal from the list of business entities with serious violations and dishonesty within 30 days after the expiration of the notice period, and the market regulation agency shall decide on the removal within 3 business days of the date of verification.

During the notice period, any organization or individual may submit a written objection to the market regulation agency. If the objection is confirmed after verification, the market regulation agency shall terminate the removal and no longer restore negative credit records.

第五十五条 有关行政许可机关在各自职责范围内，对商事主体从事取得许可方可开展的经营活动，依法进行监督管理。

第五十六条 律师事务所、会计师事务所等中介机构违反本条例规定，在代理登记业务时弄虚作假的，登记机关有权拒绝受理中介机构代理的登记业务，并定期公示中介机构代理登记业务的相关信息。

登记机关可以向有关行业主管部门、行业自律组织建议对相关中介机构进行监督检查，有关行业主管部门、行业自律组织应当自收到建议之日起三十日内予以反馈。

第五十七条 行业协会、商会和依法成立的专业服务机构应当建立会员单位信用记录，制定会员单位失信行为的惩戒清单，可以将会员单位失信信息通过企业信用信息公示系统进行公示。

第四章 法律责任

第五十八条 商事主体违反本条例第九条，提交虚假材料或者采取其他欺诈手段故意隐瞒重要事实，取得商事登记的，登记机关可以依法予以撤销，依照国家有关规定予以处罚。

商事主体违反本条例第二十七条，未按照规定办理变更登记的，由登记机关责令限期登记；逾期不登记的，依照国家有关规定予以处罚。

第五十九条 商事主体违反本条例第二十七条，未按照规定办理备案的，由登记机关责令改正；逾期未改正的，处一千元以上三万元以下的罚款。

Article 55 The appropriate administrative licensing agency shall, within the scope of their respective duties, supervise and manage the business activities that market entities can carry out only after obtaining permission pursuant to law.

Article 56 If the intermediary agency such as the law firm or accounting firm violates these Regulations and fraudulently acts as an agent for the registration business, the registering office shall have the right to refuse the registration by the intermediary agency and regularly publish the relevant information regarding the registration business of the intermediary agency.

The registering office may suggest to the relevant industry competent agency and industry self-regulatory organizations to oversight and inspect the relevant intermediary agency, and such competent agency and organizations shall reply within 30 days of the date of receiving the suggestion.

Article 57 Trade associations, chambers of commerce, and professional service organizations incorporated pursuant to the rules shall establish the credit record of the members, make disciplinary lists of members' dishonesty, and publish the dishonesty of members through the enterprise credit information publicity system.

Chapter IV Legal Liability

Article 58 If the market entity, in violation of Article 9 of these Regulations, intentionally conceals important facts by submitting false materials or adopting other fraudulent means and obtains commercial registration, the registering office may lawfully revoke it and punish pursuant to relevant national regulations.

For any commercial enterprise in violation of Article 27 and who does not register pursuant to the rules, the registering office shall demand it to register within a time limit. If overdue, such enterprise shall be punished pursuant to national regulations.

Article 59 If the market entity, in violation of Article 27 of these Regulations, does not record according to the provisions, the registering office shall demand remediation. If overdue, such entity shall be fined not less than 1,000 Yuan and not more than 30,000 Yuan.

第六十条 商事主体违反本条例第四十六条，有下列情形之一的，由县级以上人民政府市场监督管理部门责令改正；逾期不改正的，处以一万元以上五万元以下的罚款。法律、法规另有规定的，从其规定：

（一）未按照规定公示年度报告或者未按照市场监督管理部门责令改正的期限公示有关信息的；

（二）公示信息隐瞒真实情况、弄虚作假的。

第六十一条 商事主体违反本条例第四十七条，有下列情形之一的，由县级以上人民政府市场监督管理部门处以一万元以上十万元以下的罚款，构成违反治安管理行为的，由公安机关依法予以处罚：

（一）拒绝检查人员或者其委托的专业机构进入被检查场所，致使检查工作无法正常进行的；

（二）拒绝向检查人员或者其委托的专业机构提供相关材料致使检查工作无法正常进行的；

（三）提供虚假材料的；

（四）其他阻扰、妨碍检查工作，致使检查工作无法正常进行的。

第六十二条 违反本条例的行为，本条例未设定处罚但其他法律法规已设定处罚的，依照有关法律法规的规定处罚。

第六十三条 县级以上人民政府市场监督管理部门及其工作人员在商事登记管理活动中滥用职权、弄虚作假、玩忽职守、徇私舞弊的，由任免机关或者监察机关对直接负责的主管人员和其他直接责任人员依法给予处分；构成犯罪的，依法追究刑事责任。

Article 60 If the market entity violates Article 46 of these Regulations and falls under any of the following circumstances, the market regulation agency of the people's government at or above the county level shall issue an order to rectify. If overdue, such enterprise shall be fined not less than 10,000 Yuan and not more than 50,000 Yuan, unless otherwise provided by laws and regulations:

(a) fail to publish the annual report pursuant to law or fail to rectify within the given time limit provided by market regulation agency; or

(b) disclosed information conceals the reality or is falsified.

Article 61 Where the market entity violates Article 47 of these Regulations and falls under any of the following circumstances, the market regulation agency of the people's government at or above the county level shall impose the fine of not less than 10,000 Yuan and not more than 100,000 Yuan, and if in violation of public safety administration, it shall be lawfully punished by the public security agencies:

(a) refuse the inspector or the authorized professional institutions to enter the inspected places, leading to the failure of the inspection;

(b) refuse to provide relevant materials to the inspector or the professional institutions with the authorization, leading to the failure of the inspection;

(c) provide falsified materials; or

(d) other obstacles to the inspection leading to the failure of the inspection.

Article 62 Other laws and regulations shall control for any violations against these Regulations if other laws and regulations specify penalties for such violations while these Regulations do not.

Article 63 If the market regulation agency of the people's government and their employees at or above the county level are involved in the abuse of position, falsification, dereliction of duty, playing favoritism and committing irregularities in the commercial registration management, the appointment and removal agency or the oversight agency shall impose sanctions on the person directly in charge and other persons subject to direct liabilities lawfully. If a crime is constituted, it shall be held criminally in accordance with the law.

第五章 附 则

第六十四条 按照外国（地区）相关法律法规在外国（地区）设立，持续规范经营，资信状况良好的外国（地区）企业，可以在本自由贸易试验区划定的特定区域内从事除我国法律法规明令禁止之外的经营活动。具体登记管理办法另行规定。

第六十五条 海南省行政区域内非本自由贸易试验区的商事登记管理参照本条例执行。

第六十六条 本条例自 2019 年 1 月 1 日起实施。1993 年 9 月 28 日海南省第一届人民代表大会常务委员会第四次会议通过的《海南经济特区企业法人登记管理条例》同时废止。

Chapter V Supplementary Provisions

Article 64 The foreign (regional) enterprises established in foreign countries (regions) pursuant to the applicable law of foreign countries (regions), continuously operating with good credit, may engage in business activities except those expressly prohibited by the laws and regulations of China within the specific areas designated by the PFTZ. The specific commercial registration administration rules shall be enacted separately.

Article 65 In respect of the commercial registration management within the administrative area of Hainan Province but outside the PFTZ, these Regulations shall be applied *mutatis mutandis*.

Article 66 These Regulations shall come into force as of January 1, 2019. The Regulations of Hainan Special Economic Zone on the Administration of Registration of Enterprises with Legal Personality, adopted at the 4th session of the Standing Committee of the 1st Hainan Provincial People's Congress on September 28, 1993, shall be repealed simultaneously.

中国（海南）自由贸易试验区
重点园区极简审批条例

Regulations of China (Hainan) Pilot Free Trade Zone on Expedited Review for Key Parks

中国（海南）自由贸易试验区重点园区极简审批条例

（2019 年 3 月 26 日海南省第六届人民代表大会常务委员会第十次会议通过）

第一章　总　则

第一条　为了推广和深化“多规合一”下的极简审批改革，营造法治化、国际化、便利化的营商环境，加快中国（海南）自由贸易试验区和中国特色自由贸易港建设，推动重点园区建设项目尽快落地，遵循国家法律、行政法规原则，依据全国人民代表大会对海南省人民代表大会常务委员会的立法授权，结合本自由贸易试验区实际，制定本条例。

第二条　省和市、县、自治县人民政府应当按照简政放权、放管结合、优化服务的要求，遵循宽进、严管、快办、便民、诚信、公开的原则，最大限度精简审批事项、评估事项和下放审批权限，探索实施单一部门集中审批管理模式；优化审批流程，提高审批效率；推进行政审批和政务服务标准化，主动为行政管理相对人提供高效优质服务。

第三条　在重点园区逐步推行规划代立项审批、区域评估代单个项目评估，实行准入清单和告知承诺管理，组织联合验收，强化事中事后监管，以及实施其他极简审批做法。

重点园区名录由省人民政府公布。

Regulations of China (Hainan) Pilot Free Trade Zone on Expedited Review for Key Parks

(Adopted at the 10th Session of the Standing Committee of the 6th Hainan Provincial People's Congress on March 26, 2019)

Chapter I General Provisions

Article 1 These Regulations are enacted under national laws and administrative regulations pursuant to the legislative authority from the National People's Congress to the Standing Committee of Hainan Provincial People's Congress and based on the actual circumstances of the China (Hainan) Pilot Free Trade Zone (hereinafter referred to as the "PFTZ") for the purposes of promoting and deepening the expedited review reform under the "regulations in one", creating a law-based, internationalized and convenient business environment, speeding up the development of PFTZ and the free trade port with Chinese characteristics, and facilitating the implementation of key park projects as soon as possible.

Article 2 The people's governments of provinces, cities, counties and autonomous counties shall, pursuant to the devolution, integration of streamlining administration and delegating power, and upgrade service requirements, streamline examination, approval, and evaluation, devolve review authority to the maximum extent and explore the implementation of centralized review by a single-agency based on the principles of wide entry, strict management, quick processing, convenience, honesty, and openness; the governments shall also optimize the approval process and improve the approval efficiency, promote the standardization of administrative review and administrative services, and actively provide efficient and high-quality services for administrative counterparts.

Article 3 In key parks, planning shall gradually replace approval, regional evaluation for individual evaluation. The access list and notification-commitment system shall be launched, and joint acceptance, improve post-event oversight shall be organized, and other expedited review procedures shall be adopted.

The list of key parks shall be published by the provincial people's government.

第四条 博鳌乐城国际医疗旅游先行区、海口国家高新技术产业开发区、海南老城经济开发区三个产业园区（以下简称“三园”）范围内的建设项目，依照本条例第二章、第三章的规定实施特别极简审批（以下简称“三园”特别极简审批）。

在前款规定以外的其他重点园区推广适用或者部分推广适用“三园”特别极简审批的，由省人民政府评估论证后，报省人民代表大会常务委员会决定，或者另行制定经济特区法规规定。

第五条 在其他重点园区推广适用或者部分推广适用“三园”特别极简审批前，省和市、县、自治县人民政府应当依据省和市、县、自治县总体规划，做好下列基础工作：

（一）组织编制和调整完善重点园区的总体规划、控制性详细规划以及产业发展规划等规划；

（二）组织开展相关区域评估，并结合相关评估普查区域内的文物单位、历史建筑、古树名木等现状；

（三）编制并公布产业项目准入清单。

第六条 授权符合法定条件的“三园”管理机构行使本产业园区管理事项的行政审批权和相应的行政处罚权。

省和市、县、自治县人民政府及其有关部门应当根据推行极简审批的需要，充分委托前款规定以外的其他重点园区管理机构实施行政审批和行政处罚，或者在前款规定以外的其他重点园区内设点办理行政审批事项。需要授权符合法定条件的其他重点园区管理机构行使本园区管理事项的行政审批权和相应的行政处罚权的，由省人民政府报省人民代表大会常务委员会决定，或者另行制定法规规定。

Article 4 The special expedited review (hereinafter referred to as the "Special Expedited Review for the Three Parks"), subject to Chapters I and III of these Regulations, shall be implemented for construction projects within the Bo'ao Hope International Medical Tourism Pioneer Zone, Haikou National High-tech Industrial Development Zone, and Hainan Old Town Economic Development Zone (hereinafter referred to as the "Three Parks").

If, in other key parks beyond the preceding paragraph, the Special Expedited Review for the Three Parks is popularized (or partially popularized), it shall, after evaluation by the provincial people's government, be submitted to the Standing Committee of the Provincial People's Congress for approval; or the special economic zone regulations shall be enacted separately.

Article 5 Before the Special Expedited Review for the Three Parks is popularized (or partially) in other key parks, the people's governments of provinces, cities, counties, and autonomous counties shall conduct the following pursuant to the comprehensive plan of provinces, cities, counties, and autonomous counties:

(a) to organize the preparation, adjustment, and improvement of the comprehensive plan, regulatory detailed planning, and industrial development planning of key parks;

(b) to organize an appropriate regional assessment, and combine the appropriate assessment to survey the current conditions for heritage preservation, historical buildings, ancient and famous trees in the region; and

(c) to prepare and publish the industrial project access list.

Article 6 The administrative agencies of the Three Parks, pursuant to statutory conditions, are authorized to exercise the administrative review power and the corresponding administrative penalty power for the administration of this industrial park.

The people's governments of provinces, cities, counties, and autonomous counties and their appropriate agencies shall, based on the demands of implementing expedited review, fully entrust other key park administrative agencies other than those specified in the preceding paragraph to conduct an administrative review and issue administrative penalties or set up offices in other key parks other than those specified in the preceding paragraph to manage the administrative review. If it is necessary to authorize other key park administrative agencies, pursuant to statutory conditions, to exercise the power of administrative review and the corresponding power of administrative penalty on the park administration, it shall be decided by the Standing Committee of the Provincial People's Congress after submission by the provincial people's government; or regulations shall be enacted separately.

第七条　鼓励重点园区结合实际需要，探索改革做法，创新管理模式，深化本区域的极简审批改革。

第八条　在本自由贸易试验区重点园区内进行的督查、检查、巡查、考核等工作，应当适用本条例。

第九条　由国务院及其部门行使审批权的事项，依照有关法律、行政法规和国家有关规定办理，不适用本条例。

第二章　审批事项和评估事项精简

第十条　"三园"范围内的建设项目，符合省和市、县、自治县总体规划以及本园区的总体规划、控制性详细规划等规划的，下列事项不再审批：

（一）建设项目选址意见书核发；

（二）建设项目用地预审。

第十一条　"三园"范围内的建设项目，符合省和市、县、自治县总体规划以及本园区的总体规划、控制性详细规划等规划的，下列事项不再审批，改为备案管理：

（一）河道管理范围内建设项目工程建设方案审查；

（二）工程建设项目招标事项核准；

（三）省级、市县级文物保护单位建设控制地带内建设工程设计方案审批；

（四）防空地下室设计方案审核；

（五）防空地下室易地建设许可；

Article 7 Key parks are recommended to explore reform practices, innovate management patterns and deepen the reform of expedited review in this area.

Article 8 These Regulations shall apply to the oversight, inspection, patrol, and assessment carried out in the key parks of the PFTZ.

Article 9 For matters in which the State Council and its component agencies exercise the power of review, the applicable laws, administrative regulations, and state rules shall prevail, and these Regulations shall not apply.

Chapter II Simplification of Review and Approval

Article 10 For construction projects within the Three Parks, pursuant to the comprehensive plan of the province and city, county, autonomous county and the park's comprehensive plan, regulatory detailed planning, and other planning, the following no longer need to be approved:

(a) the issue of submission for construction project site; or

(b) the pre-approval of land for construction projects.

Article 11 For construction projects within the Three Parks, pursuant to the comprehensive plan of the province and city, county, autonomous county and the park's comprehensive plan, regulatory detailed planning, and other planning, the following no longer need to be approved and can be changed to a record system:

(a) the examination of the construction plan for construction projects within the scope of river management;

(b) the approval of the construction project bidding;

(c) the review of the construction project design plan within the construction regulatory zone of the organizations with cultural relics under protection at the province, city, and county levels;

(d) the audit of the air defense basement design;

(e) air-raid shelter construction permit;

（六）防雷装置设计审核；

（七）城市道路挖掘许可；

（八）城镇污水排入排水管网许可。

第十二条 在“三园”范围内，对建筑面积在一千平方米以下（含）的结构简单和功能单一的厂房、仓库、设备用房等建筑物，不再进行施工图设计文件审查。具体实施办法由省人民政府制定。

第十三条 “三园”范围内的建设项目，符合省和市、县、自治县总体规划以及本园区的总体规划、控制性详细规划等规划的，下列事项以区域审核审批替代单个项目审核审批：

（一）建设项目使用林地审核审批；

（二）建设项目压覆重要矿床审批；

（三）固定资产投资项目节能评估审查（需备案）。

第十四条 本自由贸易试验区重点园区范围内的建设项目，符合省和市、县、自治县总体规划以及本园区的总体规划、控制性详细规划等规划，对地质灾害危险性已统一组织区域评估的，不再进行单个项目评估，但具体建设项目用地位于评估划定的危险性大、中等区段的除外。

第三章 审批程序和流程优化

第十五条 “三园”范围内的建设项目，符合省和市、县、自治县总体规划以及本园区的总体规划、控制性详细规划等规划的，下列事项实行告知承诺制：

(f) the lightning protection device design review;

(g) the urban road excavation permit; or

(h) the permit for urban sewage discharged into the sewer network.

Article 12 Within the Three Parks, document review of the construction drawings and design documents for simple structure and single function, such as factories, warehouses, and equipment rooms with a building area of less than 1,000 square meters shall no longer take place. The detailed measures shall be enacted by the provincial people's government.

Article 13 For construction projects within the Three Parks, pursuant to the comprehensive plan of the province, city, county, and autonomous county, as well as the comprehensive plan and regulatory detailed planning of the park, the following shall be subject to regional review instead of individual review:

(a) the review of the use of forest land in construction projects;

(b) the approval of construction projects covering important deposits; and

(c) the energy-saving assessment and review of fixed assets investment projects (required for recordation).

Article 14 For construction projects within key parks of the PFTZ, pursuant to the comprehensive plan of provinces, cities, counties, and autonomous counties, as well as the comprehensive plan and regulatory detailed plans of this park and the regional assessment of geological hazards already uniformly organized, no individual assessment shall be conducted, except when the land for specific construction projects is located in the high-risk and medium-risk sections specified in the assessment.

Chapter III Approval Procedures and Process Optimization

Article 15 For development projects within the Three Parks, pursuant to the comprehensive plan of the province and city, county, autonomous county and the park's comprehensive plan, regulatory detailed planning, and other planning, the followings are subject to the notification-commitment system:

（一）建设用地规划许可；

（二）建设工程规划许可；

（三）建筑工程施工许可。

第十六条 尚未授权重点园区管理机构行使行政审批权的，省和市、县、自治县人民政府应当确定重点园区建设项目立项用地规划许可、工程建设许可、施工许可、竣工验收四个审批阶段的牵头部门，并由各牵头部门组织协调相关部门严格按照限定时间，完成本阶段的审批。

同一部门实施的管理内容相近或者属于同一办理阶段的多个审批事项，应当整合为一个审批事项。能够用征求相关部门意见方式替代的审批事项，可以调整为政府内部协作事项。

各审批阶段由牵头部门制定统一的办事指南和申报表格，每一个审批阶段申请人只需提交一套申报材料。不同审批阶段的审批部门应当共享申报材料，不得要求申请人重复提交。

第十七条 对基本条件具备、主要申请材料齐全且符合法定形式，但次要条件或者申请材料欠缺的审批事项，经过申请人作出相应承诺后，审批部门或者重点园区管理机构可容缺后补，先予受理，经审查后颁发相关许可证件。

按照前款规定办理审批的，审批部门或者重点园区管理机构应当当场一次性告知需要补正的材料、时限和超期补正处理办法，并要求申请人承诺在一定期限内补正全部材料。

第十八条 建设项目环境影响评价、地震安全性评价等评价事项不作为项目审批或者核准条件。地震安全性评价由建设单位在工程设计前办理完成，其他评价事项由建设单位在工程开工前办理完成。

(a) the permit of development land planning;

(b) the permit of development project planning; and

(c) the development permit.

Article 16 If the administrative agencies of key parks have not been authorized to exercise the power of administrative review, the people's governments of provinces, cities, counties, and autonomous counties shall determine the leading agencies in the four stages of review: land planning permit, engineering construction permit, construction permit, and completion acceptance. Each leading agency shall organize and coordinate the appropriate agencies to complete the review at the respective stages in strict compliance with the limited time.

The multiple review items with similar administrative contents charged by the same agency or belonging to the same stage shall be integrated into one. The review items that can be replaced by seeking the opinions of the appropriate agencies shall be changed to internal collaboration items within the government.

In each review stage, the leading agency shall draft the standardized guidelines and application forms, and the applicant shall only submit a set of application materials for each review stage. The approving agencies at different stages shall share the application materials and shall not require the applicants to repeatedly submit such.

Article 17 For review items meeting basic conditions with their main application materials and meeting the statutory format but lacking in secondary conditions or application materials, after the applicant issues the corresponding commitments, the approving agency or the administrative agency of the key parks may allow correction after application, preliminarily accept, and issue the appropriate licenses after review.

The approving agencies or the administrative agencies of the key parks shall, under the preceding paragraph for review, inform the applicant of materials in need of correction, the time limit and methods for overdue correction in one instance, and require the applicant to promise to correct all the materials within of the specified time.

Article 18 The environmental impact assessment, seismic safety evaluation, and other evaluations of the construction project shall not be used as the approval or granting requirements. The seismic safety evaluation shall be completed by the developer before the project design, and other evaluations shall be completed by the developer before the project starts.

“三园”以外的重点园区建设项目用地预审意见可以作为使用土地证明文件申请办理建设工程规划许可证，用地批准手续由建设单位在施工许可前办理完成。

第十九条 专业技术要求较高的审批事项，其技术审查可以通过政府购买服务的方式，委托具有相关资质的专业机构统一审查，并出具审查意见。具体实施办法由省人民政府制定。

委托专业机构进行技术审查的，审批部门对技术审查结果作法定要件的符合性审查。经审查符合法定要件的，审批部门依申请核发行政许可证件。

第二十条 房屋建筑工程、市政基础设施工程以及国家和本省规定的其他建设项目实行施工图联合审查，将消防设计审核、防雷装置设计、人防设计审查等技术审查并入施工图设计文件审查，分别作出审查意见。

建设项目依照本条例第十二条规定不再进行施工图设计文件审查的，其消防设计审核的技术审查依照本条例第十九条的规定办理。

第二十一条 依法应当由行政机关验收的事项，建设单位可以向省和市、县、自治县人民政府确定的牵头部门或者重点园区管理机构提出联合验收申请，由牵头部门或者重点园区管理机构统筹组织规划、消防等主管部门在规定时限内完成验收工作，统一出具验收意见。

省和市、县、自治县人民政府应当统一制定联合验收标准和验收图纸，明确验收时限，推动实现相关部门的信息互换、监管互认、执法互助。

The pre-examination opinions on land use for construction projects of key parks other than the Three Parks can be used as land use certification to apply for the construction project planning permit, and land use approval procedures shall be completed by the developer before the construction permit is granted.

Article 19 For professional and technical requirements of the review, the technical review can be processed via government service procurement, i.e., hiring professional agencies with appropriate qualifications to review and issue the opinion. The specific rules shall be enacted by the provincial people's government.

For professional agencies hired to conduct the technical review, the approving agencies shall conduct the statutory requirements compliance review for the technical review results. After review, if it meets the statutory requirements, the approving agencies shall issue the administrative license based on the application.

Article 20 Housing construction projects, municipal infrastructure projects, and other construction projects specified by the state and the province shall be subject to a joint review of construction drawings, and technical reviews, such as fire protection design review, lightning protection device design, and civil air defense design review, shall be included in the review of construction drawings and design documents, and review opinions shall be made respectively.

If the construction drawing design documents of a construction project are not reviewed pursuant to Article 12, the technical review of the fire design audit shall be managed pursuant to Article 19.

Article 21 For matters requiring approval by administrative agencies pursuant to law, the developer may apply for joint acceptance to the leading agency determined by the people's governments of provinces, cities, counties, and autonomous counties or the administrative agency of the key park, and such agency shall organize the planning, fire protection, and other competent agencies to complete the approval within the specified time limit and issue the unified approval opinions.

The people's governments of provinces, cities, counties, and autonomous counties shall uniformly draft joint approval standards and approval drawings, specify the time limit for approval, and promote the realization of information exchange, mutual recognition of oversight, and mutual law enforcement cooperation among appropriate agencies.

第二十二条 竣工验收事项和产权登记涉及的规划验收测量、人防工程测量和房产测绘，应当合并为单个综合性联合测绘项目。对于验收涉及的测绘工作，实行统一测绘、出具多套测绘成果，成果共享。

省人民政府规划主管部门会同有关部门制定联合测绘的综合技术标准，统一工程建设项目行政审批监管中建筑面积计算规则，明确联合测绘的内容、精度、成果形式等要求。

第二十三条 省和市、县、自治县总体规划和相关规划以及相关评估已明确能满足审批依据要求的指标、要素、参数等数据的建设项目，申请人在申请材料中无需再提供相关材料，即可办理相关审批手续。

第二十四条 审批部门或者重点园区管理机构对能够通过公共数据平台提取的材料，不再要求申请人提供，但可以要求申请人予以确认；申请人认为通过公共数据平台提取的材料与实际不符的，以申请人提供的材料作为申请材料。

第四章 监管和服务

第二十五条 省和市、县、自治县人民政府及其部门以及重点园区管理机构，应当建立以信用监管为核心，完善以记录、抽查和惩戒为手段的事中事后监管体系和诚信档案，建立责任追究制度，提高监管效能，保障极简审批顺利实施。

第二十六条 省和市、县、自治县人民政府有关部门和重点园区管理机构实施极简审批，应当严格履行下列重要职责：

（一）强化对项目后续建设中违法违规行为的查处；

Article 22 The planning acceptance survey, civil air defense engineering survey and real estate surveying and mapping completion approval, and property registration shall be merged into a single comprehensive joint surveying and mapping project. For the surveying and mapping involved in the approval, unified surveying and mapping shall be conducted, multiple sets of surveying and mapping results shall be issued, and the results shall be shared.

The competent planning agencies of the provincial people's government shall, together with the appropriate agencies, draft comprehensive technical standards for joint surveying and mapping, unify the calculation rules of the construction area in the administrative review oversight for engineering construction projects, and specify the content, precision, and results format requirements for joint surveying and mapping.

Article 23 If the comprehensive plan and related planning of provinces, cities, counties, and autonomous counties and related evaluations have clearly met the indexes, elements, and parameters required by the review, the applicant can go through the appropriate review without providing the necessary materials in the application materials.

Article 24 The approving agencies or administrative agencies of key parks no longer require the applicant to provide materials that can be obtained through the public data platform, but may require the applicant to confirm such; if the applicant believes that the materials obtained through the public data platform are inconsistent with the truth, the materials provided by the applicant shall be used as the application materials.

Chapter IV Oversight and Services

Article 25 The people's governments of provinces, cities, counties, and autonomous counties and their agencies, as well as the administrative agencies of key parks, shall prioritize the credit oversight, improve the post-event oversight system and credit archives by records, inspection, and penalties, establish an accountability system, improve oversight efficiency, and ensure the smooth implementation of expedited review.

Article 26 When conducting the expedited review, the provincial and municipal, county, autonomous county people's government agencies and the administrative agencies of key parks shall strictly perform the following important duties:

(a) to improve the investigation and penalties of the violations of law in the follow-up construction of the project;

（二）对承诺人履行承诺情况及时跟踪检查和处理；

（三）采取有效措施确保管理范围内生态环境质量不下降。

第二十七条 实行告知承诺制的审批事项，审批部门或者重点园区管理机构在受理时发现存在明显虚假承诺的，可拒绝接受承诺，不予办理有关审批事项。

审批部门或者重点园区管理机构对实行告知承诺制的审批事项，应当在作出批准后的二个月内，对申请人履行承诺情况进行检查，并加强后续监管。

第二十八条 省和重点园区所在地的市、县、自治县人民政府应当根据职责，对重点园区管理机构行使行政审批权和行政处罚权的情况加强监督。

行政审批的委托机关应当加强对受委托的相关管理机构的监管，指导受委托的相关管理机构实施审批。受委托的相关管理机构应当严格依法依约办理委托事项，并及时向委托机关报告实施情况。

第二十九条 对实施极简审批的审批部门、重点园区管理机构以及相关主管部门，省和市、县、自治县人民政府应当加强监管和考评。

第三十条 省和市、县、自治县人民政府及其部门和重点园区管理机构应当加强风险防控，建立和实施有关风险评估制度，制定有关风险防控预案，及时处置和化解实施极简审批过程中出现的风险和问题。

第三十一条 省和市、县、自治县人民政府相关部门应当最大限度实行网上受理、网上办理、网上反馈，逐步实现一网通办、一口办理，将重点园区政务服务事项全部纳入全省统一的在线政务服务平台办理。

(b) to track, inspect, and manage the performance of the commitment in a timely manner; and

(c) to take effective measures to ensure that the quality of the ecological environment within the scope of management does not decline.

Article 27 When implementing the review notification-commitment system, if the approving agencies or the administrative agencies of key parks finds clear false promises upon approval, they may refuse to accept the promise, and shall not process the review.

The approving agencies or the administrative agencies of key parks shall, within two months after the approval, inspect the applicant's performance of the commitment and improve the follow-up oversight.

Article 28 The people's governments of cities, counties and autonomous counties where the seat of a province and key parks are located shall, pursuant to their duties, improve oversight over the exercise of the power of administrative review and administrative penalties by administrative agencies of key parks.

The entrusting administrative review agency shall improve the oversight of the entrusted administrative agencies and guide such agencies to process the review. The entrusted administrative agencies shall process the entrusted matters in strict compliance with the law, and promptly report to the entrusting agencies.

Article 29 For the agencies conducting expedited review, administrative agencies of key parks and appropriate agencies, provincial and municipal, county, autonomous county people's government shall improve oversight and evaluation.

Article 30 The people's governments of provinces, cities, counties, and autonomous counties and their agencies and administrative agencies of key parks shall improve risk prevention and control, establish and implement appropriate risk assessment systems, draft appropriate risk prevention and control plans, and promptly process and resolve risks and problems arising from the implementation of expedited review.

Article 31 The agencies of the people's governments of provinces, cities, counties, and autonomous counties concerned shall conduct online acceptance, online processing, and online feedback to the maximum extent, and gradually achieve one website and one agency processing and integrate all the key park government affairs onto the province's unified online administrative service platform.

在线政务服务平台应当开设极简审批专项通道，允许申报材料容缺后补。

在线政务服务平台应当集中提供建设项目涉及的法律法规、办事指南、标准规范、问题解答等信息。

第三十二条 省和市、县、自治县人民政府政务服务机构、相关审批部门以及重点园区管理机构，应当在政务服务大厅为企业和个人提供综合咨询、专业咨询服务，并提供帮办服务。

支持专业咨询机构开展咨询市场化服务。

第三十三条 省和市、县、自治县人民政府应当建立不履行极简审批行为的举报投诉制度，公开举报投诉电话、邮箱，及时调查举报、投诉问题并依法依规处理。

第五章 法律责任

第三十四条 重点园区的项目建设单位有下列情形之一的，依法依约追究单位及其相关人员的责任；情节严重的，依法撤销行政许可，直至作出强制退出园区处理：

（一）未按照承诺开展投资运营等相关工作的；

（二）违反相关规划或者擅自改变土地用途的；

（三）违反施工安全或者工程质量规定的；

（四）违反生态环境保护规定的；

（五）其他违法违约行为。

The online administrative service platform shall set up a special channel for expedited review and allow for correction after application.

The online administrative service platform shall prioritize the provision of information such as applicable law, guidelines, standards and specifications, and questions-and-answers for construction projects.

Article 32 The administrative service agencies of the people's governments of provinces, cities, counties, and autonomous counties, appropriate approving agencies, and administrative agencies of key parks shall provide comprehensive consulting and professional consulting services for business entities and individuals in the administrative service hall, and provide hiring services.

Professional consulting agencies are supported to carry out market-oriented consulting services.

Article 33 The people's governments of provinces, cities, counties, and autonomous counties shall create a reporting and complaint system for the failure to perform the expedited review, publish telephone numbers and email addresses for reporting, promptly investigate reports and complaints, and resolve such pursuant to law.

Chapter V Legal Liability

Article 34 Any developer of key parks and their employees under any of the following circumstances shall be investigated for liability pursuant to law. If the circumstances are serious, the administrative license shall be revoked pursuant to law and the developer shall ultimately be forced to withdraw from the park:

(a) failure to carry out investment operations and other related work as promised;

(b) in violation of the appropriate planning or unauthorized change of land use;

(c) in violation of construction safety or engineering quality rules;

(d) in violation of the ecological environmental protection rules; or

(e) other violations and defaults.

第三十五条 申请人违反本条例有关告知承诺制规定的，审批部门或者重点园区管理机构应当责令限期改正，可以给予警告，并可处一万元以上五万元以下的罚款；情节严重的，可处五万元以上三十万元以下的罚款。逾期不改正或者整改后仍不符合规定的，依法撤销相应的行政许可。造成危害后果的，依照有关法律法规的规定处理。

第三十六条 申请人违反第十七条第二款规定，未在承诺期限内补正全部材料或者提交的材料不符合要求的，审批部门依法撤销相应的行政许可。

第三十七条 行政管理相对人存在不履行承诺或者弄虚作假等行为的，将其违法违规信息记入企业和个人诚信档案，并禁止其在二年内选择适用告知承诺制和容缺后补等规定；情节严重的，列入严重失信企业名单，实行联合惩戒。对失信企业及其法定代表人、控股股东、实际控制人、董事、监事、高级管理人员等，在土地出让、政府采购、国有产权交易、财政资金补助补贴、工程招投标、从业资格等方面，依法予以限制或者禁止。

第三十八条 审批部门或者重点园区管理机构以及相关主管部门、政务服务机构及其工作人员违反本条例的规定，有下列情形之一的，有关机关、单位应当严肃处理，对直接负责的主管人员和其他直接责任人员依法予以问责、处分：

（一）对依法不再审批的事项实施审批或者变相审批的；

（二）对依法不再评估的事项要求实施评估或者变相评估的；

（三）对依法应当办理的审批事项或者服务事项不予办理、推诿办理或者拖延办理的；

Article 35 If the applicant violates the notification-commitment system of these Regulations, the approving agencies or the administrative agencies of the key park shall require correction within a specified time limit, issue a warning, and impose a fine of not less than 10,000 Yuan and not more than 50,000 Yuan. If the circumstances are serious, a fine of not less than 50,000 Yuan and not more than 300,000 Yuan may be imposed. If overdue or correction still does not comply with the rules, the corresponding administrative license shall be revoked pursuant to law. Applicants causing any harmful consequences shall be managed pursuant to law.

Article 36 Where the applicant, in violation of Paragraph 2 of Article 17, fails to correct all materials within the promised time limit or the submitted materials do not meet the requirements, the approving agencies shall revoke the corresponding administrative license pursuant to law.

Article 37 If a counterpart of administrative management fails to fulfill their promise or commits fraud, the violation shall be recorded in the credit files of business entities and individuals, and such counterpart shall be prohibited from applying to the system of notification-commitment and correction for two years following their application. If the circumstances are serious, they shall be put on the list of seriously discredited business entities, and joint penalties shall be imposed. The discredited business entities and their statutory representative, controlling shareholders, actual controllers, directors, supervisors, and senior management employees shall be restricted or prohibited pursuant to law in terms of land transfer, government procurement, state-owned property rights transactions, financial subsidies, project bidding, and employment qualifications.

Article 38 If the approving agencies, the administrative agencies of key parks, the competent agencies, administrative service agencies, and their employees violate any of these Regulations or engage in any of the following circumstances, the appropriate agencies and organizations shall manage them sternly, and the person directly in charge and other employees directly liable shall be held accountable and penalized pursuant to law, if he:

(a) conducts a review or indirect review no longer required pursuant to law;

(b) conducts a direct or indirect assessment no longer required pursuant to law;

(c) refuses to process, avoids, or delays the processing of a review pursuant to law;

（四）不依法履行监管职责的；

（五）不依法履行有关公开职责或者告知职责的；

（六）不依法提供或者主动提供相关服务的；

（七）其他违反本条例规定的行为。

第三十九条 相关单位和个人为了推进和实施极简审批，出现一般性失误、轻微违纪违法且未造成实际损失或者恶劣影响的，酌情从轻、减轻或者免予追究相关责任。

第六章 附 则

第四十条 省和重点园区所在地的市、县、自治县人民代表大会常务委员会应当加强对同级人民政府极简审批实施情况的监督检查。

第四十一条 本条例所称告知承诺制，是指对能够通过事中事后监管纠正不符合审批条件的行为的审批事项，由公民、法人和其他组织提出行政审批申请，相关部门一次性告知其审批条件和需要提交的材料，申请人按照要求作出书面承诺，且符合基本条件的，审批部门可以直接作出审批决定的方式。

第四十二条 本条例自 2019 年 4 月 1 日起施行。

(d) does not to perform supervisory duties pursuant to law;

(e) does not perform the appropriate duties of disclosure or notification pursuant to law;

(f) does not provide appropriate services or initiatives to provide appropriate services pursuant to law; or

(g) other violations of these Regulations.

Article 39 In order to promote and implement the expedited review, liability for any organizations and individuals concerned that make common mistakes or are in slight violation of discipline and law but do not cause actual losses or adverse effects shall be mitigated, extenuated, or exempted as appropriate.

Chapter VI Supplementary Provisions

Article 40 The standing committee of the people's congresses of cities, counties, and autonomous counties where the seat of a province and key parks are located shall improve the oversight and inspection of the implementation of expedited review by the people's governments at the same level.

Article 41 "Notification and commitment system", for the purpose of these Regulations, refers to the method that citizens, juristic persons, and other organizations apply for administrative review that can be corrected by post-event oversight, and the appropriate agencies inform them of the review requirements and materials to be submitted in one instance. If the applicant issues the written commitment pursuant to the rules and meets the basic conditions, the approving agency can directly issue the review decision.

Article 42 These Regulations shall come into force as of April 1, 2019.

(8) does not, to perform [illegible] pursuant to law;

(9) does not perform the [illegible] duties of [illegible] pursuant to law;

[illegible]

海南省人民代表大会常务委员会关于海南自由贸易港洋浦经济开发区等重点园区管理体制的决定

Decision of the Standing Committee of Hainan Provincial People's Congress on the Management System of the Key Industrial Parks Including Yangpu Economic Development Zone of Hainan Free Trade Port

海南省人民代表大会常务委员会关于海南自由贸易港洋浦经济开发区等重点园区管理体制的决定

（2020年4月2日海南省第六届人民代表大会常务委员会第十九次会议通过）

按照分步骤、分阶段加快推进海南自由贸易港建设的要求，为了营造法治化、国际化、便利化的营商环境，促进和保障海南自由贸易港重点园区开发和建设，根据有关法律法规，结合海南自由贸易港建设实际，海南省人民代表大会常务委员会作出如下决定：

一、本决定所称海南自由贸易港重点园区包括洋浦经济开发区（含东方临港产业园、临高金牌港开发区）、博鳌乐城国际医疗旅游先行区、海口江东新区、海口国家高新技术产业开发区（含观澜湖旅游园区）、海口综合保税区、三亚崖州湾科技城、三亚中央商务区、文昌国际航天城、陵水黎安国际教育创新试验区、海南生态软件园等十个重点园区。

二、洋浦经济开发区（含东方临港产业园、临高金牌港开发区）、海口国家高新技术产业开发区（含观澜湖旅游园区）、海口综合保税区按照现行体制进行管理。

三、在博鳌乐城国际医疗旅游先行区、海口江东新区、三亚崖州湾科技城、三亚中央商务区、文昌国际航天城、陵水黎安国际教育创新试验区、海南生态软件园设立管理机构，作为在园区履行相应行政管理和公共服务

Decision of the Standing Committee of Hainan Provincial People's Congress on the Management System of the Key Industrial Parks Including Yangpu Economic Development Zone of Hainan Free Trade Port

(Adopted at the 19th Session of the Standing Committee of the 6th Hainan Provincial People's Congress on April 2, 2020)

Pursuant to the requirements to accelerate the phased construction of Hainan Free Trade Port (hereinafter referred to as "HFTP"), to create the law-based, internationally oriented, and convenient business environment, and to promote and guarantee the development and construction of the key industrial parks in the HFTP, the Standing Committee of Hainan Provincial People's Congress makes the following decision pursuant to law and in light of the actual circumstances of the HFTP:

I. The key industrial parks of the HFTP, for the purpose of this Decision, consist of 10 industrial parks: Yangpu Economic Development Zone (Dongfang Lingang Industrial Park and Lingao Jinpai Port Development Zone included), Boao Lecheng International Medical Tourism Pioneer Zone, Haikou Jiangdong New District, Haikou National High-tech Industrial Development Zone (Guanlan Lake Tourism Park included), Haikou Integrated Bonded Zone, Sanya Yazhouwan Science and Technology City, Sanya Central Business District, Wenchang International Aerospace City, Lingshui Li'an International Education Innovation Experimental Zone and Hainan Ecological Software Park.

II. The current system shall still be applied for the administration of Yangpu Economic Development Zone (Dongfang Lingang Industrial Park and Lingao Jinpaigang Development Zone included), Haikou National High-tech Industrial Development Zone (Guanlan Lake Tourism Park included), and Haikou Integrated Bonded Zone.

III. Administrative agencies are established as the statutory agencies in Boao Lecheng International Medical Tourism Pioneer Zone, Haikou Jiangdong New District, Sanya Yazhouwan Science and Technology City, Sanya Central Business District, Wenchang International Aerospace City, Lingshui Li'an International Education Innovation Experimental Zone, and Hainan Ecological Software Park. Such agencies may provide appropriate administrative and public services

职责的法定机构，依法具有机关法人资格，具体负责园区综合协调、开发建设、运营管理、产业发展、投资促进、制度创新、企业服务等工作。

法定机构按照精简高效的原则，在薪酬总额范围内，自主决定机构设置、岗位设置、人员聘用、薪酬标准等，依照有关规定任命的人员除外。

四、赋予重点园区更大的自主发展权。省人民政府及其有关部门应当依照本决定将有关省级管理权限下放或者委托重点园区管理机构行使，具体事项由省人民政府根据重点园区的实际需要确定，依法应当报请省人大常委会决定的除外。

重点园区所在地市、县、自治县人民政府及其有关部门可以依照本决定将本级管理权限下放或委托重点园区管理机构行使。

五、重点园区内社会管理事务原则上由所在地市、县、自治县人民政府承担，法律、法规另有规定的除外。

六、对下放或委托行使的管理权限事项，省和市、县、自治县人民政府各有关部门应当加强对重点园区的业务培训指导，强化事中事后监管，做到放管结合。承接的重点园区管理机构应当周密组织，落实责任，建立承接管理权限的有效机制，做到规范有序，确保严格依法行使职权。对实践证明不宜下放或委托行使的，及时收回相关管理权限。

七、本决定自公布之日起施行。

in the parks, and they are created as the governmental agencies with legal personality pursuant to law and are responsible for the integrated coordination, development and construction, operation management, industrial development, investment promotion, institutional innovation, and services to entities in the parks.

Pursuant to the principle of streamlining and high efficiency, the statutory agencies independently decide the institutional setup, arrangements of positions, employment, salary standards within the scope of the total payment package, those who are appointed pursuant to law are not subject to this article.

IV. The key parks shall be granted greater authority for independent development. The provincial people's government and its appropriate agencies shall, based on this Decision, devolve or delegate the appropriate provincial management authority to the administrative agencies for the key parks. Specific matters shall be determined by the provincial people's government according to the actual needs of the key industrial parks, except those subject to the decision of the Standing Committee of the Provincial People's Congress pursuant to law.

The people's governments of cities, counties, and autonomous counties and their appropriate agencies where the key industrial parks are located may devolve or delegate the management authority to the administrative agencies at the corresponding level pursuant to this Decision.

V. The people's governments at the local cities, counties, autonomous counties, in principle, are responsible for the public management in key industrial parks, except as otherwise provided by other laws and regulations.

VI. In respect of the devolved or delegated management authority, the appropriate agencies of the provincial and city, county, autonomous county people's governments shall improve the service training and guidance of the key parks, promote *ex post* oversight, and achieve the combination of delegated power and improved regulation. The administrative agencies of the key industrial parks shall develop meticulous organization, clarify the responsibility, and establish an effective mechanism to undertake the management authority to archive standardized and orderly implementation, and ensure the strict exercise of functions and powers pursuant to law. If it is proved inappropriate to devolve or delegate, the appropriate management authority shall be promptly withdrawn.

VII. This Decision shall come into force as of the issuance date.

海南省人民代表大会常务委员会关于将林业植物检疫证书核发等省级管理权限调整由海南自由贸易港重点园区管理机构实施的决定

Decision of the Standing Committee of the Hainan Provincial People's Congress on the Adjustment of Provincial Administrative Powers, Including Forest Plan Phytosanitary Certificate Issuance, to the Hainan Free Trade Port Main Zone Administrative Agencies

海南省人民代表大会常务委员会关于将林业植物检疫证书核发等省级管理权限调整由海南自由贸易港重点园区管理机构实施的决定

（2021 年 12 月 1 日海南省第六届人民代表大会常务委员会第三十一次会议通过）

为营造法治化、国际化、便利化的营商环境，促进海南自由贸易港重点园区开发建设，赋予重点园区更大的自主发展权，根据有关法律法规和《海南省人民代表大会常务委员会关于海南自由贸易港洋浦经济开发区等重点园区管理体制的决定》，结合海南自由贸易港建设实际，海南省人民代表大会常务委员会决定将 7 项省级管理权限调整由相关重点园区管理机构在重点园区范围内实施。对已调整由市、县、自治县人民政府实施的有关省级管理权限，市、县、自治县人民政府在重点园区范围内不再实施。

原实施机关应当加强对重点园区管理机构的业务培训指导，强化事中事后监管，切实做到放管结合；承接的重点园区管理机构应当周密组织，落实责任，建立承接管理权限的有效机制，做到规范有序，确保严格依法行使职权。原实施机关应当适时对调整实施事项进行评估，对实践证明可行的，继续加强事中事后监管；经评估施行效果不好的，及时按照法定程序收回相关管理权限。

本决定自公布之日起施行。

Decision of the Standing Committee of the Hainan Provincial People's Congress on the Adjustment of Provincial Administrative Powers, Including Forest Plan Phytosanitary Certificate Issuance, to the Hainan Free Trade Port Main Zone Administrative Agencies

(Adopted at the 31st Session of the Standing Committee of the 6th Hainan Provincial People's Congress on December 1, 2021)

The Standing Committee of the Hainan Provincial People's Congress decided to transfer 7 provincial-level powers and authorities to the administrative agencies of Main Zones in the Hainan Free Trade Port to institute a law-based international and convenient business environment, improve the development and establishment of Main Zones in the Hainan Free Trade Port, and grant these zones greater authority to allow them to develop in accordance with the applicable laws and regulations and the Decision of the Standing Committee of the Hainan Provincial People's Congress on the Administrative System of the Hainan Free Trade Port Yangpu Economy Development Area and actual circumstances in the Hainan Free Trade Port. The people's governments of cities, counties, and autonomous counties shall no longer exercise these powers and authorities previously exercised within the scope of the Main Zones.

The former agencies shall improve business training and guidance for the administrative agencies in Main Zones. They shall improve regulatory oversight conducted upon request to facilitate government administration and oversight pursuant to law; the administrative agencies exercising such powers and authorities shall carefully organize and perform their responsibilities, establish an effective system to assume these powers and authorities, and strict performance of functions and powers in a consistent and orderly manner in accordance with the law. The former administrative agencies shall promptly review the transfer of power and authority, and shall continue to improve regulatory oversight conducted upon request, provided that the transfer has been proven to be feasible. Otherwise, such powers and authorities shall be revoked in accordance with statutory procedures.

This Decision shall come into force as of the date of promulgation.

附　件

调整由海南自由贸易港重点园区管理机构实施的 7 项省级管理权限目录

序号	权限名称	原实施机关	承接园区	调整方式
1	林业植物检疫证书核发	省林业局	三亚崖州湾科技城	下放
2	拍卖企业设立、变更备案	省商务厅	洋浦经济开发区、海口江东新区、海口国家高新技术产业开发区、海口综合保税区、三亚崖州湾科技城、三亚中央商务区、文昌国际航天城、陵水黎安国际教育创新试验区	下放
3	从事饲料、饲料添加剂生产的企业审批	省农业农村厅	三亚崖州湾科技城	下放
4	非经营性互联网文化单位备案	省旅游和文化广电体育厅	海口江东新区、海口国家高新技术产业开发区、三亚崖州湾科技城、三亚中央商务区、文昌国际航天城、陵水黎安国际教育创新试验区、海南生态软件园	下放
5	台湾地区的投资者在内地投资设立演出场所经营单位从事演出场所经营活动审批	省旅游和文化广电体育厅	海口国家高新技术产业开发区、三亚中央商务区、陵水黎安国际教育创新试验区、海南生态软件园、文昌国际航天城	下放
6	台湾地区的投资者在内地投资设立演出经纪机构从事营业性演出活动审批	省旅游和文化广电体育厅	海口国家高新技术产业开发区、三亚中央商务区、陵水黎安国际教育创新试验区、海南生态软件园、文昌国际航天城	下放
7	香港特别行政区、澳门特别行政区服务提供者在内地设立内地方控股的文艺表演团体从事营业性演出活动审批	省旅游和文化广电体育厅	海口国家高新技术产业开发区、三亚中央商务区、陵水黎安国际教育创新试验区、海南生态软件园、文昌国际航天城	下放

Schedule

List of the 7 Provincial-Level Authorities Transferred to the Administrative Agencies of Hainan Free Trade Port Main Zones

No.	Name of Power and Authorities	Former Implementing Agencies	Zones Undertaking the Authority	Adjustment Method
1	Forest Plant Phytosanitary Certificate Issuance	Department of Forest of Hainan Province	Sanya Yazhou Bay Science and Technology City	Delegation
2	Business Incorporation and Change Filing for Auction Entities	Department of Commerce of Hainan Province	Yangpu Economic Development Zone, Haikou Jiangdong New Area, Haikou National High-Tech Industrial Development Zone, Haikou Integrated Free Trade Zone, Sanya Yazhou Bay Science and Technology City, Sanya CBD, Wenchang International Aerospace City, and Lingshui Li'an International Education Innovation Experimental Zone	Delegation
3	Business Entity Approval of Fodder and Fodder Additives Production	Department of Agriculture and Rural Affairs of Hainan Province	Sanya Yazhou Bay Science and Technology City	Delegation
4	Non-profit Internet Culture Institutions Recordings	Department of Tourism, Culture, Radio, Television, and Sports of Hainan Province	Haikou Jiangdong New Area, Haikou National High-Tech Industrial Development Zone, Sanya Yazhou Bay Science and Technology City, Sanya CBD, Wenchang International Aerospace City, Lingshui Li'an International Education Innovation Experimental Zone, and Hainan Resort Software Community	Delegation
5	Approval of Investors in the Taiwan Region to Invest in the Establishment of Performance Place Business Entities Engaged in Performance Place Business Activities	Department of Tourism, Culture, Radio, Television, and Sports of Hainan Province	Haikou National High-Tech Industrial Development Zone, Sanya CBD, Lingshui Li'an International Education Innovation Experimental Zone, Hainan Resort Software Community, and Wenchang International Aerospace City	Delegation
6	Approval of Investors in the Taiwan Region to Invest in the Establishment of Performance Brokerage Agencies Engaged in Performance Business Activities	Department of Tourism, Culture, Radio, Television, and Sports of Hainan Province	Haikou National High-Tech Industrial Development Zone, Sanya CBD, Lingshui Li'an International Education Innovation Experimental Zone, Hainan Resort Software Community, and Wenchang International Aerospace City	Delegation
7	For-profit Performance Approval for Joint Ventures Created by Hong Kong SAR and Macao SAR Service Providers and Controlling Mainland of China Entities	Department of Tourism, Culture, Radio, Television, and Sports of Hainan Province	Haikou National High-Tech Industrial Development Zone, Sanya CBD, Lingshui Li'an International Education Innovation Experimental Zone, Hainan Resort Software Community, and Wenchang International Aerospace City	Delegation

海南省人民代表大会常务委员会关于将旅行社设立审批等省级管理权限调整由海南自由贸易港重点园区管理机构在重点园区范围内实施的决定

Decision of the Standing Committee of the Hainan Provincial People's Congress on the Adjustment of Authorized Provincial Administrative Powers to Be Enforced within the Main Industrial Parks, Including Approval Power for the Incorporation of Travel Agencies, to the Main Industrial Park Administrative Agencies of the Hainan Free Trade Port

海南省人民代表大会常务委员会关于将旅行社设立审批等省级管理权限调整由海南自由贸易港重点园区管理机构在重点园区范围内实施的决定

（2021 年 7 月 27 日海南省第六届人民代表大会常务委员会第二十九次会议通过）

为营造法治化、国际化、便利化的营商环境，促进海南自由贸易港重点园区开发建设，赋予重点园区更大的自主发展权，根据有关法律法规和《海南省人民代表大会常务委员会关于海南自由贸易港洋浦经济开发区等重点园区管理体制的决定》，结合海南自由贸易港建设实际，海南省人民代表大会常务委员会决定将 17 项省级管理权限调整由相关重点园区管理机构在重点园区范围内实施。对已调整由市、县、自治县人民政府实施的有关省级管理权限，市、县、自治县人民政府在重点园区范围内不再实施。

原实施机关应当加强对重点园区管理机构的业务培训指导，强化事中事后监管，切实做到放管结合；承接的重点园区管理机构应当周密组织，落实责任，建立承接管理权限的有效机制，做到规范有序，确保严格依法行使职权。原实施机关应当适时对调整实施事项进行评估，对实践证明可行的，继续加强事中事后监管；经评估施行效果不好的，及时按照法定程序收回相关管理权限。

本决定自公布之日起施行。

Decision of the Standing Committee of the Hainan Provincial People's Congress on the Adjustment of Authorized Provincial Administrative Powers to Be Enforced within the Main Industrial Parks, Including Approval Power for the Incorporation of Travel Agencies, to the Main Industrial Park Administrative Agencies of the Hainan Free Trade Port

(Adopted at the 29th Session of the Standing Committee of the 6th Hainan Provincial People's Congress on July 27, 2021)

For the purposes of creating a rule of law, international and convenient business environment, encouraging the development and construction of major parks in the Hainan Free Trade Port, and granting main parks with greater independent development rights, the Standing Committee of the Hainan Provincial People's Congress has decided to authorize 17 provincial administrative powers to be enforced within the main parks to the main industrial park administrative agencies of the Hainan Free Trade Port pursuant to applicable laws and regulations and the Decision of the Standing Committee of the Hainan Provincial People's Congress on the Administrative System of Main Industrial Parks Including Yangpu Economic Development Zone in Hainan Free Trade Port, combined with actual developments in the Hainan Free Trade Port. The provincial administrative power implemented by the people's governments at the city, county, and autonomous county level before the adjustment, shall not be implemented in main industrial parks by such people's governments.

The former implementing agencies shall improve operational training and guidance for main industrial park administrative agencies, improve continuous oversight, and effectively delegate power and improve administration; the main industrial park administrative agencies that perform the administrative power shall be well organized, implement their responsibilities, create effective systems to exercise administrative power, be standardized and orderly, and ensure that they exercise their functions and powers in strict compliance with the law. The former implementing agencies shall promptly evaluate the amended and implemented matters, and continue to improve continuous oversight if they determined feasible in practice; the administrative agencies shall regain the administrative powers pursuant to statutory procedures if the review shows the implementation to be unsatisfactory.

The Decision shall come into force as of the date of issuance.

附　件

调整由海南自由贸易港重点园区管理机构在重点园区范围内实施的 17 项省级管理权限目录

序号	权限名称	原实施机关	承接园区	调整方式
1	旅行社设立审批	省旅游和文化广电体育厅	海口江东新区、海口国家高新技术产业开发区、博鳌乐城国际医疗旅游先行区、文昌国际航天城、陵水黎安国际教育创新试验区	下放
2	外商投资旅行社业务许可	省旅游和文化广电体育厅	海口江东新区、海口国家高新技术产业开发区、博鳌乐城国际医疗旅游先行区、文昌国际航天城、陵水黎安国际教育创新试验区	下放
3	旅行社业务经营许可证毁损换发、遗失补发	省旅游和文化广电体育厅	海口江东新区、海口国家高新技术产业开发区、博鳌乐城国际医疗旅游先行区、文昌国际航天城、陵水黎安国际教育创新试验区	下放
4	旅行社登记事项变更备案（含名称、经营场所、法定代表人、出资人变更）	省旅游和文化广电体育厅	海口江东新区、海口国家高新技术产业开发区、博鳌乐城国际医疗旅游先行区、文昌国际航天城、陵水黎安国际教育创新试验区	下放
5	旅行社终止经营备案	省旅游和文化广电体育厅	海口江东新区、海口国家高新技术产业开发区、博鳌乐城国际医疗旅游先行区、文昌国际航天城、陵水黎安国际教育创新试验区	下放

Schedule

List of 17 Authorized Provincial Administrative Powers to Be Enforced within the Main Industrial Parks by the Main Industrial Park Administrative Agencies of the Hainan Free Trade Port

No.	Authority	Former Implementing Agencies	Parks Undertaking the Authority	Adjustment Method
1	Approval of the Establishment of Travel Agencies	Department of Tourism, Culture, Radio, Television and Sports of Hainan Province	Haikou Jiangdong New Area, Haikou National High-Tech Industrial Development Zone, Boao Lecheng International Medical Tourism Pilot Zone, Wenchang International Aerospace City, Lingshui Li'an International Education Innovation Pilot Zone	Delegation
2	Foreign-invested Travel Agency Business Licensing	Department of Tourism, Culture, Radio, Television and Sports of Hainan Province	Haikou Jiangdong New Area, Haikou National High-Tech Industrial Development Zone, Boao Lecheng International Medical Tourism Pilot Zone, Wenchang International Aerospace City, Lingshui Li'an International Education Innovation Pilot Zone	Delegation
3	Renewal and Reissuance of Damaged or Lost Travel Agency Business Licesnes	Department of Tourism, Culture, Radio, Television and Sports of Hainan Province	Haikou Jiangdong New Area, Haikou National High-Tech Industrial Development Zone, Boao Lecheng International Medical Tourism Pilot Zone, Wenchang International Aerospace City, Lingshui Li'an International Education Innovation Pilot Zone	Delegation
4	Recording Travel Agency Registration Changes (Including Change of Name, Principal Place of Business Statutory Representative, or Contributor)	Department of Tourism, Culture, Radio, Television and Sports of Hainan Province	Haikou Jiangdong New Area, Haikou National High-Tech Industrial Development Zone, Boao Lecheng International Medical Tourism Pilot Zone, Wenchang International Aerospace City, Lingshui Li'an International Education Innovation Pilot Zone	Delegation
5	Recording Travel Agency Business Termination	Department of Tourism, Culture, Radio, Television and Sports of Hainan Province	Haikou Jiangdong New Area, Haikou National High-Tech Industrial Development Zone, Boao Lecheng International Medical Tourism Pilot Zone, Wenchang International Aerospace City, Lingshui Li'an International Education Innovation Pilot Zone	Delegation

续表

序号	权限名称	原实施机关	承接园区	调整方式
6	导游证核发（含换发、补发）	省旅游和文化广电体育厅	海口江东新区、海口国家高新技术产业开发区、博鳌乐城国际医疗旅游先行区、文昌国际航天城、陵水黎安国际教育创新试验区	下放
7	导游员调动所属单位变更备案	省旅游和文化广电体育厅	海口江东新区、海口国家高新技术产业开发区、博鳌乐城国际医疗旅游先行区、文昌国际航天城、陵水黎安国际教育创新试验区	下放
8	演出经纪机构从事营业性演出经营活动审批（含设立、延续、变更）	省旅游和文化广电体育厅	海口江东新区、海口国家高新技术产业开发区、博鳌乐城国际医疗旅游先行区、文昌国际航天城、陵水黎安国际教育创新试验区	下放
9	降低旅游服务质量保证金资格确认	省旅游和文化广电体育厅	海口江东新区、海口国家高新技术产业开发区、博鳌乐城国际医疗旅游先行区、文昌国际航天城、陵水黎安国际教育创新试验区	下放
10	医疗机构执业登记审批（不含互联网医院）	省卫生健康委员会	博鳌乐城国际医疗旅游先行区	下放
11	社会办医疗机构甲类大型医用设备配置许可	省卫生健康委员会	博鳌乐城国际医疗旅游先行区	委托

Continuation

No.	Authority	Former Implementing Agencies	Parks Undertaking the Authority	Adjustment Method
6	Issuance of Tour Guide Certificates (Including Renewal and Reissuance)	Department of Tourism, Culture, Radio, Television and Sports of Hainan Province	Haikou Jiangdong New Area, Haikou National High-Tech Industrial Development Zone, Boao Lecheng International Medical Tourism Pilot Zone, Wenchang International Aerospace City, Lingshui Li'an International Education Innovation Pilot Zone	Delegation
7	Recording Changes in Tour Guide Affiliation	Department of Tourism, Culture, Radio, Television and Sports of Hainan Province	Haikou Jiangdong New Area, Haikou National High-Tech Industrial Development Zone, Boao Lecheng International Medical Tourism Pilot Zone, Wenchang International Aerospace City, Lingshui Li'an International Education Innovation Pilot Zone	Delegation
8	Approval of Performance Brokerage Agency Business Activities (Including Establishment, Continuation, and Change)	Department of Tourism, Culture, Radio, Television and Sports of Hainan Province	National Hi-Tech Industrial Development Zone, Sanya Central Business District, Hainan Resort Software Community, Wenchang International Aerospace City, Lingshui Li'an International Education Innovation Pilot Zone	Delegation
9	Verification of Eligibility to Lower Tourism Service Quality Margin	Department of Tourism, Culture, Radio, Television and Sports of Hainan Province	Haikou Jiangdong New Area, Haikou National High-Tech Industrial Development Zone, Boao Lecheng International Medical Tourism Pilot Zone, Wenchang International Aerospace City, Lingshui Li'an International Education Innovation Pilot Zone	Delegation
10	Approval of Medical Institution Practice Registration (not Including Internet Hospitals)	Health Commission of Hainan Province	Boao Lecheng International Medical Tourism Pilot Zone	Delegation
11	Approval for Private Medical Institutes to Purchase Class-A Large Medical Equipment	Health Commission of Hainan Province	Boao Lecheng International Medical Tourism Pilot Zone	Authorization

续表

序号	权限名称	原实施机关	承接园区	调整方式
12	社会办医疗机构配置乙类大型医用设备备案	省卫生健康委员会	博鳌乐城国际医疗旅游先行区、海南生态软件园	下放
13	外国人野外考察国家重点保护野生植物审批	省农业农村厅	三亚崖州湾科技城	委托
14	民办普通高中、民办中等职业学校以捐赠者姓名或者名称作为校名的审批	省教育厅	洋浦经济开发区、海口江东新区	下放
15	设立普通技工学校、高级技工学校审批	省人力资源和社会保障厅	洋浦经济开发区、文昌国际航天城	下放
16	建设行业注册类人员（二级注册建筑师）执业资格的确认（初始、延续、变更注册）	省住房和城乡建设厅	洋浦经济开发区、海口江东新区、海口国家高新技术产业开发区、海口综合保税区、三亚中央商务区、海南生态软件园、陵水黎安国际教育创新试验区	委托
17	超限高层建筑工程抗震设防核准	省住房和城乡建设厅	洋浦经济开发区、海口江东新区、海口国家高新技术产业开发区、海口综合保税区、三亚崖州湾科技城、三亚中央商务区、文昌国际航天城、海南生态软件园、陵水黎安国际教育创新试验区	委托

Continuation

No.	Authority	Former Implementing Agencies	Parks Undertaking the Authority	Adjustment Method
12	Recording Private Medical Institute Purchases of Class-B Large Medical Equipment	Health Commission of Hainan Province	Boao Lecheng International Medical Tourism Pilot Zone, Hainan Resort Software Community	Delegation
13	Approval of Field Surveys of Nationally Protected Wild Plants under Special State Protection Conducted by Foreigners	Department of Agriculture and Rural Affairs of Hainan Province	Sanya Yazhou Bay Science and Technology Park	Authorization
14	Approval of the Contributor Names Being Used as School Names for Private Regular Senior Secondary Schools and Private Secondary Vocational Schools	Department of Education of Hainan Province	Yangpu Economic Development Zone, Haikou Jiangdong New Area	Delegation
15	Approval of the Establishment of Regular and Senior Technical Schools	Department of Resources and Social Security of Hainan Province	Yangpu Economic Development Zone, Wenchang International Aerospace City	Delegation
16	Qualification Verification of Registered Construction Industry (Initial, Continuing and Registration Changes) Employees (Grade-2 Certified Architects)	Department of Housing and Urban-Rural Development of Hainan Province	Yangpu Economic Development Zone, Haikou Jiangdong New Area, Haikou National Hi-Tech Industrial Development Zone, Haikou Comprehensive Bonded Zone, Sanya Central Business District, Hainan Resort Software Community, Lingshui Li'an International Education Innovation Pilot Zone	Authorization
17	Approval of Seismic Precautions for High-rise Building Project	Department of Housing and Urban-Rural Development of Hainan Province	Yangpu Economic Development Zone, Haikou Jiangdong New Area, Haikou National Hi-Tech Industrial Development Zone, Haikou Comprehensive Bonded Zone, Sanya Central Business District, Hainan Resort Software Community, Lingshui Li'an International Education Innovation Pilot Zone	Authorization

海南省大数据开发应用条例

Regulations of Hainan Province on Big Data Development and Application

海南省大数据开发应用条例

（2019 年 9 月 27 日海南省第六届人民代表大会常务委员会第十四次会议通过）

目　录

第一章　总　则

第一条　为了推动大数据的开发应用，发挥大数据提升经济发展、社会治理和改善民生的作用，促进大数据产业的发展，培育壮大数字经济，服务中国（海南）自由贸易试验区和中国特色自由贸易港建设，根据有关法律法规，结合本省实际，制定本条例。

第二条　本省行政区域内大数据开发应用及相关活动适用本条例。

本条例所称大数据，是指以容量大、类型多、存取速度快、应用价值高为主要特征的数据集合，以及对数据集合开发利用形成的新技术和新业态。

Regulations of Hainan Province on Big Data Development and Application

(Adopted at the 14th Session of the Standing Committee of the 6th Hainan Provincial People's Congress on September 27, 2019)

Contents

Chapter I General Provisions

Article 1 In order to promote the development and application of big data, fully enable big data to promote economic development, social governance, and people's well-being, facilitate the development of the big data industry, foster and strengthen the digital economy, and serve the China (Hainan) Pilot Free Trade Zone (hereinafter referred to as "HPFTZ") and the construction of a free trade port with Chinese characteristics, the Regulations of Hainan Province on Big Data Development and Application (hereinafter referred to as "these Regulations") are enacted under applicable laws and regulations and in light of the actual circumstances of this Province.

Article 2 These Regulations shall apply to the development and application of big data and related activities within the administrative area of this Province.

For the purpose of these Regulations, "big data" refers to the data collection characterized by large volume, multiple types, fast access, and high-value application, as well as the new technologies and new businesses generated by the development and utilization of the data collection.

第三条 大数据开发应用应当坚持全省统筹、依法管理、市场主导、创新引领、共享开放、保障安全的原则。

第四条 省、市、县、自治县人民政府领导本行政区域内大数据开发应用工作，协调解决大数据开发应用重大问题。

省人民政府信息化主管部门负责规划、指导、监督全省大数据开发应用工作，市、县、自治县人民政府信息化主管部门负责本行政区域内的大数据管理工作。

县级以上人民政府其他部门应当按照各自职责做好大数据开发应用相关工作。

第五条 省人民政府设立省大数据管理机构，作为实行企业化管理但不以营利为目的、履行相应行政管理和公共服务职责的法定机构。

省大数据管理机构负责组织实施大数据开发应用总体规划，统筹政务信息化项目管理和政务信息资源共享开放，管理运营政务数据资产，推进政务和社会大数据开发应用，具体实施大数据开发应用监督工作。

第六条 省人民政府信息化主管部门应当会同省大数据管理机构和有关部门，按照适度超前、合理布局、绿色集约、资源共享的原则，编制本省大数据开发应用总体规划，报省人民政府批准后公布实施。

市、县、自治县人民政府和省人民政府有关部门应当依据本省大数据开发应用总体规划，编制本区域、本部门、本行业大数据开发应用专项规划，报省人民政府信息化主管部门和省大数据管理机构备案。

Article 3 The development and application of big data shall adhere to the principles of comprehensive planning, lawful management, market-oriented, innovation prioritized, open access, and security guaranteed.

Article 4 The people's governments of provinces, cities, counties, and autonomous counties shall be responsible for the development and application of big data within the administrative areas respectively, and coordinate and resolve major problems in respect of the development and application of big data.

The competent information agency of the Provincial People's Government shall take responsibility for planning, guiding, and overseeing the development and application of big data of this Province, and the competent information agency of the people's governments of cities, counties, and autonomous counties shall be responsible for the management of big data within their respective administrative areas.

Other competent agencies of the people's governments at or above the county level shall make efforts in the development and application of big data based on their respective responsibilities.

Article 5 The Provincial People's Government shall set up the provincial big data administrative office as the statutory institution that operates as a non-profit enterprise and performs corresponding administrative and public services duties.

The provincial big data administrative office shall take charge of organizing and implementing the comprehensive plan of big data development and application, coordinating the management and the open-access of administrative information resources, managing and operating government data assets, promoting the development and application of administrative data and big data, and overseeing the big data development and application.

Article 6 The competent information agency of the Provincial People's Government shall, in collaboration with the provincial big data administrative office and appropriate agency, prepare the comprehensive plan for the development and application of big data in this Province based on the principles of moderate advance, rational layout, green and intensive and resource sharing, and submit it to the Provincial People's Government for approval before promulgation and implementation.

The people's government of cities, counties, autonomous counties governments and appropriate agency of the provincial people's government shall, based on the comprehensive plan of big data development and application of this Province, prepare detailed plans for the development and application of big data in their respective regions, competent agencies and industries respectively, and submit them to the competent information agency of the Provincial People's Government and the provincial big data administrative office for recordation.

第七条 省人民政府标准化主管部门应当会同省人民政府信息化主管部门和省大数据管理机构制定数据采集、开发、交换、共享、开放、安全等标准，实现数据准确、完整、规范，促进大数据的开发应用。

省大数据管理机构应当制定政务信息资源全过程管理规范。

第八条 任何单位或者个人采集、开发和利用数据应当遵守法律法规规定，遵循合法、正当、必要的原则，不得损害国家利益、社会公共利益和他人合法权益。

第九条 县级以上人民政府及有关部门应当加强大数据开发应用、安全等方面知识的宣传普及、教育培训，增强全社会大数据安全意识，提高大数据开发应用和安全风险防范能力。

第二章 大数据开发与共享

第十条 省人民政府应当建立跨部门、跨区域、跨行业的大数据信息资源协同推进机制，统筹规划全省信息基础设施，推进信息资源的归集整合、共享开放和融合应用。

市、县、自治县人民政府应当推进本行政区域内信息基础设施建设，提升大数据开发应用支撑能力，提高信息基础设施网络化智能化水平。

第十一条 省大数据管理机构应当建设、管理全省统一的政务数据中心、信息共享交换平台、政务大数据公共服务平台和政务数据开放平台等政务信息资源共享开放基础设施以及全省基础性、公共性政务信息化项目。

Article 7 The competent standardization agency of the Provincial People's Government shall, in collaboration with the competent information agency of the Provincial People's Government and the provincial big data administrative office, draft standards for data collection, development, exchange, sharing, access, and security, to provide accurate, complete and standardized data and promote the development and application of big data.

The provincial big data administrative office shall draft the management rules of government information resources of the whole process.

Article 8 Any entity or individual that collects, develops, and utilizes data shall abide by the laws and regulations, follow the principles of legality, appropriateness, and necessity, and not infringe upon national interests, the public interest of society, and the legal rights of others.

Article 9 The people's governments and its appropriate agency at or above the county level shall strengthen the public awareness, education, and training of big data development, application, and security, promote the awareness of big data security among the whole society, and improve the capability of big data development, application and security risk prevention.

Chapter II Big Data Development and Sharing

Article 10 The Provincial People's Government shall establish the collaborative mechanism for promoting big data information resources across competent agencies, regions, and industries, create a comprehensive plan for the information infrastructure of this Province, and promote the collection, integration, sharing, access, and integration of information resources.

The people's governments of cities, counties, and autonomous counties shall promote the construction of information infrastructure within their respective administrative areas, enhance the capability of supporting big data development and application, and improve the capability of network and intelligence of information infrastructure.

Article 11 The provincial big data administrative office shall build and manage the sharing infrastructure for administrative information resources such as the integrated government data center, information sharing and exchange platform, administrative big data public services platform, and government open data platform, as well as the basic and public administrative information projects of this Province.

已建、新建的政务信息系统，应当与全省统一的政务信息资源共享开放基础设施互联互通和信息共享。

第十二条 鼓励和支持基础电信运营商建设国际海底光缆及省内登陆点等信息基础设施，构建安全便利的国际互联网数据专用通道，提高本省的国际通信互联互通水平。

第十三条 省大数据管理机构应当统筹推动政务数据采集汇聚、登记管理、共享开放，推动社会数据汇聚融合、互联互通、开发利用。

第十四条 政务信息资源实行目录管理。

政务部门应当按照国家和本省有关规定和标准，编制、注册登记、更新、维护政务信息资源目录，并负责采集政务数据。

省大数据管理机构和市、县、自治县人民政府信息化主管部门应当按照国家有关规定，统筹确认政务信息资源共享目录和开放目录。

本条例所称政务部门，是指政府部门及法律法规授权具有行政职能的事业单位和社会组织。

第十五条 政务信息资源共享分为无条件共享、有条件共享、不予共享三种类型，实行负面清单管理，负面清单以外的政务信息资源应当共享。

凡列入不予共享类的政务信息资源，应当有法律、行政法规或者国务院政策依据。

省大数据管理机构应当会同保密等有关部门开展政务信息资源负面清单审核工作。

The administrative information system, having been built and renewed, shall be connected and accessed with the provincial integrated sharing infrastructure for administrative information resources.

Article 12 The telecommunications operators shall be encouraged and supported to build international submarine optical cables and landing points and other information infrastructure within this Province, build a safe and convenient dedicated channel for international internet data, and improve the international connectivity in this Province.

Article 13 The provincial big data administrative office shall make a comprehensive plan to promote the collection, registration management, sharing, and access of administrative data, and promote the collection, interconnection, development, and utilization of social data.

Article 14 The catalog management shall be applied to administrative information resources.

The administrative agencies shall, in accordance with the relevant national and provincial rules and standards, compile, register, update and maintain the catalog of administrative information resources, and be responsible for collecting administrative data.

The provincial big data administrative office and the competent information agency of the people's government of the cities, counties, or autonomous counties shall, in accordance with the applicable national rules, create a comprehensive plan to confirm the catalog for sharing and opening to the public the administrative information resources.

For the purpose of these Regulations, "administrative agencies" refer to institutions and social organizations with administrative authority delegated by competent government agencies and the law.

Article 15 Administrative information resources are divided into unconditional sharing, conditional sharing, and non-sharing. The negative list shall be applied, and administrative information resources beyond the negative list shall be shared.

The administrative information resources not permitted for sharing shall be subject to the statutes, administrative regulations, and State Council policies.

The provincial big data administrative office shall, in collaboration with the privacy governance and other appropriate agencies, carry out the audit of the negative list of dministrative information resources.

第十六条 政务部门应当按照采集数据类型、登记信息以及标准规范，在规定期限内将政务信息资源目录中的共享数据向全省统一的信息共享交换平台进行汇聚共享。

通过共享可获得的政务信息资源，政务部门不得向公民、法人和其他组织重复采集。

第十七条 政务部门应当按照国家和本省有关规定提供和使用共享数据，并确保其共享开放的政务信息资源准确、完整、可用、及时更新。

第十八条 政务部门通过全省统一的政务信息资源共享开放基础设施获取的政务信息资源，与纸质文书具有同等效力。

第十九条 从事数据采集、存储、清洗、开发、应用、交易、服务等大数据生产经营活动的单位（以下统称大数据生产经营单位）应当依法规范数据的采集、管理和使用，可以参照政务信息资源目录管理标准建立数据目录管理制度。

第二十条 鼓励大数据生产经营单位通过共享获得、联机验证等方式采集数据。

因商业用途需采集个人信息的，大数据生产经营单位应当申明采集的目的、用途和具体信息等，并取得被采集人的同意。被采集人要求采集人删除个人信息的，采集人应当删除。

第二十一条 大数据生产经营单位不得以改善服务质量、提升用户体验、定向推送信息、研发新产品等为由，以默认授权、功能捆绑等形式强迫、误导被采集人同意其采集个人信息。

Article 16 The administrative agencies shall, in accordance with the types of collected data, registration information, and standards, within the prescribed time limit, provide access to the shared data in the catalog of administrative information resources for the integrated information sharing and exchange platform across this Province.

The administrative agencies shall not repeatedly collect the administrative information resources that can be accessed through the sharing channels from citizens, juristic persons, and other organizations.

Article 17 The administrative agencies shall, pursuant to national and provincial provisions, provide and use the shared data, and ensure that their shared administrative information resources are accurate, complete, available, and promptly updated.

Article 18 The administrative information resources accessed through the provincial integrated open sharing infrastructure for administrative information resources by the administrative agencies shall be equally as legally binding as printed documents.

Article 19 The organization engaged in big data production and business such as data collection, storage, cleaning, development, application, transaction, and service ("the Big Data Business Organization") shall lawfully standardize data collection, management, and application, and may establish the catalog management system with reference to the management standards for the catalog of administrative information resources.

Article 20 The Big Data Business Organization shall be encouraged to collect data through data sharing and online verification.

If personal information is to be collected for commercial purposes, the Big Data Business Organization shall declare the purpose, application, and specific information of such collection, and obtain the personal consent. If such person asks the collector to delete personal information, the collector shall delete it.

Article 21 The Big Data Business Organization shall not coerce or mislead the collected party to consent to the collection of the personal information by default authorization or function binding on the grounds of improving service quality, enhancing user experience, targeted dissemination, and developing new products.

除法律法规另有规定外，大数据生产经营单位不得采集与其提供服务无关的个人信息，不得以被采集人拒绝提供相关信息而限制或者拒绝其享受普遍服务。

采集个人信息，还应当遵守本条例和有关法律法规关于个人信息保护的规定。

第二十二条 鼓励大数据生产经营单位将相关数据向全省统一的信息共享交换平台汇聚，或者开发利用政务信息资源开展业务。

第二十三条 鼓励行业协会、学会、商会等组织，医疗、教育、养老等社会服务机构以及从事供水、供电、供气、公共交通、金融、通信等公共服务的企业将依法收集、存储的相关数据，按照本省有关规定向全省统一的信息共享交换平台提供，用于数据的共享和开放。

第三章 大数据应用与产业促进

第二十四条 政务信息资源开放分为无条件开放、有条件开放、不予开放三种类型。

政务部门应当广泛征集社会公众对政务信息资源开放的需求，及时制定和调整政务信息资源开放目录，按照国家和本省有关规定将政务信息资源目录中的开放数据向全省统一的政务数据开放平台汇聚开放。

第二十五条 公民、法人和其他组织可以通过全省统一的政务数据开放平台免费获取无条件开放的政务信息资源。

Unless otherwise provided by the laws and regulations, the Big Data Business Organization shall not collect personal information irrelevant to the services and shall not restrict or reject the universal services due to the collected person's refusal to disclose certain information.

The collection of personal information shall also comply with these Regulations and applicable laws and regulations on the protection of personal information.

Article 22 The Big Data Business Organization shall be encouraged to transfer relevant data to the provincial integrated information sharing and exchange platform, or to develop and utilize administrative information resources to carry on business.

Article 23 The trade associations, academic societies, chambers of commerce and other organizations, social service institutions such as medical care, education, and elderly care, and business entities engaged in public services such as water supply, power supply, gas supply, public transportation, finance, communication, are encouraged to provide lawfully collected and stored data to the integrated information sharing and exchange platform across this Province, pursuant to the applicable data sharing and opening rules of this Province.

Chapter III Big Data Application and Industry Promotion

Article 24 Administrative information resources are divided into unconditional opening, conditional opening, and non-opening.

The administrative agencies shall solicit the public's demand for the open access of administrative information resources, formulate and adjust the open catalog of such resources in a timely manner, and transfer the open data in the catalog of such resources to the provincial integrated administrative data open platform in accordance with the national and provincial applicable rules.

Article 25 Citizens, juristic persons, and other organizations may obtain unconditional open administrative information resources free of charge through the provincial integrated administrative data open platform.

第二十六条 公民、法人和其他组织可以申请获取有条件开放的政务信息资源。申请者应当向全省统一的政务数据开放平台提交数据使用申请，说明数据用途、应用场景、使用时限和安全保障措施等。

政务部门应当自受理申请之日起五个工作日内通过全省统一的政务数据开放平台向申请者开放所需数据；不同意开放的，应当说明理由并提供依据。

第二十七条 省大数据管理机构和政务部门应当推动原始性、可机器读取、可供社会化再利用的政务信息资源向社会开放，推动政务信息资源挖掘、增值利用和大数据产业发展。

省大数据管理机构和政务部门应当优先推动信用、交通、医疗、就业、社保、教育、环境、气象、企业登记监管等民生保障服务相关领域的政务信息资源向社会开放利用。

在依法利用和保障安全的条件下，省大数据管理机构和政务部门可以通过政府采购、服务外包、合作等方式，开展政务信息资源市场化开发应用。

第二十八条 县级以上人民政府及其部门应当加强大数据在政府决策、监督管理与服务等方面的应用，推动放管服改革，优化营商环境。

第二十九条 县级以上人民政府及其部门应当推动大数据在公共安全、劳动就业、社会保障、城乡建设与管理、人口资源与环境、卫生健康、养老服务、社会救助、科技教育、文化旅游等领域的应用，优化公共资源配置，提升社会治理能力和服务民生水平。

第三十条 支持运用大数据等信息技术，加强公共信用数据与互联网、电子商务、第三方信用信息等数据的汇聚整合，推动社会信用体系建设。

Article 26 Citizens, juristic persons, and other organizations may apply for access to the conditional open administrative information resources. The applicant shall submit in writing for data use to the provincial integrated administrative data open platform; and provide information on how data is used, use cases, time limit of use, and security measures.

The administrative agencies shall, within 5 business days of the date of receiving the application, provide access to the required data to the applicant through the provincial integrated administrative data open platform. If such an application is denied, the administrative agencies shall explain the reasons and give a basis for such denial.

Article 27 The provincial big data administrative office and administrative agencies shall promote the open-access of administrative information resources that are original, machine-readable, and available for reuse, and promote the collection of administrative information resources, value-added utilization, and the development of the big data industry.

The provincial big data administrative office and administrative agencies shall prioritize the open-access of administrative information resources in respect of the people's well-being services such as credit, transportation, medical care, employment, social security, education, environment, meteorology, business entity formation, and oversight.

Under lawful use and security guarantee, the provincial big data administrative office and administrative agencies may carry out market-oriented development and application of administrative information resources through government procurement, outsourcing, and cooperation.

Article 28 The people's governments and their competent agencies at or above the county level shall strengthen the application of big data in government decision-making, oversight, management, and service, delegate governmental functions, and optimize the business environment.

Article 29 The people's governments and their competent agencies at or above the county level shall promote the application of big data in public safety, labor, and employment, social security, urban and rural development and management, population resources and environment, hygiene and health, old-age care, social assistance, science and technology education, and culture and tourism, optimize the allocation of public resources and enhance the capability of social governance and services to people's well-being.

Article 30 The information technologies like big data are supported to strengthen the collection and integration of public credit data and data such as internet, e-commerce, and third-party credit information, and promote the construction of social credit system.

第三十一条 政务部门、大数据生产经营单位应当积极运用大数据等信息技术，为人员、物资、资金自由便捷流动提供技术服务和安全保障。

第三十二条 支持运用大数据提升投资贸易自由化便利化水平，建设具有国际先进水平的国际投资、贸易“单一窗口”，推动数据协同、简化和标准化，为企业提供全程数据服务。

第三十三条 推动大数据与旅游业、现代服务业、高新技术产业和种业、医疗、教育、体育、电信、互联网、文化、维修、金融、航运等重点领域深度融合，开发新产品新服务，推动产业融合发展。

第三十四条 鼓励公民、法人和其他组织利用国内外大数据资源创新大数据产品、技术和服务。

支持大数据关键技术、解决方案、重点产品、配套服务、商业模式创新和应用研究，培育大数据骨干企业，建立大中小企业协调发展的大数据产业体系，推进大数据产业集聚。

鼓励资源丰富、技术先进的大数据企业开放大数据平台的数据、计算能力、开发环境等基础资源，推动大众创新创业。

第三十五条 鼓励和引导社会资本投资大数据发展应用；鼓励金融机构创新金融产品，完善金融服务，支持大数据发展应用；鼓励社会资金采取风险投资、创业投资、股权投资等方式，参与大数据发展应用；鼓励、支持符合条件的大数据企业依法进入资本市场融资。

第三十六条 县级以上人民政府应当制定大数据人才发展规划，培养和引进高端领军人才、急需紧缺人才，为大数据人才开展教学科研和创业创新等活动创造条件。

Article 31 The administrative agencies and the Big Data Business Organization shall actively use big data and other information technologies to provide technical services and security for the free and convenient flow of personnel, materials, and funds.

Article 32 The big data is supported to use to improve the liberalization and facilitation for investment and trade, build a "single window" for international investment and trade, promote data collaboration, streamlining, and standardization, and provide businesses with full-range data services.

Article 33 The big data is promoted to be integrated with key areas such as tourism, modern service industry, high-tech industry and seed industry, medical care, education, sports, telecommunications, internet, culture, maintenance, finance, and shipping to develop new products and services and facilitate industrial integration and development.

Article 34 Citizens, juristic persons, and other organizations are encouraged to make use of big data resources at home and abroad to innovate big data products, technologies, and services.

The innovation and application research regarding big data key technologies, solutions, key products, support services, and business model is supported to cultivate the backbone enterprises of big data, establish the big data industry system with coordinated development of large, medium, and small-sized enterprises, and promote the aggregation of the big data industry.

The big data enterprises with rich resources and advanced technology are encouraged to open access to basic resources including data, computing power and development environment of big data platform, and to promote mass innovation and start-ups.

Article 35 The social capital is encouraged and guided to invest in the development and application of big data. The financial institutions are encouraged to innovate financial products, improve financial services and support the development and application of big data. The social funds are encouraged to participate in the development and application of big data using venture capital, entrepreneurial capital, and equity capital. The qualified big data enterprises are encouraged and supported to lawfully enter the capital market for financing.

Article 36 The people's governments at or above the county level shall draft development plans for big data talents, train and introduce high-end leading talents and talents in urgent need, and facilitate big data talents to carry out teaching, scientific research, entrepreneurial innovation, and other activities.

第三十七条 鼓励和支持高等院校、科研机构、职业学校、企业开展产学研合作，建设大数据教学培训、研发孵化、创新创业基地。

鼓励引进国际和国家级大数据科研机构在本省设立研发中心。

第三十八条 推动大数据与云计算、移动互联网、物联网、卫星导航、人工智能、区块链等信息技术的融合，培育大数据服务新技术、新业态，促进数字经济创新发展。

第三十九条 依法获取的各类数据经处理无法识别特定数据提供者且不能复原的，或经过特定数据提供者明确授权的，可以交易、交换或者以其他方式开发应用。

第四十条 数据交易应当遵循自愿、公平和诚实信用原则，遵守法律法规，尊重社会公德，不得损害国家利益、公共利益和他人合法权益。

第四十一条 省大数据管理机构应当培育数据交易市场，规范交易行为，鼓励和引导数据交易主体在依法设立的大数据交易平台进行数据交易，加强对大数据交易平台的监管。

第四十二条 大数据交易平台建设单位应当制定和完善数据交易规则、信息披露规则、数据交易备案登记等管理制度。

大数据交易平台建设单位应当建立安全可信、管理可控、全程可追溯的数据生产、共享、开放、交易和流转环境，保证数据交易安全可信。

第四十三条 数据交易应当依法订立合同，明确数据质量、交易价格、提交方式、数据用途等内容。

省大数据管理机构、大数据交易平台建设单位应当推广使用数据交易合同示范文本。

Article 37 Higher learning institutions, research institutes, vocational schools, and businesses are encouraged and supported to carry out industry/academic collaboration, and to build the base for big data teaching and training, research and development incubation, innovation, and entrepreneurship.

The international and national big data research institutions are encouraged to be introduced and to set up research and development centers in this Province.

Article 38 The big data is promoted to be integrated with information technologies such as cloud computing, mobile internet, Internet of Things, satellite navigation, artificial intelligence, and blockchain to foster new technologies and business of big data services and facilitate the innovation and development of the digital economy.

Article 39 Where any types of lawfully obtained data cannot be used to identify the specific data provider or be recovered after processing, or have been explicitly authorized by such provider, such types of data can be traded, exchanged or developed, and applied in other means.

Article 40 The data transactions shall follow the principles of voluntariness, fairness and honesty, abide by the laws and regulations, respect social morality, and shall not harm national interests, public interests, and the legal rights of others.

Article 41 The provincial big data administrative office shall nurture data trading markets, standardize trading behaviors, encourage and guide data trading organizations to do data business on lawfully established big data trading platforms, and strengthen oversight over big data trading platforms.

Article 42 The construction organization of the big data trading platform shall draft and improve management systems such as data trading rules, information disclosure rules, and record and registration of data transactions.

The construction organization of the big data trading platform should establish a safe, credible, controllable and traceable data production, sharing, opening, trading, and circulation environment to ensure the safety and credibility of data transactions.

Article 43 The data transaction shall be enforceable for any lawfully implemented contract that provides for the quality, transaction price, submission method, and data use.

The provincial big data administrative office and big data trading platform construction organization shall promote the use of model data contracts.

第四章　数据安全与保护

第四十四条　县级以上有关部门按照下列规定，履行大数据安全管理职责：

（一）网信部门负责统筹协调大数据安全和相关监督管理。

（二）公安机关负责大数据网络安全等级保护工作的监督管理，依法查处相关违法行为。

（三）省大数据管理机构和市、县、自治县信息化主管部门分别负责组织实施本行政区域内政务大数据安全体系建设和安全保障工作，指导督促社会大数据开发应用的安全保障工作。

（四）国家安全、保密、密码管理、通信管理等主管部门按照各自职责范围，负责大数据安全相关监督管理。

第四十五条　政务部门和大数据生产经营单位应当制定数据安全等级、数据安全风险测评等管理制度，建立大数据安全重大风险识别处置机制，加强对大数据安全技术、设备和服务提供商的风险评估和安全管理。

第四十六条　政务部门和大数据生产经营单位应当制定数据安全应急预案，采取有效的安全保护措施，防止数据丢失、毁损、泄露和篡改，确保数据安全。发生重大数据安全事故时，应当立即采取补救措施，告知可能受到影响的用户，并按照规定向有关主管部门报告。

第四十七条　政务部门和大数据生产经营单位存储数据，应当选择安全性能、防护级别与其安全等级相匹配的存储载体，并且依法进行管理和维护。

Chapter IV Data Security and Protection

Article 44 The appropriate agency at or above the county level shall take on the following responsibilities and functions:

(a) the cyberspace administration shall be responsible for coordinating big data security and related oversight and management;

(b) the public security agencies shall be responsible for the oversight and management of the security level of big data networks and lawfully investigate and punish violations;

(c) the provincial big data administrative office and the city, county, and autonomous county competent information agencies shall be responsible for organizing the government construction for the big data security system and security affairs within their respective administrative areas, and guiding and supervising the security guarantee for the social big data development and application; and

(d) the competent agencies of national security, confidentiality, password management, and communication management shall be responsible for the oversight and management of big data security according to their respective responsibilities.

Article 45 The administrative agencies and the Big Data Business Organization shall draft management systems such as data security level and data security risk assessment, establish the mechanism for identifying and tackling major big data risks, and strengthen risk assessment and security management for big data security technologies, equipment and service providers.

Article 46 The administrative agencies and the Big Data Business Organization shall draft plans for data emergencies and take action to effectively prevent data loss, damage, breach, and tampering, and ensure data security. When the major incident occurs, remedial measures shall be taken immediately, users who may be affected shall be informed, and report made to the appropriate competent agency pursuant to the rules.

Article 47 When the administrative agencies and the Big Data Business Organization store data, they shall adopt a storage medium whose security feature and protection level correspond to their security level and manage and maintain them lawfully.

政务部门和大数据生产经营单位销毁数据，应当明确销毁对象、流程和技术等要求，以不可逆方式销毁数据内容。

第四十八条 在电子政务、电子商务、公共服务等领域推广使用电子签名、密码技术，鼓励电子签名认证数字证书在互联网上应用。

第四十九条 任何单位和个人有责任保护其采集的公民、法人和其他组织数据的安全。

在商业经营活动中采集的数据，未经被采集人同意，不得向他人提供，但是经过处理后无法识别特定单位和个人且不能复原的除外。

第五十条 省大数据管理机构应当会同有关部门建立大数据生产经营单位信用档案，记录数据生产、交易、应用、管理、安全等方面的信息，并按照有关规定纳入社会信用体系。

第五章　法律责任

第五十一条 违反本条例规定的行为，《中华人民共和国网络安全法》等法律、行政法规已设定处罚的，从其规定。

违反本条例规定的行为，本条例未设定处罚，本省其他地方性法规已设定处罚的，依照其规定处罚。

第五十二条 信息化主管部门和有关部门、大数据管理机构及其工作人员在大数据开发应用工作中滥用职权、玩忽职守、徇私舞弊，妨碍大数据开发应用工作的，视情节轻重，由任免机关或者监察机关依法给予处分。构成犯罪的，依法追究刑事责任。

When the administrative agencies and the Big Data Business Organization destroy data, they shall clarify the requirements of destruction objects, processes, and technologies, and destroy the data in an irreversible way.

Article 48 In respect of e-administration, e-commerce, public services, and others, the electronic signature and password technology are promoted, and the digital certificates for the electronic signature authentication on the internet are encouraged.

Article 49 Any entity or individual is obliged to protect the data collected by citizens, juristic persons, and other organizations.

The data collected in commercial activities shall not be provided to others without the consent from the person being collected, except that specific entity and individual cannot be identified and recovered after processing.

Article 50 The provincial big data administrative office shall, jointly with the appropriate agencies, create a credit archive for big data production and Big Data Business Organization, keep records on data production, transaction, application, management, and security, and incorporate them into the social credit system in accordance with the applicable regulations.

Chapter V Legal liability

Article 51 With regard to the violation of these Regulations, the Cybersecurity Law of the People's Republic of China and other laws and administrative regulations shall apply *mutatis mutandis* if a penalty is provided by laws and administrative regulations.

The violation of these Regulations is not subject to the punishment of these Regulations, while other local regulations of this Province will apply *mutatis mutandis* if the punishment is provided by them.

Article 52 If the competent information agency and appropriate agencies, big data administrative office and their staff abuse the position, derelict duty, or play favoritism and commit irregularities, or are noncompliant in the development and application of big data, leading to the obstruction of the development and application of big data, as the case may be, the appointment and removal agency or the oversight agency shall punish such acts lawfully. If such act constitutes a crime, criminal liability shall be investigated for in accordance with the law.

第五十三条 违反本条例规定，政务部门及其工作人员有下列行为之一的，由大数据管理机构责令限期改正；逾期未改正的，视情节轻重，由任免机关或者监察机关依法给予处分：

（一）未按本条例规定汇聚数据的；

（二）未按本条例规定编制、注册登记、更新、维护政务信息资源目录的；

（三）无故拒绝、拖延提供政务信息资源的；

（四）其他违反本条例规定的行为。

第五十四条 有本条例规定的违法行为的，依照有关规定记入信用档案，予以公示，并依照有关规定实施信用联合惩戒。

第六章 附 则

第五十五条 全部或者部分使用财政性资金建设的信息化项目和制作或者获取的各类信息资源及其次生信息资源，分别按照政务部门信息化项目和政务信息资源进行管理。

第五十六条 涉及国家秘密的数据管理，按照国家有关规定执行。

第五十七条 本条例自 2019 年 11 月 1 日起施行。

Article 53 If the administrative agencies and their staff, in violation of these Regulations, are under any of the following circumstances, the big data administrative office shall demand remediation within a specified time limit. If such remediation is late, as the case may be, the appointment and removal agency or the oversight agency shall lawfully penalize such acts:

(a) fail to aggregate data according to these Regulations;

(b) fail to compile, register, update and maintain the catalog of administrative information resources in accordance with these Regulations;

(c) refuse or delay the provision of administrative information resources without justification; or

(d) other acts in violation of these Regulations.

Article 54 The violations of these Regulations shall be recorded in the credit register in accordance with the applicable rules and made open to the public, and the joint credit punishment shall be imposed in accordance with applicable rules.

Chapter VI Supplementary Provisions

Article 55 All or part of the information projects supported by financial funds, all kinds of information resources produced or acquired and their secondary information resources shall be managed according to the information projects and administrative information resources of the administrative agencies respectively.

Article 56 The data management involving state secrets shall be subject to the applicable national regulations.

Article 57 These Regulations shall come into force as of November 1, 2019.

海南省多元化解纠纷条例

Regulations of Hainan Province on Diversified Dispute Resolution

海南省多元化解纠纷条例

（2020年6月16日海南省第六届人民代表大会常务委员会第二十次会议通过）

目　录

第一章　总　则

第一条　为了规范和促进多元化解纠纷工作，提高社会治理能力，促进社会和谐稳定，优化营商环境，服务和保障海南自由贸易港建设，根据有关法律法规，结合本省实际，制定本条例。

第二条　本条例所称多元化解纠纷，是指通过和解、调解、行政裁决、行政复议、仲裁、诉讼等多种途径，构建有机衔接、协调联动的化解纠纷机制，便捷、高效地化解当事人之间的纠纷。

第三条　多元化解纠纷工作应当坚持党委领导、政府负责、民主协商、社会协同、公众参与、法治保障、科技支撑的社会治理体系，并遵循下列原则：

（一）尊重当事人意愿；

（二）和解、调解优先，多方衔接联动；

Regulations of Hainan Province on Diversified Dispute Resolution

(Adopted at the 20th Session of the Standing Committee of the 6th Hainan Provincial People's Congress on June 16, 2020)

Contents

Chapter I General Provisions

Article 1 In order to regulate and encourage diversified dispute resolution, improve social governance capacity, improve social harmony and stability, optimize the business environment, serve and support the development of Hainan Free Trade Port (hereinafter referred to as the "HFTZ"), these Regulations are enacted pursuant to laws and regulations and in combination with the circumstances of this Province.

Article 2 "Diversified dispute resolution" (hereinafter referred to as "DDR"), for the purpose of these Regulations, refers to an integrated and coordinate dispute resolution mechanism through various methods such as reconciliation, mediation, administrative decision, administrative review, arbitration, and litigation, so as to resolve disputes between parties conveniently and efficiently.

Article 3 The work on DDR shall abide by the Party committee's leadership, government responsibility, inclusive negotiation, social coordination, public participation, rule of law, and scientific-technological support, as well as the following principles:

(a) respecting the wishes of the parties;

(b) prioritizing reconciliation and mediation involving multiple parties;

（三）遵守法律法规，尊重公序良俗，坚持公平公正；

（四）便民利民，快捷高效；

（五）预防与化解相结合。

第四条 各级人民政府及有关部门、人民法院、人民检察院、人民团体、企业事业单位、基层群众性自治组织和其他社会组织，应当按照各自职责，建立健全社会稳定风险防范、纠纷排查调处机制；坚持属地管理和谁主管谁负责，对跨区域、跨部门、跨行业，涉及人数众多、社会影响较大的纠纷，应当加强联动配合，从源头上预防和化解纠纷。

鼓励和支持公道正派、群众认可的社会人士和其他社会力量依法参与化解纠纷。

第五条 国家机关、人民团体、企业事业单位、新闻媒体等应当按照各自职责开展法治宣传教育，弘扬社会主义核心价值观，普及多元化解纠纷法律知识，引导公众以理性合法方式表达利益诉求、解决利益纠纷、维护合法权益。

第二章 职责分工

第六条 县级以上人民政府应当发挥多元化解纠纷工作的主导作用，将多元化解纠纷工作纳入法治政府建设规划，健全协调机制，督促政府有关部门建立健全化解纠纷责任制度，落实化解纠纷工作职责，引导社会力量参与化解纠纷。

乡镇人民政府、街道办事处应当组织协调辖区内公安派出所、司法所、人民法庭、派驻乡镇检察室、退役军人服务站、居民委员会、村民委员会和人民调解组织，开展纠纷预防、排查和化解。

(c) abiding by the laws and regulations, respecting public order and good morals, and respecting fairness and justice;

(d) convenience and efficiency; and

(e) the combination of prevention and resolution.

Article 4 The people's governments and appropriate agencies at all levels, people's courts, people's procuratorates, people's entities, businesses, institutions, primary-level self-governance organizations, and other social organizations shall, pursuant to their respective authorities and duties, establish and improve systems for preventing social risks and investigating and mediating disputes, and abide by territorial management and clearly identified authority and responsibility. The interconnectivity and collaboration for disputes involving a large number of people and having a significant social impact across regions, agencies, and industries shall be improved to prevent and resolve disputes at the source.

The fair and decent people and other private sectors recognized by the masses are encouraged and supported to participate in dispute resolution pursuant to law.

Article 5 The government agencies, people's entities, enterprises and institutions, and news media shall, pursuant to their authorities and duties, conduct a public awareness campaign to encourage knowledge and education on the rule of law, socialist core values, legal knowledge on diversified dispute resolution, and guide the public to raise petitions and demands, solve disputes, and safeguard their legal rights in a rational and lawful manner.

Chapter II Authorities and Duties

Article 6 The people's governments at the county level or above shall play a leading role in the DDR, incorporate it into the law-based government development plan, improve the coordination system, urge the appropriate agencies to establish and improve the accountability system for dispute resolution, specify the authorities and duties for dispute resolution, and guide the private sector to participate in the dispute resolution.

The township people's governments and local subdistrict offices shall organize and coordinate police stations, justice offices, people's courts, township procuratorates, veteran service stations, residents' committees, villagers' committees, and people's mediation organizations within their jurisdictions to carry out dispute prevention, investigation, and resolution.

第七条 人民法院应当发挥在多元化解纠纷工作中的司法引领、推动和保障作用，健全诉讼和非诉讼相衔接的化解纠纷机制，加强与行政机关、仲裁机构、公证机构和调解组织的协调配合，推动在程序安排、效力确认、法律指导等方面的有机衔接。

第八条 人民检察院应当依法履行法律监督职责，健全检察建议、检察宣告等制度，完善参与化解纠纷工作机制，引导当事人选择适宜的途径解决纠纷。

第九条 县级以上人民政府司法行政部门负责政府有关部门和其他组织多元化解纠纷工作的组织协调和督导检查；加强人民调解组织网络化建设，推动设立行业性、专业性调解组织；指导人民调解、行政调解和行业性、专业性调解工作，促进人民调解与行政调解、司法调解等衔接联动；指导行政机关完善行政裁决等工作机制；依法开展行政复议、行政应诉工作；组织、推动律师事务所、基层法律服务所、法律援助机构等参与化解纠纷。

第十条 公安机关应当依法完善治安、交通事故调解和轻微刑事案件和解工作机制，依法协调当事人和解、调解。支持和参与乡镇、街道、社区、居民委员会、村民委员会开展和解、调解工作。

第十一条 人力资源和社会保障、卫生健康、自然资源和规划、农业农村、市场监督管理、民政、住房和城乡建设、生态环境、旅游和文化、教育、交通运输、退役军人事务等行政主管部门应当按照各自职责，依法开展行政调解、行政裁决工作，推动、指导和监督本领域行业性、专业性调解组织建设。

Article 7 The people's court shall play the role of judicial guidance, promotion, and support in the DDR, improve the dispute resolution mechanism with the interconnectivity between litigation and non-litigation, improve coordination and collaboration with administrative agencies, arbitration committee, notaries, and mediation organizations, and improve the integration of procedural arrangements, validity confirmation, and legal guidance.

Article 8 The people's procuratorates shall perform their duties of legal oversight lawfully, improve the system of procuratorial recommendations and announcements, improve the system of dispute resolution participation, and guide the parties to choose the proper approaches concerning dispute resolution.

Article 9 The justice agencies of the people's governments at or above the county level are responsible for organizing, coordinating, overseeing, and inspecting the work on DDR by appropriate agencies and other organizations, improving the network of people's mediation organizations and promoting the establishment of industrial and professional mediation organizations, guiding the people's mediation, administrative mediation and industrial and professional mediation, and promoting the interconnectivity between people's mediation and administrative and judicial mediation, guiding the administrative agencies to improve the administrative decision-making system, carrying out the administrative review and administrative litigation lawfully, and organizing and promoting the participation of law firms, community-level legal services, and legal aid institutions in dispute resolution.

Article 10 The public security agencies shall improve the working system of public security, traffic accident mediation, and reconciliation of minor criminal cases lawfully, coordinate the parties' reconciliation and mediation in accordance with the law, support and participate in the reconciliation and mediation by townships, local subdistricts, communities, residents' committees, and villagers' committees.

Article 11 The administrative agencies in charge of human resources and social security, health, natural resources and planning, agriculture and rural affairs, market regulation, civil affairs, housing and urban-rural development, ecological environment, tourism and culture, education, transportation, veteran affairs shall, pursuant to their authorities and duties, carry out administrative mediation and administrative decision lawfully, and promote, guide, and oversee the development of industrial and professional mediation organizations.

第十二条 信访工作机构应当通过法定途径分类处理信访事项，理顺信访与行政裁决、行政复议、仲裁和诉讼等制度的关系，畅通信访渠道，跟踪、督促和协调信访事项的办理。

第十三条 居民委员会、村民委员会应当建立健全人民调解组织，组织人民调解员、社区工作者、法律顾问、心理工作者等及时、就地排查和化解纠纷。

人民调解员可以依照有关规定依托人民调解组织设立个人调解工作室。

第十四条 工会、共青团、妇女联合会、归国华侨联合会、残疾人联合会、工商业联合会、消费者委员会、法学会和行业协会等可以设立行业性、专业性调解组织，参与多元化解纠纷工作。

第十五条 商会、行业协会、民办非企业单位、商事仲裁机构等可以依法成立商事调解组织，在法律允许的范围内开展商事调解活动。

依法设立的国际商事调解机构可以依照章程等规定调解国内外平等主体的自然人、法人和其他组织之间发生的商事纠纷。国际商事调解机构应当制定调解规则，明确调解员任职条件，并予以公布。

境外商事调解机构可以依照国家有关规定参与商事调解。

第十六条 律师事务所、基层法律服务所、公证机构和司法鉴定机构等公共法律服务组织可以提供纠纷调解服务或者参与纠纷调解工作。

第三章 纠纷化解机制

第十七条 各级人民政府及有关部门作出涉及公民、法人和其他组织

Article 12 The public complaints and proposals administration shall classify and manage complaints and proposals through legal channels, streamline the relationship among complaints and proposals, administrative decision, administrative review, arbitration, and litigation, unbar complaints and proposals channels, and track, oversee, and coordinate the resolution of complaints and proposals.

Article 13 The residents' committees and villagers' committees shall establish and improve people's mediation organizations, and organize people's mediators, community workers, legal counsel, and psychological practitioners to investigate and resolve disputes promptly and on-site.

The people's mediators may set up individual mediation offices under the people's mediation organizations pursuant to law.

Article 14 The trade unions, the Communist Youth League of China, All-China Women's Federation, All-China Federation of Returned Overseas Chinese, disabled persons federations, federations of industry and commerce, consumer associations, law societies, and industry associations may set up industrial and professional mediation organizations to participate in the DDR.

Article 15 The chambers of commerce, trade associations, private non-corporate entities, and commercial arbitration committee may set up commercial mediation organizations pursuant to law to carry out commercial mediation lawfully.

An international commercial mediation institution established lawfully may mediate commercial disputes among natural persons, juristic persons, and other entities with an equal identity either domestically or overseas pursuant to its articles of association. The international commercial mediation institution shall draft mediation rules, specify the qualifications of mediators and publicize them.

Overseas commercial mediation institutions may participate in commercial mediation pursuant to national law.

Article 16 Public legal service organizations such as law firms, community-level legal service offices, notaries, and forensic labs may provide dispute mediation services or participate in the DDR.

Chapter III Dispute Resolution Mechanism

Article 17 If the people's governments and appropriate agencies at all levels make a major

切身利益且涉及面广、可能对社会稳定产生影响的重大行政决策，根据法律法规和其他规定，需要进行风险评估的，应当事先开展社会稳定风险评估，依照法定程序，对重大行政决策作出可实施、暂缓实施、不实施的决定，从源头上预防和化解社会稳定风险事件和重大群体性纠纷。

第十八条 各级人民政府及有关部门应当健全纠纷排查分析预警调处工作制度。

对纠纷易发多发领域，应当加强纠纷排查和调处工作。发生重大自然灾害、事故灾难、公共卫生事件和社会安全事件等突发事件时，应当同步开展纠纷排查和调处，依法启动应急预案。

第十九条 当事人可以依法自主选择下列途径化解纠纷：

（一）和解；

（二）调解；

（三）行政裁决；

（四）行政复议；

（五）仲裁；

（六）诉讼；

（七）法律法规规定的其他途径。

第二十条 当事人可以通过线下或者线上平台办理化解纠纷申请、协商、调解、行政裁决、仲裁、诉讼等事务。

在线化解纠纷，化解纠纷工作人员可以通过电话、在线文字、语音、视频等方式与当事人沟通。

第二十一条 化解纠纷单位和组织对当事人化解纠纷申请，应当进行登记，并按照下列情形分别处理：

administrative decision involving the vital interests of citizens, juristic persons, and other entities or may impact social stability, and risk assessment is required pursuant to laws, regulations and other rules, they shall initiate social stability risk assessment in advance, and consider the major administrative decision that can be implemented, suspended, or terminated pursuant to legal procedures, so as to prevent and resolve social events and major group disputes at the source.

Article 18 The people's governments and appropriate agencies at all levels shall improve the system for dispute investigation, analysis, early warning, and mediation.

The investigation and mediation of disputes in dispute-prone areas shall be improved. Dispute investigation and mediation for major natural disasters, accidents, public health emergencies, and social security incidents shall be carried out at the same time, and emergency plans shall be implemented lawfully.

Article 19 The parties concerned can independently choose the following to lawfully resolve disputes:

(a) reconciliation;

(b) mediation;

(c) administrative adjudication;

(d) administrative review;

(e) arbitration;

(f) litigation; and

(g) other methods specified by laws and regulations.

Article 20 The parties may process dispute resolution application, negotiation, mediation, administrative decision, arbitration, or litigation via offline or online platforms.

Employees involved in online dispute resolution may communicate with the parties via telephone, online text, audio, and video.

Article 21 The dispute resolution entities and organizations shall register the parties' applications for dispute resolution and resolve them separately under the following circumstances:

（一）属于其职责范围的，应当及时受理处理；

（二）不属于其职责范围的，应当做好释明、疏导、移交工作，引导当事人向有权处理的单位、组织提出申请；

（三）涉及多个单位、组织职责范围的，由与纠纷最密切的单位或者组织会同其他有关单位或者组织共同办理。

第二十二条 化解纠纷单位和组织收到化解纠纷申请，律师等法律工作者接受法律咨询、委托代理，应当告知当事人各类化解纠纷途径及其特点要求，引导当事人依法理性选择纠纷化解途径。

第二十三条 引导当事人选择纠纷解决途径，按照下列次序进行：

（一）引导和解；

（二）当事人不愿和解或者和解不成的，引导调解；

（三）当事人不愿调解或者调解不成，或者纠纷不适宜调解的，引导当事人选择其他非诉讼或者诉讼途径。

依法应当由行政机关或者仲裁机构先行处理的，告知当事人申请行政机关或者仲裁机构先行处理。

第二十四条 当事人之间涉及婚姻家庭（确认身份关系的除外）、邻里关系、人身和财产权益等民事纠纷可以向人民调解组织提出调解申请。

涉及劳动争议的，可以向企业劳动争议调解委员会、人民调解组织或者在乡镇、街道设立的具有劳动争议调解职能的组织提出调解申请。

涉及投资、贸易、金融、证券期货、保险、房地产、工程承包、运输、技术转让、电子商务、知识产权等商事纠纷的，可以向商事调解组织提出调解申请，也可以向仲裁机构提出仲裁申请。

(a) promptly accept and resolve disputes that fall within their authorities and duties;

(b) explain, guide, transfer disputes that do not fall within their authorities and duties, and guide the parties to submit the dispute to the competent entities or organizations; or

(c) the entity or organization with the closest connection shall resolve disputes involving multiple entity or organization authorities and duties in collaboration with other entities or organizations.

Article 22 If the dispute resolution entity or organization receives the dispute resolution application, or lawyers accept to provide legal advice or representation, they shall inform the parties of all kinds of dispute resolution methods and their characteristics and requirements, and guide the parties to rationally choose lawful methods.

Article 23 Parties shall be guided to resolve their disputes pursuant to the following order:

(a) guided reconciliation;

(b) mediation if the parties are unwilling to reconcile or reconciliation is unsuccessful; and

(c) other non-litigation or litigation methods if the parties are unwilling to mediate or mediation fails, or the dispute is not appropriate for mediation.

The parties shall be informed to submit the dispute to an administrative agency or arbitration committee first if such is required pursuant to law.

Article 24 Civil disputes concerning marriage and family (excluding the confirmation of identity), neighborhood relations, personal and property rights between the parties may be submitted to the people's mediation organization for mediation.

Disputing parties in labor disputes may submit the dispute to the enterprise labor dispute mediation organization, the people's mediation organization, or the organization with labor dispute mediation function in towns and local subdistricts for mediation.

Disputing parties in investment, trade, finance, securities and futures, insurance, real estate, project contracting, transportation, technology transfer, e-commerce, and intellectual property disputes may submit the dispute to the commercial mediation organization for mediation or the arbitration institution for arbitration.

涉及房屋土地征收、社会保障、治安管理等方面的行政争议和交通损害赔偿、医疗卫生、消费者权益保护等与行政管理职能有关的民事纠纷，可以向有关行政主管部门提出行政调解申请，或者依照有关规定向行业性、专业性调解组织提出调解申请。

对违法犯罪行为造成的损害赔偿纠纷可以依法申请公安机关、人民法院进行调解。

第二十五条 人民调解组织依法调解民间纠纷。

基层人民法院、公安机关或者其他国家机关对适宜通过人民调解方式解决的纠纷，可以在受理前告知当事人向人民调解组织申请调解；也可以在受理后书面委托人民调解组织调解或者邀请人民调解组织协助调解，但应当征得人民调解组织的同意。

人民调解组织调处重大疑难纠纷，可以邀请有关专家参与调解，也可以申请人民政府司法行政部门安排人民调解专家提供咨询或者参与调解。

第二十六条 行业性、专业性调解组织依照相关规定调解行业纠纷，其调解活动可以参照人民调解程序开展。法律法规另有规定的除外。

第二十七条 行政机关或者法律法规授权的具有行政管理职能的组织对与履行行政管理职责有关的民事纠纷或者行政争议，可以根据当事人的申请，依法进行行政调解。

行政机关对自然资源、生态环境、公共安全、食品药品安全等领域的纠纷，以及涉及人数较多、影响较大、可能影响社会稳定的纠纷，应当依法主动进行调解。

Administrative disputes related to eminent domain, social security, public security administration, and civil disputes related to administrative functions, such as traffic damage indemnities, medical care, and consumer rights protection, may be submitted to the appropriate administrative agencies or industrial and professional mediation organizations for mediation pursuant to law.

Disputes over indemnity for damages caused by violations of law and crime can be submitted to the public security agency or the people's court for mediation lawfully.

Article 25 The people's mediation organizations shall mediate civil disputes lawfully.

The community-level people's courts, law enforcement agency, or other government agencies may inform the disputing parties to apply to the appropriate people's mediation organization before acceptance, or delegate the people's mediation organization to mediate or invite the people's mediation organization to assist in writing after acceptance, subject to the consent of the people's mediation organization.

The people's mediation organizations may invite appropriate experts to participate in mediation or apply to the justice agency of the people's government to arrange people's mediation experts to provide advice or participate in mediation for complicated disputes.

Article 26 The industrial and professional mediation organizations shall mediate industry disputes pursuant to law, which can be carried out with reference to the people's mediation procedures, except as otherwise provided by laws and regulations.

Article 27 The administrative agencies or entities with administrative functions authorized by laws and regulations may conduct administrative mediation based on the application of the parties to civil disputes or administrative disputes related to the performance of administrative authorities and duties.

The administrative agencies shall initiate dispute mediation related to natural resources, ecological environment, public safety, food and drug safety, as well as disputes involving a large number of people, or significantly impacting or possibly affecting social stability.

第二十八条 行政机关或者法律法规授权的具有行政管理职能的组织对与行政管理活动有关的民事纠纷，可以根据当事人的申请，依照法律法规授权进行裁决。行政裁决过程中可以先行调解，调解不成的，依法作出行政裁决，并告知当事人救济途径。

第二十九条 行政复议机关对依法受理的行政复议申请，符合法定条件的，可以进行调解；调解不成的，依法作出行政复议决定，并告知当事人救济途径。

第三十条 仲裁机构对民商事纠纷作出裁决前，可以引导当事人和解或者调解。

劳动人事争议仲裁机构和农村土地承包仲裁机构对受理的争议或者纠纷，应当先行调解。

当事人不能达成和解或者调解不成的，仲裁机构依法及时作出裁决。

第三十一条 对起诉至人民法院的纠纷，适宜调解的，人民法院依法进行诉前调解，但当事人拒绝调解的除外。一方当事人明确提出终止诉前调解，或者诉前调解期限已满，当事人无法达成调解协议的，应当依法登记立案。

登记立案后，适宜调解的，人民法院可以依法进行调解或者委托调解，但当事人拒绝调解的除外。调解未达成协议或者调解书送达前一方反悔的，人民法院应当及时审理并作出裁判。

第三十二条 人民检察院办理符合和解法定条件的案件，可以建议当事人进行和解。

第三十三条 化解纠纷单位和组织调解过程中，可以邀请人大代表、政协委员、法律工作者、社区工作者、心理工作者等相关人员参与调解，也可以根据实际需要并经当事人同意，邀请与纠纷有一定关联的组织或者个人协助调解。

Article 28 The administrative agencies or organizations with administrative functions authorized by laws and regulations may issue decisions on civil disputes related to administrative activities based on the application of the parties and as authorized by laws and regulations. During the proceedings, mediation shall be carried out first. The administrative decision shall be processed lawfully if mediation fails and the disputing parties shall be informed of the remedial methods.

Article 29 The administrative review agencies shall carry out mediation after accepting applications for administrative review submitted lawfully. If such fails, the administrative review decision shall be issued lawfully, and the disputing parties shall be informed of the remedial methods.

Article 30 The arbitration institution may guide the parties to reconcile or mediate before issuing an award in civil and commercial disputes.

The labor dispute arbitration committee and rural land contract arbitration committee shall mediate the disagreement or dispute first after acceptance.

The arbitration institution shall promptly issue an award lawfully if the disputing parties fail to reconcile or mediate.

Article 31 If the dispute brought to the people's court is suitable for mediation, the people's court shall conduct pre-litigation mediation lawfully, unless the parties refuse to mediate. If one party explicitly recommends terminating the pre-litigation mediation, or if the period of pre-litigation mediation has expired and the parties cannot enter into a reconciliation agreement through mediation, the people's court shall lawfully accept the case.

If the mediation is suitable, the people's court may conduct or delegate mediation lawfully after accepting the case, except when the parties refuse mediation. If it fails to reach the agreement or the party repents before the reconciliation agreement reached through mediation is served, the people's court shall promptly try the case and issue a judgment.

Article 32 The people's procuratorate may recommend the parties settle cases that meet statutory conditions for reconciliation.

Article 33 In the proceeding of mediation, dispute resolution entities and organizations may invite NPC deputies, CPPCC members, legal professionals, community workers, and psychological practitioners to participate in mediation and may also invite organizations or individuals related to the disputes to assist based on the circumstances and with the consent of the disputing parties.

涉及盲、聋、哑等残疾当事人纠纷的和解、调解，其法定代理人、近亲属应当参加，并可以邀请残联组织代表参与。和解、调解过程中，化解纠纷单位和组织应当为残疾当事人提供手语、盲文等辅助服务。

和解、调解过程中，可以根据实际需要并经当事人同意，委托律师、有关专家或者其他中立第三方，对纠纷事实进行调查或者对纠纷处理进行评估，形成评估意见。调查结果或者评估意见供当事人和解、调解参考。

第三十四条 化解纠纷单位和组织依法调解纠纷。在不违背法律法规、国家政策和公序良俗的情况下，可以依据行业惯例、交易习惯、自治章程和村规民约进行调解。

第三十五条 建立国际商事纠纷多元化解机制，完善国际商事纠纷案件集中审判机制，利用国际商事仲裁、国际商事调解等多种非诉讼方式解决纠纷。

国际商事调解机构调解国际商事纠纷，应当依照相关法律法规，尊重国际惯例，遵守该机构的调解规则或者当事人协商确定的规则。

第三十六条 志愿者、志愿服务组织可以为化解纠纷提供志愿服务。国家机关、人民团体、企业事业单位、基层群众性自治组织和其他社会组织可以组织本单位具备专业知识、技能的工作人员为化解纠纷提供专业志愿服务。

化解纠纷单位和组织化解纠纷需要志愿服务的，可以向志愿服务组织发出邀请，并提供与志愿服务有关的信息。志愿服务组织应当对有关信息进行核实，并及时予以答复。

鼓励心理工作者参与化解纠纷志愿服务，提供免费的心理辅导、危机干预和心理救援服务。

Agents by operation of law and close relatives shall participate in dispute reconciliation and mediation involving blind, deaf, dumb, and other disabled parties, and representatives of the disabled persons federation may also be invited to participate. Entities and organizations shall provide assistance such as sign language and braille for the disabled during reconciliation and mediation proceedings.

In the proceeding of the reconciliation and mediation, lawyers, experts, or other neutral third parties may be delegated to investigate the facts of disputes or evaluate dispute proceedings in light of the circumstances and with the consent of the parties concerned to form evaluative opinions. The results or opinions can be used as references for reconciliation and mediation between the parties.

Article 34 The dispute resolution entities and organizations mediate disputes lawfully. The mediation may be processed pursuant to industry practices, trade usage, self-governing rules, and village rules without violating the law, national policies, or public order and good morals.

Article 35 The diversified dispute resolution mechanism for international business disputes is established, the centralized trial system for international business disputes is improved, and various non-litigation methods such as international commercial arbitration and international commercial mediation are used to resolve disputes.

With respect to mediating international business disputes, the international commercial mediation institution shall respect international usage pursuant to law, and abide by the mediation rules of the institution or the rules determined by the parties via negotiation.

Article 36 The volunteers and volunteer service organizations may provide volunteer service for dispute resolution. The government agencies, people's entities, enterprises, and institutions, and primary-level self-governance organizations may organize their own employees with professional knowledge and skills to provide professional volunteer services for dispute resolution.

The entities and volunteer service organizations may send invitations to volunteer service organizations and provide information related to volunteer services if required for dispute resolution. Volunteer service organizations shall verify the appropriate information and reply promptly.

Psychological practitioners are encouraged to participate in volunteer services and to provide psychological counseling, crisis intervention, and psychological rescue services free of charge.

第三十七条 当事人经人民调解组织调解达成调解协议的，可以制作调解协议书。当事人认为无需制作调解协议书的，可以采取口头协议方式，人民调解员应当记录协议内容，并由当事人签字。

当事人经行政机关、劳动争议调解组织、医疗纠纷调解组织、商事调解组织等调解达成调解协议的，行政机关或者调解组织应当制作调解协议书。

第三十八条 以给付为内容的和解协议、调解协议，当事人可以共同向公证机构申请办理具有强制执行效力的债权文书公证。

对前款规定的公证债权文书，债务人逾期不履行或者履行不适当的，债权人可以依法向人民法院申请执行。

第四章 保障与监督

第三十九条 各级人民政府应当为多元化解纠纷工作提供必要的经费保障，并纳入本级财政预算。

对人民调解委员会、公益性调解组织以及人民调解员给予适当经费补助和补贴。

第四十条 鼓励和支持在劳动争议、道路交通、医疗卫生、旅游、物业管理、消费者权益保护、土地承包、环境保护以及其他矛盾纠纷集中的领域，探索建立专业化的一站式纠纷解决服务平台，提供化解纠纷服务。

市、县、乡镇人民政府、街道办事处根据需要，可以建立综合性的一站式纠纷解决服务平台，整合政府有关部门、人民法院、人民检察院以及仲裁机构、公证机构、人民调解组织、行业性专业性调解组织等化解纠纷力量，为化解纠纷提供便利条件。

Article 37 If the parties reach a reconciliation through mediation by a people's mediation organization, they may enter into a reconciliation agreement. The parties may implement a verbal agreement if they consider a written reconciliation agreement to be unnecessary, and the people's mediator shall record the matters covered by the agreement signed by the parties.

If the parties reach a reconciliation agreement through mediation by an administrative agency, labor dispute mediation organization, medical dispute mediation organization, or commercial mediation organization, the administrative agency or mediation organization shall issue the settlement agreement.

Article 38 The parties may jointly request a notary office to notarize any enforceable creditors' rights documents for reconciliation agreement or settlement agreements reached through mediation involving specific performance.

If the debtor fails to perform the notarized creditor's rights documents specified in the above provision within a given time or fails to adequately perform such, the creditor may petition the people's court for enforcement lawfully.

Chapter IV Support and Oversight

Article 39 The people's governments at all levels shall provide the necessary funding for the DDR, which shall be included in the financial budget at the corresponding level.

Financial subsidies and allowances are properly given to the people's mediation organizations, public welfare mediation organizations, and people's mediators.

Article 40 The establishment of the professional all-in-one dispute resolution service platform is encouraged and supported to provide dispute resolution services in areas prone to disputes such as labor disputes, road traffic, medical and health care, tourism, property management, consumer rights protection, land contract, and environmental protection disputes.

The city, county, township people's governments, and local subdistrict authorities may establish a comprehensive all-in-one dispute resolution service platform based on demands and integrate the dispute resolution forces of appropriate agencies, people's courts, people's procuratorates, arbitration committee, notaries, people's mediation organizations, and professional industry mediation organizations to facilitate dispute resolution.

第四十一条 各级人民政府及有关部门、人民法院、人民检察院等应当加强信息化建设，推进大数据应用，完善信息共享平台，提高化解纠纷工作效率。

第四十二条 当事人在纠纷解决过程中符合法律援助条件的，法律援助机构应当依法提供法律援助；符合司法救助或者社会救助条件的，司法机关或者社会救助机构应当提供救助。

第四十三条 行政机关、人民团体、人民调解组织、劳动人事争议仲裁机构、农村土地承包仲裁机构化解纠纷，以及人民法院对人民调解协议进行司法确认，不得向当事人收取费用，法律法规另有规定的除外。

实行市场化运作的调解需要收取费用的，依照有关规定执行。

第四十四条 有关国家机关、人民团体、企业事业单位、基层群众性自治组织和其他社会组织应当建立健全调解组织名册和调解员名册管理制度，加强对调解组织和调解员的监督管理。

依法成立的地方性、行业性、专业性调解员协会，实行自律管理。

第四十五条 有关国家机关、人民团体、商会、行业协会和其他社会组织应当加强调解员队伍建设，组织调解员培训，提高其职业道德水平和业务能力，推动调解员专业化建设。

第四十六条 各级人民政府及有关部门、人民法院、人民检察院、人民团体、基层群众性自治组织和其他社会组织在开展多元化解纠纷工作中有下列情形之一的，依法依规追究直接负责的主管人员和其他直接责任人员的责任：

（一）未建立或者未落实化解纠纷工作责任制的；

（二）负有化解纠纷职责，无正当理由，拒不受理化解纠纷申请的；

Article 41 The people's governments and appropriate agencies at all levels, people's courts, and people's procuratorates shall improve informatization development, encourage the use of big data, improve the information sharing platform, and improve the efficiency of dispute resolution.

Article 42 Legal aid organizations shall provide legal aid pursuant to law should the disputing parties meet legal aid conditions during dispute resolution. The justice agencies or social assistance institutions shall provide assistance should the disputing parties meet the justice or social assistance conditions during dispute resolution.

Article 43 Charging the parties is prohibited when the administrative agencies, people's entities, people's mediation organizations, labor and employment dispute arbitration committee, and rural land contract arbitration committee resolve disputes, or people's courts confirm the reconciliation agreement reached through mediation unless otherwise provided by laws and regulations.

The mediation fee charged by commercial mediation organizations shall comply with the law.

Article 44 The appropriate government agencies, people's entities, enterprises and institutions, primary-level self-governance organizations, and other social organizations shall establish and improve the administration of the list of mediation organizations and mediators, and improve the oversight and administration of mediation organizations and mediators.

The local, industrial, and professional associations of mediators established lawfully shall be subject to self-regulatory administration.

Article 45 The appropriate government agencies, people's entities, chambers of commerce, trade associations, and other social organizations shall improve the development of mediators, organize mediator training, improve their professional ethics and skills, and encourage mediator professionalism.

Article 46 If the people's governments and appropriate agencies at all levels, people's courts, people's procuratorates, people's entities, primary-level self-governance organizations, and other social organizations are found to be under any of the following circumstances during DDR, the person directly in charge and other employees directly liable shall be penalized lawfully:

(a) the accountability system for dispute resolution has not been established or implemented;

(b) responsible for dispute resolution but refuse to accept the application for dispute resolution without valid cause;

（三）采取的化解纠纷措施违反法律法规及有关规定的；

（四）化解纠纷不及时，没有采取有效措施的；

（五）未履行本条例规定的其他义务的。

第四十七条 违反本条例第四十三条第一款规定，向当事人收取费用的，由有关部门责令退还，对直接负责的主管人员和其他直接责任人员依法处理。

第四十八条 违反本条例规定的行为，法律、行政法规已有处罚规定的，从其规定。

第五章 附 则

第四十九条 本条例自 2020 年 8 月 1 日起施行。

(c) the measure taken to dispute resolution violate the laws and regulations, and applicable rules;

(d) not resolve disputes promptly and not take effective measures; or

(e) fail to perform other obligations specified in these Regulations.

Article 47 Arbitration committees charging fees in violation of Paragraph 1 of Article 43 shall be required by the appropriate agencies to refund such fees, and the person directly in charge and other employees directly liable shall be penalized lawfully.

Article 48 If any violation of these Regulations is subject to penalties specified in other laws and administrative regulations, such laws and administrative regulations shall apply.

Chapter V Supplementary Provision

Article 49 These Regulations shall take effect as of August 1, 2020.

海南省反走私暂行条例

Provisional Regulations of Hainan Province on Anti-Smuggling

海南省反走私暂行条例

（2020年1月6日海南省第六届人民代表大会常务委员会第十七次会议通过）

第一章 总 则

第一条 为了预防和惩治走私，规范和推进反走私工作，维护市场秩序，保护市场公平竞争，根据《中华人民共和国海关法》等有关法律法规，结合本省实际，制定本条例。

第二条 本省反走私工作坚持打防结合、标本兼治、权责一致、统筹协调的原则，实行联合缉私、统一处理、综合治理的缉私体制和政府统一领导、部门各尽其责、企业自律配合、群众积极参与、军警民协调联动的综合治理机制，服务海南自由贸易试验区和海南自由贸易港建设。

第三条 县级以上人民政府领导本行政区域反走私综合治理工作，建立反走私综合治理工作责任制，将反走私工作纳入政府考核，完善反走私军警民协调联动综合治理机制，将所需经费列入同级财政预算，对反走私综合治理工作成绩突出的单位和个人给予表彰和奖励。

乡镇人民政府、街道办事处应当支持和配合有关部门开展反走私综合治理工作，并指导村民委员会、居民委员会做好反走私综合治理的相关工作。

村民委员会、居民委员会应当在当地人民政府指导下，支持和配合反走私综合治理工作。

Provisional Regulations of Hainan Province on Anti-Smuggling

(Adopted at the 17th Session of the Standing Committee of the 6th Hainan Provincial People's Congress on January 6, 2020)

Chapter I General Provisions

Article 1 In order to prevent and punish smuggling, regulate and promote the work on anti-smuggling, maintain market order and protect fair competition, the Provisional Regulations of Hainan Province on Anti-Smuggling (hereinafter referred to as the "Provisional Regulations") are enacted pursuant to the Customs Law of the People's Republic of China and other applicable laws and regulations, and based on the actual circumstances of this Province.

Article 2 The anti-smuggling enforcement in this Province adheres to the principle of the combining punishment and protection, addressing both the symptoms and root causes, parity of power and responsibility and coordinated plans, and enforces the joint anti-smuggling system, uniform enforcement, and integrated management, and the comprehensive governance mechanism with unified government leadership, agencies performing their respective competent agency power and duties, entities cooperating with self-regulation, active public participation, and military-police-civilian coordination, so as to serve the construction of Hainan Free Trade Zone (hereinafter referred to as the "HFTZ") and Hainan Free Trade Port.

Article 3 The people's governments at or above the county level shall lead the integrated anti-smuggling administration (hereinafter referred to as the "Administration") in their respective administrative areas, establish the accountability system for the Administration, incorporate the Administration into the government evaluation, improve the military-police-civilian coordination of the Administration, incorporate the required funds into the financial budget at the same level, and commend and reward the organizations and individuals who outstandingly contribute to the Administration.

Township people's governments and the local subdistrict competent agency shall support and collaborate with appropriate agency to carry out the Administration, and guide villagers' committees and residents' committees to make efforts to the Administration.

The villagers' committees and residents' committees shall, under the guidance of the local people's governments, support and cooperate with the Administration.

第四条 县级以上人民政府设立反走私综合治理领导机构。反走私综合治理领导机构负责做好反走私综合治理的组织、指导、协调、指挥、监督和检查等工作，具体履行下列职责：

（一）制定反走私综合治理工作规划、计划；

（二）组织、指导、协调有关部门、单位开展预防走私工作，监督、检查、考核反走私综合治理工作；

（三）组织、指挥、监督有关部门、单位开展反走私综合治理联合执法和专项执法，协调、督促查处跨地区、跨部门的重大、复杂走私案件；

（四）协调处理海关、海警查缉走私需要地方政府部门、单位配合的有关事项；

（五）开展反走私综合治理信息化建设，提高反走私综合治理工作智能化水平；

（六）组织宣传有关反走私综合治理的法律法规和方针政策；

（七）负责本级人民政府和上级反走私综合治理领导机构交办的其他事项。

第五条 海关、海警按照国家规定职责查处走私违法犯罪行为。

公安机关依法查处发生在海关监管区外的非涉税走私犯罪案件，并及时查缉其他发生在海关监管区外的走私行为；在海关等有关部门履行反走私职责遇到抗拒时，公安机关应当予以协助并依法处理。

省人民政府确定的机构负责通过港口、铁路、机场运输出岛货物的查验工作。

市场监督管理、药品监督管理、交通运输、渔业、商务、财政、应急管理、生态环境、烟草专卖、海事、税务、人民银行等有关部门和单位，应当按照各自职责做好反走私综合治理相关工作。

Article 4 The people's governments at or above the county level set up a lead agency for the Administration (hereinafter referred to as the "Lead Agency"). The Lead Agency is responsible for the organization, guidance, coordination, command, oversight, and inspection of the Administration, and specifically the following:

(a) draft the work planning and plan for the Administration;

(b) organize, guide, and coordinate the appropriate agencies and organization to prevent smuggling, and oversight, inspect, and evaluate the Administration;

(c) organize, direct, and oversee the appropriate agencies and organizations conducting joint and specific law enforcement for the Administration, and coordinate and oversee the investigation of major and complex smuggling cases across regions or agencies;

(d) coordinate and manage interdiction of smuggling cases made by customs and the coast guard;

(e) conduct the informationization of the Administration and promote the digitalization of the Administration;

(f) organize and publish management laws and regulations, and policies; and

(g) other matters designated by the people's government at the corresponding level and the Lead Agencies of the Administration at higher grades.

Article 5 The customs and coast guard investigate and manage smuggling illegal acts and crimes pursuant to their power and duties as provided by the state.

The public security agency investigates non-tax-related smuggling crime outside the customs supervision area pursuant to law, and promptly interdicts other smuggling outside the customs supervision area. If the customs and other appropriate agencies are refused during enforcement of duties, the public security agency shall assist and punish them pursuant to law.

The offices designated by the Provincial People's Government are responsible for the inspection of goods departure from the Island through ports, railways and airports.

The market regulation, medical products administration, transportation, fishery, commerce, finance, emergency management, ecological environment, tobacco, maritime affairs, taxation, the people's bank, and other appropriate agencies and organizations shall make efforts in the Administration pursuant to their respective duties.

第六条 严禁利用国家给予本省的关税优惠政策和便利条件进行走私违法犯罪活动。

第七条 省人民政府应当建立反走私省际交流合作和跨境交流合作机制，实现区域间反走私信息共享和执法协作。

第二章 预 防

第八条 省人民政府应当支持在本省的港口、码头、机场、邮件处理中心和海关监管业务集中的地点设立口岸监管机构，对相关人员、运输工具、货物、物品依法履行监管职责。

海关监管的货物、物品进出本省的，应当通过设立海关的地点或者经批准的地点进出。

第九条 省人民政府应当统筹社会管理信息化平台和物流监管平台等信息化平台建设，强化物联网、大数据、人工智能等高新技术对反走私工作的支撑。

第十条 县级以上反走私综合治理领导机构应当组织相关部门建立反走私综合治理预警监测机制和信息通报制度，及时收集、汇总、分析涉嫌走私案件信息和数据，促进资源共享、协作联动和监管互认。

第十一条 海事、渔业、交通运输等部门应当按照各自职责分工加强对船舶的管理，建立船舶信息搜集跟踪机制。

在海南水域活动的船舶，应当按照规定配备无线电通信设备、船舶定位识别等装置，并保持正常工作状态，不得擅自关闭、拆卸。船舶无线电通信设备、船舶定位识别等装置发生故障的，应当及时报告海事、渔业等主管部门并迅速修复。

Article 6 Use of preferential tariff policies and other concessions granted by the state to commit the smuggling-related illegal acts and crimes is strictly prohibited.

Article 7 The Provincial People's Government shall establish inter-provincial and cross-border anti-smuggling communication and cooperation mechanism to realize inter-regional information sharing and law enforcement cooperation.

Chapter II Prevention of Smuggling

Article 8 The Provincial People's Government shall support the establishment of port oversight agencies in ports, docks, airports, mail processing centers and places where customs supervision is carried out in this Province, and oversee personnel, means of transport, goods, and articles pursuant to law.

The goods and articles under customs supervision shall enter and exit the province through the place where the customs reside, or through the approved place.

Article 9 The Provincial People's Government shall coordinate the development of information platforms such as the social management information platform and logistics oversight platform, and improve high-tech support such as the Internet of Things, big data, and artificial intelligence for anti-smuggling.

Article 10 The Lead Agencies for the Administration at or above the county level shall organize appropriate agencies to establish the warning and monitoring system and the information notification system for the Administration, collect, aggregate, and analyze information and data of the suspected smuggling in a timely manner, and promote resource sharing, collaboration and mutual recognition of the results.

Article 11 The maritime, fishery, transportation, and other agencies shall improve the management of ships pursuant to their respective power and duties, and establish the ship information collection and tracking system.

Ships, in the waters under Hainan's jurisdiction, shall be equipped with radio communication equipment, ship positioning and identification devices pursuant to the rules, and keep them on, and not shut down or dismantle without authorization. In case of the failure of such equipment, ships shall promptly report to the competent agency of maritime affairs, fisheries, or other agencies and promptly repair such.

第十二条 市、县、自治县人民政府应当建立基层预防走私工作机制，在容易发生走私的区域设立反走私工作站（点），设置固定的反走私宣传栏、警示牌、监控设施以及其他必要的装备设备。

反走私工作站（点）负责向有关部门反映涉嫌走私的情况和问题，并配合和协助有关部门开展工作。

第十三条 县级以上反走私综合治理领导机构应当建立健全反走私应急处理机制，制定应急预案，并报本级人民政府批准。

第十四条 各级人民政府及其有关部门应当组织开展反走私宣传教育，通过新闻出版、广播电视、报刊、互联网等媒体，对反走私工作进行公益宣传和舆论引导，增强公众反走私意识。

第十五条 县级以上人民政府应当组织有关部门开展反走私领域企业和个人诚信体系建设，建立企业和个人信用管理制度。

第十六条 县级以上人民政府应当设立举报奖励资金，制定举报奖励和保密制度，建立健全举报处理机制。

反走私综合治理领导机构、海关、海警、公安机关和市场监督管理等部门应当公布举报电话、通信地址和电子信箱。

第十七条 行业协会应当建立健全行业自律机制，指导、监督本行业进出口企业的经营活动，引导企业依法建立和完善进出口经营管理工作制度，提高企业自律管理能力。

Article 12 The people's governments of cities, counties and autonomous counties shall create community-level anti-smuggling systems, set up anti-smuggling branches (offices), and set up anti-smuggling publicity bulletins, warning signs, monitoring facilities, and other necessary equipment.

The anti-smuggling branches (offices) are responsible for reporting the information of suspected smuggling to appropriate agencies and cooperating with and assisting such agencies.

Article 13 The Lead Agencies for the Administration at or above the county level shall establish and improve the system for the anti-smuggling emergency response, draft emergency plans, and submit to the people's government at the same level for approval.

Article 14 The people's governments and their appropriate agencies at all levels shall organize and carry out anti-smuggling education, and advertise in public and guide the public opinion concerning anti-smuggling management through press, radio and television, newspapers, and the internet, so as to enhance public awareness of anti-smuggling.

Article 15 The people's governments at or above the county level shall organize appropriate agencies to carry out the development of the anti-smuggling credit system for business entities and individuals, and establish the credit management system for business entities and individuals.

Article 16 The people's governments at or above the county level shall set up reward funds for reporting, enact reward and confidentiality systems for reporting, and establish and improve the reporting system.

The Lead Agency for the Administration, customs, coast guard, public security, and market regulation shall publish their phone number, mailing address, and e-mail for reporting.

Article 17 The trade associations shall establish and improve the industry self-regulatory system, guide and oversee the business activities of import and export business entities of the industry, guide business entities to establish and improve the import and export management system pursuant to the rules, and improve the self-regulatory capabilities of business entities.

第三章 查 缉

第十八条 禁止违反《中华人民共和国海关法》等有关法律、行政法规，逃避海关监管，偷逃应纳税款，逃避国家有关进出境的禁止性或者限制性管理的行为。

禁止违反国家和本省关于海南自由贸易港减免税进口货物、物品监管的有关规定，擅自将减免税进口货物、物品运输、携带、邮寄出岛销售牟利。

海南离岛免税物品按照国家有关规定监管。

海关、海警、公安机关和其他有关部门按照各自职责分工，加强对进口货物、物品的监督管理。

第十九条 禁止使用船舶、车辆、航空器等运输工具运输、收购、贩卖国家禁止或者未经许可的限制进出境的货物、物品，或者运输、收购、贩卖没有合法证明的减免税进口货物。

海关、海警、公安机关和海事、渔业等部门应当加强查缉使用无船名船号、无船舶证书、无船籍港的船舶进行走私的行为。

第二十条 省人民政府确定的机构在查验出岛货物时，发现涉嫌走私的行为，应当及时移送海关或者公安机关依法处理。具体查验办法由省人民政府制定。

第二十一条 禁止从事无合法来源证明进口货物经营行为。

经营进口货物的，应当索要或者复制进口货物的合法来源证明，建立凭证档案以及进货、销售记录制度。进口货物的合法来源证明和相关进货、销售记录保存期限不得少于货物保质期满后六个月，没有明确保质期的，保存期限不得少于二年。进口货物经营者应当建立进口货物追溯制度。

Chapter III Smuggling Interdiction

Article 18 It is prohibited, in violation the Customs Law of the People's Republic of China and other applicable laws and administrative regulations, to refuse customs supervision, evade taxes payable, and avoid the state's prohibitive or restrictive administration of entry and departure.

It is prohibited, in violation of applicable rules of the state and the Province on the oversight of duty-free imported goods and articles in the HFTZ, to transport, carry and mail the duty-free imported goods and articles departure from the Island for profit.

In respect of the offshore duty-free goods, applicable national rules shall apply.

The customs, coast guard, public security, and other appropriate agencies improve the oversight and administration of imported goods and articles pursuant to their respective duties.

Article 19 It is prohibited to use ships, vehicles, aircraft, and other means to transport, purchase, or sell goods and articles prohibited by the state or restricted from entering or leaving the state without permission, or to transport, purchase, or sell imported goods without lawful certificates for tax reduction or exemption.

The customs, coast guard, public security, maritime affairs, fisheries, and other agencies shall strengthen the interdiction of smuggling by using ships without name, number, certificate and port of registry.

Article 20 The agencies designated by the Provincial People's Government in the inspection of goods departure from the Island shall promptly transfer it to the customs or public security agency if they find any smuggling involved. The specific inspection rules are enacted by the Provincial People's Government.

Article 21 It is prohibited to engage in the business of import without a lawfully issued certificate of origin.

The lawfully issued certificate of origin for the imported goods shall be required or provided with a copy for engaging in the business of import, and the archive and records system for import shall also be established. The lawfully issued certificate of origin of imported goods and appropriate purchases and sales records shall be preserved for no less than 6 months after the expiration of the shelf-life. If the shelf-life is not specified, the preservation period shall not be less than 2 years. The operators of imported goods shall establish the traceability system for the imported goods.

市场监督管理、药品监督管理、生态环境、烟草专卖等部门应当按照各自职责分工，加强对进口货物经营行为的监督检查；对经营无合法来源证明进口货物、涉嫌走私的，应当及时移送海关或者公安机关依法处理，对不属于走私的，依照相关法律法规和本条例的规定予以查处。

第二十二条　禁止任何单位和个人为走私违法犯罪行为和无合法来源证明进口货物经营行为提供贷款、资金、帐号、发票、证明、海关单证，或者提供运输、保管、邮寄以及其他便利。

第二十三条　县级以上反走私综合治理领导机构应当协调和推动海关、海警、公安机关和其他有关部门加强沟通协作，建立完善案件协查制度，构建常态化的职能优势互补、执法信息共享的反走私联合机制。

海关、海警、公安机关和其他有关部门对查获的走私案件情况应当及时通报本级反走私综合治理领导机构。反走私综合治理领导机构应当将反走私综合治理的有关情况报告本级人民政府，并通报相关部门。

海关、海警、公安机关和其他有关部门应当建立健全反走私监督工作机制，确保执法活动规范、高效。

第二十四条　反走私综合治理领导机构、海关、海警、公安机关和其他有关部门应当利用社会管理信息化平台、物流监管平台等信息化平台，对走私活动开展态势感知、预警预测、综合研判，发现涉嫌走私线索和行为，及时组织核查处置。

第二十五条　县级以上反走私综合治理领导机构应当组织协调海关、海警、公安机关和其他有关部门，对走私高发区域、重点渠道、走私相对集中的运输工具、货物、物品集散地和经营场所，开展反走私联合执法或者专项执法。

The agencies responsible for regulatory activities including without limitation market regulation, medical products administration, ecological environment, and tobacco shall improve oversight and inspection of import pursuant to their respective powers and duties; the imported goods which have no lawfully issued certificate of origin and may constitute smuggling shall be promptly transferred to the customs or public security agencies, the imported goods not involved in smuggling shall be investigated and dealt with pursuant to applicable laws and regulations, and these Provisional Regulations.

Article 22 Any entity or individual is prohibited from providing loans, funds, account numbers, tax receipts, certificates, customs documents, or providing other conveniences including transportation, storage, mailing for smuggling-related illegal acts and crimes and business of imported goods without legally issued certificate of origin.

Article 23 The Lead Agency for the Administration at or above the county level shall coordinate and promote the customs, coast guard, public security, and other appropriate agencies to improve communication and collaboration, establish and improve the investigation system, and develop a regular joint anti-smuggling system that complements each other's advantages and law enforcement information sharing.

The customs, coast guard, public security, and other appropriate agencies shall promptly inform the Lead Agency for the Administration at the same level of the seizures. The Lead Agency for the Administration shall report the appropriate situation to the people's government at the corresponding level and inform the appropriate agencies.

The customs, coast guard, public security, and other appropriate agencies shall establish and improve the anti-smuggling oversight system to ensure the regulated and efficient law enforcement.

Article 24 The Lead Agency for the Administration, customs, coast guard, public security, and other appropriate agencies shall make use of information platforms such as social management information platform and logistics oversight platform to carry out situational awareness, prior warning and prediction, coordinated consideration and with regard to the smuggling, discover suspected indications and activities related to smuggling, and promptly organize verification and processing.

Article 25 The Lead Agency for the Administration at or above the county level shall organize and coordinate the customs, coast guard, public security, and other appropriate agencies to carry out joint or special law enforcement against smuggling in areas prone to smuggling, key channels, transportation tools, distribution centers of goods and articles and business places where smuggling are relatively concentrated.

联合执法和专项执法应当将减免税进口货物、物品走私出岛的行为作为查处重点，加强对逃避海关监管的单位和人员，以及为其提供运输、仓储等服务的单位和人员的查处。

有关部门应当对有从事走私和经营无合法来源证明进口货物违法行为等不良信用记录的企业和个人进行重点检查，并通过企业信用信息系统或者政务网站等其他信息平台，及时公开其违法行为的查处结果。

第二十六条 沿海市、县、自治县人民政府应当建立基层反走私巡查工作机制，对沿海岸线实行岸长制、网格化管理，加强对辖区内港口、码头和海湾、堤岸、滩涂等区域的日常巡查。

市、县、自治县人民政府应当在反走私重点地区组建巡查队伍，协助配合海关、海警、公安机关和其他有关部门，加强重点巡查。

第二十七条 有关部门履行反走私职责时，可以行使以下职权：

（一）询问当事人或者有关人员；

（二）查阅、复制或者登记保存与违法行为有关的合同、票据、账簿以及其他资料；

（三）检查有违法嫌疑的运输工具、货物、物品和经营场所。检查时，有关当事人应当到场；当事人未到场的，在有见证人的情况下，可以径行检查；

（四）查封、扣押涉嫌走私或者无合法来源证明的进口货物、物品、运输工具、设备以及有关合同、票据、账簿等资料；

（五）法律法规规定的其他职权。

单位和个人应当配合有关部门行使职权，并如实提供相关资料。

The joint and special law enforcement shall take the smuggling of imported goods and articles with tax reduction and exemption departure from the Island as the key target, and strengthen the investigation and punishment of organization and personnel who avoid customs supervision, and who provide transportation, warehousing and other services.

The appropriate agencies shall prioritize the inspection of business entities and individuals with negative credit records such as ever engaged in smuggling or business without a lawfully issued certificate of origin, and disclose the results in a timely manner via other information platforms such as the business credit information system or government websites.

Article 26 The people's governments of coastal cities, counties and autonomous counties shall establish the community-level anti-smuggling inspection system, enforce shore master system and grid management on coastline, and strengthen daily inspections on ports, docks, bays, embankments and tidal flats within their respective jurisdictions.

The cities, counties, autonomous county people's governments shall set up inspection teams in key areas of the anti-smuggling, assist with customs, coast guard, public security, and other appropriate agencies to strengthen key inspections.

Article 27 The appropriate agencies may exercise the following functions and powers when enforcing anti-smuggling duties:

(a) examine the party concerned or appropriate personnel;

(b) consult, copy, register, or preserve contracts, bills, account books, and other materials related to the illegal acts;

(c) check the suspected illegal means of transport, goods, articles, and business places. During the inspection, the party concerned shall be present; if not, they may conduct a spot inspection with the presence of a witness;

(d) seize and detain imported goods, articles, means of transport, equipment, appropriate contracts, bills, account books, and other materials under the suspicion of smuggling or without a lawfully issued certificate of origin; and

(e) others as provided by the laws and regulations.

The entity and individual shall cooperate with appropriate agencies to exercise their functions and powers and provide the true information.

第四章　处　理

第二十八条　有关部门查获的走私案件，依法应当给予行政处罚的，移送海关、海警依法处理；涉嫌犯罪的，应当移送海关、海警或者公安机关依据案件管辖分工和法定程序依法处理。海关查获的属于公安机关、市场监督管理部门等管辖的案件，移送有管辖权的公安机关、市场监督管理等部门依法处理。

有关部门对案件移送或者管辖有异议的，由同级反走私综合治理领导机构协调处理。

接受移送部门应当及时将案件移送情况和处理结果，报告同级反走私综合治理领导机构，处理结果同时反馈原移送部门。

第二十九条　对当事人逃逸或者所有人不明，导致违法事实无法查清、处理有争议或者需要有关部门配合的，由查获地市、县、自治县反走私综合治理领导机构协调处理；跨地域移送的，报省反走私综合治理领导机构协调处理。

第三十条　市场监督管理、药品监督管理、生态环境、烟草专卖等部门查获涉嫌无合法来源证明的进口货物以及涉案运输工具、设备，当事人无法查清的，应当在本级人民政府门户网站或者当地主要新闻媒体上发布协助调查公告，公告期限为二十日。公告期满无当事人接受调查的，查获部门应当对涉嫌无合法来源证明的进口货物以及涉案运输工具、设备予以没收。

Chapter IV Treatment

Article 28 In respect of the seizure by appropriate agencies, if the party concerned shall be given administrative punishment pursuant to law, such party shall be transferred to the customs or coast guard; if it constitutes a crime, the party concerned shall be transferred to the customs, coast guard, or public security agencies pursuant to the jurisdiction and legal procedures. In respect of the seizure by the customs under the jurisdiction of public security agencies or market regulation agency, the party concerned shall be transferred to the competent public security agency or market regulation agency.

If the appropriate agencies raise any objection to the transfer or jurisdiction, it shall be coordinated by the Lead Agency for the Administration at the same level.

The agency to which the transfer is made shall promptly report such transfer case and its result to the Lead Agency for the Administration at the same level and report to the agency from which the transfer is made.

Article 29 If the party escapes or the owner is unknown, resulting in failure to ascertain the truth and disputed treatment or the cooperation of appropriate agencies is required, it shall be coordinated by the Lead Agency for the Administration in the cities, counties and autonomous counties where the seizure is conducted; if the transfer is made across regions, the provincial Lead Agency for the Administration shall coordinate such transfer after approval.

Article 30 The agencies responsible for regulatory activities including without limitation market regulation, medical products administration, ecological environment, and tobacco, upon seizing the suspected imported goods without a lawfully issued certification of origin and transportation but with no discovered responsible party, shall issue a notice of request for assistance on the people's government website portal at the corresponding level or the local major news media, and the notice shall be on for 20 days. If no party is subject to investigation at the expiration, the seizure agency shall confiscate the imported goods, the transportation vehicles, and the equipment involved.

第三十一条 依法查封、扣押的涉嫌无合法来源证明的进口货物，属于危险化学品或者鲜活、易腐、易失效等不宜长期保存的，有关部门可以依法先行变卖、销毁。

第三十二条 县级以上反走私综合治理领导机构应当协调和推动海关、海警、公安机关和其他有关部门建立完善走私案件涉案货物、物品处理机制。

第五章 法律责任

第三十三条 违反本条例第十一条第二款，船舶未按规定配备无线电通信设备、船舶定位识别等装置，或者配备后擅自关闭、拆卸的，或者发生故障不及时报告、不修复的，由海事、渔业等主管部门或者海警、公安机关责令改正，处五千元以上三万元以下罚款。

第三十四条 违反本条例第十八条的，依照《中华人民共和国海关法》等法律、行政法规的规定处罚。

第三十五条 违反本条例第十九条第一款，使用船舶、车辆、航空器等运输工具运输、收购、贩卖国家禁止或者未经许可的限制进出境的货物、物品的，依照《中华人民共和国海关法》等法律、行政法规的规定处罚；运输、收购、贩卖没有合法证明的减免税进口货物的，由海关、海警、公安机关按照各自职责分工，没收非法运输、收购、贩卖的减免税进口货物、违法所得、专门用于掩护违法活动的货物、物品以及专门用于违法活动的运输工具、设备，并处货值金额等额以下罚款。

Article 31 If the imported goods, having been seized or detained pursuant to law and suspected of lacking a lawfully issued certificate of origin, are dangerous chemicals or not suitable for long-term preservation, such as being fresh, perishable, and ineffective, the appropriate agency may sell or destroy them pursuant to law.

Article 32 The Lead Agency for the Administration at or above the county level shall coordinate and promote the customs, coast guard, public security agencies, and other appropriate agencies to establish and improve the processing system for goods and articles involved smuggling.

Chapter V Legal Liability

Article 33 If, in violation of Paragraph 2 of Article 11 of these Regulation, the vessel is not equipped with radio communication equipment, ship positioning and identification devices pursuant to the rules or which is closed or dismantled without authorization, or fails to promptly report or repair the malfunction, the competent agencies of maritime affairs and fisheries, the coast guard, or public security agencies shall demand it to correct such, and impose a fine of not less than 5,000 Yuan and not more than 30,000 Yuan.

Article 34 Anyone in violation of Article 18 of these Regulations shall be punished pursuant to the Customs Law of the People's Republic of China, and other applicable laws and administrative regulations.

Article 35 Anyone who uses ships, vehicles, aircraft, and others to transport, purchase, or sell goods and articles prohibited by the state or restricted from entering or leaving the state without permission in violation of Paragraph 1 of Article 19 of these Regulations shall be punished pursuant to the Customs Law of the People's Republic of China, other applicable laws and administrative regulations; in case of transporting, purchasing, or selling imported goods with tax reduction or exemption without legal proof, the customs, coast guard, and public security agencies shall, pursuant to their respective functions and duties, confiscate the illegally transported, purchased, or sold imported goods with tax reduction or exemption, illegal income, goods and articles specifically used to conceal the illegal activity, and transportation and equipment specifically used for the violation, and impose a fine equal to or less than the value of the goods.

第三十六条 违反本条例第二十一条第一款，经营无合法来源证明进口货物，构成走私的，依照《中华人民共和国海关法》等法律、行政法规的规定处罚；不构成走私的，由市场监督管理、药品监督管理、生态环境、烟草专卖等部门按照各自职责分工，没收违法所得、违法经营的进口货物和专门用于违法活动的运输工具、设备，处三千元以上三万元以下罚款；情节严重的，处三万元以上三十万元以下罚款，货值金额超过三十万元的，处货值金额等额罚款，并责令停业整顿，直至依法吊销营业执照、相关许可证；经营无合法来源证明进口货物，同时违反食品安全、药品、烟草专卖、动物防疫、野生动植物及其制品管理以及固体废物污染环境防治等法律法规规定的，由市场监督管理、药品监督管理、生态环境、农业农村、烟草专卖等部门依照法律法规的规定处罚。

违反本条例第二十一条第二款，未按规定建立并遵守进口货物凭证档案以及进货、销售记录制度的，由市场监督管理、药品监督管理、生态环境、烟草专卖等部门按照各自职责分工，责令改正，给予警告；拒不改正的，处三千元以上三万元以下罚款，法律法规另有规定的，从其规定。

第三十七条 违反本条例第二十二条，与走私人通谋为走私人提供贷款、资金、帐号、发票、证明、海关单证，或者提供运输、保管、邮寄以及其他便利的，依照《中华人民共和国海关法》等法律、行政法规的规定处罚。

Article 36 The people's governments at or above the county level shall draft development plans for big data talents, train and introduce high-end leading talents and talents in urgent need, and facilitate big data talents to carry out teaching, scientific research, entrepreneurial innovation, and other activities; anyone who engages in importing goods without a lawfully issued certificate of origin which amounts to smuggling in violation of Paragraph 1 of Article 21 of these Regulations shall be punished pursuant to the Customs Law of the People's Republic of China and other applicable laws and administrative regulations; if not, the market regulation, medical products administration, ecological environment, tobacco, and other departments shall, pursuant to their respective functions and duties, confiscate the illegal income, illegally operated imported goods and transportation and equipment specially used for the violation, and impose a fine of not less than 3,000 Yuan and not more than 30,000 Yuan; if the circumstances are serious, a fine of not less than 30,000 Yuan and not more than 300,000 Yuan shall be imposed. If the value exceeds 300,000 Yuan, a fine equal to the value of the goods shall be imposed, and the party concerned shall be required to suspend for correction until its business license and appropriate licenses are voided pursuant to law; anyone, engaging in imported goods without a lawfully issued certificate and in violation of the law such as food safety, drugs, tobacco, animal epidemic prevention, management of wild animals and plants and their products, and prevention and control of environmental pollution by solid waste, shall be punished by the market regulation, medical products administration, ecological environment, agriculture and rural affairs, and tobacco agencies pursuant to law.

Anyone who fails to prepare and comply with import goods record and the purchase and sales record-keeping requirements in violation of Paragraph 2 of Article 21 of these Regulations, the market regulation, medical products administration, ecological environment, tobacco, and other agencies shall, pursuant to their respective functions and duties, require them to correct and issue a warning; if the correction is refused, a fine of not less than 3,000 Yuan and not more than 30,000 Yuan shall be imposed, unless otherwise provided by laws and regulations.

Article 37 Anyone who conspires with smugglers to provide loans, funds, account numbers, receipts, certificates, customs documents, or provide transportation, storage, mailing, and other conveniences in violation of Article 22 of these Regulations shall be punished pursuant to the Customs Law of the People's Republic of China and other applicable laws and administrative regulations.

违反本条例第二十二条，知道或者应当知道他人经营无合法来源证明进口货物，仍为其提供贷款、资金、帐号、发票、证明、海关单证，或者提供运输、保管、邮寄以及其他便利的，由市场监督管理、药品监督管理、生态环境、烟草专卖等部门按照各自职责分工，责令停止违法行为，没收违法所得和专门用于违法活动的运输工具、设备，处三千元以上三万元以下罚款；情节严重的，处三万元以上三十万元以下罚款，货值金额超过三十万元的，处货值金额等额罚款，并责令停业整顿，直至依法吊销营业执照、相关许可证。

第三十八条 违反本条例第二十七条第二款，单位或者个人拒绝配合有关部门检查，拒绝提供检查资料或者提供虚假资料的，有关部门可以责令其改正，给予警告；逾期不改正的，可以处三千元以上三万元以下罚款；情节严重的，处三万元以上二十万元以下罚款；构成违反治安管理行为的，由公安机关依法给予治安管理处罚。

第三十九条 有本条例规定的违法行为的，依照有关规定记入信用档案，予以公示；对严重失信企业和个人，由有关部门采取取消通关便利、取消减免税进口货物买卖资格等措施予以联合惩戒；联合惩戒严重失信企业时，对其相关责任人员同时采取相应的惩戒措施。

第四十条 各级人民政府、有关部门及其工作人员有下列情形之一的，由有权机关按照管理权限责令改正，对直接负责的主管人员和其他直接责任人员依法给予处分：

（一）未按照规定履行反走私综合治理职责的；

（二）对走私案件应当依法移送其他有关部门处理而不移送的；

（三）包庇、纵容走私或者本条例规定的禁止性行为的；

If anyone, in violation of Article 22 of these Regulations, knows or should have known that another person is engaged in the import of goods without a lawfully issued certificate of origin, still provides loans, funds, account numbers, invoices, certificates, customs documents, or provides transportation, storage, mailing and other conveniences, the agency responsible for activities including without limitation market regulation, medical products administration, ecological environment, and tobacco, shall intervene to stop such illegal acts pursuant to their respective functions and duties, confiscate the illegal income and the transportation and equipment specifically used for the violation, and impose a fine of more than 3,000 Yuan and less than 30,000 Yuan; if the circumstances are serious, a fine of not less than 30,000 Yuan and not more than 300,000 Yuan shall be imposed; if the value exceeds 300,000 Yuan, a fine equal to the value shall be imposed, and the party concerned shall be ordered to suspend for remediation until its business license and appropriate licenses are voided pursuant to law.

Article 38 If the entity or individual, in violation of Paragraph 2 of Article 27 of these Regulations, refuses to cooperate with the inspection of an appropriate agency, to provide inspection data or false information, the appropriate agency may require it to correct and issue the warning; if overdue, a fine of not less than 3,000 Yuan and not more than 30,000 Yuan shall be imposed; if the circumstances are serious, a fine of not less than 30,000 Yuan and not more than 200,000 Yuan shall be imposed; if in violation of public safety requirements, the party concerned shall be punished by the public security agency pursuant to law.

Article 39 Anyone, in violation of these Regulations, shall be filed in the credit records pursuant to the rules and published. In respect of the business entities' and individuals' serious dishonesty, the appropriate agencies shall take action including without limitation terminating the customs clearance conveniences and the qualifications for the purchase and sale of imported goods for tax reduction and exemption. Where jointly and several liability is imposed on business entities with serious dishonesty, the employees liable shall be subject to corresponding disciplinary measures.

Article 40 If the people's governments, appropriate agencies, and their staff members at all levels are under any of the following circumstances, the competent agencies shall require correction pursuant to their administrative functions and duties, and the person directly in charge and other employees directly liable shall be punished pursuant to law:

(a) failure to perform the duties of the Administration pursuant to the rules;

(b) failure to transfer the smuggling cases to other appropriate agencies pursuant to law, which shall be transferred;

(c) providing shelter or conniving with smuggling or prohibited matters as provided in these Regulations;

（四）泄露举报人、投诉人信息的；

（五）违法处理涉案财物的；

（六）其他滥用职权、玩忽职守、徇私舞弊的行为。

第四十一条 违反本条例的行为，根据国务院相对集中行政处罚权的规定已经确定集中由市、县、自治县综合执法部门处理的，从其规定。

第四十二条 违反本条例规定的行为，本条例未设定处罚而法律法规另有处罚规定的，从其规定。

违反本条例规定的行为，构成犯罪的，依法追究刑事责任。

第六章 附 则

第四十三条 本条例下列用语的含义：

（一）出岛，是指从海南岛到其他省、自治区、直辖市，或者从海南岛到本省其他行政区域。

（二）无合法来源证明进口货物经营行为，是指从事经营活动的单位或者个人，对其所运输、储存、销售的进口货物，在被有关部门检查之日起七个工作日内或者有关部门同意的延长期限内，不能提供进口货物合法来源证明的行为。有关部门同意延长的期限最长不得超过二十日。

进口货物合法来源证明，包括进口货物报关单、进口关税及进口环节海关代征税纳税凭证、进货发票、商业单证、运输单证、依法拍卖成交确认书或者其他可以证明合法来源的材料。

第四十四条 本条例自2020年4月1日起施行。

(d) leaking the information of the reporter and complainant;

(e) illegally processing the property involved; or

(f) others including abuse of position, dereliction of duty or playing favoritism and committing irregularities.

Article 41 If any violation of these Regulations is subject to the comprehensive law enforcement agency at the city, county or autonomous county level according to the rules of the State Council concerning the power to impose administrative penalty in a centralized manner, such rules shall prevail.

Article 42 Where there are rules provided by other laws and regulations concerning the acts that violate these Regulations, such rules shall control.

Where the violation of these Regulations amounts to a crime, criminal liability shall be imposed pursuant to law.

Chapter VI Supplementary Provisions

Article 43 The terms of these Regulations shall be subject to the following meaning:

(a) "Leaving the Island" refers to travelling from Hainan Island to other provinces, autonomous regions and municipalities directly under the Central Government, or from Hainan Island to other administrative areas of this Province.

(b) "The business of imported goods without a lawfully issued certification of origin" refers to that the entity or individual, engaged in business activities, fails to provide a lawfully issued certification of origin of the imported goods within 7 business days of the date of inspection by appropriate agencies or within the extended period granted by appropriate agencies. The extension granted by the appropriate agencies shall not exceed 20 days.

The lawfully issued certification of origin of the imported goods, including customs declaration form of imported goods, import duties, tax payment document issued by customs at import, purchase invoice, commercial document, transport document, confirmation of lawful auction or other materials that can evidence the origin pursuant to law.

Article 44 These Regulations shall come into force as of April 1, 2020.

海南经济特区律师条例

Regulations of Hainan Special Economic Zone on Lawyers

海南经济特区律师条例

（2019 年 9 月 27 日海南省第六届人民代表大会常务委员会第十四次会议通过）

第一章　总　则

第一条　为了保障律师依法执业，规范律师管理工作，维护法律服务秩序，优化营商环境，发挥律师在海南自由贸易试验区和中国特色自由贸易港建设中的作用，根据《中华人民共和国律师法》和有关法律法规，结合本经济特区实际，制定本条例。

第二条　在本经济特区从事律师执业以及与律师管理相关的活动，适用本条例。

第三条　省人民政府应当将律师工作纳入国民经济和社会发展规划，保障和促进律师工作健康发展。

第四条　县级以上人民政府司法行政部门应当依法对律师、律师事务所和律师协会进行指导、监督，并会同有关国家机关依法保障律师执业权利。

县级以上人民政府司法行政部门应当按照国家和本省有关规定对律师事务所的执业和管理活动实施年度检查考核，建立健全对律师事务所负责人谈话提醒制度和问责机制，督促律师事务所负责人加强对本所律师执业活动的日常管理监督。

Regulations of Hainan Special Economic Zone on Lawyers

(Adopted at the 14th Session of the Standing Committee of the 6th Hainan Provincial People's Congress on September 27, 2019)

Chapter I General Provisions

Article 1 With a view to ensuring lawyers practice as required by law, regulating the administration of lawyers, maintaining the order in the legal industry, optimizing the business environment, and playing the role of lawyer in the development of the Hainan Free Trade Pilot Zone and the free trade port with Chinese characteristics, the Regulations of Hainan Special Economic Zone on Lawyers (hereinafter referred to as "these Regulations") are enacted pursuant to the Law of the People's Republic of China on Lawyers and other applicable laws and administrative regulations, and based on the actual circumstances of this Special Economic Zone (hereinafter referred to as the "SEZ").

Article 2 These Regulations shall apply to the activities related to lawyers' practices and administration in this SEZ.

Article 3 The People's Government of Hainan Province (hereinafter referred to as the "Provincial People's Government") shall include lawyer administration into the national economic and social development plan, and safeguard and promote the sound development of the lawyer profession.

Article 4 The judicial administrations of people's government at or above the county level shall, in collaboration with national agencies, guide and oversee the lawyers, law firms, and lawyers' associations, and safeguard the lawyer's right to practice pursuant to law.

The judicial administrations of people's government at or above the county level shall annually assess the practices and management of law firms pursuant to applicable rules of the state and the Province, establish and improve the talk for warning and accountability systems for the responsible persons of law firms, require such responsible persons to improve the oversight over the lawyers' practices.

县级以上人民政府司法行政部门依法对本行政区域内的法律服务机构及人员实行统一管理。没有取得律师执业证书的人员，不得以律师名义从事法律服务业务；除法律另有规定外，不得从事诉讼代理或者辩护业务。

第五条　省人民政府司法行政部门应当根据海南自由贸易试验区和中国特色自由贸易港建设的法律服务需求，科学编制律师行业发展规划，实现律师行业的均衡发展和合理布局。

第六条　省人民政府司法行政部门应当加强律师行业诚信管理，建立律师和律师事务所信用信息记录和查询制度，公开律师、律师事务所基本信息，并将律师、律师事务所奖惩、失信等信息记入诚信档案。

第七条　律师应当维护宪法和法律尊严，维护当事人的合法权益，维护法律正确实施，维护社会公平和正义。在执业中，应当诚实守信，勤勉尽责，以事实为根据，以法律为准绳，恪守律师职业道德和执业纪律。

律师依法执业的权利受法律保护，任何组织和个人不得侵害律师依法执业的权利。

第八条　律师、律师事务所应当按照国家和本省有关规定履行法律援助义务，参与信访、调解、社区工作等其他公益性法律服务。

律师、律师事务所担任国家机关和人民团体法律顾问、参与信访接待和处理、参与调解等事项应当按照有关规定列入政府购买服务目录。

第九条　律师协会是社会团体法人，是律师的自律性组织，依法登记成立，为律师提供服务。

律师协会应当建立和完善内部治理结构，建立健全议事、决策、执行和监督机制。

The judicial administrations of the people's government at the county or above shall implement a unified administration system for the organizations and individuals providing legal services. Individuals who do not have a legal practice certificate shall not engage in any legal services on behalf of a lawyer; unless otherwise provided by laws, such individuals shall not be employed by any litigation agency or defense.

Article 5 The judicial administration of the Provincial People's Government shall enact a specific development plan for the legal sector based on the legal services needed for Hainan Free Trade Pilot Zone and the free trade port with Chinese characteristics to achieve balanced development and reasonable distribution.

Article 6 The judicial administration of the Provincial People's Government shall improve honesty administration of the legal sector, establish a credit record and inquiry system for lawyers and law firms, make the basic information of lawyers and law firms public, and put the information about the lawyer's and law firm's awards, penalties, and dishonesty into the credit archives.

Article 7 Lawyers shall safeguard the dignity of the Constitution and law, protect the legal rights of the client, and maintain the correct implementation of the law, social equity, and justice. Lawyers shall be honest and trustworthy, diligent and conscientious, take the facts as the basis and the law as the criterion, and abide by professional ethics and the disciplines for lawyers' practices.

A lawyer's right to practice is protected by law, and shall not be compromised by any entity or individual.

Article 8 The lawyers and law firms shall assume their obligations of legal assistance pursuant to applicable rules of the state and the Province, and provide non-profit legal services for public complaints and proposals, mediation, community affairs, and others.

Legal counseling for national agencies and people's organizations and participation in accepting and managing public complaints and proposals and mediation by the lawyers or law firms shall be included in the government procurement catalog pursuant to relevant rules.

Article 9 Lawyers' associations are juristic persons of social groups and lawyer self-regulation organizations registered pursuant to law and serving the lawyers.

The lawyers' associations shall improve the internal governance structure, and implement a sound system for deliberation, decision-making, implementation, and oversight.

律师协会对任何非法妨碍律师执业、侵犯律师合法人身权利、财产权利的行为，有权向有关部门控告和检举。有关部门对律师协会的控告和检举应当受理，并函复律师协会。

对律师协会违反法律、法规或者其章程作出的错误决定，省人民政府司法行政部门可以责令其改正或者撤销。

第十条 任何单位和个人对律师、律师事务所在执业中的违法、违反执业纪律和违背职业道德的行为，有权向县级以上人民政府司法行政部门和律师协会投诉。县级以上人民政府司法行政部门和律师协会应当及时处理，并向投诉人反馈处理结果。

第二章 律师执业许可

第十一条 申请律师执业的人员应当按照法律法规的有关规定向省人民政府司法行政部门提交下列材料：

（一）律师执业申请登记表；

（二）律师资格证书或者法律职业资格证书原件及复印件；

（三）居民身份证原件及复印件；

（四）律师协会出具的申请人实习考核合格的材料；

（五）律师事务所出具的同意接收申请人的证明。

申请特许律师执业，按照国务院有关规定办理。

第十二条 省人民政府司法行政部门应当自收到律师执业申请材料之日起二个工作日内作出是否准予执业的决定。准予执业的，应当自决定之日起二个工作日内向申请人颁发律师执业证书，并将相关信息通报律师执业所在地的司法行政部门；不准予执业的，应当通知申请人并书面说明理由。

The lawyers' associations are entitled to file complaints and report any acts that illegally obstruct the lawyers' practices or infringes upon their personal or property rights. The appropriate agencies shall accept such complaints and accusations, and respond with a letter to the lawyers' association.

The judicial administration of the Provincial People's Government may issue an order to correct or rescind any wrong decision made by the lawyers' association that violates laws, regulations, or the articles of association.

Article 10 Any entity or individual has the right to file a complaint against the lawyers and the law firms that violate the law, professional conduct rules, and ethics in their practices with the judicial administration of the people's government at or above the county level and the lawyers' association. The judicial administration of the people's government at or above the county level and the lawyers' association shall resolve such complaints in a timely manner and notify the complainant of the results.

Chapter II Legal Practice Certificate

Article 11 The applicants for practice certificates shall submit the following documents to the judicial administration of the Provincial People's Government pursuant to law:

(a) the practice certificate registration document;

(b) the original and a copy of the lawyer's qualification certificate or the legal profession qualification certificate;

(c) the original and a copy of the resident identity card;

(d) the materials provided by the lawyers' association to certify that the applicants have passed the apprenticeship assessment; and

(e) the certificate issued by the law firm agreeing to accept the applicant.

The application for a licensed practicing certificate is subject to the applicable rules of the State Council.

Article 12 The judicial administration of the Provincial People's Government shall, within 2 business days of the date of receiving the application, make a decision whether to permit practicing. If permitted, the applicant shall be granted the certificate within 2 business days from the decision, and information shall be reported to the judicial administration where the lawyer practices law; if not permitted, the applicant shall be notified of the reasons in writing.

第十三条　律师变更执业机构执业，应当向转入的律师事务所所在地人民政府司法行政部门提出申请，受理部门应当对变更申请及提交的材料审核。不准予变更的，应当通知申请人并书面说明理由；准予变更的，省人民政府司法行政部门应当自受理之日起二个工作日内为申请人换发律师执业证书。

第十四条　除《中华人民共和国律师法》规定外，律师有下列情形之一的，由省人民政府司法行政部门收回、注销其律师执业证书：

（一）受到吊销律师执业证书处罚的；

（二）原准予执业的决定被依法撤销的；

（三）因本人不再从事律师职业申请注销的；

（四）因与所在律师事务所解除聘用合同或者所在的律师事务所被注销，在六个月内未被其他律师事务所聘用的；

（五）因其他原因终止律师执业的。

因前款第（三）项、第（四）项、第（五）项规定情形被注销律师执业证书的人员，在上述情形消除后，可以按照本条例规定的程序重新申请律师执业。

律师正在接受司法机关、县级以上人民政府司法行政部门、律师协会立案调查期间，不得申请注销执业证书。

第三章　律师执业机构

第十五条　律师事务所是律师的执业机构，可以由律师合伙设立、个人设立或者由国家出资设立。鼓励具备条件的律师事务所实行公司化管理，按照国家和本省有关规定设立公司制律师事务所。

Article 13 Where the lawyer changes the organization of practicing, an application shall be made to the judicial administration where the new organization is located. The change of application and the application materials shall be reviewed by the competent agency. If not permitted, the applicant shall be notified of the reasons in writing; if permitted, the judicial administration of the Provincial People's Government shall issue a new lawyer's practicing certificate within 2 business days from the permission being granted.

Article 14 Unless otherwise provided by the Law of the People's Republic of China on Lawyers, the judicial administration of the Provincial People's Government may withdraw and deregister the lawyer's practicing certificate if:

(a) the lawyer's practicing certificate is voided;

(b) the decision to permit practicing is withdrawn pursuant to law;

(c) the deregistration application for a lawyer who no longer practices law is made;

(d) such lawyer is not employed again within 6 months from the law firm terminating the employment contract or it is deregistered; or

(e) the lawyer's practice is terminated for other reasons.

Lawyers whose practicing certificates are deregistered due to the circumstances of Subparagraph (c), (d), or (e) of the preceding paragraph may apply for practicing certificate again pursuant to the procedures of these Regulations if those frustrations are eliminated.

Lawyers under investigation by judicial agencies, judicial administration of the people's government at or above the county level, or the lawyers' association shall not apply for reregistration.

Chapter III Lawyer's Practicing Organization

Article 15 Law firms are the organizations where the lawyers practice law and are established as partnerships between lawyers, by individuals ("sole proprietorship") or through capital contribution from the state. The eligible law firms are recommended to enforce corporate management and create a corporate governance structure pursuant to relevant provisions of the state and the Province.

鼓励律师、律师事务所在欠发达地区设立律师事务所或者分所。

鼓励律师、律师事务所在国外和香港特别行政区、澳门特别行政区、台湾地区设立分支机构。

第十六条 设立个人律师事务所应当具备下列条件：

（一）有自己的名称、住所和章程；

（二）设立人应当具有高等学校法律本科以上学历；

（三）设立人应当是具有五年以上执业经历并能够专职执业的律师，且在申请设立前三年内未受过停止执业处罚；

（四）有人民币十万元以上的资产；

（五）有符合要求的公益法律服务承诺。

第十七条 设立普通合伙律师事务所应当具备下列条件：

（一）有自己的名称、住所和章程；

（二）有书面合伙协议；

（三）有三名以上合伙人作为设立人；

（四）设立人应当是具有三年以上执业经历并能够专职执业的律师，且在申请设立前三年内未受过停止执业处罚；

（五）有人民币十万元以上的资产；

（六）有符合要求的公益法律服务承诺。

第十八条 设立特殊的普通合伙律师事务所应当具备下列条件：

（一）有自己的名称、住所和章程；

（二）有书面合伙协议；

（三）有十名以上合伙人作为设立人；

（四）设立人应当是具有三年以上执业经历并能够专职执业的律师，且在申请设立前三年内未受过停止执业处罚；

Lawyers and law firms are encouraged to set up regional or satellite offices in less-developed areas.

Lawyers and law firms are encouraged to establish branches in other countries, the Hong Kong Special Administrative Region ("Hong Kong SAR"), Macao Special Administrative Region ("Macao SAR"), and Taiwan region.

Article 16 The establishment of a solo practitioner firm shall comply with the following conditions:

(a) the firm shall own its name, domicile and articles of association;

(b) the promoter shall have a bachelor's degree or above in law;

(c) the promoter shall be a lawyer with over-five-year experience and able to practice full-time, and not be penalized with the suspension of practice 3 years prior to the establishment;

(d) assets worth over 100,000 Yuan; and

(e) the firm shall promise to engage in non-profit legal services that comply with specific requirements.

Article 17 The establishment of a general partnership law firm shall comply with following conditions:

(a) the firm shall own its name, domicile, and articles of association;

(b) the firm shall own a written partnership contract;

(c) the firm shall own over three partners as promoters;

(d) the promoters shall be lawyers with over-three-year experience and able to practice full-time, and not be penalized with the suspension of practice 3 years prior to the establishment;

(e) assets worth over 100,000 Yuan; and

(f) the firm shall promise to engage in non-profit legal services that comply with specific requirements.

Article 18 The establishment of a limited liability partnership law firm shall comply with the following conditions:

(a) the firm shall own its name, domicile, and articles of association;

(b) the firm shall own a written partnership contract;

(c) the firm shall own over ten partners as promoters;

(d) the promoters shall be lawyers with over-three-year experience and able to practice full-time, and not be penalized with the suspension of practice 3 years prior to the establishment;

（五）有人民币一百万元以上的资产；

（六）有符合要求的公益法律服务承诺。

注册会计师、注册税务师、注册造价工程师、专利代理人等其他专业人员可以成为特殊的普通合伙律师事务所的合伙人，但其出资份额和人数比例不得超过25%，不得担任律师事务所负责人。

省人民政府司法行政部门应当将担任特殊的普通合伙律师事务所除律师以外其他合伙人的情况，报国务院司法行政部门备案。

第十九条 外国和香港特别行政区、澳门特别行政区、台湾地区的律师事务所在本经济特区设立代表处，以及香港特别行政区、澳门特别行政区、台湾地区的居民经国家统一考试取得律师资格或者法律职业资格，申请在本经济特区执业的，按照有关规定办理。

第二十条 外国和香港特别行政区、澳门特别行政区的律师事务所驻海南代表机构可以按照有关规定从事部分涉本省的商事非诉讼法律事务。

第二十一条 中国律师事务所与外国律师事务所，香港特别行政区、澳门特别行政区、台湾地区的律师事务所与内地（大陆）律师事务所可以按照有关规定在本经济特区通过协议约定进行联营，在各自执业范围、权限内以分工协作方式开展业务合作。

香港特别行政区、澳门特别行政区的律师事务所可以按照有关规定与内地律师事务所在本经济特区设立合伙联营律师事务所，合伙联营律师事务所的内地执业律师可以从事民商事和行政诉讼代理业务，合伙联营律师事务所的负责人应当由内地律师担任。合伙联营律师事务所管理办法由省人民政府司法行政部门另行制定。

(e) assets worth 1,000,000 Yuan; and

(f) the firm shall promise to engage in non-profit legal services that comply with specific requirements.

The certified public accountants, certified tax agents, certified cost engineers, patent agents, and other professionals may be partners with the limited liability law firms. The capital share and number of such partners shall not exceed 25% and they shall not be the responsible persons of law firms.

The judicial administration of the Provincial People's Government shall report the information about other partners, except the lawyers of the limited liability law firms, to the State Council judicial administrations.

Article 19 The establishment of representative offices in this SEZ by the law firms of foreign countries, the Hong Kong SAR, Macao SAR, and Taiwan region of China, and the applications made by the citizens of the Hong Kong SAR, Macao SAR, and Taiwan region who obtain legal qualifications or legal profession certificates after passing the national examination in this SEZ are subject to specific rules.

Article 20 The representative offices of the law firms of foreign countries, Hong Kong SAR and Macao SAR of China in this Province may engage in non-litigation commercial legal services related to this Province pursuant to applicable rules.

Article 21 The Chinese law firms and international law firms, or law firms from the Hong Kong SAR, Macao SAR, Taiwan region and mainland law firms may, based on applicable rules, establish associations through a contract in this SEZ and operate pursuant to their own scope of service and functions.

The law firms from the Hong Kong SAR and Macao SAR may establish joint partnership associations with the mainland law firms in this SEZ pursuant to applicable rules. The lawyers of such partnerships from the mainland of China may provide civil, commercial, and administrative litigation services, and the responsible persons of such partnership associations shall be the lawyers from the mainland of China. The rules on managing the partnership associations shall be separately enacted by the judicial administration of the Provincial People's Government.

第二十二条 外国律师事务所驻华代表机构可以按照有关规定与本经济特区律师事务所互派执业律师担任法律顾问。

内地律师事务所可以按照有关规定向香港特别行政区、澳门特别行政区律师事务所在本经济特区的代表机构派驻内地律师担任内地法律顾问。

本经济特区内的律师事务所可以按照有关规定聘请外籍律师担任外国法律顾问，聘请香港特别行政区、澳门特别行政区律师担任法律顾问，办理已获准从事律师执业业务的香港特别行政区、澳门特别行政区以及中国以外其他国家的法律事务。

第二十三条 设立律师事务所，由申请人按照法律法规的相关规定向省人民政府司法行政部门提交下列材料：

（一）申请书；

（二）律师事务所名称、章程；

（三）律师事务所登记表；

（四）设立人的名单、简历，身份证、律师执业证书原件及复印件；

（五）资产证明；

（六）符合要求的住所证明；

（七）公益法律服务承诺书。

设立合伙律师事务所，还应当提交合伙协议、选举负责人的决议。

第二十四条 省人民政府司法行政部门应当自收到报请审核材料之日起三个工作日内予以审核，作出是否准予设立的决定，并将相关信息通报律师事务所所在地的司法行政部门；不准予设立的，应当通知申请人并书面说明理由。

Article 22 The representative office of the law firms of foreign countries may, together with the law firms of this SEZ, appoint lawyers as legal counsels to each other's organization pursuant to applicable rules.

The mainland law firms may appoint their own lawyers as legal counsels to the representative offices of the law firms from the Hong Kong SAR and Macao SAR in this SEZ pursuant to applicable rules.

The law firms in this SEZ may appoint foreign lawyers as foreign legal counsels pursuant to applicable law, appoint the Hong Kong SAR and Macao SAR lawyers as legal counsels, and provide legal services in Hong Kong SAR, Macao SAR of China, and foreign countries where they are allowed to practice law.

Article 23 The applicants shall submit the following materials to judicial administration of the Provincial People's Government when establishing a law firm pursuant to applicable rules:

(a) application letter;

(b) name and articles of association;

(c) registration form;

(d) names, résumé, ID card, the original, and a copy of the lawyer's practicing certificate;

(e) asset certification document;

(f) domicile certification document that complies with certain requirements; and

(g) a promise letter to engage in non-profit legal services.

The establishment of a joint partnership law firm additionally requires the partnership contract and the decision on the election of responsible persons.

Article 24 The judicial administration of the Provincial People's Government shall complete the review of the application materials within 3 business days of the date it receives such materials, make a decision whether to permit the establishment or not, and report the relevant information to the local judicial administrations where the law firm is located; if not permitted, the applicant shall be notified of the reasons in writing.

第二十五条 律师事务所设立申请人应当在领取执业证书后的六十日内，按照有关规定刻制印章、开立银行账户、办理税务登记，完成律师事务所开业的各项准备工作，并将刻制的律师事务所公章、财务专用章印模和开立的银行账户报县级以上人民政府司法行政部门备案。

第二十六条 律师事务所变更名称的，应当经省人民政府司法行政部门批准，并将变更信息通报律师事务所所在地的司法行政部门。

律师事务所变更执业场所、负责人、合伙人、章程、合伙协议的，应当自变更之日起十五日内报所在地的市、县、自治县人民政府司法行政部门备案，市、县、自治县人民政府司法行政部门应当将变更信息报告省人民政府司法行政部门。

第二十七条 律师事务所变更组织形式的，应当在自行依法处理好业务衔接、人员安排、资产处置、债务承担等事务，并对章程、合伙协议作出相应修改后，按照本条例的设立程序办理。

律师事务所因分立、合并，需要对原律师事务所进行变更或者注销原律师事务所、设立新的律师事务所的，应当在自行依法处理好相关律师事务所的业务衔接、人员安排、资产处置、债务承担等事务后，提交分立协议或者合并协议等申请材料，按照本条例的设立程序办理。

第二十八条 律师事务所终止的，应当向社会公告，并妥善处理受理的法律事务，依法清算债权债务。

律师事务所解散或者终止的，应当在清算结束后十五日内向所在地的市、县、自治县人民政府司法行政部门提交解散或者终止申请书、清算报告、本所执业证书以及其他有关材料，由其出具审查意见，并连同全部注销申请材料报省人民政府司法行政部门审核，办理注销手续。

Article 25 The applicant shall, within 60 days of receiving the practicing certificate, make seals, open a bank account and complete tax registration pursuant to applicable law, finish the preparations for the establishment, and submit the corporate seal, financial seal impressions, and bank account to the judicial administration of the people's government at or above the county level for recordation.

Article 26 Where the law firm changes its name, such change shall be approved by the judicial administration of the Provincial People's Government and reported to the local judicial administrations where the law firm is located.

Where the law firm changes its domicile, responsible person, partners, articles of association, or partnership contract, such change shall be reported for recordation to the judicial administrations of the municipal, county, or autonomous county people's government within 15 days of the change taking effect and reported the judicial administration of the Provincial People's Government.

Article 27 Where the law firm changes its organization, such change shall be conducted pursuant to the procedures of these Regulations after the business, staff arrangement, assets, and debts are resolved pursuant to law and the articles of association and partnership contract are amended.

Where a law firm needs to be changed or deregistered and a new law firm established due to separation or merger, the law firm shall submit a separation or merger contract and other application materials pursuant to the procedures of these Regulations after the business, staff arrangements, assets, and debts are resolved pursuant to law.

Article 28 Where a law firm is terminated, such termination shall be announced, the remaining services properly resolved, and the obligations and debts liquidated pursuant to law.

Where a law firm is dissolved or terminated, the application letter, liquidation report, the practicing certificate of the law firm, and other materials for the dissolution or termination shall be submitted to the local judicial administrations of the municipal, county, or autonomous county's people's government within 15 days of the completion of the liquidation. Such local administration agencies shall review and submit opinions, report the opinions and all the deregistration application materials to the judicial administration of the Provincial People's Government for review, and complete the deregistration procedures.

第二十九条 律师事务所应当建立决策程序、人员管理、利益冲突审查、统一收案收费、风险控制、质量控制、收益分配等内部管理制度。

对违反法律法规和有关管理制度的律师，律师事务所可以解除聘用关系或者除名。处理结果应当报所在地县级以上人民政府司法行政部门和律师协会备案。

第三十条 律师事务所应当建立赔偿责任制度。律师违法执业或者因过错给当事人造成损失的，由其所在的律师事务所承担赔偿责任，律师事务所赔偿后，可以向有故意或者重大过失行为的律师追偿。

律师事务所与委托人签订委托协议时，应当写明过错赔偿条款，以协议中约定的赔偿条件和数额作为赔偿的依据。未约定过错赔偿条款的，不免除律师事务所应当承担的赔偿责任。

第三十一条 律师事务所按照国家有关规定实行执业责任保险制度。

鼓励律师事务所和律师就单独的法律服务项目或者其他法律服务购买保险，以降低执业风险，保障当事人利益。

第三十二条 律师事务所应当按照规定为聘用的律师和辅助人员办理失业、养老、医疗、工伤、生育等社会保险和缴存住房公积金。

符合人才引进相关规定的律师，享受人才引进的优惠政策待遇。

第三十三条 本经济特区内的律师和律师事务所可以依法选择缴纳税款的方式，并按照有关规定享受税收优惠。

Article 29 A law firm shall establish internal management rules, including for decision-making, staff management, investigation of conflicts of interest, standards for case acceptance and charges, risk control, quality control, and revenue distribution.

The law firm may terminate the employment contract of or remove lawyers who violate laws and regulations and other administrative or management rules. The result of the management of such lawyers shall be reported to the judicial administration of the people's government at or above the county level and the lawyers' association for recordation.

Article 30 Law firms shall implement indemnification systems. If a lawyer causes damages to the client due to a violation of law when practicing law or other faults, the law firm assumes the indemnification; after making the indemnification, the law firm may seek to recover such from the lawyer who commits intentional or grossly negligent acts.

When a law firm signs a contract with the client, the indemnification clause shall be clearly stated, and the conditions and amount of indemnification in the contract shall be the basis for indemnification. If such a clause is not stated in the contract, the law firm shall not be exempt from indemnification.

Article 31 Law firms shall carry liability insurance pursuant to applicable national rules.

Law firms and lawyers are encouraged to purchase insurance for separate legal service projects or other legal services to lower professional risks and ensure the interests of the clients.

Article 32 The law firms shall purchase employment pension, medical, work-related injury, maternity, pension, and other insurance and contribute to housing provident funds for the employed lawyers and support staff pursuant to law.

The lawyers that meet the conditions for talent introduction shall enjoy the corresponding benefits.

Article 33 The lawyers and law firms in this SEZ may choose their own methods of paying taxes pursuant to law and enjoy tax incentives pursuant to applicable rules.

第四章 律师业务

第三十四条 除诉讼和仲裁代理业务外，律师还可以依法接受委托办理招商引资、商标、专利、商事登记、不动产登记等各类非诉讼法律事务。律师接受委托办理的法律事务，不受地域、行业的限制。但法律、法规另有规定的除外。

第三十五条 律师承办法律事务，应当由律师事务所统一接受委托、收取费用。

律师事务所依据委托合同向委托人收取律师服务费后，应当出具税务机关监制的收费凭证。

第五章 律师的权利和义务

第三十六条 律师担任刑事辩护人，依法享有下列权利：

（一）查阅、摘抄、复制本案案卷材料；

（二）就本案事实向有关单位、个人进行调查、取证；

（三）同在押的犯罪嫌疑人、被告人会见和通信；

（四）出席法庭辩护；

（五）被告人在立案侦查、审查起诉中合法权利受到侵害，有权向法庭陈述侵害事实，出具证据材料；

（六）获得本案法律文书的副本，复制庭审笔录等庭审活动的有关材料；

（七）因不可抗力或者意外事件，可以申请人民法院在法定结案的时间内推迟开庭时间；

（八）行使法律、法规规定的其他权利。

Chapter IV The Lawyers' Services

Article 34 The lawyers may also lawfully engage in non-litigation services including investment, trademark, patent, business registration, and real estate registration in addition to litigation and arbitration services. The scope of legal services that the lawyers may provide is not subject to the limits of region and industry unless otherwise provided by laws and regulations.

Article 35 The legal services of a lawyer shall be conducted in the name of the law firm and charged pursuant to the law firm's standards.

The law firm shall issue receipts for charges produced by the tax authority after collecting the charges from the clients pursuant to the commission contract.

Chapter V Rights and Obligations of Lawyers

Article 36 The lawyer providing criminal defense has the rights to:

(a) access, or make excerpts or copies of the case files;

(b) investigate case facts and obtain evidence from appropriate agencies and individuals;

(c) meet and communicate with the suspects or the defendants;

(d) defend before the court;

(e) present the facts and produce evidence to the court if the defendants' legal rights are violated during investigation and prosecution;

(f) obtain copies of the legal documents of the case, and make copies of the transcripts and other materials of the court proceedings;

(g) apply to the court to postpone the court session within the legally specified time for closing cases due to *force majeure* or unforeseeable accidents; and

(h) other rights as prescribed by laws and regulations.

第三十七条 律师代理判决已生效的刑事、民事、行政诉讼案件的申诉，有权查阅、摘抄、复制原审案卷；代理刑事申诉时，有权同在押、服刑人员会见和通信。

第三十八条 律师办理非诉讼法律事务，凭律师执业证书、律师事务所的调查专用介绍信和当事人的授权委托书，可以向国家机关、有关单位、组织和个人调查与所承办事务有关的情况，查阅、摘抄、复制与所承办事务有关的材料，国家机关、有关单位、组织和经办人员应当予以配合，但国家秘密、商业秘密、个人隐私等不宜公开的材料除外。

对获取的材料，律师不得在该委托事务之外使用。

第三十九条 公安机关、国家安全机关、人民检察院、人民法院、司法行政部门应当尊重律师，健全律师执业权利保障制度，按照法律规定，保障律师知情权、申请权、申诉权，以及会见、阅卷、收集证据和发问、质证、辩论等方面的执业权利，不得阻碍律师依法履行辩护、代理职责。

第四十条 律师在代理刑事案件过程中，自行收集、调取证据存在困难的，可以书面申请人民检察院、人民法院收集、调取证据；人民检察院、人民法院应当在收到申请后的三日以内，作出是否同意的决定，并通知律师；不予准许的，应当书面说明理由。

律师在代理的民事案件审理、执行阶段，可以向人民法院申请签发调查令；被申请机关不予签发调查令的，应当通知律师并书面说明理由。有关单位、组织和个人应当根据调查令的调查内容及时提供有关证据。

第四十一条 律师在执业活动中，应当遵守法庭、仲裁庭纪律和有关规定，不得有下列行为：

（一）违反规定会见法官、检察官、仲裁员以及其他有关工作人员；

Article 37 Lawyers petitioning against effective criminal, civil, or administrative judgments have the right to access, make excerpts or copies of the case files; if petitioning a criminal case, the lawyers have the right to meet and communicate with the persons in custody or serving a sentence.

Article 38 The lawyer engaging in non-litigation services may, by presenting the lawyer's practicing certificate, special letter of introduction, and the power of attorney, investigate the matters related to the case with the national agencies, appropriate agencies, organizations, and individuals, and access, or make excerpts or copies of the related materials, excluding materials involving state secrets, trade secrets, and personal privacy unsuitable for disclosure; the national agencies, appropriate agencies, organizations, and individual in charge shall cooperate.

The lawyer shall not use the materials obtained for matters outside the power of attorney.

Article 39 The public security agencies, national security agencies, people's procuratorates, people's courts, and judicial administrations shall respect lawyers and implement a sound system to ensure lawyers' rights, safeguard the lawyers' right to be informed, submit an application, make a petition, meet, access to case files, obtain evidence, question, cross-examine, defend, and other rights related to the practice of law pursuant to law, and shall not hinder lawyers to lawfully perform their defense or agency duties.

Article 40 Where the lawyers have difficulty in collecting and obtaining evidence on their own when representing the criminal defendants, the lawyers may apply in writing to the people's procuratorates and the people's courts to collect and obtain evidence; the people's procuratorates and people's courts shall make a decision within 3 days after receiving the application and notify the lawyers; if not approving the application, the people's procuratorates and people's courts shall explain the reasons in writing.

The lawyers may apply to the people's court to issue an investigation order at the trial and enforcement stages of a civil case; if the issuance of the investigation order is denied, the people's court shall notify the lawyers and explain the reasons in writing. The appropriate agencies, organizations, and individuals shall provide the evidence provided by the investigation order.

Article 41 The lawyers shall abide by the disciplines and applicable rules during court proceedings or arbitration, and not:

(a) meet the judges, prosecutors, arbitrators, and other relevant staff in violation of the law;

（二）向法官、检察官、仲裁员以及其他有关工作人员行贿，介绍贿赂或者指使、诱导当事人行贿，或者以许愿、宴请、送礼等不正当方式影响法官、检察官、仲裁员以及其他有关工作人员依法办理案件；

（三）威胁、利诱他人提供虚假证据；利用他人的隐私及违法行为，胁迫他人提供与实际情况不符的证据材料；利用物质或者各种非物质利益引诱他人提供虚假证据；

（四）采取伪造证据、虚假陈述等手段，恶意串通、捏造事实，进行虚假诉讼或者虚假仲裁；

（五）在法庭、仲裁庭上发表危害国家安全、破坏民族团结、诽谤他人、扰乱庭审秩序的言论；

（六）私自接受委托承办法律事务，私自向委托人收取费用、额外报酬、财物或者可能产生的其他利益；

（七）利用提供法律服务的便利牟取当事人争议的权益；

（八）接受对方当事人的财物或者其他利益，与对方当事人或者第三人恶意串通，侵害委托人的权益；

（九）煽动、教唆当事人采取扰乱公共秩序、危害公共安全等非法手段解决争议；

（十）将因代理案件获取的案件材料在该委托事务之外使用、公开；

（十一）法律、法规规定的其他禁止性行为。

律师对其曾以司法机关、仲裁机构工作人员身份经办过的法律事务，应当自行回避。

第四十二条 律师和律师事务所在与委托人及其他人员接触中，不得采用下列不正当手段与同行进行业务竞争：

(b) bribe, introduce bribery, instigate or induce the clients to bribe the judges, prosecutors, arbitrators, and other relevant staff, or to influence judges, prosecutors, arbitrators, and other relevant staff by making promises, buying meals, giving gifts, or other improper means;

(c) threaten or induce others to provide false evidence; coerce others by taking advantage of their privacy or illegal acts to provide false evidence and materials; use the material or non-material benefits to induce others to provide false evidence;

(d) forge evidence, make false statements, or collude and fabricate facts in any other way to bring false claims or arbitration;

(e) pass remarks before the court or arbitral tribunal that endanger national security, undermine national unity, slander others, or disrupt the order of court proceedings;

(f) privately accept agency employment and collect charges, additional fees, property, or other possible benefits from the client;

(g) take advantage of the agency to obtain the rights and interests under dispute by the client;

(h) accept property or other interests from the opposing party, collude with the opposing party or a third party to infringe upon the rights and interests of the client;

(i) instigate or abet the client to settle the disputes by disrupting public order, compromising the public security, or through other means;

(j) use or disclose the case files outside the power of attorney; or

(k) other acts prohibited by laws and regulations.

The lawyers shall voluntarily recuse themselves from the legal matters that they have managed as the staff members of judicial agencies or arbitration institutions.

Article 42 The lawyers and law firms shall not by resorting to compete for business with other lawyers and law firms in their contacts with clients and other people:

（一）故意诋毁、诽谤其他律师或者律师事务所信誉、声誉；

（二）无正当理由，以在同行业收费水平以下收费为条件吸引客户，或者采用承诺给予客户、中介人、推荐人回扣，馈赠金钱、财物方式争揽业务；

（三）故意在委托人与其代理律师之间制造纠纷；

（四）向委托人明示或者暗示律师或者律师事务所与司法机关、行政机关及其工作人员具有特殊关系，排斥其他律师或者律师事务所；

（五）就法律服务结果或者司法诉讼的结果做出任何没有事实及法律根据的承诺；

（六）明示或者暗示可以帮助委托人达到不正当目的，或者以不正当的方式、手段达到委托人的目的；

（七）法律、法规规定的其他禁止性行为。

第四十三条 申请律师执业人员在实习期间，可以代为申请立案、提交和领取法律文书等；可以在律师的带领下，参加调查取证、会见犯罪嫌疑人或者被告人、庭前会议和庭审等活动。

第六章 法律责任

第四十四条 违反本条例规定的行为，《中华人民共和国律师法》等法律、行政法规已设定处罚的，从其规定。

第四十五条 违反本条例第四条第三款规定，从事法律服务的，由县级以上人民政府司法行政部门责令停止非法执业，没收违法所得，可以并处违法所得一倍以上五倍以下的罚款。

(a) intentionally slander or defame the credibility or reputation of other lawyers or law firms;

(b) attract clients by offering charges that are below the industrial standards without legitimate reason, or to solicit business by promising the clients, intermediaries, and referrals rebates, money, or other property;

(c) deliberately engineer a dispute between the client and the lawyer;

(d) explicitly or implicitly indicate that the lawyers or law firms have special connections with the judicial agencies, administrative agencies, or their employees for the purpose of excluding other lawyers or law firms;

(e) make promises on the results of legal services or judicial proceedings that have no legal or factual basis;

(f) explicitly or implicitly indicate that they can help the clients achieve improper purposes or achieve the clients' purposes through improper means; or

(g) other acts prohibited by laws and regulations.

Article 43 The applicants for practicing certificates may in their apprenticeship apply for case filing, submit and receive legal documents on the lawyer's behalf, participate in evidence investigation and collection, meet suspects or defendants, and participate in pre-trial conferences, court proceedings, and other activities under the guidance of lawyers.

Chapter VI Legal Liability

Article 44 The rules specified by the Law of the People's Republic of China on Lawyers and other laws and regulations shall apply in the event of acts that violate these Regulations.

Article 45 Where any individual provides legal services that violate Subparagraph 3 of Article 4 of these Regulations, the judicial administration of the people's government at or above the county level shall issue an order to suspend such person's illegal practice, confiscate the illegal gains, and may concurrently impose a fine of not less than one time and not more than five times the illegal gains.

第四十六条 违反本条例第四十二条规定的，由县级以上人民政府司法行政部门给予警告，可以处一万元以上十万元以下的罚款；有违法所得的，没收违法所得；情节严重的，给予停止执业三个月以上六个月以下的处罚；构成犯罪的，依法追究刑事责任。

第四十七条 外省律师在本经济特区违法执业，由县级以上人民政府司法行政部门按照有关法律、法规的规定给予处罚，并由省人民政府司法行政部门向该律师执业登记所在地的省级人民政府司法行政部门通报；应当给予停止执业、吊销律师执业证书处罚的，由省人民政府司法行政部门建议该律师执业登记所在地省级人民政府司法行政部门给予处罚。

第四十八条 律师、律师事务所违法执业，应当给予警告、罚款、没收违法所得、停止执业或者停业整顿处罚的，由县级以上人民政府司法行政部门依法作出决定。

应当给予吊销律师、律师事务所执业证书处罚的，由省人民政府司法行政部门依法作出决定。

第四十九条 律师、律师事务所对司法行政部门作出的行政许可、行政处罚决定不服的，可以依法申请复议，或者依法向人民法院提起诉讼。

律师、律师事务所对司法行政部门的处罚决定不服，但逾期不申请复议、也不向人民法院起诉，又拒不履行处罚决定的，作出处罚决定的部门可以申请人民法院强制执行。

第五十条 司法行政部门的工作人员违反本条例规定，失职渎职、徇私舞弊、索贿受贿，尚未构成犯罪的，由任免机关或者监察机关按照管理权限给予处分；构成犯罪的，依法追究刑事责任。

Article 46 Where any individual violates Article 42 of these Regulations, the judicial administrations of the people's government at the county level or above shall issue a warning and may impose a fine of not less than 10,000 Yuan and not more than 100,000 Yuan, confiscate any illegal gains if any, imposes a penalty of not less than 3 months and not more than 6 months suspension of practice if the circumstances are serious, and impose criminal liability on such individual if the violation constitutes a crime.

Article 47 Where the lawyers of other provinces illegally practice law in this SEZ, the judicial administration of the people's government at or above the county level shall impose penalties pursuant to law and the judicial administration of the Provincial People's Government shall report such illegal practice to the appropriate agency in the Province where such lawyer registers the practicing certificate; where the punishment is the suspension of practice and revocation of lawyer's practicing certificate, the judicial administration recommends such punishment to the appropriate agency of the Province where such lawyer registers the practicing certificate.

Article 48 Where the lawyers and law firms are penalized with a warning, fines, confiscation of illegal gains, suspension of practicing, or suspension of practicing for correction due to illegal practicing, the judicial administration of people's government at or above the county level makes the decision regarding the punishment pursuant to law.

Where the punishment shall be the revocation of the practicing certificates of lawyers or law firms, the judicial administration of the Provincial People's Government makes the decision regarding the punishment pursuant to law.

Article 49 The lawyers and law firms that do not accept the administrative licensing or administrative penalty decisions made by the judicial administration may apply for administrative reconsideration pursuant to law or file administrative litigation with the people's court.

The lawyers and law firms that do not accept the penalty imposed by the judicial administration but fail to apply for administrative reconsideration or file administrative litigation with the people's court and refuse to submit to the penalty, the agency that makes the penalty decision may apply to the people's court for enforcement.

Article 50 The employees of the judicial administration who neglect duty, play favoritism and commit irregularities, ask for bribes, and accept bribes that violate these Regulations but do not constitute a crime shall be penalized by the appointment and removal agency or the supervisory agency pursuant to the power and authority; if a crime is constituted, such staff shall be penalized with criminal liabilities pursuant to law.

第七章　附　则

第五十一条　公职律师、公司律师在海南经济特区范围内从事法律服务活动，按照国家有关规定执行。

第五十二条　海南经济特区以外的本省行政区域范围内的律师执业，参照本条例执行。

第五十三条　本条例的具体应用问题由省人民政府负责解释。

第五十四条　本条例自 2019 年 10 月 1 日起施行。2011 年 7 月 22 日海南省第四届人民代表大会常务委员会第二十三次会议通过的《海南经济特区律师执业条例》同时废止。

Chapter VII Supplementary Provisions

Article 51 The legal services and other activities of the public employee lawyers and corporate lawyers within this SEZ are subject to applicable national rules.

Article 52 The lawyers' practices within this Province's administrative area but outside this SEZ are subject to these Regulations *mutatis mutandis*.

Article 53 The specific matters arising from the implementation of these Regulations are construed by the Provincial People's Government.

Article 54 These Regulations shall come into force as of October 1, 2019. The Regulations of Hainan Special Economic Zone on Lawyer's Practice adopted at the 23rd Session of the Standing Committee of the 4th Hainan Provincial People's Congress on July 22, 2011 are simultaneously repealed.

Chapter VII Supplementary Provisions

海南经济特区注册会计师条例

Regulations of Hainan Special Economic Zone on Certified Public Accountants

海南经济特区注册会计师条例

（2019 年 7 月 29 日海南省第六届人民代表大会常务委员会第十三次会议通过）

目 录

第一章 总 则

第一条 为了发挥注册会计师在社会经济活动中的鉴证和服务作用，规范注册会计师的执业行为，加强对会计师事务所的管理，根据《中华人民共和国注册会计师法》和国家有关法律、法规的规定，结合本经济特区实际，制定本条例。

第二条 本条例适用于在本经济特区内从事审计及相关业务的专业机构和人员。

第三条 注册会计师是依法取得注册会计师证书并接受委托从事审计及相关业务的执业人员。注册会计师必须加入会计师事务所方可执行业务。

Regulations of Hainan Special Economic Zone on Certified Public Accountants

(Adopted at the 13th Session of the Standing Committee of the 6th Hainan Provincial People's Congress on July 29, 2019)

Contents

Chapter I General Provisions

Article 1 These Regulations are enacted under to the Law of the People's Republic of China on Certified Public Accountants and applicable national laws, and based on the actual circumstances of this special economic zone (hereinafter referred to as the "SEZ") for the purposes of giving sufficient authority to certified public accountants (hereinafter referred to as the "CPAs") for verifications and services for social and economic activities, standardizing the CPAs' performance and improving the management of accounting firms.

Article 2 These Regulations shall apply to professional institutions and personnel engaging in auditing and related business in the SEZ.

Article 3 A certified public accountant, for the purpose of these Regulations, refers to a person who has obtained the CPA certificate pursuant to law and is authorized to engage in auditing and related business. The CPAs must be in an accounting firm before practicing.

第四条 会计师事务所是依法设立并承办注册会计师业务的专业机构。

会计师事务所实行独立核算，自负盈亏，自担风险，并依法纳税。

第五条 鼓励引进国际化的会计师事务所，培育和引进国际化审计、会计专业人才。

第六条 省注册会计师协会是由注册会计师、会计师事务所组成的社会团体。省注册会计师协会依法对注册会计师和会计师事务所进行自律性管理。

省注册会计师协会依法取得社会团体法人资格。

第七条 省人民政府财政部门（以下简称省财政部门）是本经济特区注册会计师行业的主管部门，依法对注册会计师、会计师事务所和省注册会计师协会进行管理、监督、指导。

省财政部门可以委托各市、县、自治县财政部门，对本地区的注册会计师和会计师事务所进行监督和指导。

第八条 全面推行电子化注册会计师注册、会计师事务所执业许可审批，实现网上申请、网上办理全程电子化管理。

省财政部门、省注册会计师协会对能够通过公共数据平台提取的材料，不再要求申请人提供，但可以要求申请人予以确认。

第九条 注册会计师和会计师事务所执行业务，必须严格遵守法律、法规，遵守执业准则和职业道德规范，恪守独立、客观、公正的原则。

第十条 注册会计师依法出具的报告具有法定证明效力。委托人和有关部门不得拒绝接受注册会计师依法出具的报告。

Article 4 An accounting firm, for the purpose of these Regulations, is a professional institution established pursuant to law and engages in business concerning the CPAs.

An accounting firm conducts accounting, assumes profit and losses, assumes risks, and pays taxes independently pursuant to law.

Article 5 International accounting firms are recommended to settle down in order to develop and introduce international auditing and accounting professionals.

Article 6 The Provincial Association of Certificated Public Accountants (hereinafter referred to as the "PACPA") is a social organization composed of the CPAs and accounting firms. The PACPA manages the CPAs and the accounting firms with each self-regulating themselves pursuant to law.

The PACPA has obtained legal personality as a social organization pursuant to law.

Article 7 The Financial Department of the Provincial People's Government (hereinafter referred to as the "PFD") is the competent agency for the CPA sector in the SEZ, and regulates, oversees, and guides CPAs, accounting firms, and the PACPA pursuant to law.

The PFD may hire the financial agencies of the cities, counties, and autonomous counties to supervise and guide the CPAs and the accounting firms in the areas respectively.

Article 8 The electronic registration of the CPAs and electronic examination and approval of accounting firms practice application shall be completely facilitated. Online application, online processing, and the whole-procedure electronic management shall be achieved.

The PFD and the PACPA no longer require the applicant to provide materials that can be obtained from the public data platform but may request further confirmation by the applicant.

Article 9 The CPAs and accounting firms must strictly abide by laws and regulations, carry out the business-related code of conduct and professional ethics, and follow the principles of independence, objectivity, and impartiality.

Article 10 Reports lawfully issued by CPAs have certification force pursuant to law. The client and the appropriate agencies shall not refuse to accept reports lawfully issued by the CPAs.

第二章 注册会计师

第十一条 具备下列条件之一，并在中国境内从事审计业务工作二年以上者，可以向省注册会计师协会申请注册：

（一）参加注册会计师全国统一考试成绩合格；

（二）经依法认定或者考核具有注册会计师资格。

香港、澳门特别行政区会计师在向本经济特区申请中国注册会计师证书时，已在港澳从事审计业务工作时间视同在内地从事审计业务工作时间。

第十二条 申请人申请注册，应当通过其所在的会计师事务所，向省注册会计师协会提交注册会计师注册申请表。注册会计师注册申请表应当包含下列内容：

（一）申请人基本情况；

（二）申请人出具的符合注册条件的承诺；

（三）会计师事务所出具的申请人在该会计师事务所专职从业的承诺。

申请人为香港、澳门特别行政区和台湾地区居民的，应当提交港澳台居民居住证或者出入境证件信息。

申请人为外国人的，应当提交护照、签证等信息。

第十三条 省注册会计师协会受理申请后，应当在十五日内决定是否准予注册。准予注册的，向申请人颁发注册会计师证书；不予注册的，应当自决定之日起五日内书面通知申请人并说明理由；申请人有异议的，可以依法申请行政复议或者提起行政诉讼。

Chapter II The CPAs

Article 11 Anyone who meets one of the following conditions and engages in auditing within the territory of China for more than 2 years can apply for registration with the PACPA:

(a) passed the national CPA examination; and

(b) be accredited as a CPA after an accreditation test or assessment pursuant to law.

Where an accountant, from Hong Kong Special Administrative Region ("Hong Kong SAR") or Macao Special Administrative Region ("Macao SAR") applies for the Chinese CPA certificate in the SEZ, the practicing periods of auditing in Hong Kong SAR or Macao SAR shall be deemed equal to those in the Mainland of China.

Article 12 When applying for registration, the applicant shall submit to the PACPA for registration through his/her accounting firm. The submission shall include:

(a) the key information of the applicant;

(b) the promise issued by the applicant on having met the registration requirements; and

(c) the promise issued by the accounting firm for the applicant to practice full-time in the accounting firm.

If the applicant is a resident of Hong Kong SAR, Macao SAR, or Taiwan region, he/she shall submit the residence permit or entry and exit permit.

If the applicant is a foreigner, he/she shall submit a passport, visa, and other information.

Article 13 The PACPA shall decide to grant or reject the application within 15 days of its receipt. If the application is granted, the CPA certificate shall be issued to the applicant; if the application is rejected, the PACPA shall notify the applicant in writing within 5 days of the date of the decision and specify the reason; if the applicant objects, he/she may apply for administrative reconsideration or file an administrative lawsuit pursuant to law.

第十四条 申请人有下列情形之一的，省注册会计师协会不予注册：

（一）不具有完全民事行为能力的；

（二）因受刑事处罚，自刑罚执行完毕之日起至申请注册之日止不满五年的；

（三）因在财务、会计、审计、企业管理或者其他经济管理工作中犯有严重错误受行政处罚、撤职以上处分，自处罚、处分决定之日起至申请注册之日止不满二年的；

（四）受吊销注册会计师证书的处罚，自处罚决定之日起至申请注册之日止不满五年的；

（五）年龄超过七十周岁的；

（六）不在会计师事务所专职执业的；

（七）因以欺骗、贿赂等不正当手段取得注册会计师证书而被撤销注册，自撤销注册决定生效之日起至申请注册之日止不满三年的。

第十五条 已取得注册会计师证书的人员，注册后有下列情形之一的，由省注册会计师协会撤销注册，收回注册会计师证书：

（一）完全丧失民事行为能力的；

（二）受刑事处罚的；

（三）自行停止执行注册会计师业务满一年的；

（四）年龄超过七十周岁的；

（五）不在会计师事务所专职执业的；

（六）以欺骗、贿赂等不正当手段取得注册会计师证书的。

被撤销注册的当事人有异议的，可以自接到撤销注册、收回注册会计师证书的通知书之日起依法申请行政复议或者提起行政诉讼。

Article 14 No applicant shall be allowed to enroll in the PACPA, if:

(a) the applicant does not have complete civil capacity;

(b) the period between the end date of the execution of criminal penalties and the date of the application for registration is less than 5 years;

(c) the applicant committed serious errors related to financial, accounting, auditing, business entities management, or other economic management, which resulted in administrative penalties or dismissal, and the period between the date of penalty or decision to impose the penalty or disciplinary sanction and the date of application for registration is less than 2 years;

(d) the CPA certificate has been voided, and the period between the date of the decision to sanction and the date of application for registration is less than 5 years;

(e) the applicant is over 70 years old;

(f) the applicant does not practice in the accounting firm full-time; or

(g) registration is canceled out of cheating, bribery, and other illegal means to obtain the CPA certificate, and the period between the effective date of the decision to cancel and the date of application for registration is less than 3 years.

Article 15 If anyone, after obtaining the CPA certificate, is under any of the following circumstances, the PACPA shall cancel the registration and withdraw the CPA certificate:

(a) the person completely loses the civil capacity;

(b) the person is subject to criminal penalties;

(c) the person suspends the CPA business independently for 1 year or more;

(d) the person is over 70 years old;

(e) the person does not practice in the accounting firm full-time; or

(f) the person has obtained the CPA certificate via cheating, bribery, or other improper means.

If the party objects to the registration being voided, he/she may, upon the date of receiving the notification of the voiding or withdrawal of the CPA certificate, request administrative reconsideration or file an administrative lawsuit pursuant to law.

被撤销注册的人员可以重新申请注册，但必须符合本条例的有关规定。

第十六条 注册会计师实行任职资格年度检查制度。省注册会计师协会对注册会计师本年度的任职资格情况进行检查。经检查，具有本条例第十五条规定情形的，依法予以撤销。

第十七条 注册会计师离所、转所均须向省注册会计师协会办理登记手续。

第十八条 注册会计师承办下列审计业务：

（一）审查会计报表，出具审计报告；

（二）验证资本，出具验资报告；

（三）办理企业合并、分立、清算事宜中的审计业务，出具有关的报告；

（四）法律、法规规定的其他审计业务。

第十九条 注册会计师可以承办下列相关业务：

（一）参与制定财务会计制度，担任会计顾问，提供会计、财务、税务和经济管理咨询；

（二）办理代理记账业务、涉税专业服务、担任破产清算管理人；

（三）代办申请注册登记，协助拟订合同、章程和其他经济文件；

（四）参与培训财务会计、审计和其他经济管理人员；

（五）办理资产评估业务；

（六）其他相关业务。

Subject to these Regulations, he/she may re-apply for registration after the registration is voided.

Article 16 The CPAs are subject to the annual inspection system for their qualifications. The PACPA shall inspect the qualifications of the CPAs during the one-year period. If after inspection, any of the circumstances specified in Article 15 of these Regulations occur, the CPA certificate shall be voided pursuant to law.

Article 17 The CPAs must register with the PACPA when resigning from their original accounting firm or transferring to other accounting firms.

Article 18 The CPAs conduct the following audit services:

(a) to examine accounting statements and issue audit reports;

(b) to verify capital and issue capital verification reports;

(c) to audit in the merger, division, and liquidation of business entities and issue appropriate reports; and

(d) other business pursuant to laws and regulations.

Article 19 The CPAs may engage in the following practices:

(a) to participate in the creation of the financial accounting system, act as the accounting consultant to advise on accounting, finance, taxation, and economic management;

(b) to conduct bookkeeping, tax-related professional services, and act as a liquidator;

(c) to apply for registration as the agent and assist in drafting contracts, articles of association, and other financial documents;

(d) to participate in the training of financial accounting, auditing, and other economic management personnel;

(e) to conduct asset appraisals; and

(f) to conduct other related business.

第三章 会计师事务所

第二十条 会计师事务所的组织形式为个人会计师事务所、合伙会计师事务所、有限责任会计师事务所。合伙会计师事务所包括普通合伙会计师事务所和特殊普通合伙会计师事务所。

第二十一条 会计师事务所实行首席合伙人（主任会计师）负责制。

第二十二条 个人会计师事务所由个人对其债务承担无限责任；合伙会计师事务所的债务承担方式按照《中华人民共和国合伙企业法》的有关规定执行；有限责任会计师事务所以其全部资产对其债务承担责任。

第二十三条 设立会计师事务所或者分所，应当先取得营业执照，再向省财政部门申请执业许可。

第二十四条 设立会计师事务所或者分所，应当具备下列条件：

（一）个人会计师事务所由一名注册会计师设立并有二名以上注册会计师；普通合伙会计师事务所有二名以上合伙人和二名以上注册会计师；特殊普通合伙会计师事务所有十名以上合伙人和四十名以上注册会计师；有限责任会计师事务所有五名以上股东和五名以上注册会计师；会计师事务所分所有五名以上注册会计师；

（二）合伙人（股东）年龄在七十周岁以下，在中国境内专职从事与职业资格相关的工作连续五年以上，且无不良记录；

（三）合伙人（股东）在境内有稳定住所，最近五年每年在境内居留不少于六个月；

（四）有固定的办公场所及必要的办公设备；

Chapter III Accounting Firms

Article 20 The forms of an accounting firm include sole practitioner, partnership, and limited liability. Partnerships are divided into general partnerships and special general partnerships.

Article 21 The chief partner (chief accountant) is liable for an accounting firm.

Article 22 The sole-proprietorship accounting firm shall assume unlimited liability for its debts. The partnership accounting firm, subject to the Law of the People's Republic of China on Partnership, is liable for its debts. The limited liability accounting firm shall be liable for its debts with all its assets.

Article 23 To set up an accounting firm or branch, the initiator shall first obtain a business license and apply to the PFD for practice approval.

Article 24 To establish an accounting firm or branch, the following conditions shall be met:

(a) the sole practitioner accounting firm, launched by a CPA, with more than 2 CPAs; the general partnership accounting firm, with more than 2 partners and more than 2 CPAs; the special general partnership accounting firm, with more than 10 partners or more than 40 CPAs; the limited liability accounting firm, with more than 5 shareholders and more than 5 CPAs; the branch of the accounting firms, with more than 5 CPAs;

(b) the partner (shareholder), under 70 years of age, engaging in full-time business related to their professional qualifications for more than 5 consecutive years in the territory of China with no negative record;

(c) the partner (shareholder), having a stable residence in China, not less than 6 months in the last five years in the territory of China;

(d) a fixed workplace and necessary working facilities; and

（五）法律、法规规定的其他条件。

取得中国注册会计师证书的香港、澳门特别行政区永久居民申请成为会计师事务所合伙人时，已在港澳从事审计业务工作时间视同在内地从事审计业务工作时间。

第二十五条 省财政部门应当自受理会计师事务所或者分所的执业许可申请之日起十五日内作出准予许可或者不予许可的书面答复。准予许可的，应当依法颁发执业许可证书；不予许可的，应当说明理由。

第二十六条 会计师事务所或者分所未能持续符合执业许可条件的，由省财政部门责令其在六十日内整改。整改期满，仍不符合条件的，予以撤销执业许可。

第四章 执业管理

第二十七条 注册会计师承办业务，由其所在的会计师事务所统一受理并与委托人签订委托合同。

第二十八条 会计师事务所、注册会计师执行业务，应当按照执业准则、规则确定的工作程序出具报告。

第二十九条 会计师事务所、注册会计师在执行业务过程中，发现下列情况，应当向委托单位明确指出，并按照执业准则的有关要求进行披露：

（一）以隐瞒实际情况，伪造、变造凭证、帐目或者报表等手段作不实报告的；

（二）有关人员利用虚报冒领或者其他不正当手段谋取私利的；

(e) others provided by laws and regulations.

Where a permanent resident of Hong Kong SAR or Macao SAR, after obtaining the Chinese CPA certificate, applies as a partner of an accounting firm, the working period of auditing in Hong Kong SAR or Macao SAR shall be deemed equal to that in the Mainland of China.

Article 25 The PFD shall respond to an applicant in writing for approval or rejection within 15 days of the date of accepting the application for the permit of establishing an accounting firm or branch. If granted, the permit shall be issued pursuant to law; if rejected, the reasons shall be specified.

Article 26 If an accounting firm or branch fails to continuously comply with the practice permit, the PFD shall require corrections within 60 days. If such firm or branch still fails to meet the requirements after the expiration of the correction period, the practice permit shall be voided.

Chapter IV Practice Management

Article 27 An accounting firm is liable for its CPAs' business by uniform acceptance and shall execute an agency appointment contract with the principal.

Article 28 The accounting firms and CPAs, in the course of accounting performance, shall issue reports pursuant to the business code of conduct.

Article 29 The accounting firms and CPAs, in the course of accounting performance, upon the discovery of the following circumstances, shall clearly point out to the principal, and disclose such pursuant to the business code of conduct requirements:

(a) false reports involving concealment, forging or altering vouchers, accounts or statements, and other means;

(b) the appropriate personnel make false claims or use other improper means for personal benefits;

（三）在财务收支和会计处理中，有明显违反国家法律、法规和会计制度规定行为的；

（四）采取的会计政策和处理方法，有损相关方经济利益的；

（五）法律、法规规定应当指出的其他情况。

第三十条 会计师事务所、注册会计师执行业务出具报告时，不得有下列行为：

（一）明知委托人对重要事项的财务会计处理与国家有关规定相抵触，而不予指明；

（二）明知委托人的财务会计处理会直接损害报告使用人或者其他利害关系人的利益，而予以隐瞒或者作不实的报告；

（三）明知委托人的财务会计处理会导致报告使用人或者其他利害关系人产生重大误解，而不予指明；

（四）明知委托人的会计报表的重要事项有其他不实的内容，而不予指明。

对委托人有前款所列行为，会计师事务所、注册会计师按照执业准则、规则应当知道的，适用前款规定。

第三十一条 会计师事务所、注册会计师应当对所出具的报告的真实性、合法性负责。

会计师事务所应当按照有关规定建立职业风险基金、办理职业保险，用于执行业务时造成的损害赔偿。

第三十二条 会计师事务所、注册会计师对执行业务过程中知悉的商业秘密负有保密义务，但委托人同意或者法律、法规另有规定的除外。

(c) in the financial revenue and expenditure and accounting process, there are obvious violations of national laws, regulations, and the accounting system;

(d) the accounting policies and processing methods adopted are detrimental to the economic interests of interested parties; and

(e) others that should be pointed out pursuant to laws and regulations.

Article 30 No accounting firm or CPA shall be allowed to do any of the following when issuing a business report:

(a) refuse to specify after learning that the principal's financial accounting processing of important items is contrary to applicable national regulations;

(b) conceal or make a false report after learning that the financial accounting processing of the principal directly will damage the user of the report or other interested parties;

(c) refuse to specify after learning that the financial and accounting processing of the client will lead to a major misunderstanding of the user of the report or other interested parties; or

(d) refuse to specify after learning that other important items in the principal's accounting statements have been falsified.

The rules of the preceding paragraph shall apply to the circumstances listed in the preceding paragraph, which the accounting firms and CPAs shall be made aware of in the business code of conduct.

Article 31 The accounting firms and CPAs shall account for the authenticity and validity of the reports issued.

The accounting firms shall, pursuant to applicable rules, establish occupational risk funds and provide occupational insurance for indemnification against damages out of the performance.

Article 32 The accounting firms and CPAs shall keep confidential the business secrets learned in the course of performance, except as agreed by the client or otherwise provided by laws and regulations.

第三十三条 会计师事务所受理业务，不受行政区域、行业的限制，但法律、法规另有规定的除外。

第三十四条 会计师事务所不得有下列行为：

（一）向业务委托单位及其人员支付或者变相支付业务介绍费、佣金、手续费或者回扣等；

（二）采取不正当价格、诋毁同行、强迫、欺诈、贿赂等手段招揽业务；

（三）售卖注册会计师业务报告；

（四）违反法律、法规规定的其他行为。

第三十五条 注册会计师不得有下列行为：

（一）索取、收受委托合同约定以外的酬金和财物，或者利用执行业务之便，谋取其他不正当利益；

（二）允许他人以本人名义执行业务；

（三）同时在两个或者两个以上的会计师事务所执行业务；

（四）在执行审计业务期间，违反规定买卖被审计单位的股票、债券或者购买被审计单位、个人的其他财产；

（五）接受委托催收债款；

（六）对其能力进行广告宣传以招揽业务；

（七）提示、协助委托人或者被审计单位编制虚假会计资料；

（八）违反法律、法规规定的其他行为。

第三十六条 禁止国家机关和相关单位及其工作人员利用职权限定或者干预委托人委托会计师事务所办理业务。

第三十七条 会计师事务所应当建立完善的档案保管制度。

Article 33 The accounting firms' business acceptance is not subject to the limits of administrative regions and industries, except as otherwise provided by laws and regulations.

Article 34 No accounting firm shall be allowed:

(a) to pay, either directly or indirectly, brokerage fees, commissions, processing fees, or kickbacks to principals and their personnel;

(b) to solicit by unfair price, slander of peers, coercion, fraud, and bribery;

(c) to sell CPAs' reports; or

(d) other acts in violation of the laws and regulations.

Article 35 No CPA shall be allowed:

(a) to ask for and accept compensation or property other than those specified in the agency appointment contract, or seek other illegitimate interests by taking advantage of the performance;

(b) to allow others to practice on their behalf;

(c) to practice in two or more accounting firms at the same time;

(d) in violation of audit guidelines, purchase and sell stocks or bonds of the audited entity, or purchase other property belonging to an audited organization or individual;

(e) to accept authorization to collect debts;

(f) to advertise their capabilities to attract business;

(g) to prompt or assist the principal or the audited organization to prepare false accounting materials; or

(h) other acts in violation of the laws and regulations.

Article 36 The national appropriate agencies and organizations and their staff concerned are prohibited from taking advantage of their authority to determine or interfere with the business delegated by the principal to the accounting firms.

Article 37 An accounting firm shall implement a sound record-keeping system.

会计师事务所解散、撤销时，应当清理好档案，移交档案保管机构保管。

第五章 注册会计师协会

第三十八条 省注册会计师协会的主要职责：

（一）依法制定、修改注册会计师协会章程及行业管理制度；

（二）组织实施注册会计师考试工作；

（三）核准注册会计师注册；

（四）对注册会计师任职资格、执业质量进行检查，并对违反执业准则和职业道德规范的行为予以惩戒；

（五）组织开展继续教育培训；

（六）组织开展同业间的业务交流活动；

（七）支持会员依法执业，维护其合法权益；

（八）法律、法规规定的其他职责。

第三十九条 省财政、民政等相关部门应当加强对省注册会计师协会的监督管理。

省注册会计师协会作出的不符合法律、法规的决定，省财政部门有权予以撤销。

第六章 法律责任

第四十条 未取得注册会计师证书的人员、未取得会计师事务所执业许可证书的机构承办注册会计师审计业务的，其出具的报告无效，由省

If the accounting firm is dissolved or voided, it shall clean up the files and assign them to the archiving agency.

Chapter V Certificated Public Accountants Association

Article 38 The main functions and duties of the PACPA:

(a) to draft and revise the PACPA articles of association and industry management system pursuant to law;

(b) to organize and conduct the CPA examination;

(c) to approve the registration of CPAs;

(d) to review the qualifications and practices of the CPAs, and penalize violations of the business code of conducts and professional ethics;

(e) to organize further education and training;

(f) to organize business exchanges among peers;

(g) support members to practice pursuant to law and safeguard their legal rights; and

(h) other duties pursuant to the laws and regulations.

Article 39 The provincial finance, civil affairs, and other appropriate agencies shall improve the regulatory oversight of the PACPA.

The PFD is entitled to void the decisions contrary to the regulations and guidelines issued by the PACPA.

Chapter VI Legal Liability

Article 40 Where anyone who has not obtained the CPA certificate, or, an organization that has not obtained an accounting firm practice permit conducts a CPA audit, the report they issue

财政部门责令停止违法行为，没收违法所得，并处以违法所得一倍以上五倍以下的罚款。

第四十一条 会计师事务所违反本条例第二十三条规定，未经省财政部门批准，擅自设立分所的，由省财政部门责令撤销分所；情节严重的，由省财政部门责令会计师事务所暂停经营业务一至三个月。

第四十二条 注册会计师违反本条例第二十七条规定的，由省财政部门给予警告；情节严重的，由省财政部门责令暂停执行业务三至六个月或者吊销注册会计师证书。

第四十三条 会计师事务所违反本条例第二十八条、第二十九条、第三十条规定的，由省财政部门给予警告，没收违法所得，并处以违法所得一倍以上五倍以下的罚款；情节严重的，由省财政部门责令暂停经营业务或者吊销执业许可证书。

注册会计师违反本条例第二十八条、第二十九条、第三十条规定的，由省财政部门给予警告；情节严重的，由省财政部门责令暂停执行业务或者吊销注册会计师证书。

会计师事务所、注册会计师违反本条例第二十八条、第二十九条、第三十条规定，给有关单位、个人造成损失的，应当承担赔偿责任。

第四十四条 会计师事务所违反本条例第三十一条第二款规定的，由省财政部门责令改正，暂停经营业务一至三个月，并对首席合伙人（主任会计师）给予警告。

第四十五条 会计师事务所违反本条例第三十四条规定的，由省财政部门给予警告，没收违法所得，并处以违法所得一倍以上三倍以下的罚款；情节严重的，由省财政部门责令暂停经营业务一至三个月。

shall be invalid. The PFD shall require it to stop the illegal acts, confiscate the illegal income, and impose a fine of more than 1 time and less than 5 times the illegal income.

Article 41 If an accounting firm violates Article 23 and establishes a branch without the approval of the PFD, the PFD shall require it to void the branch. If the circumstances are serious, PFD shall require the firm to suspend business for 1 to 3 months.

Article 42 Any CPA who violates Article 27 shall be given a warning by the PFD. If the circumstances are serious, the PFD shall require the CPA to suspend practicing for 3 to 6 months or void the CPA certificate.

Article 43 If an accounting firm violates the rules of Article 28, 29 or 30 of these Regulations, the PFD shall issue a warning, confiscate the illegal income and impose a fine of more than 1 multiple and less than 5 multiples the illegal income. If the circumstances are serious, the PFD shall require the firm to suspend business or void its practice permit.

Any CPA who violates Article 28, 29 or 30, shall be given a warning by the PFD. If the circumstances are serious, the PFD shall require the CPA to suspend practice or void the CPA certificate.

Any accounting firm or CPA who violates Article 28, 29 or 30 and causes losses to any organization or an individual concerned shall be held liable for indemnification.

Article 44 Any accounting firm that violates Paragraph 2 of Article 31 shall be required to remediate by the PFD and suspend business for 1 to 3 months, and a warning shall be issued to the chief partner (chief accountant).

Article 45 Accounting firms who violate Article 34 shall be issued a warning by the PFD, the illegal income shall be confiscated, and a fine of more than the illegal income and less than 3 times such income shall be imposed. If the circumstances are serious, the PFD shall require it to suspend its practice for 1 to 3 months.

第四十六条 注册会计师违反本条例第三十五条规定的，由省财政部门给予警告，没收违法所得，并处以违法所得一倍以上三倍以下的罚款；情节严重的，由省财政部门责令暂停执行业务或者吊销注册会计师证书。

第四十七条 有关单位、个人违反本条例第三十六条规定的，由其上级主管部门责令改正，对直接负责的主管人员和其他直接责任人员依法给予处分；有违法所得的，由省财政部门没收违法所得。

第四十八条 注册会计师累计受两次警告处分的，由省财政部门责令暂停执行业务三至六个月；会计师事务所累计受两次警告处分的，由省财政部门责令暂停经营业务一至三个月。

第四十九条 省财政部门、省注册会计师协会及其工作人员违反本条例有关规定，不依法履行职责或者存在贪污贿赂、滥用职权、玩忽职守、权力寻租、利益输送、徇私舞弊等职务违法行为的，对直接负责的主管人员和其他直接责任人员依法给予处分。

第五十条 违反本条例规定，构成犯罪的，依法追究刑事责任。

第五十一条 违反本条例规定，本条例未设定处罚，相关法律、法规已有处罚规定的，依照其规定处罚。

第七章 附 则

第五十二条 海南经济特区以外的本省行政区域范围内的注册会计师管理工作，参照本条例规定执行。

第五十三条 本条例自 2019 年 9 月 1 日起施行。《海南省注册会计师条例》同时废止。

Article 46 Any CPA who violates Article 35 shall be given a warning by the PFD, the illegal income shall be confiscated, and a fine of more than the illegal income and less than 3 times such income shall be imposed. If the circumstances are serious, the PFD shall require the CPA to suspend practice or void the CPA certificate.

Article 47 Any entity or individual who violates Article 36 shall be required to remediate by the ranking competent agencies, and the person directly in charge and other employees directly liable shall be penalized pursuant to law. The PFD shall confiscate the illegal income (if any).

Article 48 Any CPA who receives two warnings shall be required to suspend practice for 3 to 6 months by the PFD. Any accounting firm which has been warned twice in total shall be demanded to suspend practice for 1 to 3 months by the PFD.

Article 49 Where the PFD, the PACPAs or their staff, in violation of these Regulations, do not perform their duties pursuant to law, or there are illegal acts such as corruption, bribery, abuse of position, dereliction of duty, rent seeking, *quid pro quo*, playing favoritism and committing irregularities, and other noncompliance, the person directly in charge and other employees directly liable shall be penalized pursuant to law.

Article 50 Anyone, in violation of these Regulations and committing a crime, shall assume the criminal liability pursuant to the laws and regulations.

Article 51 Applicable law shall control where these Regulations are violated but no sanctions are specified by these Regulations.

Chapter VII Supplementary Provisions

Article 52 These Regulations shall apply *mutatis mutandis* to CPAs out of Hainan SEZ but within the administrative region of this Province.

Article 53 These Regulations shall come into force as of September 1, 2019. The Regulations of Hainan Province on Certificated Public Accountants shall be repealed at the same time.

海南经济特区道路旅游客运管理若干规定

Rules of Hainan Special Economic Zone on the Administration of Road Passenger Transport

海南经济特区道路旅游客运管理若干规定

（2012 年 3 月 30 日海南省第四届人民代表大会常务委员会第二十九次会议通过　根据 2015 年 9 月 25 日海南省第五届人民代表大会常务委员会第十七次会议《关于修改海南经济特区道路旅游客运管理若干规定决定》修正　2018 年 12 月 1 日海南省第六届人民代表大会常务委员会第七次会议修订）

第一条　为了适应海南全域旅游发展的需要，维护道路旅游客运市场秩序，提高道路旅游客运服务质量，保障道路旅游客运安全和当事人的合法权益，促进道路旅游客运事业的健康发展，根据《中华人民共和国道路运输条例》等有关法律、法规，结合本经济特区实际，制定本规定。

第二条　本规定所称道路旅游客运，是指以运送进行游览、度假、休闲、商务、通勤等活动的旅客为目的，由经营者提供旅游客运车辆和驾驶劳务，按照约定的起始地、目的地和路线行驶，按行驶里程或者包用时间计费并支付费用的道路包车客运方式，包括包车客运和非定线旅游客运。

第三条　县级以上人民政府交通主管部门负责本行政区域内道路旅游客运的监督管理工作。县级以上道路运输管理机构负责具体实施道路旅游客运管理工作。

Rules of Hainan Special Economic Zone on the Administration of Road Passenger Transport

(Adopted at the 29th Session of the Standing Committee of the 4th Hainan Provincial People's Congress on March 30, 2012; revised pursuant to the Decision on Amending Rules of Hainan Special Economic Zone on the Administration of Road Passenger Transport issued at the 17th Session of the Standing Committee of the 5th Hainan Provincial People's Congress on September 25, 2015; revised at the 7th Session of the Standing Committee of the 6th Hainan Provincial People's Congress on December 1, 2018)

Article 1 These Rules are enacted pursuant to the Regulations of the People's Republic of China on Road Transport and other applicable laws and regulations, in combination with the actual circumstances of this special economic zone, in order to meet the needs of tourism development in Hainan, maintain the market order, facilitate the service, ensure the safety of road passenger transport and the legal rights of the parties concerned, and promote the sound development of road passenger transport.

Article 2 "Road passenger transport", for the purpose of these Rules, refers to the chartered road passenger transport engaged in sightseeing, vacation, leisure, business, commuting, and other activities, where the operator(s) provide(s) transport vehicles and driving services in conformity with the agreed starting place, destination, and route, and charge the fees based the mileage or time of package, including chartered passenger transport and non-scheduled passenger transport.

Article 3 The competent transportation agency of the people's governments at or above the county level shall be responsible for the regulatory oversight of road passenger transport within their respective administrative areas. Road transport administrative agencies at or above the county level shall be responsible for the specific enforcement of road passenger transport management.

旅游、公安、发展改革、市场监督管理、应急管理等有关部门应当按照各自的职责，做好道路旅游客运管理工作。

第四条 省人民政府交通主管部门应当会同有关部门组织编制全省道路旅游客运发展规划，报省人民政府批准后实施。

省道路运输管理机构应当定期向社会公布本经济特区内的道路旅游客运运力投放、主要客流流向和流量等情况。

第五条 道路旅游客运管理遵循公平、公正、公开、高效、便民、安全的原则，维护良好的市场秩序。

道路旅游客运经营者应当依法经营、诚实守信、公平竞争。任何单位和个人不得封锁或者垄断道路旅游客运市场。

第六条 从事道路旅游客运经营，应当办理商事登记，取得道路运输经营许可证，投入运营的车辆应当取得营运证。

申请从事道路旅游客运经营的，应当具备下列条件：

（一）申请人应当具有企业法人资格；

（二）有与其经营业务相适应并经检测合格的客运车辆：

1. 车辆类型等级应当达到营运客车类型划分及等级评定标准规定的中级以上，其中高一级以上的车辆使用年限不超过八年，中级车辆使用年限不超过六年；

2. 车辆技术等级应当达到道路运输车辆技术等级划分和评定要求标准规定的一级技术等级；

3. 车型的燃料消耗量限值应当符合营运客车燃料消耗量限值及测量方法标准的相关规定；

Agencies of tourism, public security, development and reform, market regulation, emergency administration, and other appropriate agencies shall enforce the management of road passenger transport based on their respective duties.

Article 4 The competent transportation agency of the provincial people's government shall, together with other appropriate agencies, organize the preparation of the provincial development plan of road passenger transport, which shall be submitted to the provincial people's government for approval before enforcement.

The provincial road transport administrative office shall periodically publish the deployment of road passenger transport capacity, the direction of the main passenger flow, and its rate in this special economic zone.

Article 5 The administration of road passenger transport follows the principles of fairness, impartiality, openness, high efficiency, convenience, and safety to maintain good market order.

Road passenger transport operators should operate pursuant to law, be honest and trustworthy, and compete fairly. No entity or individual may block or monopolize the road passenger transport market.

Article 6 Before enrolling in the road passenger transport business, the road passenger transport operator shall apply for business registration and obtain a road transport operating permit. Vehicles put into operation shall obtain business licenses.

To apply for enrolling in road passenger transport business, the following conditions shall be met:

(a) the applicant shall be a qualified organization with legal personality;

(b) the applicant shall have passenger vehicles suitable for their business and having passed the test:

(i) the type and grade of the vehicle should reach the intermediate or above level specified in the operating bus type and rating. The service life of vehicles at high or above level is no more than 8 years, and the service life of intermediate vehicles is no more than 6 years;

(ii) the technical level of vehicles should reach the level I technical standard specified in the technical standard rating and assessment requirements for road transport vehicles;

(iii) the fuel consumption limit of the vehicle type shall comply with applicable fuel consumption limit and measurement method rules for operating buses;

4. 车辆设施应当符合旅游客车设施与服务规范标准的相关规定；

5. 客运车辆数量在三十辆以上且客位三百个以上；

（三）有与其经营规模相适应的停车场地和固定办公场所；

（四）有符合规定的从事道路旅游客运经营的管理人员和驾驶员；

（五）有健全的安全生产管理制度。

经批准的道路旅游客运经营者在经营期间应当具备本条第二款规定的条件，并在许可的范围内从事经营活动。

第七条 鼓励道路旅游客运经营者实行规模化、集约化、网络化、品牌化经营。

道路旅游客运经营者应当按照本省相关规划分阶段、分步骤使用新能源汽车和清洁能源汽车。

第八条 申请在本经济特区从事道路旅游客运经营的，应当向省道路运输管理机构提出申请。省道路运输管理机构应当自受理申请之日起二十日内作出许可或者不予许可的决定。予以许可的，向申请人颁发道路运输经营许可证，注明在本经济特区范围内经营，并向申请人投入运输的车辆配发车辆营运证；不予许可的，应当书面通知申请人并说明理由。

本规定实施前依法取得包车客运经营许可证和车辆营运证的客运经营者，可以向省道路运输管理机构申请从事道路旅游客运经营。省道路运输管理机构经审核符合本规定第六条的，应当为其换发道路运输经营许可证和车辆营运证，并可以在原批准期限内在本经济特区从事道路旅游客运经营。

(iv) vehicle facilities shall comply with applicable passenger bus facility and service rules; and

(v) the number of passenger vehicles is more than 30 and the number of seats is more than 300;

(c) the applicant has a parking lot and a fixed office space suitable for its business scale;

(d) the applicant has a qualified manager and driver engaged in road passenger transport business; and

(e) a sound safety production administration system.

Approved road passenger transport operators shall meet the conditions provided in Paragraph 2 of this Article during the operation and engage in business activities within the permitted scope.

Article 7 Road passenger transport operators are encouraged to conduct large-scale, intensive, network and brand management.

Road passenger transport operators shall use new energy vehicles and clean energy vehicles in stages and steps pursuant to the applicable provincial plans.

Article 8 To apply for road passenger transport business in this special economic zone, the party concerned shall apply to the provincial road transport administrative agency. The provincial road transport administrative agency shall decide to grant or reject within 20 days of the date of accepting the application. If the application is granted, such agency shall issue the road transport operating permit to the applicant and note that the operating scope is limited within this special economic zone, and the vehicle operating license shall be distributed to the vehicles that the applicant has put into transportation. If the application is rejected, the agency shall notify the applicant in written form and specify the causes.

Any passenger transport operator, who has obtained chartered passenger transport operating permit and vehicle operating permit pursuant to law before the enforcement of the rules, may apply to the provincial road transport administrative agency for enrolling in the road passenger transport business. Where provincial road transport administrative agency considers it under Article 6 of these Rules, such agency shall renew the road transport operating permit and vehicle operating certificate, and such operator is entitled to enroll in road passenger transport business in the special economic zone within the original approval period.

第九条 道路旅游客运经营期限为六年到八年。省道路运输管理机构在作出道路旅游客运经营许可时，应当根据车辆技术和类型等级等因素明确具体的经营期限。经营期限届满需要延续经营的，道路旅游客运经营者应当在期限届满前六十日重新提出申请。

第十条 禁止未取得道路运输经营许可证和车辆营运证的经营者从事道路旅游客运经营。旅行社、其他单位或者个人（以下统称承租人）不得向未取得道路运输经营许可证或者车辆营运证的经营者租用车辆。

第十一条 道路旅游客运经营者在道路旅游客运经营期限内，应当拥有道路旅游客运车辆所有权，禁止挂靠经营、转包经营。

禁止转让、变相转让或者出租、出借道路运输经营许可证和车辆营运证。

第十二条 道路旅游客运经营者应当向旅客提供连续运输服务，不得擅自暂停、终止道路旅游客运经营。

道路旅游客运经营者需要暂停、终止经营的，应当提前三十日向原许可机关提出申请。经批准暂停经营的，道路旅游客运经营者应当在十日内将道路运输经营许可证、车辆营运证交回原许可机关；经批准终止经营的，由原许可机关注销其道路运输经营许可证、车辆营运证。

道路旅游客运经营者在取得道路运输经营许可证、车辆营运证后，无正当理由超过六个月不投入运营或者运营后连续六个月以上停运的，视为自动终止道路旅游客运经营，由原许可机关注销其道路运输经营许可证或者车辆营运证。

Article 9 Road passenger transport business period lasts for 6 to 8 years. The provincial road transport administrative agency shall clarify the specific operating period based on factors including vehicle technology and type grade upon issuing the road passenger transport operating permit. If the operation period expires and needs to be continued, the road passenger transport operator shall reapply 60 days before the expiration of the period.

Article 10 Any operator who has not obtained the road transport operating permit and vehicle business certificate is prohibited from enrolling in the road passenger transport business. Travel agencies, other organizations, or individuals (hereinafter referred to as the "lessee") shall not rent vehicles from such operators.

Article 11 Road passenger transport operator shall take the ownership of road passenger transport vehicles within the operating period of road passenger transport and is banned from affiliate operation or subcontract operation.

The transfer, assignment, or indirect lease, or lending of road transport operating permit and vehicle operating permit is prohibited.

Article 12 Road passenger transport operator shall provide continuous transport services to passengers and shall not suspend or terminate the operation of road passenger transport with no authorization.

Road passenger transport operator, in need of suspending or terminating the business, shall apply to the original permitting agency 30 days in advance. Being approved to suspend, the road passenger transport operator shall return the road transport operating permit and vehicle operating permit to the original permitting agency within 10 days. Being approved to terminate, the original permitting agency shall cancel its road transport operating permit and vehicle operating permit.

If the road passenger transport operator fails to put into operation for more than 6 months without justification after obtaining the road transport operating permit and vehicle operating permit, such operator is deemed as automatically terminating the road passenger transport business, and the original permitting agency shall cancel its road transport operating permit or vehicle operating permit.

第十三条 道路旅游客运经营者应当按照以下要求规范经营：

（一）对客运车辆和驾驶员进行统一管理和调度；

（二）通过企业银行账户统一进行收支管理和成本核算，依法缴纳税费；

（三）依法与所聘从业人员签订劳动合同，为其足额发放工资和缴纳各项社会保险费。

未经道路旅游客运经营者统一调派，驾驶员不得私自提供道路旅游运输服务。

第十四条 道路旅游客运经营者是本单位安全生产工作的责任主体，应当依法加强安全管理，遵守以下安全管理规定：

（一）完善安全生产条件，健全和落实安全生产责任制，设置安全生产管理机构或者配备专职安全生产管理人员；

（二）加强对从业人员的安全生产教育、培训和考核，未经安全生产教育和培训考核合格的从业人员不得上岗作业；

（三）依法对客运车辆、驾驶员、运营过程等进行安全隐患排查，及时消除安全隐患；

（四）加强营运车辆维护、技术状况检查、定期检测等安全检查，确保车辆符合机动车国家安全技术标准。未经安全检查或者安全检查不合格的车辆不得载客运营；

（五）按照相关规定报告道路旅游客运事故情况。

第十五条 驾驶员有下列情形之一的，道路旅游客运经营者不得聘用其驾驶客运车辆：

（一）无有效的机动车驾驶证或者从业资格证件的；

（二）运输服务诚信考核不合格或者被列入黑名单的；

Article 13 Road passenger transport operator shall standardize their operations pursuant to the following requirements:

(a) to unify management and scheduling of passenger vehicles and drivers;

(b) to unify revenue and expenditure management and cost accounting via business entity bank accounts, and pay taxes and fees pursuant to law; and

(c) to sign labor contracts with employees pursuant to law, and pay full wages and social insurance premiums for them.

Without the unified deployment by road passenger transport operators, drivers are not allowed to provide road transport services without permission.

Article 14 Road passenger transport operator takes the first account for the safety production and should strengthen safety management pursuant to law and abide by the following safety administrative regulations:

(a) to improve conditions for safe production, promote and take on a responsibility system for safe production, set up safety production administrative office or provide full-time safety production management personnel;

(b) to strengthen the safety education, training, and assessment of employees, and employees, not passing the safety education and training assessment, shall be not allowed for the posts;

(c) to remove potential safety hazards for passenger vehicles, drivers, operating processes in a timely manner after the investigation pursuant to law;

(d) improve the operation of vehicle maintenance, technical inspection, regular inspection, and other safety inspections, to ensure that vehicles meet the national security technical standards for motor vehicles. Vehicles that have not completed the safety inspection or that fail the safety inspection shall not be operated; and

(e) report the road passenger transport accidents pursuant to law.

Article 15 Any driver who is under one of the following circumstances, shall not be employed by a road passenger transport operator to drive passenger vehicles:

(a) no valid motor vehicle license or qualification certificate;

(b) the result of faith assessment for transportation service is unqualified or the driver is put onto the blacklist;

（三）三年内有重大以上交通责任事故记录的；

（四）三年内有一个记分周期交通违法记满十二分的；

（五）吸食、注射毒品或者服用依赖性精神药品成瘾尚未完全戒除的；

（六）法律法规规定其他不得驾驶客运车辆的情形。

道路旅游客运经营者发现已聘用的驾驶员具有前款规定情形的，应当调离驾驶岗位；情节严重的，应当依法予以辞退。

国家对驾驶员从事旅游客运经营有更严格规定的，从其规定。

第十六条 道路旅游客运驾驶员在执行运输任务前应当对车辆进行安全检查，禁止车辆带故障运行，严格遵守道路交通安全法律法规的相关规定。

驾驶员应当向旅客告知乘车的安全注意事项。导游应当配合驾驶员进行安全检查，指导旅客做好系安全带等安全防范工作。

发生危及旅客人身安全的情形时，驾驶员应当采取必要的措施，立即报告危险发生地道路运输管理机构和所属道路旅游客运经营者，并可以要求承租人、导游和旅客配合处理，防止人员或者客运车辆受损失。发生人身伤亡等安全事故的，驾驶员、导游或者旅客应当立即报警，并向所属道路旅游客运经营者和相关部门报告，采取应急措施，配合有关部门进行救助。

第十七条 道路旅游客运经营者应当为旅客投保承运人责任险。

鼓励道路旅游客运经营者共同建立道路旅游客运交通安全互助金，提高抵御交通事故风险的能力。

(c) recorded with major or above traffic accident within 3 years;

(d) traffic violations have been scored 12 points within a recording cycle in 3 years;

(e) addiction to smoking, injecting drugs, or taking dependent psychotropic drugs has not been completely rehabilitated; or

(f) other circumstances leading to the disqualification to drive passenger vehicles provided by laws and regulations.

Road passenger transport operator, finding that the hired driver is under the circumstances specified in the preceding paragraph, should remove such driver. If the circumstances are serious, such a driver shall be dismissed pursuant to law.

If there are stricter national regulations concerning drivers engaging in the passenger transport business, such regulations shall prevail.

Article 16 Road passenger driver should carry out safety inspections on vehicles before driving and is banned from running vehicles with faults, and shall strictly abide by applicable law on road traffic safety.

The driver should inform passengers of the safety precautions. A tour guide should cooperate with the driver to carry out safety inspections and lead passengers to do safety precautions like fastening seat belts.

When the personal safety of passengers is under threat, the driver shall take all necessary action, immediately make a report to the road transport administrative agency, and may require the lessee, the tour guide, and passengers to jointly prevent the loss of personnel or passenger vehicles. In case of safety accidents such as personal injury or death, the driver, the tour guide, or passenger shall immediately report to the police, the road passenger transport operator, and appropriate agencies, take emergency measures, and assist appropriate agencies.

Article 17 Road passenger transport operators shall ensure the carrier liability insurance for passengers.

Road passenger transport operators are encouraged to jointly establish mutual funds for road passenger transport safety and promote the capacity to downgrade traffic accident risks.

第十八条 道路旅游客运价格实行市场调节价。道路旅游客运经营者应当依据客运车辆的车型等级、社会平均成本、市场供求状况等要素，合理制定价格。

道路旅游客运经营者应当明码标价，公平交易，不得以排挤竞争对手为目的，以低于成本的价格、贿赂承租人等不正当竞争的方式从事道路旅游客运经营。

交通、旅游部门应当引导道路旅游客运经营者和承租人建立互信互认的费用结算方式。鼓励道路旅游客运行业协会和相关旅游行业协会协商建立道路旅游客运运费结算方式。

第十九条 道路旅游客运经营者应当在营运车辆外部的适当位置喷涂旅游客运标识和经营者名称或者其标识，在车厢内显著位置公示经营者和驾驶员信息、监督投诉电话。

道路旅游客运经营者应当为旅客提供良好的乘车环境，保证车辆设备、设施齐全有效，保持车辆整洁、卫生，并采取必要的措施防止在运输过程中发生侵害旅客人身、财产安全的违法行为。

营运车辆因故障不能正常行驶时，道路旅游客运经营者应当及时更换其他车辆，并不得加收任何费用。

第二十条 道路旅游客运经营者应当与承租人签订客运合同，明确起始地、目的地和线路等运行计划、服务标准、双方权利义务等内容。

道路旅游客运经营者及其从业人员应当按照客运合同提供运输服务，不得中途擅自将旅客交给他人运输或者终止运输，不得擅自变更运行计划和营运车辆。

Article 18 Road passenger transport prices are based on regulated market prices. Road passenger transport operators should reasonably set prices based on the factors such as the type grade of passenger vehicles, the average social cost, and the market supply and demand.

Road passenger transport operator shall clearly mark the price and make fair trade and shall not engage in road passenger transport business for the purpose of crowding out competitors via unfair competition like setting a price below the costs or bribing the lessee.

Transportation and tourism agencies should guide road passenger transport operators and the lessee to establish mutual trust and mutual recognition of cost settlement methods. Road passenger transport industry associations and related tourism industry associations are encouraged to negotiate the establishment of freight settlement methods concerning road passenger transport.

Article 19 Road passenger transport operator shall spray passenger transport marks and operator's name or mark at appropriate positions outside the operating vehicles, publish operator's and driver's information, and the complaint hotlines in a prominent location within the cabin.

Road passenger transport operator shall provide passengers with a good environment, ensure that the vehicles are fully and effectively equipped, keep the vehicles clean and sanitary, and take necessary measures to prevent illegality against the person and property of passengers during transportation.

Where an operating vehicle fails to run normally, road passenger transport operators should promptly replace such with another vehicle at no extra cost.

Article 20 Road passenger transport operator shall sign a passenger transport contract with the lessee, and state matters including without limitation the operation plan, service standards, rights, and obligations of both parties.

Road passenger transport operator and its employees shall provide transportation services pursuant to the passenger transport contract. Without prior authorization, such operator shall not outsource passenger transportation or terminate the transportation service and not change the operation plan and operating vehicles.

道路旅游客运经营者及其从业人员未按照约定线路运输增加运输费用的，承租人有权拒绝支付增加的运输费用。道路旅游客运经营者擅自降低营运车辆等级的，应当退还多收的费用；提高车辆等级的，不得加收费用。

旅行社和旅客经协商依法变更运行计划的，道路旅游客运经营者及其从业人员应当按照变更后的运行计划提供运输服务，所增加的费用由旅行社和旅客承担。客运合同另有约定的除外。

鼓励道路旅游客运经营者利用物联网、移动互联网技术，为承租人提供网上租车等服务。

第二十一条 道路旅游客运经营者及其从业人员在提供运输服务时，不得有下列行为：

（一）损害国家利益、民族尊严、人格尊严及违反社会公德；

（二）不尊重旅客宗教信仰和民族风俗；

（三）擅自搭载无关的人员；

（四）诱导或者安排旅客参加黄、赌、毒等活动；

（五）刁难、殴打、谩骂旅客或者导游；

（六）欺骗、胁迫旅客消费；

（七）向旅客索要小费，收取旅游景区、饭店、购物场所、娱乐场所等经营者给予的财物；

（八）法律、法规禁止的其他行为。

第二十二条 旅行社和导游应当履行旅游客运合同的约定，不得擅自变更运行计划；擅自变更的，道路旅游客运经营者及其从业人员和旅客有权拒绝，并可以向有关部门和导游所在的旅行社举报。

If the road passenger transport operator or its employees increases the transportation cost in violation of the agreed line transportation, the lessee is entitled to refuse to pay the increased transportation cost. Road passenger transport operator, downgrading the level of operating vehicles without authorization, shall refund the overcharged fees; upgrading the level of vehicles, no extra fees shall be charged.

If a travel agency and passengers change the operation plan after consultation pursuant to law, the road passenger transport operator and its employees shall provide transportation services based on the changed operation plan, and the increased expenses shall be assumed by the travel agency and passengers unless otherwise agreed in the passenger transport contract.

Road passenger transport operators are encouraged to use the Internet of Things and mobile internet technology to provide online car rental and other services for the lessee.

Article 21 Road passenger transport operator and its employees shall not engage in the following when providing transportation services:

(a) to damage the state's interests, national dignity, personal dignity, and violation of social morality;

(b) to disrespect the religious beliefs and ethnic customs of passengers;

(c) to carry unauthorized persons ;

(d) to induce or arrange passengers to participate in lewdity, gambling, drugs, and other similar activities;

(e) to make things difficult, beat or abuse passengers or tour guides;

(f) to deceive or coerce passengers to make purchases;

(g) to ask for tips from passengers or collect property given by operators of tourist attractions, restaurants, shopping malls, and entertainment places; and

(h) other acts prohibited by laws and regulations.

Article 22 Travel agencies and tour guides shall fulfill the passenger transport contract and not change the operation plan without authorization. Otherwise, the road passenger transport operator and its employees and passengers are entitled to refuse and report to the appropriate agencies and the travel agency in the location where the tour guide is located.

承租人、导游和旅客不得向道路旅游客运经营者及其从业人员提出危及行车安全、侮辱人格尊严或者违反职业道德和行业规定的不合理要求。

承租人和导游应当合理安排驾驶员的休息时间，禁止驾驶员连续驾驶超过国家规定的时间。

第二十三条 导游和旅客乘坐道路旅游客运车辆应当遵守乘车安全规则，不得有下列行为：

（一）携带易燃易爆等危险物品；

（二）擅自操作或者破坏车辆及相关设施、设备；

（三）抢夺车辆方向盘等干扰驾驶员正常工作影响行车安全；

（四）殴打驾驶员等侵害驾驶员人身安全；

（五）其他危害道路旅游客运安全的行为。

导游和旅客有前款规定行为的，任何人有权劝阻和制止。造成危及行车安全紧急情况的，驾驶员应当停车处理，不得继续危险驾驶车辆；驾驶员、导游和旅客可以对违法行为人采取必要的控制措施，并及时向公安机关等有关部门报告。

第二十四条 道路旅游客运经营者应当为其客运车辆安装符合国家规定的车载卫星定位装置和视频监控装置，并接入符合国家规定的车辆动态监控平台及全国重点营运车辆联网联控系统，对驾驶员和车辆运行过程进行实时监控，及时向驾驶员发送提示信息，监督、纠正营运车辆超员、超速、疲劳驾驶等行为。

卫星定位装置数据应当保存不少于六个月，视频监控装置数据应当保存不少于三个月。

Lessee, tour guides, and passengers shall not put forward unreasonable requirements to road passenger transport operators and their employees that endanger traffic safety, insult personal dignity, or violate professional ethics and industry regulations.

The lessee and the tour guide shall reasonably arrange the rest time for a driver. The driver is banned from continuously driving over the national time limits.

Article 23 Tour guides and passengers should abide by the safety rules when taking road passenger vehicles and shall not engage in the following activities:

(a) carry flammable and explosive dangerous goods;

(b) operate or destroy the vehicles and related facilities and equipment without authorization;

(c) interfere with the normal work of the driver and affect driving safety like grabbing the steering wheel of the vehicle;

(d) harm the drivers' personal safety like assaulting drivers; and

(e) other acts endangering the safety of road passenger transport.

Anyone is entitled to dissuade and stop any tour guide or passenger who commits any of the acts specified in the preceding paragraph. If an emergency creates dangerous driving conditions, the driver should stop the vehicle and not continue to drive the vehicle in dangerous conditions. Drivers, tour guides, and passengers should take necessary action to control violators and report to public security agencies and other appropriate agencies in a timely manner.

Article 24 Road passenger transport operator shall install vehicle-mounted satellite positioning devices and video monitoring devices in accordance with national regulations for passenger vehicles, and access the vehicle dynamic monitoring platform meeting the requirements of national regulations and the national joint online monitoring system for key operating vehicles, so as to monitor drivers and the vehicle operation process in real-time, send prompt information to the drivers in time, and supervise and correct practices including without limitation overcrowding, speeding of the operating vehicles and driving while tired.

Satellite positioning device data shall be kept for not less than 6 months and video monitoring device data shall be kept for not less than 3 months.

第二十五条 道路旅游客运经营者应当加强对车载卫星定位装置和视频监控装置的维护管理，确保正常运行。

任何单位和个人不得拆卸、破坏卫星定位装置和视频监控装置，不得恶意人为干扰、屏蔽卫星定位装置信号，不得篡改卫星定位装置和视频监控装置数据。

道路旅游客运经营者应当在客运车辆的显著位置张贴车辆视频监控标识，提示旅客已经进入视频监控区域。

第二十六条 在旅游客运高峰期或者旅游客运运力不足时，省道路运输管理机构可以临时调用符合以下条件的营运客运车辆和社会非营运客运车辆应急运输：

（一）车辆技术等级不低于二级；

（二）已购买承运人责任险。

省道路运输管理机构应当建立统一的应急调用车辆信息库并公告临时调用应急运输车辆有关事项，拥有符合前款规定条件车辆的单位可以向省道路运输管理机构提出申请。经审查符合条件的，省道路运输管理机构应当将其纳入应急调用车辆信息库，由承租人自行选择租用。被租用的车辆凭省道路运输管理机构开具的证明运行。

驾驶员有本规定第十五条第一款规定情形之一的，从事应急运输服务的单位不得聘用其驾驶应急调用车辆。

第二十七条 省人民政府交通主管部门应当会同旅游、应急管理部门制定道路旅游客运服务质量标准。

Article 25 Road passenger transport operators shall strengthen the maintenance and management of vehicle-mounted satellite positioning devices and video monitoring devices to ensure normal operation.

No entity or individual may dismantle or destroy the satellite positioning device and the video monitoring device, or maliciously interfere with or shield the signal of the satellite positioning device, or tamper with the data of the satellite positioning device and video monitoring device.

Road passenger transport operators should post vehicle video surveillance signs in a prominent place of passenger vehicles to make passengers notice their entry into the video surveillance.

Article 26 During the peak period of passenger transport or insufficient capacity of tourist passenger transport, the provincial road transport administrative agency may temporarily call for the emergency transport of operating passenger vehicles and private passenger vehicles that meet the following conditions:

(a) the technical level of the vehicle is not lower than level II; and

(b) the carrier liability insurance has been purchased.

The provincial road transport administrative agency shall establish a unified information database for emergency vehicle deployment and announce the information related to the temporary call for, and the organizations with vehicles meeting the conditions specified in the preceding paragraph may apply to the provincial road transport administrative agency. After examination, the provincial road transport administrative agency shall include it in such information database for the lessee to rent. The rented vehicle shall operate with a certificate issued by the provincial road transport administrative agency.

No driver who is under one of the circumstances specified in Paragraph 1 of Article 15 of the Rules shall be employed to drive the vehicle for an emergency call by any organization engaging in the emergency transportation service.

Article 27 The competent transportation agency of the provincial people's government shall, in conjunction with the tourism and emergency administration agencies, draft quality standards for road passenger transport services.

第二十八条 省人民政府交通主管部门和道路运输管理机构应当按照国家有关规定建立和完善道路旅游客运车辆的互联网监管服务平台，向社会公示道路旅游客运经营者、车辆和驾驶员信息，加强对道路旅游客运车辆运行状态、通行信息和服务质量信息的采集，实行动态监管，提供便捷的公共信息服务。

第二十九条 县级以上人民政府交通主管部门和道路运输管理机构应当建立健全监督检查制度，采取随机抽查、定期巡查、重点检查相结合的方式，对道路旅游客运经营者及其从业人员的经营行为、安全生产、服务质量等情况进行监督检查，定期进行考核，并将考核结果向社会公布。

第三十条 县级以上人民政府交通主管部门应当加强道路旅游客运信用管理，建立道路旅游客运经营者和从业人员信用档案，纳入信用信息平台，依法定期向社会公布，并依照有关规定对严重失信的道路旅游客运经营者和从业人员实施联合惩戒。

第三十一条 县级以上人民政府发展改革部门应当加强对道路旅游客运价格的监测分析，每月定期发布相关价格信息，引导道路旅游客运经营者合理定价。

县级以上人民政府市场监督管理部门应当依法对道路旅游客运价格活动进行监督检查，查处价格违法行为。

第三十二条 县级以上人民政府交通、旅游、公安、市场监督管理、应急管理等部门以及道路运输管理机构应当公布投诉电话、网站等，及时受理旅游客运投诉，并在投诉受理之日起三十日内，做出投诉处理决定并告知当事人。

Article 28 The competent transportation agency and road transport administrative agency of the provincial people's government shall, pursuant to national law, establish and improve the internet oversight service platform for road passenger transport vehicles, publish the information of road passenger transport operators, vehicles, and drivers, strengthen the collection of road passenger transport vehicle operation status, traffic information, and service quality information, conduct dynamic oversight and provide convenient public information services.

Article 29 The competent transportation agency and road transport administrative agency of the people's governments at or above the county levels shall establish and improve the oversight and inspection system, and conduct a randomized inspection, regular inspections, and key inspections to oversee and inspect the business behavior, safety production and service quality of road passenger transport operators and their employees, and conduct regular assessments and publish the results.

Article 30 The competent transportation agency of the people's government at or above the county level shall improve the credit administration of road passenger transport, create credit records of road passenger transport operators and their employees, include them into the credit information platform, and regularly publish pursuant to law, and enforce joint punishment for road passenger transport operators and employees who are seriously discredited pursuant to law.

Article 31 The development and reform departments of the people's government at or above the county level shall strengthen the monitoring and analysis of the price of road passenger transport, publish monthly price information, and guide the operators of road passenger transport to set reasonable pricing.

The market regulation agencies of the people's government at or above the county level shall oversee and inspect the pricing activities of road passenger transport pursuant to law, and investigate and resolve pricing violations.

Article 32 Agencies of the transportation, tourism, public security, market regulation, emergency administration, and other agencies of the people's government at or above the county level, as well as the road transport administrative office, shall publish the complaint phone number and website, accept complaints from passengers in a timely manner, and make a decision and inform the parties concerned within 30 days of the date of accepting the complaints.

第三十三条 交通、旅游、公安、发展改革、市场监督管理、应急管理等部门应当实行道路旅游客运资源共享，建立信息互通机制。

第三十四条 违反本规定，未取得道路运输经营许可擅自从事道路旅游客运经营或者超越范围经营的，依照《中华人民共和国道路运输条例》有关规定进行处罚。

违反本规定，承租人向未取得道路运输经营许可证或者车辆营运证的经营者租用车辆从事经营活动的，由县级以上道路运输管理机构或者有关主管部门责令改正，没收违法所得，并处五千元以上五万元以下罚款；违法所得五万元以上的，并处违法所得一倍以上五倍以下罚款；情节严重的，责令停业整顿或者依法吊销相关经营许可证；对直接负责的主管人员和其他直接责任人员，处二千元以上二万元以下罚款。

第三十五条 违反本规定，道路旅游客运经营者在经营期间不具备本规定第六条规定条件的，由县级以上道路运输管理机构责令限期整改，道路旅游客运经营者在整改期间不得从事道路旅游客运经营；逾期不整改或者整改不合格的，由原许可机关吊销道路运输经营许可证、车辆营运证。

第三十六条 违反本规定，道路旅游客运经营者在经营期限内擅自暂停、终止旅游客运服务的，由县级以上道路运输管理机构责令限期整改，处一万元以上五万元以下罚款；逾期不整改或者整改不合格的，由原许可机关吊销道路运输经营许可证。

第三十七条 违反本规定，道路旅游客运经营者有下列情形之一的，由县级以上道路运输管理机构责令限期整改，处一万元以上十万元以下

Article 33 Agencies of transportation, tourism, public security, development and reform, market regulation, emergency administration, and other agencies shall share resources on road passenger transport and implement an information exchange system.

Article 34 Any road passenger transport operator who, in violation of these Rules, has not obtained the road transport operator license to engage in the road passenger transport business or outside the operational scope, shall be penalized pursuant to the Regulations of the People's Republic of China on Road Transport.

Any lessee who, in violation of these Rules, rents a vehicle to an operator who has not obtained a road transport operating permit or vehicle operating permit to engage in business activities, shall be required to remediate by the road transport administrative agency at or above the county level or the competent agencies, and the illegal income shall be confiscated and the leaser shall be fined not less than 5,000 Yuan and not more than 50,000 Yuan. If the illegal income exceeds 50,000 Yuan, a fine of not less than such income and not more than five times such income shall be imposed on the leaser. If the circumstances are serious, it shall be required to suspend business for remediation or the appropriate operating permit shall be revoked pursuant to law. The person directly in charge and other employees directly liable shall be fined not less than 2,000 Yuan and not more than 20,000 Yuan.

Article 35 Any road passenger transport operator who, in violation of these Rules, does not meet the conditions provided in Article 6 during the operation period, shall be ordered to remediate within the time limit set by the road transport administrative agency at or above the county level, and shall not engage in road passenger transport business during the remediation period. If the remediation is overdue or nonconforming, the original permitting agency shall revoke the road transport operating permit and vehicle operation permit.

Article 36 Any road passenger transport operator who, in violation of these Rules, suspends or terminates passenger transport services without an authorization within the operating period, shall be ordered to remediate within the time limit by the road transport administrative agency at or above the county level, and shall be fined not less than 10,000 Yuan and not more 50,000 Yuan. If the remediation is overdue or nonconforming, the original permitting agency shall revoke the road transport operating permit and vehicle operating permit.

Article 37 Any road passenger transport operator who, in violation of these Rules, does or any of the following, shall be ordered to remediate within the time limit by the road transport administrative agency at or above the county level and shall be fined not less than 10,000 Yuan and not more than 100,000 Yuan. The illegal income of the operator, if any, shall be confiscated. If the

罚款；有违法所得的，没收违法所得；逾期不整改或者整改不合格的，由原许可机关吊销道路运输经营许可证、车辆营运证：

（一）允许挂靠经营或者转包经营的；

（二）转让、变相转让或者出租、出借道路运输经营许可证、车辆营运证的；

（三）未对客运车辆和驾驶员实行统一管理和调度的。

第三十八条 违反本规定，驾驶员未经道路旅游客运经营者统一调派私自提供道路旅游运输服务的，由县级以上道路运输管理机构责令限期改正，处五千元以上二万元以下罚款；有违法所得的，并没收违法所得。

第三十九条 违反本规定第十四条、第十六条规定的，由县级以上道路运输管理机构或者应急管理部门依照《中华人民共和国安全生产法》和《海南经济特区安全生产条例》的有关规定进行处罚。

第四十条 道路旅游客运经营者及其从业人员违反本规定第二十条第二款和第二十一条规定的，由县级以上道路运输管理机构责令改正，给予警告，处五千元以上三万元以下罚款；情节严重的，由原许可机关依法吊销道路运输经营许可证；违反治安管理规定的，由公安机关依法予以处罚；构成犯罪的，依法追究刑事责任。

第四十一条 道路旅游客运经营者违反本规定第十八条规定的，由县级以上人民政府市场监督管理部门依照《中华人民共和国价格法》等法律法规进行处罚。

第四十二条 导游和旅客违反本规定第二十三条规定的，依照《中华人民共和国道路交通安全法》和《中华人民共和国治安管理处罚法》等法律法规进行处罚；构成犯罪的，依法追究刑事责任。

remediation is overdue or nonconforming, the original permitting agency shall revoke the road transport operating permit and vehicle operating permit:

(a) allow affiliated operation or subcontracting operation;

(b) transfer, assign or indirectly lease, lend a road transport operating permit, or a vehicle operating permit; or

(c) does not conduct unified management and scheduling of passenger vehicles and drivers.

Article 38 Any driver who, in violation of these Rules, provides road transport services without the unified dispatch by road passenger transport operator, shall be ordered to remediate within the time limit by the road transport administrative agency at or above the county level and shall be fined not less than 5,000 Yuan and not more than 20,000 Yuan. The illegal income of the driver shall be confiscated (if any).

Article 39 Anyone in violation of Articles 14 and 16 of these Rules shall be penalized by the road transport administrative agency or emergency administration agencies at or above the county levels pursuant to the Law of the People's Republic of China on Safety Production and the Regulations of Hainan Special Economic Zone on Safety Production.

Article 40 If the road passenger transport operator or its employees violates Paragraph 2 of Article 20 or Article 21 of these Rules, the road transport administrative agency at or above the county level shall be ordered to remediate, deliver a warning, and impose a fine of not less than 5,000 Yuan and not more than 30,000 Yuan. If the circumstances are serious, the original permitting agency shall void the road transport operating permit pursuant to law. Any operator or its employees who violates any of the rules on the administration of public safety shall be penalized pursuant to law by the public security agencies. If a crime has been committed, criminal liability shall be assumed pursuant to law.

Article 41 Road passenger transport operators in violation of Article 18 of these Rules shall be penalized by the market regulation agencies of the people's government at or above the county level pursuant to the Price Law of the People's Republic of China and other laws and regulations.

Article 42 Tour guides or passengers in violation of Article 23 of these Rules, shall be penalized pursuant to the Law of the People's Republic of China on Road Traffic Safety and the Law of the People's Republic of China on Public Safety Administration and Punishment. If a crime has been committed, criminal liability shall be assumed pursuant to law.

第四十三条 违反本规定，有下列情形之一的，由县级以上道路运输管理机构责令改正，处一万元以上三万元以下罚款；拒不改正的，由县级以上道路运输管理机构责令停运并限期整改：

（一）未安装或者擅自拆卸车辆卫星定位装置和视频监控装置的；

（二）未将卫星定位装置和视频监控装置接入符合国家规定的车辆动态监控平台及全国重点营运车辆联网联控系统的；

（三）破坏卫星定位装置和视频监控装置或者恶意人为干扰、屏蔽卫星定位装置信号的；

（四）伪造、篡改或者删除卫星定位装置和视频监控装置数据的；

（五）使用卫星定位装置和视频监控装置不能正常运行的客运车辆从事道路旅游客运经营活动的。

第四十四条 被吊销道路运输经营许可证的道路旅游客运经营者，二年内不得申请道路旅游客运经营。

第四十五条 违反本规定，交通主管部门、道路运输管理机构及其工作人员有下列情形之一的，对直接负责的主管人员和其他直接责任人员依法给予处分；构成犯罪的，依法追究刑事责任：

（一）不依照本规定的条件、程序和期限实施行政许可的；

（二）参与或者变相参与道路旅游客运经营的；

（三）发现违法行为不及时查处的；

（四）未按规定期限处理投诉的；

（五）违法扣留运输车辆、道路运输经营许可证、车辆营运证的；

（六）索取、收受他人财物，或者谋取其他利益的；

（七）其他滥用职权、玩忽职守、徇私舞弊的行为。

Article 43 Anyone who is found to have done any of the following shall be required to remediate by the road transport administrative office at or above the county level, and shall be fined not less than 10,000 Yuan and not more than 30,000 Yuan. Anyone who refuses to remediate shall be required to suspend the business and remediate within the time limit specified by the road transport administrative agency at or above the county level:

(a) the vehicle satellite positioning device and video monitoring device are not installed or dismantled without authorization;

(b) the satellite positioning device and video monitoring device are not connected to the vehicle dynamic monitoring platform under the national regulations and the national joint online monitoring system for the key operating vehicles;

(c) destroy satellite positioning devices and video monitoring devices or willfully interfere with or shield signals of satellite positioning devices;

(d) falsify, tamper, or delete data of satellite positioning devices and video monitoring devices; or

(e) the satellite positioning devices and video surveillance devices not in good working condition are used in passenger vehicles for road passenger transport business.

Article 44 Road passenger transport operator whose road transport operating permit has been revoked shall not apply for road passenger transport business within 2 years.

Article 45 If, in violation of these Rules, the competent transportation agency, the road transport administrative agency, or any of their employees are under one of the following circumstances, the person directly in charge and other employees directly liable shall be penalized pursuant to law. If a crime has been committed, criminal liability shall be assumed pursuant to law:

(a) the administrative licensing is not carried out under the conditions, procedures, and time limits specified in these Rules;

(b) to participate in, directly or in any disguised form, the operation of the road passenger transport;

(c) any illegal act having been found is not promptly investigated;

(d) the complaint is not responded to and resolved within the specified time limit;

(e) to illegally detain transport vehicle, road transport operating permit and vehicle operating permit;

(f) to solicit or accept other people's belonging, or seek other benefits; or

(g) others like abuse of position, dereliction of duty or playing favoritism and committing irregularities.

第四十六条 违反本规定，本规定未设定处罚，相关法律、法规已有处罚规定的，依照其规定处罚。

第四十七条 在本省内经济特区以外区域的道路旅游客运管理工作，参照本规定执行。

第四十八条 本规定的具体应用问题，由省人民政府负责解释。

第四十九条 本规定自 2019 年 1 月 1 日起施行。

Article 46 The penalty provided by applicable laws and regulations shall control in the event any provisions of these Rules are violated but these Rules do not specify a penalty.

Article 47 Road passenger transport administration out of the special economic zones of this Province but within the Province shall be enforced with reference to these Rules.

Article 48 The detailed application of these Rules shall be interpreted by the Provincial People's Government.

Article 49 These Rules shall come into force as of January 1, 2019.

海南经济特区禁止一次性不可降解塑料制品规定

Rules of Hainan Special Economic Zone on Banning Single-Use Nondegradable Plastic Products

海南经济特区禁止一次性不可降解塑料制品规定

（2019 年 12 月 31 日海南省第六届人民代表大会常务委员会第十六次会议通过）

第一条　为了防治一次性不可降解塑料制品污染，保护和改善环境，推进国家生态文明试验区建设，根据有关法律法规的规定，结合本经济特区实际，制定本规定。

第二条　在本经济特区内禁止生产、运输、销售、储存、使用下列一次性不可降解塑料袋、塑料餐具等塑料制品：

（一）含有非生物降解高分子材料的一次性袋类，包括购物袋、日用塑料袋、纸塑复合袋等商品包装袋和用于盛装垃圾的塑料袋；

（二）含有非生物降解高分子材料的一次性餐饮具类，包括盒（含盖）、碗（含盖）、碟、盘、饮料杯（含盖）等；

（三）省人民政府根据实际确定的其他需要禁止的一次性不可降解塑料制品。

具体禁止的一次性不可降解塑料制品种类实行名录管理。禁止名录的制定和调整由省人民政府生态环境主管部门论证评估后提出，报省人民政府批准，并向社会公布。

第三条　县级以上人民政府应当加强对禁止生产、运输、销售、储存、使用一次性不可降解塑料制品工作的领导，制定工作计划，建立协调机制，组织、协调、督促有关部门依法履行监督管理职责，并将所需经费纳入本级财政预算。

Rules of Hainan Special Economic Zone on Banning Single-Use Nondegradable Plastic Products

(Adopted at the 16th Session of the Standing Committee of the 6th Hainan Provincial People's Congress on December 31, 2019)

Article 1 With a view to preventing pollution from single-use nondegradable plastic products, protecting and ameliorating the environment, and promoting the development of Hainan as the National Ecological Civilization Pilot Zone, these Rules are enacted pursuant to applicable laws and regulations, and based on the actual circumstances of this Special Economic Zone (hereinafter referred to as "SEZ").

Article 2 The following types of single-use nondegradable plastic bags and dinnerware are not allowed to be manufactured, transported, sold, stored, or used in this SEZ:

(a) single-use bags that contain non-biodegradable polymer materials, including shopping bags, daily-use plastic bags, paper-plastic composite bags, and other packaging bags and plastic garbage bags;

(b) single-use dinnerware that contains non-biodegradable polymer materials, including boxes (with lids), bowls (with lids), plates, utensils, beverage cups (with lids), etc.; or

(c) other single-use nondegradable plastic products that need to be banned as determined by the People's Government of Hainan Province (hereinafter referred to as the "Provincial People's Government").

The specific types of single-use nondegradable plastic products are subject to catalog administration. The creation and modification of such catalog shall be recommended by the competent agency in charge of ecological and environmental matters of the Provincial People's Government (hereinafter referred to as the "provincial ecology and environment competent agency") after assessment, reported to the Provincial People's Government for approval, and then announced to the public.

Article 3 The people's governments at the county level or above shall improve the leading role in banning the manufacturing, transportation, sales, storage, and use of single-use nondegradable plastic products, create working plans, implement coordination systems, organize, coordinate and require the appropriate agencies to accomplish their oversight and administrative responsibilities pursuant to law, and include the necessary funds into their own financial budgets.

第四条 县级以上人民政府生态环境主管部门负责禁止生产、运输、销售、储存、使用一次性不可降解塑料制品的统一监督管理工作。

县级以上人民政府市场监督管理部门根据省人民政府和本级人民政府确定的职责负责禁止生产、运输、销售、储存、使用一次性不可降解塑料制品的监督管理工作。

县级以上人民政府发展和改革、工业和信息化、农业农村、住房和城乡建设、环境卫生、财政、商务、交通运输等部门按照各自职责负责禁止生产、运输、销售、储存、使用一次性不可降解塑料制品的相关监督管理工作。

乡镇人民政府、街道办事处应当协助生态环境、市场监督管理等有关部门做好禁止生产、运输、销售、储存、使用一次性不可降解塑料制品工作。

第五条 工会、共青团、妇联等团体和居民委员会、村民委员会应当协助有关部门开展禁止生产、运输、销售、储存、使用一次性不可降解塑料制品工作。

鼓励和支持各类科研机构、生态环境保护组织和其他社会团体开展各种形式的禁止生产、运输、销售、储存、使用一次性不可降解塑料制品活动。

公众应当减少使用禁止名录之外的一次性不可降解塑料制品。

第六条 县级以上人民政府及其有关部门应当组织开展禁止生产、运输、销售、储存、使用一次性不可降解塑料制品宣传活动，引导公众增强环境保护和节约资源意识，使用全生物降解塑料制品、纸制品、布制品等替代品，积极参与一次性不可降解塑料制品污染防治，推动形成绿色生活方式。

Article 4 The competent agencies of the people's governments at the county level or above responsible for the ecological and environmental matters (hereinafter referred to as "ecology and environment agency at the county level or above") are responsible for the unified regulatory oversight of the banning of the manufacturing, transportation, sale, storage, and use of single-use nondegradable plastic products.

The competent agencies of the people's governments at the county level or above responsible for market regulation ("market regulation agencies at the county level or above") are responsible for the regulatory oversight of the banning of the manufacturing, transportation, sale, storage, and use of single-use nondegradable plastic products pursuant to the responsibilities determined by the Provincial People's Government and the people's governments at their own level.

The competent agencies in charge of development and reform, industry and information technology, agriculture and rural affairs, housing and urban-rural development, environment and health, finance, business, transportation are responsible for the appropriate work on regulatory oversight for the banning of the manufacturing, transportation, sale, storage, and use of single-use nondegradable plastic products pursuant to the division of responsibilities.

The town/township people's governments and the subdistrict offices shall assist the competent ecology and environment and market regulation agencies in the banning of the manufacturing, transportation, sale, storage, and use of single-use plastic products.

Article 5 The labor union, youth league, women's federation, the residents' committee, and the villagers' committee shall assist the appropriate agencies in the banning of the manufacturing, transportation, sale, storage, and use of single-use nondegradable plastic products.

The scientific research institutions, environmental protection organizations, and other social groups are recommended and supported to participate in various activities committed to the banning of the manufacturing, transportation, sale, storage, and use of single-use nondegradable plastic products.

The public shall reduce the use of single-use nondegradable plastic products outside the above-mentioned catalog.

Article 6 The people's governments at the county level or above and their appropriate agencies shall organize and carry out promotion activities on the banning of the manufacturing, transportation, sale, storage, and use of single-use nondegradable plastic products to improve public awareness of environmental protection and resource conservation, to advance the use of completely biodegradable plastic products, paper products, cloth products, or other alternatives, to encourage the public to actively participate in the prevention of pollution due to single-use nondegradable plastic products and promote a green lifestyle.

学校和幼儿园应当对青少年、儿童开展一次性不可降解塑料制品污染防治知识普及教育。

新闻媒体应当开展禁止生产、运输、销售、储存、使用一次性不可降解塑料制品宣传，免费刊载、播放公益广告。

第七条　经营者应当在经营场所显著位置设置禁止使用一次性不可降解塑料制品名录和提示标语。

经营者不得向消费者提供禁止名录内的一次性不可降解塑料制品。

集贸市场、超市等经营场所的管理者应当建立管理制度，及时制止在本场所内销售、使用禁止名录内的一次性不可降解塑料制品的行为；制止无效的，应当报告生态环境、市场监督管理等主管部门。

第八条　县级以上人民政府及其有关部门应当鼓励支持一次性不可降解塑料制品替代品的科学研究、生产、推广使用和一次性塑料制品的回收利用，并给予适当的资金扶持。

对生产一次性不可降解塑料制品替代品和回收利用一次性塑料制品的企业，按照有关规定减免税收或者行政事业性收费。

第九条　省人民政府工业和信息化主管部门应当会同有关部门制定全生物降解塑料产业发展规划，报省人民政府批准后实施。

县级以上人民政府应当支持和督促禁止名录内的一次性不可降解塑料制品生产项目转型。

第十条　全生物降解塑料制品应当严格执行国家标准、行业标准、地方标准。

省人民政府标准化主管部门应当根据实际情况组织制定全生物降解塑料制品的相关地方标准。

The schools and kindergartens shall educate the children and young people about preventing pollution from single-use nondegradable plastic products.

The news media shall promote the banning of the manufacturing, transportation, sale, storage, and use of single-use nondegradable plastic products, publish and broadcast public awareness advertisements on such for free.

Article 7 Business operators shall post the catalog of banned single-use nondegradable plastic products and notices of such banning in conspicuous places.

The business operators shall not provide customers with plastic products within the catalog.

The managers of wet markets and supermarkets shall establish a management system, and prohibit the sale and use of single-use nondegradable plastic products in the catalog within the markets; if the prohibition fails, they shall report to the appropriate ecology and environment and market regulation agencies.

Article 8 The people's governments at the county level or above and their appropriate agencies shall recommend and support the alternative product research, manufacturing and promotion, and the recycling of single-use plastic products and give appropriate financial support.

The organizations manufacturing alternative products and engaging in the recycling of single-use plastic products are eligible for tax or administrative fee deductions pursuant to applicable rules.

Article 9 The competent agency of the Provincial People's Government in charge of industry and information technology shall create the development plan for the full biodegradable plastic industry together with the appropriate agencies and report it to the Provincial People's Government for approval.

The people's governments at the county level or above shall support and require the transformation of single-use nondegradable plastic production projects.

Article 10 The completely biodegradable plastic products shall strictly comply with national, industrial, and local standards.

The competent agency of the Provincial People's Government in charge of standardization shall organize the creation of appropriate local standards for completely biodegradable plastic products based on actual circumstances.

鼓励社会团体、企业制定并执行高于国家标准、行业标准和地方标准相关技术要求的团体标准、企业标准。

第十一条　鼓励全生物降解塑料制品生产企业向符合条件的认证机构申请产品质量认证。

第十二条　省人民政府生态环境主管部门应当会同市场监督管理等有关部门建立全生物降解塑料制品信息平台，将全生物降解塑料制品生产企业信息和产品信息纳入平台管理，保障全流程可追溯。

生产经营者应当建立全生物降解塑料制品追溯体系，按照规定将溯源信息上传至全生物降解塑料制品信息平台。鼓励生产经营者采用信息化手段采集、留存生产经营信息。

第十三条　县级以上人民政府及其有关部门应当加强对禁止名录之外的一次性塑料制品的管理，建立和探索政府、企业、社会多元化投入、回收、利用和处理的市场化运营机制，合理安排回收网点，严格农用塑料薄膜等一次性塑料制品清理、回收的监督管理。

第十四条　县级以上人民政府应当加强禁止生产、运输、销售、储存、使用一次性不可降解塑料制品监督检查工作的组织协调，建立由市场监督管理部门牵头，生态环境、旅游文化、农业农村、交通运输、环境卫生、综合执法等有关部门参与的联合执法机制，及时查处违反本规定的行为。

第十五条　县级以上人民政府市场监督管理等有关部门应当将生产、运输、销售、储存、使用禁止名录内的一次性不可降解塑料制品的违法信息在国家企业信用信息公示系统公示，并纳入省信用信息共享平台，依法实施联合惩戒。

The social groups and organizations are recommended to create and enforce the organizational and organization standards stricter than the national, industrial, and local standards.

Article 11 The organizations manufacturing completely biodegradable plastic products are recommended to apply for product quality certification with the appropriate certification agencies.

Article 12 The provincial ecology and environment competent agency shall create an information platform for completely biodegradable plastic products together with the appropriate agencies, including the market administration agency, and add information about the organizations manufacturing the completely biodegradable plastic products and their products into the platform to ensure that the whole process is traceable.

The business operators shall create a tracing system for completely biodegradable plastic products and upload the source information to the completely biodegradable plastic products traceability platform pursuant to the rules. The business operators are recommended to use information technology to collect and store manufacturing and business operation information.

Article 13 The people's governments at the county level or above and their appropriate agencies shall improve the administration of single-use plastic products outside the catalog, explore and create a market-oriented system for the government, organizations, and the social figures to invest, recycle, use, and treat these plastic products, reasonably organize recycling stations, and strictly supervise and manage the cleaning and recycling of single-use plastic products, including agricultural films.

Article 14 The people's governments at the county level or above shall improve the organizational coordination for overseeing and inspecting the work on banning the manufacture, transportation, sale, storage, and use of single-use nondegradable plastic products, create a joint law enforcement system led by the market regulation agency and joined by the appropriate agencies, including the ecology and environment, tourism, agriculture and rural affairs, transportation, health, and coordinated administrative enforcement agencies.

Article 15 The appropriate agencies, including the market regulation agencies of the people's governments at the county level or above, shall publish information about violations of law concerning the manufacture, transportation, sales, storage, and use of single-use nondegradable plastic products on the National Enterprise Credit Information Publicity System, add such information to the provincial credit sharing platform, and jointly impose penalties pursuant to law.

第十六条 县级以上人民政府市场监督管理等有关部门履行禁止生产、运输、销售、储存、使用一次性不可降解塑料制品监督检查职责时，有权采取下列措施：

（一）查阅复制有关文件和资料；

（二）向被检查的单位和个人了解有关情况；

（三）进入现场开展检查、取样；

（四）依法查封、扣押禁止名录内的塑料制品和直接用于生产该塑料制品的原辅材料、包装物、生产工具；

（五）法律法规规定的其他措施。

第十七条 县级以上人民政府市场监督管理等有关部门依法进行监督检查时，有关单位或者个人应当配合，不得弄虚作假，不得拒绝、阻挠。

第十八条 县级以上人民政府应当对在禁止生产、运输、销售、储存、使用一次性不可降解塑料制品工作中作出显著成绩或者突出贡献的单位和个人给予表彰、奖励。

第十九条 任何单位和个人有权向生态环境、市场监督管理等有关部门举报违反本规定的行为。

生态环境、市场监督管理等有关部门应当将举报方式向社会公布。

接到举报的部门应当及时处理并将处理结果告知举报人。

对实名举报并查证属实的，由查处违法行为的部门按照有关规定对举报人给予奖励。

第二十条 违反本规定，生产禁止名录内的一次性不可降解塑料制品的，由县级以上人民政府市场监督管理部门责令停止生产，没收违法生产的一次性不可降解塑料制品，并处五万元以上二十万元以下的罚款；

Article 16 The appropriate agencies, including the market administration of the people's governments at the county level or above, shall oversee and inspect the work on banning the manufacture, transportation, sales, storage, and use of single-use nondegradable plastic products, and are authorized to take the following measures:

(a) check and make copies of relevant documents and files;

(b) inquire the organizations and individuals under inspection;

(c) conduct on-site inspection and sampling;

(d) seize or detain the plastic products within the catalog and the raw and auxiliary materials, packaging, and production tools pursuant to law; and

(e) other measures provided by laws and regulations.

Article 17 The appropriate organizations or individuals under oversight and inspection shall cooperate with the appropriate agencies, including the market regulation, of the people's governments at the county level or above, and shall not commit fraud, refuse, or obstruct such lawful oversight and inspection.

Article 18 The people's governments at the county level or above shall commend and reward the organizations or individuals that have made outstanding achievements or contributions to the banning of the manufacture, transportation, sale, storage, and use of single-use nondegradable plastic products.

Article 19 Any entity or individual has the right to report violations of these Rules to the appropriate agencies including the ecology and environment and market regulation.

The appropriate agencies, including the ecology and environment and market regulation, shall publish the reporting methods.

The agencies receiving such reports shall resolve with them promptly and inform the reporters of the results.

If the real-name reporting is verified, the agencies for reporting investigation shall reward the reporter pursuant to law.

Article 20 The market regulation agency at the county level or above shall issue an order to suspend the manufacture of single-use nondegradable plastic products within the catalog, confiscate the manufactured products, and impose a fine of not less than 50,000 Yuan and not more than 200,000 Yuan if such production violates these Rules; if the value of the products exceeds 200,000 Yuan, a fine for the equivalent amount shall be imposed; if there are gains from such illegal products, the gains shall be confiscated; if the circumstances are serious,

货值金额超过二十万元的，处货值金额等额的罚款；有违法所得的，没收违法所得；情节严重的，依法吊销营业执照。

第二十一条 违反本规定，销售禁止名录内的一次性不可降解塑料制品的，由县级以上人民政府市场监督管理部门责令改正，没收一次性不可降解塑料制品，并处三万元以上二十万元以下的罚款；货值金额超过二十万元的，处货值金额等额的罚款；有违法所得的，没收违法所得；情节严重的，依法吊销营业执照。其中零售摊贩销售禁止名录内的一次性不可降解塑料制品的，由县级以上人民政府市场监督管理部门责令改正，没收一次性不可降解塑料制品，并处一千元以下的罚款。

第二十二条 违反本规定，运输、储存禁止名录内的一次性不可降解塑料制品的，由县级以上人民政府市场监督管理部门没收运输、储存的一次性不可降解塑料制品，并处一万元以上十万元以下的罚款；货值金额超过十万元的，处货值金额等额的罚款；有违法所得的，没收违法所得。

第二十三条 违反本规定，经营者使用或者提供使用禁止名录内的一次性不可降解塑料制品的，由县级以上人民政府市场监督管理部门责令改正，没收一次性不可降解塑料制品，对单位处一千元以上十万元以下的罚款；对零售摊贩处一千元以下的罚款。

前款规定以外的单位和个人使用禁止名录内的一次性不可降解塑料制品的，由乡镇人民政府、街道办事处批评教育；拒不改正的，乡镇人民政府、街道办事处应当报告所在地市场监督管理部门，由市场监督管理部门责令改正，没收一次性不可降解塑料制品，对单位可以并处一千元以下的罚款；对个人可以并处五十元以下的罚款。

the business license shall be revoked pursuant to law.

Article 21 The market regulation agency at the county level or above shall order the correction of the sales of single-use nondegradable plastic products within the catalog, confiscate the products on the shelf, and impose a fine of not less than 30,000 Yuan and not more than 200,000 Yuan if such sales violate these Rules; if the value of the products exceeds 200,000 Yuan, fine for the equivalent amount shall be imposed; if there are gains from such sales, the gains shall be confiscated; if the circumstances are serious, the business license shall be revoked pursuant to law. If such sales are made by retail vendors, the market regulation agency at the county level or above shall issue an order to correct the retail sales of single-use nondegradable plastic products, confiscate the products, and impose a fine of less than 1,000 Yuan.

Article 22 The market regulation agency at the county level or above shall confiscate the cataloged single-use nondegradable plastic products under transportation or storage if such transportation or storage violates these Rules, and shall impose a fine of not less than 10,000 Yuan and not more than 100,000 Yuan; if the value of the products exceeds 100,000 Yuan, a fine for the equivalent amount shall be imposed; if there are gains from such transportation or storage, the gains shall be confiscated.

Article 23 The market regulation agency at the county level or above shall issue a correction order against the use or provision of the cataloged single-use nondegradable plastic products by the business operators, confiscate the products, and impose a fine of not less than 1,000 Yuan and not more than 100,000 Yuan if the business operator is an organization, and a fine of not more than 1,000 Yuan if the business operator is an individual.

The town/township people's government or subdistrict agency shall criticize and educate the organizations or individuals mentioned in the preceding paragraph; if they refuse to accept, the town/township people's government or subdistrict agency shall report to the local market regulation agency. Such market regulation agency shall issue a correction order, confiscate the products, and impose a fine of not more than 1,000 Yuan on the organizations or of not more than 50 Yuan on the individuals.

第二十四条 违反本规定，未在经营场所显著位置设置禁止使用一次性不可降解塑料制品名录和提示标语的，由县级以上人民政府市场监督管理部门责令改正。

第二十五条 生产、销售全生物降解塑料制品不符合国家标准、行业标准、地方标准的，依照相关法律法规的规定查处。

第二十六条 违反本规定，在接受监督检查时弄虚作假或者拒绝、阻挠县级以上人民政府市场监督管理等有关部门监督检查的，由履行监督检查职责的部门责令改正；拒不改正的，处一千元以上五万元以下的罚款；情节严重的，责令停业整顿，直至依法吊销营业执照；构成违反治安管理行为的，由公安机关依法给予处罚。

第二十七条 违反本规定，县级以上人民政府有关主管部门及其工作人员滥用职权、玩忽职守、徇私舞弊的，依法对直接负责的主管人员和其他直接责任人员给予处分；构成犯罪的，依法追究刑事责任。

第二十八条 违反本规定的行为，根据国务院相对集中行政处罚权的规定已经确定集中由市、县、自治县综合执法部门处理的，从其规定。

第二十九条 在本省内经济特区以外区域禁止生产、运输、销售、储存、使用一次性不可降解塑料制品，参照本规定执行。

第三十条 本规定自 2020 年 12 月 1 日起施行。2008 年 5 月 30 日海南省第四届人民代表大会常务委员会第三次会议通过的《海南经济特区限制生产运输销售储存使用一次性塑料制品规定》同时废止。

Article 24 The market regulation agency at the county level or above shall issue a correction order against the violation of these Rules by the business operators who fail to post the catalog of the banned single-use nondegradable plastic products and notices of such banning in conspicuous places.

Article 25 The production or storage of fully biodegradable plastic products that do not comply with national, industrial, and local standards shall be investigated and punished pursuant to law.

Article 26 The appropriate agencies of the people's government at the county level or above in charge of investigation and inspection shall issue a correction order against any falsification, fraud, refusal, or obstruction during investigation and inspection; if such correction order is refused, a fine of not less than 1,000 Yuan and not more than 50,000 Yuan shall be imposed; if the circumstances are serious, an order to suspend business for correction shall be issued, and the business license may be revoked if correction is not made; if such act violates the administration of public security, the public security agency will impose penalties.

Article 27 The individuals directly in charge and other directly responsible individuals shall be penalized pursuant to law if the appropriate agencies of the people's government at the county level or above and their employees commit abuse of position, dereliction of duty, or play favoritism and commit irregularities; if their act constitutes a crime, they shall be held criminally liable pursuant to law.

Article 28 If any violation of these Rules is subject to the coordinated administrative enforcement agency at the municipal, county, or autonomous county-level pursuant to the provisions of the State Council on the power to impose administrative penalties in a centralized manner, such regulations shall apply.

Article 29 The banning of the production, transportation, sales, storage and use of single-use nondegradable plastic products outside this SEZ within this Province shall be subject to these Rules *mutatis mutandis*.

Article 30 These Rules shall come into force as of December 1, 2020. The Rules of Hainan Special Economic Zone on Limiting the Manufacture, Transportation, Sales, Storage and Use of Single-Use Plastic Products adopted at the 3rd Session of the 4th Standing Committee of the Hainan Provincial People's Congress on May 30, 2008, shall be simultaneously repealed.

海南经济特区外国企业从事服务贸易经营活动登记管理暂行规定

Interim Rules of Hainan Special Economic Zone on the Registration of Trade in Service of Foreign Companies

海南经济特区外国企业从事服务贸易经营活动登记管理暂行规定

（2019 年 12 月 31 日海南省第六届人民代表大会常务委员会第十六次会议通过）

第一条 为了促进跨境服务贸易发展，规范外国企业在本经济特区从事服务贸易经营活动的登记管理，保护其合法权益，加快形成法治化、国际化、便利化的营商环境和公平开放统一高效的市场环境，遵循法律、行政法规的基本原则，制定本规定。

第二条 本规定适用于外国企业在本经济特区内从事服务贸易经营活动的登记及相关管理活动。

本规定所称外国企业，是指依照外国法律规定在中国境外设立的营利性组织。

第三条 外国企业在本经济特区从事服务贸易经营活动，应当遵守中国法律法规，不得危害中国国家安全、损害社会公共利益。

外国企业在本经济特区从事服务贸易经营活动，应当遵守国家和本经济特区跨境服务贸易管理的规定。依照有关规定禁止的领域，外国企业不得从事服务贸易经营活动；依照有关规定限制的领域，外国企业从事服务贸易经营活动应当符合规定的条件。

第四条 省人民政府市场监督管理部门负责外国企业的登记管理工作。

省和市、县、自治县人民政府相关行业主管部门按照各自职责分工对外国企业服务贸易经营活动进行监督管理。

Interim Rules of Hainan Special Economic Zone on the Registration of Trade in Service of Foreign Companies

(Adopted at the 16th Session of the Standing Committee of the 6th Hainan Provincial People's Congress on December 31, 2019)

Article 1 With a view to promoting cross-border trade in service, regulating the registration of trade in service activities of foreign companies in this Special Economic Zone (hereinafter referred to as the "SEZ"), protecting their legal rights, facilitating a convenient international business environment characterized by rule of law and a fair, open, unified, and efficient market, the Interim Rules of Hainan Special Economic Zone on the Trade in Service of Foreign Companies (hereinafter referred to as "these Rules") are enacted pursuant to the basic principles of laws and administrative regulations.

Article 2 These Rules apply to the registration and administration of the trade in service activities of the foreign companies in this SEZ.

For the purpose of these Rules, the foreign companies refer to the for-profit organizations established outside the territory of China under foreign law.

Article 3 The foreign companies engaging in trade in service in this SEZ shall abide by Chinese law and not endanger China's national security or damage public interest.

The foreign companies engaging in trade in service in this SEZ shall abide by national laws and the rules of this SEZ on cross-border trade in service administration. The foreign companies shall not engage in trade in service in the fields prohibited by applicable rules; the foreign companies shall fulfill the conditions pursuant to the rules if there are restrictions in such industry.

Article 4 The market regulation agency of the People's Government of Hainan Province (hereinafter referred to as the "Provincial People's Government") is responsible for the registration and administration of foreign companies.

The appropriate agency in charge of relevant sectors of the provincial, municipal, county, or autonomous county people's governments shall enforce regulatory oversight over the trade in service of the foreign companies based on the division of authorities and responsibilities.

第五条 外国企业在本经济特区从事服务贸易经营活动，设立经营场所的，应当依照本规定申请登记。

法律法规规定外国企业在本经济特区从事服务贸易经营活动应当在中国境内设立外商投资企业或者分支机构、子机构、代表机构的，从其规定。

第六条 在本经济特区从事服务贸易经营活动依法需要办理前置审批的，外国企业应当依法申请审批，获得批准后再向登记机关申请登记，未通过审批的不予登记。

第七条 外国企业登记后，依法需要办理后置审批方可从事服务贸易经营活动的，未经批准，不得从事服务贸易经营活动。

外国企业在所属国已获得从事相关服务贸易经营活动的资质、许可、认证，其条件和标准具有国际先进性或者不低于中国国家规定的，经本经济特区相关行业主管部门备案后予以认可，但后置审批事项依法应当由国家有关部门审批或者涉及国家安全、公共安全的除外。可以认可的资质、许可、认证事项清单由省人民政府制定并向社会公布。

第八条 外国企业在办理登记时，登记机关应当告知外国企业需要申请审批的经营项目和相应的审批部门。

涉及后置审批事项的，办理登记后，登记机关应当将外国企业登记信息通过信息共享平台告知有关行政审批部门。有关行政审批部门应当及时依法办理相关后置审批，并依法履行后续监管职责。

第九条 外国企业应当指定一个获授权代表负责提交、签收登记材料及相关法律文件。获授权代表可以是下列人员或者机构：

（一）海南省常住居民；

Article 5 Where the foreign companies engaging in trade in service in this SEZ establish a business place, they shall apply for registration pursuant to these Rules.

Where there are laws and regulations providing that the foreign companies engaging in trade in service shall establish a foreign-invested enterprise, branch, subsidiary, or representative office in China, such laws and regulations shall apply.

Article 6 Where the engagement in trade in service in this SEZ needs *ex ante* approval pursuant to law, the foreign companies shall apply for such approval pursuant to law, and then apply for registration upon approval being granted; no registration shall be made without approval.

Article 7 Where the engagement in trade in service in this SEZ requires *ex post* approval pursuant to law, the foreign companies shall apply for approval; if not approved, such foreign companies shall not engage in any trade in service.

Where the foreign companies have obtained qualifications, licenses, or certifications for trade in service in the country to which it belongs and whose requirements and standards are international or not lower than those of Chinese national regulations, the appropriate agency in charge in this SEZ may recognize such qualifications, licenses, or certifications after recordation, unless national security or public security is concerned, or the *ex post* approval shall be made by the appropriate national agency. The list of such qualifications, licenses, and certifications shall be enacted by the Provincial People's Government and publicly announced.

Article 8 The registering office shall inform the foreign companies applying for registration of the business items subject to approval and the appropriate approving agency.

For the purpose of *ex post* approval, the registering office shall inform the appropriate administrative approving agency of the registration information about the foreign companies through the information-sharing platform. Such administrative approving agency shall complete the *ex post* approval in a timely manner and perform its duty in following regulatory oversight pursuant to law.

Article 9 The foreign companies shall appoint an authorized representative to submit and receive the registration materials and appropriate legal documents. Such authorized representative may be the following person or organization:

(a) a local permanent resident in Hainan Province;

（二）在海南注册的会计师事务所；

（三）在海南注册的律师事务所。

第十条 外国企业应当在设立经营场所后三十日内，向登记机关申请登记，并通过获授权代表提交下列材料：

（一）登记申请书；

（二）企业章程（协议）；

（三）所属国政府有关部门出具的合法开业证明；

（四）负责人的任职文件和获授权代表的授权委托书；

（五）负责人和获授权代表的身份证明文件。

外国企业在申请前置审批时已经提交过的材料，在向登记机关申请登记时可以不再提交。

第十一条 登记机关对外国企业提交的申请材料实行形式审查。

外国企业应当对申请材料的真实性、合法性、完整性负责。

第十二条 外国企业申请登记时，应当使用合法开业证明载明的名称或者中文译名，也可以同时登记外文名称和中文译名。

外文名称和中文译名应当符合中国法律、法规规定和公序良俗。名称和中文译名存在与其他企业名称重名或者近似情形时，应当加注识别性的符号或者表述。

名称不符合前款规定的，应当予以纠正；未纠正的，登记机关不予登记。

第十三条 对符合登记条件的外国企业，登记机关应当自受理之日起三个工作日内颁发营业执照，并通过企业信用信息公示系统向社会公示。

外国企业应当凭营业执照申请办理社会保险、税务、海关和登记后置审批等事项，可以凭营业执照申请办理银行账户。

(b) an accounting firm registered in Hainan; and

(c) a law firm registered in Hainan.

Article 10 The foreign companies shall apply for registration and submit the following materials through the authorized representative within 30 days after establishing the business place:

(a) the registration application form letter;

(b) articles of association (contract);

(c) a certificate of legal standing issued by the appropriate agency in the country to which it belongs;

(d) the letter of appointment of the responsible person and the power of attorney for the authorized representative; and

(e) the identity certificates of the responsible person and the authorized representative.

The documents that have been submitted by foreign companies when applying for *ex ante* approval may not be submitted to the registering office when applying for registration.

Article 11 The registering office shall enforce a formal approval review for the documents submitted by the foreign companies.

The foreign companies shall be responsible for the authenticity, legality, and integrity of the submitted documents.

Article 12 When applying for registration, the foreign companies shall use the foreign name or Chinese name indicated by the certificate of legal standing or register both the foreign and Chinese name.

The foreign name and Chinese name shall conform to Chinese laws, administrative regulations and public order. If there are any overlaps or similarities in names, the foreign name and Chinese name shall be indicated with marks or notes.

The names that do not conform with the preceding paragraph shall be corrected; if not corrected, the registration shall be refused.

Article 13 The registering office shall issue the business license to the eligible foreign companies within 3 business days after the registration application is accepted, and publish it on the enterprise credit information publicity system.

The foreign companies shall apply for social security, taxes, customs, and *ex post* approval using the business license and may open banking accounts using the business license.

第十四条 外国企业登记事项包括统一社会信用代码、企业名称、企业类型、经营场所、负责人、获授权代表、经营范围、营业期限。

登记事项发生变动的，外国企业应当自变动决定作出之日起三十日内向登记机关申请办理变更登记。

第十五条 省人民政府市场监督管理部门和相关部门应当按照有关规定通过企业信用信息公示系统公示外国企业的登记、行政许可、行政处罚等相关信息，供社会公众查询。

第十六条 外国企业应当依照有关规定，通过企业信用信息公示系统向省人民政府市场监督管理部门报送上一年度的年度报告，并向社会公示。

年度报告事项包括：

（一）外国企业、负责人和获授权代表在本经济特区的联系方式等信息；

（二）外国企业在本经济特区的从业人数、营业收入、利润、纳税总额等经营情况信息；

（三）外国企业在本经济特区的出资情况、资产总额、负债总额等信息；

（四）法律法规规定的其他应当公示的信息。

前款第一项规定的信息应当向社会公示，第二项、第三项规定的信息由外国企业选择是否向社会公示。经外国企业同意，公民、法人或者其他组织可以查询外国企业选择不公示的信息。

第十七条 外国企业在本经济特区不再设立经营场所的，应当自不再设立经营场所之日起三十日内向登记机关提出退出申请。

获授权代表应当自外国企业在本经济特区不再设立经营场所之日起三十日内向登记机关报告。

Article 14 The items requiring registration for the foreign companies include the unified social credit identifier, name, type, business place, responsible person, authorized representative, the scope of business, and period of business.

Where the items requiring registration change, the foreign companies shall apply for change registration within thirty days of the commencement of the change.

Article 15 The market regulation agency of the Provincial People's Government and appropriate agencies shall publish the information about the registration, administrative licensing, and administrative penalties of the foreign companies on the enterprise credit information publicity system for public inquiries.

Article 16 The foreign companies shall report their previous year's annual reports to the market regulation agency of the Provincial People's Government through the enterprise credit information publicity system pursuant to applicable rules and make them available to the public.

The items of the annual report include:

(a) the contact information in this SEZ of the foreign companies, their responsible persons, and their authorized representatives;

(b) the number of employees, revenue, profit, the total amount of taxes paid, and other information about business operations;

(c) the information about the capital contribution, total assets, and total debts; and

(d) other information subject to announcement pursuant to laws and regulations.

The information provided in Subparagraph (a) of the preceding paragraph shall be published, and the publication of information provided in Subparagraphs (b) and (c) shall be subject to the foreign companies' discretion. With the consent of foreign companies, citizens, juristic persons, or other organizations may inquire about the information that the foreign companies choose not to publish.

Article 17 Where the foreign companies no longer establish a business place in this SEZ, such companies shall apply for withdrawal of business with the registering office within 30 days from the date such withdrawal commences.

The authorized representative shall report to the registering office within 30 days of the date of such withdrawal from this SEZ.

第十八条　登记机关应当在收到外国企业退出申请之日起三个工作日内受理，并通过企业信用信息公示系统向社会公告，公告期为七日。

公告期间，利害关系人和有关机关可以向登记机关提出异议申请。根据以下情形，登记机关分别作出决定：

（一）无异议情形的，公告期届满后予以办理退出登记；

（二）有异议情形但已消除或者异议不成立的，公告期届满后予以办理退出登记；

（三）有异议情形且未消除的，不予办理退出登记。

外国企业、利害关系人可以向登记机关申请举行听证会。听证期间不计入公告期限。

第十九条　登记机关发现外国企业在本经济特区不再设立经营场所的，可以通过获授权代表书面通知外国企业，要求外国企业在九十日内作出确认。无法联系获授权代表的，由登记机关通过企业信用信息公示系统向社会公告，要求外国企业在九十日内予以确认。

外国企业逾期未确认或者回复确认在本经济特区不再设立经营场所，并且不提出退出申请的，登记机关通过企业信用信息公示系统向社会公告拟作出除名的决定，公告期为三十日，公告期满利害关系人、有关机关没有提出异议的，登记机关对外国企业予以除名，并向社会公示。

被除名的外国企业不得继续在本经济特区从事服务贸易经营活动；需要继续从事的，应当重新申请登记取得营业执照。

第二十条　登记机关及相关行业主管部门发现外国企业在境外的运营情况和资信状况发生可能影响交易安全的变化，可以委托中介服务机构予以调查，外国企业应当配合。调查结果经认定后，及时通过企业信用信息公示系统向社会公告。

Article 18 The registering office shall process the withdrawal application within 3 business days of the date of receiving such application and announce it in the enterprise credit information publicity system for 7 days.

During the 7-day notice period, any interested party and the appropriate agency may submit an application of opposition. The registering office may make a decision based on the following circumstances:

(a) where the proof for the opposition does not exist, the withdrawal shall be registered when the notice period expires;

(b) where the proof for the opposition exists but has been eliminated or such opposition cannot be established, the withdrawal shall be registered when the notice period expires; and

(c) where the proof for the opposition exists and is not eliminated, the application for withdrawal shall be refused.

The foreign companies and the interested party may apply for a hearing with the registering office. The period for the hearing shall not be counted in the notice period.

Article 19 Where the registering office finds that the place of business of the foreign company is no longer in this SEZ, such registering office may notify the foreign company in writing through the authorized representative, requesting that the company confirm within 90 days. If the authorized representative cannot be reached, the registering office shall issue a notice through the enterprise credit information publicity system to request the company to confirm within 90 days.

Where the foreign company does not confirm within the specified period or confirms that its place of business is no longer in the SEZ and does not submit an application for withdrawal, the registering office shall issue a notice in the enterprise credit information publicity system recommending such enterprise be delisted within a period of 30 days. If the interested party and appropriate agency do not oppose the delisting by the expiration of the period, the registering office shall delist the company and announce such to the public.

The delisted foreign company shall not engage in any service trade in this SEZ; if such company chooses to continue the trade in service, it shall resubmit a registration application and obtain a new business license.

Article 20 Where the registering office and appropriate agency in charge find any change in the overseas business operations and credit of the foreign company that may influence transaction security, such agencies may appoint an agency to conduct an investigation with which such company shall cooperate. Upon confirmation, the investigation results shall be published in the enterprise credit information publicity system in a timely manner.

第二十一条 对外国企业违反本规定的行为，县级以上人民政府市场监督管理部门依照有关规定列入企业经营异常名录或者严重违法失信企业名单。

第二十二条 有下列情形之一的外国企业在本经济特区从事服务贸易经营活动的，由县级以上人民政府市场监督管理部门责令停止违法行为，没收违法所得，处以一万元以上五万元以下的罚款：

（一）依照本规定应当申请登记而未申请登记的；

（二）被登记机关除名的；

（三）已办理退出登记的。

第二十三条 外国企业提交虚假材料或者采取其他欺诈手段隐瞒重要事实取得登记的，由登记机关没收违法所得，处以一万元以上十万元以下的罚款，对负责人处以一千元以上五千元以下的罚款；情节严重的，撤销登记。

明知外国企业存在前款规定的违法行为而参与的，对担任获授权代表的海南省常住居民处以一千元以上五千元以下的罚款，对担任获授权代表的会计师事务所或者律师事务所处以一万元以上三万元以下的罚款；情节严重的，三年内不得再担任获授权代表。

第二十四条 县级以上人民政府市场监督管理部门及其工作人员在登记管理活动中滥用职权、弄虚作假、玩忽职守、徇私舞弊的，由任免机关或者监察机关对直接负责的主管人员和其他直接责任人员依法给予处分；构成犯罪的，依法追究刑事责任。

第二十五条 违反本规定的行为，本规定未设定处罚但其他法律、法规已设定处罚的，依照有关法律、法规的规定处罚。

Article 21 The market regulation agency of the people's government at the county level or above shall add the foreign companies violating these Rules to the Suspicious Activities List or the Seriously Illegal Business Entities List pursuant to the applicable rules.

Article 22 The foreign company engaging in trade in service in this SEZ may be penalized by the market regulation agency of people's government at the county level or above with an order to suspend businesses, confiscation of illegal gains, and a fine of not less than 10,000 Yuan and not more than 50,000 Yuan if any of the following circumstances occur:

(a) failure to apply for registration pursuant to these Rules;

(b) delisting by the registering office; or

(c) application for withdrawal.

Article 23 Where the foreign companies complete registration through the provision of falsified materials or other fraudulent means to conceal important facts, the registering office shall confiscate the illegal gains, impose a fine of not less than 10,000 Yuan and not more than 100,000 Yuan, and impose a fine of not less than 1,000 Yuan and not more than 5,000 Yuan on the responsible person; if the circumstances are serious, the registration shall be revoked.

Where a permanent resident of this Province acting as the authorized representative knows that the foreign company commits the illegal acts in the preceding paragraph but participates in these acts, such resident shall be penalized with a fine of not less than 1,000 Yuan and not more than 5,000 Yuan; the accounting firm or law firm committing the same shall be penalized with a fine of not less than 10,000 Yuan and not more than 30,000 Yuan; if the circumstances are serious, they shall not be permitted to serve as authorized representatives for 3 years.

Article 24 The individuals directly in charge and other individuals liable shall be penalized pursuant to law by the appointment and removal agency or the oversight agency if the market regulation agency of the people's government at the county level or above and their employees commit abuse of position, fraud, dereliction of duty, or play favoritism and commit irregularities during their work in registration; if their act constitutes a crime, they shall assume criminally liability pursuant to law.

Article 25 Where punishments are provided by other laws and regulations concerning the acts that violate these Rules, such laws and regulations shall apply.

第二十六条 香港、澳门、台湾地区企业在本经济特区从事服务贸易经营活动的，参照本规定执行。

第二十七条 本规定自 2020 年 3 月 1 日起施行。

Article 26 The service trade engaged by the organizations from Hong Kong Special Administrative Region, Macao Special Administrative Region, and Taiwan region shall be subject to these Rules *mutatis mutandis*.

Article 27 These Rules shall come into force as of March 1, 2020.

海南热带雨林国家公园特许经营管理办法

Administrative Measures of Concessions in Hainan Tropical Rainforest National Park

海南热带雨林国家公园特许经营管理办法

（2020年12月2日海南省第六届人民代表大会常务委员会第二十四次会议通过）

第一章 总 则

第一条 为了规范海南热带雨林国家公园特许经营活动，严格保护和合理利用自然资源，实行自然资源有偿使用制度，根据有关法律、法规，结合海南热带雨林国家公园实际，制定本办法。

第二条 海南热带雨林国家公园一般控制区内的经营服务活动实行特许经营，核心保护区内禁止开展经营服务活动。

本办法所称特许经营，是指海南热带雨林国家公园管理机构（以下简称国家公园管理机构）依法授权公民、法人或者其他组织在一定期限和范围内开展经营活动，特许经营者依照特许经营协议和有关规定履行相关义务的行为。

未经国家公园管理机构授权不得从事特许经营活动。

第三条 海南热带雨林国家公园内特许经营项目实行目录管理。

特许经营目录由国家公园管理机构依据海南热带雨林国家公园总体规划和专项规划以及有关产业准入政策编制，经省人民政府批准后向社会公布，并根据需要适时调整。

Administrative Measures of Concessions in Hainan Tropical Rainforest National Park

(Adopted at the 24th Session of the Standing Committee of the 6th Hainan Provincial People's Congress on December 2, 2020)

Chapter I General Provisions

Article 1 These Measures are enacted based on applicable laws and regulations and actual circumstances of the Hainan Tropical Rainforest National Park (Rainforest Park) for the purposes of regulating concession activities within the Rainforest Park, strictly protecting and reasonably utilizing natural resources, and implementing a paid use system for natural resources.

Article 2 Business and services are subject to concessions within Rainforest Park affiliated areas but are prohibited in the core protected area.

"Concession" in these Measures refers to the operator's performance of obligations in compliance with the concession agreement and applicable law after the Rainforest Park's Management Office (hereinafter referred to as the "Park Office") authorizes citizens, juristic persons, or other organizations to conduct business activities within a certain term and scope pursuant to law.

No concession activities shall be allowed without the authorization of the Park Office.

Article 3 The particular concessions in the Rainforest Park shall be administered as a list.

The list of concessions shall be prepared by the Park Office based on the Rainforest Park comprehensive and ad hoc plans and applicable industrial access policies, announced to the public after being approved by the provincial people's government, and promptly adjusted based on current requirements.

第四条 国家公园管理机构应当通过竞争方式确定特许经营者。海南热带雨林国家公园内原住居民（以下简称原住居民）利用自有或者本集体经济组织及其成员的房屋开展餐饮、住宿、商品销售等经营服务活动，以及国家和省人民政府规定的其他经营服务活动，可以不通过竞争方式确定特许经营者。

第五条 海南热带雨林国家公园内的基础设施和公用事业实行特许经营的，由国家公园管理机构和县级以上人民政府相关主管部门依照本办法和国家有关规定执行。

第六条 特许经营使用费标准由国家公园管理机构会同省财政部门制定，经省人民政府批准后施行。

特许经营使用费应当上缴省级国库，纳入财政预算管理。

第二章 特许经营范围

第七条 海南热带雨林国家公园一般控制区内可以开展下列符合海南热带雨林国家公园总体规划和专项规划的特许经营项目：

（一）建设、运营经营服务设施；

（二）销售商品；

（三）租赁设备或者场地；

（四）提供住宿、餐饮、游憩导览、解说；

（五）经营户外运动项目或者商业拍摄、商业演艺活动等文化体育服务；

（六）提供生态旅游和体验、森林康养、休闲度假服务；

（七）提供生态科普、自然教育服务；

Article 4 Park Office shall determine the operator on a competitive basis. Where the indigenous peoples in The Rainforest Park (hereinafter referred to as the "indigenous peoples") use their own houses or collective economic organizations and their members' houses to provide food service, accommodation, product sales, and other business service activities, in addition to those business service activities specified by the national and provincial people's governments, the operators may be determined without competition.

Article 5 Concessions for infrastructure and public utilities in the Rainforest Park shall be granted by the Park Office and appropriate people's government agencies at or above the county level in compliance with these Measures and applicable national provisions.

Article 6 Concession fees shall be jointly calculated by the Park Office and the provincial finance agency and implemented after being approved by the provincial people's government.

Concession fees shall be handed over to the provincial treasury and subject to financial budget management.

Chapter II Concession Scope

Article 7 The following concession projects may be performed in Rainforest Park affiliated areas in compliance with the Rainforest Park overall and special planning:

(a) constructing and operating business and service facilities;

(b) selling products;

(c) leasing equipment or sites;

(d) providing accommodation, catering, guiding tours, and interpretive guiding;

(e) operating outdoor sports or cultural and sports services such as commercial shooting and performing arts activities;

(f) providing ecological tourism and experiences, forest health, recreation, and vacation services;

(g) providing ecological science awareness and nature education services;

（八）提供旅游运输服务；

（九）生产、销售载有海南热带雨林国家公园标识的产品；

（十）其他实行特许经营的项目。

第八条　海南热带雨林国家公园内的宗教活动、原住居民开展的种养等传统生产活动以及国家和省人民政府规定的不实行特许经营的其他经营活动，不列为特许经营项目。

第九条　国家公园管理机构编制特许经营目录，应当征求海南热带雨林国家公园所在地县级以上人民政府、有关部门、专家学者、原住居民和社会公众的意见。

国家公园管理机构应当对拟实行的特许经营项目的合理性和可行性组织论证；重大项目应当委托具有相应资质的第三方机构对项目资源使用情况和生态环境保护要求等方面进行合理性和可行性评估。

第三章　特许经营者的确定

第十条　国家公园管理机构通过竞争方式确定特许经营者的，应当符合国家和本省的有关规定，具体方式包括：

（一）招标；

（二）竞争性谈判或者竞争性磋商；

（三）法律、法规规定的其他竞争方式。

具备招标条件的特许经营项目，应当优先采用招标方式确定特许经营者。

(h) providing tourism and transportation services;

(i) producing and selling products bearing the Rainforest Park logo; and

(j) other concession projects.

Article 8 Religious activities in the Rainforest Park, traditional production activities such as agricultural planting and animal husbandry by indigenous peoples, and other business activities provided by the state and provincial people's government not subject to concessions are not listed as concession projects.

Article 9 When compiling the concession list, the Park Office shall collect the opinions of the people's governments at or above the county level, applicable agencies, experts and scholars, indigenous peoples, and the public where the Rainforest Park is located.

The Park Office shall organize and demonstrate the rationality and feasibility of the proposed concession project. Third party agencies with appropriate qualifications shall be hired to evaluate the rationality and feasibility of project resource utilization and ecological environment protection requirements for major projects.

Chapter III Determination of Operator

Article 10 Where the Park Office determines the operator on a competitive basis, state and provincial regulations shall be abided by and the specific methods shall be as follows:

(a) bidding;

(b) competitive negotiation or competitive consultation; and

(c) other competitive methods provided by laws and regulations.

For concession projects with bidding conditions, priority shall be given to selecting operators through bids.

第十一条 下列特许经营项目应当依照有关规定通过招标方式确定特许经营者：

（一）利用海南热带雨林国家公园内国有自然资源资产开展特许经营活动的；

（二）租赁海南热带雨林国家公园内国有固定资产开展特许经营活动的；

（三）建设经营性服务设施开展文化体育、生态旅游和体验、森林康养、休闲度假、生态科普、自然教育、旅游运输等特许经营活动的；

（四）设立独立的经营性商业广告设施的；

（五）国家和本省规定应当招标的其他项目。

第十二条 需要授予土地等自然资源使用权、涉及固定资产投资的特许经营项目，由国家公园管理机构和所在地县级以上人民政府有关部门联合实施组合性特许，确定特许经营者。具体办法由省人民政府制定。

第十三条 依法通过竞争方式确定的特许经营者，国家公园管理机构应当向社会公示。

第十四条 申请开展本办法第四条第二款规定的经营服务活动的，应当向国家公园管理机构提交特许经营申请材料，经批准后依法签订特许经营协议，并办理相关许可手续。

具体办法由国家公园管理机构制定，报省人民政府批准后实施。

第十五条 本办法实施前海南热带雨林国家公园一般控制区内已经实施且属于特许经营目录范围内的经营项目，符合相关法律、法规规定的，应当依照本办法规定重新签订特许经营协议。

Article 11 Operators of the following concession projects shall be determined through bidding pursuant to applicable provisions:

(a) where state-owned natural resource assets in the Rainforest Park are utilized to conduct concession activities;

(b) where state-owned fixed assets in the Rainforest Park are leased to conduct concession activities;

(c) where business service facilities are constructed to conduct concession activities, such as cultural and sports, eco-tourism and experiences, forest health, recreation and vacation, ecological science awareness, nature education, tourism, and transportation;

(d) where independent commercial advertising facilities are set up; and

(e) other projects that shall be determined through bidding pursuant to national and provincial regulations.

Article 12 Where concession projects require use rights for natural resources such as land to be granted and involve investment in fixed assets, the Park Office and appropriate local people's government agencies at or above the county level shall jointly implement the combined concessions and determine the operators. Specific measures for such shall be prepared by the provincial people's government.

Article 13 The operators determined through competitive methods pursuant to law shall be announced to the public by the Park Office.

Article 14 Anyone requesting to conduct business service activities provided in Paragraph 2 of Article 4 of these Regulations shall submit their concession application materials to the Park Office, sign the concession agreement pursuant to law following approval, and complete the necessary licensing procedures.

Specific measures shall be prepared by the Park Office and implemented following approval from the provincial people's government.

Article 15 Concession agreements for projects operating in Rainforest Park affiliated areas before the implementation of these Measures, fall under the scope of the concession list, and conducted pursuant to applicable laws and regulations shall be restated and executed in compliance with these Measures.

依法应当退出的经营项目，依照有关规定办理。需要设定过渡期的，由国家公园管理机构提出具体办法，并报省人民政府批准后执行。

第四章 特许经营协议和相关义务

第十六条 国家公园管理机构应当与特许经营者签订特许经营协议。

特许经营协议应当包括以下主要内容：

（一）特许经营项目名称；

（二）特许经营方式、内容、区域、范围、期限以及资源利用限制性要求；

（三）所提供产品或者服务的数量、质量和标准；

（四）特许经营使用费的缴费标准、金额、支付方式；

（五）设施设备的维护、更新改造要求；

（六）项目的自然资源保护要求和损害治理；

（七）项目实施情况评估和方式；

（八）根据项目评估结果应采取的整改措施和整改不符合要求的退出情形；

（九）违约责任以及争议解决方式；

（十）特许经营协议的变更、解除、终止及补偿；

（十一）特许经营协议终止后，相关设施和设备资产处置、技术资料和其他相关档案资料移交方式、程序和要求等；

（十二）其他应当明确的事项。

Operating projects that need to be stopped pursuant to law shall be managed in compliance with applicable provisions. Where a transition period is required, the Park Office shall recommend specific measures and submit them to the provincial people's government for approval before implementation.

Chapter IV Concession Agreement and Obligations

Article 16 The Park Office shall sign concession agreements with operators.

A concession agreement shall contain of the following main provisions:

(a) name of the concession project;

(b) concession method, description, area, scope, term, and restrictive requirements for resource utilization;

(c) quantity, quality, and standard of the products or services provided;

(d) payment standards, amounts, and payment methods for concession fees;

(e) facility and equipment maintenance, renovation, and conversion requirements;

(f) natural resources protection requirements and damage control;

(g) project implementation evaluation and methods;

(h) corrective action to be taken based on the project evaluation results and the exit conditions when such corrective actions fail to meet the requirements;

(i) liability for breach of contract and dispute resolution methods;

(j) concession agreement amendment, cancellation, termination, and indemnification;

(k) management of facilities and equipment assets, assignment methods, procedures, and requirements of technical data and other filings following the termination of the concession agreement; and

(l) other matters that shall be explicitly provided.

第十七条 海南热带雨林国家公园特许经营项目的经营期限，应当综合考虑项目所提供产品或者服务要求、建设内容、投资额度、项目生命周期、投资回收期、经济社会和生态效益等因素确定。

授予特许经营者建设、运营涉及固定资产投资的经营服务设施的，特许经营期限一般为10年，原则上不超过20年。需要授予更长特许经营期限的，报省人民政府批准后确定。

前款规定以外的其他特许经营项目按照特许经营协议确定特许经营期限，最长不超过10年。

第十八条 特许经营者应当依照约定缴纳特许经营使用费。

符合下列情形之一的，可以免收或者减收特许经营使用费：

（一）原住居民利用自有或者本集体经济组织及其成员的房屋开展餐饮、住宿、商品销售等经营服务活动，或者从事海南热带雨林国家公园内游憩导览等微利项目的；

（二）与国家公园管理机构合作，从事自然教育等提升海南热带雨林国家公园管理成效的活动的；

（三）可以免收或者减收特许经营使用费的其他情形。

免收或者减收特许经营使用费的具体办法由国家公园管理机构会同省财政部门制定，报省人民政府批准后施行。

第十九条 特许经营者应当按照海南热带雨林国家公园有关管理要求从事特许经营活动，不得有下列行为：

（一）破坏自然资源、环境、景观；

（二）超出约定范围从事经营服务活动；

（三）违反国家、行业标准提供产品和服务，损害公众利益；

Article 17 When determining the operating period for a Rainforest Park concession project, factors including requirements for products or services provided by the project, construction descriptions, investment quota, project life cycle, investment payback period, and economic, social, and ecological benefits shall be given comprehensive consideration.

Where an operator is granted the right to build and operate business and service facilities involving investment in fixed assets, the concession period is generally 10 years and, in principle, no more than 20 years. The grant of a longer concession period shall be determined following the approval of the provincial people's government.

Concession projects other than those provided in the above paragraph shall be determined based on the concession agreement, and the concession period shall not exceed 10 years.

Article 18 Operators shall pay the concession fees subject to the agreement.

Concession fees may be exempted or reduced under any of the following circumstances:

(a) where indigenous peoples use their own houses or houses belonging to collective economic organizations and their members to conduct catering, accommodation, product sales, and other business service activities, or are involved in low-profit projects such as tour guiding and interpretive guiding within the Rainforest Park;

(b) where environmental education activities are organized to improve Rainforest Park management effectiveness in collaboration with the Park Office; or

(c) other circumstances under which concession fees may be exempted or reduced.

Specific measures for exempting or reducing concession fees shall be jointly prepared by the Park Office and the provincial finance agency and implemented after being approved by the provincial people's government.

Article 19 Operators shall conduct concession activities in compliance with the applicable Rainforest Park administration requirements and shall not commit any of the following acts:

(a) destroying natural resources, the environment, or landscape;

(b) conducting business service activities beyond the agreed scope;

(c) providing products and services in violation of national and industrial standards, and harming the public interest;

（四）以转让、出租、质押等方式处置特许经营权或者国家公园管理机构提供给特许经营者使用的资源资产、设施设备；

（五）擅自停业、歇业；

（六）其他违反法律、法规及特许经营协议约定的行为。

第二十条 鼓励特许经营者通过向原住居民分享特许经营收益、聘用原住居民等方式，促进居民增收。

第二十一条 特许经营者申请提前终止特许经营协议的，国家公园管理机构应当自收到申请3个月内作出答复。在国家公园管理机构决定终止协议前，特许经营者应当继续履行协议。

第五章 监督管理

第二十二条 国家公园管理机构及县级以上人民政府有关部门应当根据各自职责对特许经营活动进行监督管理。

第二十三条 省人民政府应当建立由县级以上人民政府有关部门参加的特许经营协调机制，协调解决海南热带雨林国家公园内特许经营活动中的重大问题。

第二十四条 国家公园管理机构应当加强对特许经营者履行特许经营协议和相关义务、利用自然资源、保护生态环境等情况的监督。

第二十五条 国家公园管理机构应当建立健全特许经营活动的社会监督机制，发挥媒体、社会监督员作用，及时处理举报和投诉，严格追究特许经营活动中破坏生态环境等方面的违法责任。

(d) assigning, leasing, or pledging the concession or any resource, asset, or facility that the park office provides the operator to a third party;

(e) suspending or temporarily closing business without authorization; or

(f) other acts in violation of the law or concession agreement.

Article 20 Operators are encouraged to increase local residents' income by sharing concession revenues with indigenous peoples or employing indigenous peoples.

Article 21 Where an operator requests the early termination of the concession agreement, the Park Office shall respond within 3 months of receiving the request. Before the Park Office decides to terminate the agreement, the operator shall continue to perform the agreement.

Chapter V Oversight and Administration

Article 22 The Park Office and appropriate agencies of the people's governments at or above the county level shall oversee and administrate concession activities in line with their duties.

Article 23 The provincial people's government shall set up a concession coordination system with the participation of agencies from people's governments at or above the county level to coordinate and solve major problems in concession activities within the Rainforest Park.

Article 24 The Park Office shall improve the oversight of operators fulfilling concession agreements and their obligations, utilizing natural resources, and protecting the ecological environment.

Article 25 The Park Office shall establish and optimize a public oversight system for concession activities, take full advantage of media and public oversight, resolve reports and complaints in a timely manner, and strictly hold those damaging the ecological environment during concession activities accountable.

第二十六条 国家公园管理机构应当依据有关规定对特许经营重大项目的社会效益和生态环境效益进行评估，并向社会公开评估结果。对评估发现问题的，责令特许经营者限期整改；整改不符合要求、严重违反有关规定和约定情形的，解除特许经营协议。

第二十七条 特许经营协议终止时，对法律、法规规定和协议约定应当移交政府的资产，国家公园管理机构和相关部门应当及时接管。

第六章 法律责任

第二十八条 特许经营者违反本办法第十九条第一项规定，破坏自然资源、环境、景观的，国家公园管理机构对价值减损等情况组织评估，责令责任人采取有效措施修复，并依照有关法律、法规予以处罚；情节严重的，解除特许经营协议。

第二十九条 特许经营者违反本办法第二条第三款和第十九条第二项规定，未经授权擅自开展特许经营活动或者超出约定范围从事经营服务活动的，责令改正，予以警告，没收非法所得，并处一万元以上五万元以下罚款；情节严重的，处五万元以上十万元以下罚款，解除特许经营协议。

第三十条 特许经营者违反本办法第十九条第四项规定，以转让、出租、质押等方式处置特许经营权或者国家公园管理机构提供给特许经营者使用的资源资产、设施设备的，责令恢复原状、赔偿损失，并处一万元以上五万元以下罚款；情节严重的，处五万元以上十万元以下罚款，解除特许经营协议。

Article 26 The Park Office shall evaluate the social benefits and ecological and environmental benefits of major concession projects pursuant to applicable regulations and publicly announce the evaluation results. Where problems are found in the evaluation, the operator shall be required to correct such within a time limit. Should the corrections fail to meet requirements and materially violate applicable regulations and agreements, the concession agreement shall be terminated.

Article 27 When the concession agreement is terminated, the Park Office and the appropriate agencies shall promptly take over the assets to be assigned to the government pursuant to law and the agreement.

Chapter VI Legal Liability

Article 28 Where the operator violates Subparagraph (a) of Article 19 of these Measures and damages natural resources or the environment and landscape, the Park Office shall organize an evaluation of the reduction in value and require the responsible person to take action to effectively correct such, as well as impose penalties pursuant to laws and regulations. The concession agreement may be terminated under serious circumstances.

Article 29 Where the operator violates Paragraph 3 of Article 2 and Subparagraph (b) of Article 19 of these Measures, conducts concession activities without authorization, or engages in business service activities beyond the agreed scope, the operator shall be ordered to correct its actions, receive warnings, have any illegal income earned confiscated, and be subject to a fine of not less than 10,000 Yuan and not more than 50,000 Yuan. A fine of not less than 50,000 Yuan and not more than 100,000 Yuan shall be imposed for material violations and the concession agreement shall be terminated.

Article 30 Where the operator violates Subparagraph (d) of Article 19 of these Measures and assign, lease, or pledge the concession or any resource, asset, or facility that the Park Office provides the operator to a third party, the operator shall be ordered to pay restitution and indemnify against losses, and be subject to a fine of not less than 10,000 Yuan but not more than 50,000 Yuan; a fine of not less than 50,000 Yuan and not more than 100,000 Yuan shall be imposed for material violations and the concession agreement shall be terminated.

第三十一条　特许经营者违反本办法第十九条第五项规定，擅自停业、歇业的，责令改正，并处三万元以下罚款；情节严重的，处三万元以上十万元以下罚款，解除特许经营协议。

提供旅游运输等对海南热带雨林国家公园管理有重大影响的特许经营者擅自停业、歇业的，从重处罚。

在海南热带雨林国家公园内开展特许经营活动的原住居民、个体工商户、小微企业擅自停业、歇业，情节轻微的，可视情况免于处罚。

第三十二条　国家公园管理机构和有关主管部门及其工作人员在特许经营监督管理活动中，不依法履行监督管理职责、违法授予特许经营权或者违法变更、解除特许经营协议，以及有其他滥用职权、玩忽职守、徇私舞弊行为的，依法予以问责、给予处分；构成犯罪的，依法追究刑事责任。

第三十三条　违反本办法规定的行为，由省人民政府确定的执法机构实施处罚。法律、法规另有规定的，从其规定。

第三十四条　违反本办法规定的行为，本办法未设定处罚但其他法律、法规已设定处罚的，依照有关法律、法规的规定处罚；有关法律、法规的处罚规定严于本办法的，适用有关法律、法规的规定。

第七章　附　则

第三十五条　海南热带雨林国家公园内的国有林业企业、农垦企业职工参照适用本办法有关原住居民的规定。

第三十六条　本办法自 2021 年 3 月 1 日起施行。

Article 31 Operators who violate Subparagraph (e) of Article 19 of these Measures and suspend or temporarily close business without authorization shall be required to make corrections and be subject to a fine of not more than 30,000 Yuan. A fine of not less than 30,000 Yuan and not more than 100,000 Yuan shall be imposed for material violations and the concession agreement shall be terminated.

Operators who provide tourism transportation and other services that have a significant impact on the administration of the Rainforest Park shall be severely penalized if they suspend or temporarily close their business without authorization.

Where the operators are indigenous people, sole proprietorships, or small and micro-sized businesses that carry out concession activities in the Rainforest Park, they may be exempted from penalties for minor violations.

Article 32 Where the Park Office and applicable agencies or their employees fail to perform their duties of oversight and administration pursuant to law, illegally grant concessions or illegally amend or terminate concession agreements, and engage in other acts of abuse of position, dereliction of duty, or playing favoritism and committing irregularities, they shall be held accountable and punished pursuant to law. Those committing crimes shall be held criminally liable pursuant to law.

Article 33 Penalties for violations of these Measures shall be issued by the law enforcement agencies determined by the provincial people's government, except as otherwise provided by laws and regulations.

Article 34 Where other laws and regulations provide penalties for violations of these Measures not provided in these Measures or provide more severe penalties than these Measures, such laws and regulations shall govern.

Chapter VII Supplementary Provisions

Article 35 State-owned forestry and agricultural reclamation business entities employees in the Rainforest Park shall refer to these Measures for matters concerning indigenous peoples.

Article 36 These Measures shall come into force as of March 1, 2021.

海南省人民代表大会常务委员会关于海南省资源税具体适用税率等有关事项的决定

Decisions of the Standing Committee of the Hainan Provincial People's Congress on Specific Applicable Resource Tax Rates in Hainan Province and Other Matters

海南省人民代表大会常务委员会关于海南省资源税具体适用税率等有关事项的决定

（2020年7月31日海南省第六届人民代表大会常务委员会第二十一会议通过）

为了保护生态环境，合理利用资源，加强资源管理，根据《中华人民共和国资源税法》（以下简称《资源税法》）规定，结合本省应税资源的品位、开采条件以及对生态环境的影响等情况，现就《资源税法》授权事项，作出如下决定：

一、《资源税法》规定实行幅度税率的，本省相关资源税的具体适用税率在国家规定的税率幅度内，具体按照《海南省资源税税目税率表》执行。

二、《资源税法》规定可以实行从价计征或者从量计征的，本省地热、石灰岩、其他粘土、矿泉水税目实行从量计征，砂石税目实行从价计征。地热水、矿泉水的水资源费并入资源税。

三、符合下列条件之一的，减征或者免征资源税：

（一）纳税人开采或者生产应税产品过程中，因意外事故或者自然灾害等原因遭受重大损失的，可以按损失金额的50%减征资源税，但减税额最高不超过其遭受重大损失当年应纳的资源税；

Decisions of the Standing Committee of the Hainan Provincial People's Congress on Specific Applicable Resource Tax Rates in Hainan Province and Other Matters

(Adopted at the 21st Session of the Standing Committee of the 6th Hainan Provincial People's Congress on July 31, 2020)

The following decisions on the matters authorized under the Resource Tax Law are made to protect the ecological environment, encourage rational resource exploitation, and improve resource management, pursuant to the Resource Tax Law of the People's Republic of China (hereinafter referred to as the "Resource Tax Law") and combined with taxable resource grade and exploitation condition, ecological and environmental impacts, and other circumstances:

I. Where a range of tax rates is provided in the Resource Tax Law, the specific applicable provincial resource tax rates shall be controlled by the Hainan Province Resource Tax Taxable Items and Tax Rates Table within the national tax rate.

II. Where resource taxes may be collected either on an ad valorem basis or volume basis, taxes for geothermal, limestone, clay, and mineral water taxable items in the Province shall be collected on a volume basis, and taxes for sandstone taxable items shall be collected on ad valorem basis pursuant to the Resource Tax Law. Geothermal water and mineral water resource fees shall be merged into the resource tax.

III. The resource tax may be reduced or exempted under any of the following circumstances:

(a) a resource tax abatement of 50% of the losses may be given should a taxpayer suffer material losses while exploiting or producing taxable products due to accidents or natural disasters, but the maximum tax abatement shall not exceed the resource tax payable for the year when the taxpayer suffered such losses;

（二）纳税人开采共生矿，共生矿与主矿产品销售额分开核算的，共生矿减征 10% 资源税；

（三）纳税人开采伴生矿，伴生矿与主矿产品销售额分开核算的，对伴生矿免征资源税；

（四）纳税人开采低品位矿减征 50% 资源税；

（五）纳税人开采尾矿免征资源税。

符合前款规定的，由纳税人申报享受各项优惠政策，相关资料留存备查。

四、根据工作需要，主管税务机关可以要求当地自然资源和规划主管部门提供共伴生矿、低品位矿、尾矿等应税矿产品的认定情况以及与减免税相关的其他信息，有关自然资源和规划主管部门应予以协助支持。

本决定自 2020 年 9 月 1 日起施行。

(b) a 10% resource tax abatement on paragenetic materials may be given to any taxpayer exploiting paragenic materials, whose sales and host mineral products are calculated separately;

(c) no resource tax shall be charged where any taxpayer exploits associated minerals and the sales of such associated minerals and host mineral products are calculated separately;

(d) a 50% resource tax abatement shall be given to any taxpayer who exploits low-grade minerals; or

(e) no resource tax shall be imposed on any taxpayer exploiting tailings.

Taxpayers may declare and benefit from several preferential policies subject to the preceding paragraphs, and related information shall be kept for future reference.

IV. The appropriate tax office may request local natural resources and planning departments to define taxable mineral products, such as associated minerals, low-grade minerals, tailings, and other information related to tax reduction and exemption based on actual needs, and the appropriate natural resources and planning department shall provide assistance and support.

These Decisions shall come into force as of September 1, 2020.

附 件

海南省资源税税目税率表

<table>
<tr><th colspan="3">税目</th><th>征收对象</th><th>税率</th></tr>
<tr><td colspan="2">能源矿产</td><td>地热</td><td>原矿</td><td>4 元 / 立方米</td></tr>
<tr><td rowspan="14">金属矿产</td><td rowspan="4">黑色金属</td><td rowspan="2">铁</td><td>原矿</td><td>9%</td></tr>
<tr><td>选矿</td><td>4%</td></tr>
<tr><td rowspan="2">钛</td><td>原矿</td><td>9%</td></tr>
<tr><td>选矿</td><td>3%</td></tr>
<tr><td rowspan="8">有色金属</td><td rowspan="2">锌</td><td>原矿</td><td>5%</td></tr>
<tr><td>选矿</td><td>3.5%</td></tr>
<tr><td rowspan="2">铝土矿</td><td>原矿</td><td>5%</td></tr>
<tr><td>选矿</td><td>3.5%</td></tr>
<tr><td rowspan="2">金</td><td>原矿</td><td>6%</td></tr>
<tr><td>选矿</td><td>3%</td></tr>
<tr><td rowspan="2">锆</td><td>原矿</td><td>10%</td></tr>
<tr><td>选矿</td><td>3%</td></tr>
<tr><td rowspan="12">非金属矿产</td><td rowspan="8">矿物类</td><td rowspan="2">高岭土</td><td>原矿</td><td>4%</td></tr>
<tr><td>选矿</td><td>3%</td></tr>
<tr><td rowspan="2">石灰岩</td><td>原矿</td><td>5 元 / 吨</td></tr>
<tr><td>选矿</td><td>5.5 元 / 吨</td></tr>
<tr><td rowspan="2">天然石英砂、脉石英、粉石英</td><td>原矿</td><td>7%</td></tr>
<tr><td>选矿</td><td>3.5%</td></tr>
<tr><td rowspan="2">其他粘土（铸型用粘土、砖瓦用粘土、陶粒用粘土、水泥配料用粘土、水泥配料用红土、水泥配料用黄土、水泥配料用泥岩、保温材料用粘土）</td><td>原矿</td><td>5 元 / 立方米</td></tr>
<tr><td>选矿</td><td>5 元 / 立方米</td></tr>
<tr><td rowspan="4">岩石类</td><td rowspan="2">大理岩</td><td>原矿</td><td>6%</td></tr>
<tr><td>选矿</td><td>6%</td></tr>
<tr><td rowspan="2">花岗岩</td><td>原矿</td><td>6%</td></tr>
<tr><td>选矿</td><td>4.5%</td></tr>
</table>

Schedule

Hainan Province Resource Tax Taxable Items and Tax Rates Table

Taxable Items			Tax Objects	Tax Rates
Energy Minerals		Geothermy	Raw Ores	4 Yuan per cubic meter
Metal Minerals	Ferrous Metals	Iron	Raw Ores	9%
			Mineral Processing	4%
		Titanium	Raw Ores	9%
			Mineral Processing	3%
	Non-ferrous Metals	Zinc	Raw Ores	5%
			Mineral Processing	3.5%
		Bauxite	Raw Ores	5%
			Mineral Processing	3.5%
		Gold	Raw Ores	6%
			Mineral Processing	3%
		Zirconium	Raw Ores	10%
			Mineral Processing	3%
Nonmetallic Minerals	Minerals	Kaolin	Raw Ores	4%
			Mineral Processing	3%
		Limestone	Raw Ores	5 Yuan per ton
			Mineral Processing	5.5 Yuan per ton
		Natural quartz sand, vein quartz, tripoli	Raw Ores	7%
			Mineral Processing	3.5%
		Other clays (clay for molding, clay for bricks and tiles, clay for ceramsite, clay for concrete batching, red earth for concrete batching, loess for concrete batching, mudstone for concrete batching, clay for thermal insulation materials)	Raw Ores	5 Yuan per cubic meter
			Mineral Processing	5 Yuan per cubic meter
	Stone	Marble	Raw Ores	6%
			Mineral Processing	6%
		Granite	Raw Ores	6%
			Mineral Processing	4.5%

续表

税目			征收对象	税率
		其他岩石类（白云岩、石英岩、砂岩、辉绿岩、安山岩、闪长岩、板岩、玄武岩、片麻岩、角闪岩、页岩、浮石、凝灰岩、黑曜岩、霞石正长岩、蛇纹岩、麦饭石、泥灰岩、含钾岩石、含钾砂页岩、天然油石、橄榄岩、松脂岩、粗面岩、辉长岩、辉石岩、正长岩、火山灰、火山渣、泥炭）	原矿	5%
			选矿	3.5%
		砂石	原矿	4%
			选矿	4%
水气矿产		矿泉水	原矿	7.2 元 / 立方米
盐		海盐		2%

Continuation

Taxable Items			Tax Objects	Tax Rates
		Other stone (dolomite, quartzite, sandstone, diabase, andesite, diorite, slate, basalt, gneiss, amphibolite, shale, pumice, tuff, obsidian, nepheline syenite, serpentine, maifan stone, marlstone, potassium-bearing rock, potassium-bearing sandshale, natural oilstone, peridotite, pitchstone, trachyte, gabbro, pyroxenite, syenite, volcanic ash, volcanic slag, peat)	Raw Ores	5%
			Mineral Processing	3.5%
		Dinas	Raw Ores	4%
			Mineral Processing	4%
Groundwater and Gas Minerals		Mineral Water	Raw Ores	7.2 Yuan per cubic meters
Salt		Sea Salt		2%

海南省人民代表大会常务委员会关于海南省契税具体适用税率和免征减征办法的决定

Decisions of the Standing Committee of the Hainan Provincial People's Congress on the Measures on Specific Tax Rates and Exemption or Abatement of Deed Tax in Hainan Province

海南省人民代表大会常务委员会关于海南省契税具体适用税率和免征减征办法的决定

（2021 年 7 月 27 日海南省第六届人民代表大会常务委员会第二十九次会议通过）

根据《中华人民共和国契税法》（以下简称《契税法》）规定，结合本省实际，现就《契税法》授权事项，对契税具体适用税率和免征减征办法作出如下决定：

一、本省契税税率为百分之三。

二、有下列情形之一的，免征或者减征契税：

（一）因土地、房屋被本省县级以上人民政府征收、征用，选择货币补偿且在本省内重新购置土地、房屋的，成交价格不超过货币补偿部分免征契税，超出部分征收契税；选择房屋产权调换、土地使用权置换且不缴纳差价的免征契税，缴纳差价的，对差价部分征收契税。

（二）因不可抗力灭失住房，在本省内重新承受住房权属的，免征契税。

三、国家另有免征、减征契税规定的，从其规定。

四、本决定自 2021 年 9 月 1 日起施行。

Decisions of the Standing Committee of the Hainan Provincial People's Congress on the Measures on Specific Tax Rates and Exemption or Abatement of Deed Tax in Hainan Province

(Adopted at the 29th Session of the Standing Committee of the 6th Hainan Provincial People's Congress on July 27, 2021)

Pursuant to the Deed Tax Law of the People's Republic of China (hereinafter referred to as the "Deed Tax Law"), and in consideration of the actual circumstances in Hainan Province, the following decisions on the measures on specific tax rates and exemption or abatement of deed tax are formulated as authorized by the Deed Tax Law:

I. The provincial deed tax rate shall be 3%.

II. Deed tax shall be exempted or abated under any of the following circumstances:

(a) Where the original land or building is under eminent domain by a government at or above the county level, and financial compensation is chosen and land or a building is re-purchased within the Province, deed tax shall be exempt provided that the transaction price does not exceed the financial compensation or shall be levied from the part exceeding the financial compensation; where housing property exchange or land use right exchange is chosen, deed tax shall be exempted if there is no price difference or shall be levied from any price difference.

(b) Deed tax shall be exempted where a new residential building ownership within the Province is accepted after the original has been destroyed in a *force majeure* event.

III. Other state regulations shall prevail if they provide otherwise for the exemption or abatement of deed tax.

IV. These Decisions shall come into force as of September 1, 2021.

《海南省人民代表大会常务委员会关于海南省契税具体适用税率和免征减征办法的决定》解读

2021 年 7 月 27 日，海南省第六届人民代表大会常务委员会第二十九次会议审议通过了《海南省人民代表大会常务委员会关于海南省契税具体适用税率和免征减征办法的决定》（以下简称《决定》），自 2021 年 9 月 1 日起施行。

一、出台《决定》的背景和依据

2020 年 8 月 11 日第十三届全国人民代表大会常务委员会第二十一次会议审议通过《中华人民共和国契税法》（以下简称《契税法》），于 2021 年 9 月 1 日起实施。其中第三条授权省人民政府在国家规定的税率幅度（百分之三至百分之五）内提出契税的具体适用税率以及提出对因土地、房屋被县级以上人民政府征收、征用，重新承受土地、房屋权属和因不可抗力灭失住房，重新承受住房权属两种情形免征或者减征契税的具体办法，报同级人民代表大会常务委员会决定。为保障《契税法》今年 9 月 1 日在我省顺利实施，我省出台《决定》，明确了授权事项。

二、《决定》的主要内容

我省按照总体税制平移的思路确定了契税税率和免征减征办法，并据实际情况，作了略微必要调整。

（一）我省契税税率为百分之三，与现行税率保持一致，维持法定税率（3%—5%）最低档不变。

Interpretation of the Decisions of the Standing Committee of the Hainan Provincial People's Congress on the Measures on Specific Tax Rates and Exemption or Abatement of Deed Tax in Hainan Province

After deliberation, the Decisions of the Standing Committee of the Hainan Provincial People's Congress on the Measures on Specific Tax Rates and Exemption or Abatement of Deed Tax in Hainan Province (hereinafter referred to as these "Decisions") are adopted at the 29th Session of the Standing Committee of the 6th Hainan Provincial People's Congress on July 27, 2021, and shall come into force as of September 1, 2021.

I. Decisions' Background and Basis

The 21st Session of the Standing Committee of the 13th National People's Congress deliberated on and passed the Deed Tax Law of the People's Republic of China (hereinafter referred to as the "Deed Tax Law") on August 11, 2020, which shall come into force on September 1, 2021. Article 3 of the Deed Tax Law authorizes the provincial people's government to recommend a specific deed tax rate within the nationally required tax rate range (3% through 5%), and recommend specific regulations for the exemption or abatement of deed tax in the event new land use rights or building ownership are accepted where the original one was under eminent domain by a government at or above the county level or a new residential building ownership is accepted after the original is destroyed in a *force majeure* event, and shall report such to the standing committee of the people's congress at the same level for decision. We issued these Decisions and clarified the authorized matters to ensure the smooth implementation of the Deed Tax Law in the Province on September 1 of the same year.

II. Description of these Decisions

The deed tax rate and exemption and abatement method shall be determined based on the concept of accepting the old tax system comprehensively in Hainan Province, and any necessary adjustments shall be made based on actual circumstances.

(a) The provincial deed tax rate is 3%, which matches the current tax rate, and the lowest statutory tax rate (3%–5%) remains unchanged.

（二）因土地、房屋被本省县级以上人民政府征收、征用，选择货币补偿且在本省内重新购置土地、房屋的，成交价格不超过货币补偿部分免征契税，超出部分征收契税；选择房屋产权调换、土地使用权置换且不缴纳差价的免征契税，缴纳差价的，对差价部分征收契税。此项优惠政策既延续了现有房屋征收、征用重新承受房屋权属的契税优惠政策(《财政部、国家税务总局关于企业以售后回租方式进行融资等有关契税政策的通知》（财税〔2012〕82 号）第三条规定），又扩展到土地征收、征用重新承受土地权属方面，将土地和房屋的优惠政策进行统一，可以减轻纳税人负担。

（三）因不可抗力灭失住房，在本省内重新承受住房权属的，免征契税。与现行规定（《海南省地方税务局关于加强契税征收管理若干规定的通知》（琼地税发〔2001〕77 号）第四条第四款）保持一致。

（四）国家另有免征、减征契税规定的，从其规定。目前，我省按照财政部、国家税务总局、住房城乡建设部发布《关于调整房地产交易环节契税营业税优惠政策的通知》(财税〔2016〕23 号，以下简称《通知》)，对房地产交易环节契税实施优惠税率。《契税法》授权了国务院根据国民经济和社会发展的需要，对居民住房需求保障等情形可以规定免征或者减征契税，因此《决定》做了衔接性规定，对国家另有免征、减征契税规定的，按照国家规定执行。

(b) Where the original land or building is under eminent domain by a government at or above the county level and financial compensation is chosen, and land or a building is re-purchased within the Province, the deed tax shall be exempted if the transaction price does not exceed the financial compensation or shall be assessed on the part exceeding the financial compensation; where housing property or land use rights exchange is chosen, deed tax shall be exempted if there is no price difference or assessed on the price difference. This preferential policy both continues the existing preferential deed tax policy applicable to the acceptance of new building ownership due to eminent domain (Article 3 of the Notice of the Ministry of Finance and State Taxation Administration of the People's Republic of China on Applicable Deed Tax Policies for Organizations Financing by Sale and Lease-back (Cai Shui [2012] No. 82)) and extends to the acceptance of new land use rights due to eminent domain, standardizing land use rights and building ownership preferential policies to reduce the burden on taxpayers.

(c) Deed tax shall be exempt where a new residential building ownership in the Province is accepted after the original is destroyed in a *force majeure* event. This provision is in line with current regulations (Paragraph 4 of Article 4 of the Notice of Improving Deed Tax Administration from Hainan Tax Authority (Qiong Di Shui Fa [2001] No. 77)).

(d) Other state regulations shall prevail if they provide otherwise for the exemption or abatement of deed tax. Pursuant to the Notice on Adjusting the Preferential Policies for Deed Tax and Business Tax in Real Estate Transactions (Cai Shui [2016] No. 23, hereinafter referred to as the "Notice") issued by the Ministry of Finance, State Taxation Administration of the People's Republic of China and the Ministry of Housing and Urban-Rural Development, preferential tax rates for deed tax in real estate transactions are currently applied within the Province. The Deed Tax Law authorizes the State Council to exempt or abate tax to meet residents' housing needs based on the national economy and social development. Therefore, these Decisions have made provision to connect them, that is where other state regulations shall control if they provide otherwise for the exemption or abatement of deed tax.

后 记

今年是“一带一路”倡议提出的第十年。“一带一路”倡议是中国旨在进一步扩大对外开放、推进全球化进程的中国方案，是旨在促进区域政治、经济、法律与文化多元发展的多边国际合作倡议，是“中国发起、各方共建、世界共享的优质公共产品”。十年来，我国与“一带一路”沿线国家的经贸往来与合作取得重大突破，我国对外贸易与对外投资额大幅上涨，基础设施建设与投资力度持续加大，贸易自由化与贸易便利化程度显著提高。

该系列图书是我作为首席专家承担的国家社会科学基金重大项目“‘一带一路’沿线国家法律文本翻译、研究及数据库建设”（批准号 18ZDA157）的最终成果。自 2018 年立项以来，为按时保质完成翻译与研究计划，我们重点翻译了东南亚、西亚北非、东欧地区约 40 个国家和地区 400 万余字法律文本，分为《世界主要自由贸易港法律选译》、《东南亚及南亚国家投资法选译》、《西亚北非东欧国家经济法选译》以及《海南自由贸易港法规（2020—2021）选编（中英对照）》，以期为相关主体提供真实可信、切合实需的法律译本，助力“一带一路”建设的长远发展。

建设海南自由贸易港，需要对标国际高水平经贸规则。《世界主要自由贸易港法律选译》聚焦自由贸易港相关的法律规定，涉及新加坡、迪拜、韩国济州等世界知名自由贸易港（区）的园区建设、市场准入、投资贸易、海关港务、数据保护、商业信托、医疗养老、国际仲裁等八个方面的立法。本卷从立法的选择、翻译到审校各环节，是在海南省人大常委会领导同志的关心支持下顺利推进的。

《东南亚及南亚国家投资法选译》以“扩大高水平对外开放”“绿色投资”“全球可持续发展”三大板块为主题，内容涉及东盟国家的重要法律法规、实施细则、命令等细化规定，主要有《新加坡反补贴反倾销法》《印度尼西亚贸易法》《越南生物多样性法》等。

《西亚北非东欧国家经济法选译》主要选取与中国双边贸易额和投资额较大的海湾阿拉伯国家和埃及的投资法、公司法进行译介。“一带一路”沿线阿拉伯国家多为发展中国家，各国在市场准入、行业监管、金融体系和税收安排、进出口管理、投资争端解决等领域存在很大差异。然而，针对具体项目开展全面、系统的法律尽职调查，对我国大多数“走出去”的企业而言，仍存在经济上和操作上的困难。译介相关阿拉伯国家的重点经济立法，将为企业提供第一手的有关外商投资、公司制度等问题的实用法律信息，为中国企业与相关阿拉伯国家贸易、投资合作保驾护航。

上述三卷是外国法汉译成果，而《海南自由贸易港法规（2020—2021）选编（中英对照）》则是中国法外译成果。本卷旨在将海南自由贸易港法规体系翻译出去，以供世界各国了解海南自由贸易港是法治的自由贸易港，进而彰显海南乃至中国的法治形象。需要特别致谢的是，该系列图书中的《世界主要自由贸易港法律选译》和《海南自由贸易港法规（2020—2021）选编（中英对照）》是我主持的重大项目课题组直接受海南省人大常委会法制工作委员会（以下简称海南省人大常委会法工委）委托翻译完成的。

除以上立法翻译成果外，课题组还围绕域外管辖、涉外法治以及立法翻译研究等主题，展开相关研究。课题组在《中国社会科学》《中外法学》《华东政法大学学报》《中国翻译》《中国外语》《外语与外语教学》等期刊发表了系列论文。此外，课题组初步建成中英、中阿多语交叉法律数据库和英汉术语表。总之，本项目是面向“一带一路”倡议、全面依法治国战略和构建人类命运共同体等国家需求展开的一项重大翻译工程。

2020 年以来，受海南省人大常委会法工委委托，我将有关海南自由贸易港建设、营商环境优化、商品贸易和服务贸易便利化、社会征信体制建设、外资准入与退出机制等 34 部重要法规进行英译。这项工作对于对外宣传海南省人民代表大会围绕海南自由贸易港建设和优化营商环境改革所作的制度创新和完成的立法工作具有重要意义。我和我的团队严谨求实、积极细致的工作态度，以及我们在法规英译工作中展现出的专业素质，获得海南省人大常委会法工委充分肯定，相关成果也得到采纳和使用。

机缘巧合，我能承担这项光荣的任务，盖得益于全国人大常委会法制工作委员会（以下简称全国人大常委会法工委）研究室夏继红处长对“海派”学者的信任。自 2019 年受聘担任全国人大常委会法工委法律英文译审专家以来，我曾先后四次受到全国人大常委会法工委表彰函谢。或许是我每次在领到指派的译审任务后，一来能够及时完成任务，二来在翻译法律术语等细节上比较顶真，给夏继红处长留下了比较可靠的印象。据她而言，我大抵有着“海派匠人”身上的某种执着，所以当海南省人大常委会法工委征询意见时，夏继红处长便推荐我作为译者人选。

翻译立法文件照理说是件苦差事，但这项任务的意义契合我的某种追求。这些年来，我始终在思考一个问题：该怎样带领法律翻译团队主动积极地服务国家需求，承担起历史赋予我们这一代法律外语人的使命，投身于建设法治中国的伟大实践。为此，我认真梳理回顾中国立法对外翻译两百余年的历史，参阅历史上留下的各种中文立法英译本。得益于我对法律史和法律翻译研究的执念和兴趣，得益于多年来从事法律翻译教学与法律翻译实践累积的经验，我基于英国小斯当东于 1810 年英译《大清律例》以来，历位法律译者在中文立法文本英译道路上所做的探索，基于立法文本和立法语言的特点，尝试总结出中文立法文本的外译宜遵循对等律、同一律与等效律三项成体系的基本原则。其中，就对等律而言，我主张中文立法文本的英译宜恪守文本类型对等、语义对等和形式对等三项次级翻译原则，以及术语对术语、通俗对通俗、准确对准确、模糊对模糊等四项翻译策略。我认为，立法文本翻译遵循的对外翻译原则体系，也适用于中国法治话语的对外翻译实践。问题是，这样抽象的理论概括，能否真正运用到立法翻译实践中？于我而言，这既是一个问题，也是一项挑战。在组织编译本书时，我试图以该立法文本翻译原则指导这次法律法规翻译实践。

在立法文本翻译实践中，我所面临的问题不仅是该确立何种翻译原则，更现实的则是立法文本的选择问题。2018 年作为首席专家承担该重大项目以来，选择怎样的立法文本进行翻译，便是一件首先要加以解决的问题。众所周知，“一带一路”沿线 64 个国家的确定标准为地理范围，主要包括北亚 1 国、中亚 5 国、南亚 8 国、东南亚 11 国、西亚北非 16 国、独联体 7 国、中东欧 16 国等七大地理方向，而“一带一路”的参与国就不限于上述地理范围内的沿线国家。近年来，与中国签署“一带一路”合作协议或备忘录的参与国仍在持续增加。质言之，“一带一路”沿线国家法律繁杂、语情多样，分属三大法系、七大法源、九大语系。综合地理、法系及语系分布等因素，加之各国在持续对其本国的法律法规规章进行着废改立工作，仅靠个体几乎无法完成翻译“一带一路”沿线国家全部法律的超大工程。

法律在世界范围传播、流动，是法律发展的规律之一。但目下，全球范围内还没有建成一个动态的，能够支撑普通法、大陆法、伊斯兰法等主要法系立法的集成式汉译法律数据库。理想的“一带一路”国家立法文本数据库，是基于多国立法的、多法系的、多语言的集成数据库，其组建难度远超“新加坡法律在线”（Singapore Statutes Online）、“电子版香港法例”（Hong Kong e-Legislation）等单体数据库。理想的“一带一路”国家立法文本数据库，可以公法、私法、社会法等主要立法文类（genre）的原文及译文为基础，以国家、地区、国际组织、区域性国际组织和法律类别为网格，既能为参与主体提供风险预防的方案，也能深化中外法律交流、法律对话，并为中国法的完善提供镜鉴。不唯此，理想的“一带一路”国家立法文本数据库应具有工具价值，可以实现多语法律术语识别与提取、术语分类，提供应用接口，供计算机辅助翻译软件或其他机器翻译系统调用，为翻译实践提供可供调用的记忆库及术语库，最终推动法律术语翻译的规范化。可是我也明白，所谓有所为而有所不为，我脑海中构画的上述图景，不是我和我的团队短期可以实现的。所以我宁愿本着有限目标原则，务实地一项一项来译。于是，在选择什么样的立法文本作为翻译对象这一问题上，我尽可能遵循译介重点国家和重点领域的立法、能够服务贸易以及服务中央和地方立法规划的立法等原则，量力而行。

因此，当海南省人大常委会法工委在征询我是否愿意承担这项意义重大的法规英译任务时，我毫不迟疑地答应下来。我和我的团队认为，海南省在“海上丝绸之路”上具有重要的历史和现实地位，是中国同东盟国家进一步开展深入合作的前沿地带。“一带一路”倡议和海南自贸区（港）建设互相成就、相生相伴、相辅相成。建设海南自由贸易港，是我国扩大对外开放和纵深推进“一带一路”倡议的重要战略举措。

基于这样的认识，我开始在工作中探索完善立法翻译的实践程序和项目管理流程，带领我的翻译团队全身心投入翻译工作中。具体到本卷，译者有四位，他们都是团队骨干成员，当时也全部是华东政法大学的在读博士研究生，具备良好的法律英文功底和法学理论素养。我在这里对四位译者及他们各自承担的工作量作简要介绍。

万立是我指导的博士研究生，与我合著《不平等与不对等：晚清中外旧约章翻译史研究》（商务印书馆 2021 年版，该书入选国家哲学社会科学成果文库）、合编《涉外法治法律英语教程》（法律出版社 2021 年版），在《世界历史》《中国翻译》《中外法学》《学术月刊》等权威刊物发表学术论文 10 余篇，以高分通过国家司法考试。万立曾作为主力队员代表华东政法大学参加“第十六届 JESSUP 国际法模拟法庭中国选拔赛”并获得亚军。万立主要承担《海南自由贸易港市场主体注销条例》《海南自由贸易港消防条例》《海南自由贸易港优化营商环境条例》《海南自由贸易港征收征用条例》《海南自由贸易港知识产权保护条例》《海南自由贸易港反消费欺诈规定》《海南自由贸易港科技开放创新若干规定》《海南自由贸易港博鳌乐城国际医疗旅游先行区条例》《中国（海南）自由贸易试验区商事登记管理条例》《中国（海南）自由贸易试验区重点园区极简审批条例》《海南省人民代表大会常务委员会关于海南自由贸易港洋浦经济开发区等重点园区管理体制的决定》《海南省大数据开发应用条例》《海南省多元化解纠纷条例》《海南省反走私暂行条例》《海南经济特区注册会计师条例》《海南经济特区道路旅游客运管理若干规定》等 16 部法规的初译工作。

曹雳是李秀清教授指导的博士研究生，硕士阶段跟随我学习，曾赴香港大学访学。他的本科和硕士专业是翻译，博士专业是法律史。曹雳主要承担《海南自由贸易港公平竞争条例》《海南自由贸易港国际船舶条例》《海南自由贸易港海口江东新区条例》《海南自由贸易港三亚崖州湾科技城条例》《海南省人民代表大会常务委员会关于将旅行社设立审批等省级管理权限调整由海南自由贸易港重点园区管理机构在重点园区范围内实施的决定》《海南热带雨林国家公园特许经营管理办法》《海南省人民代表大会常务委员会关于海南省资源税具体适用税率等有关事项的决定》《海南省人民代表大会常务委员会关于海南省契税具体适用税率和免征减征办法的决定》等 8 部法规的初译工作。

龚茁是我指导的博士研究生，现为浙江工商大学副教授，长期从事法律翻译教学与研究工作，在《辞书研究》《日语学习与研究》等期刊发表多篇论文。龚茁主要承担《海南自由贸易港企业破产程序条例》《海南自由贸易港社会信用条例》《海南自由贸易港安居房建设和管理若干规定》《海南自由贸易港免税购物失信惩戒若干规定》《海南自由贸易港闲置土地处置若干规定》《海南自由贸易港洋浦经济开发区条例》《海南省人民代表大会常务委员会关于将林业植物检疫证书核发等省级管理权限调整由海南自由贸易港重点园区管理机构在重点园区范围内实施的决定》等 7 部法规的初译工作。

詹继续是我指导的博士研究生，现为华东政法大学讲师，在《外语与外语教学》《华东政法大学学报》发表多篇论文，其中 1 篇被《新华文摘》转载，并与我合译《大智立法：新中国成立 70 年立法历程》。詹继续主要承担《海南经济特区律师条例》《海南经济特区禁止一次性不可降解塑料制品规定》《海南经济特区外国企业从事服务贸易经营活动登记管理暂行规定》等 3 部法规的初译工作。

我同上海外国语大学法律翻译专家 Adrian Dunbar（中文名李安谆）、万立、詹继续、曹霁、龚茁等承担了审校工作。华东政法大学法律学院硕士研究生韩驰完成了本卷全部译文的排版工作。

期间，我们的法律翻译、翻译研究和审校工作得到许多专家学者的支持，尤其感谢我的导师华东政法大学原校长何勤华教授，我的导师教育部长江学者、华东政法大学李秀清教授，上海交通大学法学院沈伟教授，郑州大学中国外交话语研究院院长杨明星教授，西南政法大学外语学院肖云枢教授以及华东政法大学外语学院宋丽珏副教授、国际金融法律学院丁勇教授等人所提供的各项建设性意见、承担子课题时所做的协调工作及所付出的努力。

感谢全国人大常委会法工委法规备案审查室严冬峰副主任，全国人大常委会法工委研究室五处夏继红处长、达吉副处长以及程周鲁丹、任雨婕等同志对我们工作的支持。感谢上海市哲学社会科学规划办公室李安方主任、四级调研员王云飞同志给予的支持。

感谢华东政法大学党委书记郭为禄教授、校长叶青教授对于这项工作的大力支持，感谢党委副书记应培礼教授、唐波教授的鼓励，感谢副校长韩强教授、周立志同志在我承担翻译任务时提供的工作支持。感谢华东政法大学学校办公室主任练育强教授，外语学院院长余素青教授，科研处处长陆宇峰教授，科研处副处长陈蓉、彭桂兵和科研处陈叶的细微帮助。

感谢浙江大学文科资深教授许钧先生、北京外国语大学讲席教授王克非先生、中国外文局原副局长兼总编辑黄友义译审、中国外文局原副局长兼中国翻译协会法律翻译委员会主任王刚毅先生、上海外国语大学党委书记姜锋研究员、中国外文局当代中国与世界研究院党委书记杨平编审、上海政法学院校长刘晓红教授、司法部国际合作局尹雪梅副局长、上海外国语大学副校长查明建教授、上海市人大常委会法制工作委员会阎锐主任、上海市司法局副局长罗培新教授、上海市检察院政治部荚振坤主任、上海市浦东新区司法局黄爱武局长、上海外国语大学校长助理胡开宝教授、全国翻译专业学位研究生教育指导委员会副主任委员兼广东外语外贸大学翻译学研究中心主任赵军峰教授、中国政法大学外国语学院张法连教授、浙江大学法学院程乐教授、上海市人民政府外事办公室翻译室董鹤莉主任、司法部国际合作局毛佳玲副处长、锦天城律师事务所高级合伙人叶芳律师等人在我组织本书翻译各时期给予的关注和帮助。

我要特别感谢上海市法学会专职副会长施伟东主编和孙建伟副主编同意在《上海法学

研究》集刊连载刊登我们翻译的 104 篇译文。特别感谢《外语与外语教学》原主编赵永青教授及《中国外语》常少华副主编和首席编辑艾斌刊发我谈中国法外译原则的两篇学术论文。感谢《法治日报》副总编辑张国庆、《中国社会科学报》上海站记者查建国、陈炼，《新民晚报》记者卫蔚、吴宇桢，以及《人民法院报》对于阶段性项目成果给予的支持与关注。感谢法律出版社韩泓宇、朱峰等编辑老师的细致工作。

尽管我们全力以赴，但难免翻译中有各种瑕疵，不足之处，恳请读者多批评指正。

屈文生

2023 年 4 月于上海寓所